Berlin

timeout.com/berlin

Published by Time Out Guides Ltd, a wholly owned subsidiary of Time Out Group Ltd.
Time Out and the Time Out logo are trademarks of Time Out Group Ltd.

© Time Out Group Ltd 2006
Previous editions 1996, 1998, 2000, 2002, 2004.

10 9 8 7 6 5 4 3 2 1

This edition first published in Great Britain in 2006 by Ebury Publishing
Ebury Publishing is a division of The Random House Group Ltd,
20 Vauxhall Bridge Road, London SW1V 2SA

Random House Australia Pty Limited 20 Alfred Street, Milsons Point, Sydney, New South Wales 2061, Australia
Random House New Zealand Limited 18 Poland Road, Glenfield, Auckland 10, New Zealand
Random House South Africa (Pty) Limited Isle of Houghton, Corner Boundary
Road & Carse O'Gowrie, Houghton 2198, South Africa

Random House UK Limited Reg. No. 954009

Distributed in USA by Publishers Group West
1700 Fourth Street, Berkeley, California 94710

Distributed in Canada by Penguin Canada Ltd
10 Alcorn Avenue, Toronto, Ontario, Canada M4V 3B2

For further distribution details, see www.timeout.com

ISBN
To 31 December 2006: 1-904 978-56-8
From 1 January 2007: 9781904978565

A CIP catalogue record for this book is available from the British Library

Colour reprographics by Icon, Crowne House, 56-58 Southwark Street, London SE1 1UN

Printed and bound in Germany by Appl

Papers used by Ebury Publishing are natural, recyclable products made from wood grown in sustainable forests

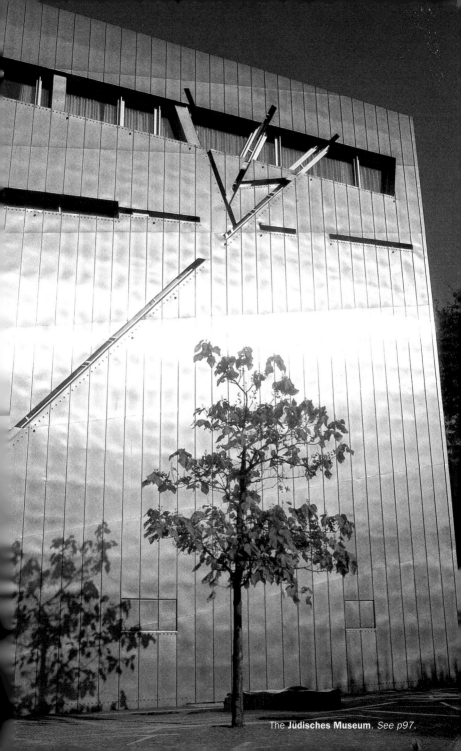

The **Jüdisches Museum**. *See p97.*

Time Out Guides Limited
Universal House
251 Tottenham Court Road
London W1T 7AB
Tel + 44 (0)20 7813 3000
Fax + 44 (0)20 7813 6001
Email guides@timeout.com
www.timeout.com

Editorial
Editor Dave Rimmer
Deputy Editor Simon Coppock
Researcher Manon Kahle
Proofreader Tamsin Shelton
Indexer Anna Norman

Editorial/Managing Director Peter Fiennes
Series Editor Ruth Jarvis
Deputy Series Editor Lesley McCave
Business Manager Gareth Garner
Guides Co-ordinator Holly Pick
Accountant Kemi Olufuwa

Design
Art Director Scott Moore
Art Editor Pinelope Kourmouzoglou
Senior Designer Josephine Spencer
Graphic Designer Henry Elphick
Digital Imaging Dan Conway
Ad Make-up Jenny Prichard

Picture Desk
Picture Editor Jael Marschner
Deputy Picture Editor Tracey Kerrigan
Picture Researcher Helen McFarland

Advertising
Sales Director Mark Phillips
International Sales Manager Ross Canadé
International Sales Executive Simon Davies
Advertising Sales (Berlin) In Your Pocket
Advertising Assistant Kate Staddon

Marketing
Marketing Director John Luck
Marketing & Publicity Manager, US Rosella Albanese

Production
Production Director Mark Lamond
Production Controller Marie Howell

Time Out Group
Chairman Tony Elliott
Managing Director Mike Hardwick
Financial Director Richard Waterlow
General Manager Nichola Coulthard
Art Director John Oakey
Online/Managing Director David Pepper
Production Director Steve Proctor
IT Director Simon Chappell

Contributors

Introduction Dave Rimmer. **History** Frederick Studemann (*Beauty and the bust* Kevin Cote; *Who wants to be a billionaire?* Dave Rimmer; *Stasiland* Kevin Cote). **Berlin Today** Kevin Cote. **Architecture** Michael Lees. **Where to Stay** Manon Kahle, Sophie Lovell (*A hotel of one's own* Rose T. Merrill). **Sightseeing** Manon Kahle, Dave Rimmer (*Monumental debate* Don Mac Coitr, Dave Rimmer; *The babes of Prenzl'berg* Kevin Cote; *The capital of Turkish Berlin* Edmund Gordon; *Hub, bub* Dave Rimmer; *Berlin by boat* Nicky Gardner; *Walking the Wall* Julie Gregson). **Restaurants** Kevin Cote, Nicky Gardner, Edmund Gordon, Andrew Horn, Patrick Lonergan, Dave Rimmer, David Strauss (*Curry on sausages* Dave Rimmer). **Cafés, Bars & Pubs** Nicky Gardner, Edmund Gordon, Dave Rimmer, David Strauss (*Where to get your early piece* Dave Rimmer). **Shops & Services** Emma Pearse (*The shop that wasn't there* Emma Pearse, *Ostalgia all over again* Susan Hanneford, Dave Rimmer). **Festivals & Events** Emma Pearse (*May Day! May Day!* Emma Pearse, Dave Rimmer). **Children** Don Mac Coitr. **Film** Andrew Horn. **Galleries** Neal Wach. **Gay & Lesbian** Nickolas Woods. **Music: Rock, World & Jazz** Tanya Ott, David Strauss (*So far so Gut* Tanya Ott). **Nightlife** Tanya Ott, David Strauss (*One Russian under a groove* Tanya Ott). **Performing Arts** Classical & Opera David Canisius; *Theatre, Cabaret* Priscilla Be; *Dance* Emma Pearse (*No ordinary opera house* Priscilla Be). **Sport & Fitness** (Don Mac Coitr). **Trips Out of Town** Peterjon Cresswell, Julie Gregson, Dave Rimmer (*The empty quarter* Nicky Gardner). **Directory** Kevin Cote, Edmund Gordon, Manon Kahle, Biba Kopf, Dave Rimmer (*Not so godless after all* Nicky Gardner; *It goes around the sausage* Dave Rimmer).

Maps JS Graphics (john@jsgraphics.co.uk).

Photography by Britta Jaschinski, except pages 10, 14, 21, 23, 184, 255 Corbis; page 12 Mary Evans Picture Library; page 13 AKG; page 183 Sebastian Bolesch; page 221 Kerstin Anders; page 227 Manhatten Verlag; page 235 Matthias Heyde; page 242 Gadi Dagon; page 246 Bytepark; pages 264, 265, 267 4Corners Images.
The following images were provided by the featured establishments/artist: pages 16, 52, 211.

The Editor would like to thank Chris Bohn, Kevin Cote, Chaos, Peterjon Cresswell, Angela Dwyer, John Fitzsimons, Edmund Gordon, Gosto Babka von Gostomski, Volker Hauptvogel, Russell King, Patrick Lonergan, Mark Reeder, Martin Rimmer, and Nicky Gardner and Susanne Kries of *Hidden Europe*.

Contents

Contents

Introduction

No city is ever complete – change is the nature of the urban beast. But after nearly two decades of major construction and reorganisation, following 40 years of being torn in two and walled into an uneasy stasis – and that after the entire place had literally been bombed into rubble – Berlin has finally arrived at a point where it can sit down for a minute and say 'phew!'

From the end of May 2006, the new Berlin Hauptbahnhof will open where the old Lehrter Bahnhof once stood (*see p102* **Hub, bub**). This doesn't just mean a humble S-Bahn station reborn as the continent's largest railway intersection and a city that spent half of the 20th century way off the map repositioned as a key hub in the north European transport network. It's also the final piece of the reunification puzzle, the completion – after the new government quarter and the area around Potsdamer Platz – of the last big initiative meant to heal the wounds of history and bring Berlin's two halves back together.

Of course, nothing's ever that easy. The German capital remains an enigmatic place and east and west still have their differences even if they do now mingle in the malls and cinemas of Potsdamer Platz. But for the visitor it means both a new point of arrival and one more piece of spectacular architecture in a new downtown cityscape that's become an attraction in itself.

Other attractions are of older vintage. A renegade underground culture still thrives on energy pent up over decades of political suppression and engagement. Division has left Berlin with twice as many orchestras and opera houses as any normal city. A fondness for shameless nightlife and no-holds-barred hedonism dates back even further, to the pre-war Weimar era, as does Berlin's role as a major gay city, a crucible of experimental art and a centre for theatre and cabaret. And the city's deserved reputation for tolerance dates back even further still, to the 19th century, and still holds true today. Berlin might not superficially be the world's most welcoming city, but whatever you want to get up to, the natives really aren't going to mind.

Meanwhile, one of the first things any visitor will notice on arriving at Berlin Hauptbahnhof is the curious lack of any connection to the U-Bahn system. Same story, strangely enough, at both Tegel and Schönefeld airports. For all the vague sense of completion, it's clear that this puzzle of a city just ain't quite finished yet.

ABOUT TIME OUT CITY GUIDES

The seventh edition of *Time Out Berlin* is one of an expanding series of around 50 Time Out guides produced by the people behind the successful listings magazines in London, New York, Chicago and other cities around the globe. Our guides are all written by resident experts who have striven to provide you with all the most up-to-date information you'll need to explore the city or read up on its background, whether you're a local or a first-time visitor.

THE LOWDOWN ON THE LISTINGS

Above all, we've tried to make this book as useful as possible. Telephone numbers, websites, transport information, opening times, admission prices and credit card details are included in our listings. And we've given details on facilities, services and events, all checked and correct at press time. However, owners and managers can change their policies with little notice. Before you go out of your way, we strongly advise you to call and check opening times, dates of exhibitions and other particulars. While every effort has been made to ensure the accuracy of the information in this guide, the publishers cannot accept responsibility for any errors it may contain.

PRICES AND PAYMENT

Our listings detail the major credit cards – American Express (AmEx), Diners Club (DC), Discover (Disc), MasterCard (MC) and Visa (V) – taken by each venue. Many will also accept travellers' cheques issued by a major financial institution, such as American Express.

The prices we've supplied should be treated as guidelines, not gospel. Fluctuating exchange rates and inflation can cause prices to change rapidly, especially in shops and restaurants. If costs vary wildly from those we've quoted, then ask whether there's a good reason – and please email us to let us know. We aim to give the best and most up-to-date advice, so we always want to know if you've been badly treated or overcharged.

The *Arkaden* near **Potsdamer Platz**.
See p102.

THE LIE OF THE LAND

Berlin is a big, sprawling city. For ease of use, we've split many chapters of this guide into districts. The first page of each sightseeing chapter contains a small locator map, so you can see how each area relates to those around it, and then there is a larger overview map of Berlin's *Bezirke*, or boroughs, on page 320.

The back of this book also includes street maps of inner Berlin, with enlarged maps of those areas most densely packed with things to see and do. The street maps start on page 300, and now pinpoint the specific locations of hotels (❶), restaurants (❶), and cafés and bars (❶). The majority of addresses fall into the area we've mapped, and we've given map references to make them easier to find.

TELEPHONE NUMBERS

The code for Berlin is 030, dialled before the relevant number when calling from within Germany. From abroad, you need to dial the international access code followed by 49 for Germany, 30 for Berlin and then the number itself. For more on telephones, *see p283*.

LANGUAGE

Many Berliners, especially younger ones, speak some English, but you can't assume you will be understood. A few basic German phrases go a long way, and you'll find some on page 286, plus some help with restaurant menus on page 134.

ESSENTIAL INFORMATION

For any practical information you might need for visiting the city, including visa and customs information, disabled access, emergency telephone numbers, a list of useful websites and the ins and outs of the local transport network, see the Directory (*pp270-289*) at the back of this guide.

LET US KNOW WHAT YOU THINK

We hope you enjoy *Time Out Berlin*, and we'd like to know what you think of it. We welcome tips for places that you believe we should include in future editions and appreciate your feedback on our choices. Please e-mail us at guides@timeout.com.

There is an online version of this book, along with guides to over 100 other international cities, at **www.timeout.com**.

In Context

Reichstag. *See p101.*

Ruins

History

From swampland to sin city in seven easy centuries.

Berlin's origins are neither remarkable nor auspicious. A settlement emerged sometime in the 12th century on swamplands that German knights had wrested from the Slavs. The name Berlin is believed to be derived from the Slav word *birl*, meaning 'swamp'.

Facing off across the Spree river, Berlin and its twin settlement Cölln (on what is now the Museumsinsel) were founded as trading posts halfway between the older fortress towns of Spandau and Köpenick. Today the borough of Mitte embraces Cölln and old Berlin, and Spandau and Köpenick are outlying suburbs. The town's existence was first recorded in 1237, when Cölln was mentioned in a church document. In the same century, construction began on the Marienkirche and Nikolaikirche, both of which still stand (for both, *see p89*).

The Ascanian family, as Margraves of Brandenburg, ruled over the twin towns and the surrounding region. To encourage trade, they granted special rights to merchants, with the result that Berlin and Cölln emerged as prosperous trading centres linking east and west . In 1307 the towns were officially united.

Early years of prosperity came to an end in 1319 with the death of the last Ascanian ruler. This opened the way for robber barons from outlying regions, eager to take control of Berlin. But, despite political upheaval and the threat of invasion, Berlin's merchants continued business. In 1359 the city joined the Hanseatic League of free-trading northern European cities.

BRUTAL BROTHERS

But the threat of invasion remained. In the late 14th century two powerful families, the Dukes of Pomerania and the brutal von Quitzow brothers, began to vie for control of the city.

Salvation came with Friedrich of Hohenzollern, a nobleman from southern Germany sent by the Holy Roman Emperor in 1411 to bring peace to the region. Initially, Friedrich was well received. The bells of the Marienkirche were melted down and made into weapons for the fight against the aggressors. (Echoing this event, the Marienkirche bells were again transformed into tools of war in 1917, during the reign of Kaiser Wilhelm II, the last of the Hohenzollerns to rule.)

Having defeated the von Quitzow brothers, Friedrich officially became Margrave. In 1416 he took the further title of Elector of Brandenburg, denoting his right to vote in the election of the Holy Roman Emperor – titular head of the German-speaking states.

Gradually, Berlin was transformed from an outlying trading post to a small-sized capital (in 1450 the population was 6,000). In 1442 foundations were laid for Berlin Castle and a royal court was established.

With peace and stability came the loss of independent traditions, as Friedrich consolidated power. Disputes rose between the patrician classes (representing trade) and the guilds (which represented crafts). Rising social friction culminated in the 'Berlin Indignation' of 1447-8 when the population rose up in rebellion. Friedrich's son, Friedrich II, and his courtiers were locked out of the city and the foundations of the castle were flooded, but it was only months before the uprising collapsed and the Hohenzollerns returned triumphant. Merchants faced new restrictions and the city lost economic impetus.

REFORMATION AND UNREFORMABLE

The Reformation arrived in Berlin and Brandenburg under the reign of Joachim I Nestor (1535-71), the first Elector to embrace Protestantism. Joachim strove to improve the cultural standing of Berlin by inviting artists, architects and theologians to work in the city.

In 1538 Caspar Theyss and Konrad Krebbs, two master builders from Saxony, began work on a Renaissance-style palace. The building took 100 years to complete, and evolved into the bombastic Stadtschloss, which stood on what is now Museumsinsel in the Spree until the East German government demolished it in 1950.

Joachim's studious nature was not reflected in the self-indulgent behaviour of his subjects. Attempts to clamp down on drinking, gambling and loose morals had little effect. Visiting the city, Abbot Trittenheim remarked that 'the people are good, but rough and unpolished; they prefer stuffing themselves to good science'.

After stuffing itself with another 6,000 people, Berlin left the 16th century with a population of 12,000.

THE THIRTY YEARS WAR

The outbreak of the Thirty Years War in 1618 dragged Berlin on to the wider political stage. Although initially unaffected by the conflict between Catholic forces loyal to the Holy Roman Empire and the Swedish-backed Protestant armies, Berlin was eventually caught up in the war, which left the German-speaking states ravaged and divided for two centuries.

In 1626 imperial troops occupied Berlin and plundered the city. Berliners were soon forced to pay special taxes to the occupying forces. Trade collapsed and the city's hinterland was laid waste. To top it all, there were four serious epidemics between 1626 and 1631 which killed thousands. By the end of the war in 1648, Berlin had lost a third of its housing and the population had fallen to less than 6,000.

RECONSTRUCTION AND REFUGEES

Painstaking reconstruction was carried out under Friedrich Wilhelm, 'the Great Elector'. He succeeded his father in 1640, but sat out the war in exile. Influenced by Dutch ideas on town planning and architecture (he was married to a Princess of Orange), Wilhelm embarked on a policy that linked urban regeneration, economic expansion and solid defence.

New fortifications were built around the city, and a garrison of 2,000 soldiers established as Friedrich expanded his 'Residenzstadt'. In the centre of town, the Lustgarten was laid out opposite the Stadtschloss. Running west from the palace, the first Lindenallee ('Avenue of Lime Trees' or *Unter den Linden*) was created.

To revive the economy, housing and property taxes were abolished in favour of a sales tax. With the money raised, three new towns were built – Friedrichswerder, Dorotheenstadt and Friedrichstadt. (Together with Berlin and Cölln, these now form the district of Mitte.) In the 1660s a canal was constructed linking the Spree and Oder rivers, establishing Berlin as an east–west trading centre.

But Friedrich Wilhelm's most inspired policy was to encourage refugees to settle. First to arrive were over 50 Jewish families from Vienna. In 1672 Huguenot settlers arrived from France. Both groups brought new skills to Berlin.

The growing cosmopolitan mix laid the foundations for a flowering of intellectual and artistic life. By the time the Great Elector's son Friedrich III took the throne in 1688, one in five Berliners spoke French. Today French words still pepper Berlin dialect, among them *boulette* ('hamburger') and *étage* ('floor').

In 1695 work commenced on Schloss Charlottenburg (*see p110*) west of Berlin. A year later the Academy of Arts was founded and, in 1700, the Academy of Sciences. The building of the Französischer Dom and Deutscher Dom (for both, *see p83*), at Gendarmenmarkt in 1701 gave Berlin one of its loveliest squares. Five years later the Zeughaus ('Armoury'), now housing the Deutsches Historisches Museum (*see p79*), was completed on Unter den Linden.

In 1701 Elector Friedrich III had himself crowned Prussian King Friedrich I (not to be confused with the earlier Elector).

Frederick
the Great.

COLLECTING SOLDIERS

The common association of Prussia with
militarism can broadly be traced back to the
18th century and the efforts of two men in
particular: King Friedrich Wilhelm I and his son
Friedrich II (also known as Frederick the Great).
Although father and son hated each other, and
had different sensibilities (Friedrich Wilhelm
was boorish and mean, Friedrich II sensitive
and philosophical), together they launched
Prussia as a major military power and gave
Berlin the character of a garrison city.

King Friedrich Wilhelm I (1713-40) made
parsimony and militarism state policy – and
almost succeeded in driving Berlin's economy
into the ground. The only thing that grew was
the army, which by 1740 numbered 80,000
troops. Many of these were deployed in Berlin
and billeted in the houses of ordinary citizens.

With a king more interested in keeping the
books than in reading them, intellectual life
began to suffer. Friedrich Wilhelm had no use
for art, so he closed down the Academy of Arts;
instead he collected soldiers, and swapped a
collection of oriental vases for one of the King
of Saxony's regiments. The Tsar, meanwhile,
received a small gold ship in exchange for
150 Russian giants.

But the obsession with all things military did
have some positive effects. The King needed
competent soldiers, so he made school
compulsory; the army needed doctors, so he
set up medical institutes. Berlin's economy
also picked up on the back of demand from the
military. Skilled immigrants arrived (mostly
from Saxony) to meet the increased demand.
The result was a population boom – from
60,000 in 1713 to 90,000 in 1740 – and a
growth in trade.

FREDERICK THE GREAT

While his father collected soldiers, Frederick
the Great (Friedrich II) deployed them – in a
series of wars with Austria and Russia (1740-
42, 1744-5 and 1756-63; the last known as the
Seven Years War) in a bid to win territory in
Silesia in the east. Initially, the wars proved
disastrous. The Austrians occupied Berlin in
1757, the Russians in 1760. However, thanks to
a mixture of good fortune and military genius,
Frederick finally emerged victorious from the
Seven Years War.

When not fighting, the King devoted his time
to forging a modern state apparatus (he styled
himself 'first servant of the state'; Berliners
called him 'Old Fritz') and transforming Berlin
and Potsdam. This was achieved partly through
conviction – the King was friends with Voltaire
and saw himself as an aesthetically minded
Enlightenment figure – but it was also a
political necessity. He needed to convince
enemies and subjects that even in times of
crisis he was able to afford grand projects.

So Unter den Linden was transformed into
a grand boulevard. At the palace end,
the Forum Fredericianum, designed and
constructed by the architect von Knobelsdorff,
comprised the Staatsoper (*see p234*), Sankt-
Hedwigs-Kathedrale (*see p79*), Prince Heinrich
Palace (now housing Humboldt-Universität;
see p283) and the Staatsbibliotek (*see p278*).
Although it was never completed, the Forum
is still one of Berlin's main attractions.

> ## 'Although father and son hated each other, together they launched Prussia as a major military power.'

To the west of Berlin, the Tiergarten was
landscaped and a new palace, Schloss Bellevue
(now the official residence of the German
president), built. Frederick also replaced a set
of barracks at Gendarmenmarkt with a theatre,
now called the Konzerthaus (*see p234*).

To encourage manufacturing and industry
(particularly textiles), advantageous excise
laws were introduced. Businesses such as
the KPM (Königliche Porzellan-Manufaktur)
porcelain works were nationalised and turned
into prestigious and lucrative enterprises.

Legal and administrative reforms also
characterised Frederick's reign. Religious
freedom was enshrined in law, torture was
abolished and Berlin became a centre of the
Enlightenment. Cultural and intellectual life
blossomed around figures such as philosopher
Moses Mendelssohn and poet Gottfried Lessing.

Borsig Werke. *See p14.*

By the time Frederick died in 1786, Berlin had a population of 150,000 and was the capital of one of Europe's great powers.

A DEBT TO ARCHITECTURE

The death of Frederick the Great also marked the end of the Enlightenment in Prussia. His successor, Friedrich Wilhelm II, was more interested in spending money on classical architecture than wasting time on political philosophy. Censorship was stepped up and the King's extravagance plunged the state into an economic crisis. By 1788 14,000 Berliners were dependent on state and church aid. The state apparatus crumbled under the weight of greedy administrators. When he died in 1797 Friedrich Wilhelm II left his son with huge debts.

However, the old King's love of classicism left Berlin with its most famous monument: the Brandenburger Tor (Brandenburg Gate; *see p76*). It was built by Karl Gottfried Langhans in 1789, the year of the French Revolution, and modelled on the Propylaea in Athens. Two years later, Johann Schadow added the Quadriga, a sculpture of Victoria riding a chariot drawn by four horses. Originally one of 14 gates, the Brandenburger Tor is now the geographical and symbolic centre of the city.

If the King did not care for intellect, then the emerging bourgeoisie did. Towards the turn of the century, Berlin became a centre of German Romanticism. Literary salons flourished; they were to remain a feature of Berlin's cultural life into the middle of the 19th century.

Despite censorship, Berlin still had a platform for liberal expression. The city's newspapers welcomed the French Revolution so enthusiastically that in the southern German states Jacobins were referred to as 'Berliners'.

THE NAPOLEONIC WARS

In 1806 Berlin came face to face with the effects of revolution in France: following the defeat of the Prussian forces in the battles of Jena and Auerstadt on 14 October, Napoleon's army headed for Berlin. The King and Queen fled to Königsberg and the garrison was removed from the city. On 27 October Napoleon and his army marched through the Brandenburger Tor. Once again, Berlin was an occupied city.

Napoleon set about changing the political and administrative structure. He called together 2,000 prominent citizens and told them to elect a new administration ('the *Comité Administratif*'), which oversaw the city's administration until the French troops left in 1808. Napoleon then decreed that property belonging to the state, the Hohenzollerns and many aristocratic families be expropriated. Priceless works of art were removed from palaces in Berlin and Potsdam and sent to France. Even the Quadriga was taken from the Brandenburg Gate and shipped to Paris, earning Napoleon the nickname *Pferdedieb* – 'horse thief'. At the same time, the city was hit by crippling war reparations.

When the French left, a group of energetic, reform-minded aristocrats, grouped around Baron vom Stein, introduced a series of reforms in a bid to modernise the moribund Prussian state. One key aspect was the clear separation of state and civic responsibility, which gave Berlin independence to manage its own affairs. A new council was elected (though only property owners and the wealthy were entitled to vote). In 1810 the philosopher Wilhelm von Humboldt founded the university. All remaining restrictions on the city's Jews were removed. Generals Scharnhorst and Gneisenau completely overhauled the army.

Although the French occupied Berlin again in 1812 on their way home from the disastrous Russian campaign, this time they were met with stiff resistance. A year later the Prussian King finally joined the anti-Napoleon coalition and thousands of Berliners signed up to fight. Napoleon was defeated at nearby Grossbeeren. This, together with a subsequent defeat in the Battle of Leipzig, marked the end of Napoleonic rule in Germany.

In August 1814 General Blücher brought the Quadriga back to Berlin, restoring it to its place on the Brandenburg Gate with one symbolic addition: an Iron Cross and Prussian eagle were added to the staff in Victoria's hand.

POLICE AND THINKERS

The burst of reform initiated in 1810 was short-lived. Following the Congress of Vienna (1814-15), which established a new order for post-Napoleonic Europe, King Friedrich Wilhelm III reneged on promises of constitutional reform. Instead of a greater unity among the German states, a loose alliance came into being; dominated by Austria, the German Confederation was distinctly anti-liberal.

In Prussia state power increased. Alongside the normal police, a secret service and a vice squad were established. The police president even had the power to issue directives to the city council. Book and newspaper censorship increased and the authorities sacked von Humboldt from the university he had created.

Otto von Bismarck. *See p15.*

With their hopes for change frustrated, the bourgeoisie withdrew to their salons. It is one of the ironies of this time that, although political opposition was quashed, a vibrant cultural movement flourished. Academics like Hegel and Ranke lectured at the university and enhanced Berlin's reputation as an intellectual centre.

The period became known as Biedermeier, after a fictional character embodying bourgeois taste, created by Swabian comic writer Ludwig Eichrodt. Another legacy of this period is the range of neo-classical buildings designed by Schinkel, such as his Altes Museum (*see p80*) and the Neue Wache (*see p78*).

For the majority, however, the post-Napoleonic era was a period of frustrated hopes and bitter poverty. Industrialisation swelled the ranks of the working class. Between 1810 and 1840 the city's population doubled to 400,000. But most of the newcomers lived in conditions that would later lead to riot and revolution.

THE INDUSTRIAL REVOLUTION

Prussia was ideally equipped for the industrial age. By the 19th century it had grown dramatically and boasted one of the greatest abundances of raw materials in Europe.

It was the founding of the Borsig Werke on Chausseestrasse in 1837 that established Berlin as the workshop of continental Europe. August Borsig was Berlin's first big industrialist. His factories turned out locomotives for the new Berlin-to-Potsdam railway, which opened in 1838. Borsig also left his mark through the establishment of a suburb (Borsigwalde) that still carries his name.

The other great pioneering industrialist, Werner Siemens, set up his electrical engineering firm in a house by Anhalter Bahnhof. The first European to produce telegraph equipment, Siemens personified the German industrial ideal, with his mix of technical genius and business savvy. And to house its workers, the Siemens company also added a new suburb, Siemensstadt, to the city.

THE PEOPLE V FRIEDRICH WILHELM

Friedrich Wilhelm IV's accession to the throne in 1840 raised hopes of an end to repression; and, initially, he did appear to share the desire for real change. He declared an amnesty for political prisoners, relaxed censorship, sacked the hated justice minister and granted asylum to refugees.

Political debate thrived in coffeehouses and wine bars. The university was another focal point for discussion. In the late 1830s Karl Marx spent a term there, just missing fellow alumnus Otto von Bismarck. In the early 1840s Friedrich Engels came to Berlin to do his military service.

The thaw didn't last long. It soon became clear that Friedrich Wilhelm IV shared his father's opposition to constitutional reform. Living and working conditions worsened for the majority of Berliners. Rapid industrialisation brought sweatshops, 17-hour days and child labour. Poor conditions were compounded in 1844 by harvest failure. Food riots broke out on Gendarmenmarkt, when a crowd stormed the market stalls.

Things came to a head in 1848, the year of revolutions. Berliners seized the moment. Political meetings were held in beer gardens and in the Tiergarten, and demands made for internal reform and a unification of German-speaking states. After one demonstration in the Tiergarten, there was a running battle between police and demonstrators on Unter den Linden.

On 18 March the King finally conceded to allowing a new parliament, and made vague promises about other reforms. Later that day, the crowd of 10,000 that gathered to celebrate the victory were set upon by soldiers. Shots were fired and the revolution began. Barricades went up throughout central Berlin and demonstrators fought with police for 14 hours. Finally, the King backed down for a second time. In exchange for the dismantling of barricades, he ordered his troops out of Berlin. Days later, he took part in the funeral service for the 'March Dead' – 183 revolutionaries who had been killed – and promised more freedoms.

Berlin was now ostensibly in the hands of the revolutionaries. A Civil Guard patrolled the city and the King rode through the streets wearing the revolutionary colours (black, red and gold), seeming to embrace liberalism and nationalism. Prussia, he said, should 'merge into Germany'.

But the revolution proved short-lived. When pressed on unification, the King merely suggested that the other German states send representatives to the Prussian National Assembly, an offer that was rebuffed.

Leading liberals instead convened a German National Assembly in Frankfurt in May 1848, while a new Prussian Assembly met in what is now the Konzerthaus (*see p234*) to debate a new constitution. At the end of 1848 reforming fervour took over Berlin.

THE BACKLASH

Winter, however, brought a change of mood. Using continuing street violence as the pretext, the King ordered the National Assembly to be moved to Brandenburg. In early November, he brought troops back into Berlin and declared a state of siege. Press freedom was once again restricted. The Civil Guard and National Assembly were dissolved. On 5 December the

King delivered his final blow by unveiling a new constitution fashioned to his own tastes.

Throughout the winter of 1848-9 thousands of liberals were arrested or expelled. A new city constitution, drawn up in 1850, reduced the number of eligible voters to five per cent of the population. The police president became more powerful than the mayor.

By 1857 Friedrich Wilhelm had gone senile. His brother Wilhelm acted as regent until becoming King on Friedrich's death in 1861.

'Shots were fired and the revolution began. Barricades went up throughout Berlin.'

Once again, the people's hopes were raised: the new monarch began his reign by appointing liberals to the cabinet. The building of the Rotes Rathaus ('Red Town Hall') gave the city council a headquarters to match the size of the royal palace. Completed in 1869, the Rathaus was named for the colour of its bricks, not (yet) the political persuasion of its members.

But by 1861 the King was locked in a dispute with parliament over proposed army reforms. He wanted to strengthen his control of the armed forces. Parliament refused, so the King went over its members' heads and appointed a new prime minister: Otto von Bismarck.

THE IRON CHANCELLOR

An arrogant genius who began his career as a diplomat, Bismarck was well able to deal with unruly parliamentarians. Using a constitutional loophole to rule against the majority, he quickly pushed through the army reforms. Extra-parliamentary opposition was dealt with in the usual manner: oppression and censorship. Dissension thus suppressed, Bismarck turned his mind to German unification.

Unlike the bourgeois revolutionaries of 1848, who desired a Germany united by popular will and endowed with political reforms, Bismarck strove to bring the states together under the authoritarian dominance of Prussia. His methods involved astute foreign policy and outright aggression.

Wars against Denmark (1864) and Austria (1866) brought post-Napoleonic order to an abrupt end. Prussia was no longer the smallest Great Power, but an initiator of geopolitical change. Austria's defeat confirmed Prussia's primacy among German-speaking states. Victory on the battlefield boosted Bismarck's popularity across Prussia – but not in Berlin itself. He was defeated in his constituency in the 1867 election to the new North German League. This was a Prussian-dominated body, linking

Beauty and the bust

The most famous pre-modern work of art, the most exactly proportioned human face in history, the best-preserved treasure of the ancient world – there's no shortage of superlatives surrounding the **bust of Queen Nefertiti**, now on display in the Altes Museum (*see p80*). The extraordinary artefact's modern story is intimately linked with the history of Berlin, making its survival over the last few decades even more of a miracle than the three millennia it persevered under Egyptian sands.

When immortalised at the age of 30, Nefertiti was so seductive she only had to sing and sway a little to get the sun god Aten to rise every morning. That was the story 3,300 years ago, shortly after Nefertiti's husband Akhenaten introduced a revolutionary, monotheistic religion based on light and love. She was probably the world's original sex goddess, presiding over a cult of femininity rather than fertility. Tuthmose, the court sculptor at Akhenaten's city of al-Amarna, did a brisk business selling small plaster images of Nefertiti.

The Berlin bust represents the apex of German archaeology. It was discovered by Ludwig Borchardt, digging at Tuthmose's workshop in 1912. At the time the Germans were preparing for war and trailing both the French and British in the ancient treasure stakes. The digs at al-Amarna put them spectacularly back in the running, some 42 years after Heinrich Schliemann uncovered Troy.

Borchardt sent the bust back to Berlin as part of a trove from Amarna, and James Simon, the cotton trader who had financed the expedition, took Nefertiti as his cut. It was temporarily exhibited in 1913, causing a sensation. The Egyptians immediately began a campaign to get her back. Simon kept the bust at home during World War I, then donated it to Berlin's original Egyptian museum on Museumsinsel in Mitte, where it was on display until 1939.

Hitler wanted Nefertiti enshrined in a new museum to be built in his grandiose fantasy world capital, Germania. So the Nazis hid her away in the vault of the Reichsbank. The bust was transferred to a flak bunker at the Zoo Station as another war approached, and then wound up in a salt mine in the Harz Mountains. There it was eventually discovered by an American army officer. He kept it in Wiesbaden instead of shipping it back to America, and in 1956 the bust was sent back to West Berlin.

Nefertiti was now displayed in the then new Dahlem museum complex. Her 'discovery' caused another sensation, and another hapless bid by the Egyptians; this time they offered to trade the staff lost by German Field Marshall Rommel in North Africa. With Museumsinsel at that time on the other side of the Wall, the bust was eventually housed in a new Egyptian museum across from Schloss Charlottenburg. Already a lot of coming and going for a woman whose name, curiously, means 'the beautiful one has arrived'. But in the summer of 2005 Nefertiti returned to Mitte for the first time since she was spirited away during the war.

the northern states, and a stepping stone towards Germany's overall unification.

Bismarck's third war – against France in 1870 – revealed his scope for intrigue and opportunism. He exploited a dispute over the Spanish succession to provoke France into declaring war on Prussia. Citing the North German League and treaties signed with the southern German states, Bismarck brought together a united German army under Prussian leadership.

> ## 'Bismarck's war against France revealed his scope for intrigue and opportunism.'

Following the defeat of the French army on 2 September, Bismarck turned a unified military into the basis for a unified nation. The Prussian king would be German emperor: beneath him would be four kings, 18 grand dukes and assorted princes from the German states, which would retain some regional powers. (This arrangement formed the basis for the modern federal system of regional *Länder*.)

On 18 January 1871 King Wilhelm was proclaimed German Kaiser ('Emperor') in the Hall of Mirrors in Versailles. In just nine years, Bismarck had united Germany and forged an empire that dominated central Europe. The political, economic and social centre of this new creation was Berlin.

IMPERIAL BERLIN

The coming of empire threw Berlin into its greatest period of expansion and change. The economic boom (helped by five billion gold francs extracted from France as war reparations) led to a wave of speculation. Farmers in Wilmersdorf and Schöneberg became millionaires overnight as they sold off their fields to developers.

During the decades following German unification, Berlin emerged as Europe's most modern metropolis. This period was dubbed the Gründerzeit ('Foundation Years') and was marked by a move away from traditional Prussian values of thrift and modesty, towards the gaudy and bombastic. The change of mood manifested itself in monuments and buildings. The Reichstag (*see p101*), the Kaiser-Wilhelm-Gedächtniskirche (*see p109*), the Siegessäule ('Victory Column'; *see p102*) and the Berliner Dom (*see p80*) were all built in this period.

Superficially, the Reichstag (designed by Paul Wallot, and completed in 1894) represented a commitment to parliamentary democracy. But in reality Germany was still in the grip of conservative, backward-looking forces. The authoritarian power of the Kaiser remained intact, as was demonstrated by the decision of Wilhelm II to sack Bismarck in 1890 following disagreements over policy.

SEEING RED

When Bismarck began his premiership in 1861 his offices on Wilhelmstrasse overlooked potato fields. By the time he lost his job in 1890 they

The Reichstag.

were in the centre of Europe's most congested city. Economic boom and growing political and social importance attracted hundreds of thousands of new inhabitants. At unification in 1871 820,000 people lived in Berlin; by 1890 this number had nearly doubled.

The working class was shoehorned into tenements – *Mietskasernen*, 'rental barracks' – that sprouted across the city, particularly in Kreuzberg, Wedding and Prenzlauer Berg. Poorly ventilated and overcrowded, the *Mietskasernen* (many of which still stand) became a breeding ground for unrest.

The Social Democratic Party (SPD), founded in 1869, quickly became the voice for the city's have-nots. In the 1877 general election it won 40 per cent of the Berlin vote. Here was born the left-wing reputation of *Rotes Berlin* ('Red Berlin') that has persisted to the present day.

In 1878 two assassination attempts on the Kaiser gave Bismarck an excuse to classify socialists as enemies of the state. He introduced restrictive laws to ban the SPD and other progressive parties. The ban lasted until 1890 – the year of Bismarck's sacking – but did not stem support for the SPD. In the 1890 general election, the SPD dominated the vote in Berlin; in 1912 it won more than 70 per cent of the vote, becoming the largest party in the Reichstag.

KAISER BILL

Famed for his ridiculous moustache, Kaiser Wilhelm II came to the throne in 1888, and soon came to personify the new Germany: bombastic, awkward and unpredictable. Like his grandmother Queen Victoria, he gave his name to an era. Wilhelm's epoch is associated with showy militarism and foreign policy bungles leading to a world war that cost the Kaiser his throne and Germany its stability.

The Wilhelmine years were also notable for the explosive growth of Berlin (the population rose to four million by 1914) and a blossoming of cultural and intellectual life. The Bode Museum (*see p80*) was built in 1904. In 1912 work began next door on the Pergamonmuseum (*see p81*) while a new Opera House was unveiled in Charlottenburg (later destroyed in World War II; the Deutsche Oper now stands on the site; *see p234*). Expressionism took off in 1910 and the Kurfürstendamm filled with galleries – Paris was still Europe's art capital, but Berlin was catching up. By Wilhelm's abdication in 1918, Berlin had become a centre of scientific and intellectual development. Six Berlin scientists, including Einstein and Max Planck, were awarded the Nobel Prize.

In the years immediately preceding World War I, Berlin appeared to be loosening its stiff collar of pomposity. The tango became all the rage in new clubs around Friedrichstrasse – though the Kaiser banned officers in uniform from joining in the fun. Yet, despite the progressive changes, growing militarism and international tension overshadowed the period.

By 1914 Europe was armed to the teeth and ready to tear itself apart. In June, the assassination of Archduke Franz Ferdinand provided the excuse. On 1 August Germany declared war on Russia, and the Kaiser appeared on a balcony of the royal palace to tell a jubilant crowd that from that moment onwards, he would recognise no parties – only Germans. At the Reichstag the deputies, who had near unanimously voted for war, agreed.

WORLD WAR I AND REVOLUTION

No one was prepared for the disaster to come. After Bismarck, the Germans had come to expect quick, sweeping victories. The armies on the Western Front settled into their trenches for a war of attrition that would cost over a million German lives. Meanwhile, the civilian population had to adapt to austerity and shortages. After the 1917 harvest failed there were outbreaks of famine. Soon dog and cat meat started to appear on the menu in the capital's restaurants.

The SPD's initial enthusiasm for war evaporated, and in 1916 the party refused to pass the Berlin budget. A year later, members of the party's radical wing broke away to form the Spartacus League. Anti-war feeling was voiced in mass strikes in April 1917 and January 1918. These were brutally suppressed, but, when the Imperial Marines in Kiel mutinied on 2 November 1918, the authorities were no longer able to stop the anti-war movement.

> ## '*Mietskasernen* became a breeding-ground for unrest.'

The mutiny spread to Berlin, where members of the Guards Regiment came out against the war. On 9 November the Kaiser was forced into abdication and, later, exile. This date is weirdly layered with significance in German history: it's the anniversary of the establishment of the Weimar Republic (1918), the Kristallnacht pogrom (1938) and the fall of the Wall (1989).

It was on this day that Philip Scheidemann, a leading SPD member of parliament and key proponent of republicanism, broke off his lunch in the second-floor restaurant of the Reichstag. He walked to a window overlooking Königsplatz (now Platz der Republik) where a crowd had massed and declared: 'The old and the rotten have broken down. Long live the new! Long live the German Republic!'

At the other end of Unter den Linden, Karl Liebknecht, who co-led the Spartacus League with Rosa Luxemburg, declared Germany a socialist republic from a balcony of the occupied Stadtschloss. Liebknecht and the Spartacists wanted a communist Germany; Scheidemann and the SPD favoured a parliamentary democracy. Between them stood those still loyal to the vanished monarchy. All were prepared to fight; street battles ensued throughout the city.

It was in this climate of turmoil and violence that the Weimar Republic was born.

THE WEIMAR REPUBLIC
The revolution in Berlin may have brought peace to the Western Front, where hostilities were ended on 11 November, but in Germany it unleashed political terror and instability. Berlin's new masters, the SPD under Friedrich Ebert, ordered renegade battalions returning from the front (known as the Freikorps) to quash the Spartacists, who launched a concerted bid for power in January 1919.

Within days, the uprising was bloodily suppressed. Liebknecht and Luxemburg were arrested on 15 January, interrogated in a hotel near the Zoo, and then murdered by the Freikorps. A plaque marks the spot on the Liechtenstein Bridge from which Luxemburg's body was dumped into the Landwehr Canal.

Four days later, national elections returned the SPD as largest party: the Social Democrats' victory over the far left was complete. Berlin was deemed too dangerous for parliamentary business, so the government decamped to the provincial town of Weimar, which gave its name to the first German republic.

Germany's new constitution ended up being full of good liberal intentions, but riddled with technical flaws, and this left the country wide open to weak coalition government and quasi-dictatorial presidential rule.

Another crippling blow to the new republic was the Versailles Treaty, which set the terms of peace. Reparation payments (set to run until 1988) blew a hole in an already fragile economy. Support for the right-wing nationalist lobby was fuelled by the loss of territories in both east and west, and restrictions placed on the German military led some on the right to claim that Germany's soldiers had been 'stabbed in the back' by Jews and left-wingers.

In March 1920 a right-wing coup was staged in Berlin under the leadership of Wolfgang Kapp, a civil servant from east Prussia. The recently returned government once again fled the city. For four days Berlin was besieged by roaming Freikorps. Some had taken to adorning their helmets with a new symbol: the *Hakenkreuz* or swastika.

Ultimately, a general strike and the army's refusal to join Kapp brought an end to the putsch. But the political and economic chaos in the city remained. Political assassinations were commonplace, and food shortages lead to bouts of famine. Inflation started to escalate (*see p21* **Who wants to be a billionaire?**).

'Political assassinations were commonplace.'

There were two main reasons for the precipitate devaluation of the Reichsmark. To pay for the war, the desperate imperial government had resorted simply to printing more money, a policy continued by new republican rulers. The burden of reparations also led to an outflow of foreign currency.

In 1923 the French government sent troops into the Ruhr industrial region to take by force reparation goods that the German government said it could no longer afford to pay. The Communists planned an uprising in Berlin for October, but lost their nerve.

In November a young ex-corporal called Adolf Hitler, who led the tiny National Socialist Party (NSDAP or Nazi Party), launched an attempted coup from a Munich beerhall. He called for armed resistance to the French, an end to the 'dictatorship of Versailles' and punishment for those – especially the Jews – who had 'betrayed' Germany at the war's end.

Hitler's first attempt to seize power came to nothing. Instead of marching on Berlin, he went to prison. Inflation was finally brought down with the introduction of a new currency. But the overall decline of moral and social values that had taken place in the five years since 1918 was not so easy to reverse.

THE GOLDEN TWENTIES
Josef Goebbels came to Berlin in 1926 to take charge of the local Nazi Party organisation. On arriving, he noted: 'This city is a melting pot of everything that is evil – prostitution, drinking houses, cinemas, Marxism, Jews, strippers, negroes dancing and all the offshoots of modern art.' Omitting the word 'evil', Goebbels's description of 1920s Berlin was not far wrong. During that decade the city overtook Paris as continental Europe's arts and entertainment capital, and added its own decadent twist. 'We used to have a first-class army,' mused Klaus Mann, the author of *Mephisto*; 'now we have first-class perversions.'

By 1927 Berlin boasted more than 70 cabarets and nightclubs. While Brecht's *Dreigroschenoper* (*Threepenny Opera*) played at the Theater am Schiffbauerdamm, Berlin's

Dadaists gathered on Tauentzienstrasse at the Romanisches Café (later destroyed by bombing – the Europa-Center mall now stands on the site). There was a proliferation of avant-garde magazines focusing on new art and literature.

But the flipside of all the frenetic enjoyment was raw poverty and glaring social tension, reflected in the works of painters like George Grosz and Otto Dix. In the music halls, Brecht and Weill used a popular medium to ram home points about social injustices.

In architecture and design, the revolutionary ideas of the Bauhaus school in Dessau (it moved to Berlin in 1932, but was closed down by the Nazis a year later) were taking concrete form in projects such as the Shell House on the Landwehr Canal, the Siemensstadt new town, and the model housing project Hufeisensiedlung ('Horse Shoe Estate') in Britz.

STREET-FIGHTING YEARS

The Wall Street Crash and the onset of global depression in 1929 ushered in the brutal end of the Weimar Republic. The fractious coalition governments that had clung to power in the prosperous late 1920s were no match for rocketing unemployment and a surge in support for extremist parties.

By the end of 1929 nearly one in four Berliners were out of work. The city's streets became a battleground for clashes between Nazis, Communists and Social Democrats. Increasingly, the police relied on water cannon, armoured vehicles and guns to quell street fighting. One May Day demonstration left 30 dead and several hundred wounded. At Bülowplatz (now Rosa-Luxemburg-Platz), where the Communist Party (KPD) had its headquarters, there were regular battles between Communists, the police and Nazi stormtroopers (the SA). In August 1931 two police officers were murdered on Bülowplatz. One of those accused of the murders (and later found guilty, albeit by a Nazi court) was Erich Mielke, a young Communist, later to become the head of East Germany's secret police, the Stasi (see p30 **Stasiland**).

In 1932 the violence in Berlin reached crisis level. In one six-week period, 300 street battles left 70 people dead. In the general election in July the Nazis took 40 per cent of the vote and became the largest party in the Reichstag. Hermann Göring, one of Hitler's earliest followers and a wounded veteran of the beerhall putsch, was appointed Reichstag president.

But the prize of government still eluded the Nazis. At the elections held in November, the Nazis lost two million votes across Germany and 37,000 in Berlin, where the Communists emerged as the strongest party.

The election was held against the backdrop of a strike by some 20,000 transport employees protesting against planned wage cuts. The strike had been called by the Communists and the Nazis, who vied with each other to capture the mass vote and bring the Weimar Republic to an end. Under orders from Moscow, the KPD shunned all co-operation with the SPD, ending any possibility of a broad left-wing front.

As Berlin headed into another winter of depression, almost every third person was out of work. A city survey recorded that almost half of Berlin's inhabitants were living four to a room, and that a large proportion of the city's housing stock was unfit for human habitation. Berlin topped the European table of suicides.

'Watching the torchlight parade, Max Liebermann remarked: "I cannot eat as much as I'd like to puke."'

The new government of General Kurt von Schleicher ruled by presidential decree. Schleicher had promised President von Hindenburg that he could tame the Nazi Party into a coalition. When he failed, his rival Franz von Papen manoeuvred the Nazi leader into power. On 30 January 1933 Adolf Hitler was named chancellor.

That evening, the SA staged a torchlight parade through the Brandenburg Gate. Watching from the window of his house, the artist Max Liebermann remarked to his dinner guests: 'I cannot eat as much as I'd like to puke.'

HITLER TAKES POWER

The government Hitler now led was a coalition of Nazis and German nationalists, led by the media magnate Alfred Hugenberg. Together their votes fell just short of a parliamentary majority, so another election was called for March, while Hitler continued to rule by decree.

The last free election of the Republic was also the most violent. Open persecution of Communists began. The Nazis banned meetings of the KPD, shut down left-wing newspapers and broke up SPD election rallies.

On 27 February a fire broke out in the Reichstag. It was almost certainly started by the Nazis, who used it as an excuse to step up the persecution of opponents. Over 12,000 Communists were arrested. Spelling it out in a speech at the Sportspalast two days before the election, Goebbels said: 'It's not my job to practise justice, instead I have to destroy and exterminate – nothing else.'

The Nazis still didn't achieve an absolute majority (in Berlin they polled 34 per cent), but that didn't matter. With the support of his coalition allies, Hitler passed an Enabling Act that gave him dictatorial powers. By summer Germany had been declared a one-party state.

Already ad hoc concentration camps – known as 'brown houses' after the colour of SA uniforms – had sprung up around the city. The SS established itself in Prinz Albrecht Palais, where it was later joined by the secret police, the Gestapo. To the north of Berlin near Oranienburg, the Sachsenhausen concentration camp was set up.

Who wants to be a billionaire?

Of all the disasters that befell 20th-century Berlin, nothing was quite as mad as the hyperinflation of 1923. It wasn't a sudden catastrophe. The German government had been dallying with inflation for years, funding its war effort by printing bonds. In 1914 a dollar was buying 4.2 marks; by late 1922 it was buying 7,000. And then the French occupied the Ruhr and things got really out of hand. By 20 November 1923 the rate had reached a boggling 4,200,000,000,000 marks to the dollar.

Images of the crisis seem vaguely comic: children using bundles of notes as building blocks, a wheelbarrow of currency for a loaf of bread. At its height, over 300 paper mills and 2,000 printing presses worked around the clock to supply the Reichsbank with notes – in denominations of one million, then one billion, then a hundred billion. Some companies paid their employees twice a day, so they could shop at lunch to beat the afternoon inflation.

A little hard currency could buy anything or anyone. Foreign visitors splashed out in an orgy of conspicuous consumption. Entrepreneurs created whole business empires from ever cheaper marks. And the homes of peasants in nearby villages filled up with Meissen porcelain and fine furniture as Berliners traded valuables for eggs or bread.

Although it was absurd, it wasn't funny. People starved as all their possessions vanished. The suicide rate shot up, as did

infant mortality. Teenagers prostituted themselves after school, often with parental approval. Nothing made sense anymore. And as the simple fabric of everyday life was seen to unravel, so did people's faith in government. Among the worst hit were those who had most trusted the idea of Germany: the middle-class patriots who had sunk their money into war bonds, only to be paid back in useless paper.

The crisis was eventually brought under control, but the result had been a mass transfer of wealth to a handful of adventurers, big business and government. And as a pauperised people wondered who to blame, the hard right found a cause. Nothing prepared the ground for Hitler better than the literal and moral impoverishment of the inflationary period.

Currency issues would continue to rumble through Berlin's 20th century. The formal division of Germany and Berlin followed the introduction of zonal currencies in 1948. The destabilisation of the Ostmark was one factor behind the later decision to build the Wall. For the rest of the Cold War, foreign visitors whooping it up on hard currency once again became a feature of city life, at least in its Eastern half. The true end of the GDR came on the July 1990 day when the Ostmark was absorbed by its Western counterpart – at a one-to-one rate so unrealistic it promptly caused the collapse of East German industry. And now, of course, everyone's moaning about the euro.

Along the Kurfürstendamm squads of SA stormtroopers would go 'Jew baiting', and on 1 April 1933 the first boycott of Jewish shops began. A month later Goebbels, who became Minister for Propaganda, organised a book-burning, which took place in the courtyard of the university on Unter den Linden. Books by Jews or writers deemed degenerate or traitors were thrown on to a huge bonfire.

With their policy of *Gleichschaltung* ('co-ordination'), the Nazis began to control public life. Party membership became obligatory for doctors, lawyers, professors and journalists. Unemployment was tackled through public works programmes, conscription to an expanding military and by 'encouraging' women to leave the workplace.

'Books by Jews or writers deemed degenerate were thrown on a huge bonfire.'

During the Night of the Long Knives in July 1934, Hitler settled old scores with opponents within the SA and Nazi Party. At Lichterfelde barracks, officers of the SS shot and killed over 150 SA members. Hitler's predecessor as chancellor, General von Schleicher, was shot with his wife at their home in Wannsee.

After the death of President von Hindenburg in August, Hitler had himself named *Führer* ('Leader') and made the armed forces swear an oath of allegiance to him. It had taken the Nazis less than two years to subjugate Germany.

DEGENERATE VICTORIES

A brief respite came with the Olympic Games in August 1936. In a bid to persuade foreign spectators that all was well in the Reich, Goebbels ordered the removal of anti-Semitic slogans from shops. 'Undesirables' were moved out of the city, and the pavement display cases for the racist Nazi newspaper *Der Stürmer* (*The Stormtrooper*) were dismantled.

The Games, centred on the newly built Olympiastadion (*see p39* **The final stadium**), were not such a success for the Nazis. Instead of blond Aryans sweeping the field, Hitler had to watch the African-American Jesse Owens clock up medals and records. The Games did work, however, as a public relations exercise. Foreign visitors left with reports of a strident and healthy nation. Few stuck around to observe the reality of Hitler's rule.

As part of a nationwide campaign to cleanse cultural life of what the Nazis considered *Entartete Kunst* ('Degenerate Art'), works of modern art were collected and brought together in a touring exhibition designed to show the depth of depravity in contemporary ('Jewish-dominated') culture. But Nazi hopes that these 'degenerate' works would repulse the German people fell flat. When the exhibition arrived at the Zeughaus in early 1938, thousands queued for admission. People loved the paintings.

After the exhibition, the paintings were auctioned in Switzerland. Those that remained unsold were burnt in the fire station on Köpenicker Strasse. More than 5,000 paintings were destroyed.

TOTALITARIAN TOWN PLANNING

After taking power, Hitler ordered that the lime trees on Unter den Linden be chopped down to give the boulevard a cleaner, more sanitised form – the first step in Nazi urban planning.

Hitler's plans for the redesign of Berlin reflected the hatred the Nazis felt for the city. Hitler entrusted young architect Albert Speer with the job of recreating Berlin as a metropolis to 'out-trump Paris and Vienna'. The heart of old Berlin was to be demolished, and its small streets replaced by two highways stretching 37 kilometres (23 miles) from north to south and 50 kilometres (30 miles) from east to west.

Each axis would be 90 metres (295 feet) wide. Crowning the northern axis would be a domed Volkshalle ('People's Hall') nearly 300 metres (1,000 feet) high, with space for 150,000 people. Speer and Hitler also had grand plans for a triumphal arch three times the size of the Arc de Triomphe, and a Führer's Palace 150 times bigger than the one occupied by Bismarck. The new city was to be called Germania.

Little of this was to be built. Hitler's new Chancellery, completed in early 1939, went up in under a year – and was demolished after the war. On the proposed east–west axis, a small section around the Siegessäule was widened for Hitler's 50th birthday in April 1939.

A PEOPLE DESTROYED

Of the half-a-million Jews living in Germany in 1933, over a third were in Berlin. For centuries, the Jewish community had played an important role in Berlin's development, especially in financial, artistic and intellectual circles.

The Nazis wiped all this out in 12 years of persecution and murder. Arrests followed the boycotts and acts of intimidation. From 1933 to 1934 many of Berlin's Jews fled. Those who stayed were subjected to legislation (the 1935 Nuremberg Laws) that banned Jews from public office, forbade them to marry Aryan Germans and stripped them of citizenship. Jewish cemeteries were desecrated and the names of Jews chipped off war memorials.

Berlin businesses that had been owned by Jews – such as the Ullstein newspaper group

Adolf Hitler at the 1936 Olympics – at least no Jesse Owens in the swimming events.

and Tietz and Wertheim department stores – were 'Aryanised'. The Nazis expropriated them or forced owners to sell at absurdly low prices.

On 9 November 1938 'Kristallnacht', a wave of 'spontaneous' acts of vandalism and violence against Jews, was staged in response to the assassination of a German diplomat in Paris by a young Jewish émigré. Jewish properties across Berlin were stoned, looted and set ablaze. A total of 24 synagogues were set on fire. The Nazis rounded up 12,000 Jews and took them to Sachsenhausen concentration camp.

WORLD WAR II

Since 1935 Berliners had been taking part in air-raid drills, but it was not until the Sudeten crisis of 1938 that the possibility of war became real. At that juncture Hitler was able to get his way and persuade France and Britain to let him take over the German-speaking areas of northern Czechoslovakia.

But a year later, his plans to repeat the exercise in Poland were met with resistance in London and Paris. Following Germany's invasion of Poland on 1 September 1939, Britain and France declared war on the Reich.

Despite the propaganda and early victories, most Berliners were horrified by the war. The first air raids came with the RAF bombing of Pankow and Lichtenberg in early 1940.

In 1941, after the German invasion of the Soviet Union, the 75,000 Jews remaining in Berlin were required to wear a yellow Star of David and the first systematic deportations to concentration camps began. By the end of the war only 5,000 Jews remained in Berlin.

Notorious assembly points for the deportations were Putlitzstrasse in Wedding, Grosse Hamburger Strasse and Rosenstrasse in Mitte. On 20 January 1942 a meeting of the leaders of the various Nazi security organisations in the suburb of Wannsee agreed on a 'final solution' to the Jewish question. They joked and drank brandy as they sat around discussing mass murder.

The turning point in the war came with the surrender at Stalingrad on 31 January 1943. Looking for a positive spin on this crushing defeat, Goebbels held a rally in the Sportpalast where he announced that Germany was now in a state of 'total war'. By summer, women and children were being evacuated from Berlin; by the end of 1943, over 700,000 people had fled.

The Battle of Berlin, which the RAF launched in November 1943, reduced much of the city centre to rubble. Between then and February 1944 more than 10,000 tonnes of bombs were dropped on the city. Nearly 5,000 people were killed and around 250,000 made homeless.

In Context

THE JULY PLOT

On 20 July 1944 a group of officers, civil servants and former trade unionists launched a last-ditch attempt to assassinate Hitler. But Hitler survived the explosion of a bomb placed at his eastern command post in East Prussia by Colonel Count von Stauffenberg.

That evening Stauffenberg was killed by firing squad in the courtyard of army headquarters in Bendlerstrasse, now Stauffenbergstrasse. The other members of the plot were rounded up and put on trial at the People's Court near Kleistpark and subsequently executed at Plötzensee Prison.

In early January 1945 the Red Army launched a major offensive that carried it on to German soil. On 12 February the heaviest bombing raid yet on Berlin killed over 23,000 people in little more than an hour.

As the Red Army moved into Berlin's suburbs, Hitler celebrated his last birthday on 20 April in his bunker behind Wilhelmstrasse. Three days later Neukölln and Tempelhof fell. By 28 April Alexanderplatz and Hallesches Tor were in the hands of the Red Army.

The next day Hitler called his last war conference. He then married his companion Eva Braun and committed suicide with her the day after. As their bodies were being cremated by SS officers, a few streets away a red flag was raised over the Reichstag. The city officially surrendered on 2 May 1945. Germany's unconditional surrender was signed on 8 May at the Red Army command centre in Karlshorst, now the Museum Berlin-Karlshorst (*see p120*).

DEVASTATION AND DIVISION

When Bertolt Brecht returned to Berlin in 1948 he found 'a pile of rubble next to Potsdam'. Nearly a quarter of all buildings had been destroyed. The human cost of the war was as startling – around 80,000 Berliners had been killed, not including the thousands of Jews who would not return from the concentration camps.

There was no gas or electricity and only the suburbs had running water. Public transport had broken down. In the first weeks after capitulation, Red Army soldiers went on a rampage of looting, killing and rape. Thousands of men were transported to labour camps in the Soviet Union. Food supplies were used up and later the harvest failed in the land around the city. Come winter, the few remaining trees in the Tiergarten and other parks were chopped down for firewood.

Clearing the rubble was to take years of dull, painstaking work. The *Trümmerfrauen* ('rubble women') cleared the streets and created literal mountains of junk – like the Teufelsberg, one of seven hills that now exist as a result.

Airlift Memorial at Platz der Luftbrücke.

The Soviets stripped factories across Berlin as part of a programme to dismantle German industry and take it back home. As reparation, whole factories were moved to Russia.

Under the terms of the Yalta Agreement, which divided Germany into four zones of control, Berlin was also split into sectors, with the Soviets in the east and the Americans, British and French in the west. A Kommandatura, made up of each army's commander and based in the building of the People's Court in Kleistpark, dealt with the administration of the city.

Initially, the administration worked well in getting basics such as public transport back in running order. But tensions between the Soviets and the Western Allies began to rise as civilian government of city affairs returned. In the Eastern sector a merger of the Communist and Social Democratic parties (both refounded in summer 1945) was pushed to form the Socialist Unity Party (SED). In the Western sector, the SPD continued as a separate party.

Events came to a head after elections for a new city government in 1946. The SED failed to get more than 20 per cent of the vote, while the SPD won nearly 50 per cent of all votes cast. The Soviets vetoed the appointment of the SPD's mayoral candidate, Ernst Reuter, a committed anti-Communist.

THE BERLIN AIRLIFT

The situation worsened in spring 1948. In response to the decision by the Western Allies to merge their respective zones in Germany into one administrative entity and introduce a new currency, the Soviets walked out of the Kommandatura. In late June all transport links to West Berlin were cut off and Soviet forces began a blockade of the city. Three 'air corridors' linking West Berlin with western Germany became lifelines as Allied aircraft transported food, coal and industrial components to the beleaguered city.

Within Berlin the future division of the city began to take permanent shape as city councillors from the West were drummed out of the town hall. They moved to Rathaus Schöneberg in the West. Fresh elections in the Western sector returned Reuter as mayor. The Freie Universität was set up in response to Communist dominance of the Humboldt-Universität in the East.

Having failed to starve West Berlin into submission, the Soviets called off the blockade after 11 months. The blockade also convinced the Western Allies that they should maintain a presence in Berlin and that their sectors of the city should be linked with the Federal Republic, founded in May 1949. The response from the East was the founding of the German Democratic Republic on 7 October. With the birth of the 'first Workers' and Peasants' State on German soil', the formal division of Germany into two states was complete.

THE COLD WAR

During the Cold War, Berlin was the focal point for stand-offs between the United States and the Soviet Union. Far from having any control over its own affairs, the city was wholly at the mercy of geopolitical developments. Throughout the 1950s the 'Berlin Question' remained prominent on the international agenda.

Technically, the city was still under Four-Power control, but since the Soviet departure from the Kommandatura, and the setting up of the German Democratic Republic with its capital in East Berlin (a breach of the wartime agreement on the future of the city), this counted for little in practice.

In principle, the Western Allies adhered to these agreements by retaining ultimate authority in West Berlin, while letting the city integrate into the West German system. (There were exceptions, such as the exemption of West Berliners from conscription, and the barring of city MPs from voting in the West German parliament.) Throughout the 1950s the two halves of Berlin began to develop separately as the political systems in East and West evolved.

In the East, Communist leader Walter Ulbricht set about creating Moscow's most hardline ally in eastern Europe. Work began on a Moscow-style boulevard – called Stalinallee – running east from Alexanderplatz. Industry was nationalised and subjected to rigid central planning. Opposition was kept in check by the new Ministry for State Security: the Stasi (*see p30* **Stasiland**).

West Berlin landed the role of 'Last Outpost of the Free World' and, as such, was developed into a showcase for capitalism. As well as the Marshall Plan, which paid for much of the reconstruction of West Germany, the US poured millions of dollars into West Berlin to maintain it as a counterpoint to communism. The West German government, which at the time refused to recognise East Germany as a legitimate state, demonstrated its commitment to seeing Berlin reinstated as German capital by holding occasional parliamentary sessions in the city. The prominence accorded West Berlin was later reflected in the high profile of its politicians (Willy Brandt, for example) who were received abroad by prime ministers and presidents – unusual for mere mayors.

Yet despite the emerging divisions the two halves of the city continued to co-exist in some abnormal fashion. City planners on both sides of the sectoral boundaries initially drew up plans with the whole city in mind.

The transport system crossed between East and West, with the underground network being controlled by the West and the S-Bahn by the East. Movement between the sectors (despite 'border' checks) was relatively normal, as Westerners went East to watch a Brecht play or buy cheap books. Easterners travelled West to work, shop or see the latest Hollywood films.

The secret services of both sides kept a high presence in the city, and there were frequent acts of sabotage. Berlin became espionage capital of the world.

RECOVERY AND RESTRICTIONS

As the effects of US money and the West German 'economic miracle' took hold, West Berlin began to recover. A municipal housing programme meant that by 1963 200,000 new flats had been built. Unemployment dropped from 30 per cent in 1950 to virtually zero by 1961. The labour force also included about 50,000 East Berliners who commuted over the inter-sector borders.

In the East reconstruction was slower. Until the mid 1950s East Germany paid reparations to the Soviet Union. To begin with, there seemed to be more acts of wilful destruction than positive construction. The old Stadtschloss, slightly damaged by bombing, was blown up in 1950 to make way for a parade ground, which later evolved into a car park.

In 1952 the East Germans sealed off the border with West Germany. The only way out of the 'zone' was through West Berlin and the number of refugees from the East rose dramatically from 50,000 in 1950 to 300,000 in 1953. Over the decade, one million refugees from the East came through West Berlin.

THE 1953 UPRISING

In June 1953, partly in response to the rapid loss of skilled manpower, the East German government announced a ten per cent increase in working 'norms' – the number of hours and volume of output that workers were required to fulfil each day. In protest, building workers on Stalinallee (now Karl-Marx-Allee) downed tools on 16 June and marched to the government offices on Leipziger Strasse. The government refused to relent, and strikes soon broke out across the city. Crowds stormed Communist Party offices and tore red flags from public buildings. By midday the government had lost control of the city and it was left to the Red Army to restore order. Soviet tanks rolled into the centre of East Berlin, where they were met by stones thrown by demonstrators.

By nightfall the uprising was crushed. Officially 23 people died, though other estimates put the figure at over 200. There followed a wave of arrests across East Berlin, with more than 4,000 people detained. Most went on to receive stiff prison sentences.

The 17 June uprising only furthered the wave of emigration. And by the end of the 1950s it seemed likely that East Germany would cease to function as an industrial state through the loss of skilled labour. Estimates put the loss to the East German economy through emigration at some DM100 billion. Ulbricht increased his demands on Moscow to take action.

In 1958 Soviet leader Nikita Khrushchev tried to bully the Allies into relinquishing West Berlin by calling for an end to military occupation and a 'normalisation of the situation in the capital of the GDR', by which he meant Berlin as a whole. The ultimatum was rejected and the Allies made clear their commitment to West Berlin. Unwilling to provoke a world war, but needing to prop up his ally, Khrushchev backed down and sanctioned Ulbricht's alternative plan for a solution to the Berlin question.

THE WALL

During the early summer of 1961 rumours spread that Ulbricht intended to seal off West Berlin with a barrier or reinforced border. Emigration had reached a high point as 1,500 East Germans fled to the West each day.

However, when in the early hours of 13 August units of the People's Police (assisted by Working Class Combat Groups) began to drag bales of barbed wire across Potsdamer Platz, Berlin and the world were caught by surprise.

In a finely planned and executed operation (overseen by Erich Honecker, then Politburo member in charge of security affairs), West Berlin was sealed off within 24 hours. As well as a fence of barbed wire, trenches were dug, the windows of houses straddling the new border were bricked up, and tram and railway lines were interrupted: all this under the watchful eyes of armed guards. Anyone trying to flee west risked being shot; in the 29 years the Wall stood, nearly 80 people died trying to escape. Justifying their actions, the East Germans said they had erected an 'Anti-Fascist Protection Rampart' to prevent a world war.

Days later the construction of a wall began. When it was completed, the concrete part of the 160-kilometre (100-mile) fortification ran to 112 kilometres (70 miles); 37 kilometres (23 miles) of the Wall ran through the city centre. Previously innocuous streets like Bernauer Strasse (where houses on one side were in the East, on the other in the West) suddenly became the location for one of the world's most deadly borders.

The initial stunned disbelief of Berliners turned into despair as it became clear that (as with the 17 June uprising) the Western Allies could do little more than make a show of strength. President Kennedy dispatched American reinforcements to Berlin, and, for a few tense weeks, American and Soviet tanks squared off at Checkpoint Charlie.

'People abseiled off buildings, swam the Spree or waded through sewers.'

Vice-President Johnson came to show moral support a week after the Wall was built. Two years later Kennedy himself arrived and spoke to a crowd of half-a-million in front of Rathaus Schöneberg. His speech linked the fate of West Berlin with that of the free world and ended with the now famous statement 'Ich bin ein Berliner!' (Literally, alas, 'I am a doughnut'.)

In its early years the Wall was the scene of many daring escape attempts. People abseiled off buildings, swam across the Spree, waded through sewers or tried to climb over. But as the fortifications were improved with mines, searchlights and guard dogs, and as the guards were given orders to shoot on sight, escape became nearly impossible. By the time the Wall fell in 1989 it had been 'updated' four times to render it more or less completely impermeable.

Layers of history: top, remains of the **Wall**; below, more Wall remains standing above the Topographie des Terror exhibition in the Gestapo's former basement.

In 1971 the Four Powers met and signed the Quadrapartite Agreement, which formally recognised the city's divided status. Border posts (such as the infamous Checkpoint Charlie) were introduced and designated to particular categories of visitors – one for foreigners, another for West Germans, and so on.

A TALE OF TWO CITIES

During the 1960s, with the Wall as infamous and ugly backdrop, the cityscape of modern Berlin (both East and West) began to take shape. On Tauentzienstrasse in the West the Europa-Center was built, and the bomb-damaged Kaiser-Wilhelm-Gedächtniskirche was given a partner – a new church made up of a glass-clad tower and squat bunker.

Hans Scharoun laid out the Kulturforum in Tiergarten as West Berlin's answer to the Museumsinsel complex in the East. The first building to go up was Scharoun's Philharmonie, completed in 1963. Mies van der Rohe's Neue Nationalgalerie was finished in 1968.

In the suburbs work began on concrete mini-towns, Gropiusstadt and Märkisches Viertel. Conceived as solutions to housing shortages, they would develop into alienating ghettos.

Alexanderplatz in the East was rebuilt along totalitarian lines and the Fernsehturm ('Television Tower'; see p89) was finished. The historic core of Berlin was mostly cleared to make way for parks (such as the Marx-Engels Forum) or new office and housing developments. On the eastern outskirts of the city in Marzahn and Hohenschönhausen work began on mass-scale housing projects.

In 1965 the first sit-down was staged on the Kurfürstendamm by students protesting low grants and expensive accommodation. This was followed by several student political demonstrations against the state in general and the Vietnam War in particular. The first communes were set up in Kreuzberg, sowing the seeds of a counterculture that would make the district famous.

The student protest movement came into violent confrontation with the police in 1967 and 1968. One student, Benno Ohnesorg, was shot dead by police at a demonstration against the Shah of Iran, who visited the city in June 1967. A year later the students' leader, Rudi Dutschke, was shot by a right-winger. Demonstrations were held outside the offices of the newspaper group Springer, whose papers were blamed for inciting the shooting. It was out of this movement that the Red Army Faction (also known as the Baader-Meinhof Gang) was to emerge. It made headlines often in the 1970s, not least through a series of kidnappings of high-profile city officials.

NORMALISING ABNORMALITY

The signing of the Quadrapartite Agreement confirmed West Berlin's abnormal status and ushered in an era of decline, as the frisson of Cold War excitement and 1960s rebellion petered out. More than ever West Berlin depended on huge subsidies from West Germany to keep it going.

Development schemes and tax breaks were introduced to encourage businesses to move to the city (Berliners also paid less income tax), but still the economy and population declined. At the same time there was growth in the number of *Gastarbeiter* ('guest workers') who arrived from southern Europe and particularly Turkey, to take on menial jobs. Today there are over 120,000 Turks in the city, largely concentrated in Kreuzberg (*see p94* **The capital of Turkish Berlin**).

'From its headquarters in Normannenstrasse, the Stasi permeated every part of East German society.'

By the late 1970s Berlin was in decline. In the West, the city government was discredited by a number of scandals, mostly connected with property deals. In East Berlin, where Erich Honecker had succeeded Ulbricht in 1971, a regime that began in a mood of reform became repressive. Some of East Germany's best writers and artists, previously supporters of socialism, left the country. From its headquarters in Normannenstrasse, the Stasi directed its policy of mass observation and permeated every part of East German society (*see p30* **Stasiland**). Between East and West there were squalid exchanges of political prisoners for hard currency.

The late 1970s and early 1980s saw the rise of the squatter movement (centred in Kreuzberg), which brought violent political protest back on to the streets.

In 1987 Berlin celebrated its 750th birthday and East and West vied to outdo each other's festivities. In the East, the Nikolaiviertel was restored, and Honecker began a programme to do the same for the few remaining historical sites that had survived both wartime bombing and post-war planning. The statue of Frederick the Great riding his horse was returned to Unter den Linden.

THE FALL OF THE WALL

Restored monuments were not enough to stem the growing discontent of East Berliners. The arrival of perestroika in the USSR had been ignored by Honecker, who stuck hard to his

Stalinist instincts. Protest was strong and only initially beaten back by the police.

By the spring of 1989 the East German state was no longer able to withstand the pressure of a population fed up with communism and closed borders. Throughout the summer thousands fled the city and the country via Hungary, which had opened its borders to the West. Those who stayed began demonstrating for reforms.

By the time Honecker was hosting the celebrations in the *Volkskammer* ('People's Chamber') to mark the 40th anniversary of the GDR on 7 October 1989 crowds were demonstrating outside, chanting 'Gorby! Gorby!' to register their opposition. Honecker was ousted days later.

Honecker's successor, Egon Krenz, could do little to stem the tide of opposition. In a bid to defend through attack, he decided to grant the concession East Germans wanted most – freedom to travel. On 9 November 1989 the Berlin Wall was opened, just over 28 years after it had been built. As thousands of East Berliners raced through to the sound of popping corks, the end of East Germany and the unification of Berlin and Germany had begun.

REUNIFYING BERLIN

With the Wall down, Berlin found itself once again at centre stage. Just as the division of the city defined the split of Europe, so the freedom to move again between East and West marked the dawn of the post-Cold War era.

For a year the city was in a state of euphoria. Between November 1989 and October 1990 the city witnessed the collapse of communism and the first free elections (March 1990) in the East for more than 50 years; economic unification, with the swapping of the tinny Ostmark for the Deutschmark (July 1990); and the political merger of East into West with formal political unification on 3 October 1990. (It was also the year West Germany won its third World Cup. The team may have come from the West, but in a year characterised by outbursts of popular celebration, Easterners cheered too.)

Unification also brought problems, especially for Berlin, where the two halves of the city now had to be welded into one whole. While Western infrastructure in the form of roads, telephones and other amenities was in decent working order, in the East it was falling apart. Challenges also came from the collapse of a command economy where jobs were provided regardless of cost or productivity. The Deutschmark put hard currency into the wallets of Easterners, but it also exposed the true state of their economy. Within months thousands of companies cut jobs or closed down altogether.

Responsibility for restructuring Eastern industry was placed with the Treuhandanstalt, a state agency that, for a while, was the world's largest industrial holding company. In Goering's old air ministry on the corner of Leipziger Strasse and Wilhelmstrasse (now the Finance Ministry), the Treuhand gave high-paid employment to thousands of Western yuppies and put hundreds of thousands of Easterners on the dole.

Easterners soon turned on the Treuhand, vilified as the agent of a brutal Western takeover. The situation escalated when Detlev Karsten Rohwedder, a Western industrialist who headed the agency, was assassinated in spring 1991 – probably by members of the Red Army Faction, the left-wing terror group.

The killing of another state employee, Hanno Klein, an influential city planner not always loved by the city's construction sector, drew attention to another dramatic change brought about by unification: the property boom. With the Wall down and – after a 1991 parliamentary decision – the federal government committed to moving from Bonn to Berlin, a wave of construction and investment swept the city.

DRIFTING TO NORMALITY

The giddy excitement of the post-unification years soon gave way to disappointment. The sheer amount of construction work, the scrapping of federal subsidies and tax breaks to West Berlin, rising unemployment and a delay in the arrival of the government all contributed to dampening spirits. In 1994 the last Russian, US, British and French troops left the city. With them went its unique Cold War status. After decades of being different, Berlin was becoming like any other big European capital.

> '**The Treuhand gave highly paid employment to western yuppies and put thousands of easterners on the dole.**'

The 1990s were characterised by the regeneration of the east. In the course of the decade the city's centre of gravity shifted towards Mitte. The government and commercial districts were revitalised. On their fringes, especially around Oranienburger Strasse, the Hackesche Höfe and into Prenzlauer Berg, trendy bars, restaurants, galleries and boutiques sprouted in streets that under communism had been grey and crumbling.

Fast-track gentrification in the east was matched by the decline of West Berlin. The proprietors of upmarket shops and bars began to desert Charlottenburg and Schöneberg. Kreuzberg, once the inelegantly wasted

Stasiland

Nobody's exactly sure how many unofficial informers were on the payroll of East Germany's Ministerium für Staatssicherheit, better known as the **Stasi**. There were something like 90,000 full-time agents, and about 175,000 *inoffizielle Mitarbeiter* – unofficial informers – otherwise known as IMs. For certain, the secret police apparatus was the most pervasive in the history of state-sponsored repression; by way of comparison, the Gestapo in its 1940s heyday only had about 30,000 members.

Though its grip on everyday life in the GDR was exhaustive, the Stasi must go down in history as a flawed institution. In spite of secret prisons, hidden cameras and microphones, and the burgeoning network of IMs, the Stasi failed to prevent the peaceful revolution of 1989. And only a few weeks after the Wall was breached, crowds fell on the Stasi headquarters at Normannenstrasse, venting anger and frustration on the offices of their former tormentors.

In the preceding days, Stasi agents were working overtime, using up to 100 shredding machines to destroy documents. But they barely put a dent in the six million or so files, which are now administered by a special authority charged with reviewing them and making them available to prosecutors and everyday people who are simply curious to know what the Stasi knew about them.

Not surprisingly, the files contained embarrassing revelations for many politicians, journalists, athletes and other folks trying to get on with life in united Germany. Most of the charges involve people being listed as IMs, a status hard to dispute or verify. West German investigative reporter Günther Wallraff and former transport minister Manfred Stolpe are among those implicated. Stolpe has explained that it was necessary to be a double agent in order to retain his contacts with the dissident movement, while Wallraff has flatly denied any Stasi connection at all. Many could have been falsely implicated by overambitious Stasi career types, whose rank and pay were pegged to their success at recruiting spies. Even former chancellor Helmut Kohl and East German figure-skater Katarina Witt have been in court fighting to have their files kept under lock and key.

There are, however, thousands of Germans who readily own up to their double lives with the Stasi. They have to, in fact, to get their pensions – one major function of the agency minding the Stasi files is to determine who qualifies for retirement payments.

One of those qualifying was Erich Meilke, the Stasi supremo. Meilke collected about €400 monthly until he died in an old people's home in May 2000 at the age of 92. Meilke was sentenced to prison in 1993 for murdering two policemen in Berlin in 1931, but was set free a few years later due to senility and declining health. His former office is now the centrepiece of the **Forschungs- & Gedenkstätte Normannenstrasse** (*see p120*), also known as the Stasi Museum.

symbol of a defiant West Berlin, in places degenerated to near slum-like conditions, while a new bohemia developed across the Spree in Friedrichshain.

Westerners did, however, benefit from the reopening of the Berlin hinterland. Tens of thousands left the city for greener suburbs in the surrounding state of Brandenburg.

THE BERLIN REPUBLIC
Having spent the best part of a decade doing what it had done so often in the past – regenerating itself out of the wreckage left by history – Berlin left the 20th century with a flourish. Many of the big, symbolic construction projects had already sprouted: the new Potsdamer Platz, a Reichstag remodelled by Sir Norman Foster. Other major landmarks such as Daniel Libeskind's Jüdisches Museum and IM Pei's extension to the Deutsches Historisches Museum on Unter den Linden soon followed.

The turn of the century also saw Berlin return to the centre of German politics. Parliament, the government and the accompanying baggage of lobbyists and journalists arrived from Bonn. From Chancellor Gerhard Schröder down, everyone sought to mark the transition as the beginning of the 'Berlin Republic' – for which read a peaceful, democratic, and above all, self-confident Germany as opposed to the chaos of the Weimar years or the self-conscious timidity of the Bonn era.

The Kosovo crisis of 1999, the attacks of 11 September 2001 and the wars in Afghanistan and Iraq all saw the Berlin government called upon to play a more active role on the international stage. With this came marked differences from the past. When President George W Bush came to Berlin in May 2002, it was a world away from previous visits by US leaders. Where Kennedy brought a boost in a time of crisis, Reagan a bit of straight talking ('Mr Gorbachev, tear down this wall!') and Bush senior a nod to Germany's emerging importance, George W came to tell the Europeans to fall into line over Iraq. He was soon to be disappointed. Schröder made opposition to military action in Iraq a centrepiece of his September 2002 re-election campaign, which helped the 'Red-Green' coalition of Social Democrats and Greens squeak back into power.

Meanwhile, Berlin's financial problems – brought on by rocketing demands on expenditure, decline in central government handouts and the collapse of traditional industries – grew steadily worse. Matching this was the ineptitude of the city's political establishment, desperate to hang on to old privileges and unwilling to face up to tough, new choices. This was all encapsulated in the collapse of the Bankgesellschaft Berlin, a bank largely owned by the city. In the summer of 2001 it was felled by a raft of dud and corrupt real-estate loans. As well as sparking further deterioration in public finances, the scandal brought down the Senate – a grand coalition of Christian Democrats and SPD that had governed since 1990.

> **'Wowereit's unapologetic homosexuality made him the first openly gay politician to be elected to high office.'**

The resulting elections went some way towards a new start. Klaus Wowereit, head of the SPD, broke one of the great post-unification taboos and invited the Party of Democratic Socialism – successor party to East Germany's Communists and winners of half the eastern vote – into a Social Democrat-led coalition. The hullabaloo all but drowned out Wowereit's other bit of taboo-breaking: his unapologetic homosexuality, which made him the first openly gay politician elected to high office.

At national level Schröder's second term was far from happy. A brave attempt to reform welfare and the labour market saw the chancellor attacked from all sides, including the left of his own SPD. Defeats in regional polls forced Schröder in May 2005 to make one last bold move: early elections. Schröder entered the bitter campaign trailing his opponent Angela

Merkel and the Christian Democrats in the opinion polls, but came within a whisker of winning the September general election.

The result was a mess. Both the main parties – CDU and SPD – lost votes; neither was able to form its preferred coalition. Instead they were forced into a CDU-led grand coalition with Merkel as chancellor.

UNITY AND DOUBT

As the first woman and first easterner to hold the chancellorship, Merkel ensured her place in the history books when she took office in November 2005. Fifteen years after unification, her appointment demonstrated that, for all the difficulties, some progress was being made in bringing east and west together. The election of Matthias Platzeck, another easterner, to chairmanship of the SPD underscored the point.

It was a development echoed on the ground in Berlin where the final pieces of the structural reunification puzzle tumbled into place. The following year was to see the colossal new Berlin Hauptbahnhof take a bow as one of Europe's largest stations (see p102 **Hub, bub**), while the renovated Olympia Stadion would play host to the World Cup Final. Peter Eisenman's Denkmal für die ermordeten Juden Europas (Memorial to the Murdered Jews of Europe) was unveiled with the usual whiff of controversy. The hexagon of Leipziger Platz took final shape as the city centre's reception room. And after years of argument for and against, demolition of the Palast der Republik was back on the cards. The former communist parliament is eventually to be replaced by a reconstruction of the old Stadtschloss that formerly stood on the site. But there is still no real idea of where the money will come from, or how the huge new building will be used.

Expectations for the Merkel government were equally fuzzy. Reformers feared that the compromises endemic to such a marriage of convenience meant that Germany would – once again – avoid taking the kind of tough decisions Merkel had promised on the campaign trail. The overbearing weight of government parties in the Bundestag – some 70 per cent of delegates – aroused memories of the time West Germany had a Grand Coalition, in the late 1960s. Back then, opposition to the government shifted to the streets and extremist parties saw a marked increase in support. Optimists hoped that at least the Merkel government would use its majority to push through fundamental constitutional reforms that had eluded nearly all its predecessors. On one thing, though, everyone could agree: for all the political coalitions and new city landmarks, Berlin hadn't quite settled down yet.

Key events

1237 Town of Cölln first mentioned in a church document.
1307 Towns of Berlin and Cölln officially united under the rule of the Ascanian family.
1319 Last of the Ascanians dies.
1359 Berlin joins the Hanseatic League.
1411 Friedrich of Hohenzollern is sent by the Holy Roman Emperor to bring peace to the region.
1447-8 The 'Berlin Indignation'. Citizens rebel and lock Friedrich II out of the city.
1535 Accession of Joachim I Nestor, the first Protestant Elector. The Reformation gains pace.
1538 Work begins on the Stadtschloss.
1618-48 Berlin and Brandenburg are ravaged by the Thirty Years War; population halved.
1640-88 Reign of Friedrich Wilhelm, the Great Elector.
1662-8 Construction of Oder–Spree canal.
1672 Huguenot refugees settle, following the arrival of Jewish immigrants.
1695 Work starts on Schloss Charlottenburg.
1701 Elector Friedrich III, son of the Great Elector, has himself crowned Friedrich I, King of Prussia. Work begins on the German and French cathedrals at the Gendarmenmarkt.
1713-40 Reign of King Friedrich Wilhelm I; Berlin becomes a garrison city.
1740-86 Reign of Frederick the Great (Friedrich II), a time of military expansion.
1756-63 Seven Years War ends triumphantly for Prussia.
1788-91 Construction of Brandenburg Tor.
1806 Napoleon marches into Berlin. Two years of French occupation. The Quadriga taken to Paris.
1813 Napoleon defeated at Grossbeeren and Leipzig.
1814 General Blücher brings the Quadriga back to Berlin; restored to Brandenburg Gate.
1837 Foundation of the Borsig Werke marks the beginning of Berlin's expansion towards becoming Europe's largest industrial city.
1838 First railway line in Germany, from Berlin to Potsdam.
1840 Friedrich Wilhelm IV accedes to the throne. With a population of around 400,000, Berlin is the fourth largest city in Europe.
1848 The 'March Revolution' breaks out. Berlin briefly ruled by revolutionaries.
1861 Accession of King Wilhelm I.
1862 Appointment of Otto von Bismarck as Prime Minister of Prussia.

1871 After victory in the Franco-Prussian war, King Wilhelm I is proclaimed German Kaiser ('Emperor'). Berlin becomes imperial capital.
1879 Electric lighting comes to Berlin, which also boasts the world's first electric railway. Telephone services arrive in 1882. Berlin becomes Europe's most modern metropolis.
1888 Kaiser Wilhelm II comes to the throne.
1890 Wilhelm II sacks Bismarck.
1894 Completion of the Reichstag.
1902 First underground line is opened.
1914-18 World War I.
1918 9 Nov: the Kaiser abdicates, Philip Scheidemann proclaims Germany a republic and Karl Liebknecht declares Germany a socialist republic. Chaos ensues.
1919 Spartacist uprising suppressed.
1923 Hyperinflation – at one point $1 is worth 4,200,000,000,000 marks.
1926 Josef Goebbels comes to Berlin to take charge of the local Nazi Party organisation.
1927 Berlin boasts more than 70 cabarets.
1933 Hitler takes power.
1936 11th Olympic Games held in Berlin.
1938 9 Nov: Kristallnacht – Jewish properties are looted and set ablaze.
1939 Outbreak of World War II, during which Berlin suffers appalling devastation.
1944 A group around Colonel Count von Stauffenberg attempts to assassinate Hitler.
1945 Germany signs unconditional surrender.
1948-9 The Berlin Blockade. The Soviets cut off all transport links to West Berlin. For 11 months city is supplied by the Allied Airlift.
1949 Foundation of Federal Republic in May and German Democratic Republic in October.
1953 17June: East Berlin uprising crushed.
1961 13 Aug: the Wall goes up.
1968 Student leader Rudi Dutschke is shot.
1971 Erich Honecker succeeds Walter Ulbricht as GDR head of state. Quadrapartite Agreement formalises Berlin's divided status.
1980-81 'Hot Winter': squatter protests.
1987 Berlin's 750th birthday.
1989 9 Nov: the Wall comes down.
1990 3 Oct: formal German Reunification.
1994 Last of the Allied military leaves Berlin.
1999 German government moves from Bonn and the 'Berlin Republic' is born.
2001 Gay Klaus Wowereit elected mayor. Boroughs merge across east–west divide.
2005 Angela Merkel becomes Germany's first female chancellor.
2006 Berlin hosts the FIFA World Cup Final.

Berlin Today

No longer a geopolitical anomaly, but not yet used to being Germany's capital, Berlin is in a budgetary pickle.

The gleaming new Berlin Hauptbahnhof (formerly the unassuming S-Bahn stop, Lehrter Bahnhof; *see p102* **Hub, bub**) is poised close to the seam of the old East and West Berlin dividing line. Completed at the end of May 2006, this is the last of the great 1990s development projects that were supposed to bind Berlin's two halves, create a new identity for the city, and define its look for the future.

Berliners will still pass through on the S-Bahn, whizzing between Mitte and the west end, but most of those using the new central station will be travellers, visitors, strangers to the city. Their first impressions from the upper tracks will include the spectacular vista to the south. The new Reichstag, the gracefully massive Bundeskanzleramt, and even the tip of the spacey Potsdamer Platz complex on the horizon. This view simply didn't exist five years ago. It is now the premier cityscape, the welcoming tableau of 21st-century Berlin. But significantly, it is a view largely being lost on the work-a-day Berliner.

One reason is that Berlin remains a city of insular neighbourhoods, in spite of the dramatic transformations that have taken place. But the neighbourhoods have evolved. Districts in the east have seen the most change. Prenzlauer Berg and Mitte are preferred by 'new Berliners'. Young families are attracted to the leafy streets and parks of Prenzlauer Berg. Young singles are drawn by the boutiques and bars of northern Mitte. Berlin's total population has not changed, but the demographics have. Within the next years around a third of the population will have rotated. Hundreds of thousands have packed up and moved out; just as many are moving in.

The upheaval keeps Berlin dynamic. The newcomers bring enthusiasm and add to the buzz. They're drawn by the arts and nightlife, as well as by cheap rents. Creative people burnt out on the pace and expense of life in London or New York increasingly find respite in Berlin.

Germans coming to Berlin mostly find a city transformed since their last visit, one that lives up to the spectacular photo spreads they've

Bundeskanzleramt.

seen in the national press. But they haven't really got used to the idea of Berlin as their capital, the central point around which the nation revolves. So far they are tolerating the prospect that this may one day be the case.

WHAT'S A CAPITAL FOR?

When Britons go to London they see the British Museum and the Crown jewels and do a bit of shopping in Harrods or Camden Lock. Americans travelling to Washington DC visit the memorials to Lincoln, Jefferson and Washington. When the French go to Paris, they stop by the Bastille, and eat in great restaurants. One of the functions of a capital city is to make you feel good about being British, American or French. But what if you're German? Why would you visit Berlin?

Begin thinking about that question, and you're carrying the baggage you need to discover the Berlin of today. First off, let's establish that the Berlin often mentioned in the same breath as London and Paris is not always the same as today's Berlin. Some of the same buildings are around, sure, but Berlin has

changed allegiances several times since the days when, like London or Paris, it was both the cradle of nationhood and the country's premier urban centre. First it was capital of Prussia, then capital of the German Reich, then of the Weimar Republic, and then of the Third Reich. After World War II half of the divided city was the capital of the German Democratic Republic, then after 1991 a united Berlin was preferred in a referendum to Bonn as the capital of an expanded Federal Republic. It's hardly surprising that Germans don't necessarily see it as the natural centre of things.

The protean nature of the city and its role in history is, of course, a part of its enduring attraction to outsiders. But among Germans it has triggered a full-blown case of national soul-searching known broadly as the *Hauptstadtdebatte* ('the capital debate'). Though the debate has many facets, it all boils down to money. Berlin remains in a major financial crisis – not that unusual for many cities, but here the debate is not just about how to solve the problem. It's also about who is responsible for solving it.

Meanwhile, the shimmering capital of Europe's biggest economy is flat out of cash. Educational standards are plummeting as a hiring freeze has left kids with ageing, jaded teachers. Civil servants are demotivated and unable to cope with new cost-saving procedures. Grass isn't cut. Roads aren't repaired. Around 250,000 manufacturing jobs have been lost since 1990 – the most recent cuts were announced by Samsung, which slashed hundreds of jobs in January 2006. Unemployment runs at nearly 20 per cent. Empty shopfronts are common on the Ku'damm, once West Berlin's glitzy shopping centrepiece. Newspaper circulations have plummeted, as have advertising revenues. Discount chains and own-brand supermarkets hold sway over the retail landscape. Berlin businesses have a harder time getting funding because creditworthiness is low.

THOSE WERE THE DAYS

It wasn't always this way, and that's part of the problem. During the Cold War days, both East and West Berlin offered fairly cushy lifestyles. Large employers were attracted to West Berlin by generous subsidies; East Berlin was kept afloat as a showcase of socialist achievement. In West Berlin, politicians and civil servants were basically charged with distributing huge monthly transfers from Bonn. The situation bred fraud and corruption. East Berlin was different, but residents had enough privileges to be resented by other East Germans living in drab villages or polluted factory towns.

When the Wall was breached in 1989, the rug was yanked from under the feet of Berliners, East and West. Initially, there was euphoria. People talked of the government moving lock, stock and moneybags into Berlin by 1995. East Berliners converted their Ostmarks to Deutschmarks at a phenomenal one-to-one rate, and the city was awash in cash. Chancellor Kohl told Germans that unification would result in a huge economic upswing – 'flourishing landscapes' were what he famously envisaged – and Berlin would be in the middle. International investors would flock to the city, building a commercial gateway to the east. Berlin would have a new international airport, dwarfing the three existing ones. Population would grow to five million by the turn of the century.

None of this happened. When the government finally did take up residence, it was in 1999 not 1995, and not all of the federal ministries and offices moved here from Bonn. East Germany turned out to have a lot fewer assets than anticipated and the one-to-one currency conversion helped bring about the near total collapse of eastern industry. Far from offering

flourishing landscapes, it turned into a bottomless pit. An end to subsidies drove out various big western employers and potential new investors got spooked by the government's delay in moving and the lack of an international airport. Today in Berlin only 15 companies employ more than 500 people. Plans to expand the airport in Schönefeld have stalled repeatedly over financing and planning issues. And the population has barely budged.

NEW REALITY

The problem for Berliners was that as the euphoria of unification wore off, as the billions from Bonn dried up and one employer after another closed shop, their elected representatives continued with business as usual. They borrowed money to replace lost subsidies and failed to make the politically sensitive cutbacks needed for the city to meet its payroll. These bureaucrats specialised in spending money, not saving it. And they got the city involved in a number of real-estate projects that have since gone bust. The bottom line is that the city is now saddled with about €58 billion of debt. New debt totalled €3.5 billion in 2005, actually less than anticipated, due to ongoing cutbacks. While Berliners struggle to come to terms with the new reality, many Germans have little sympathy.

'The shimmering capital of Europe's biggest economy is flat out of cash.'

Considering the city's ongoing corruption scandals and poor track record at cutting the fat out of bureaucracy, leaders of some German states say they no longer want to transfer part of their revenue to impoverished Berlin, as required in Germany's federal system. Berliners counter that at least some of the burdens facing the city are not of its own making, that many arise from Berlin's new status as a capital city. Those on this side of the *Hauptstadtdebatte* say Berlin needs to maintain a vibrant cultural scene, with world-class museums and concert halls. The city has to have a big police force to keep order when, say, hundreds of thousands of trade unionists from all over the nation rally at the Brandenburg Gate. Why should Berliners pay?

But Germany's national economy has been sputtering for years. With reforms in pension payments and working conditions introduced by the last government under former Chancellor Gerhard Schroeder, and the new coaltion government tackling healthcare costs, Berlin's chances of relief from the federal government are currently looking bleak.

Schinkel's **Altes Museum**. *See p40.*

Architecture

A city where builders leave no style unturned.

Berlin is an exhibition of architectural change. After nearly two decades of intense building activity the city is re-emerging as a metropolis with a mix of contemporary projects and a long history of architectural development and experimentation. During the 1910s and '20s Berlin was home to some of the century's greatest architects and designers, such as Peter Behrens, Bruno Taut, Ludwig Mies van der Rohe and Walter Gropius. But the path to modernism was launched a century earlier by Karl Friedrich Schinkel, perhaps Berlin's greatest builder. In addition, fine specimens of nearly every style since the baroque age can be found here, from neo-Renaissance to neo-rationalism, plus new buildings by just about every name architect of today.

It wasn't until the late 19th century that Berlin was able to hold its own with grander European capitals, thanks to a construction boom known as the Gründerzeit, triggered by the rapid progress in industry and technology that followed German unification in 1871. The city acquired a massive scale, with wide streets and large blocks. These followed a rudimentary geometry and were filled in with five-storey *Mietskaserne* ('rental barracks') built around linked internal courtyards. The monotony was partially relieved by a few public parks. Later apartment houses gradually became more humane and eventually got rather splendid. During the 1920s this method of development was rejected in favour of Bauhaus-influenced slabs and towers, which were used to fill out the peripheral zones at the edge of the forests. The post-war years saw even more radical departures from the earlier tradition in all sectors of the city.

The post-Wall building boom has now deposited a new layer, a mixture of contemporary international design and historic emulation of local styles. Some of it uses new environmental strategies and much of it attempts to restore a sense of continuity to an urban fabric serially ruptured by war, division and heavy-handed reconstruction.

The spirit of historic revival has even taken in the city's most famous landmark, the **Wall** itself (*see p114* **Walking the Wall**). Speedily dismantled after 1989, it is now commemorated in public art, from the **Gedenkstätte Berliner Mauer** (*see p113*) to Frank Thiel's portraits of the last Allied soldiers, suspended above Checkpoint Charlie. The former line of the Wall is marked in places by a cobblestone strip, such as that visible west of the Brandenburg Gate. But with so much new architecture, its memory is fading away.

THE FIRST FEW CENTURIES

The city began as Berlin and Cölln, two Wendish/Slavic settlements on the Spree that were colonised by Germans around 1237. Among their oldest surviving buildings are the parish churches **Marienkirche** and **Nikolaikirche** (for both, *see p89*). The latter was rebuilt in the district known as the Nikolaiviertel, between Alexanderplatz and the Spree. It's the only part of central Berlin to give any idea of how the medieval city might have felt – except it's a clumsy fake, rebuilt by the East Germans in 1987, just a few decades after they had levelled the district.

Little survives of the massive **Stadtschloss** ('City Palace', 1538-1950), other than some recently excavated foundations in the square in front of the soon-to-be-demolished Palast der Republik. The Schlossbrücke crossing to Unter den Linden, adorned with sensual figures by Christian Daniel Rauch, and the Neptunbrunnen ('Neptune Fountain', now relocated south of Marienkirche), modelled on Bernini's Roman fountains, were designed to embellish the palace.

'With so much new architecture, the memory of the Wall is fading away.'

In 1647 the Great Elector Friedrich Wilhelm II (1640-88) hired Dutch engineers to transform the route to the Tiergarten, the royal hunting forest, into the tree-lined boulevard of Unter den Linden. It led west toward **Schloss Charlottenburg** (*see p110*), built in 1695 as a summer retreat for Queen Sophie-Charlotte. Over the next century, the Elector's 'Residenzstadt' expanded to include Berlin and Cölln. Traces of the old stone *Stadtmauer* ('city wall') that enclosed them can still be seen on Waisenstrasse in Mitte. Two further districts, Dorotheenstadt (begun 1673) and Friedrichstadt (begun 1688), expanded the street grid north and south of Unter den Linden. Andreas Schlüter built new palace wings for Elector

Friedrich Wilhelm III (1688-1713, crowned King Friedrich I of Prussia in 1701) and supervised the building of the Zeughaus (Armoury; Nering and de Bodt, 1695-1706; now home to the **Deutsches Historisches Museum**; *see p79*), whose bellicose ornamentation embodies the Prussian love of militarism.

Wilhelm I, the Soldier King (1713-40), imposed conscription and subjugated the town magistrate to the court and military elite. The economy now catered to an army comprising 20 per cent of the population (a fairly constant percentage until 1918). To spur growth in gridded Friedrichstadt – and to quarter his soldiers cheaply – the King forced people to build new houses, mostly in a stripped-down classical style. He permitted one open square, Gendarmenmarkt, where twin churches were built in 1701, one of which now houses the **Hugenotten Museum** (*see p83*).

After the population reached 60,000 in 1710, a new customs wall enclosed four new districts –

Schloss Charlottenburg: Sophie's retreat.

The final stadium

From 1936 through to building works commencing in 2000, the Third Reich showpiece **Olympiastadion** (*see p42* and *p244*) held true to its original architectural image – a simple, arcaded classical oval of light-coloured Franconian stone, open to the elements. There was a certain curiosity and charm in all this, if the weather was right. You could sit back and look at a largely unchanged monument, reflect on how it was when Jesse Owen streaked round and ponder about where Hitler sat that day.

In the 1990s the debate about updating the stadium began with Germany's bid to host the 2006 World Cup finals. The stadium was out of date and wouldn't meet FIFA's technical and safety requirements. Commercially it was hopeless, with no decent facilities for food and drink, no private boxes, and a main spectator area that got soaked when it rained. Much needed to change, but the stadium and its setting were a protected historical structure. The debate raged between positions that the thing was a Nazi symbol and shouldn't be treated so carefully, and the counter-argument that despite its dodgy pedigree the whole complex was a fine piece of architecture that could and should be carefully adapted.

Von Gerkan Marg and Partners' solution was chosen from various other proposals and, after four years of phased building stages, the stadium was reopened in 2004. Their design places a delicate ring roof as an apparently hovering disc over the seating areas, leaving the central portion open to the sky. Light supports have been placed in the rake of the stadium to carry the steel canopy, and the surfaces are clad in a stretched Teflon-coated membrane that creates the illusion of floating. The inner edge is glass and the floodlights are integrated into the surface of this huge canopy. In addition to updating the access and evacuation routes, restoring the original stone building, and providing new seats, toilets, bars, restaurants and private spectator boxes, the playing surface has been lowered by some 3.5 metres (11 feet) and thereby sight lines have been improved.

The hovering roof is a classical and simple form, and sits well with the geometry of the original building. The success of the stadium is that it has become a modern facility fit to host a World Cup Final, and yet the original design of architect Werner March remains quite clear and distinct. You can still arrive at the Olympischer Platz and pass under the Olympic portal, drift through the surrounding grounds taking in the heroic statuary and cracked Olympic bell, and stroll around the arcade at the stadium's base.

---

the Spandauer Vorstadt, Königstadt, Stralauer Vorstadt and Köpenicker Vorstadt; all now parts of Mitte. The 14-kilometre (nine-mile) border remained the city limits until 1860.

Geometric squares later marked three of the 14 city gates in Friedrichstadt. At the square-shaped Pariser Platz, Langhans built the **Brandenburger Tor** (Brandenburg Gate; *see p76*) in 1789, a triumphal arch later topped by Schadow's Quadriga. The stately buildings around the square were levelled after World War II, but have now largely been reconstructed or replaced, including the **Adlon Hotel** (Patzschke, Klotz, 1997; *see p49*), on an expanded version of its original site, and the buildings flanking the gate, Haus Sommer and Haus Liebermann (Kleihues, 1998).

SCHINKEL AND CO

Even with the army, Berlin's population did not reach 100,000 until well into the reign of Frederick the Great (1740-86). Military success inspired him to embellish the city; many of the monuments along Unter den Linden stem from his vision of a 'Forum Fredericianum'. Though never completed, the ensemble of neo-classical, baroque and rococo monuments includes the **Humboldt-Universität** (Knobelsdorff/ Boumann, 1748-530; *see p283*); the **Staatsoper** (Knobelsdorff, Langhans, 1741-3; *see p234*); the Prinzessinnenpalais (1733, now the **Operncafé**; *see p146*) and the Kronprinzenpalais (Unter den Linden 3; 1663, expanded 1732). Set back from the Linden on Bebelplatz are the Alte Bibliothek, reminiscent of the curvy Vienna Hofburg (Unger, 1775-81, part of Humboldt-Universität) and the pantheon-like, copper-domed **St Hedwigs-Kathedrale** (Legeay and Knobelsdorff, 1747-73; *see p79*).

Not long after the Napoleonic occupation, the prolific Karl Friedrich Schinkel became Berlin's most revered architect under Prince Friedrich Wilhelm IV. Drawing on classical and Italian precedents, his early stage-sets experimented with perspective, while his inspired urban visions served the cultural aspirations of an ascendant German state. His work includes the colonnaded **Altes Museum** (1828; *see p80*; photo *p37*), regarded as his finest work, and the **Neue Wache** (New Guardhouse, 1818; *see p78*), whose Roman solidity lent itself well to Tessenow's 1931 conversion into a memorial to the dead of World War I.

Other Schinkel masterpieces include the Schauspielhaus (1817-21, now the **Konzerthaus**; *see p234*); the neo-Gothic brick **Friedrichwerdersche Kirche** (1830, now the Schinkel-Museum; *see p79*); and the cubic **Schinkel-Pavillon** (1825; *see p110*) at Schloss Charlottenburg. After his death in 1841, his many disciples continued working. Friedrich August Stüler satisfied the King's desire to complement the Altes Museum with the **Neues Museum** (1841-59, Bodestrasse 1-3, Mitte), mixing new wrought-iron technology with classical architecture. By 1910 Museumsinsel comprised the neo-classical **Alte Nationalgalerie** (also Stüler, 1864; *see p80*) with an open stairway framing an equestrian statue of the King; the triangular **Bode Museum** (von Ihne, 1904; *see p80*); and the sombre grey **Pergamonmuseum** (Messel and Hoffmann, 1906-9; *see p81*). These are a stark contrast to the neo-Renaissance polychromy of the **Martin-Gropius-Bau** across town (Gropius and Schmieden, 1881; *see p97*).

WILD ECLECTICISM

As the population boomed after 1865, doubling to 1.5 million by 1890, the city began swallowing up neighbouring towns and villages. Factory complexes and worker housing gradually moved to the outskirts. Many of the new market halls and railway stations used a vernacular brick style with iron trusses, such as Arminiushalle in Moabit (Blankenstein, 1892; Bremer Strasse 9) and Franz Schwechten's Romanesque Anhalter Bahnhof (1876-80, now a ruin; Askanischer Platz). Brick was also used for civic buildings, like the neo-Gothic **Berliner Rathaus** (1861-9; *see p88*), while the orientalism of the gold-roofed **Neue Synagoge** (Knoblauch and Stüler, 1859-66; *see p87*) made use of colourful masonry and mosaics.

Restrained historicism gave way to wild eclecticism as the 19th century marched on, in public buildings as well as apartment houses with plain interiors, dark courtyards and overcrowded flats behind decorative façades. This eclectic approach is also reflected in the lavish Gründerzeit villas in the fashionable suburbs to the south-west, especially Dahlem and Grunewald. In these areas the modest yellow-brick vernacular of Brandenburg was rejected in favour of stone and elaborate stucco.

THE NEW METROPOLIS

In anticipation of a new age of rationality and mechanisation, an attempt at greater stylistic clarity was made after 1900, in spite of the bombast of works such as the new **Berliner Dom** (Raschdorff, 1905; *see p80*) and the **Reichstag** (Wallot, 1894; *see p101*). The Wilhelmine era's paradoxical mix of reformism and conservatism yielded an architecture of *Sachlichkeit* ('objectivity') in commercial and public buildings. In some cases, such as Kaufmann's Hebbel-Theater (1908, now part of **HAU**; *see p238*), or the **Hackesche Höfe** (Berndt and Endell, 1906-7; Rosenthaler Strasse 40-41, Mitte), *Sachlichkeit* meant a calmer form of art nouveau (or Jugendstil); elsewhere it was more sombre, with heavy forms, vertical ribbing and low-hanging mansard roofs. One of the most severe examples is the stripped-down classicism of Messel's Pergamonmuseum.

'Schinkel's urban visions served the aspirations of an ascendant German state.'

The style goes well with Prussian bureaucracy in the civic architecture of Ludwig Hoffmann, city architect from 1896 to 1924. Though he sometimes used other styles for his schools, courthouses and city halls, his towering Altes Stadthaus in Mitte (1919; Jüdenstrasse) and the Rudolf-Virchow-Krankenhaus in Wedding (1906; Augustenburger Platz 1), epitomise Wilhelmine architecture.

Prior to the incorporation of Berlin in 1920, many suburbs had full city charters and sported their own town halls, such as the massive Rathaus Charlottenburg (1905; Otto-Suhr-Allee 100) and Rathaus Neukölln (1909; Karl-Marx-Strasse 83-5). Neukölln's Reinhold Kiehl also built the Karl-Marx-Strasse Passage (1910, now home of the **Neuköllner Oper**; *see p235* **No ordinary opera house**) and the **Stadtbad Neukölln** (1914; *see p253*), with niches and mosaics evoking a Roman atmosphere. Special care was also given to suburban railway stations of the period, such as the S-Bahnhof Mexikoplatz in Zehlendorf, on a garden square with shops and restaurants (Hart and Lesser, 1905), and the U-Bahnhof Dahlem-Dorf, in a half-timbered faux rural style.

WEIMAR'S NEW FORMS

The work of many pioneers brought modern architecture to life in Berlin. One of the most important was Peter Behrens, who reinterpreted the factory with a new monumental language in the façade of the Turbinenhalle at

Huttenstrasse in Moabit (1909) and several other buildings for the AEG. After 1918 the turbulent birth of the Weimar Republic offered a chance for a final aesthetic break with the Wilhelmine style.

A radical new architecture gave formal expression to long-awaited social and political reforms. The *Neues Bauen* ('new buildings') began to exploit the new technologies of glass, steel and concrete, inspired by the early work of Tessenow and Behrens, Dutch modernism, cubism and Russian constructivism.

Berlin architects could explore the new functionalism, using clean lines and a machine aesthetic bare of ornament, thanks to post-war housing demand, and a new social democrat administration that put planner Martin Wagner at the helm after 1925. The city became the builder of a new form of social housing. The *Siedlung* ('housing estate') was developed within the framework of a 'building exhibition' of experimental prototypes – often collaborations among architects such as Luckhardt, Gropius, Häring, Salvisberg and the brothers Taut. Standardised sizes kept costs

down and amenities such as tenant gardens, schools, public transport and shopping areas were offered when possible.

Among the best-known 1920s estates are Bruno Taut's Hufeisen-Siedlung (Bruno-Taut-Ring, Britz, 1927), arranged in a horseshoe shape around a communal garden, and Onkel-Toms-Hütte (Haring and Taut, 1928-9; Argentinische Allee, Zehlendorf), with Salvisberg's linear U-Bahn station at its heart. Most *Siedlungen* were housing only, such as the Ringsiedlung (Goebelstrasse, Charlottenburg) or Siemensstadt (Scharoun and others, 1929-32). Traditional-looking 'counter-proposals' with pitched roofs were made by more conservative designers at Am Fischtal (Tessenow, Mebes, Emmerich, Schmitthenner et al, 1929; Zehlendorf).

Larger infrastructure projects and public works were also built by avant-garde architects under Wagner's direction. Among the more interesting are the rounded U-Bahn station at Krumme Lanke (Grenander, 1929), the totally rational Stadtbad Mitte (1930; Gartenstrasse 5-6), the Messegelände (Poelzig and Wagner,

Mies van der Rohe's **Neue Nationalgalerie**, a modernist landmark. *See p43.*

1928; Messedamm 22, Charlottenburg), the
ceramic-tiled Haus des Rundfunks (Poelzig,
1930; Masurenallee 10, Charlottenburg), and
the twin office buildings on the southern corner
of Alexanderplatz (Behrens, 1932).

Beginning with his expressionist
Einsteinturm in Babelsberg (*see p260*),
Erich Mendelsohn distilled his own brand of
modernism, characterised by the rounded
forms of the Universum Cinema (1928, now the
Schaubühne; *see p238*) and the elegant corner
solution of the IG Metall building (1930; Alte
Jacobstrasse 148, Kreuzberg).

GRAND DESIGN & DEMOLITION

In the effort to remake liberal Berlin in their
image, the Nazis banned modernist trademarks
such as flat roofs and slender columns in favour
of traditional architecture. The Bauhaus was
closed down and modern architects fled Berlin
as Hitler dreamt of refashioning it into the
mega-capital 'Germania', designed by Albert
Speer. The crowning glory was to be a grand
axis with a railway station at its foot and a
massive copper dome at its head, some 16 times
the size of St Peter's in Rome. Work was halted
by the war, but not before demolition was
begun in Tiergarten and Schöneberg.

Hitler and Speer's fantasy was that Germania
would someday leave picturesque ruins as per
ancient Rome. But ruins came sooner than
expected. Up to 90 per cent of the inner city was
destroyed by Allied bombing. Rubble cleared
by women survivors formed new hills such as
the **Teufelsberg** (*see p117*) in the west and in
Volkspark Friedrichshain (*see p92*) in the
east. During bombing and reconstruction,
many apartment buildings lost their decoration,
leaving the blunted lines typical of Berlin today.

Fascism left an invisible legacy of a bunker
and tunnel landscape. The more visible fascist
architecture can be recognised by its stripped-
down, abstracted classicism, typically in
travertine: in the west, **Flughafen
Tempelhof** (Sagebiel, 1941; *see p96* and
p270) and the **Olympiastadion** (March,
1936; *see p244* and *p39* **The final stadium**);
in the east, the marble-halled
Reichsluftfahrtministerium (Sagebiel, 1936,
now the Bundesministerium der Finanzen;
Wilhelmstrasse 97, Mitte) and the downright
scary Reichsbank (Wolff, 1938, now the
Auswärtiges Amt; Werderscher Markt, Mitte).

BERLIN, BERLIN

The Berlin Wall, put up in a single night in
1961, introduced a new and cruel reality.
The city's centre of gravity shifted as the
Wall cut off the historic centre from the west,
suspending the Brandenburger Tor and

Façade of the **GSW headquarters**. *See p46.*

Potsdamer Platz in no-man's land, while the
outer edge followed the 1920 city limits.

Post-war architecture is a mixed bag, ranging
from the crisp linear brass of 1950s storefronts
to concrete 1970s mega-complexes. Early joint
planning efforts led by Hans Scharoun were
scrapped, and radical interventions cleared out
vast spaces. Among the architectural casualties
in the East were Schinkel's Bauakademie and
much of Fischerinsel, clearing a sequence
of wide spaces from Marx-Engels-Platz to
Alexanderplatz. In West Berlin, Anhalter
Bahnhof was left to stand in ruins but Schloss
Charlottenburg narrowly escaped demolition.

Though architects from East and West
shared the same modernist education, their
work became the tool of opposing ideologies,
and housing was the first battlefield. The GDR
adapted Russian socialist realism to Prussian
culture in projects built with great effort and
amazing speed as a national undertaking. First
and foremost was Stalinallee (1951-4, now Karl-
Marx-Allee, Friedrichshain). The Frankfurter

Tor segment of its monumental axis was designed by Herman Henselmann, a Bauhaus modernist who briefly agreed to switch styles. In response, West Berlin called on leading International Style architects such as Gropius, Niemeyer, Aalto and Jacobsen to build the Hansaviertel. A loose arrangement of inventive blocks and pavilions at the edge of the Tiergarten, it was part of the 1957 Interbau Exhibition for the 'city of tomorrow', which included Le Corbusier's *Unité d'habitation* in Charlottenburg (Corbusierhaus, just south of S-Bahnhof Olympiastadion).

East and West stylistic differences diminished in the 1960s and '70s, as even bigger new *Siedlungen* were built. The Gropiusstadt in Britz and Märkisches Viertel in Reinickendorf (1963-74) were mirrored in the East by equally massive (if shoddier) prefab housing estates in Marzahn and Hellersdorf.

To replace institutions now in the East, Dahlem became home to various museums and the new Freie Universität, with its rusted-steel exterior (Candilis Woods Schiedhelm, 1967-79; *see p283*). Scharoun conceived a 'Kulturforum' on the site cleared for Germania, designing two masterful pieces: the **Philharmonie** (1963; *see p234*; **photo** *p45*) and the **Staatsbibliothek**

(1976; *see p278*). The other main addition was Mies van der Rohe's **Neue Nationalgalerie** (1968; *see p105*; **photo** *p41*).

The US presented Berlin with Hugh Stubbin's Kongresshalle in the Tiergarten (1967, now the **Haus der Kulturen der Welt**; *see p101*), an entertainingly futuristic work, which rather embarrassingly required seven years' repair after its roof collapsed in 1980. East German architects brewed their own version of futuristic modernism in the enlarged Alexanderplatz with its **Fernsehturm** (TV Tower, 1969; *see p89*), the nearby Haus des Lehrers (Henselmann, 1961-4; Grunerstrasse/Karl-Marx-Allee, Mitte) with its recently restored frieze, and the impressive cinemas, Kino International (Kaiser, 1964; Karl-Marx-Allee 33, Mitte) and Kosmos (Kaiser, 1962; Karl-Marx-Allee 131, Friedrichshain).

POSTMODERN RENEWAL

Modernist urban renewal gradually gave way to historic preservation after 1970. In the West, largely in response to the squatting movement, the city launched a public-private enterprise within the Internationale Bauausstellung (IBA), to conduct a 'careful renewal' of the *Mietskaserne* and 'critical reconstruction' with

How to obey the rules but have fun with them – Wilford's **British Embassy**. *See p46.*

Daniel Libeskind leans towards scupltural symbolism at the **Jüdisches Museum**. *See p46.*

infill projects to close the gaps left in areas along the Wall. It is a truly eclectic collection: the irreverent organicism of Ballers (Fraenkelufer in Kreuzberg; 1982-4) contrasts with the neo-rationalist work of Eisenman (1988; Kochstrasse 62-3, Kreuzberg) and Rossi (1988; Wilhelmstrasse 36-8, Kreuzberg). A series of projects was also placed along Friedrichstrasse. IBA thus became a proving-ground for contemporary architectural theories.

In the East, urban renewal slowed to a halt when funds for the construction of new housing ran dry; and towards the end of the 1970s, inner-city areas again became politically and economically attractive. Most East-bloc preservation focused on run-down 19th-century buildings in Prenzlauer Berg. Some infill buildings were also added on Friedrichstrasse in grids and pastel colours, so that the postmodern theme set up by IBA architects on the street south of Checkpoint Charlie was continued over the Wall. But progress was slow, and when the Wall fell in 1989 many sites still stood half-finished.

CRITICAL RECONSTRUCTION

Rejoining east and west became the new challenge, requiring work of every kind, from massive infrastructure to commercial and residential projects. There were two key decisions. The first was to eradicate the Wall zone with projects that would link urban structures on either side. The second was to pursue a 'critical reconstruction' of the old city block structure, using a contemporary interpretation of Prussian scale and order.

The historic areas around Pariser Platz, Friedrichstrasse and Unter den Linden were peppered with empty sites and became a primary focus for critical reconstruction. The first major commercial project in Friedrichstrasse stuck with the required city scale but took the game rules lightly. The various buildings of the Friedrichstadt-Passagen (1996; Friedrichstrasse 66-75, Mitte), despite their subterranean mall link, offer separate approaches. Pei Cobb Freed and Partner's **Quartier 206** (*see p164*) is a confection of architectural devices reminiscent of 1920s Berlin, while Jean Nouvel's **Galeries Lafayette** (*see p163*) is a smooth and rounded glass form. Only the third building, Quartier 205 by Oswald Mathias Ungers, uses a current German style with its sandstone solidity and rigorous square grid. Good examples of the emerging *Berliner Architektur*, based on the solidity of the past but with modern detail and expressive use of materials, are to be found in

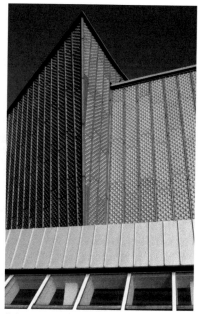

Scharoun's **Philharmonie**. *See p43.*

Thomas van den Valentyn and Matthias
Dittmann's monumental Quartier 108 (1998;
Friedrichstrasse/Leipziger Strasse, Mitte) and
in the Kontorhaus Mitte (1997; Friedrichstrasse
180-90, Mitte) by Josef Paul Kleihues, Vittorio
Magnago Lampugnani, Walther Stepp and
Klaus Theo Brenner.

On both sides of the city, much historic
substance was lost in World War II and the
sweeping changes that followed. Today the
rebuilding of the former imperial areas around
Unter den Linden, the Museumsinsel and
Schlossplatz revolve around a choice between
critical reconstruction or straightforward
replicas of the past. The Kommandenthaus,
next to the Staatsoper on Unter den Linden,
rebuilt by Thomas van den Valentyn as the
Stiftung Bertelsmann (2004), is an example
of the tendency towards historical replication,
as is the mooted reconstruction of Friedrich
Schinkel's Bauakademie next door. Thankfully,
some decisions have been taken in favour of
contemporary architecture, particularly the
new entrance building to the Auswärtiges Amt
('Foreign Office', 1999; Werdescher Markt 1) by
Thomas Müller and Ivan Reimann, and IM
Pei's triangular block for the **Deutsches
Historisches Museum** (2003; *see p79*) with
its curved foyer and cylindrical stair tower.

Berlin's return to capital-city status has
brought with it a number of interesting new
embassies and consulates in and around
a revived diplomatic quarter. Notable on
Tiergartenstrasse are the solid red-stone Indian
Embassy by Leon Wohlhage Wernik (2001),
and the extension of the existing Japanese
Embassy by Ryohei Amemiya (2000). There are
other intriguing examples around the corner in
Klingelhöferstrasse: the monumental, louvre-
fronted Mexican Embassy by Teodore Gonzalez
de Leon and J Francisco Serrano (2000); and
the encircling copper wall of the five Nordic
Embassies, containing work by various
Scandinavian architects after a plan by Alfred
Berger and Tiina Parkkinen (1999).

LINKING THE CITIES

There are four main initiatives intended to link
east and west: the area around Potsdamer Platz
and Leipziger Platz; the government quarter
and the 'Band des Bundes'; the new Berlin
Hauptbahnhof; and the reinstatement of the
Reichstag and Pariser Platz, the historical
formal entrance to the city. These are mostly
stand-alone projects outside the discussion on
critical reconstruction; their architecture reflects
this in a greater freedom of approach.

Potsdamer Platz (*see p102*) was the first of
the four, designed as a new urban area based on
the old geometries of Potsdamer and Leipziger
Platz. This former swathe of no-man's land was
redeveloped not only to link Leipziger Strasse to
the east and the Kulturforum to the west, but
also to supply Berlin with a new central focus in
an area formerly neither one side or the other.

The twin squares of Potsdamer Platz and
Leipziger Platz have been reinstated and five
small quarters radiate to the south and west.
Leipziger Platz has risen again as an enclosed
octagonal set piece, with modern terrace
buildings. Potsdamer Platz is by contrast once
more an open intersection, entrances to the
various quarters beyond staked out with major
buildings by Hans Kollhoff; Hilmer, Sattler
and Albrecht; Helmut Jahn; Renzo Piano; and
Schweger and Partner (1999-2003). The closed
metal and glass block of Helmut Jahn's **Sony
Center** (2000; *see p103*) is a singular piece,
organised around a lofty central forum with a
tented glass and textile roof as its spectacular
focus. Offices and apartments overlook an oval
public space with cinemas, bars, restaurants
and the remnants of the old Esplanade Hotel.

The DaimlerChrysler area on the other side of
Potsdamer Strasse, largest of the new quarters,
is a network of tree-lined streets with squares
and pavement cafés. It's also the work of
various architects, though Renzo Piano got all
the key pieces, notably the Arkaden shopping

mall, the Debis headquarters, and the Musicaltheater and Spielbank on Marlene-Dietrich-Platz (all 1999), all in a language of terracotta and glass. The quarter's south-west flank facing on to Tilla-Durieux-Park is a rich architectural mix, with Richard Rogers's two buildings of cylinders, blocks and wedges, and Arata Isozaki's concoction of ochre and brown stripes topped with a wavy glass penthouse (1998, all Linkstrasse).

'When Leipziger Platz is filled in, all the major symbolic linking projects will be complete.'

The 'Band des Bundes', the linear arrangement of new government buildings north of the Reichstag, is another project linking east and west. The result of a competition won by Axel Schultes and Charlotte Frank, it straddles the Spree and the former border, resembling a giant paper clip that binds the two halves of the city.

The centrepiece is the Bundeskanzleramt ('Federal Chancellery', Schlutes and Frank, 2000; Willi-Brandt-Strasse, Tiergarten), flanked by buildings with offices for parliamentary deputies. The arrangement reads like a unity thanks to a common and simple language of concrete and glass.

North of this across the Spree is the new central station, **Berlin Hauptbahnhof** (Von Gerkan Marg, 2006; *see p102* **Hub, bub**), which will open as Europe's largest rail intersection in May 2006. The 321-metre (1,053-foot) east–west overground platforms are to be covered by a barrel vault of delicately gridded glass. This will be crossed in a north–south direction by a station hall 180 metres long and 40 metres wide (590 feet by 131 feet), giving access to the trains on each intersecting level and to the shopping centre. Each side of the station hall is framed by buildings that span the east–west vault. The building has been designed to stand as a functional and symbolic link between east and west Germany, and as a hub of the whole European rail network.

Finally, there are the historical links. To the south of the Bundeskanzleramt is the **Reichstag** (*see p101*), sitting on the old threshold to the East, gutted, remodelled and topped with a new glass dome by Norman Foster (1999) to bring a degree of public access and transparency to a building with a dark past. **Pariser Platz** (*see p76*) has been almost entirely built to its old proportions. The US Embassy, long delayed but now

emerging in the south-west corner, will complete the set piece. Some of the buildings are a pale blend of modern and historic but there are exceptions such as the DG Bank by Frank Gehry (2000; Pariser Platz 3, Mitte) with its witty use of a rational façade in front of the spectacular free forms in its internal court, or Christian Portzamparc's French Embassy (2002; Pariser Platz 5, Mitte), which plays with classical composition but uses contemporary materials. In the opposite corner is the Akademie der Künste (2005; Behnisch and Partner), an exception to its neighbours with a welcoming and open glass façade. Round the corner in Wilhelmstrasse, Michael Wilford's **British Embassy** (2000; *see p275*; **photo** *p43*) also came to terms with the city's strict planning limitations by raising a conformist punched stone façade, which he then broke open to expose a rich and colourful set of secondary buildings in the central court.

FILLING IN THE BLANKS

When the last bits of Leipziger Platz and Pariser Platz are filled in, all the major symbolic linking projects planned in the Reunification period will be complete. While they wait for the urban fabric to gel around them, building on a smaller scale continues.

The last decade has also produced work that had nothing to do with Reunification. Daniel Libeskind's **Jüdisches Museum** (1999; *see p97*; **photo** *p44*) is a symbolic sculpture in the form of a lightning bolt, and Peter Eisenmann's controversial **Denkmal für die ermordeten Juden Europas** (2005; *see p78*) is a departure from a traditional memorial, with its open and sunken grid of 2,700 stelae.

Nicholas Grimshaw's Ludwig-Erhard-Haus for the stock exchange (1998; Fasanenstrasse 83-4) breaks with convention by taking the form of a glass and steel armadillo, though a city-required fire wall obscures the structure. On the corner at Kantstrasse 55, Josef Paul Kleihues's Kant-Dreieck (1995) extends the sculptural response with its huge metal weather vane. Dominique Perrault's **Velodrom** (1997; *see p244*) sinks into the landscape in the form of a disc and a flat rectangular box of glass, concrete and gleaming steel mesh.

Sauerbruch and Hutton's striking 21-storey headquarters for the GSW (1999; Kochstrasse 22A, Kreuzberg; **photo** *p42*), with its translucent sailed top and colourful and constantly changing façade, shows how singular buildings can raise the city's urban quality. Now that the major projects are all finished, it's time to let spontaneity return to the business of filling in the remaining blanks.

Where to Stay

Hotel-Pension Funk. *See p66.*

Where to Stay

Hotels that range from artfully weird to high-class and dignified.

As we go to press, the latest news is that in June 2006 the Rocco Forte group is due to open a fancy new joint called the Grand Hotel de Rome. It's right in the middle of Mitte, just behind Unter den Linden in the building that was once the East German central bank. Board members' offices are being converted into suites; the jewel room will house the pool; the colonnaded Palm Court ballroom will accommodate up to 350 people; a presidential suite has a balcony the length of the building overlooking Bebelplatz.

Of course, there are also openings at the other end of the market. Friedrichstrasse features several new backpacker hostels, including **Eastern Comfort**, on a boat moored on the river with easy access to Berlin's post-industrial nightlife district. And there always seems to be room for a few more art and design hotels, such as the new **Lux 11** or **Ku'damm 101**.

One way or another, the number of hotel beds in Berlin has almost tripled since 1992 – there are now almost 80,000. And a steadily increasing flow of visitors (there were around 6.7 million overnight stays within the first half of 2005, according to Berlin Tourismus Marketing) continues to encourage heavy investment. The good news for those visitors is that the average price of a Berlin hotel room is, at €143 per night (2003 figures, Berlin Tourismus Marketing), lower than in most other European cities; you would pay a lot more in Rome (€210), Paris (€231) or London (€349).

But don't be lulled into a false sense of security. A new hotel doesn't necessarily mean a good hotel, and good hotels have a tendency to be full. So book ahead, especially at times when there are major cultural events such as the **Berlin Marathon** (*see p185*) in September or the **FilmFest** (*see p186*) in February.

Most hotels have websites, which are worth checking for information about deals. Many, for example, offer cheaper rates at weekends. The concept of bed and breakfast is also catching on and many small *Pensionen*, especially in the Charlottenburg area, offer good value.

Hotels are mainly concentrated around the Gendarmenmarkt and Potsdamer Platz in the eastern city centre and around the Zoo and Savignyplatz in the west end. The selection of cheaper options in the east side of the city has dramatically improved in the last few years with hotels such as the **Honigmond** alongside all the new backpacker hostels. While it's good to stay in a central location, Berlin's public transport is excellent – so, unless you really are out in the suburbs, you're rarely more than half an hour from anywhere you might want to be.

The best Hotels

Ackselhaus & Bluehome
Self-catering in style. See p55.

Hotel Art Nouveau
Our favourite small hotel in Berlin. See p63.

Hotel Brandenburger Hof
Luxury meets hospitality. See p67.

CityStay Hostel
A great budget option. See p55.

Honigmond Restaurant-Hotel
Friendly staff, good restaurant, beautiful building. See p54.

Propeller Island City Lodge
Where weird is wonderful. See p68.

> ▶ ❶ Blue numbers given in this chapter correspond to the location of each hotel or hostel as marked on the street maps. *See pp300-312.*

PRICES

Our price categories work from the price of the cheapest double room: in a Deluxe hotel it will cost more than €170 per night; at an Expensive hotel it costs €120 to €170; Moderate is €70 to €119; and in a Cheap hotel or hostel it costs under €70. All prices given are room prices, unless specified. Note that rates tend to drop at weekends. Be wary of cancellation policies; it's best to ask before you book, just in case.

We've indicated where breakfast is included in the room price. Most hotels offer it as a buffet, which can be as simple as coffee and rolls (called *Schrippen* in Berlin) with cheese and salami, or the full works complete with smoked meats, muesli with fruit and yoghurt, and even a glass of sparkling wine. For hotels catering to a predominantly gay clientele, *see p208*.

Stepping into the calming colour scheme of the **Dorint Sofitel**. *See p51*.

Berlin Tourismus Marketing

Europa-Center, Budapester Strasse, Charlottenburg, 10787 (reservations/information 250 025/fax 2500 2424/www.berlin-tourist-information.de). U2, U9, S3, S5, S7, S9, S75 Zoologischer Garten. **Open** 10am-7pm Mon-Sat; 10am-6pm Sun. **Map** p305 G8.

This privatised tourist information service can sort out hotel reservations as well as tickets for shows and travel arrangements to Berlin. It provides a free listings booklet of over 400 hotels – but note that the hotels therein have paid to be included. It also has lists for campsites, apartments and holiday homes (the latter costs €1.50). Its website is quite comprehensive and you can download most information as PDF files, although they're often in German. It contains no phone numbers or direct links to the hotels, though – you have to book through BTM. But this can work to your advantage as it makes deals with hotels and often offers discounts. Allow plenty of time if you decide to visit one of the Berlin BTM branches: staff are notoriously inattentive. Booking online or by telephone is therefore recommended and saves you a €3 fee.

Other locations: Brandenburger Tor, Pariser Platz, Mitte; Fernsehturm, Alexanderplatz, Mitte; Tegel airport.

Mitte

Mitte is still a work in progress and new hotels are springing up all the time. The first wave of post-Wall, five-star establishments is now obliged to compete with assorted newcomers around Potsdamer Platz and the freshly renovated standards in the Zoo area. For the smaller, independent places, it's simply a case of adapt or die. You won't find much of the historic pension charm of, for example, Charlottenburg (*see p61*) aroumd here, but for shopping and sightseeing it's the most exciting part of Berlin to stay in.

Deluxe

Hotel Adlon Kempinski Berlin

Unter den Linden 77, 10117 (226 10/fax 2261 2222/www.hotel-adlon.de). S1, S2 Unter den Linden. **Rates** €320-€440 single; €370-€490 double; €650-€8,500 suite; €32 breakfast. **Credit** AmEx, DC, MC, V. **Map** p302/p311 L6 ❶

The original Hotel Adlon, renowned across the world for its luxurious interiors and discreet atmosphere, opened back in 1907. That version burned down after World War II. The new Adlon, rebuilt by the Kempinski group on the original site, opened in 1997. Located right next to the Brandenburg Gate and handy for the diplomatic quarter, it's the first choice for heads of state, movie stars and anyone who is keen to make an impression. The 409 rooms are decorated in a sort of international executive style; there are even three bulletproof presidential suites that look like a cross between the White House and a set from *Dallas*. The staff can be a little frosty if you don't look the part and the lobby sometimes gets a bit crowded with gawkers.

Bar. Disabled-adapted rooms (2). Gym. Internet (wireless). Parking (free). Pool (indoor). Restaurants (3). Room service. Spa. TV.

Dorint Sofitel

*Charlottenstrasse 50-52, 10117 (203 750/fax
2037 5100/www.sofitel.com). U2, U6 Stadtmitte.*
Rates €230-€250 single; €260-€280 double; €310-
€600 suite; €13-€23 breakfast. **Credit** AmEx, DC,
MC, V. **Map** p306/p310 M7 ❷
It's not easy to get a room at the Dorint Sofitel and
for good reason: it really is a very lovely hotel. A
great deal of attention has been paid to detail, from
the calming colour scheme to the excellent lighting.
The atmosphere is intimate and each room is beautifully styled, with perhaps the best-looking bathrooms in Berlin. Conference rooms are superb and
the hotel's 'wellness' area is a delight, complete
with plunge pools and picturesque views across the
Gendarmenmarkt. **Photo** *p49.*
*Bar. Business centre. Gym. Internet (wireless).
Parking (€16). Restaurants (2). Room service.
Spa. TV.*

Expensive

Hotel Albrechtshof

*Albrechtstrasse 8, 10117 (308 860/fax 3088 6100/
www.albrechtshof-hotels.de). U6, S1, S2, S5, S7, S9,
S75 Friedrichstrasse.* **Rates** (incl breakfast) €119-
€169 single; €149-€199 double; €230-€281 suite.
Credit AmEx, DC, MC, V. **Map** p302/p310 M6 ❸
Although it doesn't make a song and dance about it,
this place is a member of the Verband Christlicher
Hotels (Christian Hotels Association). Naturally,
then, it's got its own chapel. There's also a pleasant
courtyard garden, where breakfast is served during
the summer, and a newly renovated restaurant that
specialises in Berlin cuisine. The hotel is in the government quarter, close to Friedrichstrasse station
and several of the city's theatres. The decor isn't
much to write home about, but the place is agreeably smart and clean, and staff are friendly. The
owners have another two other hotels nearby, the
Augustinenhof and the Allegra – both can also be
booked at the above number.
*Bar. Disabled-adapted rooms. No-smoking rooms.
Parking (€12). Restaurant. TV.*

Alexander Plaza Berlin

*Rosenstrasse 1, 10178 (240 010/fax 2400 1777/
www.alexander-plaza.com). S5, S7, S9, S75
Hackescher Markt.* **Rates** €140 single; €150
double; €155-€215 suite; €15 breakfast buffet.
Credit AmEx, DC, MC, V. **Map** p303/p310 N6 ❹
Set in a handy location between Hackescher Markt,
Alexanderplatz and Museumsinsel, this handsome
building has been renovated as a comfortable modern establishment. Despite its proximity to one of
the liveliest parts of Mitte, the hotel stands in an
oasis of quiet. It is also quite close to the river. Staff
are polite and the decor isn't bad. There are 92
rooms, 32 of which are non-smoking. Each room has
a wireless network and there is also a fitness centre
and 'wellness landscape'.
*Gym. Internet (wireless). No-smoking rooms. Parking
(€15). Restaurant. Spa. TV (pay movies).*

Boardinghouse Mitte

*Mulackstrasse 1-2, 10119 (2804 5306/fax
2804 5308/www.boardinghouse-mitte.com).
U8 Weinmeisterstrasse or S5, S7, S9, S75
Hackescher Markt.* **Open** 9am-6pm daily. **Rates**
from €120 single apartment; from €135 double
apartment; from €150 maisonette; €6 breakfast.
Credit AmEx, DC, MC, V. **Map** p303/p310 O5 ❺
More of a place to stay for a week or more, offering
small, German designer-style serviced apartments
that are modern and fully kitted out, even offering
babysitting services. The Boardinghouse isn't
cheap, but prices get lower the longer you stay and
it's well located in the pretty Scheunenviertel and at
the heart of the fashion district. If you don't want to
cook for yourself, there are lots of good cafés and
restaurants just around the corner, and you'll be only
a short walk from Hackescher Markt. It's quite a hot
spot, so make sure to book well in advance.
Internet (high-speed). Parking (€9). TV/VCR.

Dietrich-Bonhoeffer-Haus

*Ziegelstrasse 30, 10117 (284 670/fax 2846 7145/
www.hotel-dbh.de). U6, S1, S2, S5, S7, S9, S75
Friedrichstrasse or S1, S2 Oranienburger Strasse.*
Rates (incl breakfast) €85 single; €120 double; €140
triple. **Credit** AmEx, MC, V. **Map** p302 M5 ❻
Built in 1987 as a meeting place for Christians from
East and West, this hotel is named after a theologian
executed by the Nazis for alleged participation in the
Hitler assassination attempt of 1944. The building
is centrally located in a quiet side street near the
Museumsinsel, and there's a friendly atmosphere –
everyone says hello and smiles a lot, which is unusual in this town. Rooms are enormous, the breakfast
is good and the day's weather forecast is helpfully
posted in the lift. A good place to stay.
Internet (dataport in some rooms). Restaurant. TV.

Hotel Garni Gendarm

*Charlottenstrasse 61, 10117 (206 0660/fax
2060 6666/www.hotel-gendarm-berlin.de). U2,
U6 Stadtmitte.* **Rates** €124 single; €149 double;
€164-€250 suite; €10 breakfast. **Credit** AmEx,
DC, MC, V. **Map** p306/p311 M7 ❼
If you fancy a five-star location but don't want to
blow a fortune, then this place is just the ticket. It
hasn't got a lot of extras except for a few pink frills,
but the rooms are smart and it's close to the
Gendarmenmarkt and an assortment of top restaurants. The Staatsoper is just down the road, too, so
it's well placed for cultural visits. Costing half as
much as the nearby Dorint or Hilton, you can't go
wrong – unless you decide to bring the car. In this
neighbourhood parking could end up costing as
much as your room.
Bar. Gym. TV.

Hotel Hackescher Markt

*Grosse Präsidentenstrasse 8, 10178 (280 030/fax
2800 3111/www.loock-hotels.com). S5, S7, S9, S75
Hackescher Markt.* **Rates** €120-€150 single; €130-
€180 double; €175-€205 suite. **Credit** AmEx, DC,
MC, V. **Map** p303/p310 N5 ❽

An elegant hotel in a nicely renovated townhouse that solves the noise problem at its Hackescher Markt location by having many rooms face inwards on to a tranquil green courtyard. Some rooms have balconies, all have their own bath with heated floor, and the suites are spacious and comfortable. The staff speak good English and are kind and helpful. Not cheap, though.

Bar. Internet (wireless). No-smoking floor. Parking (€15). TV.

Hotel-Pension Kastanienhof

Kastanienallee 65, 10119 (443 050/fax 4430 5111/ www.hotel-kastanienhof-berlin.de). U8 Rosenthaler Platz or U2 Senefelderplatz/tram M1, 12. **Rates** (incl breakfast) €93 single; €128 double; €138 apartment. **Credit** AmEx, MC, V. **Map** p303/p312 O4 **⑨**

If you can handle the pastel peach and pink decor, rooms here are generously proportioned and well equipped. Staff are friendly and there are three breakfast rooms (for smokers or non-smokers) and a bar. The hotel is well situated for exploring both Prenzlauer Berg and Mitte, as it lies on the border between the two districts. Up the street is a slew of cafés where the people-watching is excellent.

Bar. Internet (web TV). Parking (€7). TV.

Lux 11

Rosa-Luxemburg-Strasse 9-13 (936 2800/fax 9362 8080/www.lux-eleven.de). U2 Rosa-Luxemburg-Platz.

Lux 11 – from Stasi to stylish.

Rates €115-€125 apartment; €135-€185 suite; €25 extra bed. **Credit** AmEx, MC, V. **Map** p303/p310 O5 **⑩**

Opened in July 2005 in a building that once contained apartments for the secret police, these no-nonsense hotel-apartments are quite stylish, comfortable and well located for the fashionable parts of Mitte. Every apartment has a queen- or king-sized bed, a sitting area, a kitchen complete with microwave and dishwasher, and a raised shower up a couple of steps. Minty-white walls create a cool but clean atmosphere and you have your own intercom system to let guests in. The longer you stay, the cheaper it gets. There's an in-house Aveda salon and, as we went to press, there was talk of opening an Italian-Japanese fusion restaurant under the same management as Kuchi (*see p123*). There are no facilities for the disabled.

Bar. Café. Internet (wireless). No-smoking floors. Parking (€15). Restaurant. Spa. TV/DVD.

Maritim proArte Hotel Berlin

Friedrichstrasse 151, 10117 (203 35/fax 2033 4209/www.maritim.de). U6, S1, S2, S5, S7, S9, S75 Friedrichstrasse. **Rates** €149-€265 single; €168-€278 double; €300-€1,900 suite; €19 breakfast. **Credit** AmEx, DC, V, MC. **Map** p302/p311 M6 **⑪**

This gleaming edifice was one of the first of Berlin's 1990s 'designer hotels' and though since somewhat eclipsed by more recent arrivals, it's still a decent place with a central location. Adorned with huge paintings and designer furniture, the foyer, three restaurants and bar are pretty swish. The 403 rooms, apartments and suites all have fax and PC connections, air-conditioning and marble bathrooms. Staff are polite and helpful. The Brandenburg Gate and Reichstag are within walking distance, as are Unter den Linden, the swanky shops of Friedrichstrasse, and the bars and galleries of the Scheunenviertel.

Bar. Disabled-adapted rooms. Gym. Internet (dataport, wireless in some rooms). Parking (€15). Pool (indoor). Restaurants (3). Room service. TV (pay movies).

Radisson SAS Berlin

Karl-Liebknecht-Strasse 5, 10178 (238 280/fax 238 2810/www.berlin.radissonsas.com). S5, S7, S9, S75 Hackescher Markt. **Rates** €160-€235 single/double; €230-€650 suite; €21 breakfast buffet. **Credit** AmEx, DC, MC, V. **Map** p303/p311 N6 **⑫**

The world's largest free-standing aquarium (*see p88*) is in the middle of the atrium and many bedrooms have a 'sea view' on to the breathtaking 25m-high (82ft) tank, which houses 2,500 varieties of fish in over a million litres of salt water. For guests longing to dip their own toes, the hotel also has a large spa complete with swimming pool and sauna, and you can wet your whistle in the Aqua Lounge bar and restaurant. German-born designer Yasmine Mahmoudieh (she also did the new Airbus A380 interiors) has worked wonders with the 427 rooms, which are fresh, uncluttered and free of the blandness so typical of big chain hotels.

Bar. Disabled-adapted rooms. Gym. Internet (high-speed). Parking (free). Pool (indoor). Restaurants (2). Room service. Spa. TV (pay movies).

Westin Grand

Friedrichstrasse 158-64, 10117 (202 70/fax 2027 3362/www.westin.com/berlin). U6 Französische Strasse. **Rates** €131-€350 single; €165-€375 double; €397-€1,930 suite; €25 breakfast buffet. **Credit** AmEx, DC, V. **Map** p302/p311 M6 **13**

Just around the corner from Unter den Linden, the Westin Grand is pure five-star international posh (the Stones stay here when they are in town). Despite prefabricated East German construction, the hotel lives up to its name rather well: the decor is gratifyingly elegant with lots of glass and polished brass. The staircase and foyer are especially bombastic. The Grand's 35 suites are individually furnished with period decor themed after their names (try the Schinkel or Lessing suites); the regular rooms, meanwhile, are decorated in a tasteful, traditional style. Some rooms have wireless internet access. There's also a lovely garden and patio, plus a bar and restaurant. On the negative side, the claustrophobic corridors seem to go on for ever.

Bar. Business centre. Disabled-adapted rooms (2). Gym. Internet (dataport, wireless in some rooms). No-smoking floor. Pool (indoor). Restaurants (3). Room service. Spa. TV (pay movies).

Moderate

Hotel Am Scheunenviertel

Oranienburger Strasse 38, 10117 (282 2125/2830 8310/fax 282 1115/www.hotelamscheunenviertel.de). U6 Oranienburger Tor or S1, S2 Oranienburger Strasse. **Rates** (incl breakfast) €70 single; €80 double. **Credit** AmEx, DC, MC, V. **Map** p302/p310 M5 **14**

In the historical heart of town and the old Jewish Quarter, this 18-room hotel is a good base for exploring Berlin. The Museumsinsel, Friedrichstrasse and Hackesche Höfe are all close by, and by night the area is alive with bars and restaurants. Rooms are clean and comfortable, if a bit dark; each has a WC and good shower. On the downside, the bar below can get a bit noisy, but you can request a quieter room in the back. Staff are friendly and helpful. *TV.*

Art'otel Berlin Mitte

Wallstrasse 70-73, 10179 (240 620/fax 2406 2222/www.artotel.de). U2 Märkisches Museum. **Rates** €70-€180 single; €100-€210 double; €240-€260 suite; €4 breakfast. **Credit** AmEx, DC, MC, V. **Map** p307/p311 O7 **15**

On the banks of the Spree, this is a delightful fusion of old and new, housing both immaculately restored rococo reception rooms and ultra-modern bedrooms designed by Nalbach & Nalbach. The hotel is a showcase for the work of artist Georg Baselitz: all the rooms and corridors contain originals of his work, as well as work by AR Penck. Besides the art, every detail of the decor has been meticulously

attended to, from Philippe Starck bathrooms to the Marcel Breuer chairs in the conference rooms. Service is friendly and the views from the top suites across Mitte are stunning.

Bar. Disabled-adapted rooms. Internet (wireless). No-smoking rooms. Parking (€15). Restaurant. TV (pay movies).

Honigmond Garden Hotel

Invalidenstrasse 122, 10115 (2844 5577/fax 2844 5588/www.honigmond-berlin.de). U6 Oranienburger Tor. **Rates** (incl breakfast) €89-€109 single; €109-€159 double. **Credit** V. **Map** p302/p310 M4 **16**

Why doesn't Berlin have more hotels like this? The sister to Honigmond Restaurant-Hotel up the road (*see p54*), this place is charming and doesn't cost an arm and a leg. Choose between big rooms facing the street (loud if you open your windows) or smaller cabin-like ones facing the fish pond and Tuscan-style garden. There are also spacious apartments. Rooms are furnished with attention to detail: pine floors, iron bedsteads, oil paintings and antiques. There's also a sitting room for putting your feet up at the end of the day. The breakfast room has just been expanded, and there's an intimate conference loft over the bar for extra privacy. As the brochure points out, 'all the sights worth seeing in East Berlin can be reached by foot from here'.

Parking (€7). TV.

The charming **Honigmond Garden Hotel**.

Honigmond Restaurant-Hotel

Tieckstrasse 12, 10115 (284 4550/fax 2844 5511/
www.honigmond-berlin.de). U6 Oranienburger Tor.
Rates (incl breakfast) €59-€109 single; €79-€149
double. **Credit** V. **Map** p302/p310 M4 ⑰
The 40 rooms in this 1899 building are attractive and
spacious. Half of them were added in 2004 and the
rest were renovated. Some of the less expensive ones
lack their own shower and WC, but don't let that put
you off: this is probably the best and prettiest mid-
price hotel east of the Zoo. The beautiful new reception area has comfy chairs around a gas fireplace.
Breakfast is served in the Honigmond restaurant
(*see p53*), running since 1920. The friendly staff are
helpful and speak English. The Honigmond is also
within walking distance of the Scheunenviertel,
Museumsinsel, Friedrichstrasse and Hackescher
Markt. Highly recommended.
Bar. Disabled facilities. Parking (€7).
Restaurant. TV.

Künstlerheim Luise

Luisenstrasse 19, 10117 (284 480/fax 280 6942/
2844 8448/www.kuenstlerheim-luise.de). U6, S1, S2,
S5, S7, S9, S75 Friedrichstrasse. **Rates** €48-€115
single; €79-€150 double; €130-€175 suite; €8
breakfast. **Credit** MC, V. **Map** p302/p311 L6 ⑱
This 'artist home' deserves its reputation as one of
the city's most imaginative small hotels, with 50
rooms each decorated by a different artist. These
range from Dieter Mammel's room containing an
invitingly larger-than-life bed to a golden room
spray-painted with bananas by graffiti artist
Thomas Baumgärtel, or Angela Dwyer's 'Room Like
Any Other', whose surfaces are covered in stream-
of-consciousness scrawlings. Some rooms get a
little noise from the S-Bahn trains, but don't be put
off: this is a great place.
Bar. Disabled-adapted rooms. Restaurant.

Hotel Märkischer Hof

Linienstrasse 133, 10115 (282 7155/fax 282 4331/
www.maerkischer-hof-berlin.de). U6 Oranienburger
Tor. **Rates** (incl breakfast) €50-€60 single; €70-€80
double; €108 triple; €3 breakfast. **Credit** MC, V.
Map p302/p310 M5 ⑲
This quiet, family-run hotel is within walking dis-
tance of assorted cultural attractions, including the
Berliner Ensemble, the Metropoltheater and the
Staatsoper. It's an unremarkable place with a pen-
sion atmosphere, a good location and comfortable
rooms in an apricot hue.
Parking (free). TV.

mitArt Pension

Linienstrasse 139-40, 10115 (2839 0430/fax 2839
0432/www.mitart.de). U6 Oranienburger Tor. **Rates**
(incl breakfast) €88-€110 single; €105-€140 double.
Credit AmEx, MC, V. **Map** p302/p310 M5 ⑳
This elegant pension recently moved two blocks
from its former location to this beautifully restored
printing house. It's a good base for gallery-hopping:
Auguststrasse is around the corner and the owner
knows the art scene. The rooms themselves get their

character from an ever-changing international
gallery of works that range from sculpture to paintings to quilts such as those made by the octogenar-
ian Gerhard Knodel. Rooms are all warm and bright.
Breakfast, included in the price, is served in the
organic café on the ground floor. There aren't any
phones or TVs in the rooms, so you're pretty much
forced to kick back and relax.
Café.

Park Inn Hotel

Alexanderplatz 8, 10178 (238 90/fax 2389 4305/
www.parkinn.de). U2, U5, U8, S5, S7, S75, S9
Alexanderplatz. **Rates** €99-€250 single; €99-€240
double; €150-€335 suite; €15 breakfast. **Credit**
AmEx, MC, V. **Map** p303/p311 O5 ㉑
If you're in Berlin on a business trip, this place isn't
too bad. It's right on Alexanderplatz, so it has good
access to public transport, and the views are stunning (especially above the 16th floor) – rooms facing south or east overlook the Fernsehturm and
Karl-Marx-Allee. Ask for one of the recently renovated rooms (about half have been spruced up)
where extra windows have been added to make
them seem more spacious. There are good deals for
convention groups, but it's otherwise pretty impersonal and a bit heavy on the wallet.
Bar. Disabled-adapted rooms. Gym. Internet
(wireless). No-smoking floors. Parking (€15).
Restaurants (2). TV (pay movies).

Hotel Taunus

Monbijouplatz 1, 10178 (283 5254/fax 283 5255/
www.hotel-taunus.de). S5, S7, S9, S75 Hackescher
Markt. **Rates** €88 single; €99 double; €10 breakfast.
Credit AmEx, DC, MC, V. **Map** p303/p310 N5 ㉒
Tucked away behind Hackescher Markt S-Bahn
station, this small hotel has a great location, being
both close to the Museumsinsel and ideally placed
for exploring Mitte's bars and boutiques. It's a little
too near to the main tram terminus to be recommended for light sleepers during the summer and
the single rooms are a bit cramped, but you can't
beat it for city hustle and bustle. Ask for a room with
a view of the Dom.
Bar. Parking (€15). TV.

Cheap

Circus Hostel

Weinbergsweg 1A, 10119 (2839 1433/fax 2839
1484/www.circus-berlin.de). U8 Rosenthaler Platz.
Rates (per bed) €15 6- or 7-bed room; €18 4- or
5-bed room; €20 triple; €24-€60 twin; €32-€45 single;
€75-€130 2- to 4-bed apartment with balcony; €2
bedlinen (obligatory); €2-€4.50 breakfast. **No**
credit cards. **Map** p303/p310 N4 ㉓
The Circus now has two locations (the other is on
nearby Rosa-Luxemburg-Strasse). Both are a short
walk from Mitte's best bars and clubs. They're
friendly hostels with clean and bright rooms – a
rarity for backpacker places. The owners are young
travellers themselves and work hard to offer value

for money. Staff can arrange discount club and concert tickets, travel cards and tours of Berlin. You can also rent bicycles. For longer stays, the apartments on the top floor are well priced and have fine views. Single-sex rooms are also available. But be sure to book ahead: this place is deservedly popular.
Bar. Café. Disabled-adapted rooms. Internet (wireless in reception & café). TV room.
Other locations: Rosa-Luxemburg-Strasse 39, Mitte (2839 1433).

CityStay Hostel

Rosenstrasse 16, 10718 (2362 4031/www.city stay.de). S5, S7, S9, S75 Hackescher Markt. **Rates** (per bed) €15 dorm; €20 quad; €24 twin; €34 single; €2.50 bedlinen (obligatory); €4 breakfast. **Credit** MC, V. **Map** p311 O6 ㉔
This place is just about perfect for the price range. It's sparkling clean. The location is as central as can be, but it's on a quiet, pedestrianised street. Rooms are spacious and even dorm beds have their own reading lights. Large showers with lockable doors are on every floor and some rooms have their own shower and toilet. The cosmopolitan staff includes a lot of artists and writers and photographers. Security's pretty high for a hostel; you need an access card to get into the video-monitored building and on to your floor. The breakfast buffet features fresh organic bread and the kitchen staff will make your eggs however you want. Recommended.
Café. Internet (shared high-speed terminal).

ClubHouse Hostel

Kalkscheunenstrasse 4, 10117 (2809 7979/fax 2809 7977/www.clubhouse-berlin.de). U6, S1, S2, S5, S7, S9, S75 Friedrichstrasse. **Rates** (per bed) €13-€17 dorm; €17-€20 quad; €18-€21 triple; €22-€25 double; €32 single; €2 bedlinen (obligatory). **No credit cards. Map** p302/p310 M5 ㉕
If you want a relaxed, community feeling, try this place. The location is central, up a couple of flights in a historic building and cultural centre, the Kalkscheune ('chalk barn'). Rooms are curiously decorated with everything from an upside-down ceiling pool table to a sort of Legoland-ish map carpet. The international staff are amiable and they speak English; they can also arrange guided tours. No smoking except in the communal room, where there are also kitchen facilities. Apartments are available for longer stays.
Internet (shared terminal). No-smoking rooms.

Mitte's Backpacker Hostel

Chausseestrasse 102, 10115 (2839 0965/fax 2839 0935/www.backpacker.de). U6 Zinnowitzer Strasse. **Rates** (per bed) €12-€18 dorm; €19-€20 quad; €20-€21 triple; €22-€27 twin; €29-€30 single; €2.50 bedlinen (optional); €3 breakfast. **Credit** AmEx, MC, V. **Map** p302 L4 ㉖
Here since 1994, this is the oldest backpacker hostel in Mitte. It has a cosy, student-digs kind of atmosphere and can house up to 120 guests. The rooms are all decorated by artistically minded former guests and have been named accordingly. The

'Berlin Room' is amusing, with light fittings in the shape of the Fernsehturm and Funkturm; the 'Green Poem Room' may suit insomniacs, with walls covered in lengthy verses. There's a kitchen, bike rental and a video room with English films. Staff are multilingual and helpful.
Internet (shared terminal). TV/VCR/DVD room.

Prenzlauer Berg

This charming neighbourhood has a surprising dearth of decent accommodation. But atmospheric buildings and lively bars and cafés make it one of Berlin's most desirable places to live – especially for young families (*see p91* **The babes of Prenzl'berg**). If you intend to stay a while, try renting a private apartment or room from an accommodation agency (*see p68*).

Expensive

Ackselhaus & Bluehome

Belforter Strasse 21, 10405 (4433 7633/fax 441 6116/www.ackselhaus.de). U2 Senefelderplatz. **Rates** *Ackselhaus* €66-€95 single; €136 double; €105 suite. *Bluehome* €145 large bedroom; €150 bedroom & living room; €160 2 rooms; €30 extra person. *Breakfast* €7.50. **No credit cards. Map** p303/p312 P4 ㉗
Originally one house, now two buildings just doors apart – Bluehome is at No.24. What ties them together is their 'modernised colonial style', aqua colour scheme and shared reception at the original address. In Ackselhaus each apartment has a bedroom, sitting room, bathroom and kitchenette, with lovely old wooden floorboards, white walls, antique furniture and a Mediterranean feel. The blue and white 'maritime apartment', with mahogany furniture and seafaring paintings, is a particular gem. Most rooms have two beds, and one larger apartment is suitable for four to five people. The pricier Bluehome, with its blue façade, has balconies looking over Belforter Strasse and its Club de Mar restaurant, which offers a breakfast buffet and open fireplace. There's a delightful back garden with a large balcony you can lie out on in summer, complete with lawn chairs. Recommended, but book ahead.
Internet (wireless). Restaurant. TV.

Moderate

Hotel Greifswald

Greifswalder Strasse 211, 10405 (442 7888/ fax 442 7898/www.hotel-greifswald.de). Tram M4 Hufelandstrasse. **Rates** (incl breakfast) €65-€78 single; €78-€88 double. **Credit** AmEx, DC, MC, V. **Map** p303 Q4 ㉘
A clean, friendly, no-nonsense hotel that is near Kollwitzplatz and merely a short tram hop from Alexanderplatz. The rooms are cheerful, with colourful curtains and good-sized beds, and the staff

are bright and helpful. In the foyer you'll find an interesting collection of signed photographs from bands and musicians (Mitch Ryder is a regular); the hotel is also handy for the clubs Knaack and Magnet (*see chapter* **Music: Rock, World & Jazz**). In summer, breakfast is served in the courtyard. Apartments are available for longer stays. *Parking (free). TV.*

Myer's Hotel

Metzer Strasse 26, 10405 (440 140/fax 4401 4104/www.myershotel.de). U2 Senefelderplatz. **Rates** (incl breakfast) €85-€135 single; €110-€175 double. **Credit** AmEx, MC, V. **Map** p303 P4 ㉙
This renovated 19th-century townhouse is on a very quiet street. There's a garden and a glass-ceilinged gallery, and the big leather furniture in the smoking room invites you to light up a big, fat cigar. But as far as the rooms go, it seems a bit overpriced. The lovely Kollwitzplatz is around the corner and the hotel is within walking distance of Mitte.
Bar. Disabled-adapted rooms (3). Internet (dataport in most rooms). TV.

Cheap

Hotel Garni Transit Loft

Greifswalder Strasse 219, 10405 (4849 3773/fax 4405 1074). Tram M4 Hufelandstrasse. **Rates** (incl breakfast) €59 single; €69 double; €90 triple; €120 quad; €150 5-bed room; €19 (per person) dorm. **Credit** AmEx, MC, V. **Map** p303 Q4 ㉚
In an old, renovated factory (the entrance is at Immanuelkirchstrasse 14), this newish loft hotel caters for backpackers and groups of young travellers. The rooms all have en suite bathrooms, which means no wandering up and down the corridor in your towel, bumping into strangers. In the same building are a sauna, gym and billiard salon, which all offer special rates to guests of the hotel. There's good wheelchair access, an all-night bar and a cinema at street level.
Bar. Disabled-adapted rooms. Internet (shared high-speed terminal). TV.

Lette'm Sleep Hostel

Lettestrasse 7, 10437 (4473 3623/fax 4473 3625/ www.backpackers.de). U2 Eberswalder Strasse. **Rates** (per bed) €15-€19 3- to 7-bed room; €48 double; €59-€80 apartment; €3 bedlinen (optional). **Credit** MC, V. **Map** p303/p312 P2 ㉛
This small hostel is slap in the middle of Prenzlauer Berg, just off the Helmholtzplatz, which means greenery and lots of cafés. Breakfast is not provided, but you can make your own in the kitchen. The bathrooms and floors in the rooms have just been redone, which brightens the place up a bit. A newly renovated Biergarten is in the back, and should soon include a barbecue. Three new apartments have been added to the hostel and can sleep up to ten people each. There are special rates offered for those making longer stays.
Disabled-adapted rooms. Internet (shared terminal).

Hotel Greifswald – no nonsense. *See p55.*

Friedrichshain

Friedrichshain is the city's new bohemia, as students and creative types colonise the area between Karl-Marx-Allee's Stalinist architecture and the old industrial area around the Warschauer Brücke. With its decent transport connections, 'Eastie' feel, fantastic café breakfasts, reasonably priced bars and cafés, clubs and live music venues, it's a great area to stay in, especially if you're on a budget.

Moderate

East Side Hotel

Mühlenstrasse 6, 10243 (293 833/fax 2938 3555/ www.eastsidehotel.de). U1, S3, S5, S7, S9, S75 Warschauer Strasse. **Rates** (incl breakfast) €59-€65 single; €79-€85 double. **Credit** AmEx, MC, V. **Map** p308 R8 ㉜
This is a modest, simply decorated hotel, but with a great view of one of the last remaining stretches of the Berlin Wall. Get a room at the back if you want peace and quiet, but then you'll miss the sunset across the old red-brick factory buildings and the Oberbaumbrücke. Each double room comes with a large bathroom and bath. Easy access to public transport and a huge breakfast buffet. **Photo** *p58.*
Bar. Internet (shared wireless access). Parking (free). Restaurant. TV.

Cheap

A&O Backpackers

Boxhagener Strasse 73, 10245 (297 7810/fax 297 7820/www.aohostel.com). U5 Samariter Strasse or S3, S5, S7, S8, S9, S41, S42, S75, S85 Ostkreuz. **Rates** (per bed) €10 dorm; €16-€18 8- to 10-bed room; €24 4- to 6-bed room; €22 quad; €28-€32 twin (incl breakfast); €51-€59 single (incl breakfast); €3 bedlinen (optional); €5 breakfast buffet. **Credit** MC, V. **Map** p308 U8 ③

This hostel has a bit of a school camp atmosphere, but rooms are clean and the pine furniture is attractive. There is also the budget 'easy dorm': no locker, no shower, no booking, just a bed. There are cooking facilities and you can rent bicycles. In summer, guests hang out in the courtyard.
Internet (pay terminal, €1/20mins). No-smoking rooms. TV/DVD room.

Eastern Comfort

Mühlenstrasse 73-7, 10243 (6676 3806/fax 6676 3805/www.eastern-comfort.com). U1, S3, S5, S7, S9, S75 Warschauer Strasse. **Rates** (per bed) €17 4-bed cabin; €19 3-bed cabin; €23-€36 2-bed cabin; €58 single; €5 bedlinen & towel (optional); €3 breakfast. **Credit** MC, V. **Map** p308 R8 ③

East Side Hotel – modest. *See p57.*

Berlin's only 'hostel boat' opened in June 2005 at a mooring on the Spree just behind the East Side Hotel (*see p57*) and over the river from Kreuzberg. The rooms are clean and pretty spacious considering it's a boat, and all have their own shower and toilet. The four-person rooms could feel a bit cramped but if you need to stretch (or smoke) there are two common rooms, one lounge and three terraces offering beautiful river views. Weekly concerts in the lounge.
Internet (wireless in reception). No-smoking rooms (all). TV room.

Odyssee Globetrotter Hostel

Grünberger Strasse 23, 10243 (2900 0081/fax 2900 3311/www.hostel-berlin.de). U5 Frankfurter Tor. **Rates** (per person per night) €10 dorm; €13 8-bed room; €13-€15 6-bed room; €17 quad; €19 triple; €45-€52 double; €35 single; €3 breakfast buffet. **No credit cards. Map** p308 S7 ③

Walk along a long, dark corridor to the back yard, turn right, go up the stairs and you'll find the dimly lit reception, complete with billiards and table football. The hostel is clean and the showers have good water pressure, but if you're not into metal and tattoos, the common area may not suit you. There are lots of good alternative clubs and bars in the area and, for longer stays, there's a dorm with its own kitchen. Bedlinen is free and there are discounts for large groups and extended stays.
Bar. Internet (shared high-speed terminal). TV room.

Kreuzberg

Before the Wall came down, Kreuzberg was Berlin's alternative place to be. Now most people tend to overlook the area's charms in their rush for the 'new Mitte'. But they are making a mistake. Kreuzberg has some of Berlin's most picturesque streets, liveliest markets, coolest cafés and most interesting alternative venues.

Expensive

Hotel Riehmers Hofgarten

Yorckstrasse 83, 10965 (7809 8800/fax 7809 8808/www.hotel-riehmers-hofgarten.de). U6, U7 Mehringdamm. **Rates** (incl breakfast) €98-€108 single; €123-€138 double. **Credit** AmEx, MC, V. **Map** p306 M10 ③

In an historic building with 22 rooms, all newly renovated, and one of Berlin's prettiest courtyards, this place is wonderful. The styling is exquisite, the staff are charming, the rooms airy and well furnished, and the prices are pretty reasonable for what you get. The location is just a little off the beaten track, but Viktoriapark and the shops and cafés of Bergmannstrasse are nearby, Mitte is only ten minutes away by U-Bahn, and there are a couple of decent bars on the block. **Photo** *p59.*
Bar. Disabled-adapted rooms. Internet (wireless). Parking (€8). Restaurant. TV.

Cheap

BaxPax Berlin

Skalitzer Strasse 104, 10997 (6951 8322/fax 6951
8372/www.baxpax.de). U1 Görlitzer Bahnhof. **Rates**
(per person) €12-€17 dorm; €17-€18 quad; €19-€20
triple; €22-€23 double; €29-€30 single; €4 breakfast;
€2.50 bedlinen (optional). **Credit** AmEx, MC, V.
Map p307 Q9 **37**
Opened in 2001, Baxpax belongs to the same people
as Mitte's Backpacker Hostel (*see p55*). It follows the
usual Berlin backpacker formula: there are friendly,
English-speaking staff, a young, party atmosphere
and a self-service kitchen with a barbecue balcony.
There's also a good pool nearby, which is a boon in
summer after a hard morning of sightseeing. In one
of the dorms there's a bed made from a converted
Volkswagen Beetle. Female-only dorms need to be
booked in advance.
Bar. Internet (shared terminal). TV/VCR/DVD room.

Die Fabrik

Schlesische Strasse 18, 10997 (611 7116/fax 618
2974/www.diefabrik.com). U1 Schlesisches Tor.
Rates €34-€38 single; €40-€64 double; €58-€69
triple; €80-€84 quad; €16-€18 (per person) dorm.
No credit cards. Map p308 R9 **38**
Fabrik is German for 'factory' and this hostel, like
most others in Berlin, is in a renovated industrial
building. There's no kitchen, TV room or billiards.
It's just a bed and a locker; breakfast in the café next
door costs extra. The best feature is the solar power
that provides hot water and heating for the building. Children under six stay for free, under-12s get
a 50% discount, and bedlinen is free. It's a good location for fast food and funky bars.
Internet (shared terminal).

Pension Kreuzberg

Grossbeerenstrasse 64, 10963 (251 1362/fax
251 0638/www.pension-kreuzberg.de). U6, U7
Mehringdamm. **Rates** (incl breakfast) €40-€55
single; €52-€65 double; €22.50-€25 (per person) 3-
to 5-bed room. **No credit cards. Map** p306 M10 **39**
A small, friendly 12-room pension in a typical old
Berlin building. It's not for the lazy or infirm, as
there are four steep flights of stairs up to reception.
Only half the rooms have their own bathrooms
(there's a communal one on each floor), although
they all have washbasins. There's a cheap and cheerful vibe, and a breakfast room with buffet. Definitely
worth considering if you're a family travelling on a
budget.

Hotel Transit

Hagelberger Strasse 53-4, 10965 (789 0470/
fax 7890 4777/www.hotel-transit.de). U6, U7
Mehringdamm. **Rates** (incl breakfast) €50-€59
single; €60-€69 double; €90 triple; €120 quad;
€150 5-bed room; €19 (per person) dorm. **Credit**
AmEx, MC, V. **Map** p306 M10 **40**
Another converted factory, another budget hotel.
This one is very bright and airy, and located in one
of the most beautiful parts of Kreuzberg, handy for

Hotel Riehmers Hofgarten. *See p58.*

Viktoriapark and a variety of cafés and restaurants.
The 49 rooms are basic but clean, and the €19 dor-
mitory is pretty good value (book in advance;
women-only dorms are also available). All rooms
have showers and toilets, staff speak good English
and there's a 24-hour bar.
Bar. Internet (shared terminal).

Tiergarten

Tiergarten is now officially part of Mitte, but
nobody seems to pay much attention apart
from civil servants. Some of the following
establishments are dotted around the edge of
the huge park that gives this district its name.
Tiergarten also contains a whole bunch of
embassies, cultural institutions and, of course,
Potsdamer Platz, where various glitzy five-star
palaces are now clustered.

Deluxe

Berlin Marriott Hotel

Inge-Beisheim-Platz 1, 10785 (220 000/fax 220 001
000/www.marriott.de/BERMC). U2, S1, S2, S9, S26
Potsdamer Platz. **Rates** from €189 single/double;
€229-€1,800 suite; €23 breakfast buffet. **Credit**
AmEx, DC, MC, V. **Map** p306/p311 L7 **41**
Opened in 2004 and more modest than the Ritz-
Carlton (*see p60*) next door, the Marriott also has

five stars. It is more reasonably priced than its competitor, and decorated in what is called a 'modern designer' style. The cool white interior of the enormous atrium is impressive and the rotating globe fountain is mesmerising. By contrast, the rooms are pretty bland. The restaurant isn't too bad, though, and the hotel's proximity to the Tiergarten means you can go for a spectacular run past the Reichstag and Brandenburg Gate.

Bar. Business centre. Gym. Internet (high-speed). Parking (€24). Pool (indoor). Restaurant. Room service. TV.

Grand Hotel Esplanade

Lützowufer 15, 10785 (254 780/fax 254 788 222/ www.esplanade.de). U1, U2, U3, U4 Nollendorfplatz. **Rates** €170-€280 single; €195-€305 double; €420-€2,300 suite; €20 breakfast. **Credit** AmEx, DC, MC, V. **Map** p306 J8 **42**

One of Berlin's better luxury hotels, next to the Landwehr Canal and close to the Tiergarten. The entrance lives up to the name, with a huge, gushing wall of water and hundreds of lights glittering overhead. The lobby is spacious and beautifully decorated; art exhibitions adorn some of the walls. The rooms are tasteful and gratifyingly free of frilly decor; three floors have been set aside for non-smokers. There's a fitness centre and a triangular swimming pool. An added benefit of staying here is being within stumble-back-to-bed distance of Harry's New York Bar – it's on the ground floor,

Ritz-Carlton: butlers for every occasion.

underlining the distinctly American feel of the place. There are also three restaurants: gourmet, traditional Berlin and the Orangerie breakfast restaurant. *Bars (2). Disabled-adapted rooms. Internet (wireless). No-smoking rooms. Parking (free). Pool (indoor). Restaurants (3). Spa.*

Grand Hyatt

Marlene-Dietrich-Platz 2, 10785 (2553 1234/fax 2553 1235/www.berlin.grand.hyatt.com). U2, S1, S2, S9, S26 Potsdamer Platz. **Rates** (incl breakfast) €235 single; €265 double; €520-€3,335 suite. **Credit** AmEx, DC, MC, V. **Map** p306/p311 K8 **43**

A classy hotel. The lobby is all matt black, slick surfaces and wood panelling with the odd minimalist art touch – a refreshing change from the usual five-star marble or country mansion look. The rooms are spacious and elegant without a floral print in sight; the internet TV is also a nice touch. The rooftop spa and gym has a splendid pool with views across the city. The lobby restaurant, the Tizian Lounge, is truly excellent, with a menu of international classics and a good wine list.

Bar. Disabled-adapted rooms. Gym. Internet (wireless, web TV). Parking (€20). Pool (indoor). Restaurants (3). Spa. TV.

Hotel Intercontinental

Budapester Strasse 2, 10787 (260 20/fax 2602 2600/www.interconti.com). U2, U9, S5, S7, S9, S75 Zoologischer Garten/bus 200. **Rates** from €290 single/double; €374-€2,100 suite; €22 breakfast. **Credit** AmEx, DC, MC, V. **Map** p305 H8 **44**

Overlooking the Zoo and on the western edge of the new diplomatic quarter, the extremely plush and spacious 'Interconti' exudes luxury. The rooms are large, tastefully decorated and graced with elegant bathrooms. The airy lobby, with its soft leather chairs, is ideal for reading the paper. Thomas Kammeier of the hotel restaurant, Hugo's, became the Berlin Masterchef of 2004. The whopping gym and spa measure over 1,000sq m (nearly 11,000sq ft). Visiting heads of state take note: management claims its President Suite is the safest in the city. *Bar. Gym. Internet (high-speed). No-smoking rooms. Parking (€19.50). Pool (indoor). Room service. Spa. TV.*

Ritz-Carlton

Potsdamer Platz 3, 10785 (337 777/fax 337 775 555/www.ritzcarlton.com). U2, S1, S2, S9, S26 Potsdamer Platz. **Rates** €250-€280 single; €280-€310 double; €305-€5,000 suite; €28 breakfast. **Credit** AmEx, DC, MC, V. **Map** p306/p311 L7 **45**

It's flashy, it's trashy, it's Vegas-meets-Versailles. The 2004 Ritz-Carlton is so chock-a-block with black marble, gold taps and taffeta curtains that the rooms seem stuffy, small and cramped. It's supposedly art deco style, but overall seems rather more upmarket shopping mall. Still, the oyster and lobster restaurant is deliciously decadent, and the service fantastic: the technology butler will sort out bugs in your computer connection and the bath butler will run your bath. Bring a fat wallet, and get ready to be pampered.

*Bar. Disabled-adapted rooms. Gym. Internet
(wireless). Parking (€28). Pool (indoor). Restaurants
(2). Room service. TV (pay movies, DVD).*

Moderate

Hotel Alt Berlin
*Potsdamer Strasse 67, 10785 (260 670/fax 2606
7445/www.altberlin-hotel.de). U1 Kurfürstenstrasse.*
Rates (incl breakfast) €85-€110 single; €99-€145
double; free under-12s. **Credit** AmEx, DC, MC, V.
Map p306 K8 ⓐ
This 'turn-of-the-century-Berlin' hotel actually
opened just a few years ago – the furnishings might
look retro, but they're actually modern. The restaurant downstairs resembles a cluttered museum and
serves up hearty, traditional Berlin food. The hotel
is within walking distance of Potsdamer Platz, the
Wintergarten variety theatre, the Nationalgalerie
and the Philharmonie. If you need wireless internet
access, ask to be put on the first or second floor.
*Bar. Internet (wireless in some rooms). Parking (€7).
Restaurant. TV.*

Charlottenburg

You may not find the hippest nightlife or cafés
around here, but there's plenty of fine dining
and elegant shopping in Berlin's west end, plus
an assortment of museums and attractions.

This is the smart end of town, within easy reach
of anything you might want to do, and you can
expect to find five-star luxury hotels alongside
the traditional charms of many great little
pensions, often housed in grand *Gründerzeit*
townhouses.

Deluxe

Kempinski Hotel Bristol Berlin
*Kurfürstendamm 27, 10719 (884 340/fax
883 6075/www.kempinskiberlin.de). U1, U9
Kurfürstendamm.* **Rates** €270-€350 single;
€330-€420 double; €480-€2,500 suite; €45 extra
bed; €23 breakfast buffet. **Credit** AmEx, DC,
MC, V. **Map** p305/p312 F8 ⓐ
Probably Berlin's most famous hotel, this is the well-
aged mother of all Kempinskis and was a famous
restaurant before it became a hotel in 1951. The
rooms aren't as plush as one might expect at these
prices, but the original Berlin artwork, wonderful
pool and saunas make up for it. It's well situated and
the staff are helpful and nice. The Kempinski Eck
restaurant will have been newly refurbished by the
time this edition comes out. It will have its normal
street-side seating plus an old-style balcony overlooking the Ku'damm.
*Bar. Business centres (2). Gym. Internet (wireless).
Parking (€18). Pool (indoor). Restaurants (2). Room
service. Spa. TV (pay movies).*

Hotel Art Nouveau: One of Berlin's loveliest small hotels. *See p63.*

Swissôtel Berlin

*Augsburger Strasse 44, 10789 (220 100/fax
220 102 222/www.swissotel.com). U2, U9, S3,
S5, S7, S9, S75 Zoologischer Garten or U1, U9
Kurfürstendamm.* **Rates** €160-€590 single; €180-
€610 double; €260-€700 suite; €21 breakfast. **Credit**
AmEx, DC, MC, V. **Map** p305/p312 G8 ❹❸
The hotel's styling is elegant and the second-floor
foyer – away from the frantic Ku'damm – is architectural genius. Rooms overlook the inner courtyard
or the Ku'damm; choose the latter, on a high floor,
for a great sunset view. The Restaurant 44 (*see p142*)
is one of Berlin's top gourmet spots; restaurant guide
Gault Millau awarded chef Tim Raue 'Shooting Star
of the Year 2005'. There's no pool, but the option of
a massage in your room may compensate.
*Bar. Disabled-adapted rooms (3). Gym. Internet
(wireless). Parking (€18). Restaurant. Room
service. TV (pay movies).*

Expensive

Hotel Art Nouveau

*Leibnitzstrasse 59, 10629 (327 7440/7434/fax 3277
4440/www.hotelartnouveau.de). U7 Adenauerplatz or
S5, S7, S9, S75 Savignyplatz.* **Rates** (incl breakfast)
€95-€140 single; €120-€170 double; €165-€230 suite.
Credit AmEx, DC, MC, V. **Map** p305/p312 E8 ❹❾
This is one of the loveliest small hotels in Berlin.
The rooms are decorated with flair in a mix of
Conran-modern and antique furniture. The en suite
bathrooms are well integrated into the rooms with-
out disrupting the elegant townhouse architecture.
Even the TVs are stylish. The breakfast room has a
cooking area and a refrigerator full of goodies if
you should you feel peckish in the wee hours. Highly
recommended. **Photo** *p61*.
*Internet (dataport). No-smoking rooms. Parking (€4).
TV.*

Hotel Bleibtreu

*Bleibtreustrasse 31, 10707 (884 740/fax 8847 4444/
www.bleibtreu.com). U1 Uhlandstrasse or S5, S7,
S75 Savignyplatz.* **Rates** (incl breakfast) €122-€222
single; €132-€232 double; €40 extra bed. **Credit**
AmEx, DC, MC, V. **Map** p305/p312 E9 ❺⓪
The Bleibtreu is a cosy and smart establishment popular with media and fashion visitors. Renovated for
its tenth birthday in 2005, the rooms are a little on
the small side but they're all individually and lovingly decorated with environmentally friendly materials. A pleasant relief from the posh-bland look of
so many hotels in this category. The restaurant here
has been winner of *Bio Food Guide*'s Fit Food Award
each year from 2003 to 2005; it features speciality
low-fat foods prepared without sugar, no-sugar
bread, fresh fruit and veggie juices. The hotel also
offers private yoga classes as well as reflexology. A
wonderful choice for the health-conscious, then, but
good service with lots of pampering and attention
means it should appeal to everyone.
*Disabled-adapted rooms. Internet (wireless). Parking
(€15). Restaurant. TV.*

Concept Hotel

*Grolmanstrasse 41-3, 10623 (884 260/fax 8842
6500/www.concept-hotel.com). U1 Uhlandstrasse or
S5, S7, S9, S75 Savignyplatz.* **Rates** (incl breakfast)
€115-€145 single; €145-€180 double; €180-€260 suite.
Credit AmEx, DC, MC, V. **Map** p305/p312 F8 ❺❶
Generally pretty smart. Be sure to ask for a room in
the new wing if you want internet access and air-
conditioning in your room. There are conference
facilities and a restaurant and bar. The bar's pretty
boring and the lobby's not the most exciting either
(except for the Buddy Bear), but the hotel is quiet
and on a lovely street in the smart shopping area
with a good selection of restaurants nearby.
*Bar. Disabled-adapted rooms. Internet (some rooms).
No-smoking floors. Parking (€10.50). Restaurants
(2). TV.*

Hecker's Hotel

*Grolmanstrasse 35, 10623 (889 00/fax 889 0260/
www.heckers-hotel.com). U1 Uhlandstrasse or S5,
S7, S9, S75 Savignyplatz.* **Rates** €150-€170 single;
€120-€190 double; €310-€350 suite; under-12s free;
€15 breakfast. **Credit** AmEx, DC, MC, V. **Map**
p305/p312 F8 ❺❷
A smart, high-quality hotel with a stylish lobby and
an air of privacy. The recently renovated rooms are
spacious and comfortable, especially the suites; the
latter come with air-conditioning and Bang &
Olufsen DVD TVs. Bathrooms are clean and well lit,
with marble tiling. Single rooms have a shower and
doubles have a bath. Other highlights include the
roof terrace and the Cassambalis House restaurant,
which serves decent Mediterranean cuisine.
*Bar. Disabled-adapted room. No-smoking floors.
Parking (€12). Restaurant. TV.*

Q!

*Knesebeckstrasse 67, 10623 (810 0660/fax 810 066
666/www.loock-hotels.com). U1 Uhlandstrasse or S5,
S7, S9, S75 Savignyplatz.* **Rates** €130 single; €150
double; €200 studio; €300 penthouse. **Credit** AmEx,
MC, V. **Map** p305/p312 F8 ❺❸
It's almost worth staying here just for the beautiful
spa downstairs, complete with a Japanese washing
room, two saunas, a sand lounge and optional massage. Rooms have their own temperature control and
are wonderfully crafted; both bed and bath are part
of the same wooden unit, meaning you can literally
roll into bed after a comforting soak. Rooms have
separate shower and toilet as well. The floor, ceiling
and walls of the bar are red, the furniture blue-grey
and organically shaped. Despite winning the Travel
& Leisure Design Award 2005, Q! is no stiff magazine feature – it's young and friendly. Recommended.
Bar. Internet (wireless). Restaurant. Spa. TV.

Savoy Hotel Berlin

*Fasanenstrasse 9-10, 10623 (311 030/fax 3110
3333/www.hotel-savoy.com). U2, U9, S3, S5, S7,
S9, S75 Zoologischer Garten.* **Rates** (incl breakfast)
€142-€292 single; €152-€295 double; €202-€355
suite; €40 extra bed; €19 breakfast. **Credit** AmEx,
MC, V. **Map** p305/p312 F8 ❺❹

This smart, stylish hotel is set back from the hustle and bustle around Zoologischer Garten. Erected in 1929, it was the hotel of choice for author Thomas Mann and continues to impress. The rooms have recently been renovated; there's a new Greta Garbo suite in complete white and a Henry Miller suite in black marble. The beautiful restaurant, the Weinrot, serves South American cuisine. Best of all is the fabulous Times Bar, with its own library and excellent collection of Cuban cigars. The Savoy lives up to its name both in decor and service, and it is well situated for business visitors on a tight schedule who may need to meet and wine and dine clients on site. There's also a lovely back patio and babysitting and a range of alternative healing services on offer.
Internet (wireless). Restaurant. Room service. TV (pay movies).

SORAT Art'otel Berlin

Joachimstaler Strasse 29, 10719 (884 470/ fax 8844 7700/www.sorat-hotels.com). U1, U9 Kürfurstendamm. **Rates** (incl breakfast) €118-€168 single; €138-€188 double. **Credit** AmEx, DC, MC, V. **Map** p305/p312 G8 ⑤⑤

Just off the Ku'damm in the heart of the west end, this hotel is art-mad, with collages and prints of work by Fluxus artist Wolf Vostell adorning its walls. The place has lost a bit of its shine and the Sottsass-like styling is now somewhat dated, but the rooms are still comfortable. Ask to see a couple of them first, because they range from good to great with no apparent relation to the price – the *Eckzimmer* ('corner rooms') are the best. The breakfast room is very pleasant: the buffet is splendid and the room opens on an attractive garden in summer. The bar recently got a facelift and offers wireless internet access.
Bar. Disabled-adapted rooms (4). Internet (wireless in some rooms). No-smoking floors. Parking (€11). Restaurant. TV (pay movies).

Moderate

Askanischer Hof

Kurfürstendamm 53, 10707 (881 8033/8034/ fax 881 7206/www.askanischer-hof.de). U7 Adenauerplatz or S5, S7, S9, S75 Savignyplatz. **Rates** (incl breakfast) €95-€110 single; €117-€145 double; €200 suite. **Credit** AmEx, DC, MC, V. **Map** p305/p312 E9 ⑤⑥

One of the city's best-kept secrets, despite its location on one of Berlin's best-known streets, this friendly place has hosted visiting actors and literary types since long before World War II. The breakfast room doesn't seem to have changed since 1910 and each room spans a century of European interiors: 1970s chrome standard lamps teamed with overstuffed leather chesterfields, heavy Prussian desks and 1940s wallpaper. Full of atmosphere and in dodgy taste, this is vintage Berlin. And if you're feeling peckish in the middle of the night, the staff will make breakfast 24 hours a day. Recommended.
Bar. Internet (wireless). Parking (free). TV.

Berlin Plaza Hotel

Knesebeckstrasse 62, 10719 (884 130/fax 8841 3754/www.plazahotel.de). U1 Uhlandstrasse. **Rates** (incl breakfast) €80-€150 single; €105-€180 double. **Credit** AmEx, DC, MC, V. **Map** p305/p312 F9 ⑤⑦

Rooms are either decorated in grey and white or maroon and white, and are rather plain. Still, they're clean, and all doubles and some singles come equipped with both shower and bath. The breakfast buffet is good, particularly the mix-your-own muesli and fresh bread, which is baked on the premises regularly. German specialities, meanwhile, are served in the restaurant and bar. Children under 16 stay in their parents' room for free and the rooftop view on the seventh floor is lovely.
Bar. Internet (wireless). Parking (€10). Restaurant. TV (pay movies).

Hotel Pension Castell

Wielandstrasse 24, 10707 (882 7181/fax 881 5548/ www.hotel-castell.de). U1 Uhlandstrasse or U7 Adenauerplatz. **Rates** (incl breakfast) €65-€80 single; €85-€110 double; €105-€120 triple/quad; €15 extra bed. **Credit** AmEx, V. **Map** p305/p312 E9 ⑤⑧

Tucked away just off the Ku'damm, this 30-room pension has friendly, if somewhat haphazard, staff and clean, tidy, good-sized rooms. There's no danger of it gracing the pages of an interiors magazine, though – you need to be quite keen on the colour tangerine to stay here. Almost all rooms have a shower and TV, but some lack a WC.
Parking (€3). TV.

Hotel-Pension Dittberner

Wielandstrasse 26, 10707 (884 6950/fax 885 4046/ www.hotel-ditterberner.de). U7 Adenauerplatz or S5, S7, S9, S75 Savignyplatz. **Rates** (incl breakfast) €67-€88 single; €92.50-€107.50 double; €118 suite; €23 extra bed. **No credit cards. Map** p305/p312 E9 ⑤⑨

Stylish, eclectic and grand, this pension is full of fine original artworks from the gallery downstairs. It has enormous crystal chandeliers and comfortable rooms furnished with love and care. Owner Frau Lange is friendly and helpful, going out of her way to make guests feel at home, which is a rare treat in Berlin. What's more, some of the rooms and suites are truly palatial. One of the best pensions in the city. Delightful breakfast room.
Internet (shared terminal). TV.

Hotel Gates

Knesebeckstrasse 8-9, 10623 (311 060/fax 312 2060/www.hotel-gates.de). U2 Ernst-Reuter-Platz. **Rates** €85-€190 single; €110-€120 double; €35 extra bed. **Credit** AmEx, DC, MC, V. **Map** p305 F7 ⑥⓪

We were ready to be critical here just because of the name, but this actually turns out to be a pretty good four-star – particularly for business travellers who use Windows. There's a PC in every room with unlimited free internet access. The superior and deluxe rooms are especially comfortable, offering huge bathrooms and plenty of work space. The hotel is a great place to stay if you are in town for one of the trade fairs at the Messegelände and there's also

a fine selection of restaurants around nearby Savignyplatz. Discounts are available at weekends. Note: there are no disabled facilities.
Internet (computer provided). Parking (€15). TV.

Hotel-Pension Modena

Wielandstrasse 26, 10707 (885 7010/fax 881 5294/www.hotel-modena.de). U7 Adenauerplatz or S5, S7, S9, S75 Savignyplatz. **Rates** €55-€70 single; €75-€100 double. **Credit** AmEx, DC, MC, V. **Map** p305/p312 E9 ⓰

Taking the 1912 elevator up to the Modena is an experience in itself. The 19-room pension is sweet, clean and cheap. Staff are very friendly, accommodating and can speak English. A good place if you're travelling as part of a group and want to be in the heart of the west end. The price even gets lower the longer you stay.
Internet (wireless). TV room.

Cheap

Hotel Bogota

Schlüterstrasse 45, 10707 (881 5001/fax 883 5887/ www.hotelbogota.de). S5, S7, S9, S75 Savignyplatz. **Rates** (incl breakfast) €44-€72 single; €69-€98 double; €87-€120 triple; €134 quad. **Credit** AmEx, DC, MC, V. **Map** p305/p312 E9 ⓱

The stylish and attractive foyer of this characterful two-star belies rooms more functional than fancy. That said, this place is terrific value with a great atmosphere, wonderfully friendly staff and an interesting history. The fashion and portrait photographer Else Simon, who worked under the name Yva, had her apartment and studio in this building. Helmut Newton learned his craft here as her assistant before fleeing Germany in 1938. Yva herself died at the Majdanek concentration camp in 1942. Some of her photos are displayed in her former studio, now a fourth-floor hallway. There is a variety of rooms available, hence the wide price range. About half of the doubles have their own showers and toilets, and all have at least a washbasin.
TV (TV room, some individual rooms).

Hotel Charlot am Kurfürstendamm

Giesebrechtstrasse 17, 10629 (327 9660/fax 3279 6666/www.hotel-charlot.de). U7 Adenauerplatz or S3, S5, S6, S7, S9 Charlottenburg. **Rates** €52-€75 single; €62-€118 double. **Credit** MC, V. **Map** p305/p312 E9 ⓲

This is a moderately priced hotel that your mum might like to stay in. It's in a nice residential area full of chic shops and good cafés. The historical Jugendstil building has been carefully restored and has friendly management. The 42 bedrooms are spotless, although the decor is quite pink and frilly. Not all rooms have showers and toilets, but the communal facilities aren't too bad. Despite its name, the hotel is about five minutes' walk from the Ku'damm.
Bar. Parking (€6.50). TV.

Hotel-Pension Columbus

Meinekestrasse 5, 10719 (881 5061/fax 881 3200). U1, U9 Kurfürstendamm or U2, U9, S3, S5, S7, S9, S75 Zoologischer Garten. **Rates** (incl breakfast) €35-€55 single; €65-€85 double. **Credit** AmEx, MC, V. **Map** p305/p312 F9 ⓳

Hotel-Pension Funk: sleep like a star of silent movies. *See p66.*

This hotel is right next to the Ku'damm. The rooms are charming and unique. There are two larger rooms with an optional adjoining two-bed room, which can be quite practical for families travelling together. Prices are unbeatable for the area and the owners extremely kind. The breakfast room is a quaint place in which to enjoy the home-made yoghurt. TV.

Hotel-Pension Funk

Fasanenstrasse 69, 10719 (882 7193/fax 883 3329/www.hotel-pensionfunk.de). U1 Uhlandstrasse. **Rates** (incl breakfast) €34-€82 single; €52-€113 double; €23 extra bed. **Credit** AmEx, MC, V. **Map** p305/p312 F9 ⑥⑤

Despite fancy surroundings, this pension offers extremely good value. Built in 1895, it's actually the former apartment of Danish movie star Asta Nielsen, who starred in a number of silent films, including a gaucho-dancing femme fatale in *Afgrunden* (*The Abyss*) from 1910. The charming proprietor does his best to maintain the ambience of a graceful pre-war flat. The 14 large and comfortable rooms are furnished to cosy effect with elegant pieces from the 1920s and 1930s: satinwood beds and matching wardrobes. The large family room is in the former salon. The only niggle is that some of the showers are somewhat antiquated, but that's also part of the charm. Recommended. **Photo** *p65.*
Internet (shared terminal). Room service.

Pension-Gästezimmer Gudrun

Bleibtreustrasse 17, 10623 (881 6462/fax 883 7476). S5, S7, S9, S75 Savignyplatz. **Rates** (incl breakfast) €47.50 single; €67.50-€72.50 double. **No credit cards. Map** p305/p312 E8 ⑥⑥

A hotel of one's own

Is it a surprise that Berlin is home to the world's oldest women-only hotel? If so, the surprise shouldn't lie in the fact that Berlin claims this honour. After all, even before the late 1940s, when the *Trümmerfrauen* ('rubble women') rebuilt the devastated city, Berlin women had gained a reputation internationally for their strength, innovations and independent spirit. No, the real surprise is that the world's oldest women-only hotel is a mere 16 years of age and, rather than a Kreuzbergian castle of rainbow flags and butch bellhops, or a Prenzl'bergian paradise of daycares and organic beauty salons, this ground-breaking institution is tucked away on an anonymous street off the Ku'damm, in the top two floors of a residential apartment building.

Indeed, the **Hotel Artemisia** (*see p68*) – named for the Italian painter – leaves an impression more institutional than institution. There are no leather sofas or deep-pile rugs. A glossy, cream-coloured, wooden staircase curving down into the brightly lit reception area suggests that at any minute a swarm of giggling schoolgirls will descend. Communal fridges in the hallways reveal sealed stashes of apples and soya milk. The 12 bedrooms (all but two are en suite, sizes vary from palatial to tiny) are cheerful, clean and pragmatically furnished – like dorm rooms put together from high-quality donations. Each bedroom features work by a different Berlin-based woman artist, and off the breakfast room there's a pretty, west-facing roof terrace. These unpretentious touches all lend Hotel Artemisia a distinctly welcoming, relaxing atmosphere, but don't really distinguish it: so why stay in a women-only hotel?

Years of experience booking women-only tours throughout Europe made Artemisia's founders, Manuela Polidori and Renate Bühler, aware of the demand for 'women-friendly hotels'. It was only after extensive fundraising, both public and private, that they were able to make their dream a reality. Whether 'women-friendly' means a place where lesbian couples can shack up without being leered at, where a business woman can enjoy her morning cup of coffee without sleazy comments on her outfit, a mother can get away and contemplate her existence in sympathetic peace or a young adventuress can sleep one night without the pong of a male hostel roommate's armpits – is entirely open to interpretation, and the diversity of Artemisia's guests reflects these differing needs.

In pondering why she had to suffer stringy prunes at a girls' school 100 years ago, Virginia Woolf stumbled on a basic economic truth that, alas, still holds true today: women are poorer than men. Renate Bühler offers this same statement in answer to the question: 'Why is the oldest women-only hotel in the world only 16 years old?' Her answer could also be applied to the hotel guest's query as to why there are no complimentary soaps or little touches of elegance at Hotel Artemisia. As Virginia Woolf's headmistress said, 'The amenities will have to wait.' In the meantime, you'll find service, respect, comfort and a lot more than a room of your own at Hotel Artemisia.

Where to Stay

This tiny pension has huge rooms and friendly, helpful owners who speak English, French, Arabic and German. The rooms are decorated with lovely turn-of-the-century Berlin furniture and, for families or small groups travelling together, they are really good value. Nice place. *TV.*

Pension Kettler

Bleibtreustrasse 19, 10623 (883 4949/5676/fax 882 4228/www.kurfuerstendamm.de). U1 Uhlandstrasse or S5, S7, S9, S75 Savignyplatz. **Rates** (incl breakfast) €50-€72.50 single; €60-€90 double. **No credit cards. Map** p305/p312 E8 ⑰
Owner Isolde Josipovici can tell you some captivating stories of Berlin and has imbued this small hotel with her own distinctive style over the past 33 years. The four rooms are a cosy blend of art deco and Gründerzeit, with a touch of hippie. Rooms are named after famous folk such as Maria Callas and Toulouse-Lautrec, and have shrines to their dedicates outside. Corridor walls are otherwise festooned with mixed-media art, including a chunk of Berlin Wall.

Pension Viola Nova

Kantstrasse 146, 10623 (315 7260/fax 312 3314/www.violanova.de). S5, S7, S9, S75 Savignyplatz. **Rates** €35-€55 single; €55-€75 double. **No credit cards. Map** p305/p312 F8 ⑱
An old, converted Berlin house, the Viola Nova is particularly notable for its friendly owners and for being good value for money. It now has a variety of 20 clean, spacious rooms ranging from good backpacker standards to a couple of doubles decorated with antique furniture. Ask about prices for large rooms with several beds; these are good for small groups of travellers. Breakfast is included in the room price if you're staying for more than one night. *TV.*

Other districts

Wilmersdorf may not be the most interesting of areas, but it's not far from the rest of town and can proudly claim to host Berlin's most decadent luxury hotel (**Schlosshotel Vierjahreszeiten Berlin**), its most discreet hotel (**Hotel Brandenburger Hof**), the coolest designer hotel (**Ku'damm 101**), its wackiest hotel (**Propeller Island**) and the world's oldest women-only hotel (*see p66* **A hotel of one's own**). So it can't be all bad.

Deluxe

Hotel Brandenburger Hof

Eislebener Strasse 14, Wilmersdorf, 10789 (214 050/fax 2140 5100/www.brandenburger-hof.com). U3 Augsburger Strasse. **Rates** (incl breakfast) €170-€260 single; €245-€295 double; €325-€655 suite; €60 extra bed. **Credit** AmEx, DC, MC, V. **Map** p305/p312 G9 ⑲

Privately owned, this is a discreet jewel tucked in a quiet side street behind KaDeWe. From the moment you set foot inside the foyer you know that you are going to love this place. Staff are friendly and not at all aloof, a rarity in luxury hotels. There's a pretty winter garden and six uniquely decorated, intimate salon rooms for family gatherings, interviews or small meetings. The 72 rooms are spacious and decorated in a warmed-up Bauhaus style, and the eight new suites are located in the quietest section of the hotel. For a binge, get fully pampered by the hotel's 'Exquisit Program', which includes limo pick-up from the airport, flowers, afternoon tea and a limousine ride to any other Berlin destination. Oh, and the Quadriga restaurant is Michelin-starred. Highly recommended.
Bar. Internet (wireless). Parking (€20). Restaurant. Spa. TV/VCR.

Schlosshotel Vierjahreszeiten Berlin

Brahmsstrasse 10, Wilmersdorf, 14193 (895 840/fax 8958 4800/www.schlosshotelberlin.com). S7, S9 Grunewald. **Rates** €275-€305 single; €295-€375 double; €460-€3,000 suite; €23 breakfast. **Credit** AmEx, DC, MC, V. **Map** p304 A12 ⑳
If you are not the potentate of a small country, an industry mogul or a titled aristocrat, you won't feel at home in this place. Designed down to the smallest detail by Karl Lagerfeld, the Schlosshotel is a restored 1914 villa on the edge of the Grunewald – about 15 minutes' drive from the Ku'damm. It has a swimming pool, a couple of restaurants, a golf course, tennis, and dining on the beautiful lawn in summer. There are 12 suites and 54 rooms, a limousine and butler service, elegant marble bathrooms and flocks of well-trained staff running around after you. A beautiful place in a beautiful setting, but so exclusive that it might as well be on another planet. Check the internet for deals.
Bar. Disabled-adapted rooms. Gym. Internet (wireless). Parking (free). Pool (indoors). Restaurants (2). Spa. TV/VCR.

Expensive

Ku'damm 101

Kurfürstendamm 101, Wilmersdorf, 10711 (520 0550/fax 520 055 555/www.kudamm101. com). U7 Adenauerplatz or S41, S42, S45, S46 Halensee. **Rates** €101-€195 single; €118-€215 double; €14 breakfast. **Credit** AmEx, DC, MC, V. **Map** p304 C9 ㉑
Part of the small chain that owns the Bleibtreu and the Savoy (for both, *see p63*), this 2003 designer hotel is a huge hit with style-conscious travellers. The funky lobby, the work of Berlin designers Vogt and Weizenegger, is more like a cool club than a hotel. The rooms, meanwhile, were designed by Swiss interior designer Franziska Kessler, whose mantra is clarity and calm. It works well. The 170 rooms are simply decorated with linoleum floors and bespoke contemporary furniture; the colour scheme is cho-

sen strictly from Le Corbusier's palette. Added bonuses include high-speed wireless internet access and a breakfast terrace garden. The Lounge 101 is good for a variety of occasions: a quick breakfast, daytime snacks, and cocktails with the occasional DJ by night.

Bar. Disabled-adapted rooms. Internet (wireless). No-smoking floors. Parking (€13). Spa. TV.

Moderate

Hotel Artemisia
Brandenburgische Strasse 18, Wilmersdorf, 10707 (873 8905/fax 861 8653/www.frauenhotel-berlin.de). U7 Konstanzer Strasse. **Rates** (incl breakfast) €52-€79 single; €82-€104 double. **Credit** AmEx, DC, MC, V. **Map** p305 E10 ⑫
See p66 **A hotel of one's own.**
Internet (wireless). No-smoking rooms. TV.

Hotel-Pension München
Güntzelstrasse 62, Wilmersdorf, 10717 (8579 120/fax 8579 1222/www.hotel-pension-muenchen-in-berlin.de). U9 Güntzelstrasse. **Rates** (incl breakfast) €40-€65 single; €70-€80 double; €75-€105 apartment. **Credit** AmEx, MC, V. **Map** p305 G10 ⑬
This pension is a really charming place. The artist owner has decorated the rooms beautifully and there are original prints all over the clean white walls. Double rooms come with shower and WC, and single room facilities are in the hall. It's well located, too: a five-minute walk will connect you to the U-Bahn. A welcome change from the average pension.
Parking (€5). TV.

Propeller Island City Lodge
Albrecht Achilles Strasse 58, Wilmersdorf, 10709 (891 9016/fax 892 8721/www.propeller-island.com). U7 Adenauerplatz. **Rates** €75-€200; €7 breakfast. **Credit** MC, V. **Map** p304 D9 ⑭
Propeller Island is a guesthouse straight out of *Alice in Wonderland*. More than just a hotel, it's a work of art. Designed by artist owner Lars Stroschen, the 30 rooms are a collection of jaw-dropping theatre sets. The Upside Down Room, for example, has all of its furniture on the ceiling. The Flying Room has tilted walls and floor, and a double bed seemingly suspended in thin air. Other highlights include the disorienting Mirror Room for narcissists and a Prison Cell for those who feel the need to be punished. There are few of the usual accoutrements, such as room service or telephones. The reservation process is also surreal. View the rooms on the website, and then choose your three favourites. Bookings are taken only by fax or through the website, and your expected time of arrival must be included. There is no reception and the office is only officially open from 8am until noon. Check-in is generally until 11.30am and payment is normally by cash on arrival. A new gallery opens in 2006, showing works by one of the artists featured in the guesthouse. Highly recommended. **Photo** *p69.*
Internet (wireless). TV (some rooms).

Camping
If you want to explore the campsites of Berlin or surrounding Brandenburg, ask for a camping map from the **BTM** information offices in Berlin (*see p49*) or download a PDF from its website. The campsites are located far out of the city, so check timetables for last buses if you plan to enjoy the nightlife. Prices don't vary much between sites: for tents, you'll pay about €4-€5.60; for caravans €7.10, plus €4.95 per person (€2.50 for 6-14s). More information can be obtained from the **German Camping Club** (Deutscher Camping Club).

Landesverband des DCC (Deutscher Camping Club)
Kladower Damm, Gatow, 14089 (218 6071/6072/www.dccberlin.de). **Open** 10.30am-6pm Mon; 8am-4pm Wed; 8am-1pm Fri.

Youth hostels
Official youth hostels in Berlin – there are three: **Jugendgästehaus-International** (261 1097), **Jugendgästehaus am Wannsee** (803 2034) and **Jugendherberge Ernst Reuter** (404 1610) – are crammed most of the year so be sure to book ahead.

You can book online or call the hostels direct. You have to be a member of the YHA to stay in them and they all have single-sex dormitories. To obtain a YHA membership card, go to the **Mitgliederservice des DJH Berlin International** (also known as the Jugend-Zentrale). Remember to take your passport and a passport-sized photo. If you can't be bothered with the whole membership palaver, individual youth hostels also have a day membership deal – you simply pay an extra €3.10 per day. Check the website address below for further information.

Mitgliederservice des DJH Berlin International
Kluckstrasse 3, 10785 (261 1097/fax 265 0383/www.djh.de). U1, U7 Möckernbrücke or U1, U2 Gleisdreieck. **Open** 24hrs daily. **Map** p306 L9.

Longer stays
For a longer stay, try calling a *Mitwohnagentur* (flat-seeking agency) to see what it has on offer, but remember to ask what the total price will be, including agency fees. The agencies listed below can find you a room in a shared house or a furnished flat for anything from a week to a couple of years. In summer, when Berlin is crowded, they are useful for finding short-term accommodation. Most agencies accept advance bookings and you may want to consider

different offers, so start looking a month ahead, especially at busy holiday times. Don't forget that this is all private accommodation: you will be living in someone's home, often with their books, furniture and belongings. This can be a great way to get to know people, but take your time talking to the owners and looking at the places before you choose. For student accommodation, look on the noticeboards in the foyer of the **Hochschule der Kunst** (Hardenbergstrasse 33, Charlottenburg) or pin up your own notice there. Prices vary wildly, but if you look for something *auf Zeit* (for a limited period) you can often get something quite reasonable.

If you're staying for a couple of weeks and manage to find something through a *Mitwohnagentur*, you will probably pay €30-€50 a night. For longer stays, agencies charge different rates. It is always a good idea to ask for the total figure for comparison. Another alternative is looking at ads in *Zweite Hand*, *tip*, *Zitty* and the *Berliner Morgenpost*. Expect to pay €400-€700 per month for a two-bedroom flat in the more central districts of Kreuzberg, Prenzlauer Berg and Schöneberg; Mitte can be more pricey, but sometimes you can get lucky. There's an English-language flat-finding service at **www.roomwithaloo.com**, or you can try one of the following.

Erste Mitwohnzentrale

Sybelstrasse 53, Charlottenburg, 10629 (324 3031/fax 324 9977/www.mitwohn.com). U7 Adenauerplatz. **Open** 9am-7pm Mon-Fri; 10am-3pm Sat. **No credit cards. Map** p305/p312 E8.

fine + mine Internationale Mitwohnagentur

Neue Schönhauser Strasse 20, 10178 (235 5120/ fax 2355 1212). U8 Weinmeisterstrasse or S5, S7, S9, S75 Hackescher Markt. **Open** 10am-7pm Mon-Fri; 10am-6pm Sat. **Credit** AmEx, MC, V. **Map** p303/p310 O5.

Freiraum

Wiener Strasse 14, Kreuzberg, 10999 (618 2008/ fax 618 2006/www.frei-raum.com). U1 Görlitzer Bahnhof. **Open** 9am-7pm Mon-Fri; 10am-2pm Sat. **Credit** AmEx, MC, V. **Map** p307 Q9.

HomeCompany

Joachimstalerstrasse 17, Charlottenburg, 10719 (194 45/fax 882 6649/www.homecompany.de). U1, U9 Kurfürstendamm. **Open** 9am-6pm Mon-Thur; 9am-5pm Fri; 11am-2pm Sat. **Credit** AmEx, V. **Map** p305/p312 G8/G9.

Zeitraum Wohnkonzepte (Agentur Streicher & Burg Immobilien)

Immanuelkirchstrasse 8, 10405 (441 6622/fax 441 6623/www.zeit-raum.de). Tram M2 Knaackstrasse. **Open** 10am-1pm, 3-6pm Mon-Thur; noon-6pm Fri; by appointment Sat. **Credit** MC, V. **Map** p303 P4.

The Symbol Room at **Propeller Island City Lodge**. *See p68.*

www.berlinside-out.com

Another group travel?
or Berlinside Out

We offer the extra bit - guided tours, special trips and tailor - made programs!
Call +49 (0)30 44 77 405

One city.
One history.
One exhibition.

THE STORY OF BERLIN
The Capital's Exhibition with an Original Radiation-Proof Bunker
Kurfürstendamm 207-208 Info + Reservation 030 / 887 20 100

Sightseeing

Funkturm. *See p112*.

Introduction

All the scattered remnants of Berlin's turbulent past.

Threadbare remains of the Wall – now just another part of the cityscape.

Not the most ancient of cities and never a particularly beautiful one, Berlin is not a conventional sightseeing destination in the same way as Paris or Rome. But that isn't to say that there's nothing to see. Berlin's turbulent history has left scars and reminders all over this huge town, while the city's increasing confidence in its role as capital of the unified Germany is signalled by a growing number of architectural landmarks and memorials – even a brand new train station (*see p102* **Hub, bub**).

Most Berlin sights that could properly be described as unmissable – either because you really ought to see them or simply because you couldn't avoid them if you tried – are in and around the central **Mitte** district. But this is only a small segment of this enormous,

sprawling city – carved up by rivers and canals, and fringed with lakes and forest.

After Mitte, **Prenzlauer Berg** and **Friedrichshain** are the two districts of former East Berlin that have changed most. The former retains pockets of radical energy but is now mostly gentrified. There are few conventional sights here, but it's a relaxed place for a meal or drink. Friedrichshain is Berlin's new bohemia, managing both a firm connection with the old East and a forward-looking, youthful scene.

Kreuzberg has correspondingly lost its monopoly on the arty and anarchic, but remains fascinatingly diverse and is currently staging a recovery. Neighbouring **Schöneberg** is quiet and residential, but has some great bars and cafés, and is a major hub of the city's gay scene.

Tiergarten is dominated by the park of the same name. Along its southern fringe are some fine museums, the zoo, the reborn diplomatic quarter and the new Potsdamer Platz.

Charlottenburg has a lot to offer visitors. The shop-rich area around Bahnhof Zoo and the Ku'damm was the centre of old West Berlin, and, to the west, Schloss Charlottenburg and its surrounding museums are a major draw.

Attractions in **other districts** beyond the centre include the Dahlem museums complex, the vast Grunewald woods and the Havel river in the south-west; the proud town of Spandau in the north-west; and the villagey charms of Köpenick and Müggelsee in the south-east.

A 2001 administrative rejig amalgamated many of Berlin's historic districts into larger political units. But no Berliner would say that they live in 'Friedrichshain-Kreuzberg', so in this guide we use the old district names in the same way as the locals.

For ideas on how to spend your time in the city, *see p75* **Essential Berlin**.

MUSEUMS & GALLERIES

If you're planning to do a lot of sightseeing and museum-visiting, then you may want to invest in a discount card. Many museums and galleries are administered by the **Staatliche Museen zu Berlin (SMPK)**, including the Altes Museum, the Pergamonmuseum, the Gemäldegalerie and the Ethnologisches Museum. SMPK offers a **three-day card** (€15, €7.50 concessions), available from any of its museums (it does not, however, cover entry to temporary exhibitions). Most are closed on Mondays but open until 10pm on Thursdays, when they are free after 6pm. For more information, see the SMPK website www.smb.spk-berlin.de.

Another deal is the **WelcomeCard** (two days, €16; three days, €22; valid for one adult and up to three children under 14), which combines free public transport with reduced or free walks, tours, boat trips, and entry to museums, theatres and attractions in Berlin and Potsdam. Cards are available from BTM (*see p284*), S-Bahn offices and many hotels.

Tours

On foot

If you're pushed for time but want a good overview of the city, go for an **Insider Tour** (692 3149, www.insidertour.com) or try **The Original Berlin Walks** (301 9194, www. berlinwalks.com), whose three-and-a-half-hour Discover Berlin tour expertly whips through some 700 years of history.

If you've more time and want more detail, the seven-hour walking tour by **Brewer's Best of Berlin** (www.brewersberlintours.com) explores the city's history in depth (there is also a tour of Potsdam). **Berlin Sightseeing Tours** (7974 5600, www.berlin-sightseeing-tours.de) has come up with an interactive five-kilometre (three-mile) walking tour that takes in all major sights, plus many lesser-known ones.

By bike

Largely flat, Berlin is perfect for getting around by bike. **Fat Tire Bike Tours** (2404 7991, www.fattirebiketoursberlin.com) organises an assortment of tours, including a four- to five-hour tour along the former line of the Wall. **Fahrradstation** (*see p273*) offers themed city tours including 'Cold War Berlin', 'Architecture in Berlin' and a Sunday trip to the countryside. **Insider Tour** (*see above*) offers four-hour bike excursions covering similar ground to its walking tours. **Pedalpower** (*see p273*) organises tours for two people at a time.

Remember that most firms require you to leave some form of ID as deposit when you hire a bicycle from them.

By bus

A cheap and flexible option is **bus 100**, a standard public transport route running from Zoo to Prenzlauer Berg, passing major sights along the way. **Berolina** (8856 8030, www. berolina-berlin.com), on the other hand, offers the works – wraparound windows, commentary in a choice of languages and a handy 'hop on hop off' arrangement. **Top Tour Berlin** (0185 443 188) is just as flexible but uses open-top buses, and **Zille Bus** (2652 5569) operates tours on vintage open-top buses.

By boat/ship

Reederei Bruno Winkler (3499 5935) tours ply the Spree, the Wannsee and venture as far west as Brandenburg. If you haven't got time for a leisurely cruise, then **Historical City Tour** (536 3600) covers a fair few sights in just an hour, including the Reichstag, Palast der Republik and the Berliner Dom. **Berliner Wassertaxi-Stadtrundfahrten (BWTS)** (6588 0203, www.berlinerwassertaxi.de) does tours on Amsterdam-style 'Grachten' boats.

From Berlin's neighbour, Potsdam (*see p257*), there are more opportunities for sightseeing by boat; for instance, **Havel Dampfschifffahrt** (0331 275 9210) organises 90-minute cruises on the Havel river.

See also p272 and *p108* **Berlin by boat**.

Specialist

City Guide Tour (0332 961 4397) operates tailor-made tours, for which you can choose both theme and mode of transport, including trips by helicopter, aeroplane or balloon. **Berlin Starting Point** (306 272 1303, www.berlin-starting-point.de) also devises customised tours.

Susanne Oschmann (782 1202) focuses on the musical history of Berlin. **Milch & Honig** runs tailor-made tours of Jewish Berlin for individuals or groups (6162 5761, www.milch-und-honig.com). **Sta* Tours** (3010 5151, www.sta-tours.de) shows you the houses of famous people. And **Berliner Unterwelten** (4991 0517, www.berliner-unterwelten.de) organises tours of subterranean sites.

Essential Berlin

... in one day
The key sights
● Pick a café for breakfast in the **Scheunenviertel** area of Mitte (*see p85*).
● Get your bearings from the top of the **Fernsehturm** on Alexanderplatz (*see p89*).
● Walk across to Museumsinsel and check the architectural treasures at the **Pergamonmuseum** (*see p81*).
● Stroll along Unter den Linden (*see p76*), detouring to the **Gendarmenmarkt** (*see p83*) along the way, ending at the **Brandenburger Tor** (*see p76*).
● Ascend the dome of the **Reichstag** (*see p101*).
● Walk south to **Potsdamer Platz** (*see p102*), taking in the **Denkmal für die ermordeten Juden Europas** (*see p78*).
● Head west, either through **Tiergarten** (*see p100*), ending up at the **Zoologischer Garten & Aquarium** (*see p105*), or via the **Kulturforum** complex (lovers of Old Masters should take in the **Gemäldegalerie**, modern art fans will want to head for the **Neue Nationalgalerie** – for both, *see p105*).
● Late afternoon shopping on and around the **Ku'damm** (*see p106*).
● Take the U-Bahn to Kreuzberg to see the extraordinary **Jüdisches Museum** (*see p97*).
● Evening: sample the restaurants and bars of rejuvenated **Mitte** (*see chapters* **Restaurants** and **Cafés, Bars & Pubs**).

... in two days
Museums, palaces, greenery and a beach
● Head for **Schloss Charlottenburg** (*see p110*). Apart from the palace and grounds, there are first-rate museums in the area, including the **Bröhan-Museum** and the **Sammlung Berggruen** (for both, *see p110*).
● Then, on a fine day, escape to the leafy surrounds of the **Grunewald** (*see p117*) and/or the watery pleasures of the **Wannsee** (*see p118*).

● Evening: experience the laid-back cafés and nightlife of **Prenzlauer Berg** (*see chapters* **Cafés, Bars & Pubs** and **Nightlife**).

... in three days
Great escapes
● If you've had enough of museums, take a boat trip from Mitte through the old East down to the **Müggelsee** (*see p73, p120, p272* and *p108* **Berlin by boat**).
● If you want more culture, the museum complex at Dahlem includes the brilliant **Ethnologisches Museum** (*see p117*), and the **Brücke-Museum** (*see p118*) and **Alliierten Museum** (*see p118*) are nearby.
● Head on to the parks and palaces of **Potsdam** (*see p257*).
● Evening: try the youthful nightlife of **Friedrichshain** or decent dining in **Kreuzberg** or **Schöneberg** (*see chapters* **Nightlife** and **Restaurants**).

... in four days
Wartime and Cold War Berlin
● Get a historical overview at the **Deutsches Historisches Museum** (*see p79*) or the **Story of Berlin** (*see p109*).
● Those interested in Nazi architecture should head for the **Olympiastadion** (*see p39* **The final stadium**) or **Flughafen Tempelhof** (*see p96* and *p270*). For an insight into the Nazi terror machine, check out the **Topographie des Terrors** (*see p98*), the **Gedenkstätte Plötzensee** (*see p112*) or **Sachsenhausen** (*see p262*), a former concentration camp north of Berlin.
● If the Cold War is more alluring, make for the **Gedenkstätte Berliner Mauer** (*see p113* and *p114* **Walking the Wall**) to see a stretch of Wall, or go to the **Haus am Checkpoint Charlie** (*see p97*). The **Stasi Museum** and the **Museum Berlin-Karlshorst** (for both, *see p120*) also offer fascinating insights.
● Evening: return to your favourite bar – you'll certainly have one by now.

Sightseeing

Mitte

The sights, the shops, the scene – it's all happening in Berlin's historic centre.

Mitte means 'middle' and this is the borough where Berlin was born, on sandy islands in the Spree river, where Museumsinsel is today. The hub of the city before World War II, Mitte was of diminished importance during the Cold War as the off-centre centre of East Berlin – and they still hadn't dealt with all the wartime damage when the Wall came down in 1989. But in the last 15 years Mitte has regained its position as the centre of the city, culturally, scenically and administratively. With its historic buildings scrubbed up, a load of stylish new construction, and an influx of energy from young, moneyed settlers (especially in the once-ratty north part), Mitte is very much back at the centre of things.

Unter den Linden

Maps p302 & p311

From before the Hohenzollern dynasty through the Weimar Republic, and from the Third Reich to the GDR, the entire history of Berlin can be found on or around this celebrated street.

Laid out to connect the town centre with the Tiergarten, Unter den Linden, running east from the Brandenburger Tor to Museumsinsel, got its name from the *Linden* (lime trees) that shaded its central walkway. Hitler, concerned that the trees obscured the view of his parades, had them felled, but they were later replanted.

During the 18th and 19th centuries the Hohenzollerns erected no-nonsense baroque and neo-classical buildings along their capital's showcase street. (Most of these were rubble after World War II, but many were restored.) The grid of side streets was laid out by the Great Elector for his Friedrichstadt (*see p11*).

Brandenburger Tor & Pariser Platz

The focal point of Unter den Linden's western end is the **Brandenburger Tor** (Brandenburg Gate). Constructed in 1791, and designed by Carl Gotthard Langhans after the Propylaea gateway into ancient Athens, the Gate was built as a triumphal arch celebrating Prussia's capital city. It was initially called the Friedenstor ('Gate of Peace') and is the only gate that remains out of Berlin's original 18, though a few U-Bahn station names (Frankfurter Tor, Schlesisches Tor) serve as reminders.

The **Quadriga** statue, a four-horse chariot driven by Victory and designed by Johann Gottfried Schadow, sits on top of the gate. It has had an eventful life. When Napoleon conquered Berlin in 1806 he carted the Quadriga off to Paris and held it hostage until his defeat in 1814. The Tor was later badly damaged during World War II, and during subsequent renovations, the GDR removed the Prussian Iron Cross and turned the Quadriga around so that the chariot faced west. The current Quadriga is actually a 1958 copy of the 18th-century original, and was stranded in no-man's land for 30 years. The Tor was the scene of much celebration while the Wall came down, and after that there had to be further repairs. The Iron Cross was replaced and the Quadriga was turned back to face into Mitte again.

West of the Gate stretches the vast expanse of the **Tiergarten** (*see p100*), Berlin's central park. Just to the north is the reborn **Reichstag** (*see p101*), while ten minutes' walk south is the even more dramatically reconceived **Potsdamer Platz** complex (*see p102*).

Immediately east of the Brandenburger Tor is **Pariser Platz**, given its name in 1814 when Prussia and its allies conquered Paris. This square, enclosed by embassies and banks, was once seen as Berlin's *Empfangssaal* (reception room). Foreign dignitaries would ceremoniously pass through on their way to visit tyrants and dictators in the palaces downtown. In 1993 plans were drawn up to revive Pariser Platz, with new buildings on the same scale as the old ones, featuring conservative exteriors and contemporary interiors. Some old faces are back on the sites they occupied before World War II: the reconstructed **Adlon Hotel** (*see p49*) is now at its old address, as is Michael Wilford's new British Embassy, at Wilhelmstrasse 70-1. The building going up on the south-west corner of the square – and the last one to complete the Pariser Platz puzzle – is the US Embassy. Since a return to its old address was announced in 1993, construction was delayed first by budgetary miscalculation, then by new US State Department stipulations of a minimum 30-metre (98-foot) security zone around US embassies. Now designs have been adjusted, streets have been moved, and America should be securely back on the block in spring 2008. Meanwhile, Wilhelmstrasse is closed to traffic for a block south of the square because of security provisions for the British Embassy.

While outwardly conforming to the aesthetic restrictions, many of the straightforward exteriors front flights of fancy within. Frank Gehry's DG Bank at No.3 has a huge, biomorphic interior dome hidden behind its regular façade. The Dresdner Bank opposite is virtually hollow, thanks to another interior atrium. Next door, Christian de Portzamparc's French Embassy features a space-saving 'vertical garden' on the courtyard wall, and 'french windows' extending over two storeys.

Directly to the south of Pariser Platz is the huge, new **Denkmal für die ermordeten Juden Europas** ('Memorial to the Murdered Jews of Europe'), a city-block-size field of concrete slabs. The project has been mired in controversy since it was conceived in 1993. The winning design of an initial competition was rejected by then Chancellor Kohl, and there was no end of argument over the second competition, including rows over location (the site has no particular link to the Holocaust), function (should such a monument draw a line under history or seek to stimulate debate?) and content (many feel the memorial should honour all victims of the Holocaust, not only Jewish ones). In the wake of this one, there are now plans for assorted other victim memorials (*see p82* **Monumental debate**).

Between the Denkmal and Potsdamer Platz complex is an area filled with representations from Germany's various *Länder*.

East along Unter den Linden

Heading east along Unter den Linden, passing the 1950s monolithic, Stalinist wedding cake-style Russian Embassy on your right, and, on the next block, the box office of the **Komische Oper** (*see p234*), you reach the crossroads with Friedrichstrasse, once a café-strewn focus of Weimar Berlin.

On the other side of the junction, on the right, housed in the ground floor of a 1920 building occupied by Deutsche Bank, is the **Deutsche**

Guggenheim Berlin, somewhat more modest in size and scope than those in New York and Bilbao. Facing the art gallery across Unter den Linden stands the grandiose **Staatsbibliotek** (open to all, with a small café), usually filled with students from the next-door **Humboldt-Universität** (*see p283*). The university's grand old façade has been restored, as have the two statues of the Humboldts (founder Wilhelm and his brother Alexander), between which booksellers set up tables in good weather.

Across the street is **Bebelplatz**, site of the notorious Nazi book-burning. Micha Ullmann's monument to the event is set into the Platz, but it can be hard to see through the scratched glass. Dominating the eastern side is the **Staatsoper** (*see p234*), built in neo-classical style by Georg Wenzeslaus von Knobelsdorff in 1741-3. The present building dates from 1955, but is faithful to the original. Established as Frederick the Great's Royal Court Opera, it is now one of Berlin's three major opera houses.

Just south of the Staatsoper (and also designed by Knobelsdorff, in 1747) is **Sankt-Hedwigs-Kathedrale** (*see p79*), a curious circular Roman Catholic church, inspired by the Pantheon in Rome. A minute's walk east from here brings you to another church, **Friedrichswerdersche Kirche**, which is now a museum paying homage to its architect, Karl Friedrich Schinkel.

The best Views

Fernsehturm
Berlin's most dramatic view, but also its most detached. See p89.

Kreuzberg
The city centre spreads below the peak of Viktoriapark's 'cross hill'. See p95.

Panoramapunkt
The postmodern lookout point at Potsdamer Platz. See p105.

Reichstag
The city's new buildings from Foster's democratic dome. See p101.

Siegessäule
An angel's eye over the Tiergarten. See p102.

Teufelsberg
The Grunewald and western lakes from the city's biggest rubble-mountain. See p117.

IM Pei's cylindrical stairwell for the **Deutches Historiches Museum** extension...

The west side of Bebelplatz is taken up by the late 18th-century **Alte Bibliotek**, commonly known as the 'Kommode', after its resemblance to a curvy piece of baroque furniture. Alongside, in the centre of Unter den Linden, stands a restored equestrian statue of Frederick the Great, originally removed by the GDR, and then replaced one night when the Party line changed on Prussian history.

On the north side of Unter den Linden, the **Neue Wache** (New Guardhouse), constructed by Schinkel in 1816-18, today houses a hauntingly plain memorial to the 'victims of war and tyranny', centred on an enlarged reproduction of a Käthe Kollwitz sculpture, *Mother with Dead Son*. Beneath this are the remains of an unknown soldier and an unknown concentration camp victim, surrounded by earth from World War II battlefields and concentration camps.

Next to it to the east is the baroque Zeughaus, a former armoury with a peaceful pink façade. With renovations completed in June 2006, it once again houses the **Deutsches Historisches Museum** (*see p79*). The new wing by IM Pei hosts changing exhibitions, and has a fine café.

This whole last eastern stretch of Unter den Linden is soon to undergo further heritage restoration. The road will be narrowed to make the area feel more like a square, and to help revive the idea of the Forum Fredericanum, as this ensemble was known, period lamp-posts and other historical details will be installed.

Denkmal für die ermordeten Juden Europas

Cora-Berliner-Strasse 1 (2639 4336/www.holocaust-denkmal.de). U2, S1, S2, S26 Potsdamer Platz. **Open** *Field of stelae* 24hrs daily. *Information centre* 10am-8pm daily. **Admission** free. **Map** p306/p311 L7.

After years of controversy, Peter Eisenmann's 'field of stelae' – 2,711 of them, arranged in undulating rows over 19,704sq m (more than 212,000sq ft) – with its attendant information centre to memorialise 'the Murdered Jews of Europe', was opened on 10 May 2005. Each of the concrete slabs has its own foundation, and they tilt at differing angles. The effect is reminiscent of the packed headstones in Prague's Old Jewish Cemetery. There's no vantage point or overview – to engage with the thing you need to walk into it. The gaps between the stelae are wide enough for a wheelchair, but not for two people walking side by side; you are meant to explore its deliberate ambiguities on your own. It's spooky in places, especially on overcast days and near the middle, where many feel a sense of confinement.

The information centre is at the south-east corner, mostly underground and accessed by staircases from among the stelae. It's like a kind of secular crypt, containing a sombre presentation of facts and figures about the Holocaust's Jewish victims.

Deutsche Guggenheim Berlin

Unter den Linden 13-15 (202 0930/www.deutsche-guggenheim.de). U6 Französische Strasse. **Open** 11am-8pm Mon-Wed, Fri-Sun; 11am-10pm Thur. **Admission** €4; €3 concessions; free Mon, under-12s. **No credit cards**. **Map** p302/p311 M6.

...and a pleasingly forward-looking interior for an institution so historical.

In partnership with the Deutsche Bank (and housed in one of its buildings), this is the least impressive European branch of the Guggenheim. Big bucks, big names, big boring: glossy corporate art that you can take your granny to. In 2006-7 the disappointingly small exhibition space hosts shows from Cai Guo-Qiang and Jeff Koons, and themed expos on the Art of Tomorrow and Divisionism/Neo-Impressionism.

Deutsches Historisches Museum
Zeughaus, Unter den Linden 2 (203 040/www.dhm. de). U6 Französische Strasse. **Open** 10am-6pm Mon, Tue, Fri-Sun; 10am-10pm Thur. **Admission** €4; free under-18s. **No credit cards**. **Map** p303/p311 N6.
In a former armoury, the revamped Museum of German History is unveiled in June 2006, which meant we hadn't seen it at press time. It extends over three floors and focuses on crucial points in German history. There are also 'topic rooms' dealing with such subjects as 'The Relationship between the Sexes' or 'Changes in Work and Profession'. Temporary exhibitions are held in the splendid new wing by IM Pei on the west side of the complex. The shop has an excellent selection of historical postcards and reproduction posters.

Friedrichswerdersche Kirche
Werderscher Markt (208 1323/www.smb.spk-berlin.de). U2 Hausvogteiplatz. **Open** 10am-6pm Tue-Sun. **Admission** free. **No credit cards**. **Map** p303/p311 N6.
This brick church, designed by Karl Friedrich Schinkel, was completed in 1831. Its war wounds were repaired in the 1980s and it reopened in 1987 as a homage to its architect. Inside are statues by Schinkel, Schadow and others, bathed in soft light from stained-glass windows. Pictures of Schinkel's works that didn't survive the war (like the Prinz-Albert-Schloss) are also displayed.

Sankt-Hedwigs-Kathedrale
Hinter der katholischen Kirche 3 (203 4810/www. hedwigs-kathedrale.de). U2 Hausvogteiplatz or U6 Französische Strasse. **Open** 10am-5pm Mon-Fri; 10am-4.30pm Sat; 1-4.30pm Sun. **Admission** free. *Guided tour* €1.50. **Map** p303/p311 N6.
Constructed in 1747 for Berlin's Catholic minority, this circular Knobelsdorff creation was bombed out during the war and only reconsecrated in 1963. Its modernised interior contains a split-level double altar. The crypt contains the remains of Bernhard Lichtenberg, who preached here against the Nazis, was arrested, and died on the way to Dachau in 1943.

Museumsinsel

Maps p303 & p311
The eastern end of Unter den Linden abuts the island in the Spree where Berlin was born (*see p10*). The northern part, with its museums and galleries, is known as Museumsinsel (Museum Island). The southern half (much enlarged by landfill) was once a neighbourhood for the city's fishermen (and known as Fischerinsel); it is now dominated by a clutch of grim tower blocks.

The five Museumsinsel museums (the Pergamonmuseum, Altes Museum, Alte Nationalgalerie, Neues Museum and Bode Museum) have been undergoing a massive restoration programme for many years; the first three are open, while work remains to be done on the latter two. Such is the importance of the site that it was added to UNESCO's World Cultural Heritage list in 1999.

The **Pergamonmuseum**, one of Berlin's main attractions, is a showcase for three huge and important examples of ancient architecture: the Hellenistic Pergamon Altar, the Babylonian Gate of Ishtar and the Roman Market Gate of Miletus. It also contains the Museum für Islamische Kunst (Museum of Islamic Art).

Schinkel's superb **Altes Museum** (Old Museum), from 1830, has a small permanent collection, hosts some excellent temporary exhibitions, and for now houses the collection of the Ägyptisches Museum (Egyptian Museum). And since December 2001 the renovated **Alte Nationalgalerie** (Old National Gallery) has again been home to a wide-ranging collection of 19th-century painting and sculpture.

The **Bode Museum** is scheduled to reopen sometime in early summer 2006, and will house the collection of the Museum für Byzantinisches Kunst (Museum of Byzantine Art) and the Skulpturensammlung (Sculpture Collection). The **Neues Museum** is finally having its severe wartime bomb damage repaired – and should reopen in October 2009 as a home for the Ägyptisches Museum (currently at the Altes Museum) and Charlottenburg's **Museum für Vor- und Frühgeschichte** (Primeval and Early History Museum; *see p110*).

Dominating the Museumsinsel skyline is the the huge, bombastic **Berliner Dom**. It's worth climbing up to the cathedral's dome for the fine city views. In front, bounded on one side by the neo-classical colonnade of the Altes Museum, is the Lustgarten, an elegant green square.

Across the main road bisecting the island, demolition of the poor old Palast der Republik was set to begin early in 2006. During the Cold War, the Palast contained the main parliamentary chamber of the GDR, but also discos, bars and a bowling alley. It had replaced the remains of the war-ravaged Stadtschloss, residence of the Kaisers, demolished by the GDR in 1952. Arguments have rumbled on for years about whether or not to rebuild the Stadtschloss. At the end of 2003 it was decided to demolish the Palast and leave a green space here until funding for a rebuilt Stadtschloss (or Stadtschloss-style façade over a more modern structure) could be found.

Alte Nationalgalerie

Bodestrasse 1-3 (2090 5801/www.smb.spk-berlin.de). S5, S7, S9, S75 Hackescher Markt. **Open** 10am-6pm Tue, Wed, Fri-Sun; 10am-10pm Thur. **Admission** €8; €4 concessions. **No credit cards. Map** p303/p311 N6.

With its ceiling and wall paintings, fabric wallpapers and marble staircase, the Old National Gallery is a sparkling home to one of the largest collections of 19th-century art and sculpture in Germany. Among the 440 paintings and 80 sculptures, German artists such as Adolph Menzel, Caspar David Friedrich, Max Liebermann and Carl Spitzweg are well represented. There are also some first-rank early Impressionist works from Manet, Monet and Rodin. Although it's worth a visit, don't expect to see the definitive German national collection: you would also have to take in the vast museums of Stuttgart, Weimar, Munich and Hamburg to get a true overall view. Recent temporary exhibitions included shows on Goya, Rodin and Max Beckmann.

Altes Museum

Lustgarten (2090 5245/www.smb.spk-berlin.de). S5, S7, S9, S75 Hackescher Markt. **Open** 10am-6pm Tue, Wed, Fri-Sun; 10am-10pm Thur. **Admission** €8; €4 concessions. **No credit cards. Map** p303/p311 N6.

Opened as the Royal Museum in 1830, the Old Museum originally housed all the art treasures on Museumsinsel. It was designed by Schinkel and is considered one of his finest buildings, with a particularly magnificent entrance rotunda, where vast neon letters declare that 'All Art has been Contemporary'. This place is home to the Ägyptisches Museum (Egyptian Museum), whose most celebrated exhibit is the bust of Nefertiti, dating from around 1350 BC (*see p16* **Beauty and the bust**). The portrayal of the human face is one of the most compelling aspects of the collection, which includes a series of characterful model faces, and the vivid 'Berlin Green Head', which may date from around 500 BC and looks like a pugnacious nightclub bouncer. Another unique treasure is a piece of papyrus with the only known example of Cleopatra's handwriting, and there are mummies and statuary aplenty. The museum's normal exhibit has been pared down to a minimum to make room for all this, but there are still temporary exhibitions. When the Egyptian stuff moves to the Neues Museum in 2009, a vast exhibit on the Etruscans will take its place.

Berliner Dom

Lustgarten 1 (2026 9133/guided tours 2026 9119/ www.berliner-dom.de). S5, S7, S9, S75 Hackescher Markt. **Open** *Apr-Sept* 9am-8pm Mon-Sat; noon-8pm Sun. *Oct-Mar* 9am-7pm Mon-Sat; noon-7pm Sun. **Admission** €5; €3 concessions; free under-14s. **No credit cards. Map** p303/p311 N6.

The dramatic Berlin Cathedral is now finally healed of its war wounds and celebrated its centenary in 2005. Built in Italian Renaissance style, it was destroyed during World War II and remained a ruin until 1973, when extensive restoration work began. It has always looked fine from the outside, but now that the internal work is complete, it is fully restored to its former glory. Crammed with Victorian detail, and containing dozens of statues of eminent German Protestants, it is now holding weekly services after several decades of existing in the face of GDR dis-pleasure. Its lush 19th-century interior is hardly the perfect acoustic space for the frequent concerts, but it's worth a visit to see the crypt containing around 90 sarcophagi of notables from the Hohenzollern dynasty, or to clamber up for splendid views from the cupola. There are guided tours every 45 minutes from 10.30am to 3.30pm; call to book.

Pergamonmuseum

Am Kupfergraben (2090 5566/www.smb.spk-berlin. de). U6, S1, S2, S5, S7, S9, S75 Friedrichstrasse. **Open** 10am-6pm Tue, Wed, Fri-Sun; 10am-10pm Thur. **Admission** €8; €4 concessions. **No credit cards. Map** p303/p311 N6.

One of the world's major archaeological museums, the Pergamon shouldn't be missed. Its treasures are made up of the Antikensammlung (Collection of Classical Antiquities) and the Vorderasiatisches Museum (Museum of Near Eastern Antiquities) and contain three big draws. The first is the Hellenistic Pergamon Altar. This dates from 170-159 BC, when Pergamon was one of the major cities of Asia Minor (now western Turkey); huge as it is, the museum's partial re-creation represents only one third of its original size. The altar's outstanding feature is the stunning original frieze that once wound 113m (371ft) around its base. A remarkable proportion of it survives, and depicts the epic battle between Gods and Titans with a vividness and vitality that make the frieze one of the greatest artistic legacies of classical antiquity. In an adjoining room, and even more architecturally impressive, is the two-storey Roman Market Gate of Miletus (29m/95ft wide and almost 17m/56ft high), erected in AD 120. This leads to the third big attraction – the blue- and ochre-tiled Gate of Ishtar and Babylonian Processional Street, dating from King Nebuchadnezzar's reign (605-562 BC). There are other gems, including some stunning Assyrian reliefs, but it's an admirably digestible and focused place.

The Pergamon is also now home to the Museum für Islamische Kunst (Museum of Islamic Art), which takes up 14 rooms in the southern wing. The collection is wide-ranging, including applied arts, crafts, books and architectural details (the latter are particularly notable) produced by Islamic peoples from the eighth to the 19th century. Entrance is included in the overall admission price.

An excellent audio guide (included in the price of entrance) gives plenty of interesting, non-patronis-ing background info on the exhibits throughout the museum. The Pergamon is scheduled for renovation, which will happen in stages, beginning in 2008.

South of Unter den Linden

Maps p306 & p311

What the Kurfürstendamm was in post-war West Berlin, **Friedrichstrasse** had been and may be again: the city's glitziest shopping

Quartier 206 on **Friedrichstrasse**.

Monumental debate

Of all the debates about the intersection of history, architecture and the form of Berlin's unified cityscape, few lasted so long or conjured so much controversy as that over the memorial to Jewish Holocaust victims – the **Denkmal für die ermordeten Juden Europas** (*see p78 – pictured*).

The idea of a central memorial to recall national shame rather than national glory had been around since the 1980s opening of the site of the former Gestapo HQ – now known as the **Topographie des Terrors** (*see p98*).

In 1993 the **Neue Wache** (*see p78*), a monument to the 'victims of fascism and militarism' under the Communists, was recast as one to the 'victims of war and tyranny'. This involved installing an enlarged replica of Käthe Kollwitz's statue *Mother with Dead Son*. There were immediate protests that the new name put murdered victims on the same level as dead perpetrators, and that the statue memorialised them in a form contrary to Jewish tradition. In response, then Chancellor Kohl promised a memorial solely for Jewish victims of the Holocaust.

The winning design of a 1995 competition was a huge concrete slab, the size of two football fields, bearing the names of all 4.2 million identified Holocaust victims. But the cliché of equating the immensity of the crime with the vastness of the memorial was widely criticised. Kohl rejected the design. A second competition in 1998 produced a design by Peter Eisenmann and Richard Serra involving 4,000 columns – and what eventually got built is a scaled-down version of that.

Meanwhile, debates rumbled on about the remembrance of other victims. Groups representing Gypsies, gays, the handicapped, prisoners of war, blacks, political prisoners and forced labourers all pointed to the inadequacy of a memorial for Jewish victims alone. Roma groups argued that the extermination of their people should not be separated from that of the Jews, but refused to share a memorial with gays. Was Berlin to end up with a landscape of segregated victims' memorials, divided according to the dismal categories of the Nazis themselves?

The answer, bizarrely, seems to be yes. The Jewish Denkmal is now firmly established as one of Berlin's main monuments. A site for a memorial to Sinti and Roma victims is tucked away in the corner of the Tiergarten closest to the Reichstag, not far from the **Sowjetisches Ehrenmal** (Soviet War Memorial; *see p100*). Groups representing gays persecuted by the Nazis have been promised another patch of the Tiergarten, over the road from the Jewish memorial. And there is already a pathetically unobstrusive plaque for the victims of the Nazi euthanasia campaign in the forecourt of the nearby **Philharmonie** (*see p234*).

Predictably, not everyone is satisfied. Representatives of Germans expelled from territories now part of Poland or the Czech Republic have been demanding their own 'information centre'. This has sparked protests from Warsaw and Prague. The monumental debate looks set to lumber on – and perhaps the debate itself is the true Holocaust memorial.

street. Like Unter den Linden, the north–south street (starting at Mehringplatz in Kreuzberg and ending at Oranienburger Tor in Mitte) was laid out as part of the baroque late 17th-century expansion of the city.

The liveliest, sleekest stretch of the street is that between **Checkpoint Charlie** (*see p97*) and Friedrichstrasse station. A huge amount of money has been poured into redevelopment here, with office buildings and upmarket shopping malls galore, though opinions differ as to the effectiveness of the architecture.

Look out for the all-glass façade of the modernist-style **Galeries Lafayette** (No.75; *see p163*), the acute angles of the expressionist **Quartier 206** (Nos.71-4; **photo** *p81*) and the monolithic geometric mass of **Quartier 205** (Nos.66-70). Otherwise, there are auto showrooms for Rolls-Royce, Bentley, Volkswagen, Audi and Mercedes-Benz, boutiques for Mont Blanc, Cartier and DKNY, and countless other high-class concerns.

Just to the east of this stretch lies the square of **Gendarmenmarkt**, one of the high points of Frederick the Great's vision for the city. Here two churches, the **Französischer Dom** ('French Cathedral'; home of the Hugenottenmuseum) and the **Deutscher Dom**, frame the **Konzerthaus** (*see p234*).

Just west of Friedrichstrasse on Leipziger Strasse is the **Museum für Kommunikation**. There are many other interesting sights close by in Kreuzberg; for these, *see p93*.

Deutscher Dom

Gendarmenmarkt, entrance in Markgrafenstrasse (2273 0431/www.deutscherdom.de). U2, U6 Stadtmitte. **Open** 10am-6pm Tue; 10am-6pm Wed-Sun. *Guided tours* 11am, 1pm daily. **Admission** free. **Map** p306/p311 M7.

Both this church and the Französischer Dom were built in 1780-85 by Carl von Gontard for Frederick the Great, in imitation of Santa Maria in Montesanto and Santa Maria dei Miracoli in Rome. The Deutscher Dom was intended for Berlin's Lutheran community. Its neo-classical tower is topped by a 7m (23ft) gilded statue representing Virtue. Inside is a permanent exhibition on the history of Germany's parliamentary system, from the 1848 revolution through the suspension of parliamentary politics by the Nazis, right up to the present day. The visitor is encouraged to consider the role of parliaments not just in Germany but throughout the modern world; since there are no translations, you'll need good German to get much out of it without a guided tour.

Französischer Dom/ Hugenottenmuseum

Gendarmenmarkt (229 1760/www.franzoesische-kirche.de). U2, U6 Stadtmitte. **Open** noon-5pm Tue-Sat; 11am-5pm Sun. **Admission** €2; €1 concessions. **No credit cards.** **Map** p306/p311 M7.

Built in the early 18th century for Berlin's 6,000-plus-strong French Protestant community (known as Huguenots), the church was later given a baroque tower, which offers fine views. The tower is purely decorative and unconsecrated – and, therefore, not part of the church (open noon-5pm Mon-Sat, after service-5pm Sun).

An exhibition on the history of the French Protestants in France and Berlin-Brandenburg is displayed within the building (the modest church itself has a separate entrance at the western end). The museum chronicles the religious persecution suffered by Calvinists (note the bust of Calvin on the outside of the church) and their subsequent immigration to Berlin, at the behest of the Hohenzollerns, after their expulsion from France in 1685. The development of the Huguenot community is detailed with paintings, documents and artefacts. One part of the museum is devoted to the church's history, particularly the effects of World War II – it was bombed during a Sunday service in 1944 and remained a ruin until the mid 1980s.

Museum für Kommunikation

Leipziger Strasse 16 (202 940/www.museums stiftung.de/berlin). U2 Mohrenstrasse or U2, U6 Stadtmitte. **Open** 9am-5pm Tue-Fri; 11am-7pm Sat, Sun. **Admission** €3; €1.50 concessions. **Map** p306/p311 M7.

A direct descendant of the world's first postal museum (founded 1872), this once-dispersed collection only reopened in 2000 and covers a bit more than mere stamps. It traces the development of telecommunications up to the internet era, though philatelists might head straight to the basement and the 'Blue Mauritius', one of the world's rarest stamps. The lovely, airy interior is worth a look in itself. Three robots welcome visitors in the main atrium.

North of Unter den Linden

Maps p302 & p311

The continuation of Friedrichstrasse north of Unter den Linden is less appealingthan its southern stretch. Friedrichstrasse station has been turned into a shopping mall, the building having been totally gutted in the process. The station interior was once notable for its ability to confuse, since its role as the only East–West border crossing point open for all categories of citizen (East and West Germans, West Berliners, citizens of Allied countries, and other foreigners) involved a warren of passageways.

Following the line of the train tracks east along Georgenstrasse, you come upon the **Berliner Antik & Flohmarkt** (*see p176*) – a row of antiques stores, bookshops and cafés in the Bogen ('arches'), under the railway.

The building just to the north of the train station is known as the **Tränenpalast** ('Palace of Tears'; *see p222 and p242*), since it was the

Sightseeing (vertical tab)

H.Budzislawski
Geflügelhändlerin

A.Porteset
Angestellter

G. Jacobi
Kaufmann

The Missing House.
See p86.

checkpoint where departing visitors left their Eastern friends and relations who could not follow them through the border. It is now a concert and cabaret venue, with a bit of the Wall in its beer garden.

Across Friedrichstrasse, the landmark **Admiralspalast** is reopening in April 2006 after eight years of being dark. First opened in 1910, a survivor of wartime bombing, the building contains a 1,600-seat theatre used over the decades for everything from Broadway transplants to the Staatsoper. There are also two smaller performance spaces and a restored Roman-style bathhouse turned 'wellness spa'.

Crossing the river on the wrought-iron Weidendammer Brücke, a left turn on Schiffbauerdamm brings you to the **Berliner Ensemble** (*see p237*), with its bronze statue of Bertolt Brecht, who directed the company from 1948 to 1956, surrounded by quotations from his works. *Die Dreigroschenoper* (*The Threepenny Opera*) was premiered here on 31 August 1928. There are various congenial bars and restaurants along the riverfront, beyond which this neighbourhood begins to merge into what is now the government quarter.

Back on Friedrichstrasse stands the **Friedrichstadtpalast** (*see p241*), a large cabaret venue that was an entertainment hotspot during the days of the GDR, since it took hard currency; it still pulls the crowds today. Further north is the **Brecht-Weigel-Gedenkstätte**, home to Bertolt Brecht (until his death in 1956) and his wife Helene Weigel. Both are buried in the Dorotheenstädtische Friedhof (open 8am-dusk daily) next door, along with the architect Schinkel, the author Heinrich Mann and the philosopher Hegel.

Two worthwhile museums are five and ten minutes' walk from here: the **Museum für Naturkunde** (Natural History Museum) and the **Hamburger Bahnhof, Museum für Gegenwart** (Hamburg Station Museum of Contemporary Art), which puts on temporary exhibitions in a converted railway station.

Brecht-Weigel-Gedenkstätte

Chausseestrasse 125 (283 057 044/www.adk.de). U6 Oranienburger Tor. **Open** *Guided tours* Every 30mins 10-11.30am Tue, Wed, Fri; 10am-noon, 5-6.30pm Thur; 9.30am-1.30pm Sat. Every hr 11am-6pm Sun. **Admission** €3; €1.50 concessions. **No credit cards**. **Map** p302 M5.

of whose past members were tainted with Nazi-era controversy, has paid for the refurbishment of the Rieckhalle – an adjacent 300sq m (3,230sq ft) warehouse – to accommodate the works from his collection, many of them large-scale, as they are doled out in temporary, themed exhibitions. There are other exhibitions, too, plus a great art bookshop.

Museum für Naturkunde

Invalidenstrasse 43 (2093 8591/www.museum.hu-berlin.de). U6 Zinnowitzer Strasse. **Open** 9.30am-5pm Tue-Fri; 10am-6pm Sat, Sun. **Admission** €3.50; €2 concessions; €7 family; free under-6s. **No credit cards. Map** p302 L4.

Berlin's Natural History Museum is one of the world's largest and best organised – it's also one of the oldest: the core of the collection dates from 1716. Five exhibition halls are undergoing much-needed renovation until mid 2007, and meanwhile many of the larger dinosaur skeletons that are the museum's principal draw, including the magnificent Brachiosaurus, are languishing in storage. The Primates section is also closed for now. Most other rooms are still open, though, and there are fossils, stuffed animals and exotic minerals aplenty from the museum's collection of over 60 million items.

The Scheunenviertel

If the area south of Friedrichstrasse station is the new upmarket face of Mitte, the Scheunenviertel (stretching around the curving north bank of the Spree, running east from Friedrichstrasse to Hackescher Markt) is the face of its moneyed bohemia.

This is Berlin's main nightlife district and art quarter, littered with bars and galleries. Once so far out of town that it was safe to build the highly flammable hay barns (*Scheunen*) here, this was also historically the centre of Berlin's immigrant community, including many Jews from eastern Europe. During the 1990s it again began to attract Jewish immigrants, including both young Americans and Orthodox Jews from the former Soviet Union.

In the 1990s the Scheunenviertel became a magnet for squatters with access to the list of buildings supposedly wrecked by lazy urban developers, who had checked them off as gone in order to meet quotas – but had actually left them standing. With many other buildings in disrepair, rents were cheap, and the new residents soon learned how to take advantage of city subsidies for opening galleries and other cultural spaces. Result: the Scheunenviertel became Berlin's hot cultural centre.

The first of these art squats was **Tacheles** on Oranienburger Strasse, the spine of the Scheunenviertel. The building, built in 1907, originally housed the Friedrichstrasse Passagen, an early attempt at a shopping mall.

Brecht's home from 1948 until his death in 1956 has been preserved exactly as he left it. Tours of the house last about half an hour and give interesting insights into the life and reading habits of the playwright. The window at which he worked overlooked the grave of Hegel in the neighbouring cemetery. Brecht's wife, actress Helene Weigel, continued living here until she died in 1971. The Brecht archives are kept upstairs. Phone ahead for a tour in English. The Kellerrestaurant (*see p125*) is near the exit.

Hamburger Bahnhof, Museum für Gegenwart

Invalidenstrasse 50-51 (397 8340/www.smb.spk-berlin.de). S5, S7, S9, S75 Lehrter Bahnhof. **Open** 10am-6pm Tue, Wed, Fri; 10am-10pm Thur; 11am-8pm Sat; 11am-6pm Sun. **Admission** €8; €4 concessions. **No credit cards. Map** p302 K5.

The Hamburg Station Museum of Contemporary Art, housed within a huge and expensive refurbishment of a former railway station, opened with much fanfare in 1997. The exterior features a stunning fluorescent light installation by Dan Flavin; inside, the biggest draw is currently the gradual unveiling of the Friedrich Christian Flick Collection – a staggering 2,000 works from around 150 artists, mostly of the late 20th century. Flick, from a steel family some

It had stood vacant for years – the GDR tried to demolish it but, so the story goes, ran out of dynamite halfway through the job – and was falling apart when it was squatted by artists after the fall of the Wall. It then became a rather arrogant arbiter of hip in the neighbourhood, offering studio space to artists, performance spaces for music, a cinema, and several bars and discos. In 1997 the city presented the squatters with an opportunity to buy it cheaply and was spurned. In 1998 Tacheles was bought by a German company, which has reconstructed a big portion of the building, now housing new galleries and an 'office of cultural marketing'.

Across Tucholskystrasse at Oranienburger Strasse 32 is an entrance to the **Heckmann Höfe** (the other is on Auguststrasse), a series of restored courtyards formerly belonging to an engineering firm. The courtyards have been delightfully restored to accommodate shops and restaurants. The free-standing building with the firm's coat of arms in the pavement in front of it was once the stables, as indicated by the sculpture of a horse's head, positioned as if peering out of the building.

A little further down the block stands the **Neue Synagoge**, with its gleaming golden Moorish-style dome. Turning into Grosse Hamburger Strasse, you find yourself surrounded by Jewish history. On the right, there is a memorial to the thousands of Berlin Jews who were forced to congregate here before being shipped off to concentration camps. Following Jewish tradition, many visitors put a stone on the memorial in remembrance of those who died. Behind it is a park that was once Berlin's oldest Jewish cemetery; the only gravestone left is of the father of the German Jewish renaissance, Moses Mendelssohn, founder of the city's first Jewish school, next door at No.27. That the school has heavy security fencing and a permanent police presence, even today, only adds to the poignancy of this place.

Across the street at Nos.15-16 is **The Missing House** (photo *p84*), an artwork by Christian Boltanski, in which the walls of a bombed-out house have the names and occupations of former residents inscribed on the site of each one's apartment. A little further on, the **Sophienkirche**, from which nearby Sophienstrasse gets its name, is one of Berlin's few remaining baroque churches. It is set back from the street behind wrought-iron fences, and is one of the city's prettiest architectural sites. The interior is a little disappointing, though.

At the end of Oranienburger Strasse, at the corner of Rosenthaler Strasse, is the famous **Hackesche Höfe**. Built in 1906-7 by some young Jewish idealists, these form a complex of nine interlinking Jugendstil courtyards with elegant ceramic façades. The Höfe symbolise Berlin's new Mitte: having miraculously survived two wars, the forgotten, crumbling buildings were restored in the mid 1990s using the old plans. Today they house upmarket shops, galleries, theatres, cafés, restaurants and cinemas – and are just about Berlin's top tourist attraction. Try to avoid visiting at the weekend.

A few doors up Rosenthaler Strasse is a tumbledown alley alongside the Central cinema, in which a workshop for the blind was located during World War II. Its owner managed to stock it fully with 'blind' Jews, and helped them escape or avoid the camps. Now it houses alternative galleries, bars and shops. Across the street from the Hackesche Höfe, and under the S-Bahn arches, there is a welter of bars, restaurants and shops as well as the British Council building in the Neue Hackesche Höfe, which has a great library and internet lounge.

There are still more fashionable bars and shops further along Rosenthaler Strasse and around the corner on Neue Schönhauser Strasse as well as some good sandwich and coffee bars. This area has settled into being Berlin's hip centre with many cool little shops. Most of the original houses have now been renovated and the gaps left by wartime bombing have had some extensive dental treatment in the form of slick new buildings. Even the *Plattenbauten*, the East German prefabs, have been spruced up. The pavements still have craters, though.

Leading off Rosenthaler Strasse, **Sophienstrasse** is Mitte's most picturesque road. Built in the 18th century, it was restored in 1987 for the city's 750th anniversary, with craftworkers' ateliers that have replicas of old merchants' metal signs hanging outside them. This pseudo-historicism has now become part of a more interesting mix of handcraft shops: the excellent woodwind-instrument makers, a traditional wooden toy and figurine shop, a whisky and cigar shop, bakers and a number of art galleries (including **Alexander Ochs Galleries**, *see p197*, and **Contemporary Fine Arts**, *see p198*). The brick façade of the Handwerker Verein at No.18 is particularly impressive. If you wander into the courtyard, you'll find the **Sophiensaele** (*see p240*), an interesting performing arts space in an old ballroom. It was also the location of the first German Communist Party HQ.

At Nos.20-21 are the **Sophie-Gips Höfe**, which came into being when wealthy art patrons Erika and Rolf Hoffmann were denied permission to build a gallery in Dresden for their huge collection of contemporary art. Instead, they bought this complex between Sophienstrasse and Gipsstrasse, restored it and installed the art here, along with their spectacular private residence. Tours of the **Sammlung Hoffmann** are available on Saturdays, by appointment. There are also text, earth and light artworks integrated into the building complex (which can be seen until 10pm), as well as galleries, cafés and offices.

Running between the west end of Oranienburger Strasse and Rosenthaler Strasse, **Auguststrasse** is the core of Berlin's eastern gallery district; it was here that the whole Mitte scene originated less than a decade ago, with such important venues as **Eigen + Art** (*see p199*) and **Kunst-Werke** (*see p200*). This became known as Mitte's 'Art Mile', and the street still makes a good afternoon's stroll, although many of the cutting-edge galleries have moved on. If you're lucky, you might catch a *Rundgang* or 'walkaround' (check in the galleries for details). Pleasant on summer evenings, these crawls see galleries open their doors late and sometimes serve wine.

Neue Synagoge

Centrum Judaicum, Oranienburger Strasse 28-30 (8802 8451/www.cjudaicum.de). S1, S2 Oranienburger Strasse. **Open** *Sept-Apr* 10am-6pm Mon-Thur, Sun; 10am-2pm Fri. *May-Aug* 10am-8pm Mon, Sun; 10am-6pm Tue-Thur; 10am-5pm Fri. **Admission** €3; €2 concessions. **No credit cards**. **Map** p303/p310 N5.
Built in 1857-66 as the Berlin Jewish community's showpiece (and inaugurated in the presence of Bismarck), it was the New Synagogue that was attacked during Kristallnacht in 1938, but not too badly damaged – Allied bombs did far more harm in 1945. The façade remained intact and the Moorish dome has been rebuilt. Inside is a permanent exhibition about Jewish life in Berlin and a glassed-in area protecting the ruins of the sanctuary. The dome is also open to visitors in summer.

Sammlung Hoffman

Sophienstrasse 21 (2849 9121/www.sophie-gips.de). U8 Weinmeisterstrasse. **Open** (by appointment only) 11am-4pm Sat. **Admission** €6. **No credit cards**. **Map** p303/p310 N5.
This is Erika and Rolf Hoffmann's private collection of international contemporary art, including a charming floor installation work by Swiss video artist Pipilotti Rist and work by Douglas Gordon, Felix Gonzalez-Torres and AR Penck. The Hoffmans offer guided tours through their apartment every Saturday by appointment – felt slippers supplied.

Alexanderplatz & around

Maps p303 & p310

Visitors who have read Alfred Döblin's *Berlin Alexanderplatz* or seen the television series by Fassbinder may wonder what has happened. In the early 1970s Erich Honecker decided that

Fernsehturm. *See p89.*

this historic area should reflect the glories of socialism, tore it all down, and replaced it with a masterpiece of commie kitsch: wide boulevards, monotonous white buildings filled with cafés and shops, and, of course, the impressive golf-ball-on-a-knitting-needle, the **Fernsehturm** (Television Tower; *see p89*).

At ground level, capitalism's neon icons sit incongruously on Honecker's erections. The goofy clock topped with the 1950s-style atom design signals the time in (mostly) former socialist lands; water cascades from the Brunnen der Völkerfreundschaft ('Fountain of the Friendship of Peoples'); at the Markthalle you can sink a beer or bite into a brand-name burger. There are plans to replace most of Alexanderplatz with a dozen or so skyscrapers, among which the Fernsehturm will remain standing, but it's not at all certain when, or if, such plans will come to fruition. For now, the Kaufhaus department store on the eastern side of the square has been expanded and lost its 1970s façade, and renovation proceeds.

One of the few survivors from pre-war Alexanderplatz sits in the shadow of the Fernsehturm: the **Marienkirche**, Berlin's oldest parish church, dating from the 13th century. Later 15th-century (the tower) and 18th-century (the upper section) additions enhance the building's harmonious simplicity.

Just south of here stands the extravagant **Neptunbrunnen**, an 1891 statue of the trident-wielding sea god, surrounded by four female figures representing the most important German rivers – the Elbe, Rhine, Oder and Vistula. This was moved here from the Stadtschloss when the Communists demolished it in 1950. Overlooking Neptune from the south-east is the huge red-brick bulk of the **Berliner Rathaus** (Berlin Town Hall), while to the south-west is the open space of Marx-Engels Forum, one of the few remaining monuments to the old boys – the huge statue of Karl and Fred begs you to take a seat on Marx's lap. On Spandauer Strasse, behind the Radisson Hotel, is the entrance to the **AquaDom & Sea Life**, one of Mitte's more eccentric new attractions.

For a vague impression of what this part of the city might have looked like before Allied bombers and the GDR did their work, stroll in the Nikolaiviertel, just south of Alexanderplatz. This is Berlin's oldest quarter, centred around **Nikolaikirche**. The GDR's reconstruction involved bringing the few undamaged buildings from this period together into what is essentially a fake assemblage of history. There are a couple of historic residences, including the **Knoblauchhaus**, and the **Ephraim-Palais**, which once belonged to the court jeweller. You'll also find Gottfried Lessing's house, restaurants, cafés (including a reconstruction of Zum Nussbaum, a contender for the oldest bar in Berlin) and overpriced shops. On the southern edge of the district is the **Hanf Museum** (Hemp Museum).

Long before the infamous Wall, Berlin had another one: the medieval **Stadtmauer** (City Wall) of the original 13th-century settlement. There's almost as much left of this wall (a couple of minutes' walk east of the Nikolaiviertel, on Littenstrasse/Waisenstrasse) as there is of the more recent one. Built along the wall by the junction with Parochialstrasse is the old (and extremely popular) restaurant Zur Letzten Instanz. It takes its name from the neighbouring law court, from which there was no further appeal. There has been a restaurant on this site since 1525, Napoleon among its customers. The building is one of four old houses that have been reconstructed.

Just over the Spree from here is the church-like red-brick **Märkisches Museum**, which houses a rambling, but not uninteresting, collection tracing the history of the city, and the small neighbouring Köllnischer Park. You'll see multi-hued bear statues all over the city, but the park's bearpit is home to Schnute, Maxi and Tilo, Berlin's trio of flesh-and-blood brown bears – and official symbols of the city. Around the corner on Wallstrasse is the not very thrilling **Museum Kindheit & Jugend**.

AquaDom & Sea Life

Spandauer Strasse 3 (992 800/www.sealife.de). S5, S7, S9, S75 Hackescher Markt. **Open** 10am-6pm daily. **Admission** €13.50; €12.60 concessions; €10 under-14s. **No credit cards. Map** p303/p311 O6.
Billed as two attractions in one, but both of them involving lots of water and plenty of fish. Sea Life leads visitors through 13 themed aquariums offering fish in different habitats, starting with what you'd find in the nearby Spree, then in the Wannsee, next in Hamburg harbour, and finally beyond in the North Sea and Atlantic Ocean. The AquaDom is the world's largest free-standing aquarium – a spacey stucture that looks like it just landed from some very watery planet. You take a lift up through the middle of this giant cylindrical fishtank – a million litres (nearly 220,000 gallons) of salt water, home to 2,500 colourful creatures – and enfolded by the atrium of the Radisson hotel (*see p52*).

Berliner Rathaus

Rathausstrasse 15 (902 60/guided tours 9026 2523). U2, U5, U8, S5, S7, S9, S75 Alexanderplatz. **Open** 9am-6pm Mon-Fri. *Tours* by appointment. **Admission** free. **Map** p303/p311 O6.
This magnificent building was built of terracotta brick during the 1860s. The history of Berlin up to that point is illustrated in a series of 36 reliefs on the façade. During Communist times, it served as East Berlin's town hall – which made its old nickname, Rotes Rathaus ('Red Town Hall'), after the colour of the façade, doubly fitting. West Berlin's city politicians moved here from their town hall, Rathaus Schöneberg, in 1991. For security reasons, admission is restricted to specific areas; bring some ID.

Ephraim-Palais

Poststrasse 16 (2400 2121/www.stadtmuseum.de). U2, U5, U8, S5, S7, S9, S75 Alexanderplatz. **Open** 10am-6pm Tue-Sun. **Admission** €3; €1.50 concessions; free Wed. *Combined ticket* (with Knoblauchhaus & Nikolaikirche) €5; €3 concessions. **No credit cards. Map** p303/p311 O6.
Built in the 15th century, remodelled in the 18th century, demolished by the Communists, and then rebuilt by them close to its original location for the 750th anniversary of Berlin in 1987, the Ephraim-Palais is today home to temporary exhibitions drawn from the city's collection. Recent ones have

featured antique Berlin silver, the work of stage-set designer Wolf Leder, and expressionist paintings by Wilhelm Kohlhoff. Soft, chandelier lighting and parquet floors add a refined touch to the exhibitions.

Fernsehturm

Panoramastrasse 1A (242 3333/www.berliner fernsehturm.de). U2, U5, U8, S5, S7, S9, S75 Alexanderplatz. **Open** *Mar-Oct* 9am-1am daily. *Nov-Feb* 10am-midnight daily. **Admission** €6.80; €3.50 concessions; free under-3s. Last entry 30mins before closing. **Credit** AmEx, DC, MC, V. **Map** p303/p311 O6.

Built in the late 1960s at a time when relations between East and West Berlin were at their lowest ebb, the 365m (1,198ft) Television Tower – its ball-on-spike shape visible all over the city – was intended as an assertion of Communist dynamism and modernity. A shame, then, that such television towers were a West German invention. A shame, too, that the authorities had to get Swedish engineers to build the thing. The Communists were also displeased to note that when the sun shines on the tower, reflections on the ball form the shape of a cross: Berliners dubbed this 'the Pope's revenge'. Nevertheless, the authorities were proud enough of their tower to make it one of the central symbols of the East German capital, and today it is one of Berlin's most popular graphic images. Take an ear-popping trip in the lift to the observation platform at the top: a great way to orient yourself early on a visit to Berlin. The view is unbeatable by night or day – particularly looking westwards, where you can take in the whole of the Tiergarten and surrounding area. If heights make you hungry, take a twirl in the revolving restaurant. There are usually queues, though. **Photo** *p87.*

Hanf Museum

Mühlendamm 5 (242 4827/www.hanfmuseum.de). U2, U5, U8, S5, S7, S9, S75 Alexanderplatz. **Open** 10am-8pm Tue-Fri; noon-8pm Sat, Sun. **Admission** €3; free under-10s. **No credit cards. Map** p303/p311 O6.

The world's largest hemp museum aims to teach the visitor about the uses of hemp throughout history, as well as touching on the controversy surrounding the herb today. There are a few booklets to leaf through in English. The café (doubling as a video- and reading-room) has cakes made with and without hemp. Everything, though, is THC-free.

Knoblauchhaus

Poststrasse 23 (2345 9991/www.stadtmuseum.de). U2, U5, U8, S5, S7, S9, S75 Alexanderplatz. **Open** 10am-6pm Tue-Sun. **Admission** *Combined ticket* (with Ephraim-Palais & Nikolaikirche) €5; €3 concessions; free Wed. **No credit cards. Map** p303/p311 O6.

This neo-classical mid 18th-century townhouse was home to the influential Knoblauch family and contains an exhibition about some of the more prominent members. But the real draw is the striking haute bourgeoise interior. The first floor contains an exhibition on 'Domestic Living in the Biedermeier Era', with a living room, salon, bedroom and library. The second floor hosts temporary exhibitions about 19th-century cultural history.

Marienkirche

Karl-Liebknecht-Strasse 8 (242 4467/www.marienkirche-berlin.de). U2, U5, U8, S5, S7, S9, S75 Alexanderplatz. **Open** *Apr-Oct* 10am-6pm daily. *Nov-Mar* 10am-4pm daily. **Admission** free. **Map** p303/p311 O6.

Begun in 1270, this is one of Berlin's few remaining medieval buildings. Just inside the door is a wonderful Dance of Death fresco dating from 1485, and the 18th-century Walther organ is considered that famous builder's masterpiece. Marienkirche hit the headlines in 1989 when the civil rights movement chose it for one of their first sit-ins, since churches were among the few places where people could congregate without state permission. Tours available.

Märkisches Museum

Am Köllnischen Park 5 (3086 6215/www.stadt museum.de). U2 Märkisches Museum. **Open** 10am-6pm Tue-Sun. **Admission** €4; €2 concessions; free Wed. **Map** p307/p311 O7.

This extensive, curious and somewhat old-fashioned museum traces the history of Berlin through a wide range of historical artefacts. Different sections examine themes such as Berlin as newspaper city, women in Berlin's history, intellectual Berlin and the military. There are models of the city at different times, and some good paintings, including works by members of the Brücke group, such as Kirchner and Pechstein. Some sections have captions in English.

Museum Kindheit & Jugend

Wallstrasse 32 (275 0383/www.berlin-kindheitund jugend.de). U2 Märkisches Museum. **Open** 9am-5pm Tue-Fri; 10am-6pm Sat, Sun. **Admission** €2; €1 concessions; free Wed; €2.50 family. **No credit cards. Map** p307/p311 O7.

The place to come if you want to show kids how lucky they are to be going to school today and not 50 years ago. Apart from old toys, it displays artefacts from classrooms during the Weimar Republic, the Nazi era and under Communism.

Nikolaikirche

Nikolaikirchplatz (2472 4529/www.stadtmuseum.de). U2, U5, U8, S5, S7, S9, S75 Alexanderplatz. **Open** 10am-6pm Tue-Sun. **Admission** €1.50; free Wed. **Combined ticket** (with Knoblauchhaus & Ephraim-Palais) €5; €3 concessions. **No credit cards. Map** p303/p311 O6.

Inside Berlin's oldest congregational church, from which the Nikolaiviertel takes its name, is an interesting historical collection chronicling Berlin's development from its founding (c1230) until 1648. Old tiles, tapestries, carvings and weapons are on display, as are photos of wartime damage, plus examples of how the stones melted together in the heat of bombardment. Reconstruction was completed in 1987 for Berlin's 750th anniversary.

Prenzlauer Berg & Friedrichshain

Bohemian enclave seeks escape from gentrification.

Abutting Mitte to the north-east and south-east respectively, the districts of Prenzlauer Berg and Friedrichshain present very different faces of east Berlin. The former is now largely gentrified, with tree-lined and café-studded streets, evoking something of pre-war Berlin. The latter, stretching out from the Stalinist spine of Karl-Marx-Allee into waterfront and post-industrial quarters, feels more a product of the communist era. Both districts have lively bar and club scenes; neither offer much in the way of conventional sightseeing.

Prenzlauer Berg

Maps p303 & p312

Once thought of as a grey, depressing working-class district, in the last decade and a half Prenzl'berg (as the locals call it) has had its façades renovated, its streets cleaned and its buildings newly inhabited by everyone from Russian artists to west German office workers. Galleries and cafés have sprouted, and century-old buildings have finally had central heating, bathrooms and telephones installed. Hardcore alternative types might now have moved back to Kreuzberg or out to rawer Friedrichshain, feeling the district has lost its edge, but, for many Berliners, there's no cooler part of town.

Laid out at the turn of the 20th century, Prenzlauer Berg has wider streets and pavements than most part of town, giving the area a distinctive, open look. Although a few

buildings still await restoration, the newly scrubbed and painted streets give the impression of a 19th-century boulevard.

The district's focal point is pretty **Kollwitzplatz**, named after the artist Käthe Kollwitz, who lived much of her life around here. It is lined with bars, cafés and restaurants, and hosts an organic-type market (*see p178*). It was here in the Café Westphal (now a Greek restaurant) that the first meetings of East Berlin dissidents were held in the early 1980s.

Knaackstrasse, heading south-east from Kollwitzplatz, brings you to one of the district's main landmarks, the **Wasserturm**. This circular water tower, constructed by English architect Henry Gill in 1852-75, provided running water for the first time in Germany. During the war the Nazis used its basement as a prison and torture chamber. A plaque commemorates their victims; the tower has now been converted into apartments.

Opposite the Wasserturm on Rykestrasse is the **Synagoge Rykestrasse**, a neo-Romanesque turn-of-the-century structure that was badly damaged during Kristallnacht in 1938. After renovation in 1953, it was the only working synagogue in old East Berlin. Now it stands peacefully in gentrified surrounds. Nearby, to the south-west of Kollwitzplatz, is the **Jüdischer Friedhof**, Berlin's oldest Jewish cemetery and a fairly gloomy place due to its closely packed stones and canopy of trees. If you want to know more about the district's history, look in at the **Prenzlauer Berg Museum**.

From the other side of Kollwitzplatz, Knaackstrasse extends north-west to the vast complex of the **Kulturbrauerei** (*see p219*), an old brewery that now houses a concert space, mostly used for world music shows, plus galleries, artists' studios, a food market and a cinema. South-west from here, Kastanienallee and the area around it has plenty of good bars, restaurants and funky shops. And to the north-east, the so-called 'LSD' area around Lychener Strasse, Stargarder Strasse and Dunckerstrasse, leading up to Helmholtzplatz, is another of Prenzlauer Berg's hotspots.

The babes of Prenzl'berg

In the village of Woltersdorf, south-east of Berlin, there's an old spring – the Liebesquelle, or Love Spring – gurgling behind an iron gate. The story goes that in the Middle Ages the village produced so many little kids that they thought there must be something in the water. Now there aren't many springs in Berlin's Prenzlauer Berg, but there must be something in the air. It has the highest concentration of babies in all of Berlin. Maybe in all of Europe.

It's a rare trip to the supermarket when you don't meet a couple of pregnant women; an unusual visit to a café on Helmholtzplatz when you don't have to avoid a pushchair on your way to the bar. The playgrounds are packed, the streets throng with buggies and prams, and all the talk is about baby gymnastics or kindergarten waiting lists.

Prenzlauer Berg has the fastest-growing number of children under three in Berlin, up by as much as 31 per cent to over 5,000 between 2003 and 2004. And this is during a period when the number of kids was contracting in the rest of Berlin, the worst time for new births in Germany since the end of World War II. Prenzlauer Berg's birth rate comes in at a fecund 2.1 kids per woman of childbearing age, compared to a national average of about 1.36 kids per woman, and an EU average of 1.5.

Demographers refer to Prenzlauer Berg as a rare 'birth cluster', and point to the extraordinarily high number (39 per cent) of women between the ages of 20 and 25 who live here. But that's only part of the story, because many of the new mothers in Prenzlauer Berg are substantially older, women who moved here ten years ago as students when rents were cheap and are just now starting families. It has also benefited from a sort of inner-city 'white flight'. Many young professional couples who wanted to procreate moved here to do so because it's a nice, fashionable area that isn't grey and full of tower blocks like most of east Berlin, and where their kids won't have to share the schoolroom with lots of Turks, as they might in west Berlin.

Curiously, the area's reputation as a trendy district, full of laid-back cafés, design shops and nice restaurants, has not suffered from the onslaught of toddlers. It defies the 'boring but safe' status that would be accorded to a neighbourhood for young families in any other large city. Instead, Prenzlauer Berg seems to have stumbled on its own fountain of youth: the notion of kids as a lifestyle accessory.

East of here, over on the other side of Prenzlauer Allee, is **Ernst-Thälmann-Park**, named after the leader of the pre-1933 German Communist Party. In its north-west corner stands the **Zeiss-Grossplanetarium**, a fantastic GDR interior space that once hymned Soviet cosmonauts and still runs programmes on what's up there in space. Over on the Greifswalder Strasse side of the park, just north of the Danziger Strasse corner, is a giant statue of Ernst Thälmann himself, raising a communist fist – one of Berlin's few remaining socialist realist monuments.

Prenzlauer Berg Museum

Prenzlauer Allee 227 (902 953 916/www.kulturamt-pankow.de). U2 Senefelderplatz. **Open** 9am-6pm Mon-Fri. **Admission** free. **Map** p303/p312 P4.
A small but interesting permanent exhibit on the history and culture of the neighbourhood – lots of old photographs – with temporary exhibitions too.

Zeiss-Grossplanetarium

Prenzlauer Allee 80 (4218 4512/www.astw.de). S41, S42, S8, S85 Prenzlauer Allee. **Open** 8am-noon, 1-4pm Mon-Fri. **Admission** varies.
No credit cards. Map p303/p312 Q2.
This vast planetarium was built in the 1980s. Though changing exhibitions are in German only, the shows in the auditorium are entertaining for all.

Art on the frontier: **East Side Gallery**.

Friedrichshain

Maps pp307-9

As Prenzlauer Berg and Mitte became gentrified, Berlin's bohemia edged south-east into Friedrichshain. Much of the area remains bleakly dominated by communist-era housing blocks – more than half of its buildings were destroyed during World War II – and slashed through by the railway tracks that lead in through Ostbahnhof. This was historically an industrial district, with Berlin's central wheat and rye mill, its first hospital and Osthaven, its eastern port. Much of the district's southern portion, bordering the Spree, contains the remains of industrial buildings.

The best way to get a feeling for both Friedrichshain and the old GDR is to walk east from Alexanderplatz down Karl-Marx-Allee – a broad boulevard built in Stalinist style. It's from Lichtenberger Strasse onwards that the street truly shows its socialist past, with endless rows of Soviet-style apartment blocks stretching beyond the twin towers of Frankfurter Tor. The **Internationales Berliner Bierfestival** (*see p185*) is held on the street every August, a good time to see the neighbourhood come out in force.

To the south and east of Frankfurter Tor there is an agglomeration of bars, clubs and restaurants on **Simon-Dach-Strasse** and the surrounding streets, plus a growing number of interesting fashion and second-hand shops, and the excellent weekly **Trödelmarkt Boxhagener Platz** (*see p178*). This is the lively centre of Berlin's new bohemia, slowly growing eastwards towards Ostkreuz. North of Frankfurter Allee is another concentration of hangouts in the Rigaer Strasse area.

To the south, on Mühlenstrasse (the name means 'Mill Street'; the old mill is at No.8) along the bank of the Spree is the **East Side Gallery**, a stretch of former Wall given over to international artists. The industrial buildings hereabouts have been renovated and rechristened Oberbaum City, and now host loft spaces, offices and studios. Both Universal Music and MTV-Europe have moved their German headquarters to this area. This is also now Berlin's main clubbing area, with venues occupying a variety of post-industrial spaces.

Green relief can be found at the district's far north-west corner in the **Volkspark Friedrichshain**. This huge park is scattered with socialist realist art, and has a couple of hills, a fountain of fairytale characters and the popular **Café Schönbrunn** (*see p151*). The graves of those who fell in the battle for German unity in March 1848 are here. It's also a popular gay cruising zone (*see p215*).

Kreuzberg & Schöneberg

Come here to find queers, Turks, anarcho-punks and some of Berlin's most beautiful streets.

Bordering Mitte to the south is the district of Kreuzberg. Though now administratively joined to Friedrichshain across the Spree, it maintains some of the independence of spirit that characterised its Cold War role as the centre of alternative politics and lifestyle. It's also the capital of Turkish Berlin. To its west lies the wealthier, largely residential district of Schöneberg. Much of Berlin's irrepressible gay life is focused in its northern reaches.

Kreuzberg

Maps pp306-7 & p311

These days the Oberbaumbrücke, renovated in the 1990s by Santiago Calatrava, is just the bridge carrying traffic across the Spree between Kreuzberg and its adminstrative other half, Friedrichshain. During the Cold War it was a more serious crossing: a border post and spy-exchange venue between East and West Berlin. Kreuzberg is not the end of the world these days, and life is even washing back the other way into the borough's eastern reaches.

East Kreuzberg

In the 1970s and 1980s the eastern half of Kreuzberg north of the Landwehrkanal was off at the edge of inner West Berlin. Enclosed on two sides by the Wall, on a third by the canal, and mostly ignored by the rest of the city, its

decaying tenements came to house Berlin's biggest, and most militant, squat community. The area was full of punky left-wing youth on a draft-dodging mission and Turks who came here because the rents were very cheap and people mostly left them alone.

No area of west Berlin has changed quite so much since the Wall came down. This once-isolated pocket found itself recast as desirable real estate. Much of the alternative art scene shifted north to the Scheunenviertel in Mitte, and even the May Day Riots – long an annual Kreuzberg tradition (*see p184* **May Day! May Day!**) – began taking place in Prenzlauer Berg. Oddly enough, gentrification never really took off in this end of Kreuzberg, but it did in Prenzl'berg, so the riots have now moved back.

Though Kreuzberg is no longer a magnet for young bohemia, enough of the anarchistic old guard stayed behind to ensure that the area still has a distinct atmosphere. It's an earthy kind of place, full of cafés, bars and clubs, dotted with independent cinemas, and is an important nexus for the city's gay community.

And it's still the capital of Turkish Berlin, the world's fifth-largest Turkish city. The scruffy area around Kottbusser Tor bustles with kebab shops and Anatolian travel agents. The open-air **Türkischer Markt** (*see p178*) stretches along the Maybachufer every Tuesday and Friday. Görlitzer Park, once an important train station, turns into a huge Turkish barbecue on fine weekends. *See p94* **The capital of Turkish Berlin**.

Oranienstrasse is the area's main drag, dotted with bars and clubs, and the blocks to the north and west of here are home to even more places to booze and behave badly. South across Skalitzer Strasse, Oranienstrasse changes into Wiener Strasse, running alongside the old Görlitzer Bahnhof, where more bars and cafés welcome what's left of the Kreuzberg crowd. A couple of blocks further south lies Paul-Linke-Ufer, lined with canalbank cafés that provide a favourite spot for weekend brunch.

The U1 line runs overhead through the neighbourhood along the middle of Skalitzer

The capital of Turkish Berlin

For many Berliners, a greasy kebab is the only way to finish a good night out. Turkish food is a Berlin staple, but not many realise that the doner kebab is no import from Turkey. It was actually invented here in Kreuzberg – in 1971, by one Mehmet Aygun, these days proprietor of the **Hasir** (*see p136*) restaurant chain.

But Turkish culture stretches further than street food. In Kreuzberg, the mosques now attract more worshippers than the churches. Outside Turkey itself, Berlin has become home to the largest Turkish community in the world. The hubs are in Kreuzberg and Neukölln, where one in three residents is of Turkish origin.

The meeting of cultures has had a difficult history. The rapid flow of immigration began in 1961 as a direct consequence of the Berlin Wall. With East German workers suddenly cut off from jobs in the West, the FDR government grasped about for another source of cheap labour. Thousands of *Gastarbeiter* ('guest workers') were hurriedly recruited from Turkey, and crammed together in purpose-built blocks such as the shabby, hive-like structure at Kotbusser Tor.

The West German authorities proved ungracious hosts. The 'guest workers' were considered no more than a temporary necessity, and in time it was felt that they had outstayed their welcome. When large numbers stayed put, the government

made their displeasure clear. The Nationality Act (or 'Blood Law') of 1913, according to which German citizenship was based on heredity, was rigorously upheld. No person born of Turkish parents could be granted a German passport.

The Turkish community thus remained quite isolated from mainstream society. As recently as 2004, a report found that up to 60 per cent of children in Kreuzberg nursery schools were unable to speak a single word of German. Popular antagonism to the immigrant community reached a peak in 1990, when it was felt that large numbers of foreign settlers would destabilise Germany's national identity, and hinder the chances of successful reunification. Ex-Chancellor Helmut Kohl declared that Germany was 'not a land of immigration', thus blithely ignoring, and further alienating, the nine per cent of the country's population who had been born abroad.

But attitudes are beginning to soften. In recent years, the basis of nationality on blood has come to be seen as inappropriate for a Germany that wants to leave behind the less savoury aspects of its history. The new law implemented on 1 January 2001 (following a determined campaign by the Green Party) grants citizenship to any child born on German soil, provided their parents have been legally resident in the country for at least eight years.

In Kreuzberg, at least, a genuine desire for multiculturalism has taken hold. Turkish families, living side by side with punks and squatters, have developed into a uniquely indigenous community. The torrential sound of *Turkendeutsche* – a hybrid language spoken by the immigrant population – fills the air around Oranienstrasse, while Turkish-German rappers like Cartel and Azziza-A spit lyrics on bar stereos. The weekly **Türkischer Markt** (*see p178*) on the Maybachufer showcases the settlers' more traditional side, while regular Turkish gay nights at **S036** (*see p208*) reveal a contrasting cosmopolitanism. Turkish-born, Kreuzberg-bred comedian Kaya Yana is one of the biggest sensations on German TV – quoting his catchphrase, 'Was guckst du?' ('What are you looking at?'), has become an annoyingly regular national joke. And you can still purchase that local invention, the doner kebab, at any time of the day or night.

Sightseeing

Strasse. The onion-domed Schlesisches Tor station was once the end of the line. These days the train continues one more stop across the Spree to Warschauer Strasse. You can also walk across the Oberbaumbrücke into Friedrichshain and the post-industrial nightlife district around Mühlenstrasse. But nowadays traffic is also coming the other way. Courtesy of riverside development on the Spree and of an overspill from Friedrichshain, the area around Schlesisches Tor station and along Schlesische Strasse towards Treptow is Berlin's newest hotspot. Cafés and bars are opening up, property prices are creeping up, and Kreuzberg looks to be regaining some of its old atmosphere.

Schlesische Strasse leads over the canal and into the borough of Treptow (*see p120*). There are several cafés and venues along Puschkinallee, and Treptower Park lies beyond.

South-west Kreuzberg

The southern and western part of Kreuzberg contains some of the most picturesque corners of west Berlin, including in Viktoriapark the 'cross hill' (the literal meaning of 'Kreuzberg') after which the borough is named.

Viktoriapark is the natural way to enter the area. In summer it has a cheery, fake waterfall cascading down the Kreuzberg, and paths wind their way to the summit, where Schinkel's 1821 monument (the hill's cross is on top of it) commemorates victories in the Napoleonic Wars – many of the streets nearby are named after battles and generals of that era. From this commanding view over a mainly flat city, the landmarks of both east and west spread out before you: Friedrichstrasse dead ahead, the Europa-Center off to the left, the Potsdamer Platz high-rises in between, the Fernsehturm over to the right. The view is clearer in winter, when the trees are bare.

Back on ground level, the streets north of the park lead to one of Berlin's most picturesque courtyard complexes. Riehmers Hofgarten is cobbled, closed to traffic and often used as a film location for its 19th-century feel. It's also home to one of Berlin's nicest small hotels, the **Hotel Riehmers Hofgarten** (*see p58*).

Around the corner on Mehringdamm is the **Schwules Museum** (Gay Museum). Bergmannstrasse, which runs to the east from here, is the main hub of local activity. Bucking the tendency for everything to move eastwards, this street of cafés, junk shops, bookstores and record shops is livelier than ever by day, although the area is relatively lacklustre at night. The street leads to Marheinekeplatz, site

City views and Schinkel's war memorial on top of the Kreuzberg in **Viktoriapark**.

Sightseeing

In plane view, the **Deutsches Technikmuseum**. *See p97.*

of one of Berlin's busiest district market halls. Zossener Strasse (north from here) also bustles.

Bergmannstrasse continues east past a large cemetery to Südstern. Here is the entrance to the **Volkspark Hasenheide**, the other of the neighbourhood's large parks, with the top of Rixdorfer Höhe offering more good views.

The streets just south of Bergmannstrasse are like another movie set. Many buildings survived wartime bombing and the area around Chamissoplatz has been immaculately restored. The cobbled streets are lined with houses still sporting their Prussian façades and illuminated by gaslight at night. This is one of the most beautiful parts of this largely unbeautiful city.

South of here, just across the border into the borough of the same name, stands the enormous **Flughafen Tempelhof**. Once the central airport for the city, it was begun in the 1920s and later greatly expanded by the Nazis. The largest building in Berlin – and one of the largest in the world – its curving bulk looms with an authoritarian ominousness.

Tempelhof airport's place in the city's affections was cemented during the Airlift of 1948-9, when it served as the base for the 'raisin-bombers', which flew in and out at a rate of one a minute, bringing supplies to the blockaded city and tossing sweets and raisins to waiting kids. The monument forking towards the sky on Platz der Luftbrücke commemorates those who flew these missions, as does a photorealist painting in the terminal. In the early 1970s Tempelhof became the US Air Force base in Berlin. Today it's once more a civil airport, catering to small airlines running small planes on short-hop European routes.

This facility uses only a tiny fraction of the Tempelhof's enormous structure, some other parts of which have been converted into entertainment venues. On the other side of Columbiadamm are the **Columbiahalle** and **Columbiaclub** concert venues (for both, *see p218*). The latter was actually built by the US Air Force as a cinema for use by their personnel, and is a classic example of 1950s cinema architecture.

North-west Kreuzberg

The north-west portion of Kreuzberg, bordering Mitte, is where you will find most of the area's museums and tourist sights. The most prominent is the extraordinary **Jüdisches Museum** on Lindenstrasse, an example of architecture at its most cerebral. West of here, close to the Landwehrkanal, is the quirky and enjoyable **Deutsches Technikmuseum Berlin** (German Museum of Technology).

Over the canal to the north is the site of Anhalter Bahnhof, once the city's biggest and busiest railway station. Only a tiny piece of façade remains, preserved in its bombed state near the S-Bahn station that bears its name. The **Gruselkabinett**, a chamber of horrors, occupies an old air-raid shelter on the Schöneberger Strasse side of the area where the platforms and tracks once stood.

On Stresemannstrasse, the Bauhaus-designed Europahaus was heavily bombed during World War II, but the lower storeys remain. Nearby, on the north side of the street, Berlin's parliament, the **Abgeordnetenhaus von Berlin** (Berlin House of Representatives), meets in what was formerly the Prussian parliament. Dating from the 1890s, the building was renovated in the early 1990s. Opposite stands the **Martin-Gropius-Bau**, a venue for major art shows. The building was modelled on London's South Kensington museums – the figures of craftspeople on the external reliefs betray its origins as an applied arts museum.

Next to it is a deserted patch of ground that once held the Prinz Albrecht Palais, which the Gestapo took over as its headquarters. In the basement's 39 cells, political prisoners were held, interrogated and tortured. The land was flattened after the war. In 1985, during an acrimonious debate over the design of a memorial to be placed here, a group of citizens staged a symbolic 'excavation'. To their surprise, they hit the Gestapo's basement, and plans were then made to reclaim the site. Today, while the authorities remain mired in indecision about the site, there is an open-air exhibition known as the **Topographie des Terrors**. Along its northern boundary is a surviving stretch of the Berlin Wall, pitted and threadbare after thousands of 1990 souvenir-hunters pecked at it with hammers and chisels.

From here, it's a short walk down Kochstrasse – once Berlin's Fleet Street – to Friedrichstrasse, where Checkpoint Charlie once stood and where the **Haus am Checkpoint Charlie** documents the history of the Wall. Most of the space where the border post once stood has been claimed by new buildings. The actual site of the borderline itself is memorialised by Frank Thiel's photographic portraits of an American and a Soviet soldier. The small white building that served as gateway between East and West is now in the **Alliierten Museum** (*see p118*) – the one in the middle of the street is a replica.

Deutsches Technikmuseum Berlin

Trebbiner Strasse 9 (902 540/www.dtmb.de). U1, U7 Möckernbrücke. **Open** 9am-5.30pm Tue-Fri; 10am-6pm Sat, Sun. **Admission** €4.50; €2.50 concessions. **Map** p306 L9.
Opened in 1982 in the former goods depot of Anhalter Bahnhof, the German Museum of Technology is an eclectic and often eccentric collection of new and antique industrial artefacts. The rail exhibits have pride of place, with the station sheds providing an ideal setting for locomotives and rolling stock from 1835 to the present. Also on view are exhibitions about the Industrial Revolution; street, rail, water and air traffic; computer technology and printing technology. Behind the main complex is an open-air section with two functioning windmills and a smithy. Oddities, such as vacuum cleaners from the 1920s, make this a fun place for implement enthusiasts. The Maritime wing has

ships and displays on both inland waterways and international seafaring. In April 2005 a new wing was opened for aviation and space travel. There are models and original designs, and electronic information points offer commentaries in English and German on subjects from the slave trade to space stations. The Spectrum annexe at Möckernstrasse 26 houses over 200 interactive devices and experiments. **Photo** *p96*.

Gruselkabinett

Schöneberger Strasse 23A (2655 5546/www.gruselkabinett-berlin.de). S1, S2, S26 Anhalter Bahnhof. **Open** 10am-3pm Mon; 10am-7pm Tue, Thur, Sun; 10am-8pm Fri; noon-8pm Sat. **Admission** €7; €5 concessions. **No credit cards**. **Map** p306 L8.
This chamber of horrors is housed in the city's only visitable World War II air-raid shelter. Built in 1943, the five-level bunker was part of an underground network connecting various similar concrete structures throughout Berlin, and today houses both the Gruselkabinett and an exhibit on the bunker itself. The latter includes a few personal effects found here after the war and a video documentary in German only. The actual structure is the most interesting thing. The 'horrors' begin at ground level with an exhibit on medieval medicine (mechanical figures amputate a leg to the sound of canned screaming). Elsewhere there's a patented coffin designed to advertise your predicament should you happen to be buried alive. Upstairs is scarier: a musty labyrinth with a simulated cemetery, strange cloaked figures, lots of spooky sounds and a few surprises. Kids love it, but not those under ten.

Haus am Checkpoint Charlie

Friedrichstrasse 43-5 (253 7250/www.mauermuseum.de). U6 Kochstrasse. **Open** 9am-10pm daily. **Admission** €9.50; €5.50 concessions. **No credit cards**. **Map** p306/p311 M8.
A little tacky, but essential for anyone interested in the Wall and the Cold War. This private museum opened not long after the GDR erected the Berlin Wall in 1961 with the purpose of documenting the events that were taking place. The exhibition charts the history of the Wall, and gives details of the ingenious and hair-raising ways people escaped from the GDR – as well as exhibiting some of the actual contraptions that were used, such as rigged suitcases and a weird car with a propeller.

Jüdisches Museum

Lindenstrasse 9-14 (2599 3300/guided tours 2599 3305/www.juedisches-museum-berlin.de). U1, U6 Hallesches Tor. **Open** 10am-10pm Mon; 10am-8pm Tue-Sun. Closed Jewish holidays & Christmas Eve. **Admission** €5; €2.50 concessions; €10 family. **No credit cards**. **Map** p307 N8.
The idea of a Jewish museum in Berlin was first mooted in 1971. In 1975 an association was formed to acquire materials for eventual display. In 1989 the Jewish Department of the Berlin Museum held a competition for designs for an extension to house

these materials. Daniel Libeskind emerged as the winner, the foundation stone was laid in 1992, the building was completed in 1998 and, on 9 September 2001, the permanent exhibition finally opened. The ground plan of the building is partly based on an exploded Star of David, in part on lines drawn between the site and former addresses of figures in Berlin's Jewish history, such as Mies van der Rohe, Arnold Schönberg and Walter Benjamin. The entrance is via a tunnel from the Kollegienhaus next door. The underground geometry is startlingly independent of the above-ground building. One passage leads to the exhibition halls, two others intersect en route to the Holocaust Tower and the ETA Hoffmann Garden, a grid of 49 columns, tilted to disorientate. Throughout, diagonals and parallels carve out surprising spaces, while windows slash through the structure and its zinc cladding like the knife-wounds of history. Then there are the 'voids', negative spaces that can be viewed or crossed but not entered, standing for the emptiness left by the destruction of German Jewish culture.

The permanent exhibition struggles in places with such powerful surroundings. And the problem with telling the story of German Jewish history is that we all know only too well what it was leading up to. What makes the exhibit engaging is its focus on the personal. It tells the stories of prominent Jews, what they contributed to their community and to the cultural and economic life of Berlin and Germany. After centuries of prejudice and pogroms, the outlook for German Jews seemed to be brightening and full civil equality had been achieved under the Weimar Republic. Then came the Holocaust. This part of the exhibit is the most harrowing. Indeed, the emotional impact of countless stories of the eminent and ordinary, and the fate that almost all shared, is hard to convey adequately in print.

There are also temporary exhibitions. These have recently included 'Chrismukkah', on the relationship between Christmas and Hanukkah, and 'On the Accursed German Soil', about Jewish survivors in Germany after 1945. The museum is a must-see, but expect long queues and big crowds. Last entrance is one hour before closing.

Martin-Gropius-Bau

Niederkirchnerstrasse 7 (254 860/www.gropiusbau. de). S1, S2, S26 Anhalter Bahnhof. **Open** 10am-8pm Mon; 10am-8pm Wed-Sun. **Admission** varies. **Credit** AmEx, MC, V. **Map** p306/p311 L8.
Cosying up to where the Wall once ran (there is still a short, pitted stretch running along the south side of Niederkirchnerstrasse), the Martin-Gropius-Bau is named after its architect, one of the more famous Walter. Built in 1881, it has been renovated and serves as a venue for an assortment of art exhibitions and touring shows, ranging from a show about Stanley Kubrick's movies to an exhibition about art in the Vatican. It's also a venue for the Berlin Biennale and assorted other festivals. No permanent exhibition, but there's a decent bookshop.

Schwules Museum

Mehringdamm 61 (6959 9050/www.schwules museum.de). U6, U7 Mehringdamm. **Open** 2-6pm Mon, Wed-Sun. *Tours* 5pm Sat. **Admission** €5; €3 concessions. **No credit cards. Map** p306 M10.
The Gay Museum, opened in 1985, is still the only one in the world dedicated to the research and public exhibition of homosexual life in all of its forms. The museum, its library and archives are staffed by volunteers and function thanks to private donations and bequests (such as the archive of GDR sex scientist Rudolf Klimmer). On the ground floor is the actual museum, housing permanent and temporary exhibitions. The third-floor library and archive houses around 8,000 books (500 or so in English), 3,000 international periodicals, collections of photos, posters, plus TV, film and audio footage, all available for lending. Information is available in English.

Topographie des Terrors

Niederkirchnerstrasse 8 (2548 6703/www. topographie.de). S1, S2, S26 Anhalter Bahnhof. **Open** *Oct-Apr* 10am-dusk daily. *May-Sept* 10am-8pm daily. **Admission** free. **Map** p306/p311 M8.
Essentially a piece of waste ground where once stood the Prinz Albrecht Palais, headquarters of the Gestapo, and the Hotel Prinz Albrecht, which housed offices of the Reich SS leadership. This was the centre of the Nazi police state apparatus and it was from here that the Holocaust was directed, and the Germanisation of the east dreamt up. Not much here now except an open-air exhibition about the baleful history of the site – placards and photos using the walls of the excavated basement and hoardings at ground level – and a temporary building where you can buy publications, including the excellent catalogue (available in English; €7), and pick up a free audio guide (also in English; leave ID as security). Plans for a documentation centre have been mired in indecision and financial trouble – building started in the 1990s, but it was all dismantled in 2005. At press time they had invited entries for a new architectural competition to help determine what to do with the site, much of which is overgrown and closed to the public. A surviving segment of the Berlin Wall runs along the site's northern boundary. The main entrance is where that meets the north-east corner of the Martin-Gropius-Bau (*see above*).

Schöneberg

Maps p305 & p306

Geographically and atmospherically, Schöneberg lies between Kreuzberg and Charlottenburg. It's a diverse and vibrant part of town, mostly built in the late 19th century. Though largely devoid of conventional sights, it's rich in reminders of Berlin's recent history.

Schöneberg means 'beautiful hill' – oddly, because the borough is flat. It does have an 'island', though: the triangular **Schöneberger Insel**, carved out by the two broad railway

Rathaus Schöneberg.

near Alexanderplatz in 1910. The mansion in the park was originally a law court, and during the Cold War became headquarters for the Allied Control Council. After the 1972 treaty that formalised the separate status of East and West Germany, the building stood virtually unused. But there were occasional Allied Council meetings, before which the Americans, British and French would observe a ritual pause, as if expecting the Soviet representative, who had last attended in 1948, to show up. In 1990 a Soviet finally did wander in and the Allies held a last meeting to formalise their withdrawal from the city in 1994. This may be the place where the Cold War officially ended.

On the north-west corner of Potsdamer Strasse's intersection with Pallasstrasse stood the Sportpalast, site of many Nazi rallies and the scene of Goebbels's famous 'Total War' speech of 18 February 1943. In its place stand shabby blocks of flats. One part of the complex straddles Pallasstrasse and rests on the huge concrete hulk of a Nazi air-raid shelter, which planners were unable to destroy. This featured in Wim Wenders's 1987 film *Wings of Desire*.

At the west end of Pallasstrasse stands **St-Matthias-Kirche**. South from here, Goltzstrasse is lined with cafés, bars and interesting shops. To the north of the church is Winterfeldtplatz, site of bustling Wednesday and Saturday morning markets, engendering lively café life by day and lively eating-out by night.

Nollendorfplatz to the north is the hub of Schöneberg's nightlife. The theatre on the square has had many incarnations. In the Weimar era it was home to experimental director Erwin Piscator; under the Third Reich Hitler came here to watch Zara Leander shows; in the 1980s it was the infamous Metropol disco; and in December 2006 it reopened as the upmarket dine and dance complex **Goya** (*see p230*). Outside Nollendorfplatz U-Bahn, recently crowned with a new cupola, the small memorial to homosexuals killed in concentration camps is a reminder of the area's history. Christopher Isherwood chronicled Berlin from his rooming house at Nollendorfstrasse 17; Motzstrasse has been a major artery of Berlin's gay life since the 1920s. Gay Schöneberg continues around the corner and straddles Martin-Luther-Strasse along Fuggerstrasse.

Schöneberg's most famous daughter is screen icon Marlene Dietrich, now buried just over the district's southern boundary, in the tiny **Friedhof Friedenau** on Fehlerstrasse (*see map p305 G12*). Nico grew up around here too, and launched her career by hanging around long enough to be 'discovered' outside the department store **KaDeWe** (*see p163*), which stands at the borough's north-west corner.

cuttings that carry S-Bahn line 1 and lines 2 and 26, with an elevated stretch of lines S41, 42 and 45 providing the southern boundary. In the 1930s the area was known as Rote Insel ('Red Island'): socialistically inclined and easy to defend, it was one of the last bits of Berlin to resist Nazification. There's a fine view of central east Berlin from Monumentenbrücke, on the east side of the island going towards Kreuzberg's Viktoriapark. On the north-west edge of the island is **St-Matthäus-Kirchhof**, a large graveyard and last resting place of the Brothers Grimm.

At the Kleistpark intersection, Schöneberg's main street is called Hauptstrasse to the south and Potsdamer Strasse to the north. Hauptstrasse leads south-west in the direction of Potsdam. David Bowie and Iggy Pop once resided at No.155. Further south, the **Dominicuskirche** is one of Berlin's few baroque churches. North-west along Dominicusstrasse is **Rathaus Schöneberg**, outside of which John F Kennedy made his famous 'Ich bin ein Berliner' speech. The square now bears Kennedy's name. This was West Berlin's town hall during the Cold War, and the place where Mayor Walter Momper welcomed East Berliners in 1989.

From here, Belziger Strasse leads back in the direction of **Kleistpark**. The entrance to Kleistpark from Potsdamer Strasse is an 18th-century double colonnade, moved here from

Tiergarten

A central park, an almighty zoo, and lots of political animals.

The huge, green Tiergarten – Berlin's central park – dominates, divides and gives its name to this district. The Wall once ran along the park's eastern edge, but now Tiergarten again forms the link between Mitte and Charlottenburg, stretching from the Reichstag in the north-east to the Zoo in the south-west. Along the park's northern boundary the Spree meanders (above this is drab, residential Moabit and the new Berlin Hauptbahnhof), while south of the park the many cultural, architectural and commercial attractions include the reborn Potsdamer Platz and the Kulturforum's museums and galleries.

The park & the Reichstag

Maps p302, p305 & p311

A hunting ground for the Prussian Electors since the 16th century, **Tiergarten**, the park that stretches west from the Brandenburg Gate, was opened to the public in the 18th century. During World War II it was badly damaged, and, in the desperate winter of 1945-6, almost all surviving trees were cut down for firewood. It wasn't until 1949 that Tiergarten started to recover – towns from all over Germany donated trees (as did Queen Elizabeth II). Today joggers, gay cruisers and picnickers pour into the park in fine weather, yet its 1.7 square kilometres (0.6 square miles), much of which feels quite wild, rarely seem crowded.

All roads entering the Tiergarten lead to the park's largest monument, the **Siegessäule** (Victory Column), which celebrates the last wars Germany managed to win. The park's main thoroughfare, Strasse des 17. Juni (the date of the East Berlin workers' strike of 1953),

is one of the few pieces of Hitler's plan for Germania that got built – a grand east–west axis, lined with Nazi lamp-posts, linking Unter den Linden to Neu-Westend. The Siegessäule was moved here from its original position in front of the Reichstag.

Towards the eastern end of Strasse des 17. Juni, just west of the Brandenburger Tor, stands the **Sowjetisches Ehrenmal** (Soviet War Memorial). Once the only piece of Soviet property in West Berlin, it was built in 1945-6 out of granite and marble from the ruins of Hitler's Neue Reichskanzlei and posed something of a political problem. Standing in the British Zone, it was surrounded by a British military enclosure, which was in turn guarded by Berlin police, and all to protect the monument and the two Soviet soldiers who stood 24-hour guard. The tanks flanking the monument are said to have been the first Soviet tanks into Berlin, but this is probably a myth.

At the north-eastern corner of the park, just north of the **Brandenburger Tor** (see p76), stands the **Reichstag**. Described by Kaiser Wilhelm II as the 'Imperial Monkey House', scene of Weimar squabblings, left as a burnt-out ruin during the Third Reich, regarded by the Red Army as its main prize, and stranded for forlorn decades beside the Wall that divided the Deutsches Volk whose representatives it was intended to house, the Reichstag hasn't exactly had a happy history.

In 1995 the artist Christo wrapped it in aluminium-coated fabric, drawing a somewhat ironic line under all that, and then in 1999 Sir Norman Foster's brilliant refitting of the building was unveiled to the public. Its most crowning achievement is the glass cupola – a trip to the top should be a must-do for visitors.

With the decision to make Berlin the German capital, the area north of the Reichstag was picked for new government buildings. Designed by Axel Schultes and Charlotte Frank, the immense Spreebogen complex, also known as the Band des Bundes, is built over a twist in the River Spree (*Bogen* means 'bend'). It crosses the river twice and the old east–west border once, symbolising the reunion of Berlin. Its most notable building is the **Bundeskanzleramt** (Federal Chancellery; **photo** *p101*).

Across the river to the north stands, from June 2006, the new **Berlin Hauptbahnhof** (*see*

Sculpture by Eduardo Chillida in front of the **Bundeskanzleramt**. *See p100.*

p102 **Hub, bub**). Berlin never had a central station before. Now it has the biggest and most futuristic in Europe. At press time the builders were rushing to get it finished.

South of the Bundeskanzleramt's western end is the **Haus der Kulturen der Welt**, an impressive piece of modern architecture whose reflecting pool contains a Henry Moore sculpture. Formerly known as the Kongresshalle, the HdKdW opened in 1957 and hosts exhibits from cultures around the world.

Also on the park's northern boundary, further west, stands **Schloss Bellevue**, a minor palace from 1785, now official residence of the German president. Across the river, a serpentine 718-apartment residence for Federal employees, nicknamed 'Die Schlange' (the snake), winds its way across land formerly used as a goods yard. West of Schloss Bellevue is the **Englischer Garten**, laid out on the theory that the lack of revolutions in England was due to the abundance of green spaces.

Just north of here the **Akademie der Künste** (*see p236*) offers a varied programme of arts events and classical concerts. The district between the Akademie and the loop of the Spree is known as the **Hansaviertel**, a post-war housing project whose high-rise buildings were designed by a Who's Who of architects as part of the 1957 Interbau Exhibition for the 'city of tomorrow'.

Haus der Kulturen der Welt

John-Foster-Dulles-Allee 10 (397 870/www.hkw.de). S5, S7, S9, S75 Bellevue/bus 100. **Open** 10am-9pm Tue-Sun. **Admission** varies. **No credit cards**. **Map** p302 K6.
The House of World Cultures was set up in 1989 to promote artists from developing countries, and

mounts spectacular large-scale exhibitions on subjects such as contemporary Indian art, Bedouin culture or the Chinese avant-garde. Recent exhibitions have focused on Asia, notably a massive multimedia show called 'China: Between Past and Future'. In summer 2006 'Copa da Cultura' is a festival of Brazilian culture. The HdKdW's programme also involves film festivals, readings, lectures, discussions, concerts and dance performances. Hugh Stubbins's oyster-like building was America's contribution to the Interbau Exhibition. A unique Berlin cultural institution. Decent café too.

Reichstag

Platz der Republik (2270). S1, S2 Unter den Linden. **Open** *Dome* 8am-midnight daily; last entry 10pm. **Admission** free. **Map** p302/p311 L6.
The imposing Reichstag was controversial from the beginning. Architect Paul Wallot struggled to find a style that would symbolise German national identity at a time – 1884-94, shortly after unification – when no such style (or identity) existed. It was burned on 17 February 1933 – an event the Nazis blamed on a Dutchman and used as an excuse to suspend basic freedoms. Today, after its renovation by Sir Norman Foster, the Reichstag is again home to the Bundestag (the German parliament), and open to the public. Foster conceived it as a 'dialogue between old and new'. Graffiti scrawled by Russian soldiers in 1945, for example, has been left in view and there has been no attempt to deny the building's turbulent history. No dome appeared on his original competition-winning plans, but the German government insisted upon one. Foster, in turn, insisted that, unlike the structure's original dome (damaged in the war and demolished in the 1950s), the new one should be a public space, open to visitors.

A trip to the top is a must, but beware of queues: come first thing or in the evening if possible. A lift whisks you to the roof, and from there ramps lead to the top of the dome, affording fine city views. At the centre is a funnel of mirrors, angled so as to shed light on the workings of democracy below. Viewed from the spiral walkways, they also have an almost funhouse effect. Foster has created a space that's open, playful and defiantly democratic.

Siegessäule

Strasse des 17. Juni (391 2961). S5, S7, S9, S75 Bellevue. **Open** *Summer* 9.30am-6.30pm Mon-Thur; 9.30am-7pm Fri, Sat. *Winter* 9.30am-5pm Mon-Thur; 9.30am-6pm Fri, Sat. **Admission** €2.20; €1.50 concessions. **No credit cards. Map** p305 H7.
Tiergarten's biggest monument was built in 1871-3 to commemorate Prussian campaigns against Denmark (1864), Austria (1866) and France (1870-71). Originally planted in front of the Reichstag, it was moved here by Hitler to form a centrepiece for the east–west axis connecting western Berlin with Mitte. On top of the column is an 8m (26ft) gilded Goddess of Victory by Friedrich Drake; captured French cannons and cannonballs, sawn in half and gilded, provide the decoration of the column proper. It's 285 steps up to the viewing platform.

Maps pp305-6 & p311

At the south-east corner of the Tiergarten is the reborn **Potsdamer Platz** (photo *p104*), intended as the reunified city's new commercial centrepiece. In the 1920s Potsdamer Platz was reckoned to be one of Europe's busiest squares. The first ever traffic lights stood here (a replica can be seen on the south side of the square). Then it was bombed flat in World War II and during the Cold War became a no-man's land bisected by the Wall. Fierce debate ensued over whether the redevelopment should adopt the typical scale of a 'European' city or go for an 'American' high-rise approach. The result was a compromise, with medium-height development except on Potsdamer Platz itself, where high-rises up to 90 metres (295 feet) were allowed.

Opinions are mixed as to the success of the finished article. Neither east nor west of the city, it sounded like a good candidate for a

Hub, bub

In 1989 the desire of East Germans to travel was the motor of events leading to the reunification of Berlin and Germany. Now the final piece of the structural reunification puzzle is, fittingly, a new transport hub – not just for the city or the region, not even just for Germany, but for the whole of northern Europe. When **Berlin Hauptbahnhof** opens in May 2006, it will be Europe's largest rail station, crossing point for lines running north and south to Scandinavia and the Balkans, east and west to Brussels and Moscow.

Berlin never had one central station, just separate terminuses for different lines. Many were destroyed in the war and never rebuilt because the Wall meant there was no longer anywhere for the lines to go. Anhalter Bahnhof and Görlitzer Bahnhof are two such former stations, their names surviving as stops on the U- or S-Bahn.

Lehrter Bahnhof was another, built in 1871 as the terminus for trains to Hanover. Heavily damaged in World War II, the main structure was demolished in 1957, leaving only a station on the east–west S-Bahn. In 1987 that was listed and renovated to the tune of 10 million Deutschmarks. Then the Wall fell. City planners peered at the map and came up with the so-called *Pilzkonzept* ('mushroom concept'), which involved a new north–south line tunnelling under the Tiergarten and

intersecting the east–west lines. The name came from the vaguely 'shroom-like shape formed by the new and existing lines. At the cap of the mushroom was Lehrter Bahnhof.

In 2002 the listed structure was torn down to make room for a fancy new station in steel and glass, and the following year its name was changed to Hauptbahnhof-Lehrter Bahnhof. On opening, it becomes Berlin Hauptbahnhof, a five-level interchange for all long-distance and regional trains, and built to handle around 300,000 passengers a day.

The *Pilzkonzept* has knock-on effects. Gesundbrunnen and Papestrasse S-Bahn stations become Nordkreuz and Südkreuz, handling intercity trains on their way in and out of town. The casualty is Bahnhof Zoo, downgraded from intercity to local status. At press time, there are protests against that decision, fuelled by both business and the irritation of ordinary citizens.

Thing is, Lehrter Bahnhof might be a logical place for lines to intersect, but it's pretty inconvenient for just about everything else, surrounded by waterways, parks and disused industrial land, far from the commercial hotspots. Ridiculously, it's not even on the U-Bahn network, although a short and for the time being isolated stretch of new line – the U55, running two stops to Unter den Linden – will supposedly open in late 2007.

Sightseeing

unifying centre. But it's an isolated island of redevelopment, not yet connecting to any area around it, still neither one thing nor the other. That said, it's beginning to feel worn in – a natural part of a disjointed urban landscape.

Helmut Jahn's soaring **Sony Center** (**photo** *p104*), surprisingly light in steel and glass, contains the Forum, conceived as an urban entertainment complex. In this, at least, it has succeeded, containing the **CineStar** multiplex (*see p193*), the more offbeat **Arsenal** cinema (*see p193*) and the **Filmmuseum Berlin**. (There's another multiplex – the **CinemaxX**, *see p193* – over the road in the DaimlerChrysler quarter.) Served also by a clutch of new five-star hotels, including the **Ritz-Carlton** (*see p60*) and the **Hyatt** (*see p59*), Potsdamer Platz is also now the main venue for the film festival (*see p194* **Berlin International Film Festival**). But there is sadly little to recommend around here in terms of eating, drinking or shopping. It's all franchise culture.

One of only two Potsdamer Platz buildings to survive World War II and the subsequent clearout was here on the Sony site: the **Kaisersaal Café** from the former Grand Hotel Esplanade. When plans for the area solidified, the café was found to be in a bad position and was moved 75 metres (246 feet) to its present location on the north side of the Sony Center.

The other major corporate presence at Potsdamer Platz is DaimlerChrysler, responsible for most of the development south of the Sony Center. This includes buildings by Richard Rogers, Renzo Piano and Hans Kollhof. One of the most admired buildings is Kollhof's triangular, brick-clad tower at Potsdamer Platz 1, which, together with the curved Deutsche Bahn tower over the road, forms the gateway to the area. It's the tallest building around here, and you can ride to the **Panoramapunkt** viewing platform up top.

A few doors down the road at Alte Potsdamer Strasse 5 is **Haus Huth**, the only other building that survives from before World War II. For decades a lonely structure in the middle of wasteland, now it stands next to the three-storey Arkaden shopping mall. At ground level, Haus Huth hosts **Diekmann's** restaurant (*see p138*). At the top of the building is **DaimlerChrysler Contemporary**, a gallery for works from the auto manufacturer's big-name abstract art collection. Planners have also positioned various pieces of contemporary sculpture about the quarter, including work by Jeff Koons, Robert Rauschenberg, Keith Haring and Nam June Paik.

Immediately west of the Potsdamer Platz development is one of the city's major concentrations of museums, galleries and cultural institutions. Collectively known as the **Kulturforum** and built in anticipation of reunification, this quarter was based on the designs of Hans Scharoun (1946-57). Scharoun himself designed the **Staatsbibliotek** (State Library) and the unmistakeable gold **Philharmonie** (*see p234*), home to the Berlin Philharmonic Orchestra. Adjacent is the **Musikinstrumentenmuseum** (Musical Instrument Museum).

One block to the west is a low-rise museum complex. Its biggest draw is the wonderful collection of 13th- to 18th-century art in the **Gemäldegalerie** (Picture Gallery). The **Kunstgewerbemuseum** (Museum of Decorative Art) is also worth a peek. Here, too, is the **Kunstbibliotek** (Art Library) and a decent café and shop. Next door stands the **Matthäuskirche** (Matthias Church) and, to the south, the bold glass cube of the **Neue Nationalgalerie** (New National Gallery).

Between the north flank of the Kulturforum and the south flank of Tiergarten runs Tiergartenstrasse, main drag of Berlin's revived diplomatic quarter. Part of Albert Speer's plan for Germania, the original embassy buildings were designed by German architects. Damaged by bombing, they were largely abandoned, and Tiergartenstrasse became an eerie walk past decaying grandeur. But with the land often still the property of the respective governments, embassies were reconstructed at their old addresses during the diplomatic relocation from Bonn. Now this area is embassy row again.

The **Gedenkstätte Deutscher Widerstand** (Memorial to the German Resistance) is south on Stauffenburgstrasse – a street named after the leader of the July 1944 plot to kill Hitler. At the corner of this street and Reichpietschufer is **Shell House**, a curvaceous expressionist masterpiece by Emil Fahrenkamp (1932). Five minutes' walk further west along the Landwehrkanal is the gleaming white **Bauhaus Archiv – Museum für Gestaltung**; another ten minutes' walk leads to less highbrow attractions in the **Zoologischer Garten** and to the hub of west Berlin around Bahnhof Zoo and the Ku'damm (*see p106*).

Bauhaus Archiv

Klingelhöferstrasse 13-14 (254 0020/www.bauhaus. de). Bus 100, 129, 187, 341. **Open** 10am-5pm Mon, Wed-Sun. **Admission** *Mon, Wed-Fri* €7; €4 concessions. *Sat, Sun* €6; €3 concessions. **No credit cards. Map** p306 J8.
Walter Gropius, founder of the Bauhaus school, designed the elegant white building that now houses this absorbing design museum. The permanent exhibition presents furniture, ceramics, prints, sculptures, photographs and sketches created in the Bauhaus workshop between 1919 and 1933 (when

Sightseeing

Potsdamer Platz scrapes the sky. *See p102.*

Kaisersaal Café and **Sony Center** canopy. *See p103.*

the school was closed down by the Nazis). There are also first-rate temporary exhibitions, such as a recent show of photomontages by Marianne Brandt. The interesting gift shop offers 250 items for the home or office, including design icons such as the Bauhaus lamp by Wilhelm Wagenfeld.

DaimlerChrysler Contemporary

Alte Potsdamer Strasse 5 (2594 1420/www. sammlung.daimlerchrysler.com). U2, S1, S2, S26 Potsdamer Platz. **Open** 11am-6pm daily. *Guided tours* 3pm Sat. **Admission** free. *Guided tours* €2.50. **Map** p306/p311 L8.

As you'd expect, DaimlerChrysler's collection is serious stuff. It has stuck to the 20th century, and covers abstract, conceptual and minimalist art; its collection numbers around 1,300 works from artists such as Josef Albers, Max Bill, Walter de Maria, Jeff Koons and Andy Warhol. The gallery rotates themed portions of the collection, typically 30-80 works at a time: 'Classical: Modern' runs until September 2006. It's followed by an exhibition of work from Sylvie Fleury and Shilpa Gupta. And from December 2006 to March 2007 is the fourth in its series 'Private/Corporate' juxtaposing items from its collection with those of a private collector, this time Anupam Poddar from Dehli.

Filmmuseum Berlin

Sony Center, Potsdamer Strasse 2 (300 9030/www. filmmuseum-berlin.de). U2, S1, S2, S26 Potsdamer Platz. **Open** 10am-6pm Tue, Wed, Fri-Sun; 10am-8pm Thur. **Admission** €6; €4 concessions. **No credit cards. Map** p306/p311 L7.

Since 1963 the Deutsche Kinemathek has been amassing a collection of films, memorabilia, documentation and antique film apparatus. In 2000 all this stuff finally found a home in this roomy, well-designed exhibition space on two floors of the Filmhaus in the Sony Center. It chronicles the history of German Cinema. Comprehensive, striking exhibits include the two-storey-high video wall of disasters from Fritz Lang's adventure films and a morgue-like exhibition space devoted to films from the Third Reich. On a lighter note, there's the collection of claymation figures from Ray Harryhausen films. The main attraction, though, is the Marlene Dietrich collection – personal effects, home movies, designer clothes and correspondence. There are regular exhibitions, often with accompanying films at the Arsenal cinema (*see p193*) downstairs.

Gedenkstätte Deutscher Widerstand

Stauffenbergstrasse 13-14 (2699 5000/www.gdw-berlin.de). U2, S1, S2, S26 Potsdamer Platz. **Open** 9am-6pm Mon-Wed, Fri; 9am-8pm Thur; 10am-6pm Sat, Sun. **Admission** free. **Map** p306 K8.

The Memorial of the German Resistance chronicles the German resistance to National Socialism. The building is part of a complex known as the Bendlerblock, owned by the German military from its construction in 1911 until 1945. At the back is a memorial to the conspirators killed during their attempt to assassinate Hitler at this site on 20 July 1944. Also occasional temporary exhibitions, and Sunday morning film programmes starting at 11am.

Gemäldegalerie

Stauffenbergstrasse 40 (266 2101/www.smb.spk-berlin.de). U2, S1, S2, S26 Potsdamer Platz. **Open** 10am-6pm Tue, Wed, Fri-Sun; 10am-10pm Thur. **Admission** €8; €4 concessions. **No credit cards. Map** p306 K8.

The Picture Gallery's first-rate early European painting collection features a healthy selection of the biggest names in Western art. Although many fine Italian, Spanish and English works are on display, highlights are the Dutch and Flemish pieces. There are around 20 Rembrandts – the best of which are the portrait of preacher and merchant Cornelis Claesz Anslo and his wife, and an electric Samson confronting his father-in-law. Two of Franz Hals's finest works are here – the wild, fluid, almost impressionistic *Malle Babbe* ('Mad Babette') and the detailed portrait of the one-year-old Catharina Hooft and her nurse. Other highlights include a couple of unflinching portraits by Robert Campin (early 15th century), a version of Botticelli's *Venus Rising* and Correggio's brilliant *Leda with the Swan*. Look out also for a pair of Lucas Cranach Venus and Cupid paintings and his *Fountain of Youth*. Pick up the excellent (free) English-language audio guide.

Kunstgewerbemuseum

Kulturforum, Matthäikirchplatz (266 2902/www.smb.spk-berlin.de). U2, S1, S2, S26 Potsdamer Platz. **Open** 10am-6pm Tue-Fri; 11am-6pm Sat, Sun. **Admission** €8; €4 concessions. **No credit cards. Map** p306 K8.

The Museum of Decorative Art contains a frustrating collection of European arts and crafts, stretching from the Middle Ages through Renaissance, baroque and rococo to Jugendstil and art deco. There are some lovely pieces on display, particularly furniture and porcelain, but labelling is only in German and the layout of the building is confusing.

Musikinstrumentenmuseum

Tiergartenstrasse 1 (254 810/www.sim.spk-berlin.de). U2, S1, S2, S26 Potsdamer Platz. **Open** 9am-5pm Tue, Wed, Fri; 9am-10pm Thur; 10am-5pm Sat, Sun. **Admission** €4; €2.50 concessions; free under-12s, 1st Sun of mth. **No credit cards. Map** p306 J7.

Over 2,200 string, keyboard, wind and percussion instruments dating back to the 1500s are crammed into this small museum next to the Philharmonie. Among them are rococo musical clocks, for which 18th-century princes commissioned jingles from Mozart, Haydn and Beethoven. Museum guides play obsolete instruments such as the Kammerflugel. On Saturdays at 11am the wonderful Wurlitzer organ – salvaged from an American silent movie house – is cranked up for a performance.

Neue Nationalgalerie

Potsdamer Strasse 50 (266 2651/www.smb.spk-berlin.de). U2, S1, S2, S26 Potsdamer Platz. **Open** 10am-6pm Tue, Wed; 10am-10pm Thur; 10am-8pm Fri; 11am-8pm Sat, Sun. **Admission** €8; €4 concessions. *Special exhibitions* varies. **No credit cards. Map** p306 K8.

The building was designed in the 1960s by Mies van der Rohe, and houses German and international paintings from the 20th century. It's strong on expressionism, with key works by Kirchner, Heckel and Schmidt-Rottluff. There are Cubist pieces from Picasso, Gris and Léger. The Neue Sachlichkeit is well represented by paintings from George Grosz and Otto Dix, while the Bauhaus contributes work from Paul Klee and Wassily Kandinsky. There are also lesser-known artists such as Ludwig Meidner, whose apocalyptic post-World War I landscapes exert a garish, comic-book power. The permanent collection is sometimes put into storage for big shows, such as 2005's 'Private Picasso' exhibition or the recent installation by Jörg Immendorff.

Panoramapunkt

Potsdamer Platz 1 (2529 4372/www.panoramapunkt.de). U2, S1, S2, S26 Potsdamer Platz. **Open** 11am-8pm daily. **Admission** €3.50; €2.50 concessions. **No credit cards. Map** p306/p311 L7.

What's billed as 'the fastest elevator in Europe' shoots up 100m (nearly 330ft) to the viewing platform. The building's north-east corner is precisely at the point where the borders of Tiergarten, Mitte and Kreuzberg all meet – and also on what was the line of the Wall. From this vantage you can peer through railings at the neighbouring postmodern high-rises at the landmarks of new Berlin. There are particularly good views to the south and west; looking north, the Sony Center gets in the way. Dodgy souvenir shop, but sadly no refreshments.

Zoologischer Garten & Aquarium

Hardenbergplatz 8 (254 010/www.zoo-berlin.de). U2, U9, S5, S7, S9, S75 Zoologischer Garten. **Open** *Zoo* 9am-6.30pm daily in summer; 9am-5pm daily in winter. *Aquarium* 9am-6pm daily. **Admission** *Zoo* €11; €5.50-€8 concessions. *Aquarium* €9; €4.50-€7 concessions. *Combined admission* €16.50; €8.50-€13 concessions. **No credit cards. Map** p305 H8.

Germany's oldest zoo was opened in 1841 to designs by Martin Lichtenstein and Peter Joseph Lenné. With almost 14,000 creatures, it's one of the world's largest and most important zoos, with more endangered species in its collection than any in Europe save Antwerp's. It's beautifully landscaped, with lots of architectural oddities, and there are plenty of places for a coffee, beer or snack. A new bear enclosure (the old one really did seem too small) was finished in late 2004 – the bears now share space with the wolves. Birds of prey also now have more room. The aquarium can be entered either from within the zoo or from its own entrance on Olof-Palme-Platz by the Elephant Gate. More than 500 species are arranged over three floors, and it's a good option for a rainy day. On the ground floor are the fish (including some impessive sharks); on the first you'll find reptiles (the crocodile hall is the highlight); while insects and amphibians occupy the second. The dark corridors and liquid ambience, with colourful tanks lit from within and curious aquarian creatures floating by, are as absorbing as an art exhibit.

Charlottenburg

Culture, commerce and the Kurfürstendamm.

This huge swathe of the city, once the centre of West Berlin, stretches from the Tiergarten to Spandau, from Tegel airport in the north down to Wilmersdorf to the south. It has two main focal points – the commercial cauldron around Bahnhof Zoo and along the Kurfürstendamm, and the cluster of cultural treasures in and around Schloss Charlottenburg.

Bahnhof Zoo & the Ku'damm

Map p305 & p312

Hymned by U2 and centrepiece of the film *Christiane F*, **Bahnhof Zoo** (Zoo Station or Bahnhof Zoologischer Garten, to give it its full name) was long the entry point to this part of Berlin. During the Cold War it was a spooky anomaly – slap in the middle of West Berlin but policed by the East, which controlled the intercity rail system – and a seedy hangout for junkies and winos. In the 1990s it was spruced up into a thoroughly modern station full of chain stores and fast-food outlets. Now, with the opening of the new Berlin Hauptbahnhof (*see p102* **Hub, bub**), it is being downgraded into just another station for local trains – rather like Friedrichstrasse station across town.

The original building was designed in 1882 by Ernst Dircksen; the modern glass sheds were added in 1934. The surrounding area, with its sleaze and shopping, cinemas and bustling crowds, is gateway to the Kurfürstendamm, the main shopping street of western Berlin. The discos and bars along Joachimstaler Strasse are best avoided – the opening of the **Beate-Uhse Erotik-Museum** (*see p109*) actually added a touch of class to the area. On the other side of Hardenbergplatz – the square outside Bahnhof Zoo – is the entrance to the **Zoologischer Garten** (*see p105*) itself.

The most notable nearby landmark is the fractured spire of the **Kaiser-Wilhelm-Gedächtniskirche** (Kaiser Wilhelm Memorial Church; *see p109*) in Breitscheidplatz. Close by is the 22-storey **Europa-Center**, whose Mercedes star can be seen across the city. It was built in 1965 and looks it. Intended as the anchor for the development of a new western downtown, it was the first of Berlin's genuinely tall buildings; now it's the grande dame of the city's shopping malls. Its exterior looks best when neon-lit at night. The strange sculpture in front was erected in 1983. It is officially called *Weltenbrunnen* ('Fountain of the Worlds'), but, like almost everything else in Berlin, it has a nickname: *Der Wasserklops* ('Water Meatball').

Running along the south of the Europa-Center, **Tauentzienstrasse** is the westernmost piece of the Generalzug, a sequence of streets laid out by Peter Joseph Lenné to link the west end with Kreuzberg and points east. Constructed around 1860, they are all named after Prussian generals from the Napoleonic Wars: Tauentzien, Kleist, Bülow, Yorck and Gneisenau. The tubular steel sculpture in the central reservation along Tauentzienstrasse was commissioned for the city's 750th anniversary and represents the then divided city in that the two halves twine around each other but never meet.

The street continues east past **KaDeWe** (*see p163*), the largest department store in continental Europe. Its full title is Das Kaufhaus des Westens (Department Store of the West), and it was founded in 1907 by Adolf Jandorf, acquired by Herman Tietz in 1926 and later 'Aryanised' and expropriated by the Nazis. KaDeWe is the only one of Berlin's famous turn-of-the-century department stores to survive the war intact, and has been extensively modernised over the last decade. Its most famous feature is the sixth-floor food hall.

Tauentzienstrasse ends at Wittenbergplatz. The 1911 neo-classical U-Bahn station here (by Alfred Grenander) is a listed building and has been wonderfully restored with wooden kiosks and old ads on the walls. A block further is the huge steel sculpture at An der Urania, with its grim monument to children killed in traffic by

Berlin's drivers. This marks the end, or the beginning, of the western 'downtown'.

Leading south-west from the Kaiser-Wilhelm-Gedächtniskirche, the **Kurfürstendamm** (or Ku'damm, as it's universally known), west Berlin's tree-lined shopping boulevard, is named after the Prussian Kurfürst ('Elector') – and for centuries it was a track leading from the Elector's residence to the royal hunting palace in the Grunewald. In 1881 Bismarck insisted it be widened to 5.3 metres (17 feet).

To the south of the street, many villas were erected. Few survive today, but one sizeable exception contains the **Käthe-Kollwitz-Museum** (*see p109*), the Villa Griesbach auction house and the Literaturhaus Berlin with its **Wintergarten am Literaturhaus** café (*see p157*) on Fasanenstrasse. The villas were soon replaced by upmarket tenement buildings with huge apartments – sometimes upwards of ten large rooms. About half of the original buildings were destroyed in the war and replaced by functional offices, but many bombastic old structures remain.

The ground-level Ku'damm soon developed into an elegant shopping boulevard. It remains so today with cinemas (mostly showing dubbed Hollywood fare), restaurants (from the classy to burger joints) and upmarket fashion shops – the Ku'damm is dedicated to separating you from your cash. If you tire of shopping, check out the **Story of Berlin** (*see p109*), an entertaining trip through the history of the city.

Side streets to the south are quieter but even more upmarket, and Bleibtreustrasse to the north has more shops and a number of outrageous examples of 19th-century Gründerzeit architecture.

At the north-west corner of the intersection of Ku'damm and Joachimstaler Strasse is the **Neues Kranzler-Eck**, a Helmut Jahn-designed ensemble built around the famous old Café Kranzler, with a 16-storey tower and pedestrian courtyards including a habitat for various exotic birds.

Other notable new architecture in the area includes Josef Paul Kleihues's Kant-Dreieck (Fasanenstrasse/Kantstrasse), with its large metal 'sail', and Nicholas Grimshaw's Ludwig-Erhard-Haus for the Stock Exchange (Fasanenstrasse 83-4). Back towards the Kurfürstendamm end of Fasanenstrasse is the Jüdisches Gemeindehaus (Jewish Community House), and, opposite, the **Zille-Hof** flea market (*see p178*).

Kantstrasse runs more or less parallel to the Ku'damm at the Zoo end, and contains the grandiloquent **Theater des Westens** and more shops. Since the opening of the **stilwerk** design centre (*see p166*), the stretch between Fasanenstrasse and Savignyplatz has become a centre for designer homeware stores. The environs of leafy **Savignyplatz**, meanwhile, are dotted with numerous chic restaurants, cafés and shops, particularly on Grolmanstrasse and in the Savignypassage. Nearby

Sightseeing

Kaiser-Wilhelm-Gedächtniskirche – west Berlin's signature sight. *See p109.*

Berlin by boat

Berlin's claims to be 'the Prussian Venice' may meet with deserved scepticism, but the German capital is still an engagingly watery place. The Spree meanders through the city on its way from the Czech Republic to the Elbe. Beyond that, the entire city and its surrounding region is a maze of inter-fingering rivers, lakes and canals. For many parts of the city, boats are the ideal form of transport. Indeed, in north-west Berlin, in and around Tegeler See, there are isolated houses on islands that can only be reached by ferry.

Even the regular BVG local transport tickets include ferry services across various lakes. For visitors on a budget, a normal AB zone ticket is enough to get you on the hourly year-round ferry link from Wannsee to Kladow. There's even a decent pub by the pier in quasi-rural Kladow.

For those with a larger budget, there is a fine range of city-centre tours offered by **Stern & Kreisschiffahrt** (www.sternundkreis.de), **Reederei Winkler** (www.reedereiwinkler.de), **Reederei Riedel** (www.reederei-riedel.de) and **Star-Line** (www.starlineschifffahrt.de). All four operators offer circular tours, usually lasting three to four hours, that take in the Spree and the Landwehrkanal. Passengers can hop on and off at will at landing stages en route. For a complete tour that takes in many of the city centre's main sights from the water, look

for prices starting at about €11 per adult. There are convenient landing stages at the **Schlossbrücke** in Charlottenburg, at the **Haus der Kulturen der Welt** (*see p101*) in Tiergarten, at Märkisches Ufer, at Jannowitzbrücke and in the Nikolaiviertel. It is worth checking schedules in advance; note that many services operate only from mid March to late November.

A short train journey to Wannsee (13mins by Regional Bahn from Zoo Station) presents more opportunities. Stern & Kreis's Seven Lakes Trip (Sieben-Seen-Rundfahrt) gives you the chance to ogle some of Berlin's poshest backyards as you slide past the handsome mansions surrounding the **Kleiner Wannsee** (*see p118*). The same tour takes in the Glienicker Brücke, cruises the Havel and stops at the **Pfaueninsel** (*see p118*). This two-hour tour has six intermediate stops and passengers can alight and rejoin at will. The service runs daily from late March to mid October, with departures hourly from 10.30am.

A longer trip from Wannsee pier (daily during the summer and less frequently in other seasons) runs to Werder via Potsdam. Werder is one of the most beautiful of Brandenburg villages, a place of cobbled quaintness with a cluster of fish restaurants around the quay.

11 35   Reederei Hadynski   1 Std. Schiffsrundfah
341   Abfahrt gleic

Knesebeckstrasse is the place to come for bookshops, including the excellent **Marga Schoeller Bücherstube** (*see p161*).

Beate-Uhse Erotik-Museum

Joachimstaler Strasse 4 (886 0666/www.beate-uhse-filialen.de). U2, U9, S5, S7, S9, S75 Zoologischer Garten. **Open** 9am-midnight Mon-Sat; 1pm-midnight Sun. **Admission** €5; €4 concessions. **Credit** AmEx, MC, V. **Map** p305/p312 G8.

The three floors of this collection (housed above a flagship Beate-Uhse retail outlet offering the usual videos and sex toys) contain oriental prints, some daft showroom-dummy tableaux, and glass cases containing such delights as early Japanese dildos, Andean penis flutes, Javanese erotic dagger hilts, 17th-century chastity belts, a giant coconut that looks like an arse and a vase used in the film *Caligula*. There's a small exhibit on pioneering sex researcher Magnus Hirschfeld, sadly comprising nothing more than a few boards of dry documentary material. The only other things with any connection to Berlin are an inadequate item on Heinrich Zille and a corner documenting the career of Frau Uhse herself, who went from Luftwaffe pilot and post-war potato-picker to annual sex-aid sales of €50 million. All oddly respectable, given the subject.

Kaiser-Wilhelm-Gedächtniskirche

Breitscheidplatz (218 5023/www.gedaechtnis kirche.com). U2, U9, S5, S7, S9, S75 Zoologischer Garten. **Open** 9am-7pm daily. *Guided tours* 1.15pm, 2pm, 3pm Mon-Sat. **Admission** free. **Map** p305/p312 G8.

The Kaiser Wilhelm Memorial Church is one of Berlin's best-known sights, and one of its most dramatic at night. The neo-Romanesque church was built in 1891-5 by Franz Schwechten in honour of – you guessed it – Kaiser Wilhelm I. Much of the building was destroyed during an Allied air raid in 1943. These days the church serves as a stark reminder of the damage done by the war, although some might argue that the bombing has improved what was originally a profoundly ugly structure. Inside the rump of the church is a glittering art nouveau-style ceiling mosaic depicting members of the House of Hohenzollern going on pilgrimage towards the cross. Here, you'll also find a cross made from nails from the destroyed cathedral at Coventry, and photos of the church before and after the war. The ruin of the tower is flanked by drab concrete extensions, yet inside the chapel the wraparound blue stained glass in the windows is quite stunning. **Photo** *p107*.

Käthe-Kollwitz-Museum

Fasanenstrasse 24, Wilmersdorf (882 5210/ www.kaethe-kollwitz.de). U1, U9 Kurfürstendamm. **Open** 11am-6pm Mon, Wed-Sun. **Admission** €5; €2.50 concessions. **No credit cards.** **Map** p305/p312 F9.

Käthe Kollwitz's powerful, deeply empathetic work embraces the full spectrum of life, from the joy of motherhood to the pain of death (with rather more emphasis on the latter than the former). The collection includes her famous lithograph *Brot!*, as well as charcoal sketches, woodcuts (a medium particularly suited to her style) and sculptures, all displayed to good effect in this grand villa off the Ku'damm. Some labelling is in English.

Museum für Fotografie

Jebensstrasse 2 (266 2188/www.smb.spk-berlin.de). U2, U9, S5, S7, S9, S75 Zoologischer Garten. **No credit cards.** **Map** p305/p312 G7.

Shortly before his death in 2003, Berlin-born Helmut Newton, who served his apprenticeship elsewhere in Charlottenburg at the studio of Yva (now the Hotel Bogota; *see p65*), donated over 1,000 of his nude and fashion photographs to the city and provided funds toward the creation of a new gallery. The new Museum of Photography was the result. In a former casino behind Bahnhof Zoo, it's now the largest photographic gallery in the city. The first two floors are given over to a permanent exhibition of Newton's work – six colossal nudes, modelled on Nazi propaganda photos from the 1930s, glare down at you on entering the building, and set the tone for the big, garish, confrontational pieces that dominate the exhibition. A further space displays the work of Alice Springs, Newton's wife, including some moving images of the photographer on his deathbed. A collection of young German photographers is currently confined to a top-floor annexe, but will be spreading across two floors by the end of 2006.

Story of Berlin

Kurfürstendamm 207-8 (8872 0100/www.story-of-berlin.de). U1 Uhlandstrasse. **Open** 10am-8pm daily; last entry 6pm. **Admission** €9.30; €7.50 concessions. **No credit cards.** **Map** p305/p312 F8.

If you're interested in the city's history, the Story of Berlin should not be missed. The huge floor space is filled with well-designed rooms and multimedia exhibits created by authors, designers and film and stage specialists, telling Berlin's story from its founding in 1237. The 20 themed displays are labelled in both German and English. Underneath all this is a massive nuclear shelter. Built by the Allies in the 1970s, the low-ceilinged, oppressive bunker is still a fully functional shelter and can hold up to 3,500 people. Guided tours can be booked ahead and are included in the price of the ticket.

Schloss Charlottenburg & around

Map p300

The palace that gives Charlottenburg its name lies about three kilometres (two miles) northwest of Bahnhof Zoo. In contrast to the commercialism and crush of the latter, this part of the city is quiet, wealthy and serene. **Schloss Charlottenburg** (*see p110*) was built in the 17th century as a summer palace for Queen Sophie-Charlotte, wife of Friedrich III (later King Friedrich I), and was intended as Berlin's answer to Versailles. It's not a very convincing answer, but there's plenty of interest in the buildings and grounds of the palace – the apartments of the New Wing and the gardens are the main attractions.

Next to the palace's west wing is the **Museum für Vor- & Frühgeschichte** (Primeval & Early History Museum). In front of the Schloss entrance is the **Sammlung Berggruen: Picasso & seine Zeit** (Berggruen Collection: Picasso & His Time) and the art nouveau and art deco collection of the **Bröhan-Museum**.

There are few eating, drinking or shopping opportunities in the immediate vicinity of the palace, but if you head down Schlossstrasse and over Bismarckstrasse, the streets south of here, particularly those named after philosophers (Leibniz, Goethe), have a lot of interesting small shops selling antiques, books and the fashions that well-to-do residents sport around Charlottenburg's cafés and restaurants.

Bröhan-Museum

Schlossstrasse 1A (3269 0600/www.broehan-museum.de). U2 Sophie-Charlotte-Platz or U7 Richard-Wagner-Platz. **Open** 10am-6pm Tue-Sun. **Admission** €5; €4 concessions. Free 1st Wed of mth. *Guided tours* call for details. **No credit cards.** **Map** p301 C6.

This quiet, private museum contains three well-laid-out levels of international art nouveau and art deco pieces that businessman Karl Bröhan began collecting in the 1960s and donated to the city of Berlin on his 60th birthday. The wide array of paintings, furniture, porcelain, glass, silver and sculptures dates from 1890 to 1939. Hans Baluschek's paintings of social life in the 1920s and 1930s, and Willy Jaeckel's series of portraits of women are the pick of the fine art bunch; the furniture is superb too. The third floor hosts special exhibitions, such as a recent one on art deco in Sweden. Labelling is only in German. Good website, though.

Museum für Vor- & Frühgeschichte

Langhansbau, Schloss Charlottenburg (3267 4840/ www.smb.spk-berlin.de). U2 Sophie-Charlotte-Platz or U7 Richard-Wagner-Platz. **Open** 9am-5pm Tue-Fri; 10am-5pm Sat, Sun. **Admission** €3; €1.50 concessions. **No credit cards.** **Map** p301 C6.

The Primeval and Early History Museum – spread over six galleries – traces the evolution of Homo sapiens from 1,000,000 BC to the Bronze Age. The highlights are the replicas (and some originals) of Heinrich Schliemann's famous treasure of ancient Troy, including works of ceramics and gold, as well as weaponry. Keep an eye out also for the sixth-century BC grave of a girl buried with a gold coin in her mouth. Information is available in English.

Sammlung Berggruen: Picasso & seine Zeit

Westlicher Stülerbau, Schlossstrasse 1 (3269 5815/ www.smb.spk-berlin.de). U2 Sophie-Charlotte-Platz or U7 Richard-Wagner-Platz. **Open** 10am-5pm Tue-Sun. **Admission** €6; €3 concessions. **No credit cards.** **Map** p301 C6.

Heinz Berggruen was an early Picasso dealer in Paris, and the subtitle of this museum, 'Picasso and His Time', sums up the satisfying and important collection. Displayed over a digestible three circular floors, it's inevitable that Pablo's works dominate (taking up much of the ground floor, and almost all of the first); his astonishingly prolific and diverse output is well represented. There are also works by Braque, Giacometti, Cézanne and Matisse, and most of the second floor is given over to wonderful paintings by Paul Klee. Audio guide available.

Schloss Charlottenburg

Luisenplatz & Spandauer Damm (320 911/www.spsg.de). U2 Sophie-Charlotte-Platz or U7 Richard-Wagner-Platz. **Open** *Old Palace* 9am-5pm Tue-Fri; 10am-5pm Sat, Sun. Last tour 4pm. *New Wing* Apr-Oct 10am-5pm Tue-Sun; Nov-Mar 11am-5pm Tue-Sun. *New Pavilion* 10am-5pm Tue-Sun. *Mausoleum* Apr-Oct 10am-noon, 1-5pm Tue-Sun. Last entrance 4.30pm. *Belvedere* Apr-Oct 10am-5pm Tue-Fri; noon-5pm Sat, Sun. Nov-Mar noon-4pm Tue-Sun. **Admission** *Combination tickets* €8; €5 concessions. *Individual sights* call for details. **No credit cards.** **Map** p301 C6.

Queen Sophie-Charlotte was the impetus behind this sprawling palace and garden complex (and gave her name to both the building and the district) – her husband Friedrich III (later King Friedrich I) built it in 1695-9 as a summer home for his queen. Later kings also summered here, tinkering with and adding to the buildings. It was severely damaged during World War II, but has now been restored, and stands as the largest surviving Hohenzollern palace.

There are a number of parts of the palace to which the public are admitted, though the bafflingly complicated individual opening times and admission prices have many visitors scratching their heads. The easiest option is to go for the combination ticket that allows entrance to all parts of the palace, with the exception of the state and private apartments of King Friedrich I and Queen Sophie-Charlotte in the Altes Schloss (Old Palace), which are only accessible on a guided tour (€8; €5 concessions; in German only). This tour, through more than 20 rooms, some of staggering baroque opulence, has its highlights (particularly the Porcelain Cabinet), but can be skipped – there's plenty of interest elsewhere. The upper apartments in the Old Palace can be visited without a guided tour, but, frankly, they are really only of interest to silver and porcelain junkies.

The one must-see is the Neue Flügel (New Wing). Also known as the Knobelsdorff Wing (after its architect), the upper floor contains the State Apartments of Frederick the Great and the Winter Chambers of his successor King Friedrich Wilhelm II. The

Funkturm. *See p112*.

Sightseeing

contrast between the two sections is particularly interesting – Frederick's rooms are all excessive rococo exuberance (the wildly over-the-top Golden Gallery literally drips gilt), while Friedrich Wilhelm's far more modestly proportioned rooms reflect the more restrained classicism of his time. Frederick the Great was a big collector of 18th-century French art, and some choice canvases hang from the walls, including Watteau's masterpiece *The Embarkation for Cythera*. Also worth a look are Friedrich Wilhelm III's apartments in the New Wing.

By the east end of the New Wing stands the Neue Pavillon (New Pavilion). Also known as the Schinkel Pavilion, it was built by Schinkel in 1824 for Friedrich Wilhelm III – the King liked it so much that he chose to live here in preference to the grandeur of the main palace.

The huge gardens are one of the palace's main draws. Laid out in 1697 in French style, they were reshaped in a more relaxed English style in the 19th century. Within them you'll find the Belvedere, a three-storey structure built in 1788 and containing a collection of Berlin porcelain. Also in the gardens is the sombre Mausoleum, with the tombs of Friedrich Wilhelm III, his wife Queen Luise, Kaiser Wilhelm I and his wife. The café and restaurant are at the front of the palace. Note: the entire palace is closed on Mondays.

Elsewhere in Charlottenburg

Map p300

About three kilometres (two miles) north-east of Schloss Charlottenburg is a reminder of the terror inflicted by the Nazi regime on dissidents, criminals and anybody else they deemed undesirable. The **Gedenkstätte Plötzensee** (Plötzensee Memorial) preserves the execution shed of the former Plötzensee prison, where more than 2,500 people were killed between 1933 and 1945.

A couple of kilometres south-west of Schloss Charlottenburg, at the western end of Neue Kantstrasse, stands the futuristic International Conference Centre (ICC). Built in the 1970s, it is used for pop concerts, political rallies and the like. Next door, the even larger Messe- & Ausstellungsgelände (Trade Fair & Exhibition Area) plays host to trade fairs. In the complex, the **Funkturm** (Radio Tower) offers panoramic views. Nearby, Hans Poelzig's Haus des Rundfunks (Masurenallee 9-14) is an expressive example of monumental brick modernism.

Another couple of kilometres north-west is the **Olympiastadion**. One of the few pieces of fascist architecture still intact in Berlin, it was recently renovated to host the 2006 World Cup Final. Immediately south of Olympiastadion S-Bahn station is a huge apartment block designed by Le Corbusier. The Corbusierhaus, with its multicoloured paint job, was

constructed for the International Building exhibition of 1957. From here, a ten-minute walk along Sensburger Allee brings you to the sculptures of the **Georg-Kolbe-Museum**.

Funkturm
Messedamm (3038 1905). U2 Theodor-Heuss-Platz or Kaiserdamm. **Open** 10am-9pm Mon; 10am-11pm Tue-Sun. Closed July. **Admission** €4; €2 concessions. **No credit cards. Map** p304 A8/B8.
The 138m-high (453ft) Radio Tower was built in 1926 and looks a bit like a smaller Eiffel Tower. The Observation Deck stands at 126m (413ft); vertigo sufferers should seek solace in the restaurant, only 55m (180ft) from the ground. You get a free snack with your admission price. **Photo** *p111*.

Gedenkstätte Plötzensee
Hüttigpfad (344 3226/www.gedenkstaette-ploetzensee.de). Bus 123. **Open** *Mar-Oct* 9am-5pm daily. *Nov-Feb* 9am-4pm daily. **Admission** free. **Map** p301 F3.
This memorial stands on the site where the Nazis executed over 2,500 (largely political) prisoners. In a single night in 1943, 186 people were hanged in groups of eight. In 1952 it was declared a memorial to the victims of fascism, and a memorial wall was constructed. There is little to see today, apart from the execution area, behind the wall, with its meat hooks from which victims were hanged (many were also guillotined), and a small room with an exhibition. Booklets in English are available. The stone urn near the entrance is filled with earth from concentration camps.

Georg-Kolbe-Museum
Sensburger Allee 25 (304 2144/www.georg-kolbe-museum.de). S5, S75 Heerstrasse/bus X34, X49, 149. **Open** 10am-5pm Tue-Sun. **Admission** €4; €2.50 concessions. *Special exhibitions* €5; €3 concessions. **No credit cards.**
Georg Kolbe's former studio has been transformed into a showcase for his work. The Berlin sculptor, regarded as Germany's best in the 1920s, mainly focused on naturalistic human figures. The museum features examples of his earlier, graceful pieces, as well as his later sombre and larger-than-life works created in accordance with the ideals of the Nazi regime. One of his most famous pieces, *Figure for Fountain*, is outside in the sculpture garden.

Olympiastadion
Olympischer Platz 3 (300 688 100/tickets 018 9200/www.olympiastadion-berlin.de). U2 Olympia-Stadion or S5, S75 Olympiastadion. **Open** varies.
Admission varies. **No credit cards.**
Designed by Werner March for the 1936 Olympics, the 74,000-seat stadium has undergone a major refitting for the 2006 World Cup, including better seats and a roof over the whole lot. Home of Hertha BSC (*see p245*), it also hosts the German Cup Final, plus other sporting events and concerts. Both the Rolling Stones and Robbie Williams have performed here. *See p39* **The final stadium.**

Other Districts

Areas of lake and forest, fascinating museums and the grim legacy of communism – all within city limits.

The largest city between Paris and Moscow, Berlin sprawls for miles in every direction. But the city's historical expansion into a hinterland of lakes and forest coincided with the age of railways, so public transport can whisk you to most lesser-known neighbourhoods. Here are some suggestions for further exploration.

North of the centre

It's hard to summon much enthusiasm for districts such as Wedding, though some may find the area's industrial legacy interesting.

Wedding

Map p301 & p302

The working-class industrial district of Wedding, formerly on the western side of the Wall, is now politically part of Mitte. Apart from a couple of low-key attractions – the **Anti-Kriegs-Museum** (Anti-war Museum) and the nearby **Zucker-Museum** (Sugar Museum) – in this largely grim fastness, there is also one of the few remaining stretches of the Wall at the **Gedenkstätte Berliner Mauer** (Berlin Wall Memorial; *see also p114* **Walking the Wall**).

Anti-Kriegs-Museum

Brüsseler Strasse 21 (4549 0110/tours 402 8691/ www.anti-kriegs-museum.de). U9 Amrumer Strasse. **Open** 4-8pm daily. **Admission** free. **Map** p301 H2.
The original Anti-war Museum was founded in 1925 by Ernst Friedrich, author of the book *War Against War*. It was destroyed in 1933 by the Nazis, and Friedrich fled to Brussels. There he had another museum from 1936 to 1940, at which point Nazis once again destroyed his work. In 1982 a group of teachers, including Friedrich's grandson Tommy Spree, re-established the museum. It now hosts films, discussions, lectures and exhibitions as well as a permanent display including World War I photos and artefacts from the original museum, children's war toys, information on German colonialism in Africa and pieces of anti-Semitic material from the Nazi era. Copies of *War Against War* are available in English, but exhibitions are only in German. Call ahead to arrange a tour in English.

Gedenkstätte Berliner Mauer

Bernauer Strasse 111 (464 1030/www.berliner-mauer-dokumentationszentrum.de). U8 Bernauer

Strasse or S1, S2, S25 Nordbahnhof. **Open** *Documentation centre* Nov-Mar 10am-5pm Wed-Sun; Apr-Oct 10am-6pm Wed-Sun. **Admission** free. **Map** p302 M4.
On unification, the city bought this stretch of the Wall to maintain as a memorial; it was finally dedicated in 1998. Impeccably restored (graffiti disappears overnight), it is as sterile a monument as any in Berlin, with a (regularly defaced) brass plaque decrying the communist 'reign of terror'. The documentation centre, featuring displays on the Wall and a database of escapees, is across the street, and from its roof you can view the Wall and the Kapelle der Versöhnung (Chapel of Reconciliation) – built on the site of a church destroyed by the East Germans. *See p114* **Walking the Wall**.

Zucker-Museum

Amrumer Strasse 32 (3142 7574/www.dtmb.de). U6 Seestrasse or U9 Amrumer Strasse. **Open** 9am-4.30pm Mon-Thur; 11am-6pm Sun. **Admission** free. **No credit cards. Map** p301 H2.
A museum devoted to the chemistry, history and politics of sugar doesn't sound very entertaining, but this place, opened in 1904, does contain an unusual collection of sugar paraphernalia. Most interesting is a slide show on the slave trade, on which the sugar industry was so dependent.

West of the centre

To the west of the city is the once-independent settlement of Spandau. The district of the same name stretches from the Tegeler See in the north to the Havel in the south.

Spandau

Berlin's western neighbour and eternal rival, Spandau is a little baroque town that seems to contradict everything about the city of which it is now, reluctantly, a part. Spandauers still talk about 'going into Berlin' when they head off to the rest of the city. Berliners, for their part, basically consider Spandau to be part of west Germany, though travelling there is easy (take the U7 to either Zitadelle or Altstadt Spandau). None of the sights are thrilling, but they make for a low-key escape from the city.

The **Zitadelle** (Citadel) contains Spandau's original town charter. The fact that the charter dates from 1232 has been used by Spandauers ever since to argue their historical primacy over

Walking the Wall (what's left of it)

Most of the Berlin Wall was demolished between June and November 1990. The symbol of the inhumanity of the East German regime was prosaically crushed and reused for road fill. This walk traces the course of a small stretch of the Wall on the southern border of Wedding. Along the way you can see some of the remnants – including the restored segment at the **Gedenkstätte Berliner Mauer** (see p113) – and gain an impression of how brutally the border carved its way through the city.

The starting point, Berlin's new central station, is just north of the Tiergarten. Known as Berlin Hauptbahnhof, it is one of the final reunifying projects to be completed. See p102 **Hub, bub**. Turn right from the station into Invalidenstrasse. Continue eastwards, passing on your left a Wilhelmine building, now a regional court, and the railway station turned contemporary art gallery, **Hamburger Bahnhof, Museum für Gegenwart** (see p85).

A little further on is the **Sandkrugbrücke**, located on a former border crossing into East Berlin. A stone by the bridge commemorates Günter Litfin, the first person to be shot dead attempting to escape to West Berlin. The Invalidenhaus on the eastern side long predates the Cold War. Built in 1747 to house disabled soldiers, it was used in East German times as a military and government hospital, as well as the state's Ministry of Health and Supreme Court. Today it houses the **Bundesministerium für Wirtschaft und Arbeit** (Federal Ministry of Economics and Labour). Keeping this complex on your right, turn down the promenade by the canal, continuing to the **Invalidenfriedhof**.

The Wall once ran through this graveyard – and a section remains. Headstones of graves in the 'death strip' were removed so as not to impair the sightlines of border guards. The graveyard, more evidence of the area's military links, is a fascinating microcosm of Berlin history. Metres from the splendid 18th-

century tombs of Prussian generals, there is a plaque commemorating the anti-Hitler resistance. Victims of air raids and the Battle of Berlin are buried in an adjacent mass grave. And it was here in 1962 that West Berlin police shot dead an East Berlin border guard to save a 15-year-old boy who was in the process of escaping.

Just outside the graveyard, you will find a former **watchtower** improbably nestling in front of a new apartment building at the corner of Kieler Strasse. Opening times are unpredictable, but sometimes you can look inside the observation post. Between here and the corner of Chausseestrasse there are few traces left of the Wall, which ran roughly parallel to the canal before veering right close to the present helipad. At the end of Boyenstrasse, pavement markings indicating the Wall's former course briefly appear before vanishing under the new corner building.

Looking down Chausseestrasse, note the line of powerful street lights indicating the site of another checkpoint. The **Liesenstrasse Friedhof** is the graveyard where 19th-century writer Theodor Fontane is buried. It was also part of East Berlin's border strip. A short section of the Wall appears before the railway bridge at the junction with Gartenstrasse.

Follow Gartenstrasse south-east and turn left on to Bernauer Strasse, the last leg of our walk. Desperate scenes took place here in August 1961 as people leaped – three of them to their deaths – from windows of the houses that then stood on the street's eastern side. The buildings were in East Berlin, but the pavement before their doors was in the West. The iconic photo of a guard leaping over barbed wire into the West was snapped days earlier at the street's northern end. In the 1960s and 1970s a number of tunnels were dug from cellars in this area and dozens escaped this way.

Berlin. Spandau's old town centre is mostly pedestrianised, with 18th-century townhouses interspersed with burger joints and department stores. One of the prettiest is the former Gasthof zum Stern in Carl-Schurz-Strasse; older still are houses in Kinkelstrasse and Ritterstrasse; but perhaps the best-preserved district is north of Am Juliusturm in the area bounded by Hoher Steinweg, Kolk and Behnitz. Steinweg contains

a fragment of the old town wall from the first half of the 14th century; Kolk has the Alte Marienkirche (1848); and in Behnitz, at No.5, stands the elegant baroque Heinemannsche Haus. At Reformationsplatz, the brick nave of the Nikolaikirche dates from 1410-50; the west tower was added in 1468.

One of the most pleasant times to visit is at Christmas, when the market square houses a

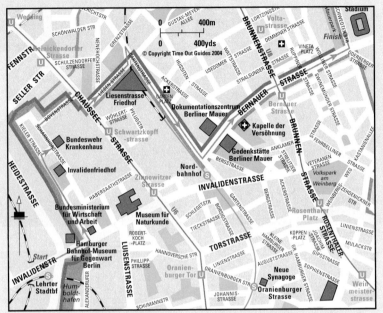

At the **Gedenkstätte Berliner Mauer** (*see p113*), on your right, you can gain an impression of what the border installation looked like. The **Dokumentationszentrum** opposite, an information centre about the Wall, has a viewing platform. A little further on is the oval **Kapelle der Versöhnung** (Chapel of Reconciliation), built on the site of an older church that was stranded in the death strip until the East Germans blew it up in 1985.

The former borderland beyond remains undeveloped, despite a prime location – there have been legal challenges to its appropriation by the Federal government. The old tarmacadam patrol road remains in places

as do some of the border illuminations. Note the lights on Swinemünder Strasse 20. The plasterwork on the building at the corner of Wolliner Strasse reveals where the eastern side of the Wall abutted existing houses.

Between Wolliner and Schwedter Strasse, you can still see the turning circle once used by West Berlin buses. On the eastern side, the tram still halts in Eberswalder Strasse. Even so, it's hard to believe that this area was once part of the world's most heavily fortified border. In the **Mauerpark**, with its popular Sunday flea market (*see p176*), you can have one last stroll along the Wall before heading to Eberswalder Strasse U-Bahn.

life-size Nativity scene with real sheep and the Christmas market is in full swing. The café and bakery on Reformationsplatz are excellent.

Many will know the name Spandau from its association with Rudolf Hess. Hitler's deputy was held in the Allied jail here after the Nuremberg trials, and remained here (alone after 1966) until his suicide at the age of 93 on 17 August 1987. Once he'd gone, the 19th-

century brick building at Wilhelmstrasse 21-4 was demolished to make way for a supermarket for the (also departed) British forces. Some way south of Spandau is the **Luftwaffenmuseum**.

Luftwaffenmuseum

Gross Glienicker Weg, Gatow (811 0769/www. luftwaffenmuseum.de). U7 Rathaus Spandau, then bus 135 to Luftwaffenmuseum/Seekorso. **Open** 9am-5pm Tue-Sun. **Admission** free.

Alliierten Museum – the exhibit that came in from the cold. *See p118.*

On the very western fringes of the city at what was formerly the RAF base in divided Berlin, this collection of more than 150 aircraft is housed in an old hangar. There's information on the history of the Luftwaffe plus fighter and surveillance planes from the early 20th century through to 1970s NATO equipment. There's a World War I triplane, a restored Handley Page Hastings (as used in the Airlift) and an Antonov An-2 from the GDR Air Force. There are also uniforms and personal equipment, and more recent aircraft outside. English guided tours by prior arrangement.

Zitadelle

Am Juliusturm (354 944 200/tours 334 6270/www. zitadelle-spandau.net). U7 Zitadelle. **Open** 9am-5pm Tue-Fri; 10am-5pm Sat, Sun. **Admission** €2.50; €1.50 concessions. **No credit cards**.
The oldest structure inside the citadel (and the oldest secular building within the city borders of Berlin) is the Juliusturm, which probably dates back to an Ascanian fortress from about 1160. The present tower was home until 1919 to 120 million Goldmarks, stored in 1,200 boxes, the reparations paid by France to Germany in 1874 after the Franco-Prussian War. (In German financial circles, state reserves are still referred to as Juliusturm.) The bulk of the Zitadelle was designed in 1560-94, in the style of an Italian fort, to dominate the confluence of the Spree and Havel rivers. Since that time it has been used as everything from garrison to laboratory. There are two museums. One tells the story of the citadel with models and maps; the other is a museum of local history and of limited interest.

South-west of the centre

The wealthy residential district of Zehlendorf is chiefly of interest for the cluster of museums in Dahlem, and the bucolic and aquatic attractions of the Grunewald, Wannsee and Glienecke.

Zehlendorf & the Dahlem museums

One major draw among these pricey suburbs is the clutch of museums at Dahlem, including the **Ethnologisches Museum** (Museum of Ethnology), which is one of the world's finest such collections. The **Museum für Indische Kunst** (Museum of Indian Art) and the **Museum für Ostasiatische Kunst** (Museum of East Asian Art) are in the same building. Not far away is the **Museum Europäischer Kulturen** (Museum of European Cultures).

Dahlem is also home to the **Freie Universität** (*see p283*), one of Germany's largest universities. North-west of the U-Bahn station, opposite the Friedhof Dahlem-Dorf (cemetery), is the **Domäne Dahlem** working farm – a great place to take kids.

Ten minutes' walk east from Dahlem along Königin-Luise-Strasse brings you to the **Botanischer Garten & Botanisches Museum** (Botanical Garden & Museum). The same street reaches the edge of the **Grunewald** (*see p117*) a kilometre or so west of Dahlem.

Botanischer Garten

Königin-Luise-Strasse 6-8 (8385 0100/www.bgbm.
fu-berlin.de). S1 Botanischer Garten. **Open** *Garden*
9am-dusk daily. *Museum* Nov-Jan 9am-4pm daily;
Feb-Oct 9am-dusk daily. **Admission** *Combined* €5;
€2.50 concessions. *Museum only* €2; €1 concessions.
No credit cards.
The Botanical Garden was landscaped at the beginning of the 20th century. Home to 18,000 plant
species, 16 greenhouses and a museum, the gardens
make a pleasant stroll. The museum is a bit dilapidated and there's no information in English, but
it's the place to come for advice on whether those
mushrooms you found in the forest are delectable or
deadly. The S-Bahn is just 15 minutes' walk away.

Domäne Dahlem

Königin-Luise-Strasse 49 (666 3000/www.domaene-
dahlem.de). U3 Dahlem-Dorf. **Open** 10am-6pm
Wed-Sun. *Shop* 10am-6pm Mon-Fri; 8am-1pm Sat.
Admission *Museum* €2; €1 concessions. Free on
Wed. **No credit cards.**
On this organic working farm, children can see how
life was lived in the 17th century. Craftspeople –
blacksmiths, carpenters, bakers and potters – pre-
serve and teach their skills. Best to visit during one
of several festivals held during the year, when children can ride ponies, tractors and hay-wagons.

Ethnologisches Museum

Lansstrasse 8 (830 1438/www.smb.spk-berlin.de).
U3 Dahlem-Dorf. **Open** 10am-6pm Tue-Fri; 11am-
6pm Sat, Sun. **Admission** €6; €3 concessions. **No**
credit cards.
The Ethnological Museum is a stunner – extensive,
authoritative, beautifully laid out and lit. It encompasses cultures from Oceania to Central America to
Africa to the Far East. Only the true ethno-fan
should attempt to see it all, but no one should miss
the Südsee (South Sea) room. Here you'll find New
Guinean masks and effigies, and a remarkable collection of original canoes and boats. The African
rooms are also impressive – look out for superb carvings from Benin and the Congo, and beaded artefacts
from Cameroon. An enlightening small exhibit
explores the influence of African art on the German
expressionists. The museum can only exhibit 2% of
its 500,000 items, but hopes to move into more space
in the Stadtschloss when that is rebuilt.

There are three other museums housed in the
same building. The **Museum für Indische Kunst**
(Museum of Indian Art) represents more than 3,000
years of Indian culture and is strong in terracottas,
stone sculptures, and bronzes, Central Asian wall
paintings and sculptures from Buddhist cave tem-
ples along the Silk Route. The **Museum für**
Ostasiatische Kunst (Museum of East Asian Art)
features archaeological objects and works of fine art
from Japan, China and Korea from the early Stone
Age to the present. The **Museum Europäischer**
Kulturen (Museum of European Cultures) contains
exhibits about European everyday culture from the
18th century to the present. One of the highlights is

a mechanical model of the Nativity, made in the
Erzgebirge region on the German–Czech border,
which is displayed each year in the Advent period.
Audio guides in English are available.

Grunewald

The western edge of Zehlendorf is formed by
the Havel river and the extensive Grunewald,
largest of Berlin's many forests. On a fine
Sunday afternoon, its lanes and pathways can
get busy with walkers, runners, cyclists, horse
riders and dog walkers. This is because it's so
easily accessible by S-Bahn. There are several
restaurants next to Grunewald S-Bahn station,
and over the motorway at Schmetterlingsplatz,
open April to October.

One popular destination is the **Teufelsee**, a
tiny lake packed with bathers in summer,
reached by heading west from the station along
Schildhornweg for 15 minutes. Close by is the
mound of the **Teufelsberg**, a product of
wartime devastation – a railway was laid from
Wittenbergplatz to carry the rubble that forms
it. Great views can be enjoyed from the summit.
There is talk of replacing the disused American
electronic listening post that stood on the top
with some kind of hotel and conference centre.

South of the station, at the far end of the
Grunewaldsee, the 16th-century Jagdschloss
Grunewald (Grunewald Hunting Lodge) is an
example of the kind of building that once
maintained the life of the landed gentry, the
Prussian Junkers. You can bathe in the lake in
summer. The Grunewaldsee is also a favourite
promenade for dogs and their owners.

A further kilometre south-east through the
forest, you'll find **Chalet Suisse**, an over-the-
top Swiss-themed restaurant popular with
families because of its playground and petting
zoo. A further ten-minute walk takes you to the
Alliierten Museum (Allied Museum). A
kilometre north of here is the **Brücke-**
Museum, housing expressionist paintings and
prints from the likes of Ernst Ludwig Kirchner,
Erich Heckel and Karl Schmidt-Rottluff.

Further south, **Krumme Lanke** and
Schlachtensee are pleasant urban lakes along
the south-eastern edge of the Grunewald,
perfect for picnicking, swimming or rowing –
and each with its own station: U3 for Krumme
Lanke, S1 for Schlachtensee.

On the west side of the Grunewald, halfway up
Havelchaussee, is the **Grunewaldturm (photo**
p119), built in 1897 in memory of Wilhelm I. It
has an observation platform 105 metres (344 feet)
above the lake, with views as far as Spandau and
Potsdam. There is a restaurant at the base, and
another over the road, both with garden terraces.
A short walk south along Havelufer leads to the

Sightseeing

ferry to **Lindwerder Insel** (island), which also has a restaurant. To the north, a little way into the forest, the singer Nico, who grew up in Schöneberg, is buried in the **Friedhof Grunewald-Forst**.

Alliierten Museum

Clayallee 135, corner of Huttenweg (818 1990/www.alliiertenmuseum.de). U3 Oskar-Helene-Heim. **Open** 10am-6pm Mon, Tue, Thur-Sun. **Admission** free.
The Allies arrived as conquerors, kept West Berlin alive during the 1948 Airlift and finally went home again in 1994. In what used to be a US Forces cinema, this museum is mostly about the period of the Blockade and Airlift, documented with photos, tanks, jeeps, planes, weapons and uniforms. Outside is the building that was once the stop-and-search centrepiece of Checkpoint Charlie. Guided tours in English can be booked in advance. It's ten minutes' walk from the U-Bahn station. **Photo** *p116*.

Brücke-Museum

Bussardsteig 9 (831 2029/www.bruecke-museum.de). U3 Oskar-Helene-Heim, then bus 115 to Pücklerstrasse. **Open** 11am-5pm Mon, Wed-Sun. **Admission** €4; €2 concessions. *Special exhibitions* €5. **No credit cards.**
This small but satisfying museum is dedicated to the work of Die Brücke ('The Bridge'), a group of expressionist painters founded in Dresden in 1905 before moving to Berlin. Oils, watercolours, drawings and sculptures from the authoritative collection of works by the main members – Schmidt-Rottluff, Heckel, Kirchner, Mueller and Pechstein – are rotated in temporary exhibitions.

Wannsee & Pfaueninsel

At the south-west edge of the Grunewald, you'll find boats and beaches in summer, castles and forests all through the year. **Strandbad Wannsee** is the largest inland beach in Europe. Between May and September, there are boats and pedalos and hooded, two-person wicker sunchairs for hire, a playground and a separate section for nudists. Service buildings house showers, toilets, cafés, shops and kiosks.

The waters of the Havel (the Wannsee is an inlet of the river) are extensive and in summer warm enough for comfortable swimming; there is a strong current, so do not stray beyond the floating markers. The rest of the water is in constant use by ferries, sailing boats, speedboats and waterskiers.

A small bridge north of the beach leads to Schwanenwerder, once the exclusive private island retreat of Goebbels and now home to international think-tank the Aspen Institute.

The town of Wannsee to the south is clustered around the bay of the Grosser Wannsee and is dominated by the long stretch of promenade, Am Grossen Wannsee, scattered

with hotels and fish restaurants. On the west side of the bay is the **Gedenkstätte Haus der Wannsee-Konferenz**. At this elegant Gründerzeit mansion, now a museum, a January 1942 meeting of prominent Nazis laid out plans for the extermination of the Jews.

A short distance from S-Bahn Wannsee along Bismarckstrasse is a little garden where German dramatist Heinrich von Kleist shot himself in 1811; the beautiful view of Kleiner Wannsee was the last thing he wanted to see.

On the other side of the railway tracks is **Düppler Forst**, a forest including a nature reserve at Grosses Fenn at the south-western end. Travelling three stops on the S1 to Mexikoplatz, then taking the 629 or 211 bus, brings you to the reconstructed 14th-century village at **Museumsdorf Düppel**.

From Wannsee, bus 218 scoots through the forest to a ferry pier on the Havel, and then it's a brief ferry ride to **Pfaueninsel** (Peacock Island). This 98-hectare (242-acre) island was inhabited in prehistoric times, but isn't mentioned in archives until 1683. Two years later the Grand Elector presented it to Johann Kunckel von Löwenstein, a chemist who experimented with alchemy but instead of gold produced 'ruby glass', examples of which are on view in the castle.

Only at the start of the Romantic era did the island's windswept charms begin to attract serious interest. In 1793 Friedrich Wilhelm II purchased it and built a Schloss for his mistress, but died in 1797 before they could move in. Its first residents were the happily married Friedrich Wilhelm III and Queen Luise, who spent much of their time together on the island, even setting up a working farm there.

A royal menagerie was later developed. Most of the animals were moved to the newly built Tiergarten Zoo in 1842, and only peacocks, pheasants, parrots, goats and sheep remain. Surviving structures include the Jakobsbrunnen (Jacob's Fountain), a copy of a Roman temple; the Kavalierhaus (Cavalier's House), built in 1803 from a design by Schinkel; and the Swiss cottage, also based on a Schinkel plan. All are linked by winding, informal paths laid out in the English manner by Peter Joseph Lenné. A walk around the island, with its monumental trees, rough meadows and views over the Havel, provides a complete sensation of escape.

Back on the mainland, a short walk south is the **Blockhaus Nikolskoe**, a huge wooden chalet built in 1819 by Friedrich Wilhelm II for his daughter Charlotte, and named after her husband, the future Tsar Nicholas of Russia. There is a magnificent view from the terrace, where you can enjoy mid-priced Berlin cuisine or coffee and cakes.

Gedenkstätte Haus der Wannsee-Konferenz

Am Grossen Wannsee 56-8 (805 0010/www. ghwk.de). S1, S7 Wannsee, then bus 114. **Open** 10am-6pm daily. **Admission** free.

On 20 January 1942 a meeting here of prominent Nazis, chaired by Heydrich, drew up plans for the Final Solution, making jokes and sipping brandy as they sorted out the practicalities of genocide. Today this infamous villa has been converted into the Wannsee Conference Memorial House, a place of remembrance, with a photo exhibit on the conference and its consequences. Call in advance if you want to join an English-language tour; otherwise all information is in German. Renovations, ongoing at press time, were due to be finished in early 2006; phone ahead to check the exhibition is open.

Museumsdorf Düppel

Clauertstrasse 11 (802 6671/www.dueppel.de). S1 Mexikoplatz, then bus 211, 629. **Open** early Apr-late Oct 3-7pm Thur; 10am-5pm Sun (last entry 4pm). **Admission** €2; €1 concessions. **No credit cards**.

At this 14th-century village, reconstructed around archaeological excavations, workers demonstrate handicrafts, medieval technology and farming techniques. Ox-cart rides for kids. Small snack bar.

Glienicke

West of Wannsee, and only a couple of kilometres from Potsdam, Glienicke was once the south-westernmost tip of West Berlin. The suspension bridge over the Havel here was named **Brücke der Einheit** ('Bridge of Unity')

because it joined Potsdam with Berlin. After the building of the Wall, it was painted different shades of olive green on the East and West sides and used only by Allied soldiers and for top-level prisoner and spy exchanges – Anatoly Scharansky was one of the last in 1986.

The main reason to come here is **Park Glienicke**. Its centrepiece is Schloss Glienicke (not open to the public), originally a hunting lodge designed by Schinkel for Prinz Carl von Preussen, who banned all women visitors, adorned the garden walls with ancient relics collected on his Mediterranean holidays, and decided to simulate a walk from the Alps to Rome in the densely wooded park, laid out by Pückler in 1824-50. The summer houses, fountains and follies are all based on original Italian models, and the woods and fields surrounding them make an ideal place for a Sunday picnic, since this park is little visited.

A restaurant, in the 1842 hunting lodge at the nearby inlet of Moorlake, is good for game dishes or afternoon coffee and cakes.

East & south-east of the centre

Much of the eastern city remains a depressing wasteland of decaying communist blocks, but there's still a lot of the flavour of old Berlin. There are a few things to see in Lichtenberg and Treptow, but the most rewarding day out in the east is to characterful Köpenick.

Grunewaldturm: lakeside folly. *See p117.*

Sightseeing

Lichtenberg & Treptow

East of Prenzlauer Berg and Friedrichshain, Lichtenberg isn't very appealing, though it does contain the **Tierpark Berlin-Friedrichsfelde** (Berlin-Friedrichsfelde Zoo) and the **Forschungs- & Gedenkstätte Normannenstrasse,** otherwise known as the Stasi Museum. Further south is the **Museum Berlin-Karlshorst,** documenting Russian–German relations in the 20th century.

South of Lichtenberg and bordering Neukölln, Treptow is chiefly of note for **Treptower Park,** containing the massive Sowjetisches Ehrenmal (Soviet War Memorial). From here, several boats leave in the summer for trips along the Spree. The park continues to the south, where it becomes the **Plänterwald** and houses a big amusement park.

Forschungs- & Gedenkstätte Normannenstrasse (Stasi Museum)

Ruschestrasse 103 (553 6854/www.stasimuseum.de). U5, S41, S42, S8, S85 Frankfurter Allee or U5 Magdalenenstrasse. **Open** 11am-6pm Mon-Fri; 2-6pm Sat, Sun. **Admission** €3.50; €2.50 concessions. **No credit cards.**

In what used to be part of the headquarters of the Ministerium für Staatssicherheit (the Stasi), you can look round the old offices of secret police chief Erich Mielke – his uniform still hangs in his wardrobe – and see bugging devices and spy cameras concealed in books, plant pots and Trabant car doors. There's also a lot of communist kitsch, including banners and busts of Lenin. Documentation is in German, but tours in English can be booked in advance.

Museum Berlin-Karlshorst

Zwieseler Strasse 4, corner of Rheinsteinstrasse (5015 0810/www.museum-karlshorst.de). S3 Karlshorst. **Open** 10am-6pm Tue-Sun. **Admission** free.

After the Soviets took Berlin, they commandeered this former German officers' club as headquarters for the military administration and it was here, on the night of 8-9 May 1945, that German commanders signed the unconditional surrender. The museum looks at the German–Soviet relationship over 70 years. Divided into 16 rooms including the one where the Nazis surrendered, it takes you through two world wars and one cold one, plus assorted pacts, victories and capitulations. Exhibits include photos, memorabilia, maps, videos and propaganda posters. Buy a guide in English; exhibits are labelled in German and Russian. English tours can be booked in advance.

Tierpark Berlin-Friedrichsfelde

Am Tierpark 125 (515 310/www.tierpark-berlin.de). U5 Tierpark. **Open** Jan, Feb, Oct-Dec 9am-4pm daily. Mar, Sept 9am-5pm daily. Apr-Aug 9am-6pm daily. **Admission** €10; €7 concessions; €16.50-€26.50 family. **No credit cards.**

Spread over 1.6sq km (0.6sq miles), this is one of Europe's largest zoos, with plenty of roaming space for herd animals, though some others are still kept in distressingly small cages. Resident beasts include bears, elephants, big cats and penguins. The zoo also has one of the Continent's biggest snake farms and, in its north-west corner, Schloss Friedrichsfelde.

Köpenick

The name Köpenick is derived from the Slavonic *copanic,* meaning 'place on a river'. The old town, around 15 kilometres (nine miles) south-east of Mitte, stands at the confluence of the Spree and Dahme. Having escaped bombs, decay and development by the GDR, it retains much of its 18th-century character. The handsome shops, cafés and restaurants of the old centre, and an extensive riverfront, make it a fine place for a Sunday afternoon wander.

The imposing **Rathaus** (Town Hall) is a good example of Wilhelmine civic architecture. It was here in 1906, two years after the building's completion, that Wilhelm Voigt, an unemployed cobbler who'd spent half his life in jail, dressed up as an army captain and ordered a detachment of soldiers to accompany him into the Treasury, where they emptied the town coffers. He instantly entered popular folklore, Carl Zuckmeyer immortalised him in a play as *Der Hauptmann von Köpenick (Captain of Köpenick),* and the Kaiser pardoned him because he had shown how obedient Prussian soldiers were. His theft is re-enacted every June during the Köpenicker summer festival.

Close by on Schlossinsel, **Schloss Köpenick,** with its medieval drawbridge, Renaissance gateway and baroque chapel, contains the **Kunstgewerbemuseum** (Museum of Applied Art, 266 2902; an outpost of its namesake in Tiergarten, *see p105*). Open-air concerts are held in the Schloss in summer.

Friedrichshagen & the Müggelsee

A couple of kilometres east of Köpenick, the village of Friedrichshagen has retained its independent character. The main street, **Bölschestrasse,** is lined with steep-roofed Brandenburg houses, and ends at the shores of a large lake, the **Grösser Müggelsee.**

Friedrichshagen is particularly enjoyable when the **Berliner Burgerbräu** brewery, family-owned since 1869, throws open its gates for the annual summer celebration. Stalls line Bölschestrasse, the brewery lays on music, and people lounge about on the lake shore with cold beer. Boat tours are available, and the restaurant Braustubl, next to the brewery, serves good Berlin cuisine.

Eat, Drink, Shop

Café Einstein. *See p138* and *p156*.

Restaurants

A dreary gastronomic tradition doesn't mean a dearth of decent dining.

There are many reasons to come to Berlin, but unless you're looking for the perfect Currywurst (*see p142* **Curry on sausages**), researching the origins of the doner kebab, or find nothing finer than a large hunk of pig, eating is unlikely to be one of them.

That's not to say you can't dine well here. In fact, with the arrival of the government to stimulate the high end, and an increasingly cosmopolitan population to encourage ethnic variety at street level, you can dine better than ever. Restaurants tend to be relaxed and roomy, and there are interesting options at all price levels. But you can still feel the lack of any indigenous gastronomic tradition.

As the French would say, the cuisine is in the soil. Round here the soil is sandy, and not much good for anything but cabbages and potatoes. Along with pork, they're the staples. Berlin's signature dish is Eisbein – leathery-skinned and extremely fatty pig's trotter, sometimes marinated, and served with puréed peas – but you'll find this served in only the most doggedly old-school of places.

That half the city spent most of the last 50 years cut off from gastronomic trends and deprived of exotic ingredients hardly helped to eradicate a certain culinary conservatism. The brevity of Germany's colonial experience has meant no deep-rooted link with a foreign cuisine, such as Britain with India's, or

Morocco's with France. There's no great ethnic presence here beside the Turks, who prefer to cook at home and sell snacks to the public.

But Reunification has meant both a better travelled population with a more adventurous palate, and lots of cheap real estate where young restaurateurs have been able try out their ideas. This has led to lighter, healthier and better seasoned eating. Things have also improved for vegetarians, with most decent restaurants now including a couple of options on the menu.

On the other hand, there's still plenty missing. Chinese food is rare; good Chinese even rarer. The same for Mexican. Indian restaurants are everywhere, but all seem to have the same, Germanised menu. Sushi places have erupted, but it's hard to find any other kind of Japanese food. And Americans are well within their rights to decry what's sold as American cuisine.

For snacking on the hoof, bakeries usually offer a desultory selection of bread rolls filled with cheese or ham. For something more, try an *Imbiss*. The term embraces just about anywhere you get food but not table service, from stand-up street-corner stalls to self-service snack bars offering exotic cuisines. Quality varies wildly, but some excellent, cheap food can be found. Turkish places offer the ubiquitous Kebap, Turkish 'pizza', half chickens and salads. The traditional German *Imbisse* will tempt you various kinds of sausage (*see p142* **Curry on sausages**).

In restaurants, a service charge of 17 per cent is added to the bill, but unless the service has been awful (not impossible in Berlin), diners

---

❶ Purple numbers given in this chapter correspond to the location of each restaurant as marked on the street maps. *See pp300-312.*

The best Restaurants

Abendmahl
Gourmet vegetarian cooking. *See p137.*

Hugo's
Top-flight food with views to match. *See p140.*

Le Cochon Bourgeois
Pig out on excellent French food. *See p134.*

Storch
The finest flavours of the Alsace. *See p137.*

Vau
For inventive top-notch nosh. *See p126.*

Witty's
Local street food that's a cut above the usual. *See p143.*

Cheap, chic, cheery and Vietnamese: the institution that is **Monsieur Voung**. *See p125.*

usually round up the bill or, in classier joints, add ten per cent. Tips are handed directly to the server (or you tell staff how much to take) rather than left on the table. When you hand over the cash, never say *danke* unless you want staff to keep the change.

Mitte

Americas

¡Viva México!

Chausseestrasse 36 (280 7865). U6 Zinnowitzer Strasse. **Open** noon-11pm Mon-Fri; 5pm-midnight Sat, Sun. **Main courses** €3-€11. **No credit cards.** **Map** p302 L4 **❶**
A Mexican woman and her family prepare authentic food from the Mexican interior. Highlights include the home-made refried beans and at least four salsas (three of which are good and spicy) to put on tacos, burritos and tortas. This place would be good in Mexico, let alone Germany.

Asian

Good Time

Chausseestrasse 1 (2804 6015/www.goodtime-berlin.de). U6 Oranienburger Tor. **Open** noon-midnight daily. **Main courses** €8.50-€29. **Credit** AmEx, MC, V. **Map** p311 M5 **❷**
Indonesian food is rare in Berlin, and this friendly place does it well. The rijstafel, the soup and the rendang (a beef dish) are all excellent. German tastes are catered to with a wide range of noodle dishes and there are Thai specialities too.

Ishin Mitte

Mittelstrasse 24 (2067 4829/www.ishin.de). U6, S1, S2, S5, S7, S9, S75 Friedrichstrasse. **Open** 11am-8pm Mon-Fri; 11am-6pm Sat. **Main courses** €5-€14. **No credit cards. Map** p311 M6 **❸**
Roomy but crowded, with a constant stream of happy hour-style discounts (starting at €5), this is probably the best money-for-quality sushi deal in Berlin. The fish is fresh, with authentic specials and steam trays offered daily, and portions are generous: when was the last time you actually received more food than the photos on the menu suggested?
Other locations: Galleria Steglitz, Schlossstrasse 101, Steglitz (797 1049); Berlinickestrasse 1A, Steglitz (8182 7071).

Kuchi

Gipsstrasse 3 (2838 6622/www.kuchi.de). U8 Weinmeisterstrasse. **Open** noon-midnight Mon-Thur; 12.30pm-12.30am Fri, Sat; 6pm-midnight Sun. **Main courses** €7-€16. **Credit** AmEx, MC, V. **Map** p310 N5 **❹**
It's the quality of the ingredients at this Japanese that makes the food special. And it isn't just fish that you'll find in the sushi rolls: one maki is filled with chicken, mandarin oranges and poppy seeds. Delicate tempura, yakitori chicken hearts or shiitake mushrooms are all excellently served by a young, cool and multinational team. It gets packed at lunchtime. The other branch has a takeaway next door which also delivers.
Other locations: Kantstrasse 30, Charlottenburg (3150 7815/delivery service 3150 7816).

Manngo

Mulackstrasse 29 (2804 0558/www.manngo.de). U8 Weinmeisterstrasse. **Open** noon-midnight Mon-Fri;

YOU KNOW WHO YOU ARE.

BERLIN • MEINEKESTRASSE 21
+49-30-884-620 • hardrock.com

Hard Rock
CAFE

4pm-midnight Sat. **Main courses** €5. **No credit cards. Map** p310 O5 ❺

A Vietnamese that, by accident or design, is well positioned to catch the overspill from Monsieur Vuong (*see p125*) around the corner. More relaxed than its neighbour, it's worth a visit for restrained but commendable noodle dishes. Stand-up and sit-down sections have separate entrances, but both are served by the same kitchen.

Mirchi

Oranienburger Strasse 50 (2844 4480/www. mirchi.de). U6 Oranienburger Tor. **Open** noon-1am Mon-Thur, Sun; noon-2am Fri, Sat. **Main courses** €7-€14. **Credit** AmEx, MC, V. **Map** p310 N5 ❻

An ambitious 'Singapore fusion' concept sees Indian, Chinese, Thai and Malay ideas mingling on a longish, creative menu. The hearty Thai-Indian soups, based on coconut and curry spices, show the kitchen at its simple, tasty best. Nice entrance, lots of space, useful location.

Monsieur Vuong

Alte Schönhauser Strasse 46 (3087 2643/www. monsieurvuong.de). U2 Rosa-Luxemburg-Platz. **Open** noon-midnight Mon-Sat; 2pm-midnight Sun. **Main courses** €5-€9. **No credit cards. Map** p310 O5 ❼

Something of an institution now, serving fresh and tasty Vietnamese soups and noodles. A couple of daily specials supplement a handful of regular dishes. Once you've tried the glass noodle salad, you'll understand why less is more. Chic, cheap and cheery, but often packed to the rafters. **Photo** *p123*.

Pan Asia

Rosenthaler Strasse 38 (2790 8811/www.panasia. de). U8 Weinmeisterstrasse or S5, S7, S9, S75 Hackescher Markt. **Open** noon-1am daily. **Main courses** €6-€14. **Credit** AmEx, DC, MC, V. **Map** p310 N5 ❽

Hidden in a pleasant courtyard off busy Rosenthaler, with tables outside in summer, this is a fashionably minimalist place to see, be seen and eat modern Asian food. Japanese beers and Chinese teas complement excellent wun tun, kimchi salad and a variety of soups and wok dishes. Self-conscious crowd, unbelievable bathrooms, inconsistent service.

French

Entrecôte Fred's

Schutzenstrasse 5 (2016 5496/www.entrecote.de). U2, U6 Stadtmitte. **Open** noon-midnight Mon-Fri; 6pm-midnight Sat. **Main courses** €12-€24. **Credit** AmEx, DC, MC, V. **Map** p311 M7 ❾

Steak and frites in a brasserie ambience close to Checkpoint Charlie. The food is simple but well prepared and Fred's Special Sauce, a mixed herb remoulade, is excellent. The extensive wine list encompasses all French regions, and there are half bottles. Professional service, classic desserts and plenty of room.

German, Austrian & Swiss

Borchardt

Französische Strasse 47 (8188 6262). U6 Französische Strasse. **Open** 11.30am-late daily. **Main courses** €16-€22. **Credit** AmEx, MC, V. **Map** p311 M7 ❿

In the late 19th century the original Borchardt opened next door at No.48. It became the place to be for politicians and society folk, but was destroyed in World War II. But now Roland Mary and Marina Richter have reconstructed a highly fashionable, Maxim's-inspired bistro that serves respectable French food. So why not snorkel down a dozen oysters and tuck into a fillet of pike-perch or beef after a cultural evening nearby?

Gambrinus

Linienstrasse 133 (282 6043/www.gambrinus-berlin-mitte.de). U6 Oranienburger Tor/bus N6. **Open** noon-4am daily. **Main courses** €6-€16. **No credit cards. Map** p310 M7 ⓫

Traditional local, serving variations on the meat, potato and cabbage theme, and usefully open late.

Honigmond

Borsigstrasse 28 (2844 5512/www.honigmond-berlin.de). U6 Zinnowitzer Strasse. **Open** 7.30am-1am daily. **Main courses** €6-€13.50. **No credit cards. Map** p310 M4 ⓬

This quiet, neighbourhood place serves up traditional German food alongside an innovative menu that ranges from kangaroo to Swiss fondue. Noteworthy are the Königsberger Klöpse (east Prussian meatballs in a creamy caper sauce) and a very good Caesar salad. Excellent wine list and remarkable home-made bread (and butter!). Small hotel upstairs too (*see p54*).

Kellerrestaurant im Brecht-Haus

Chausseestrasse 125 (282 3843/www. brechtkeller.de). U6 Oranienburger Tor. **Open** 6pm-1am daily. **Main courses** €9-€15. **No credit cards. Map** p310 M5 ⓭

Bertholt Brecht got that sleek, well-fed look from the cooking his partner Helene Weigel learned in Vienna and Bohemia. This atmospheric place, crammed with model stage sets and Brecht memorabilia, serves a number of her specialities, including Fleischlabberln (spicy meat patties) and a mighty Wiener Schnitzel. In summer, the garden more than doubles capacity.

Lutter & Wegner

Charlottenstrasse 56 (202 9540/www.lutter-wegner-gendarmenmarkt.de). U2, U6 Stadtmitte. **Open** 11am-3am daily. **Main courses** €14-€25. **Credit** AmEx, MC, V. **Map** p311 M7 ⓮

This place has it all: history (an early Berlin wine merchant, its sparkling wine became known as *Sekt*, now the common German term); atmosphere in its airy, elegant rooms; great German/Austrian/French cuisine; and excellent service. The wine list

Eat, Drink, Shop

is justifiably legendary, and if the prices look high, head for the bistro, where the same list holds sway along with perfect salads, cheese and ham plates.

Margaux

Unter den Linden 78 (2265 2611/www.margaux-berlin.de). S1, S2 Unter den Linden. **Open** 7-10.30pm Mon-Thur; noon-2pm, 7-10.30pm Fri, Sat. **Main courses** €30-€50. **Credit** AmEx, DC, MC, V. **Map** p311 L6 ⑮

The ultimate 'new Berlin' dining temple, this top-flight restaurant features Michael Hoffman's slightly avant-garde take on classic French cooking, exemplified by dishes such as stewed shoulder of venison seasoned with coriander, anise and saffron. The spacious interior is lit by glowing columns of honey-hued onyx, which reflect in the black marble floors. The restaurant is named after its extraordinary wine list, which includes around 30 vintages of Château Margaux. Service is first-rate.

Nola's am Weinberg

Veteranenstrasse 9 (4404 0766/www.nola.de). U8 Rosenthaler Platz. **Open** 10am-2am daily. **Main courses** €7.50-€18.50. **Credit** MC, V. **Map** p310 N4 ⑯

Swiss food in a former park pavilion, with a quiet terrace as well as a spacious bar and dining room. It's hearty fare, such as venison goulash with mushrooms and spinach noodles, or rösti with spinach and cheese with fried eggs. The goat's cheese mousse with rocket starter is big enough for two, and it's worth noting that, with a little thought, it's possible to eat quite cheaply here. The kitchen can sometimes drag its feet.

Schwarzwaldstuben

Tucholskystrasse 48 (2809 8084/www. schwarzwaldstuben-berlin.de). S1, S2 Oranienburger Strasse. **Main courses** €4.90-€12.90. **Open** 9am-11pm Mon-Fri; 9am-midnight Sat, Sun. **No credit cards. Map** p310 M5 ⑰

Some of the best German cuisine comes from Swabia, but Swabian restaurants tend to be filled with silly knick-knacks. But this place is a casually chic affair, and wears its mounted deer head ironically. The food is excellent. The soups are hearty, standout entrées include the Schäuffele with sauerkraut, and the Flammkuchen is good. Try the Rothaus Tannenzapfle beer on tap.

Vau

Jägerstrasse 54-5 (202 9730/www.vau-berlin.de). U6 Französische Strasse. **Open** noon-2.30pm, 7-10pm Mon-Sat. **Menus** €78-€110. **Credit** AmEx, DC, MC, V. **Map** p311 M7 ⑱

Love of innovation and inspiration from all corners of the globe make chef Kolja Kleeberg's menu one of the best in town. His lobster with mango and black olives with a tapenade, and braised pork belly with grilled scallops, are complemented by an extensive wine list (bottles from €30). Downstairs, the fake-library bar (the 'books' are bricks of coal) is terrific for occasions. Booking essential.

Weinbar Rutz

Chausseestrasse 8 (2462 8760/www.rutz-weinbar.de). U6 Zinnowitzer Strasse. **Open** 5pm-midnight Mon-Sat. **Main courses** €19.50-€24. **Credit** AmEx, DC, MC, V. **Map** p310 M5 ⑲

The impressive ground-floor bar has a whole wall showcasing wines from around the globe – not obscure New World vintages, but the best of the best. No tasting notes on the exhaustive list, though. The second-floor restaurant serves a limited nouvelle menu, all of it beautifully presented. Snacks downstairs. Booking essential.

Imbiss/fast food

Dolores

Rosa-Luxemburg-Strasse 7 (2809 9597). U2, U5, U8, S5, S7, S9, S75 Alexanderplatz. **Open** 10am-9pm Mon-Fri; 12.30pm-late Sat. **Main courses** €3.50-€4.60. **No credit cards. Map** p310 O5 ⑳

For fans of the Northern California-style burrito, this is a true haven. Black beans and lime rice mix with fresh greens and a choice of fillings, such as grilled chicken, marinated beef and tofu. The guacamole is always fresh and perfectly spicy. Delivery service, too, or you can call in your order and collect.

Der Imbiss W

Kastanienallee 49 (4849 2657). U8 Rosenthaler Platz. **Open** *Winter* 12.30-11.30pm daily. *Summer* noon-midnight daily. **Main courses** €4-€6.50. **No credit cards. Map** p312 O4 ㉑

Owned by 103 (*see p146*), the bar next door, this vogueish place is named for Gordon W, a minor celebrity chef from Canada, who devised its wacky fusion menu of 'naan pizzas', 'rice shells' and international 'dressings'. The food is clever but it's not always that well executed and, with a few wok dishes in preparation, the open kitchen can be a bit much in the small space. **Photo** *p127.*

RNBS

Oranienburger Strasse 27 (0179 540 2505/www. rnbs.de). S1, S2 Oranienburger Strasse. **Open** noon-midnight daily. **Main courses** €2.50-€3.90. **No credit cards. Map** p310 N5 ㉒

Vogueish eau de Nil and orange interior for a New Agey selection of pan-Asian ricepaper rolls, noodles, meat- and fishballs, and soups. Fast food with no artificial ingredients or flavourings.

International

Urban Comfort Food

Zionskirchstrasse 5 (4862 3131). U8 Rosenthaler Platz. **Open** 7pm-late Mon-Sat; 10.30am-5pm, 7pm-late Sun. **Main courses** €8.50-€19. **No credit cards. Map** p312 M4 ㉓

A sort of designer diner serving hearty, consoling dishes such as ravioli variations or spiced soups based on potato or pumpkin, plus home-baked bread that's crispy on the outside and slightly gooey in the middle. During the day, there are classic Italian-

Wacky fusion at **Der Imbiss W**. *See p126.*

American deli sandwiches made with fresh ingredients; in the evenings, there are soups, salads and meat, fish and veggie dishes.

Italian

C-Matto
Rosenthaler Strasse 44 (2838 5170/www.c-matto.de). S5, S7, S9, S75 Hackescher Markt. **Open** 9am-late daily. **Main courses** €10-€21. **Credit** MC, V. **Map** p310 N5 ㉔
Decent food in a blandly fashionable setting just over the road from the entrance to the Hackesche Höfe. The menu is intelligent Italian with lightly seasoned fish and fowl, and by far the best bet is the daily lunch special including a starter for about €6.90. Cocktail lounge off to the side of the bar; great summer terrace in the back.

Malatesta
Charlottenstrasse 59 (2094 5071/www.ristorante-malatesta.de). U2, U6 Stadtmitte. **Open** noon-midnight Mon-Sat; noon-10pm Sun. **Main courses** €7-€21. **Credit** AmEx, MC, V. **Map** p311 M7 ㉕
This nicely located, first-rate Italian is spread out over two floors. Downstairs there's a small bar for an aperitif or coffee. Starters such as grilled artichoke hearts or antipasto misto, familiar home-made pastas, daily fish specialities and meat dishes such as oxtail filled with truffles, are among the reasons to linger upstairs. Service is attentive but not intrusive. This is the third of Piero De Vetis's Italian restaurants in Berlin (following Osteria No.1 and Sale e Tabacchi; for both, *see p136*) and it's definitely the best.

Salumeria Culinario
Tucholskystrasse 34 (2809 6767). S1, S2 Oranienburger Strasse. **Open** 10am-midnight Mon-Fri; 11am-late Sat; 11am-midnight Sun. **Main courses** €8-€19. **No credit cards**. **Map** p310 M5 ㉖
The daily lunch menu is a great way to recharge after a morning of shopping or gallery-hopping. Pick up a bottle of wine, some cheese, olives and salami, or ponder the panettones in the Italian import section, or simply grab a plate to go. There is space for 60 at the busy beer tables on the pavement.

Schwarzenraben
Neue Schönhauser Strasse 13 (2839 1698/ www.schwarzenraben.de). U8 Weinmeisterstrasse. **Open** *Café* 11.30am-2am Mon-Sat; 2pm-2am Sun. *Restaurant* 6.30pm-midnight daily. **Main courses** €13-€23. **Credit** AmEx, MC, V. **Map** p310 N5 ㉗
Some contend that so many of Berlin's young film and theatre stars eat here because they're non-paying bait to draw other punters to owner Rudolf H Girolo's restaurant. The chicest of Berlin's Italo-Mediterranean joints. Popular but overrated.

North African & Middle Eastern

Al Rai
Grosse-Hamburger-Strasse 20-21 (2809 8355/ www.al-rai.de). S5, S7, S9, S75 Hackescher Markt or U8 Weinmeisterstrasse. **Open** 10.30am-2am Mon-Fri; 10.30am-3am Sat, Sun. **Main courses** €6-€12. **No credit cards**. **Map** p310 N5 ㉘
Reliable and self-consciously downbeat North African restaurant that's good for everything from tea to a three-course meal, offering the full range of Maghreb cuisine from falafel to couscous. Try the home-made merguez sausages and full-bodied Algerian wines. Or just sip mint tea and share a hookah around one of the low-slung couches. Service is as laid-back as the mixed clientele. Breakfast and omelettes served until 4pm. **Photos** *pp128-129.*

Fanous
Brunnenstrasse 3 (4435 2503). U8 Rosenthaler Platz/bus N2, N8. **Open** 11am-1am Mon-Thur, Sun;

Eat, Drink, Shop

11am-3.30am Fri, Sat. **Main courses** €4.50-€6.50.
No credit cards. **Map** p310 N4

This is a Moroccan snack bar convenient for the Rosenthaler Platz nightlife neighbourhood. Deep-fried halloumi with salad in pitta, topped with mango or sesame sauce, is the best vegetarian bet. Carnivores should try the merguez (lamb sausages). Also couscous, served warm and as tabbouleh salad. Free tea with meals.

Prenzlauer Berg

African

Massai
Lychener Strasse 12 (4862 5595/www.massai-berlin. de). U2 Eberswalder Strasse. **Open** 4pm-midnight daily. **Main courses** €7-€25. **No credit cards**. **Map** p312 P3

This warm and friendly restaurant is decked out in traditional Eritrean colours and serves exquisite and tasty East African dishes that use a lot of palmnut oil, peanut sauce, paprika, and berbere sauce made from hot cayenne pepper, sweet paprika and ginger. The highlights include agbisa (West African aubergines in palmnut sauce with onions and paprika) and kilwa (tender lamb fried in spicy butter). The lentil soup is masterful, and you can try things like ostrich and crocodile. It's all surprisingly light and pleasantly spicy.

Asian

Bangkok
Prenzlauer Allee 46 (443 9405). Tram M2 Marienburger Strasse. **Open** noon-11pm daily. **Main courses** €4-€8. **No credit cards**. **Map** p312 P4

This popular little Thai, with beach-hut decor and authentic dishes, is a firm local favourite. Informal, friendly and fun. Booking recommended.

China-Wok
Prenzlauer Allee 226 (4404 2563). Tram M2 Knaackstrasse. **Open** noon-midnight daily. **Main courses** €3.50-€7.50. **No credit cards**. **Map** p312 P4

Most budget Chinese places in Berlin offer only limited variations of beef, pork and chicken dishes, but this unassuming neighbourhood place actually has a real menu including steamed trout, a broccoli platter and home-made sesame balls. It's all tasty stuff.

Chinggis-Khan
Bornholmer Strasse 10 (4471 5604). S1, S2, S8, S25, S85 Bornholmer Strasse/tram 50. **Open** 4.30pm-midnight Mon-Fri; noon-midnight Sat, Sun. **Main courses** €5-€10. **No credit cards**. **Map** p303 O1

Mongolian restaurant that's off the beaten path but worth seeking out: the ample helpings of rice, fried beef and vegetarian dishes can fuel hordes. one delicacy is the pelmeni-like ravioli filled with meat.

Al Rai. *See p127.*

Mao Thai

Wörther Strasse 30 (441 9261). U2 Senefelderplatz.
Open noon-midnight daily. **Main courses** €10-€20.
Credit AmEx, DC, MC, V. **Map** p312 P3 ㉞
Charming service and excellent food comes with a
'to whom it may concern' testimonial from the Thai
ambassador, framed on the stairs down to the lower
level. Classics such as tom kai gai, vegetarian spring
rolls, green papaya salad with peanuts and sweet
vinegar dressing, and glass noodle salad with
minced pork are all spectacular. Comfortable, well
established and friendly.
Other locations: Toans Hütte, Dirkstenstrasse 40,
Mitte (283 6940).

Oki

*Oderberger Strasse 23 (4985 3130). U2 Eberswalder
Strasse.* **Open** 3-11pm Tue-Sun. **Main courses** €9-
€16.50. **No credit cards**. **Map** p312 O3 ㉟
This small, bright local successfully fuses north
German food with Japanese delights in dishes such
as potato soup with shiitake mushrooms or
Tafelspitz with stir-fried vegetables and rice. It
sounds odd but it's excellent. Traditional sashimi,
sushi, tempura and udon noodles can also be found
on the small menu.

Sumo Sushi

*Kastanienallee 24 (4435 6130). U2 Eberswalder
Strasse.* **Open** noon-midnight Mon-Fri; 3pm-
midnight Sat, Sun. **Main courses** €9-€12.
No credit cards. **Map** p312 O3 ㊱

Stands out for its sashimi, made with really fresh-
tasting tuna or salmon, and California maki, rice
rolls with crabmeat and avocado rolled in red caviar.
Other locations: Chausseestrasse 19, Mitte
(2404 8910).

Suriya Kanthi

*Knaackstrasse 4 (442 5301). U2 Senefelderplatz/
tram M2 Knaackstrasse.* **Open** noon-1am daily.
Main courses €5-€10. **No credit cards**.
Map p312 P4 ㊲
Authentic Sri Lankan and south Indian food. Dishes
include fiery curries, many involving exotic vegeta-
bles such as jackfruit, some with organic meat. Try
hoppers – similar to crêpes – instead of rice.
Other locations: Chandra Kumari,
Gneisenaustrasse 4, Kreuzberg (694 3056).

German, Austrian & Swiss

Entweder Oder

*Oderberger Strasse 15 (448 1382/www.cafe-eo.de).
U2 Eberswalder Strasse.* **Open** 10am-late daily.
Main courses €6-€14. **No credit cards**.
Map p312 O3 ㊳
German food with a light touch: roasts, grilled fish
and the occasional schnitzel cosy up to fresh salads
and simple potato side dishes. The menu changes
daily and everything is organic. Connected to the
underground art scene back in the days of the Wall,
this place still rotates new work by local artists.

Eat, Drink, Shop

Characterful charcuterie at **Gugelhof**.

Gugelhof

*Knaackstrasse 37 (442 9229/www.gugelhof.de). U2
Senefelderplatz.* **Open** 4pm-1am Mon-Fri; 10am-1am
Sat, Sun. **Main courses** €11.50-€20. **Credit** AmEx,
MC, V. **Map** p312 P3 ㊴

A mature Alsatian restaurant that pioneered the
Kollwitzplatz scene in the 1990s. The food is refined
but filling, the service formal but friendly, and the
furnishings comfortably worn in. The choucroute
contains the best charcuterie in town, and the
Backöfe – lamb, pork and beef marinated in riesling
and stewed and served in an earthware pot with root
vegetables and a bread-crust lid – shows the kitchen
at its most characterful. There's also a selection of
Alsatian tartes flambées and a very decent wine list.
Reservations recommended. Breakfast is served
until 4pm at weekends.

Café Oberwasser

*Zionskirchstrasse 6 (448 3719). U8 Bernauer
Strasse/tram M1 Zionskirchplatz.* **Main courses**
€4-€13.50. **Open** 5pm-late daily. **No credit cards**.
Map p312 N4 ㊵

This cosy bistro-type restaurant with dim lighting
and overstuffed furniture may look a bit second-
hand but after a drink or two it feels like having dinner in the attic of some faded aristocrat. The food is
a combination of Russian and non-Russian cuisine,
freshly prepared to order by a hostess who seems to

be the only person on the job. Things go slow, but
plan to make an evening of it and you won't be sorry.

Offenbach-Stuben

*Stubbenkammerstrasse 8 (445 8502/www.offenbach
stuben.de). S8, S41, S42, S85 Prenzlauer Allee.*
Open 6pm-late daily. **Main courses** €10-€15.
Credit AmEx, DC, MC, V. **Map** p312 P3 ㊶

An eccentric survivor from the old East Berlin, this
was a non-state-owned restaurant catering to the
GDR theatre crowd – and it has made the transition
to capitalism with considerable grace. There's nothing fancy in the kitchen, just classic German cuisine
prepared with top-notch ingredients and the skill
that comes from long practice. A fine Saxon wine
list helps the food down.

Imbiss/fast food

Konnopke's Imbiss

*Under U-Bahn tracks, corner of Danziger Strasse/
Schönhauser Allee (442 7765). U2 Eberswalder
Strasse.* **Open** 6am-8pm Mon-Fri; noon-7pm Sat.
Main courses €1.50-€3.50. **No credit cards**.
Map p312 O3 ㊷

This justly famous sausage stand under the U2 line
has been managed by the Ziervogel family since
1930 and introduced the Currywurst to East Berlin
in 1960. *See p142* **Curry on sausages**. **Photo** *p136.*

Salsabil

Wörther Strasse 16 (4404 6073). U2 Senefelderplatz. **Open** noon-midnight Tue-Sun. **Main courses** €2-€5. **No credit cards.** Map p312 P3 **43**

This Arabic/North African *Imbiss* has all the usual trappings of tabbouleh, falafel, houmous, schwarma as well as lamb sausage, shredded chicken, lots of fried vegetables and some kind of balls made of fried egg and courgette (Eiji). It's all very tasty and reasonably priced to eat there or take out. The Salsabil assorted platter for two is mammoth (€10). Also a nice choice of desserts.

Sezarmeze

Prenzlauer Allee 197 (4403 4280). U2 Eberswalder Strasse. **Open** 11am-2am daily. **Main courses** €1.80-€5. **No credit cards.** Map p312 P3 **44**

This welcome alternative to the typical Turkish *Imbiss* features home-made Anatolian snacks. The prerequisite falafel and schwarma are prepared with sheep cheese spreads flavoured with garlic and herbs, as well as freshly grilled vegetables, all wrapped up in durum bread. Meals can be ordered by phone so it's ready to eat when you arrive.

Italian

I Due Forni

Schönhauser Allee 12 (4401 7333). U2 Senefelderplatz. **Open** noon-1am daily. **Main courses** €6-€8.40. **No credit cards.** Map p310 O4 **45**

The punky staff look more likely to throw you out of a club than tease your tastebuds. But in a city of cheap pizzas baked by Turks or Palestinians pretending to be Italian, the stone-oven pizza here is authentic and excellent. A bit pricier than elsewhere, a meal can still run under €10, and there are also daily pasta specials and a salad that's essentially a head of lettuce you have to chop up yourself. The smaller, sister pizzeria is almost as good.
Other locations: Il Casolare, Grimmstrasse 30, Kreuzberg (694 3968).

La Focacceria

Fehrbelliner Strasse 24 (4403 2771). U8 Rosenthaler Strasse. **Open** 11am-late daily. **Main courses** €1.50-€8. **No credit cards.** Map p312 N4 **46**

Delicious, thin-crust pizzas baked on the spot with fresh toppings such as tuna and rocket, spinach and white cheese, or prawns, artichokes and chilli. This bustling *Imbiss* and café is run by old-school Italians who speak little German and pride themselves on classic dishes such as lasagne and a perfect tiramisu.

Trattoria Paparazzi

Husemannstrasse 35 (440 7333). U2 Eberswalder Strasse. **Open** 6pm-1am daily. **Main courses** €8.60-€18.90. **No credit cards.** Map p312 P3 **47**

Behind the daft name and ordinary façade is one of Berlin's best Italians. Cornerstone dishes are mal-

fatti (pasta rolls seasoned with sage) and strangolapretti ('priest stranglers' of pasta, cheese and spinach with slivers of ham), but pay attention to the daily specials. House wines are excellent, though there are few other choices. Booking essential.

Portuguese

A Cabana

Hufelandstrasse 15 (4004 8508/www.bistro-cafe-acabana-berlin.de). Tram M4 Hufelandstrasse. **Open** 4pm-midnight daily. **Main courses** €6-€8. **No credit cards.** Map p303 Q4 **48**

A bit further east than the fashionable parts of this borough, but convenient for Magnet and the Knaack Club (for both, *see p219*), this friendly, family-run Portuguese is a great place to relax over a big bowl of home-made soup, assorted fresh fish or paella. It specialises in home-style cooking and the menu changes frequently. Occasional live music.

Russian

Pasternak

Knaackstrasse 22-4 (441 3399/www.restaurant-pasternak.de). U2 Senefelderplatz. **Open** 10am-1am daily. **Main courses** €12-€15. **Credit** MC, V. Map p312 P4 **49**

Small bar and Russian restaurant that's often crammed, which can be irritating at some tables – try for one in the small side room. The atmosphere is friendly and the food fine and filling. Kick off with borscht or the ample fish plate, then broach the hearty beef stroganoff.

Turkish

Miro

Raumerstrasse 29 (4473 3013). S8, S41, S42, S85 Prenzlauer Allee. **Open** 10am-late daily. **Main courses** €8-€17. **Credit** MC, V. Map p312 P3 **50**

Named, they say, not after the painter but in honour of a 'Mesopotamian natural philosopher', this cool, roomy place serves Anatolian specialities and well-priced drinks. The menu is long and intriguing, with many vegetarian possibilities, legions of starters and a good salad selection – all of which arrive in generous proportions. Friendly service.

Friedrichshain

Czech

Prager Hopfenstube

Karl-Marx-Allee 127 (426 7367). U5 Weberwiese. **Open** 11am-midnight daily. **Main courses** €7-€22. **Credit** MC. Map p309 S6 **51**

All the faves from your last Prague holiday appear here: svickova (roast beef), veprova pecene (roast pork), knedliky (dumplings) and the lone vegetarian prospect: smazeny syr or breaded and deep-fried

Eat, Drink, Shop

THE WORLD'S YOUR OYSTER

Amsterdam

Andalucía

Athens

Bangkok

Barcelona

Berlin

Boston

Brussels

Budapest

Buenos Aires

California

Cape Town

Chicago

Copenhagen

Croatia

Dubai

Dublin

Edinburgh

Florence

Havana

Hong Kong

Istanbul

Las Vegas

Lisbon

London

Los Angeles

Madrid

Mallorca

Marrakech

Miami

Milan

Mumbai & Goa

Naples

New Orleans

New York

Paris

Patagonia

Prague

Rome

San Francisco

Shanghai

South of France

Stockholm

Sydney

Tokyo 東京

Toronto

Turin

Venice

Vancouver

Vienna

Washington, DC

Available at all good bookshops
and at www.timeout.com/shop

Time Out

hermelin cheese served with remoulade and fries. Sluice down this heavy fare with mugs of Staropramen beer; afterwards, a Becherovka herbal digestif might help stave off indigestion. Fast and friendly service is a pleasingly inauthentic touch.

Imbiss/fast food

Frittiersalon

Boxhagener Strasse 104 (2593 3906/www.frittier salon.de). U5 Frankfurter Tor. **Open** 6pm-late Mon; noon-late Tue-Fri; 1pm-late Sat, Sun. **Main courses** €2.20-€6. **No credit cards. Map** p308 T7 ➅②

Organic burgers, bratwurst and fries are flipped with attitude and served with home-made ketchup, sauces and dips in this 'multikulti' gourmet chip shop. Burgers of the week involve some curious clashes of culture – a Middle East-influenced 'halloumi burger', for example, where fried cheese is embellished with yoghurt sauce, sesame dip and salad. For vegetarians there are also soya and camembert burgers, plus a meat-free Currywurst.

Meyman

Krossener Strasse 11A (6165 2673). U1, S3, S5, S7, S9, S75 Warschauer Strasse or U5 Samariterstrasse. **Open** 11am-2am Mon-Thur, Sun; 11am-4am Fri, Sat. **Main courses** €2.70-€6.80. **No credit cards. Map** p308 T7 ➅③

Moroccan, North African and Arabic specialities plus fresh fruit shakes and pizza are served in this warm and comfortable *Imbiss*, where there are usually plenty of tables. It's a bit pricier than comparable places, but fresh ingredients and a wide variety of dishes keep them coming – and few others are open this late.

Nil

Grünberger Strasse 52 (2904 7713). U1, S3, S5, S7, S9, S75 Warschauer Strasse or U5 Frankfurter Tor. **Open** 11am-1am daily. **Main courses** €2.50-€4.50. **No credit cards. Map** p308 S7 ➅④

Friendly Sudanese *Imbiss* offering good-value lamb and chicken dishes and an excellent vegetarian selection, including falafel, halloumi and aubergine salad. Hot peanut sauces are the tasty but sloppy speciality. Grab an extra napkin.

International

Pi Bar

Gabriel-Max-Strasse 17 (2936 7581). U1, S3, S5, S7, S9, S75 Warschauer Strasse or U5 Samariterstrasse. **Open** 4pm-late Mon-Fri; 10am-midnight Sat, Sun. **Main courses** €6-€18.50. **No credit cards. Map** p308 T7 ➅⑤

An amazing variety of seafood and vegetarian dinners are served at this restaurant and bar, and this is the only place in the area where you can find crab or scampi. Many customers, however, appear less interested in the seafood selection than in the 6-8.30pm happy hour featuring around 70 different cocktails and long drinks.

Italian

Kingston Pizzerei & Cocktail Bar

Simon-Dach-Strasse 12 (2977 6494). U1, S3, S5, S7, S9, S75 Warschauer Strasse or U5 Samariterstrasse. **Open** noon-10pm daily. **Main courses** €2.20-€8.90. **No credit cards. Map** p308 S7 ➅⑥

There are only five dishes on the menu and two of them are pizza, which comes in mini (€1.50) and biggie (€3) sizes. The ultra-thin, crispy crust is a welcome change for this district, and you can pile on as many of the 18 toppings as you like for no extra charge. Tables are limited, but in summer there's plenty of outdoor seating.

North African & Middle Eastern

Shisha

Krossener Strasse 19 (2977 1995). U1, S3, S5, S7, S9, S75 Warschauer Strasse or U5 Samariterstrasse. **Open** 10am-late daily. **Main courses** €5-€13. **No credit cards. Map** p308 T7 ➅⑦

Arabic restaurant/bar serving exotic vegetarian and meat dishes from Lebanon, Syria and Iraq. Hookahs are the real attraction for the twentysomething crowd: take advantage of the ten flavoured tobaccos and huge elevated couch to smoke yourself silly at €3.50 per hookah (€4.50 after 8pm).

Vegetarian

Volkswirtschaft

Krossener Strasse 17 (2900 4604). U1, S3, S5, S7, S9, S75 Warschauer Strasse or U5 Samariterstrasse. **Open** 6pm-midnight Mon-Wed; 1pm-midnight Thur-Sat; 11am-late Sun. **Main courses** €5.20-€14.10. **No credit cards. Map** p308 T7 ➅⑧

A little of everything here: occasional live music, film nights, readings, vegetarian and vegan Sunday brunches and Pinkus, a seldom-found organic beer. As a restaurant, it prides itself on healthy, hearty dishes and an extensive menu that changes daily. Every day of the week has a culinary theme: Friday's fish and Tuesday's creative home cooking are especially good.

Kreuzberg

Americas

Kreuzburger

Oranienstrasse 190 (2558 8465). U1, U8 Kotbusser Tor. **Open** 11.30am-3am daily. **Main courses** €2.30-€4.10. **No credit cards. Map** p307 P9 ➅⑨

A rough-and-ready Kreuzberg take on the American burger bar, this brick-walled diner seems aggressively stripped of decorative frills. But the burgers, made with Neuland organic beef and ranging from

Eat, Drink, Shop

Understanding the menu

USEFUL PHRASES

I'd like to reserve a table for... people. **Ich möchte einen Tisch für... Personen reservieren.**
Are these places free? **Sind diese Plätze frei?**
The menu, please. **Die Speisekarte, bitte.**
I am a vegetarian. **Ich bin Vegetarier.**
I am a diabetic. **Ich bin Diabetiker.**
We'd/I'd like to order. **Wir möchten/ Ich möchte bestellen.**
We'd/I'd like to pay. **Bezahlen, bitte.**

BASICS

Frühstück breakfast. **Mittagessen** lunch. **Abendessen** dinner. **Imbiss** snack. **Vorspeise** appetiser. **Hauptgericht** main course. **Nachspeise** dessert.
Brot/Brötchen bread/rolls. **Butter** butter. **Ei/Eier** egg/eggs. **Spiegeleier** fried eggs. **Rühreier** scrambled eggs. **Käse** cheese. **Nudeln/Teigwaren** noodles/pasta. **Sosse** sauce. **Salz** salt. **Pfeffer** pepper. **gekocht** boiled. **gebraten** fried/roasted. **paniert** breaded/battered.

SOUPS (SUPPEN)

Bohnensuppe bean soup. **Brühe** broth.
Erbsensuppe pea soup. **Hühnersuppe** chicken soup. **klare Brühe mit Leberknödeln** clear broth with liver dumplings. **Kraftbrühe** clear meat broth. **Linsensuppe** lentil soup.

MEAT, POULTRY AND GAME (FLEISCH, GEFLÜGEL UND WILD)

Boulette meatball. **Ente** duck. **Gans** goose.
Hackfleisch ground meat/mince. **Hirsch** venison. **Huhn/Hühnerfleisch** chicken.
Hähnchen chicken (when served in one piece). **Kaninchen** rabbit. **Kohlrouladen** cabbage-rolls stuffed with pork. **Kotelett** chop. **Lamm** lamb. **Leber** liver. **Nieren** kidneys. **Rindfleisch** beef. **Sauerbraten** marinated roast beef. **Schinken** ham.
Schnitzel thinly pounded piece of meat, usually breaded and sautéed.
Schweinebraten roast pork.
Schweinefleisch pork. **Speck** bacon.
Truthahn turkey. **Wachteln** quail.
Wurst sausage.

---

the lavish and ornate Tex Burger to the humble and straightforward Hamburger, soon drag attention from the furnishings. Pavement tables in summer.

Asian

Pagoda

Bergmannstrasse 88 (691 2640). U7 Gneisenaustrasse. **Open** noon-midnight daily. **Main courses** €5.50-€9.50. **No credit cards**. **Map** p306 M10 ⑥⓪
You can watch the Thai ladies whipping up your meal behind the counter and ensure that everything is fresh and authentic. Red and green curries here are sensational and the pad thai is heavenly. There are a few tables with stools on the ground floor but if the place looks crowded, don't worry: there's extra seating in the basement where you can watch the residents of a huge fish tank.

Sumo

Bergmannstrasse 89 (6900 4963/www.s-u-m-o.com). U7 Gneisenaustrasse. **Open** noon-midnight daily. **Main courses** €7-€16. **No credit cards**. **Map** p306 M10 ⑥①
Quick, fresh Japanese food and intense flavours in a well-lit modern interior spread over two floors. The sushi is masterful but you can also enjoy standards such as tempura udon soup, warm bean salad, chicken yakitori or grilled tuna on rice. The feeling is modern Japanese toned down for German tastes.

French

Le Cochon Bourgeois

Fichtestrasse 24 (693 0101/www.le-cochon.de). U7 Südstern. **Open** 6pm-1am Tue-Sat. **Main courses** €17-€22. **No credit cards**. **Map** p307 O10 ⑥②
A calm oasis of excellent French cuisine tucked away in a quiet and unassuming corner of Kreuzberg. People come here from all over Berlin to sample dishes such as perch with a lentil salad, followed by quail with wild mushroom risotto, or guineafowl with winter vegetables and a saffron ginger sauce. There are fantastic wines from the Alsace, plus a good selection of digestifs, to round off an evening of quiet piano music and attentive service.

German, Austrian & Swiss

Austria

Bergmannstrasse 30, on Marheineke Platz (694 4440). U7 Gneisenaustrasse. **Open** 6pm-1am daily. **Main courses** €13.50-€17.50. **Credit** AmEx, MC, V. **Map** p307 N10 ⑥③
With a collection of antlers, this place does its best to look like a hunting lodge. The meat is organic, and there's a list of organic wines. Austria also offers Kapsreiter or Zipfer beer on tap, and a famously over-the-top schnitzel. Outdoor seating on a tree-lined square makes it a pleasant summer venue too. Book at weekends and in summer.

FISH (FISCH)
Aal eel. **Forelle** trout. **Garnelen** prawns. **Hummer** lobster. **Kabeljau** cod. **Karpfen** carp. **Krabbe** crab or shrimp. **Lachs** salmon. **Makrele** mackerel. **Matjes/Hering** raw herring. **Miesmuscheln** mussels. **Schellfisch** haddock. **Scholle** plaice. **Seezunge** sole. **Thunfisch** tuna. **Tintenfisch** squid. **Venusmuscheln** clams. **Zander** pike-perch.

HERBS AND SPICES (KRÄUTER UND GEWÜRZE)
Basilikum basil. **Kümmel** caraway. **Mohn** poppyseed. **Nelken** cloves. **Origanum** oregano. **Petersilie** parsley. **Thymian** thyme. **Zimt** cinnamon.

VEGETABLES (GEMÜSE)
Blumenkohl cauliflower. **Bohnen** beans. **Bratkartoffeln** fried potatoes. **Brechbohnen** green beans. **Champignons/Pilze** mushrooms. **Erbsen** green peas. **Erdnüsse** peanuts. **grüne Zwiebel** spring onion. **Gurke** cucumber. **Kartoffel** potato. **Knoblauch** garlic. **Kichererbsen** chick peas. **Knödel** dumpling. **Kohl** cabbage. **Kürbis** pumpkin. **Linsen** lentils. **Möhren** carrots. **Paprika** peppers. **Pommes** chips. **Rosenkohl** Brussels sprouts. **Rösti** roast grated potatoes. **rote Bete** beetroot. **Rotkohl** red cabbage. **Salat** lettuce. **Salzkartoffeln** boiled potatoes. **Sauerkraut** shredded white cabbage. **Spargel** asparagus. **Tomaten** tomatoes. **Zucchini** courgettes. **Zwiebeln** onions.

FRUIT (OBST)
Ananas pineapple. **Apfel** apple. **Apfelsine** orange. **Birne** pear. **Erdbeeren** strawberries. **Heidelbeeren** blueberries. **Himbeeren** raspberries. **Kirsch** cherry. **Limette** lime. **Zitrone** lemon.

DRINKS (GETRÄNKE)
Bier beer. **dunkles Bier/helles Bier** dark beer/lager. **Glühwein** mulled wine. **Kaffee** coffee. **Mineralwasser** mineral water. **Orangensaft** orange juice. **Saft** juice. **Tee** tea. **Wein** wine.

Grossbeerenkeller
Grossbeerenstrasse 90 (251 3064). U1, U7 Möckernbrücke. **Open** 4pm-1am Mon-Fri; 6pm-1am Sat. **Main courses** €7-€14.50. **No credit cards.** Map p307 P9 **64**
In business since 1862, Grossbeerenkeller serves good home cooking of a solid Berlinisch bent. The Hoppel Poppel (*see p152* **Where to get your early piece**) breakfast is legendary.

Henne
Leuschnerdamm 25 (614 7730/www.henne-berlin. de). U1, U8 Kottbusser Tor. **Open** 7pm-1am Tue-Sun. **Main courses** €2.50-€6. **No credit cards.** Map p306 M9 **65**
Only one thing on the menu – half a roast chicken – but Henne's birds are organically raised and milk-roasted. The only decisions are whether to have cabbage or potato salad, and which beer to wash it down with (try the Monchshof). Check the letter from JFK over the bar, regretting that the President missed dinner here.

Markthalle
Pücklerstrasse 34 (617 5502). U1 Görlitzer Bahnhof. **Open** 9am-2am Mon-Fri; 10am-late Sat, Sun. **Main courses** €8-€14. **Credit** MC, V. Map p307 Q8 **66**
This unpretentious schnitzel restaurant and bar, with chunky tables and wood-panelled walls, has become a Kreuzberg institution. Breakfast is served until 5pm, salads from noon, and, in the evening, a selection of filling and reasonably priced meals. It's also fun just to sit at the long bar and sample the selection of grappas. After dinner, see what's on downstairs at the Privat Club (*see p229*).

Imbiss/fast food

Bistro Yilmaz Kardesler
Kottbusser Damm 6 (no phone). U8 Schönleinstrasse. **Open** 10am-1am daily. **Main courses** €2.50-€3.50. **No credit cards.** Map p307 P10 **67**
It's crowded, it's nondescript, but this humble *Imbiss* sells one of the best doner kebabs in Turkish Berlin. Crammed full of salad and seasoned with a startling array of spices, this is the Turkish fast food icon at its addictive best. And if you're turned off by that great slab of meat slowly sweltering on the spit, there's also a good selection of grilled kebabs.

International

Knofi
Bergmannstrasse 11 (6956 4359/www.knofi.de). U7 Gneisenaustrasse. **Open** 7am-9pm daily. **Main courses** €5. **No credit cards.** Map p306 M10 **68**
Connected to the Mediterranean speciality store across the street, Knofi is cosy and not much larger than an *Imbiss*, but it boasts a cheap and delicious speciality in the form of crêpe-like gosses – both vegetarian or filled with schwarma – and generous portions of soup. It's also a top-notch bakery.

Konnopke's Imbiss – a name close to the heart of all sausage-lovers. *See p130.*

Svevo

Lausitzer Strasse 25 (6107 3216/www.restaurant-svevo.de). U1 Görlitzer Bahnhof. **Open** 6pm-late Mon-Sat. **Main courses** €12-€20. **Credit** AmEx, MC, V. **Map** p307 Q9 **69**

Once this place was a well-kept secret, now you have to call days in advance for the faintest chance of getting a table. It's no wonder. Chef Claudio Andretta successfully balances the best elements of European cuisine. Imagine mountain trout wrapped in bacon and chopped egg on a bed of peppery cress, or beef fillet poached in sour cream served on black salsify and potato gnocchi, and a pyramid of rich chocolate with cassis sauce for dessert. The interior is simple but does get cramped. Good service.

Italian

Osteria No.1

Kreuzbergstrasse 71 (786 9162). U6, U7 Mehringdamm. **Open** noon-2am daily. **Main courses** €7.50-€19. **Credit** AmEx, DC, MC, V. **Map** p306 M10 **70**

Most of Berlin's best Italian chefs paid their dues at this well-worn 1977-founded establishment, learning their lessons from a family of restaurateurs who emigrated from Lecce. Osteria is run by Fabio Angilè, nephew of the owner of Sale e Tabacchi (*see below*). There's an excellent three-course lunch menu and, in summer, you can eat in one of Berlin's loveliest garden courtyards. Staff are super-friendly. Booking recommended.

Sale e Tabacchi

Kochstrasse 18 (252 1155). U6 Kochstrasse. **Open** 9am-2am Mon-Fri; 10am-2am Sat, Sun. **Main courses** €7-€20. **Credit** MC, V. **Map** p311 M8 **71**

Well known for fish dishes (tuna and swordfish carpaccio or loup de mer) and for the pretty courgette flowers filled with ricotta and mint, not to mention its large, impressive selection of Italian wines. The interior design is meant to reflect a time when salt (*sale*) and tobacco (*tabacchi*) were sold exclusively by the state. In summer, enjoy a leisurely lunch or dinner in the garden under lemon, orange and pomegranate trees.

North African & Middle Eastern

Baraka

Lausitzer Platz 6 (612 6330). U1 Görlitzer Bahnhof. **Open** noon-midnight Mon-Thur, Sun; noon-1am Fri, Sat. **Main courses** €5-€10. **No credit cards**. **Map** p307 Q9 **72**

North African and Egyptian specialities such as couscous and foul (red beans and chickpeas in sesame sauce) enhance a menu also including standards such as falafel, schwarma and kofte. You can take away your meal or eat in the cavernous restaurant with its cosy seating on embroidered cushions.

Turkish

Hasir

Adalbertstrasse 10 (614 2373/www.hasir.de). U1, U8 Kottbusser Tor. **Open** 24hrs daily (often closes

2-3hrs early morning). **Main courses** €8. **No credit cards**. Map p307 P9 ⑦
You thought the Turks had been chewing doner since time immemorial? Sorry, it was invented in Germany in 1971 by Mehmet Aygun, who eventually opened this highly successful chain of Turkish restaurants. While you'll get one of the best doners in Berlin here, you owe it to yourself to check out the rest of the menu, which involves various other skewered meats in sauce, and some agreeably addictive bread rolls. The dessert menu is also a winner – especially the rice pudding.
Other locations: Nürnberger Strasse 46, Wilmersdorf (217 7774); Maasenstrasse 10, Schöneberg (215 6060); Oranienburger Strasse 4, Mitte (2804 1616).

Vegetarian

Abendmahl
Muskauer Strasse 9 (612 5170/www.abendmahl-berlin.de). U1 Görlitzer Bahnhof. **Open** 6pm-1am Wed-Sun. **Main courses** €8-€16. **No credit cards**. Map p307 Q9 ⑭
The name means 'last supper' and, decked out in a little catholic kitsch, this is Berlin's temple of vegetarian gastronomy – although there is fish on the menu too. Dishes change according to the seasons and the weird and wonderful names they're given are part of the offbeat charm: I Shot Andy Warhol for dessert, anyone? A thai fish curry is one of the few things that's always on the menu. Otherwise, the soups are wonderful, great things are done with seitan, and creativity is at a high level throughout. The dessert selection looks so mouth-watering it's even available as a postcard series. Booking recommended.

Lon Men
Grossbeerenstrasse 57A (7700 8037/www.lon-men-vegetarisch.de.vu). U6, U7 Mehringdamm. **Open** 6pm-midnight daily. *Buffet* €6.90 Mon-Thur; €8.90 Fri-Sun. **Credit** AmEx, MC, V. Map p306 L10 ⑮
Simply excellent all-you-can-eat Asian vegetarian buffet. No frills, no waiting and plenty of tables to eat at, including some outside in summer.

Schöneberg

African

Bejte-Ethiopia
Zietenstrasse 8 (262 5933/www.bejte-ethiopia.de). U1, U2, U3, U4 Nollendorfplatz. **Open** 4pm-1am Mon-Fri; 2pm-2am Sat, Sun. **Main courses** €6-€10. **Credit** DC, MC, V. Map p306 J9 ⑯
Ethiopian home cooking in a no-frills atmosphere. The food is essentially a variety of spiced meats and vegetables in varying states of stewedness, which are scooped on a piece of enjera bread and shovelled to the mouth. The waitstaff are unobtrusive but happy to show the uninitiated the ropes.

French

La Cocotte
Vorbergstrasse 10 (7895 7658/www.lacocotte.de). U7 Eisenacher Strasse. **Open** 6pm-1am Tue-Sun. **Main courses** €7.50-€14. **No credit cards**. Map p306 J10 ⑰
Friendly, gay-owned French restaurant where good cooking is enhanced by a sense of fun and occasional themed events – such as the Beaujolais nouveau being welcomed by a 'rustic chic' buffet and a programme of accordion music and 1980s French pop. Vegetarians aren't forgotten, there's a nice terrace and the toilets are absolutely beautiful.

German, Austrian & Swiss

Storch
Wartburgstrasse 54 (784 2059/www.storch-berlin.de). U7 Eisenacher Strasse. **Open** 6pm-1am Mon-Sat. **Main courses** €8-€22. **Credit** AmEx, MC, V. Map p306 J11 ⑱
One of our favourite places. The Alsatian food – soup and salad starters, a sausage and sauerkraut platter, plus a daily selection of meat and fish dishes from the place where German and French cuisines rub shoulders – is finely prepared and generously proportioned. House speciality is the Alsatian pizza variant, tarte flambée: a crisp pastry base baked in a special oven and topped with either cheese, onion and bacon or (as dessert) with apple, cinnamon and flaming Calvados. Long wooden tables are shared by different parties and the atmosphere usually buzzes. Booking recommended. **Photo** *p139*.

Imbiss & fast food

Habibi
Goltzstrasse 24, on Winterfeldtplatz (215 3332). U1, U2, U3, U4 Nollendorfplatz. **Open** 11am-3am Mon-Thur, Sun; 11am-5am Fri, Sat. **Main courses** €4-€11. **No credit cards**. Map p306 J9 ⑲
Freshly made Middle Eastern specialities including falafel, kibbeh, tabbouleh and various combination plates. Wash it all down with freshly squeezed orange or carrot juice, and finish up with a complimentary tea and one of the wonderful pastries. The premises are light, bright and well run. Deservedly popular, it can get very full.
Other locations: Akazienstrasse 9, Schöneberg (787 4428); Körtestrasse 35, Kreuzberg (692 2401); Oranienstrasse 30, Kreuzberg (6165 8346).

Indian

India Haus
Feurigstrasse 38 (781 2546/www.restaurant-india haus.de). U4, S41, S42, S45, S46 Innsbrucker Platz. **Open** 2pm-midnight Mon-Fri; noon-midnight Sat, Sun. **Main courses** €5.50-€11. **Credit** AmEx, DC, V. Map p305 H11 ⑳

Proximity to the English-language Odeon cinema (see p196) round the corner redeems an out-of-the-way location, but food is good here and a long menu offers many vegetarian choices. The almond soup is excellent and the Malay kofta delicious. Weekend buffets for around €7. Cheaper *Imbiss* attached.

Italian

Petite Europe
Langenscheidtstrasse 1 (781 2964). U7 Kleistpark. **Open** 5pm-1am daily. **Main courses** €7-€13. **Credit** MC, V. **Map** p306 J10 ⓺
You may have to wait for a table in this popular, friendly place, but the turnover's fast. Weekly specials are first-rate, as are the pasta dishes. Salads could be better and none of this is haute cuisine, but it's all well made, hearty and inexpensive.

Norwegian

Munch's Hus
Bülowstrasse 66 (2101 4086/www.munchshus.de). U2 Bülowstrasse. **Open** 10am-1am daily. **Main courses** €5-€14. **Credit** AmEx. **Map** p306 K9 ⓺
In a corner of town bereft of good places to eat, Berlin's only Norwegian restaurant is frequented by businessmen and artists from the neighbourhood. Daily specials are a bit like the rounded German meal – potatoes and greens accompany most dishes – but with a twist that usually involves dill. Creamy, fresh soups and delicious fish dishes are their speciality, but light sandwiches and salads are also available.

Tiergarten

American

Andy's Diner & Bar
Potsdamer Strasse 1 (2300 4990/www.andys-diner-bar.sportkneipe.de). U2, S1, S2, S26 Potsdamer Platz. **Open** 10am-6am daily. **Main courses** €7.50-€17.50. **Credit** AmEx, MC, V. **Map** p311 L7 ⓺
American-style sports bar where a wide but averagely rendered assortment of burgers, potato skins, chicken wings and steaks is augmented by more interesting weekly specials. Best for egg breakfasts and brunches, it fills at night due to its highly visible Potsdamer Platz location. Not bad for a burger, but avoid the shakes and watch the match elsewhere. **Other locations**: Im Domaquarée, Karl-Liebknecht-Strasse 5, Mitte (9789 4120); Körtestrasse 38, Kreuzberg (6950 8899).

Asian

Edd's
Lützowstrasse 81 (215 5294). U1 Kurfürstenstrasse. **Open** 11.30am-3pm, 6pm-midnight Mon-Fri; 5pm-midnight Sat; 2pm-midnight Sun. **Main courses** €14-€21. **No credit cards**. **Map** p306 J8/K8 ⓺
Known and loved by many, so bookings are essential for this comfortable, elegant Thai, where a husband-and-wife team please their guests with well balanced but somewhat spicy creations. Try the banana flower and prawn salad or duck No.18, double cooked and excellent.

Sushi Express
Potsdamer Platz 2, Passerelle (2575 1863). U2, S1, S2, S26 Potsdamer Platz. **Open** 11.30am-8pm Mon-Sat. **Main courses** €2.50-€4. **Credit** MC, V. **Map** p312 K7/L7 ⓺
Not the easiest place to find, it is under the courtyard of the Sony Center in a passage to the S-Bahn, accessible from a stairway next to the video display for the Filmmuseum (see p104). But the hunt is worth it for tasty sushi, sashimi and assorted delicacies to be plucked off the conveyor belt cycling past you at the counter. The temptation is to just keep grabbing things, but don't worry, Mon-Fri from noon-6pm all sushi and rolls are half price. Hot dishes and lunchboxes are also available, as is takeaway.

Australian

Corroboree
Sony Center, Bellevuestrasse 5 (2610 1705). U2, S1, S2, S26 Potsdamer Platz. **Open** 10am-1am daily. **Main courses** €7-€17. **Credit** MC, V. **Map** p312 K7/L7 ⓺
Big, noisy and one of the only decent places to eat in the Sony Center. It's hearty stuff, including kangaroo steak and crocodile tournedos as well as burgers and noodle dishes, a small list of Aussie wines, and macadamia nuts with everything. Not too exciting for vegetarians, though. **Photos** p140.

French

Diekmann im Weinhaus Huth
Alte Potsdamer Strasse 5 (2529 7524/www.j-diekmann.de). U2, S1, S2, S26 Potsdamer Platz. **Open** noon-1am daily. **Main courses** €14-€19. **Credit** AmEx, MC, V. **Map** p311 L8 ⓺
Decent, stylish dining in the only surviving pre-war structure on Potsdamer Platz. The staff are well drilled, there's a small terrace to complement the smart dining room, the wine list has around 120 vintages, and the food is good for the price. A changing menu offers decent lunch deals and accommodates familiar Gallic favourites. There are few decent places round here, so it's best to book. **Other locations**: Meinekestrasse 7, Charlottenburg (883 3321); Clayallee 99, Dahlem (832 6392).

German, Austrian & Swiss

Café Einstein
Kurfürstenstrasse 58 (261 5096/www.cafeeinstein.com). U1, U2, U3, U4 Nollendorfplatz. **Open** 9am-1am daily. **Main courses** €9-€20. **Credit** AmEx, DC, MC, V. **Map** p306 J8 ⓺

Eat, Drink, Shop

The venerable **Storch**. *See p137.*

Crocodile tournedos and macadamia nuts with everything at **Corroboree**. *See p138.*

Red leather banquettes, parquet flooring and the crack of wooden chairs all contribute to the old Viennese café experience at Einstein. Fine Austrian cooking is produced alongside several nouveau cuisine specialities. Alternatively, order Apfelstrudel and coffee and soak up the atmosphere of this elegant 1878 villa. The other location is more functional and has less charm, but the food is just as good. The garden out back is a wonderful spot for breakfast or lunch in summer.

Other locations: Unter den Linden 42, Mitte (204 3632).

Hugo's

Hotel Intercontinental, Budapester Strasse 2 (2602 1263/www.hugos-restaurant.de). U2, U9, S5, S7, S9, S75 Zoologischer Garten. **Open** 6-10.30pm Mon-Sat. **Main courses** €32-€39. **Credit** AmEx, DC, MC, V. **Map** p305 H8 ➌
Probably Berlin's best restaurant right now, and with all the awards to prove it. Chef Thomas Kammeier juxtaposes classic haute cuisine with an avant-garde new German style. Dishes such as cheek of ox with beluga lentils and filled calamares, goose liver with mango, and Canadian lobster salad bring out the best of a mature kitchen and well-balanced menu. The beautiful room occupies the entire top floor of the Hotel Intercontinental (*see p60*) with absorbing views over in all directions across the Tiergarten and central Berlin.

Weizmann

S-Bahnbogen 390, Lüneberger Strasse (394 2057). S5, S7, S9, S75 Bellevue. **Open** *Winter* 6pm-midnight Mon-Fri, Sun. *Summer* 6pm-midnight daily. **No credit cards. Map** p301 J6 ➌
Lovely little place serving the pastas of Swabia, including Spätzle (a dish with Bratwurst, lentils or meatballs), Käsespätzle (with cheese), Maultaschen (like giant ravioli) and Schupfnudelen (a cross between pasta and chips). Wash it down with a dark Berg beer.

Charlottenburg & Wilmersdorf

Americas

Julep's

Giesebrechtstrasse 3 (881 8823/www.juleps-berlin. de). U7 Adenauerplatz. **Open** 5pm-1am Mon-Thur, Sun; 5pm-2am Fri, Sat. **Main courses** €9-€15. **Credit** MC, V. **Map** p304 D8 ➌
Gets the fusion flavours of contemporary American cuisine just right with dishes such as duck prosciutto or quesadillas with rhubarb and apple chutney, teriyaki chicken with lemongrass and basmati rice or Cajun-style red snapper. The Caesar salad is a classic, and desserts include chocolate brownies made with Jack Daniels. Happy Hour is 5-8pm and all night Sunday.

Asian

Sachiko Sushi

*Grolmanstrasse 47 (313 2282). S5, S7, S9, S75
Savignyplatz.* **Open** noon-midnight daily. **Main
courses** €12-€24. **Credit** MC, V. **Map** p312 F8 **92**
This was Berlin's first kaiten (conveyor belt) sushi
joint. It's still invariably packed with upmarket
Charlottenburg thirtysomethings, snatching the
scrummy morsels as they circumnavigate a chrome
and black stone bar.

Tai Ji

*Uhlandstrasse 194 (313 2881). U2, U9, S5, S7,
S9, S75 Zoologischer Garten.* **Open** noon-midnight
daily. **Main courses** €8-€14. **Credit** MC, V.
Map p312 F8 **93**
Fashionable folk cluster at the better known Good
Friends around the corner, but the Chinese food is
actually far better and more authentic in this place.
The room – a peaceful, semi-circular pavilion overlooking a garden courtyard – is showing its age, but
starters such as daugoo and button mushrooms and
onion, or wun tun in a red chilli sauce, are simply
sensational. The main courses have been given
bizarre names such as Meeting on a Magic Bridge
or Eight Drunken Immortals Cross the Sea, but don't
let that put you off. Note: half the Beijing-Sichuan
dishes are vegetarian.

French

First Floor

*Hotel Palace, Budapester Strasse 45 (2502 1020/
www.firstfloor.palace.de). U2, U9, S5, S7, S9, S75
Zoologischer Garten.* **Open** noon-3pm, 6-10.30pm
Mon-Sat. **Main courses** €32.50-€36.50. **Menu** €71-
€105. **Credit** AmEx, DC, MC, V. **Map** p305 G8 **94**
Now under hot young chef Mathias Bucholz, this is
the place to come for refined French/European cuisine such as Bresse pigeon served with chanterelles
and a ragout of potatoes, venison stuffed with foie
gras, or loup de mer and Breton lobster served with
saffron and tomato confit. Three menus are offered
daily. One of Berlin's top tables.

Paris Bar

*Kantstrasse 152 (313 8052). S5, S7, S9, S75
Savignyplatz.* **Open** noon-2am daily. **Main courses**
€9-€25. **Credit** AmEx. **Map** p312 F8 **95**
Owner Michel Wurthle's friendship with Martin
Kippenberger and other artists is obvious from the
art hanging on every available inch of wall. Paris
Bar, with its old-salon appeal, is one of Berlin's tried
and true spots. It attracts a crowd of rowdy regulars, and newcomers can feel left out when seated in
the rear. The food, to be honest, isn't nearly as good
as the staff make out. To experience the often rude
service and pricey food, you'll need to book.

Florian. See p142.

Eat, Drink, Shop

Curry on sausages

Politicians pose with it, pop stars sing songs about it, great cities vie to claim the honour of its invention. The **Currywurst** is more than just a street snack. It's Germany's premier pop culture item. If Warhol was a Berliner, he would have painted a Bratwurst drenched in lurid red ketchup and liberally sprinkled with curry powder.

Germany is proud of its sausages and boasts more than 1,200 different varieties, all prepared and classified in deeply traditional ways. So how on earth did the Germans get around to putting curry powder on them?

In Hamburg, where the Currywurst is served swimming in a sweet brown sauce, they claim to have invented it in 1947. Germans from the Ruhr area have their own creation myth, in which an Essen sausage-seller accidentally drops a can of curry powder into some ketchup. But Berliners know this is nonsense, and there's

a commemorative plaque on the corner of Kantstrasse and Kaiser-Friedrich-Strasse in Charlottenburg to prove it.

On the afternoon of 4 September 1949 – a rainy day, by all accounts – 36-year-old Herta Heuwer grew bored with waiting for customers at her humble sausage stand, and began to experiment with

Georgian

Genazvale

Windscheidstrasse 14 (4508 6026). S5, S7, S9, S75 Charlottenburg. **Open** 5pm-midnight daily. **Main courses** €8-€9. **Menu** €26 for 2 people. **No credit cards**. **Map** p304 C8/D8 **96**

A decent, upmarket Georgian restaurant that draws a mixed crowd of both Georgian and Russian expats, with a few Germans and visitors from abroad for good measure. Expect to find plum sauces, walnuts and coriander as a backdrop to mega-portions of meat. Georgian kitsch is everywhere, but this is easily ignored after a vodka or three. Try the lamb khinkali and anticipate honey and pomegranates aplenty. There is also a small range of first-class Georgian wines.

German, Austrian & Swiss

Alt Luxemburg

Windscheidstrasse 31 (323 8730/www.altluxemburg. de). U2 Sophie-Charlotte-Platz. **Open** 5pm-late Mon-Sat. **Main courses** €24-€27. **Credit** AmEx, DC, V. **Map** p304 D8 **97**

Karl Wannemacher combines classic German and French flavours with Asian influences in a wonderfully romantic dining room. Sample such wonders as horseradish terrine with smoked eel, or monkfish with a succulent saffron sauce informed with tomato. The wine list could do with more moderately priced bottles, though.

Florian

Grolmanstrasse 52 (313 9184/www.restaurant-florian.de). S5, S7, S9, S75 Savignyplatz. **Open** 6pm-3am daily. **Main courses** €10-€18. **Credit** MC, V. **Map** p312 F8 **98**

Florian has been serving fine south German food for a couple of decades now. The cooking is hearty, the service impeccable. Yes, staff will put you in Siberia if they don't like your looks, but they'll also welcome you back if you're good. **Photo** *p141.*

Marjellchen

Mommsenstrasse 9 (883 2676). S5, S7, S9, S75 Savignyplatz. **Open** 5pm-midnight daily. **Main courses** €10-€20. **Credit** AmEx, DC, MC, V. **Map** p312 E8 **99**

There aren't many places like this around any more. It serves specialities from East Prussia, Pomerania and Silesia in an atmosphere of old-fashioned *Gemütlichkeit*. Beautiful bar, great service. Larger-than-life owner recites poetry and sometimes sings.

Restaurant 44

Swissôtel, Augsburger Strasse 44 (2201 02288). U1, U9 Kurfürstendamm. **Open** noon-2.30pm, 6-10.30pm daily. **Main courses** €15-€34. **Credit** AmEx, DC, MC, V. **Map** p312 G8 **100**

Chef Tim Raue offers two separate menus: one traditional French, the other radical Neue Deutsche Kuche. The latter includes the likes of sandalwood goat's cheese with lobster tail, or schnitzel with apple and beetroot salad and a remoulade of white truffle. Cool and comfortable room, elegantly framed desserts, and a fine selection of wines by the glass.

experiment with spices and seasonings. Some chilli powder in the ketchup… perhaps some Worcester sauce, too… pour it all over a skinless pork Bratwurst… scatter curry powder on top… Lo, the Currywurst was born! And quickly patented under number 721319.

Sliced up on a paper plate, often served with chips and mayonnaise, and designed to be consumed standing up with a beer, the Currywurst sallied forth in conquest. In the 1950s *Currywurstbuden* sprang up on every corner, scenting West Berlin with the aroma of hot fat, warm ketchup and Indian spices. By the time the Wall went up in 1961, the Currywurst had already crossed into the East, though to this day it is still often served on that side of town with a skin of pig's intestine, while in western Berlin it is usually skinless. (If you want it without intestine, ask for it *ohne Darm*).

In East Berlin the Currywurst held its own through the communist period, most notably at **Konnopke's Imbiss** (*see p130*), serving sausages since 1930 under the U2 tracks south of Eberswalder Strasse station. In West Berlin the Currywurst had to fight a war on two fronts against Italian pizza slices and that other Berlin street-food invention, the doner kebab. Though beaten back for a time, in today's conservative climate the Currywurst is perhaps making a comeback, celebrated as classless, authentic and German.

Konnopke's is not the only celebrated Currywurst stand. The sausages at **Ku'damm 195** (Kurfürstendamm 195, Charlottenburg) are pricey but crisp. The perennial queue at **Curry 36** (Mehringdamm 36, Kreuzberg) testifies to the quality of its Wurst. If caught in need of a Currywurst at the opposite end of that borough, try **Curry 7** (Schlesische Strasse 7, Kreuzberg). But our favourite place is the organic vendor **Witty's** (*see below*), serving classic Currywurst and fantastic chips directly opposite KaDeWe.

Imbiss & fast food

Ashoka

Grolmanstrasse 51 (3180 8154). S5, S7, S9, S75 Savignyplatz. **Open** noon-midnight daily. **Main courses** €2.50-€7. **No credit cards**. **Map** p312 F8 ❶

Most Berlin Indians seem to serve up more or less the same Germanised menu. This one can be forgiven, as it was the first to open. Over two decades later and Indian restaurants are ubiquitous in Berlin but Ashoka remains one of the best, offering decently priced and nicely prepared dishes in quiet and tasteful surroundings. There are plenty of vegetarian options and also some inventive weekly specials.

Witty's

Wittenbergplatz (no phone). U1, U2, U3 Wittenbergplatz. **Open** 11am-1am daily. **Main courses** €2.50. **No credit cards**. **Map** p305 G8 ❷

There are *Imbiss* stands on every corner of Wittenbergplatz, but this one, on the north-west side of the square just over the road from KaDeWe, is the best in the neighbourhood and quite possibly the best in the whole city. It's a friendly and courteous operation, serves only Neuland organic meat, has stunning thick-cut chips with a variety of sauces to choose from (chilli, satay, garlic mayo), and always has a queue of well-dressed folk eager to snack on a sausage that's as good as anything to be found in the food hall over the road. Wash it down with an organic Asgard beer.

Italian

XII Apostoli

Savigny Passage, Bleibtreustrasse 49 (312 1433). S5, S7, S9, S75 Savignyplatz. **Open** 24hrs daily. **Main courses** €10-€20. **No credit cards**. **Map** p312 F8 ❸

It's overcrowded, cramped and rather pricey, the service varies from rushed to rude, the music is irritating – but the pizzas are excellent and the place is never closed. Breakfast buffet at weekends. **Other locations**: S-Bahnbogen 177-80, Georgenstrasse, Mitte (201 0222); Frankfurter Allee 108, Friedrichshain (2966 9123).

Jewish

Gabriel

Jüdisches Gemeindehaus, Fasanenstrasse 79-80 (882 6138). U1, U9 Kurfürstendamm. **Open** 11.30am-3.30pm, 6.30-9.30pm Mon-Thur, Sun. **Main courses** €5-€29. **No credit cards**. **Map** p312 F8 ❹

Enter the Jewish Community Centre through airport-style security and head one floor up to this excellent kosher restaurant. On offer is a full range of Jewish central and east European specialities, including some of the best pierogi in Berlin. There's also a limited range of beers and Israeli wines to wash it down. On Tuesday from 6pm Gabriel hosts – in an adjacent room in the Centre – a mixed buffet that provides a good introduction to Jewish cuisine.

Cafés, Bars & Pubs

From breakfast to breakfast, if the bars ever close then the cafés are open.

Life in Berlin may be increasingly less leisurely, but people still find time to linger at café tables and spread out the daily papers – often provided free for your perusal. Afternoon *Kaffee und Kuchen* (coffee and cakes) remains a widely observed ritual, though the American way of coffee is making incursions.

In Berlin it's often a blurry line that separates the café from the bar. You can sometimes get breakfast, lunch, *Kaffee und Kuchen*, cocktails, dinner, and then horribly drunk into the small hours, all in the same place. But then there's also a blurry line dividing bars from clubs – if late drinking is your objective, further options will be found in the **Nightlife** chapter – and sometimes bars and/or cafés from restaurants. Many places where you might go out for dinner will also have a decent bar, and there's no law that says you have to eat to have a drink there. And just about anywhere that's open in the morning will serve some kind of breakfast (*see p152* **Where to get your early piece**), unless it's one of those places where the night before stretches well into the morning after.

Berlin is justly famous for its bars, and the inhabitants do like a drink. The capital's changing social composition means that cocktails are on the increase, and there have always been plenty of wine bars. But this is Germany and beer remains the main tipple, even though local brews are a sorry substitute for those of Bavaria and Bohemia.

People tend to pay their own way and drink at their own pace – partly because in many places bills are only totted up as you leave – but ceremonial rounds of vodka, Jägermeister or tequila are a feature of the Berlin night.

Even though the general tendency is for bars to close earlier than they used to, few places close before 1am and however late the place you're in is closing, there's bound to be somewhere else still open nearby. Just ask the bar staff – it's probably where they're going.

Mitte

Squatters in Oranienburger Strasse were the first to open cafés in the 1990s, but today it's the tourist industry that dictates the pace. Things are quieter and funkier on Auguststrasse, and the Tucholskystrasse corner bustles of an evening, but Gipsstrasse is probably the most happening nexus in this neighbourhood.

Hackescher Markt draws a lot of tourists. The restored courtyards across from the S-Bahn station are impressive, but their renovation has chased out the offbeat and left behind too many polite and over-designed bars.

Torstrasse and the Mitte-Nord area – especially around Veteranenstrasse, Rosenthaler Platz and the beginning of Kastanienallee – are happier hunting grounds and home to an assortment of eccentric establishments.

Café Aedes East

Hof II, Hackesche Höfe, Rosenthaler Strasse 40-41 (285 8271). S5, S7, S9, S75 Hackescher Markt/bus N2, N5, N8, N48, N54, N65, N92. **Open** *Summer* 10am-10pm Mon-Thur, Sun; 10am-1am Fri, Sat. *Winter* 11am-10pm Mon-Thur, Sun; 11am-midnight Fri, Sat. **Credit** AmEx, MC, V. **Map** p310 N5 ❶
This small and stylish Hackesche Höfe café fills with insiders who know that the food here is better – and better-priced – than the stuff in the larger places in the first Hof. Aedes attracts a mixture of people from the nearby theatres, bars and offices.
Other locations: Savignyplatz, S-Bahn Bogen 599, Charlottenburg (3150 9535).

Altes Europa

Gipsstrasse 11 (2404 8650/www.alteseuropa.com). U8 Weinmeisterstrasse/bus N2, N5, N8. **Open** noon-1am daily. **No credit cards. Map** p310 N5 ❷
The gentle minimalism of the decor – big picture windows, basic furnishings and nothing but a few old maps and prints on the walls – is a relief in this increasingly pretentious neighbourhood, and this spacious place is good for anything from a party to a private conversation. The bar serves light meals (€4.50-€9.50), Ukrainian vodka and draught Krusovice to a mixed, youngish crowd. The sounds are cool and the staff have a twinkle in their eye.

Barcomi's

Sophienstrasse 21, Sophie-Gips-Höfe, 2 Hof (2859 8363/www.barcomi.de). U8 Weinmeisterstrasse. **Open** *Winter* 9am-8pm Mon-Thur; 10am-9pm Fri-Sun. *Summer* 9am-10pm Mon-Thur; 10am-10pm Fri-Sun. **No credit cards. Map** p310 N5 ❸
Prominent in the renovated courtyard downstairs from the Sammlung Hoffmann (*see p87*), and serving American-style coffee and snacks and light meals,

> ❶ Pink numbers given in this chapter correspond to the location of each bar, café or pub as marked on the street maps. *See pp300-312.*

this is a popular stop for lunch or an afternoon break. Decent, but overrated and often packed. **Other locations**: Bergmannstrasse 21, Kreuzberg (694 8138).

Bergstübl

Veteranenstrasse 25 (4849 2268). U8 Rosenthaler Platz/ bus N2, N8, N84. **Open** 4pm-4am Mon-Fri; noon-late Sat, Sun. **No credit cards**. **Map** p310/p312 N4 ❹
Perhaps the most popular spot on popular Veteranenstrasse and certainly the oddest. A former fascist hangout, with old wood panelling still intact, it's now owned by an African and is strangely popular with a cruisy gay crowd. But the clientele is resolutely mixed, with hipsters sharing small tables with hardcore alkies and neighbourhood eccentrics, while an eclectic selection of DJs spin over a lousy sound system. Try a bottle of Tannenzapfel, one of Germany's best beers, but difficult to find in Berlin.

Erdbeer

Max-Beer-Strasse 56 (no phone). U2 Rosa-Luxemburg-Platz/bus N2, N54. **Open** *Summer* 2pm-late daily. *Winter* 6pm-late daily. **No credit cards**. **Map** p310 O5 ❺
The name means 'strawberry' in German, and this dark, spacious (and a bit dingy) bar off Rosa-Luxemburg-Platz has earned a reputation for its powerful and delicious fresh fruit drinks. There are other eccentric mixtures on offer, as well as the usual beers, both bottled and from the *Fass* (pump). Nightly DJs are of wildly differing styles and quality.

FC Magnet

Veteranenstrasse 26 (no phone/www.fcmagnet.de). U8 Rosenthaler Platz/bus N2, N8, N84. **Open** 8pm-late daily. **No credit cards**. **Map** p310/p312 N4 ❻
A few years ago, Berliners began transforming old-style East Berlin social clubs into fancy new bars. The slacker entrepreneurs behind FC Magnet have taken it a step further, creating a fashionable football bar complete with its own team. Though the drinks aren't exceptional, people pack in at weekends to play Kicker (table football) under a giant photograph of Franz Beckenbauer.

Galão

Weinbergsweg 8 (4404 6882/www.galao-berlin.de). U8 Rosenthaler Platz/bus N2, N8, N84. **Open**

Summer 7.30am-8pm Mon-Fri; 8am-8pm Sat, Sun. *Winter* 7.30am-7pm Mon-Fri; 8am-7pm Sat, Sun. **No credit cards**. **Map** p310 N4 ❼
Serves the best panini in the area, with delicious Milchkaffee to accompany. It's small but makes a virtue of it by tossing a few cushions on to the steps, transforming what could be a cramped, tableless restaurant into an outdoor meeting place in summer.

Gorki Park

Weinbergsweg 25 (448 7286/www.gorki-park.de). U8 Rosenthaler Platz/bus N2, N8, N84. **Open** 9.30am-2am daily. **No credit cards**. **Map** p310 N4 ❽
Tiny Russian-run café with surprisingly tasty and authentic snacks – blini, borscht and the like. Guests range from students and loafers to the occasional guitar-toting Ukrainian and scenesters having a quiet coffee before heading down to pose at more centrally located bars. Interesting weekend brunch buffet includes a selection of warm dishes, but the vodka selection is strangely disappointing.

Greenwich

Gipsstrasse 5 (2809 5566). U8 Weinmeisterstrasse/ bus N2, N5, N8. **Open** 8pm-6am daily. **No credit cards**. **Map** p310 N5 ❾
It's not long since east Berlin nightlife was mostly squats serving cheap beer and industrial vodka. But when club pioneer Cookie opened this place, still referred to as 'Cookie's Bar', the city began its half-hearted romance with glam-flecked exclusivity. Of course, this being Berlin, an Adidas jacket and an ironed shirt will probably get you in. The interior looks like a set from *Barbarella*. Increasingly a yuppie hangout, but the cocktails are top notch and the clientele is easy on the eyes. **Photo** *p147*.

Hackbarth's

Auguststrasse 49A (282 7704). U8 Weinmeisterstrasse/bus N2, N5, N8. **Open** 9am-3am daily. *Breakfast* 9am-2pm daily. **No credit cards**. **Map** p310 N5 ❿
Popular for leisurely breakfasts among ex-squatters, art-world scenesters and other long-time residents of Scheunenviertel. By night, it's less a café than a local wine bar, where the large intruding V-shaped brass counter gives the place the feel of a landlocked ship. The golden light can flatter the pale, and facilitates the pick-up tendency of late-night fun-seekers.

Eat, Drink, Shop

The best Cafés, bars & pubs

Altes Europa
A blank page to write your night on. *See p144.*

Bergstübl
Mixed, hip and really quite peculiar. *See above.*

Café Einstein
Classy breakfasts, legendary strudel. *See p156.*

Prater
A large, lusty beer garden. *See p149.*

Schwalbe
Catch the match in swish surrounds. *See p149.*

Tadschikische Teestube
A little piece of Tajikistan in Berlin. *See p146.*

Kapelle

Zionskirchplatz 22-4 (4434 1300/www.cafe-kapelle.de). U8 Rosenthaler Platz/bus N2, N8, N84. **Open** 9am-3am daily. **No credit cards**. **Map** p312 N4 ⓫

A comfortable, high-ceilinged café/bar across from the Zionskirch, Kapelle takes its name from Die Rote Kapelle, 'the Red Orchestra'. This was a clandestine anti-fascist organisation and in the 1930s and '40s the Kapelle's basement was a secret meeting place for the resistance. The regularly changing menu features organic meat and vegetarian dishes, and the proceeds are donated to local charities and social organisations.

KMA 36

Karl-Marx-Allee 36 (no phone). U5 Schillingstrasse/bus N5. **Open** 6.30pm-2am Mon-Thur, Sun; 6.30pm-6am Fri, Sat. **No credit cards**. **Map** p303 P6 ⓬

If it must, this bar with no name will answer to the above abbreviation of its official street address. In part of the GDR-constructed Café Moskau (*see p224*), it makes excellent use of the building's retro design without pandering to the banalities of Ostalgie. The decor unites communist-era wooden panelling and a wondrous glass façade that lets in city lights and allows you to observe the flotsam and jetsam on Karl-Marx-Allee. It's a snooty place, though, and rather too far up its own arse.

103

Kastanienallee 49 (4849 2651). U8 Rosenthaler Platz/bus N2, N8, N84. **Open** 9am-2am Mon-Fri; 10am-2am Sat, Sun. **No credit cards**. **Map** p312 O4 ⓭

Well-lit and airy (for Berlin), this L-shaped bar competes with Schwarz Sauer (*see p149*) to be the primary Kastanienallee hangout. The food is generally excellent, an odd mix of Asian and Italian. But more importantly, it's the perfect summer location to sit outside with a beer and watch well-coiffed local freaks strut their stuff.

Operncafé im Opernpalais

Unter den Linden 5 (2026 8433/www.opernpalais.de). U6 Französische Strasse/bus N6. **Open** 8am-midnight daily. **Credit** AmEx, MC, V. **Map** p311 N6 ⓮

A traditional coffee-and-cake stop in literally palatial surrounds. Choose from a huge selection of beautifully displayed cakes, then relax over a Milchkaffee in the elaborate interior, or sit outside in summer and watch Unter den Linden go by.

Pony Bar

Alte Schönhauser Strasse 44 (no phone). U8 Weinmeisterstrasse/bus N2, N5, N8. **Open** noon-late Mon-Sat; 6pm-late Sun. **No credit cards**. **Map** p310 O5 ⓯

This austere and edgy watering hole is an ideal place to end an evening with affordable cocktails, but it's often quiet as the grave by day. Electrolounge sounds provide a stylish soundtrack but don't drown conversation.

Roberta

Zionskirchstrasse 7 (4405 5580/www.bar-roberta.de). U8 Bernauer Strasse/bus N8, N42. **Open** 6pm-4am daily. **No credit cards**. **Map** p312 N4 ⓰

All the elements seem to be here – high ceilings, apricot walls, civilised prices and DJs playing house, easy listening, funk, soul and other music dear to the pleasantly mixed, straight and gay crowd's heart. Yet there's still something hip-bar-by-numbers about it.

Café Rosa

Rosa-Luxemburg-Strasse 41 (0172 390 6752/www.cafe-rosa.com). U2 Rosa-Luxemburg-Strasse. **Open** 9am-midnight daily. **No credit cards**. **Map** p310 O5 ⓱

Anglo-German husband-and-wife team Fiona and Rusta run this tiny, cosy café/performance space decked with vintage couches and salon-style lighting. Mornings, they serve breakfast to backpackers from the nearby Circus Hostel (*see p54*). By night they host events such as English-language readings, singer-songwriter performances and creative-writing classes. The second Thursday of the month is Talk to Strangers night, in which ordinary folk interview ordinary folk on stage.

Strandbad Mitte

Kleine Hamburger Strasse 16 (283 6877). S1, S2 Oranienburger Strasse/bus N84. **Open** 9.30am-late daily. **No credit cards**. **Map** p310 N5 ⓲

Strandbad means 'bathing beach', and this café adds a touch of seaside resort to this dead-end street off Auguststrasse. In summer, beach chairs strewn on the pavement in front of the entrance are great to sink in to – if you can get one. If not, try to grab a seat on the divan inside to sip your Milchkaffee or enjoy one of the hearty breakfasts (served till 4pm).

Tadschikische Teestube

In the Palais am Festungsgraben, Am Festungsgraben 1 (204 1112). U6, S1, S2, S5, S7, S9, S75 Friedrichstrasse. **Open** 5pm-midnight Mon-Fri; 3pm-midnight Sat, Sun. **No credit cards**. **Map** p311 N6 ⓳

An improbable gift from the Soviet Union to the people of the GDR in the early 1980s, the Tajik Tearoom is an extraordinary throwback. Sip exotic teas while lounging on the floor with samovars, low tables, plentiful rugs and cushions. It's a little faded nowadays, but worth the detour. Excellent snacks and light meals, and for less agile guests, there are a few conventional tables. Booking recommended. In the same building as the Maxim Gorki Theater (*see p238*).

3

Weydingerstrasse 20 (2804 6973). U2 Rosa-Luxemburg-Platz. **Open** 7pm-late Tue-Sat. **No credit cards**. **Map** p310 O5 ⓴

The tubas have, thankfully, been left behind, but the Kölsch culture of the Rhineland comes to Berlin in this unfinished space that serves the traditional tiny glasses of Kölsch beer on tap, as well as a few more common offerings. It's become increasingly popular with the gallery crowd from both Plattform (the artspace next door), and nearby Linienstrasse.

Space-age gin joint **Greenwich**. *See p145.*

Trommel

Kastanienallee 58 (no phone). U8 Rosenthaler Strasse. **Open** 8pm-late daily. **No credit cards.** **Map** p312 O4 ㉑
A dark neighbourhood hole with surly, educated bartenders, cheap drinks, and table football in the back. A place to meet punks and misanthropes alike.

Prenzlauer Berg

The one truly bohemian district in communist East Berlin, Prenzlauer Berg takes its cultural status perhaps a little too seriously. Kollwitzplatz is a leafy square fringed with cafés and bars. There is more of the same around the Wasserturm, at the junction of Rykestrasse and Knaackstrasse.

The cafés near Helmholtzplatz (in the so-called 'LSD' neighbourhood – the initials of Lychener Strasse, Schliemannstrasse and Dunckerstrasse) stray a bit further downmarket, stay open later and are more spontaneous than those around Kollwitzplatz. The **Prater** beer garden in nearby Kastanienallee is great on a warm summer evening, and a good starting point for crawls down Kastanienallee and into Mitte.

Café Anita Wronski

Knaackstrasse 26-8 (442 8483). U2 Senefelderplatz/ bus N2. **Open** 9am-2am daily. **No credit cards.** **Map** p312 P4 ㉒
Friendly café on two levels, with scrubbed floors, beige walls, hard-working staff and as many tables crammed into the space as the laws of physics allow. Excellent brunches, and plenty of other cafés on this stretch if there's no room here. Quiet in the afternoon, making it a good spot to sit and read.

Anna Blume

Kollwitzstrasse 83 (4404 8749/www.cafe-anna-blume.de). U2 Eberswalder Strasse. **Open** 8am-2am daily. **No credit cards.** **Map** p312 P3 ㉓
Café and florist rolled into one and named after a dada poem by Kurt Schwitters. The pastries are expensive but of high quality, the terrace is a good spot in summer, and the subdued interior, not surprisingly, smells of flowers.

Becketts Kopf

Pappelallee 64 (0162 237 9418). U2 Eberswalder Strasse. **Open** 8pm-4am Tue-Sun. **No credit cards.** **Map** p312 P2 ㉔
The head of Samuel Beckett stares from the window of this red-walled, intimate spot, which prides itself on expert cocktails and a variety of scotches and whiskeys. Prices are about average for mixed drinks in Berlin (around €7.50) but quality is several notches above. Occasional DJs play avant-jazz.

Dr Pong

Eberswalder Strasse 21 (no phone/www.drpong.de). U2 Eberswalder Strasse/bus N42. **Open** 8pm-late Mon-Sat; 2pm-late Sun. **No credit cards.** **Map** p312 O3 ㉕
Bring your table tennis bat and prepare for ping-pong madness. The action doesn't start until around midnight, but when it does you can expect around 30 players – some good, some bad – circling around

Eat, Drink, Shop

Prater. *See p149.*

the table in a game of Chinese table tennis. Beer, soda, tea and juice are available, and sometimes cakes or pastries, but otherwise no food. No tables either. Just a bunch of chairs and two couches in a smoked-out, garage-like room. Lots of fun. Be warned that opening hours are unreliable.

Eckstein

Pappelallee 73 (441 9960). U2 Eberswalder Strasse/ bus N42. **Open** 9am-1am Mon-Thur, Sun; 9am-2am Fri, Sat. **No credit cards**. **Map** p312 O2 ㉖
This beautiful café, with its broad corner front and deco-ish look, draws a mixed crowd but maintains a following among less well-scrubbed locals, adding a pleasingly bohemian feel to a place otherwise clean enough to take your parents.

8mm

Schönhauser Allee 177B (4050 0624/www.8mmbar. com). U2 Senefelderplatz/bus N2. **Open** 9pm-late daily. **No credit cards**. **Map** p310 O4 ㉗
This purple-walled dive exists to remind travellers that Berlin isn't Stuttgart. The attractive, young and poor go for that fifth nightcap into incoherence around 6am, and local scenesters rub shoulders with anglophone expats. There seems to be more hard alcohol consumed here than in your average Berlin hangout and, yes, sometimes films are shown, should anyone still be in a fit state to watch.

EKA

Dunckerstrasse 9 (4372 0612/www.eka-leka.de). U2 Eberswalder Strasse/bus N42. **Open** noon-late daily. **No credit cards**. **Map** p312 P3 ㉘
This comfortable café looks something like a 1940s American soda shop reimagined as a livery stable. Berlin always finds a way to sneak beer into an afternoon of coffee and cake, and EKA is no exception, serving both Bock and Portuguese brews.

Although in no way set up for it, it also manages to sneak in a DJ sometimes. In short, this inexpensive spot is the apotheosis of Berlin casual.

Gagarin

Knaackstrasse 22-4 (442 8807/www.bar-gagarin. de). U2 Senefelderplatz/bus N2. **Open** 10am-2am daily. **Credit** AmEx, V. **Map** p312 P4 ㉙
Brought to you by the folks who run Gorki Park (*see p145*) and Pasternak (*see p131*), adding a bar to their troika of Russian hospitality. Vogue-ish retro futurist space-age decor (colourful planets and Yuri's likeness adorn the walls) and cool electronic sounds provide the backdrop for Baltika beer and a selection of tasty Russian pub grub.

Hausbar

Rykestrasse 54 (no phone). U2 Senefelderplatz/ bus N2. **Open** 7pm-5am daily. **No credit cards**. **Map** p312 P4 ㉚
Bright red and gold, with a glorious cherub-filled sky on the ceiling, this small pocket of fabulousness seats about 15 people at a push. Hausbar is much more fun than all the wanky cafés with Russian literary names you'll find around the corner, and it's particularly inviting at three or four in the morning.

Kakao

Dunckerstrasse 10 (4403 5653/www.intveld.de). U2 Eberswalder Strasse/bus N42. **Open** noonlate daily. **No credit cards**. **Map** p312 P2 ㉛
Kitted out in standard retro orange and brown, floor-lit, and with a muted soundtrack of the laziest funk and soul, Kakao at first seems a few shades too mellow for its own good. But the glorious selection of cocoas and other hot drinks more than compensates for any heavy-handedness in the styling, and after a mug or two of thick, creamy chocolate (try it with orange, almonds or cinnamon) it's hard not to feel that this really is the most relaxing place in Berlin.

Klub der Republik

Pappelallee 81 (no phone). U2 Eberswalder Strasse/ bus N42. **Open** 8pm-4am daily. **No credit cards**. **Map** p312 O2 ㉜
Above a music school and accessed via a wobbly staircase in the courtyard, this spacious bar manages to mix the best of the retro design craze with the sort of lively revelry associated with the east in the mid 1990s. The range of beers is gratifyingly wide – try the Augustiner, one of Munich's best brews. The DJs are top notch, playing anything from 1960s soul to jazz fusion to electronica.

Laub & Frey

Kastanienallee 79 (4403 4484). U2 Eberswalder Strasse. **Open** 10am-1am Mon-Wed; 10am-late Thur-Sun. **No credit cards**. **Map** p312 O3 ㉝
A relatively plain spot resembling its Kastanienallee neighbour Schwarz Sauer (*see p149*), though not as crowded. It carries a couple of uncommon Bavarian specialities: Andechser Helles on tap, and Schamel Meerrettichschnaps. Breakfast is available until 3pm, as well as other light eats.

Looking in on **Schwarz Sauer**.

Café November

Husemannstrasse 15 (442 8425/www.cafe-november. de). U2 Eberswalder Strasse/bus N42. **Open** 9am-2am daily. **No credit cards**. **Map** p312 P3 ❸
A friendly place that's especially nice during the day when light floods in through picture windows offering views of beautifully restored Husemannstrasse. Weekend breakfast buffet (until 3pm Sat, 4pm Sun).

Prater

Kastanienallee 7-9 (448 5688/www.pratergarten.de). U2 Eberswalder Strasse/bus N42. **Open** 6-11pm Mon-Sat; 10am-11pm Sun. **No credit cards**.
Map p312 O3 ❸
Almost any evening this huge and immaculately restored swing-era bar, across the courtyard from the theatre of the same name (*see p238*), attracts a smart, high-volume crowd. The beer-swilling lustiness, big wooden tables and primeval platefuls of meat and veg (main courses €7-€15) can almost make you feel like you've been teleported to Munich. In summer the shady beer garden makes for an all-day buzz. Brunch is served from 10am to 4pm on Saturdays and Sundays. **Photo** *p148*.

Rakete

Schönhauser Allee 39A (0177 309 2249). U2 Eberswalder Strasse/bus N2. **Open** 8pm-late Mon-Sat. **No credit cards**. **Map** p312 O3 ❸
Small, white and bright, with minimalist furnishings and playing minimal techno, this has become a casual hangout for music and film scenesters, though it's just as likely to be almost empty. No draught beer, but the bartenders know how to mix a drink.

Razzia in Budapest

Oderberger Strasse 38 (4862 3620/www.razzia-in-budapest.de). U2 Eberswalder Strasse. **Open** 6pm-late daily. **No credit cards**. **Map** p312 O3 ❸

East Berlin not Ost enough for you? This wood-panelled spot boasts a 'Hungarian' feel that veers from cosy to crazed. There's Böhmisches dark beer on tap, and the bartenders pride themselves on their ten house cocktails with names such as 'Sommer in Budapest' and 'Razzia'. At weekends the DJs serve up a diet of oldies.

Schwalbe

Stargarder Strasse 10 (4403 6208/www.schwalbe berlin.de). U2, S8, S41, S42, S85 Schönhauser Allee. **Open** 4pm-2am Mon-Fri; 3pm-4am Sat; 3pm-2am Sun. **No credit cards**. **Map** p303 P2 ❸
Unwilling to endure identikit Irish pubs or brave surly local *Eck-Kneipen* (corner pubs)? Schwalbe is about as chi-chi as a football bar gets, offering German and Italian league games in a fashionable café environment where you can grab a coffee and cake instead of a beer. Downstairs there are three weirdly crowded Kicker (table football) tables and DJs on Saturday.

Schwarz Sauer

Kastanienallee 13 (448 5633). U2 Eberswalder Strasse/bus N42. **Open** 8am-6am daily. **No credit cards**. **Map** p312 O3 ❸
Possibly the most popular bar on Kastanienallee and currently the main meeting place for those who inhabit the twilight zone between Prenzlauer Berg and Mitte. Strangely, its ambience is sort of plain, its waitstaff Berlin surly, and its food and drink of only adequate quality. But in summer the outside tables overflow day and night. In winter a tolerance for cigarette smoke is helpful.

Villa Orange

Eberswalder Strasse 35 (0163 742 4944/www. villaorange.com). U2 Eberswalder Strasse/bus N42. **Open** *Winter* 6.30pm-late Mon-Fri; noon-late Sat,

Sun. *Summer* 3pm-late Mon-Fri; noon-late Sat, Sun. **No credit cards. Map** p312 O3 ⓭

A pleasant alternative to the more hectic side of Berlin's nightlife, this relaxed and stylish little bar never seems to get too full. Jumble-sale furniture and a small warren of interconnecting spaces lend it a comfortably ramshackle feel and movies are sometimes shown in the larger of two main rooms.

Wohnzimmer

Lettestrasse 6 (445 5458). U2 Eberswalder Strasse/ bus N42. **Open** 10am-4am daily. **No credit cards. Map** p312 ⓮

Immediately behind the door of this shabbily elegant 'living room' there's a suspiciously bar-like structure made from an inspired ensemble of kitchen cabinets. Threadbare divans and artsy bar girls make this the perfect place to discuss Dostoevsky with career students over a tepid borscht. Evening light from candelabra reflects on gold-sprayed walls as students and maudlin poets chase brandies with Hefeweizen. Daytimes can be sluggish.

Zum Goldenen Hirschen

Lychener Strasse 43 (5471 4680). U2 Eberswalder Strasse. **Open** 7pm-3am Mon-Thur, Sun; 7pm-4am Fri, Sat. **No credit cards. Map** p312 P2 ⓯

This strikingly modernist glass box of a bar is an anomaly in the Helmholtzplatz area. It's not particularly popular, but mixes a decently priced and above-average cocktail, offers exotic snacks and has DJs several nights a week. It can feel a bit like sitting in an aquarium, but that makes a nice change of pace from the usual smoke-and-cellar experience. Happy hour from 7pm to 8.30pm.

Friedrichshain

The area around Simon-Dach-Strasse is ground zero for Berlin's young bohemia, full of fun bars, cheap cafés and ethnic takeaways. But it's also begun to acquire a settled feel as its orbit expands east towards Ostkreuz.

Rigaer Strasse and Mainzer Strasse were once hubs of the militant squatting scene, and an element of disgruntled radicalism persists. Locals may sneer if you wear your designer togs or attempt to pay with a credit card.

Down by the Spree, bars give way to clubs and Friedrichshain begins to connect with a reviving Kreuzberg on the opposite bank. Meanwhile, the socialist showcase boulevard Karl-Marx-Allee also has its watering holes, but more as an eastern extension of the Mitte scene than a western outpost of Friedrichshain's.

Conmux

Simon-Dach-Strasse 35 (291 3863). U5 Frankfurter Tor or U1, S3, S5, S7, S9, S75 Warschauer Strasse/ bus N5, N29. **Open** *Summer* 9am-late daily. *Winter* 10am-late daily. **No credit cards. Map** p308 S7 ⓭

For those into sitting outside, there are pavement tables here even in winter, when the waiters will

light big gas heaters to warm you up. Inside there are sewing-machine tables and pieces of scrap-metal art. The menu offers well-priced light meals. Service is at best monosyllabic, at worst totally indifferent.

Ehrenburg

Karl-Marx-Allee 103A (4210 5810). U5 Weberwiese/ bus N5. **Open** 10am-late daily. **No credit cards. Map** p309 R6 ⓭

Named after Russian-Jewish novelist Ilja Ehrenburg, a dedicated socialist, this café and espresso bar, with its sober, geometric decoration, is one of the few stylish places around Weberwiese U-Bahn station. Although the library looks like it's part of the decorative style, you're free to pick up a book and study the works of Ehrenburg, Lenin, Stalin, Engels or Marx as you enjoy a latte macchiato and other capitalist achievements.

Fargo

Grünberger Strasse 77 (2900 5720). U5 Frankfurter Tor or U1, S3, S5, S7, S9, S75 Warschauer Strasse/ bus N5, N29. **Open** 5pm-late Mon-Fri; 10am-late Sat, Sun. **No credit cards. Map** p308 T7 ⓭

Any place with a happy hour and a 'hungry hour' can't be bad. From 6pm to 8pm every day you can buy cheap drinks and also get a hearty meal for just €2.90. Fargo also features an ample Sunday brunch buffet from 10am to 4pm. The pool table and amiable waitstaff should keep you entertained, and the modest late-night kitchen (open until midnight) will leave you satisfied. Happy hour also all Monday; Tuesday is Caipirinhas at €3.60 a pop. **Photo** *p151.*

Intimes

Boxhagener Strasse 107 (2966 6457). U5 Samariterstrasse/bus N5. **Open** 10am-late daily. **No credit cards. Map** p308 T7 ⓭

Next to the cinema of the same name, decorated with painted tiles and offering a good variety of Turkish and vegetarian food, as well as breakfast at reasonable prices. Pleasures can be as simple as fried potatoes with garlic sausage; best deal is the Wednesday special. Decent selection of beers, friendly service.

Kuntsliche BEATmung

Simon-Dach-Strasse 20 (0176 2334 8125). U1, S3, S5, S9, S75 Warschauer Strasse/bus N5, N29. **Open** 7.30pm-late daily. **No credit cards. Map** p308 S7 ⓭

The low-domed ceiling, plastic furniture and coloured neon can make this trendy cocktail bar feel like the inside of a space capsule – and slightly weird before the crowds arrive. Around midnight, though, the beautiful young things start dribbling in, and any oddness is soon swallowed in the crush. The elaborate drinks menu provides hundreds of lurid opportunities for experimental boozing.

Café 100Wasser

Simon-Dach-Strasse 39 (2900 1356). U5 Frankfurter Tor or U1, S3, S5, S7, S9, S75 Warschauer Strasse/bus N5, N29. **Open** 9.30am-late daily. **No credit cards. Map** p308 T7 ⓭

The all-you-can-eat brunch buffet (€8.50, 9.30am-4pm daily) has a cult following among students and other late risers. Take your time over the food and don't start to panic as the buffet gets plundered: for just when the food seems to be finished, out comes loads of new stuff.

Paule's Metal Eck

Krossener Strasse 15 (291 1624). U5 Frankfurter Tor or U1, S3, S5, S7, S9, S75 Warschauer Strasse/bus N5, N29. Open Winter 7pm-late daily. Summer 5pm-late daily. No credit cards. Map p308 S7 ⓵

Neither a typical heavy metal bar, nor remotely typical for this area, the Egyptian-themed Eck attracts a young crowd with relentless metal videos, a decent selection of beers, and both pool and table football. Inoperative disco balls, mummy overhead lamps and formidable dragon busts deck an interior that is half designed like a mausoleum, and half in gloomy medieval style. A small menu changes weekly and there's live Bundesliga football on weekends.

Café Schönbrunn

Am Schwanenteich, im Volkspark Friedrichshain (4679 3893). Bus 200. Open 10am-1am Mon-Fri; 10am-2am Sat, Sun. Credit V. Map p303 Q5 ⓾

Not for those afraid to walk in the park at night, but for everyone else it's a favoured hangout. A couple of years ago, this place by the lake sold coffee and snacks to an elderly crowd. With a change of management, the music and food improved dramatically. The unspectacular concrete front was left as it was, and the (new) lounge furniture is pure 1970s. On a sunny afternoon, older park-goers take their first afternoon beer on the terrace next to the in-crowd having breakfast. For your first visit come in daytime – just to make sure you find it.

Supamolly

Jessnerstrasse 41 (2900 7294). U5, S4, S8, S85 Frankfurter Allee/bus N5. Open 8pm-late Tue-Sun. No credit cards. Map p308 U7 ⓾

Having opened in the early 1990s as a semi-legal bolthole fronting a lively squat, Supamolly (or Supamolli) is a miracle of survival. The frequent live punk and ska shows in the club behind the bar dictate only some of the clientele; a healthy mix of young and ageing punks, unemployed activists and music lovers of all types gather in this dim, mural-smeared, candlelit watering hole until the early morning. DJs at weekends.

Tagung

Wühlischstrasse 29 (2977 3788). U5 Samariterstrasse/bus N5. Open 7pm-4am Mon-Fri; 7pm-5am Sat, Sun. No credit cards. Map p308 T7 ⓾

Small bar decked in GDR memorabilia and still serving things like Club Cola, the old Eastern brand. The patrons are twenty- and thirtysomethings and the place seems to provide good laughs and drunken nights for all. The small club downstairs is likewise 'ostalgically' decorated and offers mainstream dance music and occasional one-off events.

Kreuzberg

Enough ageing scenesters and alternative types have hung on in west Berlin's former art and anarchy quarter to ensure some kind of atmosphere. And there has been a revival in the area around Schlesisches Tor, where Kreuzberg faces off against Friedrichshain across the Spree.

The district around Oranienstrasse and Wiener Strasse offers a variety of opportunities for drinking, partying or breakfasting, and is also one of the city's gay hubs.

Though well supplied with cafés and lively by day, the Bergmannstrasse neighbourhood offers little in the way of partying after dark – except for a bit of life on the gay scene.

Café Adler

Friedrichstrasse 206 (251 8965). U6 Kochstrasse/bus N29, N84. Open 10am-midnight Mon-Sat; 10am-7pm Sun. Credit AmEx, MC, V. Map p311 M8 ⓾

'Hungry hour' at **Fargo**. *See p150.*

Where to get your early piece

Breakfast is a big thing in Berlin, especially at weekends, when people still have time to make a meal of it. Germans invite each other around for *Frühstück* (literally 'early piece') the way other cultures stage dinner parties, or go out to meet friends and linger over brunch in their favourite café.

Scrambled eggs (*Rühreier*) are often on the à la carte part of the breakfast menu – the **Atlantic** (*see p152*) offers them scrambled in 11 different ways – and some old-school places will offer a Hoppel Poppel (also known as a *Bauernfrühstück*), which is a kind of hearty ham and potato omelette. But otherwise a German *Frühstück* has little in common with a British fry-up or an American diner breakfast. The basic deal is cold rather than cooked: an assortment of bread rolls, cold cuts, cheeses, jam or honey, and maybe a soft-boiled egg.

Pretty much any café that's open in the morning will offer something of the sort. At the budget end there is usually a *kleines Frühstück* – a roll or two with jam or honey, what anglophones call a 'continental breakfast'. At the other there are grandiose productions involving *Sekt* (sparkling wine) and smoked salmon. At weekends, many places offer elaborate brunch buffets, such as those at **Café 100Wasser** (*see p150*), **Prater** (*see p149*), **XII Apostoli** (*see p143*) or **Café November** (*see p149*). In summer many places have pavement tables, and at **Café Einstein** (*see p156*) or **Café Schönbrunn** (*see p151*) you can eat surrounded by greenery.

In between, there are variations. A *Käse Frühstück* will offer a selection of cheeses to go with a basket of rolls. A *Fitness Frühstück* involves yoghurt, muesli and fruit. Breakfasts often take on national themes. A French one will have a croissant or two. An Italian one will involve mozzarella and tomatoes. At **Gorki Park** (*see p145*) you can try a Russian breakfast. **Tim's Canadian Deli** (*see p156*), **Andy's Diner** (*see p138*) or **Barcomi's** (*see p144*) offer North American breakfasts. And most of the city's Irish pubs can rustle up a recognisably 'English' breakfast. Other places theme breakfasts according to their name or function: **Potemkin** (*see p155*) does breakfasts themed on the titles of Eisenstein films.

In deference to long Berlin nights, most places that serve breakfast carry on doing so until mid-afternoon or later. And for those whose sense of time becomes totally dislocated by too much clubbing and carousing, the **Schwarzes Café** (*see p157*) serves breakfast day and night.

You could have watched history in the making from your seat at a table in this elegant corner café, which is next to what used to be Checkpoint Charlie. Today it's a bustling and business-like corner, with Café Adler remaining a well-lit oasis of calm, coffee and decent light meals.

Anker-Klause

Kottbusser Brücke/corner of Maybachufer, Neukölln (693 5649/www.ankerklause.de). U8 Schönleinstrasse/bus N8. **Open** 4pm-late Mon; 10am-late Tue-Sun. **No credit cards. Map** p307 P9 🟢
Although looking over Kreuzberg's Landwehrkanal, the only thing nautical about this 'anchor den' is the midriff-tattooed, punk-meets-portside swank of the bar staff. A slamming jukebox (rock, sleaze, beat), a weathery terrace and good sandwich melts offer ample excuse to dock here from afternoon until whenever the staff decide to close. Convivial during the week, packed at weekends.

Atlantic

Bergmannstrasse 100 (691 9292). U6, U7 Mehringdamm/bus N19. **Open** *Winter* 9am-1.30am daily. *Summer* 9am-2am daily. **No credit cards. Map** p306 M10 🟢

On the south side of the street, the pavement café thrives in the summer, and a beer as late as 8pm will still have you sitting in a ray of light, if you're lucky enough to get a table. Breakfast, including 11 different ways to have your eggs scrambled, is served until 5pm. There are also daily lunch specials, and dinner is a cheap but decent affair.

Barbie Deinhoff's

Schlesische Strasse 16 (no phone/www.bader-deinhoff.de). U1 Schlesisches Tor/bus N29. **Open** 6pm-2am Mon-Thur, Sun; 6pm-6am Fri, Sat. **No credit cards. Map** p308 R9 🟢
Run by celebrity drag queen Lena Braun (star of the fashionable documentary *Gender X*), this lively and unusual bar attracts both the more bourgeois members of Berlin's cross-dressing community and the loucher denizens of the Kreuzberg mainstream. The look is pitched somewhere between tacky kitsch and futuristic chic. Often lectures and art events in the early evening, before the debauchery kicks off.

Cake

Schlesische Strasse 32 (6162 4610/www.cake-bar.de). U1 Schlesisches Tor/bus N29. **Open** 4pm-late daily. **No credit cards. Map** p308 R9 🟢

A diverse crowd in age and nationality – the hostel across the street lends a youthful international air – mills about in this lounge equipped with old easy chairs, sofas, art-bedecked walls and a dark red, musty interior. Music gently hums overhead, providing a great atmosphere for relaxing and conversing. There's even a vintage jukebox equipped with a variety of oldies. DJs most weekends for free. Happy hour from 7pm to 9pm daily.

Careca Bar & Café

Falkenstein 42 (2501 1293). U1 Schlesisches Tor/bus N29. **Open** 6pm-4am daily. **No credit cards**. **Map** p308 R9 🖲

This modern cocktail bar and café offers a comprehensive selection of cocktails, long drinks and wines, as well as tea and excellent coffee. Don't come for the three types of bottled beer, though, or the desultory snack selection. Women often dominate the scene, possibly because this is one of the few bars in the area that isn't dark and dingy. Sit at petite, low, well-lit tables in the front room or lounge on couches in the side room. Sometimes there are DJs.

Haifischbar

Arndtstrasse 25 (691 1352/www.haifischbar-berlin.de). U6, U7 Mehringdamm/bus N19. **Open** 8pm-3am Mon-Thur, Sun; 8pm-5am Fri, Sat. **No credit cards**. **Map** p306 M10 🖲

Well-run and friendly bar where the staff are expert cocktail-shakers, the music's hip and tasteful in a trancey kind of way, and the back room, equipped with a sushi bar, is a good place to chill out at the end of an evening. Certainly the most happening place in the Bergmannstrasse area, and with some kind of crowd any night of the week.

Madonna

Wiener Strasse 22 (611 6943). U1 Görlitzer Bahnhof/bus N29, N44. **Open** 3pm-late daily. **No credit cards**. **Map** p307 Q9 🖲

With over 100 whiskies, and frescoes detailing a lascivious pageant of falling angels and clerical inebriation, this bar and café offers a friendly vantage on the debauched, counter-culture erudition of Kreuzberg thirtysomethings. Particularly interesting as neutral ground for subcultures that, until Berlin's modernisation frenzy gave them common cause, had differing opinions on the proper way to burn a car, squat a building or play a guitar.

Milagro

Bergmannstrasse 12 (692 2303/www.milagro.de). U7 Gneisenaustrasse/bus N4, N19. **Open** 9am-1am Mon-Thur, Sun; 9am-2am Fri, Sat. **No credit cards**. **Map** p306 M10 🖲

Friendly café, known for excellent breakfasts (until 4pm). Other cheap but classy dishes (soups, pasta) are served until midnight. Disorienting stairs lead to hospital-like toilets. A lot of the light in the front room comes from big picture windows – great in summer, but it can get too dim to read on winter afternoons.

Café Bar Morena

Wiener Strasse 60 (611 4716/www.morena-berlin. de). U1 Görlitzer Bahnhof/bus N29, N44. **Open** 9am-late daily. **No credit cards**. **Map** p307 Q9 🖲

Famous breakfasts are served to people who wake up at all hours. In the evening the place bustles and service can be slow. The music isn't overpowering, and half-tiled walls and parquet flooring lend an art deco feel. Outside tables in summer – and a couple of other decent cafés up the road when these get full.

The **Old Emerald Isle**. *See p154.*

Mysliwska
Schlesische Strasse 35 (611 4860). U1 Schlesisches Tor/bus N29, N65. **Open** 6pm-late daily. **No credit cards. Map** p308 R9 ⓒ
This small, dark bar draws a mixed local crowd and doesn't get going until late. The spartan interior boasts old, small, poker-like tables and stiff wooden chairs. Except for a pistachio dispenser and a frequently unpopulated, disco-balled side room, frills are kept to a minimum. Live music once or twice a month and DJs most weekends (for which there's no entrance fee).

The Old Emerald Isle
Erkelenzdamm 49 (615 6917/www.old-emerald-isle.de). U1, U8 Kottbusser Tor/bus N8, N29. **Open** noon-2am Mon-Thur, Sun; noon-4am Fri, Sat. **No credit cards. Map** p307 O9 ⓒ
Decent all-purpose Irish pub with draught Guinness and Kilkenny, a big selection of hearty meals, plenty of televisions for watching British and Irish football and rugby matches, a pleasant beer garden on the quiet street outside and a cheerfully rowdy atmosphere throughout. **Photo** *p153*.

Wiener Blut
Wiener Strasse 14 (618 9023). U1 Görlitzer Bahnhof/bus N29, N44. **Open** 6pm-late Mon-Fri, Sun; 3.30pm-late Sat. **No credit cards. Map** p307 Q9 ⓒ

A narrow, darkish bar equipped with lazy booths and a well-abused table football table, Wiener Blut sometimes features DJs who pack the place with wild beats and wild friends. Otherwise it's just another red bar. Tables out front in the summer are a good alternative to the overcrowded terrace of Morena (*see p153*) up the street.

Würgeengel
Dresdener Strasse 122 (615 5560). U1, U8 Kottbusser Tor/bus N8. **Open** 7pm-late daily. **No credit cards. Map** p307 P9 ⓒ
Red walls and velvet upholstery convey an atmosphere aching for sin, while well-mixed cocktails and a fine wine list served by smartly dressed waiting staff make this a place for the more discerning drinker. The glass-latticed ceiling and a 1920s chandelier elegantly belie the fairly priced drinks and tapas on offer. Nice in summer, when a canopy of greenery curtains outdoor picnic tables.

Schöneberg

Civilised, tolerant and cosmopolitan, the gentrified borough of Schöneberg retains a hint of its more radical past and, along Motzstrasse and Fuggerstrasse, has possibly the world's oldest – and certainly the city's biggest – gay quarter. You'll find numerous

The night is still young at the **Pinguin Club**. *See p155.*

bars and shops there, catering to all tastes and fetishes. Around Winterfeldtplatz there is a concentration of lively cafés, especially so on market days (which are Wednesday and Saturday). Bars can be crawled on and around Goltzstrasse and the junction with Hohenstaufenstrasse.

Green Door

Winterfeldtstrasse 50 (215 2515/www.greendoor.de). U1, U2, U3, U4 Nollendorfplatz/bus N2, N5, N19, N26. **Open** 6pm-3am Mon-Thur; 6pm-4am Fri, Sat; 8pm-3am Sun. **No credit cards**. **Map** p306 J9
It really does have a green door, and behind it there's a whole lotta cocktail shaking going on – the drinks menu is impressively long. There's also a nice long and curvy bar, perhaps a few too many yuppies, and a good location off Winterfeldtplatz.

Mutter

Hohenstaufenstrasse 4 (216 4990). U1, U2, U3, U4 Nollendorfplatz/bus N2, N5, N19, N26. **Open** 10am-4am daily. **Credit** AmEx, MC, V. **Map** p306 J10
'Mother' tries to do everything at once: two bars; an enormous selection of wines, beers and cocktails; breakfasts until 6pm; a sushi bar from 6pm, plus other snacks throughout the day. It's a big place, but it can be difficult to find a seat on weekend nights, when trancey house plays in the front bar (there are more sedate sounds in the café area at the back). It's

roomy, the decor is heavy on gold paint and the spectacular corridor to the toilets is worth a visit in itself.

Pinguin Club

Wartburgstrasse 54 (781 3005/www.pinguin-club.de). U7 Eisenacher Strasse/bus N4, N48. **Open** 9pm-4am daily. **No credit cards**. **Map** p306 J11
Though a little past its heyday, this speakeasy-style bar remains one of Berlin's finest and friendliest institutions. It's decorated with original 1950s Americana and rock 'n' roll memorabilia, the owners all have punk roots and good sounds are a feature. Take your pick from 156 spirits, and don't be surprised if everyone begins to dance to disco or sing along to Nick Cave tunes. **Photo** *p154.*

Potemkin

Viktoria-Luise-Platz 5 (2196 8181). U4 Viktoria-Luise-Platz/bus N46. **Open** 8am-1am Tue-Sun. **No credit cards**. **Map** p305 H9
Film stills and the likeness of *Battleship Potemkin* director Sergei Eisenstein adorn the wall, and the red and black decor has an appropriately constructivist feel. Breakfasts also sport titles of Eisenstein films, from the basic 'Ivan the Terrible' to 'Viva Mexico' with marinated chicken breast served with pineapple and cheese on toast. There's also a daily lunch special and snacks such as mozzarella rolls stuffed with serrano ham.

Eat, Drink, Shop

Schleusenkrug – the place for a canalside tipple in the Tiergarten. *See p156.*

Savarin

Kulmer Strasse 17 (216 3864). U7, S1, S2, S26 Yorckstrasse/bus N19. **Open** 10am-10pm Tue-Fri; 10am-8.30pm Sat, Sun. **No credit cards. Map** p306 K10 ⓱

Cosy café with a sophisticated edge and famously excellent cakes and pies. On Sundays it's not just that you can't find a seat – you can't even get in the door for all the people queuing to take away cheesecake slices and apple tarts. Vegetarian snacks too.

Suzy's

Hohenstaufenstrasse 69 (0160 9147 8364). U1, U2, U3, U4 Nollendorfplatz/bus N2, N5, N19, N26. **Open** 8pm-late Tue-Thur; 9pm-late Fri, Sat. **No credit cards. Map** p306 J10 ⓲

Friendly neighbourhood bar that often fills its two-room space with readings, DJs, performances and themed events, but is just as good for nursing a drink into the small hours at the counter, where the amiable owner holds court.

Tim's Canadian Deli

Maassenstrasse 14 (2175 6960). U1, U2, U3, U4 Nollendorfplatz/bus N2, N5, N19, N26. **Open** 1am Mon-Fri; 8am-late Sat; 9am-1am Sun. **Credit** AmEx, MC, V. **Map** p306 J9 ⓳

Against the odds, this place seems to have conquered the Winterfeldtplatz area, though there's not a café round here that's not full on a market day. Lots of bagels and muffins, egg breakfasts until 4pm, various light meal options.

Zoulou Bar

Hauptstrasse 4 (7009 4737). U7 Kleistpark/bus N4, N48. **Open** 8pm-6am daily. **No credit cards. Map** p306 J10 ⓴

Small bar with a funky vibe and occasional DJs. It can get packed between 10pm and 2am; after that the crowd thins and late is the best time for a visit.

Tiergarten

The area around Potsdamer Strasse is kind of a northern Schöneberg, its scene overlapping with that of the neighbouring borough. Around Lützowplatz it's rather more upmarket. We can sadly find little to recommend among all the shiny new franchises of Potsdamer Platz.

Bar am Lützowplatz

Lützowplatz 7 (262 6807/www.baramluetzowplatz. com). U1, U2, U3, U4 Nollendorfplatz/bus N2, N5, N19, N26. **Open** 2pm-late daily. **Credit** AmEx, MC, V. **Map** p306 J8 ⓱

Long bar with a long drinks list and classy customers in Chanel suits sipping expensive, well-made cocktails as they compare bank balances.

Café Einstein

Kurfürstenstrasse 58 (261 5096/www.cafeeinstein. com). U1, U2, U3, U4 Nollendorfplatz/bus N2, N5, N19, N26. **Open** 9am-1am daily. **Credit** AmEx, DC, MC, V. **Map** p306 J8 ⓲

Viennese-style coffeehouse with waiters in bow ties, international papers to read and an Apfelstrudel of legend. In summer you can enjoy a leisurely garden breakfast (served all day).

Other locations: Unter den Linden 42, Mitte (204 3632).

Joseph Roth Diele

Potsdamer Strasse 75 (2636 9884). U1 Kurfürstenstrasse. **Open** 10am-midnight Mon-Fri. **No credit cards. Map** p306 K8 ⓱

A traditional Berlin book café, just a stroll south of Potsdamer Platz, that pays homage to the life and work of inter-war Jewish writer Joseph Roth. Decorated in ochre tones, it's an amiable place with comfy seating, offering teas, coffees, wines, beers, snacks and stunning value light meals. Look for lunchtime specials from just €3; limited menu on Friday evening.

Kumpelnest 3000

Lützowstrasse 23 (261 6918). U1 Kurfürstenstrasse/ bus N2, N5, N48. **Open** 5pm-5am Mon-Thur, Sun; 5pm-late Fri, Sat. **No credit cards. Map** p306 K8 ⓳

This perennially popular and studiedly tacky establishment is at its best at the end of a long Saturday night, when it's crowded and chaotic and everyone is attempting to dance to disco classics.

Schleusenkrug

Müller-Breslau-Strasse/Unterschleuse (313 9909/www.schleusenkrug.de). S5, S7, S9, S75 Tiergarten/bus N9. **Open** *Winter* 10am-6pm daily. *Summer* 10am-1am daily. **No credit cards. Map** p305 G7 ⓴

Bar and beer garden directly on the canal in the Tiergarten, with easy listening, mod and indie pop nights. During the day the place retains much of its original flavour, hingeing on nautical themes and large glasses of Pils. **Photo** *p155*.

Victoria Bar

Potsdamer Strasse 102 (2575 9977/www.victoriabar. de). U1 Kurfürstenstrasse/bus N2, N5, N48. **Open** 6.30pm-3am Mon-Thur, Sun; 6.30pm-4am Fri, Sat. **No credit cards. Map** p306 K9 ⓴

Funky, grown-up cocktail bar for a relaxed, mixed crowd. The low-key concept – long bar, subdued lighting, restrained colours, muffled funk, and staff who work well together and know what they're mixing – is successful enough that this place feels like it's been here for ever. But actually it opened as recently as 2003.

Charlottenburg & Wilmersdorf

There are pockets of café life around Karl-August-Platz, Ludwigkirchplatz and Savignyplatz, but the last decent club checked out sometime in the early 1990s and the ageing bars are no match even for those in neighbouring Schöneberg, never mind in Mitte.

Galerie Bremer.

Galerie Bremer

Fasanenstrasse 37 (881 4908). U3, U9
Spichernstrasse/bus N9. **Open** *Gallery* 2-6pm Tue-Fri; 11am-1pm
Sat. **No credit cards. Map** p312 F9 ⓷
In the back room of a tiny gallery, this bar has the
air of a well-kept secret. The room is painted in deep,
rich colours and has a beautiful ship-like bar
designed by Hans Scharoun, architect of the
Philharmonie (*see p234*) and Staatsbibliothek. When
the assistant barman takes your coat and welcomes
you, it's meant to make you feel at home, and it's also
the done thing to make a little conversation with the
majestically bearded owner – he'll remember next
time you drop in. Then you can sit back, feel privi-
leged, and watch the odd member of parliament
entering incognito.

Diener

Grolmanstrasse 47 (881 5329). S5, S7, S9, S75
Savignyplatz/bus N27, N49. **Open** 6pm-2am daily.
No credit cards. Map p312 F8 ⓷
Diener is an authentically old-style Berlin bar. The
place is named after a famous boxer, and the walls
are adorned with faded murals showing hunting
scenes and photographs of famous Germans you
won't recognise. Enter here and you could almost be
in 1920s Berlin. Almost.

Café Hardenberg

Hardenbergstrasse 10 (312 2644/www.cafe-
hardenberg.de). U2 Ernst-Reuter-Platz/bus N45.
Open 9am-1am daily. **Credit** V. **Map** p312 F7 ⓷

Across from the Technical University and usually
packed with students drinking coffee. Simple, decent
pasta, salads and sandwiches at reasonable prices.

Leysieffer

Kurfürstendamm 218, Wilmersdorf (885 7480). U1
Uhlandstrasse. **Open** 9am-7pm Mon-Sat; 11am-5pm
Sun. **Credit** AmEx, DC, MC, V. **Map** p312 F8 ⓷
Exquisite tortes and fruitcakes are served upstairs
in the high-ceilinged café. Tempting mounds of truf-
fles and bonbons are sold downstairs in the shop.

Café im Literaturhaus

Fasanenstrasse 23 (882 5414/www.literatur-berlin.
de). U1 Uhlandstrasse/bus N10, N19, N21, N27.
Open 9.30am-1am daily. **No credit cards. Map**
p312 F8 ⓷
The café of the Literaturhaus, which has lectures,
readings and a bookshop. The greenhouse-like winter garden or salon rooms are great for tucking into
a book over breakfast or a snack.

Schwarzes Café

Kantstrasse 148 (313 8038). S5, S7, S9, S75
Savignyplatz/bus N27, N49. **Open** 24hrs daily;
closed for cleaning 6-10am Tue. **No credit cards.**
Map p312 F8 ⓷
Open all hours for breakfasts and meals, it was once
all black and anarchistically inclined (hence the
name) but the political crowd moved on decades ago
and the decor has been brightened. Service can get
overstretched if it's crowded, such as early on a
weekend morning when clubbers stop for breakfast
on their way home.

Eat, Drink, Shop

Shops & Services

Retail opportunities that are idiosyncratic, individualistic and irreducibly Berlin.

While it also boasts upmarket centres with every international chain from agnès b to Zara, what Berlin does best is offer both space and independence to small, idiosyncratic businesses. Scattered across the city, in backyards and sometimes otherwise barren streets, in neighbourhoods from the punky bohemia of Friedrichshain to the well-heeled pavements of Charlottenburg, are individual fashion labels and design boutiques, second-hand shops and eccentric specialists. If you're prepared to put in the footwork, shopping in Berlin can be more akin to a day on the set of an indie art film than a crude consumerist activity.

Conventional shopping can be found in abundance on Tauentzienstrasse and Kurfürstendamm in the west end, and along Friedrichstrasse in Mitte. The former has the **KaDeWe**, continental Europe's biggest department store, and blocks of everyday and upmarket chains. Interior design and household goods can be found in abundance between the Ku'damm and Kantstrasse. Luxury brands cluster around Fasanenstrasse.

Across town, on Friedrichstrasse, is some slightly funkier shopping, with department stores such as **Galeries Lafayette** and **Quartier 206** rubbing shoulders with the cultural cornucopia that is **Dussmann das KulturKaufhaus**. Potsdamer Platz is stuck

on its own in between these two centres, with an unremarkable but useful arcade full of chain stores (and some of the best ice-cream in Berlin).

The edgier cultural experience starts… well, wherever you choose. Music and fashion are huge here and, in keeping with the emphasis on the individual and entrepreneurial, you'll find gems and bargains that reflect a city keyed into, and determined to forge an identity within, the vinyl and streetwear revolution. Start in the upper price ranges with the polished but cutting-edge boutiques around Alte and Neue Schönhauser Strasse and the Hackesche Höfe in Mitte. Then move to the elegant bohemian assortments on and around Kastanienallee in Prenzlauer Berg. Friedrichshain has recently started to boom, with the Boxhagener/Simon-Dach-Strasse axis now unfolding to include music shops and streetwear boutiques around Grünberger Strasse and Wülischstrasse. Across the river, the area around Kreuzberg's Oranienstrasse is pumping with both local and national designers, and reworked vintage wares. The same borough's Bergmannstrasse area is a rich seam for books and music. Further west, in Schöneberg, is the lively **Winterfeldt Markt**, and good antique and curiosity shops abound on Winterfeldtstrasse and Goltzstrasse.

OPENING HOURS

Shops can sell goods until 8pm on weekdays and 6pm Saturdays (8pm for department stores and supermarkets). Those in central areas keep these hours, but shops in residential areas begin shutting at 6pm on weekdays and 3pm on Saturday. But the general tendency is for more shops to stay open longer. On Sundays, only shops in stations are allowed to stay open, although late-night delis (*Spätkauf*) have begun to find loopholes and many bakeries open for a couple of hours on Sunday afternoon to satisfy indigenous demand for cake. Most big stores open between 8.30am and 9am, newsagents and bakeries as early as 6am, and smaller or independent shops around 10am or later.

Antiques

Collectors and browsers with an interest in the 18th and 19th centuries will find many of the better dealers on **Keithstrasse** and **Goltzstrasse** in Schöneberg. The streets around **Fasanenplatz** in Wilmersdorf are

The best | Shops

Claudia Skoda Level
Designer clothes combining graceful lines and innovative fabrics. *See p167.*

IrieDaily
Skate style with an *Ost* flavour. *See p172.*

Marga Schoeller Bücherstube
Independently run and helpful to a fault. All bookshops should be like this. *See p161.*

Mondos Arts
Buy some of the East – the western conglomerates all have. *See p180.*

Weichardt-Brot
Love bread? Feed that passion. *See p175.*

good, as is **Suarezstrasse** in Charlottenburg. In the east, **Grünberger Strasse** in Friedrichshain and **Kollwitzstrasse** and **Husemannstrasse** in Prenzlauer Berg are home to small, unpretentious Antiquariäten. *See also* **Souvenirs** and **Flea markets**.

Deco Arts
Motzstrasse 6, Schöneberg (215 8672). U1, U2, U3, U4 Nollendorfplatz. **Open** 3-6.30pm Wed-Fri; 11am-3pm Sat. **No credit cards. Map** p306 J9.
Shell-shaped 1930s sofas and other deco furniture at fair prices, the odd piece by Marcel Breuer and Carl Jacobs, and some 1950s and '60s treasures. If a sofa's too big to get home, pick up a stylish ashtray or vase.

Emma Emmelie
Schumannstrasse 15A, Mitte (2838 4884). U6 Oranienburger Tor. **Open** 1-7.30pm Tue-Fri; or by appointment. **Credit** AmEx, DC, MC, V. **Map** p302/p311 L5.
This subterranean gem has the atmosphere of a lost era, with antique linens and clothes from the early 20th century, plus dolls, jewellery, glasses and china.

Fingers
Nollendorfstrasse 35, Schöneberg (215 3441). U1, U2, U3, U4 Nollendorfplatz. **Open** 2.30-6.30pm Tue-Fri; 11am-2.30pm Sat. **No credit cards. Map** p306 J9.
Splendid finds from the 1940s, '50s and '60s, including lipstick-shaped cigarette lighters, vintage toasters, weird lighting and eccentric glassware.

Radio Art
Zossener Strasse 2, Kreuzberg (693 9435/www. radio-art.de). U7 Gneisenaustrasse. **Open** noon-6pm Thur, Fri; 10am-1pm Sat. **Credit** AmEx, MC, V. **Map** p307 N10.
A fine collection of antique radios, ranging from big wooden 1930s sitting-room centrepieces to tiny 1970s transistors in shocking pink plastic. Half a century of receivers in perfect working order.

Beauty salons

Marie France
Fasanenstrasse 42, Charlottenburg (881 6555). U1 Uhlandstrasse. **Open** 9am-6pm Mon-Fri; 9am-2pm Sat. **Credit** MC, V. **Map** p305 F9.
The cosmeticians speak reasonable English and use luxurious French products at this clean, pleasant salon, which has been glamming up Berliners for over 30 years. Hot-wax depilation is a speciality.

Tietgen & Kahlcke: Friseure & Spa
Rosa-Luxemburg-Strasse 11-13, Mitte (2809 1918/ www.cutandcure.de). U2 Rosa-Luxemburg-Platz. **Open** 11am-8pm Mon-Fri; noon-6pm Sat. **Credit** MC, V. **Map** p303/p310 O5.
This new salon operates in conjunction with Aveda and the new hotel Lux 11 (*see p52*) next door. Its internationally trained hairdressers and stylists are personable and savvy; therapists offer body wraps, massage, and skin and nail care. Reasonable prices.

Books

Although the chains are spreading, Berlin still has a lively independent bookshop scene. For gay bookshops, *see p215*.

Berlin Story
Unter den Linden 40, Mitte (2045 3840/www.berlin story.de). U6 Französische Strasse. **Open** 10am-7pm daily. **Credit** AmEx, MC, V. **Map** p302/p311 M6.
You won't find a better stock of Berlin-related books in German and English: everything from novels with Berlin settings to non-fiction volumes on history and culture. Also historical maps, posters, videos, CDs, postcards and souvenirs.

Bücherbogen
Savignyplatz Bogen 593, Charlottenburg (3186 9511/www.buecherbogen.com). S3, S5, S7, S9, S75 Savignyplatz. **Open** 10am-8pm Mon-Fri; 10am-6pm Sat. **Credit** MC, V. **Map** p305/p312 F8.
The store for all manner of art books. This branch stocks international magazines and books on painting, sculpture, photography and a little architecture; the branch at S-Bahnbogen 585 does film; and round the corner in Knesebeckstrasse there's a good selection of discounted art books and remainders.
Other locations: S-Bahnbogen 585, Charlottenburg (312 1932); Knesebeckstrasse 27, Charlottenburg (8868 3695).

Hammett
Friesenstrasse 27, Kreuzberg (691 5834/www. hammett-krimis.de). U7 Gneisenaustrasse. **Open** 10am-8pm Mon-Fri; 9am-4pm Sat. **Credit** MC, V. **Map** p307 N10.
Small, friendly store specialising in crime and mystery novels, new and second-hand. Plenty in English.

Kohlhaas & Company
Fasanenstrasse 23, Wilmersdorf (882 5044). U1 Uhlandstrasse. **Open** 10am-8pm Mon-Fri; 10am-6pm Sat. **Credit** AmEx, MC, V. **Map** p305/p312 F9.
German literature predominates in this elegant little highbrow bookshop under the Literaturhaus.

Modern Graphics
Oranienstrasse 22, Kreuzberg (615 8810/www. modern-graphics.de). U1, U8 Kottbusser Tor. **Open** 10am-8pm Mon-Fri; 10am-6pm Sat. **Credit** MC, V. **Map** p307 P9.
Large selection of imported and alternative comics. Also T-shirts, graphic novels, anime and calendars. **Other locations:** Bundesallee 83, Friedenau (8599 9054).

ProQM
Alte Schönhauser Strasse 48, Mitte (2472 8520/ www.pro-qm.de). U8 Weinmeisterstrasse. **Open** noon-8pm Mon-Fri; noon-6pm Sat. **Credit** MC, V. **Map** p303/p310 O5.
Artist owners offer a well-informed and cosmopolitan selection of new and used books and mags on architecture, art, design, pop culture, town planning and cultural theory – including many in English.

Antiquarian & second-hand books

There are small antiquarian booksellers all over Berlin, and many have a shelf or two of English books along with whatever else they specialise in. The areas around **Knesebeckstrasse** in Charlottenburg, **Winterfeldtstrasse** in Schöneberg and **Kollwitzstrasse** and **Husemannstrasse** in Prenzlauer Berg all offer decent literary pickings.

English-language books

Another Country
Riemannstrasse 7, Kreuzberg (6940 1150/www. anothercountry.de). U7 Gneisenaustrasse. **Open** 11am-8pm Mon-Fri; 11am-6pm Sat. **No credit cards**. **Map** p306 M10.
Spacious, welcoming premises housing an ambitious bookshop and private library stocked with over 10,000 English-language titles – a lot of them science fiction – from the collection of British owner Alan Raphaeline. A small membership fee allows you to use the reading room downstairs and help yourself to tea and coffee, or borrow books for varying fees. Return them to recoup a deposit, or hang on to the book. Also readings and other activities.

Books in Berlin
Goethestrasse 69, Charlottenburg (313 1233/www. booksinberlin.de). S3, S5, S7, S9, S75 Savignyplatz. **Open** noon-8pm Mon-Fri; 10am-4pm Sat. **Credit** V. **Map** p305/p312 E7.
Run by a Bostonian and stocking a dynamic selection of new and used history and politics, classical and modern fiction, reference and travel books, this is something of a Berlin institution.

East of Eden
Schreinerstrasse 10, Friedrichshain (423 9362). U5 Samariterstrasse. **Open** noon-7pm Mon-Sat. **No credit cards**. **Map** p309 T6.
The owners of this old-school second-hand shop shuttle to London in search of paperback staples and rare editions. Books are also available to borrow at a small fee. Readings and concerts too.

Fair Exchange
Dieffenbachstrasse 58, Kreuzberg (694 4675). U8 Schönleinstrasse. **Open** 11am-7pm Mon-Fri; 10am-6pm Sat. **No credit cards**. **Map** p307 P10.
Big selection of second-hand English-language books, with an emphasis on literature.

Hugendubel
Tauentzienstrasse 13, Charlottenburg (214 060/ www.hugendubel.de). U1, U2, U3 Wittenbergplatz. **Open** 9.30am-8pm Mon-Fri; 9am-4pm Sat. **No credit cards**. **Map** p305 G8.
Berlin's largest bookshop houses more than 140,000 books, including a big English-language section. **Other locations**: Friedrichstrasse 83, Mitte (2063 5100).

English books at **St Georges**.

Le Matou
Husemannstrasse 29, Prenzlauer Berg (2809 9601). U2 Eberswalderstrasse. **Open** 10am-6.30pm Mon-Fri; 10am-2pm Sat. **No credit cards**. **Map** p303/p312 P3.
International books for children and young people in English, French, Italian, Spanish, Arabic and Russian, with some 3,000 titles in stock.

Marga Schoeller Bücherstube
Knesebeckstrasse 33, Charlottenburg (881 1112/ 1122). S3, S5, S7, S9, S75 Savignyplatz. **Open** 9.30am-7pm Mon-Wed; 9.30am-8pm Thur, Fri; 9.30am-4pm Sat. **Credit** MC, V. **Map** p305/p312 F8.
Rated as Europe's fourth-best independent literary bookshop by *Bookseller*, this excellent establishment, founded in 1930, includes a self-contained English-language section that's one of Berlin's most interesting. Staff are sweet, helpful, know the stock and will track down anything not on their shelves.

St Georges
Wörther Strasse 27, Prenzlauer Berg (8179 8333). Tram M2 Marienburger Strasse. **Open** 1-8pm Mon-Fri; 11am-6pm Sat. **No credit cards**. **Map** p303/p312 P3.
Comfortable leather couches are provided for browsing a decent and reasonably priced selection of second-hand English-language books. Lots of biographies and contemporary lit, and a good turnover of dog-eared classics.

Storytime Books
Schmargendorfer Strasse 36-7, Friedenau (8596 7004/www.storytime-books.com). U9 Friedrich-Wilhelm-Platz. **Open** 10am-6pm Mon-Fri; 9.30am-1.30pm Sat. **Credit** AmEx, MC, V.

Owner Diane Pentaleri-Otto specialises in children's books and works hard to make the shop child- and parent-friendly. There are many events for kids (a weekly story time in English, singalongs in English and German), and coffee and muffins for grown-ups.

Children's clothes & toys

Wooden toys are a German speciality. Puppets from the Dresdener puppet factory and tiny wooden figures from Erzgebirge are distinctive. Stuffed toys are another traditional offering: Steiff (which claims to have invented the teddy bear) and its rival Sigikid offer beautifully made cuddly animals. **Storytime Books** and **Le Matou** (*see p161*) are great kids' bookshops.

Emma & Co

Niebuhrstrasse 2, Charlottenburg (8867 6787). S3, S5, S7, S9, S75 Savignyplatz. **Open** 11am-7pm Mon-Fri; 11am-4pm Sat. **Credit** MC, V. **Map** p305/p312 E8.
Melanie Waltje's charming shop within Bramigk & Breer (*see p165*) offers well-made but not exorbitant children's wear, bedding, toys and gift items such as name books and terry-cloth teddies.

Heidi's Spielzeugladen

Kantstrasse 61, Charlottenburg (323 7556). U7 Wilmersdorfer Strasse. **Open** 9.30am-6.30pm Mon-Fri; 9.30am-2pm Sat (until 4pm at Christmas time). **Credit** MC, V. **Map** p304 D8.
Wooden toys, including cookery utensils and child-sized kitchens, are the attraction here. Also a good selection of books, puppets and wall-hangings.

H&M Kids

Kurfürstendamm 237, Charlottenburg (884 8760/ www.hm.com). U1, U9 Kurfürstendamm. **Open** 10am-8pm Mon-Sat. **Credit** AmEx, DC, MC, V. **Map** p305/p312 G8.
The place for cute, cheap clothes for kids up to 14. This branch has the largest children's department.

Michas Bahnhof

Nürnberger Strasse 24A, Schöneberg (218 6611/ www.michas-bahnhof.de). U3 Augsburger Strasse. **Open** 10am-6.30pm Mon-Fri; 10am-4pm Sat. **Credit** AmEx, DC, MC, V. **Map** p305 G8.
Small shop packed with model trains, old and new, and everything that goes with them.

Nix Design

Heckmann Höfe, Oranienburger Strasse 32, Mitte (281 8044/www.nix.de). S1, S2 Oranienburger Strasse. **Open** noon-8pm Mon-Fri; noon-6pm Sat. **Credit** AmEx, MC, V. **Map** p303/p310 N5.
In addition to her women's collection, avant-garde designer Barbara Gebhardt does a great kids' line.

Peekaboo Kindermoden

Prenzlauer Allee 213, Prenzlauer Berg (4849 6092/www.peekaboo-kindermoden.de). Tram M2 Marienburger Strasse. **Open** 10am-6.30pm Mon-Fri; 10am-2pm Sat. **Credit** AmEx, MC, V. **Map** p303/p312 P4.

A wonderful selection of classy designer handbags for little girls and beautiful clothing for boys and girls up to age five.

Tam Tam

Knesebeckstrasse 59-61, Charlottenburg (882 1454). S3, S5, S7, S9, S75 Savignyplatz. **Open** 10am-7.30pm Mon-Fri; 10am-7pm Sat. **Credit** MC, V. **Map** p305/p312 F9.
A bright, charming shop filled with stuffed animals and wooden toys, including building blocks, trains, trucks, dolls' houses, plus child-sized wooden stoves.

v.Kloeden

Wielandstrasse 24, Charlottenburg (8871 2518/ www.vonkloeden.de). U7 Adenauerplatz. **Open** 10am-7pm Mon-Fri; 10am-4pm Sat. **Credit** AmEx, DC, MC, V. **Map** p305/p312 E9.
The oldest and friendliest toy store in town stocks children's books in English, toys and reading material from the Montessori and Steiner schools, building blocks by German aviator Otto Lilienthal, handmade Käthe Kruse dolls, Erzgebirge wooden figures, and all kinds of modern fare.

Cosmetics

Belladonna

Bergmannstrasse 101, Kreuzberg (694 3731/www. bella-donna.de). U7 Gneisenaustrasse. **Open** 10am-7pm Mon-Fri; 10am-6pm Sat. **Credit** AmEx, MC, V. **Map** p306 M10.
Natural and flower-essence products from Logona, Lavera, Dr Hauschka and Weleda, plus Primavera essential oils and lamps to burn them in, jostle with brushes, make-up and baby clothes.

MAC

Rosenthaler Strasse 36, Mitte (2404 8730/www. maccosmetics.com). U8 Rosenthaler Platz. **Open** 11am-8pm Mon-Fri; 11am-6pm Sat. **Credit** MC, V. **Map** p303/p310 N5.
A mirror-lined cosmetic wonderland. This stuff is worn by every star who graces a red carpet, but the shop doesn't feel too exclusive: personal attention is excellent and you are encouraged to try products. Splurge on some serious make-up drama, but save money and buy your sponges at Woolworths.

Department stores

There is little to distinguish the four main chains: **Hertie**, **Karstadt**, **Kaufhof** and **Wertheim** all offer decent quality at similar prices.

Dussmann das KulturKaufhaus

Friedrichstrasse 90, Mitte (202 50/www.kultur kaufhaus.de). U6, S1, S2, S3, S5, S7, S9, S75 Friedrichstrasse. **Open** 10am-10pm Mon-Sat. **Credit** AmEx, MC, V. **Map** p302/p311 M6.
Intended as a 'cultural department store', this spacious four-floor retailer mixes books with CDs, videos with magazines, and has internet terminals, an interactive video-viewing room and a DVD shop.

Galeries Lafayette

*Französische Strasse 23, Mitte (209 480/www.
galerieslafayette.de). U2, U6 Stadtmitte.* **Open**
10am-8pm Mon-Sat. **Credit** AmEx, DC, MC, V.
Map p306/p311 M7.

This Jean Nouvel glass block houses a refreshing
shopping experience: great clothes, frequent sales
on the upper floors, a good selection of accessories
and cosmetics at street level and, best of all, a
basement food hall where you'll feel transported
to Paris among fresh cheeses, chocolates, wines,
breads and condiments.

KaDeWe

*Tauentzienstrasse 21-4, Schöneberg (212 10/
www.kadewe.de). U1, U2, U3 Wittenbergplatz.*
Open 10am-8pm Mon-Fri; 9.30am-8pm Sat.
Credit AmEx, DC, MC, V. **Map** p305 H9.

The largest department store in continental Europe
celebrates its 100th birthday in 2007. It carries name
brands in all departments, though the merchandise
can be hit and miss. KaDeWe is most famous for its
lavish food hall, which takes up the entire sixth floor.
The delicatessen is known for its specialities, the
gourmet bars offer everything from oysters and
champagne to beer and smoked sausage, and phone
orders can be made for more outré items (2121 1700).

Kaufhof

*Alexanderplatz 9, Mitte (247 430/www.galeria-
kaufhof.de). U2, U5, U8, S5, S7, S9, S75
Alexanderplatz.* **Open** 9am-8pm Mon-Sat. **Credit**
AmEx, DC, MC, V. **Map** p303/p310 O5.

The Kaufhof group bought the old GDR Centrum
stores and so dominates the eastern market. Once
the retail showpiece of communist East Berlin, this

Window shopping **Galeries Lafayette**.

Eat, Drink, Shop

Furniture through the looking-glass. *See p165.*

busy, utilitarian megastore was undergoing massive renovation and expansion at press time and had sadly already lost its 1970s façade.

Naturkaufhaus

Schlossstrasse 101, Steglitz (797 3716/www. naturkaufhaus-berlin.de). U9 Schlossstrasse. **Open** *Summer* 10am-8pm Mon-Fri; 10am-6pm Sat. *Winter* 10am-8pm Mon-Fri; 10am-8pm Sat. **Credit** AmEx, MC, V.

Berlin's first department store for organic goods spreads over two floors of the Galleria mall. The stock ranges from the usual foodstuffs you find in local healthfood shops to eco-friendly clothes, shoes and cosmetics, and a selection of wines.

Quartier 206

Friedrichstrasse 71, Mitte (2094 6240/www.quartier 206.de). U2, U6 Stadtmitte. **Open** 10.30am-7.30pm Mon-Fri; 10am-6pm Sat. **Credit** AmEx, DC, MC, V. **Map** p306/p311 M7.

Reminiscent of New York's Takashimaya and designed by that city's Calvin Tsao, this upmarket store offers not just the most lusted-after designers, but the definitive items from those labels. Cult cosmetics and centuries-old perfumes are on the ground floor; upstairs is devoted to women's and men's fash-

ion, lingerie, jewellery and shoes – with a Manolo Blahnik department – plus a home-living section stocked with sinfully expensive design items.

Design & household goods

Interior design has stormed the city since **stilwerk** appeared on Kantstrasse. Both **Alte** and **Neue Schönhauser Strasse** are good for neo-cool eastern and western designs from the 1950s to 1970s. **Grünberger Strasse** in Friedrichshain is good for funky antiques and well-kept furniture stores.

Bramigk & Breer

Niebuhrstrasse 1, Charlottenburg (882 7373). S3, S5, S7, S9, S75 Savignyplatz. **Open** 11am-7pm Mon-Fri; 11am-4pm Sat. **Credit** MC, V. **Map** p305/p312 E8.

Bramigk & Breer strikes a good balance between Mediterranean and Brandenburg country style with stripped-down furniture, warm lighting and irresistible ornaments. Highlights include natural linens, hand-blown drinking glasses in elegant colours and realistic silk flowers. Also houses Emma & Co (*see p162*).

Big bag in the foreground, more in the **BagGround**. *See p166*.

Coldampf's

Uhlandstrasse 54-5, Charlottenburg (883 9191/
www.coledampfs.de). U3 Hohenzollernplatz. **Open**
10am-8pm Mon-Fri; 10am-4pm Sat. **Credit** MC, V.
Map p305 F9.

An impressive 7,000 products to equip any kitchen,
from high-tech utensils to sturdy cocktail glasses.
Other locations: Wörtherstrasse 39, Prenzlauer
Berg (4373 5225).

DIM

Oranienstrasse 26, Kreuzberg (2850 30121/www.
blindenanstalt.de). U1, U8 Kottbusser Tor. **Open**
10am-7pm Mon-Fri; 10am-2pm Sat. **No credit**
cards. Map p307 P9.

A Design Institute initiative for the blind. Witty,
high-style brushes and wicker items, all handmade.

dopo_domani

Kantstrasse 148, Charlottenburg (882 2242/www.
dopo-domani.com). S3, S5, S7, S9, S75 Savignyplatz.
Open 10.30am-7pm Mon-Fri; 10am-6pm Sat. **Credit**
AmEx, MC, V. **Map** p305/p312 E8.

A temple for design aficionados. Combining an interior design practice with a well-stocked shop, the
focus is on Italian outfitters and the presentation creates an environment you'll dream of calling your own.

Furniture

Sredzkistrasse 22, Prenzlauer Berg (4434 2157).
U2 Eberswalder Strasse. **Open** 12.30-7pm Tue,
Fri; 2-7pm Wed; 12.30-8pm Thur; 12.30-4pm Sat.
No credit cards. Map p303/p312 P3.

This is a reasonably priced and well-thought-out
selection of retro furniture, TVs, radios and lamps.
Lots of plastic in burnt orange and brown and lus-
cious olive green, and a huge, enjoyable range of
wallpaper from the 1960s and '70s. **Photo** *p164*.

Leinenkontor

Tucholskystrasse 22, Mitte (2839 0277/www.
leinenkontor.com). S1, S2 Oranienburger Strasse.
Open 10am-6pm Tue-Sat. **Credit** MC, V. **Map**
p302/p310 M5.

Textile designer Eva Endruweit's shop has linens
for table and bed, drawn from her own no-frills
collection, the exquisite Austrian company Leitner
and Sweden's royal purveyor Ekelund.

Ruby

Oranienburger Strasse 66, Mitte (2838 6030).
S1, S2 Oranienburger Strasse. **Open** 11am-8pm
Mon-Fri; 11am-6pm Sat. **Credit** AmEx, MC, V.
Map p302/p310 M5.

Flying the minimalist flag, this small shop in a beautifully restored courtyard offers Spencer Fung's architectural furniture, Bowls & Linares lamps and Henry Dean glass, as well as rugs, fabrics, candles and an alluring selection of ceramics in earth tones.

Schlafwandel
Kantstrasse 21, Charlottenburg (312 6523/www. schlafwandel.de). S3, S5, S7, S9, S75 Savignyplatz. **Open** 10am-6.30pm Mon-Fri; 10am-4pm Sat. **No credit cards. Map** p305/p312 F8.
Top brands in towelling and linen for bath and bed, plus a huge selection of robes and pyjamas.

stilwerk
Kantstrasse 17, Charlottenburg (315 150/www. stilwerk.de). S3, S5, S7, S9, S75 Savignyplatz. **Open** 10am-8pm Mon; 10am-6pm Sat. **Credit** AmEx, MC, V. **Map** p305/p312 F8.
This huge, glassy haven of good taste was opened in 1999 as a theme mall for high-end products and continues to anchor the Kantstrasse area. There are over 50 retailers, purveying modern furnishings, state-of-the-art kitchens, high-tech lighting and luxurious bathroom fittings among a vast assortment of interior items by every major player from Alessi to Zanussi. There's also a fourth-floor showcase for the work of local craftspeople and designers.

Claudia Skoda Level. *See p167.*

Fashion

Major international names cluster along the **Kurfürstendamm** and **Friedrichstrasse**, with traditional luxury brands focused on **Fasanenstrasse** in Charlottenburg. Local innovations can be found in and around the **Hackesche Höfe** and **Heckmann Höfe** in Mitte. This is where younger designers tend to have their ateliers and outlets. Innovative local labels also set up shop on **Kastanienallee** in Prenzlauer Berg, **Boxhagener Strasse** and **Wülischstrasse** in Friedrichshain, and **Schlesiche Strasse** and **Oranienstrasse** in Kreuzberg. The best of these places carry a smart mix of local and international labels that sit somewhere between office and street, and together create a distinctly Berlin style.

Accessories

BagGround
Gipsstrasse 23B, Mitte (2758 3177/www.bag-ground. com). U8 Weinmeisterstrasse. **Open** noon-8pm Mon-Sat. **Credit** MC, V. **Map** p303/p310 N5.
This small, colourful shop is full of handbags hip and bright, plain or nightclubby, from classic to extraordinary, from €35 to €300. **Photo** *p165.*

Blush
Rosa-Luxemburg-Strasse 22, Mitte (2809 3580/ www.blush-berlin.com). U2 Rosa-Luxemburg-Platz. **Open** noon-7pm Mon-Wed; noon-8pm Thur, Fri; noon-6pm Sat. **Credit** MC, V. **Map** p303/p310 O5.
Beautiful lingerie in lace and silk. Imports from France and Italy, as well as German brands.

Fiona Bennett
Grosse Hamburger Strasse 25, Mitte (2809 6330/ www.fionabennett.com). S3, S5, S7, S9, S75 Hackescher Markt. **Open** 10am-6pm Mon-Fri; noon-6pm Sat; or by appointment. **Credit** AmEx, DC, MC, V. **Map** p303/p310 N5.
British-born Fiona Bennett's hats are works of art. She has mastered the sloping, wide brim, and crafts horned headdresses, feathered fedoras, hats reminiscent of insects or sea urchins, and delicate hairpieces made of a single feather shaped into a curl or of simple stars that frame the cheekbones. For all their theatrics, these hats are classic and beautiful.

Fishbelly
Sophienstrasse 7A, Mitte (2804 5180/www.fish belly.de). U8 Weinmeisterstrasse. **Open** 12.30-7pm Mon-Fri; noon-6pm Sat. **Credit** AmEx, DC, MC, V. **Map** p303/p310 N5.
Often compared to London's Agent Provocateur, this tiny Hackesche Höfe shop is licensed to thrill with extravagant undergarments by designers such as Dolce & Gabbana Intimo, Capucine Puerari and Christian Dior. Also be sure to check out Fishbelly's own-brand line of imaginative lingerie.

Les Dessous

Fasanenstrasse 42, Wilmersdorf (883 3632/ www.les-dessous.de). U3, U9 Spichernstrasse. **Open** 11am-7pm Mon-Fri; 10am-3pm Sat. **Credit** AmEx, DC, MC, V. **Map** p305 F9.

A beautiful shop featuring luxurious lingerie, silk dressing gowns and striking swimwear by Eres, Capucine, Dior, La Perla and Andres Sarda. **Other locations**: Schlüterstrasse 36, Charlottenburg (881 3660).

Mane Lange Korsetts

Hagenauer Strasse 13, Prenzlauer Berg (4432 8482/ www.manelange.de). U2 Eberswalder Strasse. **Open** 2-7pm Wed-Fri; noon-6pm Sat; or by appointment. **No credit cards**. **Map** p303/p312 P3.

Lovely original corsets in lush materials, handmade on the premises by local designer Mane Lange. Bustiers come off the rack, otherwise custom orders require a fitting but are completed in 24 hours.

Knopf Paul

Zossener Strasse 10, Kreuzberg (692 1212/www. paulknopf.de). U7 Gneisenaustrasse. **Open** 9am-6pm Tue, Fri; 2-6pm Wed, Thur. **No credit cards**. **Map** p307 N10.

A Kreuzberg institution that stocks thousands of buttons in every shape, colour and style. Whatever you're seeking, Paul Knopf ('button') will help you find it. His patient and amiable service is remarkable considering most transactions are for tiny sums.

Designer: international

Antonie Setzer

Bleibtreustrasse 19, Charlottenburg (883 1350/www. antoniesetzer.de). S3, S5, S7, S9, S75 Savignyplatz. **Open** 10am-7pm Mon-Fri; 10am-6pm Sat. **Credit** AmEx, DC, MC, V. **Map** p305/p312 E8.

Stock and labels change seasonally, but the fashion for women is intelligently selected from the likes of Prada, D&G, Miu Miu, Coach and Maliparmi.

Harvey's

Kurfürstendamm 56, Charlottenburg (883 3803/ www.harveys-berlin.de). U7 Adenauerplatz. **Open** 11am-8pm Mon-Sat. **Credit** AmEx, DC, MC, V. **Map** p305/p312 E9.

Frieder Bahnisch has been selling cutting-edge men's labels for 20 years. He stocks Japanese designers, both established and up-and-coming (UnderCover and Number 9); Belgian labels, such as Bikkembergs and Martin Margiela; and the Italian Carpe Diem.

Mientus Studio 2002

Wilmersdorfer Strasse 73, Charlottenburg (323 9077/www.mientus.com). U7 Wilmersdorfer Strasse. **Open** 10am-7pm Mon-Sat. **Credit** AmEx, DC, MC, V. **Map** p304 D8.

Clean cuts for sharp men from a range of collections including Dsquared, Neil Barrett, Helmut Lang, Miu Miu, Andrew Mackenzie and German rave labels. **Other locations**: Schlüterstrasse 26, Charlottenburg (323 9077); Ku'damm 52, Charlottenburg (323 9077).

Patrick Hellmann

Bleibtreustrasse 36, Charlottenburg (882 6961/ www.patrickhellmann.com). S5, S7, S9, S75 Savignyplatz. **Open** 9.30am-8pm Mon-Fri; 9.30am-6pm Sat. **Credit** AmEx, DC, MC, V. **Map** p305/p312 E8.

Prolific Berlin retailer with five other stores to his name, specialising in international chic for men and women. A bespoke tailoring service offers men the choice of the Hellmann design range in a variety of fabrics, including some by Italian textile maestro Ermenegildo Zegna. **Other locations**: Fasanenstrasse 29, Wilmersdorf (881 1985); Kurfürstendamm 53, Charlottenburg (882 2565).

T&G

Rosenthaler Strasse 34-5, Mitte (2809 2790). U8 Weinmeisterstrasse or S5, S7, S9, S75 Hackescher Markt. **Open** 11am-8pm Mon-Fri; 10am-6pm Sat. **Credit** MC, V. **Map** p303/p310 N5.

Kai Angladegies is not the first to fuse fashion and fine art, but 'Tools & Gallery' is a bold and enjoyably pretentious attempt. The interior is rococo, with candelabras and muslin-draped cubicles. Names for men and women include Givenchy, Alexander McQueen and Vivienne Westwood, with menswear especially strong. The gallery is accessed via a beautiful 1860 wrought-iron staircase and features exhibitions of fine art, design and haute couture.

Designer: local

Claudia Skoda Level

Linienstrasse 156, Mitte (280 7211). U6 Oranienburger Tor. **Open** noon-8pm Mon-Fri; noon-7pm Sat. **Credit** AmEx, MC, V. **Map** p303/p310 N5.

Berlin's most established womenswear designer has extended her range to include men – designs for both sexes are showcased in this loft space. Using high-tech yarns and innovative knitting techniques, the collections bear her signature combination of stretch fabrics and graceful drape effects. **Photo** *p166*.

Elternhaus

Alte Schönhauser Strasse 14, Mitte (2759 6900/ www.elternhaus.com). U8 Weinmeisterstrasse. **Open** 1-7pm Mon-Fri; noon-6pm Sat. **No credit cards**. **Map** p303/p310 O5.

Elegant streetwear created by an artist and design collective out of Hamburg. Witty German slogans are printed across beautifully tailored T-shirts for men, women and children. Also keyrings, bags and beautiful military-style jackets.

Killerbeast

Schlesische Strasse 31, Kreuzberg (9926 0319/ www.killerbeast.de). U1 Schlesisches Tor. **Open** 3-7.30pm Mon; noon-7.30pm Tue-Fri; 11am-5pm Sat. **Credit** MC, V. **Map** p308 R9.

Old things are turned new again by designer Claudia Weiler, who sits in the shop and sews solid and stylish jackets, shirts and skirts that sit nicely between office-suitable and street savvy. A children's line called Schnüllerbeast is her latest innovation.

Lisa D

Hackesche Höfe, Rosenthaler Strasse 40-41, Mitte (282 9061/www.lisad.com). U8 Weinmeisterstrasse or S3, S5, S7, S9, S75 Hackescher Markt. **Open** 11am-7.30pm Mon-Sat. **Credit** AmEx, MC, V. **Map** p303/p310 N5.

Long, flowing womenswear in subdued shades from this avant-garde designer. Austrian-born Lisa D is well known on the Berlin fashion scene and was one of the first to move into the Hackesche Höfe.

Molotow

Gneisenaustrasse 112, Kreuzberg (693 0818/ www.molotowberlin.de). U7 Mehringdamm. **Open** 2-8pm Mon-Fri; noon-4pm Sat. **Credit** AmEx, MC, V. **Map** p306 M10.

Showcasing local talent, Molotow sells fashion and millinery for men and women. Clothes are fresh and eye-catching, ranging from futuristic creations to classical sharp tailoring. Custom tailoring available.

RespectMen

Neue Schönhauser Strasse 14, Mitte (283 5010). U8 Weinmeisterstrasse. **Open** noon-8pm Mon-Fri; noon-6pm Sat. **Credit** AmEx, MC, V. **Map** p303/p310 O5.

Dirk Seidel and Karin Warburg's menswear seems traditionally tailored on the rail, yet shows a body-conscious, contemporary cut when worn. Trousers, jackets, suits and coats can be made to order. Also stocks Bikkembergs and Paul Smith.

Yoshiharu Ito

Rosa-Luxemburg-Strasse 5, Mitte (4404 4490/ www.itofashion.com). U2, U5, U8, S5, S7, S9, S75 Alexanderplatz. **Open** noon-8pm Mon-Sat. **Credit** AmEx, MC, V. **Map** p303/p310 O5.

Tokyo-born Ito's showroom offers his purist collections for men, which are in the tradition of Asian designers like Yamamoto but with strong European influences. His styles are practical, with great attention to details like perfectly worked pockets and seams in unusual places. With a nod to the avant-garde, Ito mixes a futuristic style with classic wool or lacquered cotton for fun and wearable clothes.

Fetish

For quality rubber and latex clobber, visit **Black Style** (*see p215*); **Leathers** (*see p215*) produces excellent leather and SM gear.

Schwarze Mode

Uhlandstrasse 71, Wilmersdorf (784 5922/www. schwarze-mode.de). U7 Kleistpark. **Open** 10am-8pm Mon-Fri; 10am-6pm Sat. **Credit** AmEx, DC, MC, V. **Map** p305 F10.

Leatherette, rubber and vinyl are among the delicacies stocked here for *Gummi* enthusiasts. As well as fetish fashions, next door in Schwarze Medien you'll find erotic and SM books, DVDs, CDs and mags.

Mid-range

Luzifer

Alte Schönhauser Strasse 33, Mitte (2804 2335/ www.luzifer.com). U8 Weinmeisterstrasse. **Open** noon-8pm Mon-Fri; 11am-6pm Sat. **Credit** AmEx, MC, V. **Map** p303/p310 O5.

Natural hemp and linen clothing for men and women, mostly unstructured and in simple shapes. **Other locations**: Adalbertstrasse 89, Kreuzberg (615 2239).

To Die For

Neue Schönhauser Strasse 10, Mitte (2838 6834). U8 Weinmeisterstrasse. **Open** noon-8pm Mon-Fri; 11am-7pm Sat. **Credit** AmEx, MC, V. **Map** p303/p310 O5.

Slip into instant party mode with ready-to-wear collections from the likes of D&G. **Other locations**: Alte Schönhauser Strasse 41, Mitte (2463 9643).

Second-hand clothes & shoes

Berlin's thrift-store aesthetic means that the city has busy flea markets and a profusion of junk shops and second-hand stores. There are particularly happy hunting grounds for used clobber around **Mehringdamm** in Kreuzberg and **Grünberger Strasse** in Friedrichshain, but idiosyncratic outlets can be found in most inner-city neighbourhoods. Look out also for branches of **Humana**, the super-cheap charity chain, which has its biggest outpost at Frankfurter Tor in Friedrichshain (2315 335).

Anziehend

Niederbarnimstrasse 16, Friedrichshain (2936 7829). U5 Frankfurter Tor. **Open** 11am-7pm Mon-Fri; 11am-4pm Sat. **No credit cards**. **Map** p308 T7.

This sweet store buys and sells well-maintained clothes and accessories, most with a modern twinge. Lots of elegant and playful scarves and neckwear, plus vintage H&M.

Calypso – High Heels For Ever

Rosenthaler Strasse 23, Mitte (2854 5415/www. calypsoshoes.com). U8 Weinmeisterstrasse. **Open** noon-8pm Mon-Fri; noon-4pm Sat. **No credit cards**. **Map** p303/p310 N5.

Hundreds of stilettos, wedges and platforms in vivid shades and exotic shapes from the 1930s to 1980s, almost all in fine condition. Also a selection of thigh-high, stilettoed fetish boots, some in men's sizes. **Other locations**: Oderberger Strasse 61, Prenzlauer Berg (281 6165).

Colours

1st courtyard, Bergmannstrasse 102, Kreuzberg (694 3348/www.kleidermarkt.de). U7 Gneisenaustrasse. **Open** 11am-7pm Mon-Fri; 11am-6pm Sat. **Credit** MC, V. **Map** p307 M10.

The shop that wasn't there

In the winter of 2004, just a few weeks before Christmas, there appeared a mysterious but in no way inconspicuous kind of storefront on Rosenthaler Strasse in Mitte. Bang in the middle of a cutting-edge shopping area, the place was large and light and looked more like a designer's showroom than a shop. Two long hangers ran along concrete walls; dangling from them, the works of young Berlin designers and new fashion labels. Passing tourists and clued-up Berliners began to visit and browse through jackets with frayed edges, dresses with large pockets and floral designs, lots of pin stripes, women's shirts cut for a woman's body but resembling a man's shirt (and vice versa), suits combining cotton with jersey material, classic black pants, reworked denim...

Six weeks after it opened, the showroom disappeared. The lights were turned off and the concrete crackled back into itself. Outside it was February and grey and people wondered if this was another case of the Berlin Blues – another idea fizzling out for lack of funds or enthusiasm.

But the philosophy behind **Berliner Klamotten**, as the come-and-go shop was known, was to keep moving and keep reinventing a reason to be. Four months later, rumours began. Another such space had appeared off Friedrichstrasse – a step upmarket from the original location. Once again, it was a concrete space kitted out with long hangers and a variety of accessories such as mix-and-match bags and witty, sweet

underwear. Again, it lasted only a few months before winking back out of existence, more like an underground club than a clothes shop.

The word *Klamotten* means clothes and related stuff. You might translate it as 'clobber' or 'duds'. It's not a word used by people in the fashion business, but Berliner Klamotten's founders were keen to do things differently. Lennart Jondral, Eike Wendl and Birgit Kaulfuss are three industry insiders who saw that Berlin designers needed a more visible and dynamic showcase. 'Berlin had so many good designers, but nobody knew where to find them,' says Jondral.

The assortment on their rails came from designers who were cutting and stitching in basements and living rooms around Berlin. Some were born and educated here, others had relocated to a city where design and the demand for it were booming. While at Friedrichstrasse, Berliner Klamotten gave space to labels such as Animo, Candee & Lacee and Anne Schmuhl, plus streetwear labels Mazooka and Picnic Industries – something of a shock to a street more used to, say, Gucci than the stripy, 1980s-inspired designs of Prenzlauer Berg's Blitz.

Berliner Klamotten is no longer at that location, but continues to open and close at a variety of spaces around the city – always secret, but revealed online at **www.berlinerklamotten.de**. The team is also thinking of opening an online shop, and taking the company abroad. But for now it's unique to Berlin – if you can find it.

Rows of jeans, leather jackets and dresses, including party stunners and fetching Bavarian dirndls, plus the odd gem from the 1950s or '60s.

Garage
Ahornstrasse 2, off Einemstrasse, Schöneberg (211 2760/www.kleidermarkt.de). U1, U2, U3, U4 Nollendorfplatz. **Open** 11am-7pm Mon-Fri; 11am-6pm Sat. **Credit** MC, V. **Map** p306 J8.
Cheap second-hand clothing, priced by the kilo, in a barn-like location. It's all well organised for rooting out cheap, last-minute party outfits.

Made in Berlin
Potsdamer Strasse 105, Tiergarten (262 2431/www. kleidermarkt.de). U1 Kurfürstenstrasse. **Open** 10.30am-7pm Mon-Fri; 11am-6pm Sat. **Credit** DC, MC, V. **Map** p306 K9.
Sister store of Garage (*see above*), where the 'better stuff' supposedly goes. It's still pretty cheap, though.

NYX
Zionskirchstrasse 40, Prenzlauer Berg (0177 928 1005). U8 Rosenthaler Platz. **Open** 1-8pm Tue-Fri; noon-5pm Sat. **No credit cards**. **Map** p303/p312 N4.
Good for last-minute needs such as braces or fancy gloves, plus old chain labels in abundance.

Sgt Peppers
Kastanienallee 91-2, Prenzlauer Berg (448 1121/ www.sgt-peppers-berlin.de). U2 Eberswalder Strasse. **Open** 11am-8pm Mon-Sat. **Credit** MC, V. **Map** p303/p312 O3.
Vivid and colourful gear from the 1960s to 1980s. You'll find some great T-shirts and airline bags.

Sterling Gold
Oranienburger Strasse 32, Mitte (2809 6500/www. sterlinggold.de). S1, S2 Oranienburger Strasse. **Open** noon-8pm Mon-Fri; noon-6pm Sat. **Credit** AmEx, MC, V. **Map** p303/p310 N5.

Eat, Drink, Shop

Michael Boenke couldn't believe his luck when he was offered a warehouse full of 'prom' dresses during a trip to America. He shipped them to Berlin and this shop in the Heckmann Höfe was the result. The fabulous ball- and cocktail gowns, in every conceivable shade and fabric from the 1950s to the 1980s, are in terrific condition.

Waahnsinn

Rosenthaler Strasse 17, Mitte (282 0029). U8 Weinmeisterstrasse. **Open** noon-8pm Mon-Sat. **Credit** AmEx, V. **Map** p303/p310 N5.
An extensive and diverse collection of hip and retro clothing makes this a great place to put together a costume or reinvent yourself on a budget. Beautiful vintage hats, sunglasses, accessories and furniture.

Shoes & leather goods

Bleibgrün

Bleibtreustrasse 29-30, Charlottenburg (882 1689/ www.bleibgruen.de). S3, S5, S7, S9, S75 Savignyplatz. **Open** 10.30am-6.30pm Mon-Fri; 11am-6pm Sat. **Credit** AmEx, DC, MC, V. **Map** p305/p312 E8.
Some regard this as Berlin's best designer shoe shop, with a nifty selection from the likes of Lagerfeld, Maud Frizon and Jan Jansen.

Budapester Schuhe

Kurfürstendamm 43, Charlottenburg (8862 4206). U1 Uhlandstrasse. **Open** 10am-7pm Mon-Fri; 10am-6pm Sat. **Credit** AmEx, DC, MC, V. **Map** p305/p312 F8.

Once it sold ice, but nowadays **Eisdieler** is merely cool. *See p172.*

This is the largest of four Berlin branches, offering the latest by the likes of Prada, D&G, Sergio Rossi, JP Tod's and Miu Miu. At Kurfürstendamm 199, across the street, you'll find a conservative range for men, including handmade classics from Austrian Ludwig Reiter. At the Bleibtreustrasse branch, prices are slashed by up to 50% for last year's models, remainders and hard-to-sell sizes.

Other locations: Bleibtreustrasse 24, Charlottenburg (881 7001); Friedrichstrasse 81, Mitte (2038 8110); Kurfürstendamm 199, Charlottenburg (8811 1707).

Penthesileia

Tucholskystrasse 31, Mitte (282 1152/www. penthesileia.de). S1, S2 Oranienburger Strasse. **Open** 10am-7pm Mon-Fri; 10am-4pm Sat. **Credit** MC, V. **Map** p302/p310 M5.

Showroom, shop and workspace for Sylvia Müller and Anke Runge, who design and make an imaginative range of handbags and rucksacks. Shapes are novel and organic – sunflowers, cones, shells and hearts, crafted from calfskin and nubuck.

Riccardo Cartillone

Savignyplatz 4 & 5, Charlottenburg (3150 3327/ www.riccardocartillone.com). S3, S5, S7, S9, S75 Savignyplatz. **Open** 10am-8pm Mon-Sat. **No credit cards.** **Map** p305/p312 F8.

For both women and men, probably the most popular international shoe designer in Berlin. No.4 stocks last season's styles at reduced prices; No.5 sports the newest collections. Cartillone's winter boots – some classic and sturdy, others with sleek lines and in risqué shades – are notoriously comfortable. There are also soft leather summer shoes, heeled and flat, in elegant, original colours.

Other locations: Kurfürstendamm 200, Charlottenburg (8892 6189); Oranienburger Strasse 85, Mitte (281 2821); Dircksenstrasse 48, Mitte (2804 0711); Rosenthaler Strasse 36, Mitte (2809 9636).

Trainer – Sole Box

Alte Schönhauser Strasse 50, Mitte (9789 4610/ www.solebox.de). U8 Weinmeisterstrasse. **Open** 1-7.30pm Mon-Thur; 1-8pm Fri; 1-6pm Sat. **Credit** MC, V. **Map** p303/p310 O5.

Trainer is the place for rare and collectable limited-edition Pumas, Nikes or Adidas, shoes that are no longer available in New York or London. Japanese tour groups have been known to descend like locusts and buy out the entire store. Sales staff are helpful and well informed.

Other locations: Oderberger Strasse 13, Prenzlauer Berg (9120 6690).

Walking Large

Rosenthaler Strasse 32, Mitte (2804 1751/www. walking-large.de). U8 Weinmeisterstrasse. **Open** noon-8pm Mon-Fri; 11am-8pm Sat. **No credit cards.** **Map** p303/p310 N5.

This minimalist shoebox of a shop stocks sleek urban brands Gola, Vans, Triple5Soul, PF Flyers, Bikkembergs, Asics and Converse.

Shoemakers

Breitenbach

Bergmannstrasse 30, Kreuzberg (692 3570/www. schuhzauber.de). U7 Gneisenaustrasse. **Open** 9am-6.30pm Mon-Fri; 10am-2pm Sat. **Credit** AmEx, MC, V. **Map** p306 M10.

This respected men's shoe- and bootmaker also does first-class repairs on men's and women's footwear.

Massschuhmacherei

Sophienstrasse 28-29, Mitte (4004 2861/www. massschuhmacherei.de). S5, S7, S9, S75 Hackescher Markt. **Open** noon-7pm Tue-Fri; 11am-4pm Sat. **No credit cards.** **Map** p303/p310 N5.

Handmade shoes in understated, classic designs. Also does repairs.

Sports gear

Karstadt Sport

Joachimstaler Strasse 5-6, Charlottenburg (8802 4153/www.karstadtsport.de). U2, U9, S5, S7, S9 S75 Zoologischer Garten. **Open** 10am-8pm Mon-Sat. **Credit** AmEx, DC, MC, V. **Map** p305/p312 G8.

Three-level megastore with a wide selection of both name brands and cheaper alternatives in international sportswear, German football paraphernalia and kids' clothes. There's also a skating area, a ski simulator, internet terminals and a restaurant.

MontK

Kastanienallee 83, Prenzlauer Berg (448 2590/ www.mont-k.de). U2 Eberswalder Strasse. **Open** 10am-8pm Mon-Fri; 10am-4pm Sat. **Credit** AmEx, MC, V. **Map** p303/p312 O3.

If you are a serious camper, skier, canoeist or climber, MontK can outfit you with the proper equipment, outerwear and footgear.

Niketown Berlin

Tauentzienstrasse 7B-7C, Schöneberg (250 70). U1, U2, U3 Wittenbergplatz. **Open** 10am-8pm Mon-Sat. **Credit** AmEx, DC, MC, V. **Map** p305 G8.

Monster retail outlet for the monster US company, in state-of-the-art glass and neon design, stocks everything imaginable with the branded swoosh.

Street/clubwear

Berlin has an unusually strong contingent of streetwear labels operating independently and under some charmingly idealistic business philosophies. Such labels are justly rewarded with fiercely loyal customers. The two closest to Berliners' hearts (both listed below) are **IrieDaily** and **FourAsses.**

Big Brobot

Kopernikusstrasse 19, Friedrichshain (7407 8388/ www.bigbrobot.com). U5 Frankfurter Tor. **Open** 11am-8pm Mon-Fri; 11am-6pm Sat. **Credit** MC, V. **Map** p308 S7.

Eat, Drink, Shop

The first German home for British label Fenchurch. Big Brobot also stocks Boxfresh and Motel, and US classics Stüssy and X-Large. There are all sorts of cultish accessories, as well as comics and small-edition publications. Staff are friendly and know their urban brands.

Cherrybomb
Oranienstrasse 32, Kreuzberg (614 6151). U1 Görlitzer Bahnhof. **Open** 11am-8pm Mon-Fri; 11am-6pm Sat. **Credit** AmEx, MC, V. **Map** p307 P9.
German labels such as Blutsgeschwister, Boogaloo and Berlin's own Volksmarke, plus Holland's King Louis and Colcci from Brazil, rub shoulders in this lowlit storefront. Although popular with women, there's plenty of streetwear for men too. The aesthetic is classic and functional.

Eisdieler
Kastanienallee 12, Prenzlauer Berg (2839 1291/ www.eisdieler.de). U2 Eberswalder Strasse. **Open** noon-8pm Mon-Fri; noon-7pm Sat. **Credit** AmEx, MC, V. **Map** p303/p312 O3.
Five young designers pooled resources to transform this former ice shop and each manages a label under the Eisdieler banner – clubwear, second-hand gear, casualwear and street style. Till Fuhrmann's jewellery, crafted from silver and wood, is particularly distinctive; his spiky ironwork adorns the façade. *Photo p170.*

FourAsses Clothing
Lietzenburger Strasse 56, Charlottenburg (7889 8317/www.fourasses.com). U1 Kurfürstendamm or U1, U9 Spichernstrasse. **Credit** MC, V. **Map** p305/p312 F9.
Comfy clothes in earthy colours and often geometric styles. Lots of slinky, strong shirts for women and baggy but well-cut men's duds.

IrieDaily
Depot 2, Oranienstrasse 9, Kreuzberg (611 4655/ www.iriedaily.de). U1 Görlitzer Bahnhof. **Open** 11am-8pm Mon-Fri; 11am-6pm Sat. **Credit** MC, V. **Map** p307 P9.
Eastern earthiness combined with a skater/hip hop aesthetic has made IrieDaily one of the most popular local brands. This is the company's flagship. Girls' tops and pants are flattering and edgy, the hoodies slinky and cosy; men's cargo pants are classy and velvety. Innovative accessories include belts and bags.

Planet
Schlüterstrasse 35, Charlottenburg (885 2717). U1 Uhlandstrasse. **Open** 10.30am-7.30pm Mon-Fri; 11am-6pm Sat. **Credit** AmEx, MC, V. **Map** p305/p312 E8.
Owners Wera Wonder and Mik Moon have been kitting out Berlin's club scene since 1985. Their DJ friends pump out deafening music to put you in club mode, and the shop brims with sparkling spandex shirts, fluffy vests and dance-durable footwear.

Skunkfunk
Kastanienallee 19 & 20, Prenzlauer Berg (4403 3800/www.skunkfunk.com). U2 Eberswalder Strasse. **Open** noon-8pm Mon-Fri; noon-7pm Sat. **Credit** AmEx, MC, V. **Map** p303/p312 O3.
Spanish urban label with adjacent stores that house men's and women's wear in lush cotton, fruity to earthy colours, and asymmetric styles. Jackets are streamlined and men's jeans baggy and beautifully tailored. The name is on everything, sometimes a little obvious, sometimes within a charming detail.

Food & drink

Supermarket shopping is slowly improving, with competition from a booming organic market prodding otherwise complacent chains such as **Kaiser's** and **Bolle**. Credit cards are usually not accepted. *Bioläden* (healthfood shops) proliferate in most areas, and organic produce is subject to strict controls. There are also plenty of speciality stores, from ethnic to gourmet, Italian to Australian. The best department store foodhalls are at **Galeries Lafayette** and **KaDeWe** (for both, *see p163*).

Australia Shopping World
Wallstrasse 66, Mitte (9700 5251/www.australia shop.com). U2 Märkisches Museum. **Open** 11am-7pm Mon-Fri; 11am-3pm Sat. **Credit** MC, V. **Map** p307/p311 O7.
Stocks an extensive range of Australian essentials such as Vegemite, Milo, macadamia nuts and, of course, wines. Huge selection of honeys too.

Broken English
Körtestrasse 10, Kreuzberg (691 1227/www.broken english.de). U7 Südstern. **Open** 11am-6.30pm Mon-Fri; 10am-4pm Sat. **Credit** MC, V. **Map** p307 O10.
Caters for UK expats with teas, scones, crisps and sweets; ingredients such as self-raising flour and clotted cream; a selection of cheeses and deep-frozen pies; basics (Heinz baked beans, Marmite); and a gift section with mugs and malts. Pricey, though.
Other locations: British Shop, Sophienstrasse 10, Mitte (2859 9307).

Königsberger Marzipan
Pestalozzistrasse 54A, Charlottenburg (323 8254). S3, S5, S7, S9, S75 Charlottenburg. **Open** 11am-6pm Mon, Wed; 2-6pm Tue, Thur, Fri; 11am-2pm Sat. **No credit cards**. **Map** p305/p312 E8.
Irmgard Wald and her late husband arrived from Kaliningrad after the war and began again in the confectionery trade. With her smiling American-born granddaughter, Frau Wald still produces fresh, soft, melt-in-your-mouth marzipan. Small boxed assortments make great gifts.

Leysieffer
Kurfürstendamm 218, Charlottenburg (885 7480/ www.leysieffer.de). U1 Uhlandstrasse. **Open** 10am-7pm Mon-Sat; 10am-4pm Sun. **Credit** AmEx, DC, MC, V. **Map** p303/p312 F8.

Ostalgia all over again

The plot of the movie *Good Bye Lenin!* made much of the difficulty of finding old GDR products. That story was set not long after Reunification, when the economy of East Germany had been rolled over and its citizens were snapping up fancy new western goods. Now the wheel has come full circle. Communist brands are a mark of eastern identity, retro GDR styling is cool, and a jar of Spreewald pickles is probably easier to find now than ten years ago.

In fact, you can find said pickles at **Ostkost** (Lychener Strasse 54, Prenzlauer Berg, 4465 3623, www.ostkost.de), next to Bautzener mustard, Werder ketchup, Othello chocolate biscuits and assorted other communist-era comestibles. If it's old GDR cosmetics, sweets or wine that you're after, **M Koos Ostprodukte** (in Alexanderplatz U-Bahn station, 242 5791) will sell you not only those, but also a GDR trade fair bag to carry them home. Even ordinary supermarkets often have display cases of eastern jams and honeys labelled 'Ost-Power!'.

The old east is on sale all over the place. **DaCapo** (*see p178*) on Kastanienallee has a huge selection of old vinyl from the GDR state-owned record label, Amiga. But you don't need to pay collectors' prices to hear some Ostrock. **Saturn** (*see p179*) at Alexanderplatz has a binful of CDs by old GDR bands right next to the cashier. And if you want something to read while you're listening,

Antiquariat Revers (Gabelsbergerstrasse 5, Friedrichshain, 422 7133) has shelves full of used books from East German publishers.

Street vendors at Checkpoint Charlie can supply hats, badges, binoculars and other paraphernalia from the days of the Volksarmee. Most of it is authentic, if grossly overpriced, but steer clear of the 'Wall' chunks. For the connoisseur, **Intershop 2000** (Ehrenbergstrasse 3-7, Friedrichshain, 495 6371, www.ddr-alltagskultur.de), housed in an old GDR *Raumerweiterungshalle* – a sort of telescoping container building – has items such as miniature editions of Marx, orange plastic chicken-shaped egg cups and Mitropa coffee pots. The display is assembled by a society devoted to preserving artefacts from East German daily life.

But the iconography of the communist era has become fair game for all. The young designers at **Eastberlin** (Kastanienallee 13, Prenzlauer Berg, 4404 6090, www.eastberlin. net) happily desecrate the symbolism of Germanies east and west on new clothes and jewellery. **Berlin Story** (*see p160*) is full of east-inspired souvenirs, from card games to 'GDR kits'. And both **Mondos Arts** (*see p180*) and **Ampelmännchen Galerie** (Hof 5, Rosenthaler Strasse 40-41, 4404 8801, www.ampelmann.de) sell a huge variety of stuff emblazoned with the old east's enduring symbol: the jaunty red and green traffic-light men.

Eat, Drink, Shop

JonnyCut. *See p175.*

Beautifully packaged confitures, teas and handmade chocolates from German fine food company make perfect gifts. Café upstairs and bakery attached.

Lindenberg
Morsestrasse 2, Charlottenburg (3908 1523). U9 Turmstrasse then bus 245. **Open** 8am-7pm Mon; 8am-8pm Tue-Fri; 8am-2pm Sat. **No credit cards.** **Map** p301 F6.

Wholesaler where pro and amateur chefs stock up on live lobster, fresh seafood, New Zealand lamb, local ducks, out-of-season fruit and veg, French cheeses, wines and spirits. Anyone can walk in, but most things are sold only in industrial quantities.

Mitte Meer
Invalidenstrasse 50-51, Mitte (398 0163/www.mitte-meer.de). S5, S7, S9, S75 Hauptbahnhof-Lehrter Bahnhof. **Open** 9am-8pm Mon-Fri; 9am-4pm Sat. **No credit cards.** **Map** p302 L5.

Wholesaler and retailer offering Spanish and Italian imports in industrial quantities. There's a huge Spanish wine selection, two large refrigerated rooms of sausages and cheeses, and another with fresh Mediterranean seafood. Also a vast frozen selection.

Vinh-Loi
Ansbacher Strasse 16, Schöneberg (235 0900). U1, U2, U3 Wittenbergplatz. **Open** 9am-7pm Mon-Fri; 9am-5pm Sat. **No credit cards.** **Map** p305 H8.

Asian groceries, including Thai fruit, veg and herbs, fresh from the airport on Mondays and Thursdays. Plus woks, rice steamers and Chinese crockery.

Weichardt-Brot
Mehlitzstrasse 7, Wilmersdorf (873 8099/www.weichardt.de). U7, U9 Berliner Strasse. **Open** 7am-6.30pm Tue-Fri; 7am-1pm Sat. **No credit cards.** **Map** p305 F11.

The very best bakery in town, Weichardt-Brot grew out of a Berlin collective from the 1960s. Stoneground organic flour and natural leavens make this a mecca for bread lovers.

Wine & spirits

Absinthe Depot Berlin
Weinmeisterstrasse 4, Mitte (281 6789/www.erstesabsinthdepotberlin.de). U8 Weinmeisterstrasse. **Open** 4pm-midnight Mon-Sat. **No credit cards.** **Map** p303/p310 O5.

Potent absinthes, mainly from western Europe (no Czech stuff), line the walls. The smiling owner may invite you for a tasting session and history lesson. Also boutique bottles that can be consumed at the counter or at a tall table in the middle of the shop.

Das Blaue Wunder
Seumestrasse 12, Friedrichshain (2576 8900). U5 Samariterstrasse. **Open** 4-8pm Mon-Fri; 10am-4pm Sat. **No credit cards.** **Map** p308 T7.

This neighbourhood treasure stocks organic wines from all over Germany – and beyond. Owner Klaus loves to sit you down for a chat and some tasting.

Getränke Hoffmann
Kleiststrasse 23-6, Schöneberg (2147 3096/ www.getraenke-hoffmann.de). U1, U2, U3 Wittenbergplatz. **Open** 8am-8pm Mon-Fri; 8am-6pm Sat. **No credit cards. Map** p305 H9.

Branches all over town offer a wide range of everyday booze at everyday prices. Call 2147 3096 to place an order for delivery anywhere in Berlin. **Other locations**: across the city.

Klemke Wein & Spirituosenhandel
Mommsenstrasse 9, Charlottenburg (8855 1260). S3, S5, S7, S9, S75 Savignyplatz. **Open** 9am-7pm Mon-Fri; 8am-2.30pm Sat. **No credit cards. Map** p305/p312 E8.

Respected specialists in French and Italian wines from the tiniest vineyard to the grandest chateau. Also digestifs and whiskies. Free delivery in Berlin.

Whisky & Cigars
Sophienstrasse 23, Mitte (282 0376/www.whisky-cigars.de). S3, S5, S7, S9, S75 Hackescher Markt. **Open** noon-7pm Mon-Fri; 11am-4pm Sat. **Credit** MC, V. **Map** p303/p310 N5.

Two friends with a love of single malts are behind this shop, which stocks 450 whiskies, and cigars from Cuba, Jamaica and Honduras. They hold regular tasting and smoking evenings and will deliver.

Hair salons

There are plenty of so-called 'no-name salons', where you take a number and wait your turn for a hip, cheap haircut, on and around **Kastanienallee**. **Notaufnahme** (Nos.29-30, 3011 2460, www.notaufnahme-berlin.de, closed Sun) is the best of these, but avoid the endlessly layered Berlin haircut that can look great at first but soon turns suspiciously mullet-like.

Beige
Auguststrasse 83, Mitte (2759 4051/www.salon-beige.de). U6 Oranienburger Tor. **Open** by appointment only, noon-9pm Tue-Sat. **No credit cards. Map** p302/p310 M5.

Exclusive salon on the garden level of a private apartment building. The waiting room doubles as a gallery space, and two client rooms are decorated in 1960s and baroque styles respectively. Hair designer Oliver Weidner specialises in modern colours and cuts. Reasonably priced, but by appointment only.

Dermot O'Dyna
Torstrasse 147, Mitte (2804 0800/www.dermot-o-dyna.de). U8 Rosenthaler Platz. **Open** 11am-7pm Mon; 10am-8.30pm Tue, Wed, Fri; 10am-10pm Thur; 11am-6pm Sat. **No credit cards. Map** p303/p310 N4.

The cuts by Dermot and his three friendly female stylists nicely straddle the divide between hip Berlin and lasting classic 'dos.

JonnyCut
Yorckstrasse 43, Schöneberg (217 0941/www.jonnycut.de). U7, S1, S2, S26 Yorckstrasse.

Open 11am-8pm Tue-Fri; 11am-5pm Sat. **Credit** MC, V. **Map** p306 K10.

Jonny Pazzo is a versatile stylist who shuttles from shoots for magazines and record covers to appointments in his small salon, decked out with pictures of angels, Buddhas, reggae musicians and children. **Photos** *p174*.

Shift
Neue Schönhauser Strasse 8, Mitte (280 9977/ 9978/www.shift-friseure.de). U8 Weinmeisterstrasse. **Open** noon-8pm Mon; 10am-8pm Tue, Thur, Fri; 2-8pm Wed; 10am-7pm Sat. **No credit cards.** **Map** p303/p310 O5.

Popular with a young, designery crowd for its personalised service and entertaining salons. A lot of the stylists from here move on to higher-end salons, locally and internationally.

Other locations: Grolmanstrasse 36, Charlottenburg (341 8545).

Udo Walz
Kempinski-Plaza, Uhlandstrasse 181-3, Charlottenburg (882 7457/www.udo-walz.de). U1 Uhlandstrasse. **Open** 9am-7pm Tue-Fri; 9am-3pm Sat. **Credit** AmEx, MC, V. **Map** p305/p312 F8.

Udo Walz is the darling of the Berlin hair brigade, and likes to have his picture taken with the likes of Claudia Schiffer. His stylists are well trained, imaginative and friendly.

Other locations: Hohenzollerndamm 92, Wilmersdorf (826 6108).

Jewellery

Fritz
Dresdener Strasse 20, Kreuzberg (615 1700). U1, U8 Kottbusser Tor. **Open** 10am-7pm Tue-Fri; 11am-3pm Sat. **Credit** AmEx, MC, V. **Map** p307 P9.

Bold designs by the Berliner owner are sold alongside interesting work in a range of materials by smiths based elsewhere in Germany and Europe. The selection of rings attracts many brides and grooms-to-be, with prices ranging from hundreds to thousands of euros.

Glanzstücke
Sophienstrasse 7, Mitte (208 2676). S3, S5, S7, S9, S75 Hackescher Markt. **Open** noon-7pm Mon-Fri; noon-6pm Sat. **Credit** AmEx, MC, V. **Map** p303/p310 N5.

Original 20th-century costume jewellery, with a strong emphasis on art nouveau and art deco. Owner Kirstin Pax hunts down glittering treasures in rhinestone and glass.

Philos
Kantstrasse 146, Charlottenburg (3180 7077). S3, S5, S7, S9, S75 Savignyplatz. **Open** 11am-8pm Mon-Fri; 11am-6pm Sat. **Credit** AmEx, MC, V. **Map** p305/p312 F8.

Small, friendly workshop and store for elegant and sometimes retro pieces, somewhere between street style and dinner party.

Rio
Bleibtreustrasse 52, Charlottenburg (313 3152). S3, S5, S7, S9, S75 Savignyplatz. **Open** 11am-6.30pm Mon-Wed; 11am-7pm Thur; 11am-6.30pm Fri; 10am-4pm Sat. **Credit** V. **Map** p305/p312 E8.

Most of the jewellery is from owner Barbara Kranz's collection; about 30% comes from up-and-coming French and Italian designers.

Scuderi
Wörther Strasse 32, Prenzlauer Berg (4737 4240). U2 Senefelderplatz. **Open** 11am-7pm Mon-Fri; 11am-3pm Sat. **Credit** MC, V. **Map** p303/p312 P3.

The four women who share this space work magic with gold, silver, pearls, stones and hand-rolled glass, creating lightweight ornaments that make a strong statement.

Markets

Flea markets

Berliners love flea markets and just about every neigbourhood has its own. For a full list, go to www.Berlin.de/senwiarbfrau/markt/floh.html.

Berliner Antik- & Flohmarkt
Bahnhof Friedrichstrasse, S-Bahnbogen 190-203, Mitte (208 2655/www.antikmarkt-berlin.de). U6, S1, S2, S3, S5, S7, S9, S75 Friedrichstrasse. **Open** 11am-6pm Mon, Wed-Sun. **Map** p302/p311 M6.

Over 60 dealers, in renovated arches under the S-Bahn tracks, selling furniture, jewellery, paintings and vintage clothing, some of it from the 1920s and '30s.

Flohmarkt am Mauerpark
Bernauer Strasse 63-4, Mitte (0176 2925 0021). U2 Eberswalder Strasse. **Open** 7am-5pm Sun. **Map** p303/p312 N3.

One of the biggest and busiest flea markets for everything from cheap Third World fashion to cardboard boxes of black-market CDs. It's probably better for household knick-knacks and local delicacies than it is for vintage finds. Family vibe.

Kunst & Nostalgie Markt
Museumsinsel, by Deutsches Historisches Museum (0171 710 1662). U6, S1, S2, S5, S7, S9, S75 Friedrichstrasse. **Open** 11am-5pm Sat, Sun. **Map** p303/p311 M6.

One of the few places you can still find true GDR relics, with anything from old signs advertising coal briquettes to framed pictures of Honecker. *See also p173* **Ostalgia all over again.**

Strasse des 17. Juni
Strasse des 17. Juni, Tiergarten (2655 0096). U2 Ernst-Reuter-Platz or S3, S5, S7, S9, S75 Tiergarten. **Open** 10am-5pm Sat, Sun. **Map** p305 G7.

On the stretch west of the S-Bahn station. High-quality, early 20th-century objects with prices to match, alongside a jumble of vintage and alternative clothing, old furniture, second-hand records and books. Interesting stuff, but cramped, single-file aisles.

Mr Dead & Mrs Free. *See p179.*

Scheisse happens

Even on holiday, laptops explode, keys get lost, pipes burst and shoes develop holes. Berlin boasts surprisingly few 24-hour repair services. In a water or gas emergency, try **Meisterbetrieb** (703 5050), **Ex-Rohr** (6719 8909) or **Kempinger** (851 5111). If you need a locksmith, try **Schlossdienst** (834 2292) at any time of day or night. **Breitenbach** (see *p171*) will perform top-quality shoe repairs, though branches of **Picobello** (found in most department stores) will suffice for routine

re-heeling. That broken PC can be repaired at **JE** (Grünerstrasse, Mitte, 2472 1741, www.je-computer.de), while malfunctioning Macs will be ably diagnosed and treated by the English-speaking **Petra Koch** (2403 5999, www.homepage.mac.com/macpet). And if your luggage decides to come apart at the seams, **Witt** (Hauptstrasse 9, Schöneberg, 781 4937, www.kofferhaus-witt.de) has the city's biggest stock of suitcase spare parts and can complete most repairs in a day.

Trödelmarkt Boxhagener Platz

Boxhagener Platz, Friedrichshain (0177 827 9352). U1, S3, S5, S7, S9 Warschauer Strasse. **Open** 10am-6pm Sun. **Map** p308 T7.

A lot of local young artists and T-shirt designers set up stalls at this overflowing market, while punky types and bohemian mothers shop for vintage sunglasses and unusual crockery.

Zille-Hof

Fasanenstrasse 14, Charlottenburg (313 4333). U1 Uhlandstrasse. **Open** 8am-5.30pm Mon-Fri; 8am-1pm Sat. **Map** p305/p312 F4.

Almost next door to the Kempinski Hotel (see *p49*), a tidy junk market. The better bric-a-brac is indoors, while the real bargains lurk in the courtyard outside.

General markets

Berlin's many *Wochenmärkte* usually sell cheaper, fresher produce than regular shops.

Farmers' Market

Wittenbergplatz, Schöneberg. U1, U2, U3 Wittenbergplatz. **Open** 8am-2pm Tue, Wed, Fri; 10am-7.30pm Thur. **Map** p305 H8.

Predominantly organic produce, including cheese, bread, fresh pasta and meat, plus fruit and vegetables from regions in the region. Also inedible items such as wooden brushes and sheepskins.

Kollwitzplatz

Kollwitzplatz, Prenzlauer Berg. U2 Senefelderplatz. **Open** 11am-4pm Thur, Sat. **Map** p303/p312 P3.

Open-air food markets are still rare in the east. This one is a small, unassuming organic market. Steaming punch and wholegrain cinnamon waffles make it gemütlich in winter, but it's more lively in summer.

Türkischer Markt

Maybachufer, Neukölln. U1, U8 Kottbusser Tor. **Open** noon-6.30pm Tue, Fri. **Map** p307 P9/P10.

A noisy, crowded market just across the canal from Kreuzberg, meeting the needs of the local Turkish community. Fresh vegetables, great spices.

Winterfeldt Markt

Winterfeldtplatz, Schöneberg. U1, U2, U3, U4 Nollendorfplatz. **Open** 8am-2pm Wed, Sat. **Map** p306 J9.

Saturday's multicultural experience. Everybody shows up to buy their vegetables, cheese, wholegrain breads, wurst, meats, flowers, clothes, pet supplies and toys; or simply to meet over a coffee, beer or falafel at one of the many cafés off the square.

Music: CDs & records

Berlin is a haven for vinyl collectors and indie and electronic music junkies. **Kastanienallee** in Prenzlauer Berg, **Boxhagener Strasse** and **Grünberger Strasse** in Friedrichshain, and **Bergmannstrasse** and **Zossener Strasse** in Kreuzberg are the main veins; **Dussmann das KulturKaufhaus** (see *p163*) also has a good selection. Go to www.platten.net for a complete guide to every record shop in Berlin.

DaCapo Records

Kastanienallee 96, Prenzlauer Berg (4434 0290). U2 Eberswalder Strasse. **Open** 11am-7pm Tue-Fri; 11am-4pm Sat. **Credit** MC, V. **Map** p303/p312 O3.

Pricey but wide selection of used vinyl, releases on GDR label Amiga plus rare 1950s 10-inch records and jazz singles.

D-Fens

Greifswalder Strasse 224, Prenzlauer Berg (4434 2250/www.d-fens-berlin.de). Tram M4 Am Friedrichshain. **Open** noon-7pm Mon-Fri; noon-3pm Sat. **No credit cards. Map** p303 Q4.

A small DJ shop in a revamped garage, specialising in house, trance, electro, techno and disco. Owner Ralph Ballschuh, a DJ himself, is happy to turn up the volume on any track you wish. D-Fens is tricky to find – your best bet is to follow the signs for the Knaack club (see *p219*).

DNS

Eberswalder Strasse 30, Prenzlauer Berg (247 9835/ www.dns-music.com). U2 Eberswalder Strasse. **Open**

11am-8pm Mon-Fri; 11am-6pm Sat. **Credit** AmEx, MC, V. **Map** p303/p312 O3.
Old vinyl, including some rare finds, as well as the latest pressings in the world of techno.

Gelbe Musik
Schaperstrasse 11, Wilmersdorf (211 3962). U3 Augsburger Strasse. **Open** 1-6pm Tue-Fri; 11am-2pm Sat. **Credit** MC, V. **Map** p305/p312 G9.
One of Europe's most important avant-garde outlets has racks stacked with minimalist, electronic, world, industrial and extreme noise. Rare vinyl and import CDs, music press and sound objects make for absorbing browsing.

Mr Dead & Mrs Free
Bülowstrasse 5, Schöneberg (215 1449/www. deadandfree.com). U1, U2, U3, U4 Nollendorfplatz. **Open** 11am-7pm Mon-Fri; 11am-4pm Sat. **Credit** V. **Map** p306 G9.
Long Berlin's leading address for independent and underground rock, Mr Dead & Mrs Free has bucketloads of British, US and Australian imports, a large vinyl section, and staff who know and love their music. Small but choice selection of books and mags too. **Photos** *p177.*

Musikalienhandlung Hans Riedel
Uhlandstrasse 38, Wilmersdorf (882 7395/www. musik-riedel.de). U1 Uhlandstrasse. **Open** 8am-6.30pm Mon-Fri; 9am-2pm Sat. **Credit** MC, V. **Map** p305 F9.
Probably the best address for classical music in Berlin, this huge, old-fashioned shop stocks string and brass instruments as well as CDs, and has one of the largest selections of sheet music in Europe.

Neurotitan
Rosenthaler Strasse 39, Mitte (3087 2573/www. neurotitan.de). S3, S5, S7, S9, S75 Hackescher Markt. **Open** noon-8pm Mon-Sat. **No credit cards.** **Map** p303/p310 N5.
At the end of an alley on the second floor, one of Berlin's most interesting art book and record stores. Featuring handmade and small-press art books, original artwork, and small label CDs and vinyl.

Pigasus – Polish Poster Gallery
Torstrasse 60, Mitte (2849 3697/www.pigasus-gallery.de). U2 Rosa-Luxemburg-Platz. **Open** 4-8pm Mon-Thur; 4-10pm Fri, Sat. **Credit** MC, V. **Map** p303/p310 O5.
Near the Club der polnischen Versager (*see p225f*) and Kaffee Burger (*see p224*), host to the infamous Russian Disco (*see p227* **One Russian under a groove**), this shop offers an extensive range of Polish, Russian and Ukrainian disco, plus classical music and a wonderful selection of old film and propaganda posters.

Space Hall
Zossener Strasse 33, Kreuzberg (694 7664/www. space-hall.de). U7 Gneisenaustrasse. **Open** 11am-8pm Mon-Fri; 10.30am-5pm Sat. **Credit** MC, V. **Map** p307 N10.

Now complemented by massive new premises in a former supermarket building round the corner on Bergmannstrasse, Space Hall offers a huge range of new and second-hand CDs and vinyl. Techno, house and electronica are the emphasis, but there's also a lot of hip hop, indie and rock. Prices are competitive and the staff know and love their stuff. There are several other good music shops in the vicinity.
Other locations: Bergmannstrasse 5-7, Kreuzberg (6273 5518).

Chain stores

MakroMarkt
Kurfürstendamm 206, Charlottenburg (886 886/ www.makromarkt.de). U1 Uhlandstrasse. **Open** 10am-8pm Mon-Fri; 10am-6pm Sat. **Credit** AmEx, V. **Map** p305/p312 F8.
This branch has a big selection of just about everything electronic and musical.
Other locations: across the city.

Saturn
Alexanderplatz 8, Mitte (247 516). U2, U5, U8, S5, S7, S9, S75 Alexanderplatz. **Open** 9.30am-8pm Mon-Sat. **Credit** AmEx, DC, MC, V. **Map** p303/p311 O6.
One of the cheapest chains in town, with stacks of new releases and a good back catalogue. CDs only. Also offers a range of photo-processing services.
Other locations: Potsdamer Platz Arkaden, Alte Potsdamer Strasse 7, Tiergarten (3025 9240).

Opticians

Brille 54
Friedrichstrasse 71, Mitte (2094 6060/www.brille 54.de). U6 Französische Strasse. **Open** 10am-8pm Mon-Fri; 10am-6pm Sat. **Credit** AmEx, DC, MC, V. **Map** p306 M7.
A small but functionally sleek space in Quartier 206, designed by hot young Berlin architects Plajer & Franz. All the international names can be found, including Armani, Gucci, Oliver Peoples, Lunor, Paul Smith, Prada and Miu Miu.
Other locations: Rosenthaler Strasse 36, Mitte (2804 0818); Kurfürstendamm 54, Charlottenburg (882 6696).

Fielmann
Passage, Alexanderplatz, Mitte (242 4507). U2, U5, U8, S5, S7, S9, S75 Alexanderplatz. **Open** 9am-8pm Mon-Fri; 9am-6pm Sat. **Credit** AmEx, DC, MC, V. **Map** p303/p311 O6.
Germany's biggest chain of opticians offers a large selection of frames at competitive prices.
Other locations: across the city.

ic!
Max-Beer-Strasse 17, Mitte (2472 7200/www.ic-berlin.de). U8 Weinmeisterstrasse. **Open** 11am-7pm Mon-Sat. **Credit** AmEx, DC, MC. **Map** p303/p310 O5.
This is probably the hippest eyewear store for adults and children, with a diverse range of designer prescription glasses and renowned sunglasses.

Photography

Everyday developing can be done at branches of **Rossmann** and **Schlecker**; branches of **Saturn** (see *p179*) provide processing services.

Fix Foto
Kurfürstendamm 213, Charlottenburg (882 7267).
U1 Uhlandstrasse. **Open** 9am-8pm Mon-Sat; 11am-7pm Sun. **Credit** AmEx, MC, V. **Map** p305/p312 F8.
Half-hour developing from black and white or colour film or slides, enlargements, CD-Rom and other fast services at unusually generous opening hours.
Other locations: across the city.

PPS
Alexanderplatz 2, Mitte (726 109 209). U2, U5, U8, S5, S7, S9, S75 Alexanderplatz. **Open** 9am-7pm Mon-Fri; noon-5pm Sat. **Credit** AmEx, DC, MC, V. **Map** p303/p311 O6.
Professional colour lab offering digital services, black-and-white hand-developed enlargements, scanning, two-hour developing, large-format print and other services. Also sells cameras, rents out sophisticated equipment and sends off repairs.

Souvenirs

Communist relics and alleged Wall chunks are sold at stalls near Checkpoint Charlie and the Brandenburg Gate. The **Haus am Checkpoint Charlie** (see *p97*) sells key rings, lighters and mouse pads on a 'You Are Leaving The American Sector' theme. Most **flea markets** (see *p176*) have stalls devoted to old East artefacts. **Berlin Story** (see *p160*) has a big selection of toy Trabbies, historical maps, mounted Wall chunks and other souvenirs. *See also p173* **Ostalgia all over again**.

Berliner Zinnfiguren Kabinett
Knesebeckstrasse 88, Charlottenburg (315 7000/www.zinnfigur.com). S3, S5, S7, S9, S75 Savignyplatz. **Open** 10am-6pm Mon-Fri; 10am-3pm Sat. **Credit** AmEx, MC, V. **Map** p305/p312 F8.
Home to armies of handmade tin soldiers, farm animals and historical characters, all painted in incredible detail. You could take home an entire battalion of Prussian Grenadiers.

Fanshop
Wittstocker Strasse 24, Tiergarten (294 7691). U9 Birkenstrasse. **Open** 11am-6pm Mon-Wed, Fri; 4-6pm Thur; 11am-1pm every 2nd Sat. **No credit cards**. **Map** p301 F4.
Should either of Berlin's major soccer clubs have captured your heart, this is the place to stock up on Hertha or Union caps, shawls and T-shirts.

Mondos Arts
Schreinerstrasse 6, Friedrichshain (4201 0778/ www.mondosarts.de). U5 Samariterstrasse. **Open** 10am-7pm Mon-Fri; 11am-4pm Sat. **Credit** AmEx, MC, V. **Map** p309 T6.

The best of what's left of the East. All types of GDR memorabilia, including flags, posters, clocks, border signs and various products embossed with the endangered *Ampelmännchen* – the characterful stop-and-go men on a dwindling number of traffic lights.

Stationery & art supplies

Ferdinand Braune
Grunewaldstrasse 87, Schöneberg (7870 3773/ www.braune-kuenstlerbedarf.de). U7 Kleistpark. **Open** 10am-6.30pm Mon-Fri; 10am-2pm Sat. **Credit** AmEx, MC, V. **Map** p306 J10.
Berlin's painters all come for Herr Braune's hand-blended oil paints, sketchbooks and canvas stretches.

Grüne Papeterie
Oranienstrasse 196, Kreuzberg (618 5355). U1 Görlitzer Bahnhof or U1, U8 Kottbusser Tor. **Open** 10am-7pm Mon-Fri; 10am-4pm Sat. **No credit cards**. **Map** p307 P9.
Eco-friendly stationery, wrapping paper and wooden fountain pens, as well as small gifts and toys.

Hauptsache
Rosenthaler Strasse 32, Mitte (2478 1126/www. hauptsache-berlin.net). U8 Weinmeisterstrasse. **Open** 10am-7pm Mon-Fri; noon-4pm Sat. **Credit** AmEx, MC, V. **Map** p303/p310 N5.
Big, bright shop full of fancy and colourful brands, including MontBlanc, Moleskine and ClaireFontaine.

Künstler Magazin
Kastanienallee 33, Prenzlauer Berg (448 4447/www. kuenstlermagazin.de). U2 Eberswalder Strasse. **Open** 9am-8pm Mon-Fri; 10am-6pm Sat. **No credit cards**. **Map** p303/p312 O3.
Full selection of art supplies including canvas, paint, brushes, paper and easels at reasonable prices.

Otto Ebeling
Fuggerstrasse 43-5, Schöneberg (211 4627/www. otto-ebeling.de). U1, U2, U3 Wittenbergplatz. **Open** 8.30am-7pm Mon-Fri; 10am-4pm Sat. **Credit** AmEx, MC, V. **Map** p305 G9.
Excellent selection of art supplies, paper and portfolios. Carries Schmincke Artist Colours in oil and watercolours and ships German brands abroad.

Propolis
Oranienstrasse 19A, Kreuzberg (615 2464). U1, U8 Kottbusser Tor. **Open** 10am-6pm Mon-Fri. **No credit cards**. **Map** p307 P9.
Carries over 300 pigments, plus recipes and ingredients for wall finishes. Also available are paints, resins, gold and silver leaf, brushes and canvases.

RSVP
Mulackstrasse 14, Mitte (2809 4644/www.rsvp-berlin.de). U8 Weinmeisterstrasse. **Open** noon-7pm Tue-Fri; noon-4pm Sat. **Credit** AmEx, MC, V. **Map** p303/p310 O5.
Stationery for the aesthete: fine notebooks, exotic erasers, almond glue from Italy, art deco scissors, Japanese clips and Kaweco Sport cartridge pens.

Arts & Entertainment

Features

Kunst-Werke. *See p200.*

Festivals & Events

Enjoy a day of riotous assembly or simply stay up late at the museums.

Berlin may be broke but the city still manages to host an impressive portfolio of themed events, cultural extravaganzas and colourful carnivals. Though the summer **Loveparade** has officially faded into history, the **Karneval der Kulturen** has grown to celebrate the city's cultural diversity. The **Berlin International Film Festival** brings a welcome bit of glitz to winter. Throughout the year, an assortment of trade fairs such as the **International Tourism Fair** or **Popkomm** rotate through Messegelände. At the other end of town, the **May Day Riots** are Kreuzberg's rite of spring. Twice annually, the **Lange Nacht der Museen** brings to life the exhibits in Berlin's museums. In summer, the city buzzes with open-air concert programmes and parades celebrating (or protesting) everything from hemp to gay life. And at Christmas, ice-skating rinks and seasonal markets spring up all over, lending Berlin a traditional, old-fashioned air.

Spring

Zeitfenster – Biennale für alte Musik
Konzerthaus, Gendarmenmarkt 2, Mitte (203 090/ www.konzerthaus.de). U2, U6 Stadtmitte. **Tickets** varies. **Credit** AmEx, MC, V. **Map** p306/p311 M7. **Date** 1wk in Apr 2008.
The Biennial Festival of Early Music focuses on works from the 16th and 17th centuries.

Deutschland Pokal-Endspiele
Olympiastadion, Olympischer Platz 3, Charlottenburg (300 633). U2 Olympia-Stadion or S5, S75 Olympiastadion. Info & tickets: Deutscher Fussball-Bund (tickets@dfb.de/fax 069 678 8266). **Tickets** varies. **No credit cards. Date** late Apr/early May.
The domestic football cup final has been taking place at the Olympiastadion every year since 1985. It regularly attracts some 65,000 football fans.

May Day Riots
Around Kottbusser Tor, Kreuzberg. U1, U8 Kottbusser Tor. **Map** p307 P9. **Date** 1 May.
An annual event since 1987, when Autonomen engaged in violent clashes with police. The riots have quietened in recent years, but are still worth checking out (*see p184* **May Day! May Day!**).

International Aerospace Exhibition
Flughafen Schönefeld (3038 2014/www.ila-berlin.de). S9, S45 Flughafen Berlin-Schönefeld. **Tickets** varies. **No credit cards. Date** 1wk in May 2006, 2008.

This increasingly popular biennial event, held at Schönefeld airport, features some 1,000 exhibitors from 40 countries, with aircraft of all kinds on display, as well as a serious focus on space.

Qatar Total Ladies German Open
LTTC Rot-Weiss, Gottfried-von-Cramm-Weg 47-55, Grunewald (box office 4430 4430/www.german-open. org). S7, S9 Grunewald. **Tickets** varies. **Credit** AmEx, DC, MC, V. **Date** 1st or 2nd wk in May.
The world's fifth largest international women's tennis championship. After match point, the focus switches to a gala ball and other glitzy social affairs. Tickets are hard to come by.

Theatertreffen Berlin
Organisers: Berliner Festspiele, Schaperstrasse 24, Charlottenburg (2548 9100/www.berlinerfestspiele. de). **Tickets** varies. **Credit** AmEx, MC, V. **Date** 3wks in May.
A jury chooses ten of the most innovative and controversial new theatre productions from companies in Germany, Austria and Switzerland, and the winners come to Berlin to perform their pieces.

Karneval der Kulturen
Kreuzberg (6097 7022/www.karneval-berlin.de). **Tickets** free. **Date** 4 days in May/June.
Inspired by the Notting Hill Carnival and intended as a celebration of Berlin's ethnic and cultural diversity, the long weekend (always Pentecost) includes a street festival, parties and a 'multi-kulti' parade involving dozens of floats, hundreds of musicians and thousands of spectators. The route changes every year, so check the website.

Museumsinselfestival
Museumsinsel, Mitte (www.museumsinselfestival. info). S5, S7, S9, S75 Hackescher Markt. **Map** p303/p311 N6. **Date** May-Sept.
An open-air season of high-quality rock and classical concerts, readings, plays and film screenings, with events staged not only on Museumsinsel but also at the Kulturforum complex near Potsdamer Platz. Events in summer 2005 ranged from Serbian Gypsy orchestras to a screening of *Battleship Potemkin* with live soundtrack by the Pet Shop Boys and Dresdner Sinfoniker.

Summer

In Transit
Haus der Kulturen der Welt, John-Foster-Dulles-Allee 10, Tiergarten (397 80/www.hkw.de). Bus 100. **Tickets** varies. **Credit** DC, MC, V. **Map** p302 K6. **Date** 3wks in early summer.

Tanz im August

Dance and performance artists from beyond Europe. Audiences can watch artists prepare their pieces, or wait for the resulting evening performances.

Berlin Philharmonie at the Waldbühne

Waldbühne, Am Glockenturm, Charlottenburg (box office 01805 332 433/administration 810 750/ www.berlin-philharmonic.com). S5 Pichelsberg, then shuttle bus. **Tickets** €18-€46. **Credit** AmEx, MC, V. **Date** 1 day in June.

The Philharmonie ends its season with an open-air concert. Over 20,000 Berliners light the atmospheric 'forest theatre' with candles once darkness falls.

Fête de la Musique

Various venues (4171 5289/www.fetedela musique.de). **Tickets** free. **Date** 21 June.

A regular summer solstice happening since 1995, this music extravaganza of bands and DJs takes place all over town. The music is mixed, with DJs playing everything from heavy metal to *Schlager*.

Deutsch-Französisches Volksfest

Zentraler Festplatz am Kurt-Schumacher-Damm, Kurt-Schumacher-Damm 207-245, Reinickendorf (213 3290/www.deutsch-franzoesisches-volksfest.de). U6 Kurt-Schumacher-Platz. **Tickets** €1.50. **No credit cards. Date** 4wks in June/July.

A survivor from the days when this was the French Sector, the German-French Festival offers rides, French music and cuisine, and Bastille Day fireworks.

Classic Open Air

Gendarmenmarkt, Mitte (Media On-Line 315 7540/ www.classicopenair.de). U6 Französische Strasse, U2, U6 Stadtmitte or U2 Hausvogteiplatz. **Tickets** €30-€81. **Credit** AmEx, MC. **Map** p306/p311 M7. **Date** 4-7 days in early July.

Big names usually open this concert series held in one of Berlin's most beautiful squares.

Loveparade

2570 0625/www.loveparade.de. **Date** 2nd Sat in July.

The notorious techno carnival, which at its late 1990s peak attracted over a million ravers, is now officially dead and buried. Unofficially, however, there are moves to revive it and the weekend will probably see a cluster of parties and club events.

Schwul-Lesbisches Strassenfest

Nollendorfplatz, Schöneberg (2147 3586/ www.regenbogenfonds.de). U1, U2, U3, U4 Nollendorfplatz. **Tickets** free. **Map** p306 J9. **Date** wknd before Christopher Street Day.

The Gay and Lesbian Street Fair takes over Schöneberg every year, filling several blocks in west Berlin's gay quarter. Participating bars, clubs, food stands and musical acts make this a dizzying, non-stop event that also serves as kick-off for the following week's Christopher Street Day Parade.

Christopher Street Day Parade

2362 8632/www.csd-berlin.de. **Date** Sat in late July.

Originally organised to commemorate the 1969 riots at the Stonewall Bar on Christopher Street in New York, the fun and flamboyant parade has become one of the summer's most enjoyable and inclusive street parties, attracting straights as well as gays.

Deutsch-Amerikanisches Volksfest

Truman Plaza, Hüttenweg/Clayallee, Zehlendorf (213 3290/www.deutsch-amerikanisches-volksfest.de). U3 Oskar-Helene-Heim. **Tickets** €1.50; children free. **No credit cards. Date** 4wks in July/Aug.

Originally established by the US forces stationed in West Berlin, the German-American Festival offers a tacky mix of carnival rides, cowboys doing lasso tricks, candy floss, hot dogs and Yankee beer.

HeimatKlänge

Kulturforum, Potsdamer Platz (318 6140/www. piranha.de). U2, S1, S2, S26 Potsdamer Platz. **Tickets** €5. **No credit cards. Date** 1wk in Aug.

Berlin's biggest world music festival, featuring acts from around the globe. Expect anything from Balkan brass bands to Indonesian jazz.

Tanz im August

Organisers: HAU, Hallesches Ufer 32, Kreuzberg (2590 0441/www.tanzimaugust.de). **Tickets** varies. **Credit** varies. **Date** 3wks in Aug.

May Day! May Day!

In the post-war period, on both sides of the Wall, May Day resumed its significance as a day of peaceable parades – until the events of 1987. Kreuzberg had by this date long established itself as the city's 'alternative' district. Made a geographical backwater by the Wall, the neighbourhood was soon known for its poor quality but affordable housing, which attracted Turkish immigrants and draft-dodging German youth, and gave rise to a highly politicised squatting movement. The area had the biggest concentration of black-clad, punky Autonomen anywhere in Europe.

It's an annual event as indelibly inked into the Berlin calendar as the Film Festival. Since 1987, when a peaceful demonstration in Kreuzberg's Lausitzer Platz erupted into a violent confrontation between left-wingers and police, May Day has consistently seen riots in that borough.

The international association of the first of May with labourism dates back as far as 1884, when the American Federation of Organized Trades and Labour Unions demanded an eight-hour working day with effect from 1 May 1886.

In Berlin, the date's strongest historical association is with the events of what became known as Blutmai ('Blood May') in 1929. That year, the governing Social Democrats (SPD) prohibited the traditional May Day marches. The Communist Party (KPD), strongest party in the city, called for them to proceed regardless. The result was bloody chaos. By the day's end, the police had reportedly fired 11,000 rounds of live ammunition and 32 citizens had been killed.

The events also deepened the split between the parties of the left, which gave the Nazis a boost, as the workers' movement was unable to form an anti-Hitler coalition. The Nazis adapted the first of May to their own agenda, christening it the Tag der Arbeit ('day of work'), still its official name today. Ironically, on 2 May 1933, Hitler's government then outlawed all free trade unions and independent workers' organisations.

And when heavy-handed policing sparked the 1987 riots, it wasn't just self-styled anarchists who engaged in running battles with the cops. It was also disaffected Turks. When the ruling Christian Democrats surveyed the wreckage – a supermarket was torched and there was widespread looting – they commented on the 'extraordinary merger of different problem groups'.

In the years since, the Kreuzberg riots have become strangely ritualised. It seems that both demonstrators and police come out looking for a fight. Rocks are thrown and cars overturned. Tear gas and water cannon are a regular feature. Enterprising Turks sell cans of beer from shopping trolleys. Tourists show up to watch or join in. It's almost as if it wants to be a kind of violent carnival.

There are periodic attempts to ban the event – most recently in 2001 – but it always goes ahead anyway. Since then, the authorities have instead looked for ways to minimise the violence. Their strategies seem to be working, as the 2005 riots were the most peaceable for years. Still, the tendency of fascist groups to march on the same day means there is always the possibility of violence. And it's not just confined to Kreuzberg these days, as things sometimes kick off in Friedrichshain and Prenzlauer Berg.

Germany's leading dance festival, with big-name participants and an international reputation. An annual showcase for global dance trends. **Photo** *p183*.

Hanfparade

Hallesches Tor to Rotes Rathaus (0178 659 4399/ www.hanfparade.de). **Tickets** free. **Date** 5 Aug 2006.
Celebrating the varied utility of the fibrous weed, organisers of the Hemp Parade seek total legalisation of the use and possession of cannabis. The route sometimes changes; check local press for details.

Internationales Berliner Bierfestival

Karl-Marx-Allee, from Strausberger Platz to Frankfurter Tor, Friedrichshain (508 6822/ www.bierfestival-berlin.de). U5 Frankfurter Tor. **Map** p309 R6/S6. **Date** 1wknd in Aug.
The annual Berlin International Beer Festival showcases hundreds of beers from over 60 countries.

young.euro.classic

Konzerthaus, Gendarmenmarkt 2, Mitte (tickets & information 5302 6060/www.young-euro-classic.de). U6 Französische Strasse. **Tickets** €9. **No credit cards**. **Map** p306/p311 M7. **Date** 2wks in Aug.
This annual summer concert programme brings together youth orchestras from around Europe.

Lange Nacht der Museen

902 699 444/www.lange-nacht-der-museen.de. **Tickets** €12; €8 concessions. **Date** 1 evening in late Aug.
Twice a year 80 museums stay open into the early hours. The 'Long Night of the Museums' also offers concerts, readings and stage acts. It's a huge and popular event, with museum-hoppers shuttling between venues by bus, tram or boat. *See also p186*.

Kreuzberger festliche Tage

Viktoriapark, Kreuzbergstrasse, Kreuzberg (4340 7905/www.kreuzberger-festliche-tage.de). U6, U7 Mehringdamm. **Tickets** free. **Map** p306 L10. **Date** 2wks in late Aug/early Sept.
This annual late summer festival in Kreuzberg's Viktoriapark offers music, games, beer and food.

Musikfest

Organisers: Berliner Festspiele, Schaperstrasse 24, Charlottenburg (2548 9244/www.berlinerfestspiele. de). **Tickets** varies. **Credit** varies. **Date** 1wk in late Aug/early Sept.
A new classical music festival. The Berlin Symphony Orchestra collaborates with the Berlin Philharmonic and its conductor, Sir Simon Rattle, in a week of orchestral and chamber music, plus some musical theatre. Orchestras from London, New York and around Europe also participate.

Autumn

International Literature Festival

2787 8620/www.literaturfestival.com. **Tickets** varies. **Date** 2wks mid Sept.

Major literary event with readings, symposiums and discussions attended by both major authors and rising stars. In 2005 the likes of Doris Lessing, Tariq Ali, Joachim Fest, Peter Schneider and Kazuo Ishiguro rubbed shoulders with up-and-coming writers from all over the world.

Popkomm

Messe Berlin, Messedamm 22, Charlottenburg (3038 3009/www.popkomm.de). U2 Kaiserdamm, S5, S75 Messe Süd or S41, S42, S45, S46 Messe Nord. **Tickets** varies. **Map** p304 A8. **Date** 3 days in Sept.
Europe's largest domestic music industry trade fair moved to Berlin from Cologne in 2004, bringing three days of business schmoozing and lots of music. As well as the trade-only conference, the city hosts myriad showcases and live events.

Berlin Marathon

Organisers: Berlin-Marathon SCC Running Events GmbH, Glockenturmstrasse 23, 14055 (3012 8810/ www.berlin-marathon.com). **Admission** €50-€90. **Credit** call for details. **Date** last Sun in Sept.
The city's biggest sporting event takes 30,000 participants from around the world, including wheelchair racers and in-line skaters, past most of the city's landmarks on its trek through seven boroughs.

Art Forum Berlin

Messegelände am Funkturm, Messedamm 22, Charlottenburg (3038 2076/www.art-forum-berlin.de). U2 Kaiserdamm, S5, S75 Messe Süd or S41, S42, S45, S46 Messe Nord. **Map** p304 A8. **Date** 5 days in late Sept/early Oct.
Since 1996 the Art Forum Berlin has sought to bring together gallery-owners and artists for this trade fair of contemporary art. The event attracts many of Europe's leading galleries plus thousands of lay enthusiasts. It also coincides with Berliner Liste (www.berliner-liste.org) and Preview Berlin (www. previewberlin.de), for newer galleries and artists.

Berlin Photography Festival

2007 4990/www.berlin-photography-festival.de. **Tickets** varies. **Credit** varies. **Date** late Sept-mid Nov.
A new festival of international photography. The Martin-Gropius-Bau (*see p98*) houses the main exhibit, under the festival's driving theme, while galleries across town participate with individual shows.

Spielzeiteuropa

Schaperstrasse 24 (2548 9100/www.berliner festspiele.de). **Tickets** varies. **Credit** AmEx, MC, V. **Date** Oct-Feb.
A new forum for theatre and dance from around Europe, supplemented by German co-productions and showcasing theatre that incorporates new political and aesthetic ideas from a specifically European perspective. Shows run on and off for five months.

JazzFest Berlin

Organisers: Berliner Festspiele, Schaperstrasse 24, Charlottenburg (254 890/www.berlinerfestspiele.de). **Tickets** varies. **Date** 4 days late Oct/early Nov.

Arts & Entertainment

A wide spectrum of jazz from an array of internationally renowned artists, and a fixture since 1964. The concurrent Fringe Jazz Festival (organised by JazzRadio) showcases less established acts.

Winter

Berliner Märchentage

3470 9479/www.berliner-maerchentage.de. **Tickets** varies. **Credit** varies. **Date** 3wks in mid Nov.
The Berlin Fairytale Festival celebrates tales from around the world each year with some 400 storytelling and music events, in a carnival atmosphere.

Christmas Markets

Kaiser-Wilhelm-Gedächtniskirche, Breitscheidplatz, Charlottenburg (213 3290/www.weihnachtsmarkt-deutschland.de). U2, U9, S3, S5, S7, S9, S75 *Zoologischer Garten.* **Open** 11am-8pm Mon-Thur, Sun; 11am-10pm Fri, Sat. **Map** p305 G8.
Traditional markets spring up across Berlin during the Christmas season, offering toys, mulled wine and gingerbread. This is one of the biggest.

Berliner Silvesterlauf

Grunewald (3012 3012/www.berlin-marathon.com/events/index.php). S5, S75 *Messe Süd.* **Tickets** free. **Date** 31 Dec.
A local tradition for decades, the New Year's Eve Run (aka the 'pancake run') starts in Grunewald at the intersection of Waldschulallee and Harbigstrasse.

Silvester

Date 31 Dec.
With Berliners' enthusiasm for tossing firecrackers and launching rockets from windows, New Year's Eve is always vivid, noisy and hazardous. Thousands celebrate at the Brandenburger Tor. Thousands more trek up to the Teufelsberg at the northern tip of Grunewald or the Viktoriapark in Kreuzberg to watch the fireworks across the city.

Tanztage

Sophiensaele, Sophienstrasse 18, Mitte (283 5266/www.tanztage.de). U8 *Weinmeisterstrasse* or S3, S5, S7, S9, S75 *Hackescher Markt.* **Tickets** €13; €8 concessions. **No credit cards.** **Map** p303/p310 N5. **Date** 2wks in early Jan.
New talent featured in a fortnight of dance events.

Internationale Grüne Woche

Messegelände am Funkturm, Messedamm 22, Charlottenburg (3038 2267/www.gruenewoche.de). U2 *Kaiserdamm,* S5, S75 *Messe Süd* or S41, S42, S45, S46 *Messe Nord.* **Open** 1-6pm daily. **Tickets** €10-€16. **No credit cards.** **Map** p304 A8. **Date** 10 days in Jan.
An orgy of food and drink from the far corners of Germany and across the world.

UltraSchall

Organisers: DeutschlandRadio Berlin, Hans-Rosenthal-Platz, Schöneberg (850 30/www.dradio.de/dlr). **Tickets** varies. **Credit** varies. **Date** 10 days in mid Jan.

New music presented in high-profile venues by some of the world's leading specialist ensembles. Concerts are often broadcast live by DeutschlandRadio and Rundfunk Berlin Brandenburg.

BREAD & butter

Kabelwerke, Gartenfelderstrasse 14-28, Siemensstadt (400 440/www.breadandbutter.com). **Date** 3 days in late Jan.
A cutting-edge fashion fair for independent professionals, with satellite events open to everyone.

Transmediale

Akademie der Künste, Hanseatenweg 10, Tiergarten (2474 9739/www.transmediale.de). S5, S7, S9, S75 *Bellevue* or U9 *Hansaplatz.* **Tickets** €5; €2 concessions. *Day pass* €15; €10 concessions. *Festival pass* €60; €30 concessions. **Credit** AmEx, MC, V. **Map** p301 H6. **Date** 3-5 days in early Feb.
One of the world's largest international festivals for media art and digital culture, presenting exhibitions and screenings from artists working with video, television, computer animation, internet and other visual media and digital technologies. The satellite event Club Transmediale takes place at Maria am Ostbahnhof and offers performances, discussions and media art about electronic music.

Lange Nacht der Museen

2839 7444/www.lange-nacht-der-museen.de. **Tickets** €12; €8 concessions. **Date** 1 evening in Feb.
Popular late-night museum opening; *see p185.*

Berlin International Film Festival

Potsdamer Platz, Tiergarten & other venues (259 2000/www.berlinale.de). U2, S1, S2, S26 *Potsdamer Platz.* **Tickets** €7-€16. *Festival pass* €140. **Credit** call for details. **Date** 1-2wks in mid Feb.
Now approaching 60 years old, this is one of the world's major cinema festivals, featuring over 300 movies from all five continents. It is centred at the Potsdamer Platz cinemas and attended by international stars, providing this normally glamour-proof city with a bit of glitz in the dead of winter. *See p194.*

MaerzMusik – Festival für aktuelle Musik

Organisers: Berliner Festspiele, Schaperstrasse 24, Tiergarten (2548 9100/www.berlinerfestspiele.de). **Tickets** varies. **Credit** varies. **Date** 2-3wks in Mar.
A holdover from the more culture-conscious days of the old East Germany, this annual contemporary music festival invites international avant-garde composers and musicians to present new works.

International Tourism Fair

Messegelände am Funkturm, Messedamm 22, Charlottenburg (3038 2275/www.itb-berlin.de). U2 *Kaiserdamm,* S5, S75 *Messe Süd* or S41, S42, S45, S46 *Messe Nord.* **Open** 10am-6pm daily. **Tickets** varies. **No credit cards.** **Map** p304 A8. **Date** 5 days in mid Mar.
Tourism boards, travel agents and hotels satisfy Berliner wanderlust at this trade fair.

Children

A great big playground for little people.

For such a big city, Berlin is remarkably child-friendly. Its many parks nearly all have swings and roundabouts; some have fantastic adventure playgrounds. Most of the museums have children's sections. The city has superb indoor and outdoor swimming pools (*see p252*) and well-equipped commercial indoor playgrounds.

Public transport with children is a dream compared to most cities. Kids under six travel for free. The main U- and S-Bahn stations have lifts, and buses allow easy rear-door entry for prams and buggies.

Mitte

There's no problem keeping children busy in Mitte. **Museumsinsel** (*see p79*), with its museums and weekend flea market, is a lively spot. Nearby **Monbijou Park** on Oranienburger Strasse has playgrounds and, in summer, a great wading pool, the Kinderbad Monbijou. For a different perspective on Berlin, try a boat tour, many of which operate from the Museumsinsel and nearby. For a bird's-eye view, scan the city from the **Fernsehturm** (TV Tower; *see p89*) on Alexanderplatz. Down below, kids cool off in the **Neptunbrunnen** (*see p88*) in summer.

Children will enjoy the dinosaur skeletons at the **Museum für Naturkunde** (Museum of Natural History; *see p85*), the mummies at the **Ägyptisches Museum** (currently housed at the Altes Museum; *see p80*) and the interactive exhibits at the **Museum für Kommunikation** (*see p83*). The **Museum Kindheit & Jugend** (Museum of Childhood and Youth; *see p89*) has toys and other childhood artefacts from days of old. The **Hackesches Hof Theater** (Rosenthaler Strasse 40-41, 283 2587) puts on an enjoyable Sunday brunch show, with clowns and puppets, from 10am onwards.

The new **Potsdamer Platz** complex contains three multiplex cinemas, which show children's and family films (dubbed into German) each afternoon. Many of the movies at the **Kinderfilmfest**, an offshoot of the annual grown-up FilmFest (*see p186*), are screened around here. Every February there are about 25 new children's films from around the world, and the best one is chosen by a jury of kids aged between 11 and 14.

Many restaurants in Mitte have children's menus, but the area around Hackesche Höfe and Rosenthaler Strasse offers the richest pickings. Try the **Hackescher Hof** (Rosenthaler Strasse 40, 283 5293), American at **Catherine's** (Friedrichstrasse 90, 2025 1555) or regional German food at **Der Kartoffelkeller** (Albrechtstrasse 14B, 282 8548).

AquaDom & Sealife (*see p88*) on Spandauer Strasse has 13 aquariums and plenty of hands-on gadgetry to mess about with. The centrepiece is the mighty AquaDom itself, a cylindrical, salt-water tank with a glass lift rising through the middle, from which you can view some of the thousands of exotic fish. Expect a long queue.

Prenzlauer Berg & Friedrichshain

Prenzlauer Berg has enjoyed a baby boom in recent years (*see p91* **The babes of Prenzl'berg**), but there are few specific attractions for kids. There are, however, plenty of cafés, restaurants, squares and playgrounds, particularly in the area around Kollwitzplatz. Among the restaurants offering children's menus are the Italian **Istoria** (Kollwitzstrasse 64, 4405 0208), **Zander** (Kollwitzstrasse 50, 4405 7678) and **Prater** (Kastanienallee 7; *see p149*) serving German food, and the Indian **Maharadsha 2** (Schönhauser Allee 142, 448 5172).

Die Schaubude (Greifswalder Strasse 81-4, 423 4314) is a high-quality puppet theatre, used by a variety of local and visiting troupes. **Volkspark Friedrichshain** has half-pipes and skater routes, and the Märchenbrunnen ('fairytale fountain') features figures from stories by the Brothers Grimm.

Kreuzberg

This vibrant borough has lots of small shops, plenty of good, cheap restaurants, and a child-friendly atmosphere. Older children will enjoy the **Haus am Checkpoint Charlie** (*see p97*), containing the old cars and balloons that people used to circumvent the Wall. And they'll love the **Gruselkabinett** (*see p97*), a spooky chamber of horrors in an old World War II bunker. The **Deutsches Technikmuseum Berlin** (*see p97*) has vintage locomotives and

Arts & Entertainment

Paradise regained

Berlin's plentiful public parks are remarkably safe and clean, but they do have their perils, especially for those travelling with small children. Watch out for bicycles hurtling by, and not everyone heeds official instructions to keep dogs on a leash – even fewer do their duty when it comes to cleaning up after them.

If you really want to get away from it all, Berlin has some wonderful enclosed parks. For a small fee, you can spend anything from a couple of hours to a whole day in serene surroundings, with no crazy cyclists or doggy do. Further information on these urban oases can be found at www.gruen-berlin.de.

One of Berlin's most interesting enclosed parks is **Naturpark Schöneberger Südgelände**. This nature reserve encapsulates the soul of a city that keeps having to reinvent itself. It's a disused railway marshalling yard, most of which has been left for nature to reclaim. Some facilities, including a 50-metre-high (164-foot) water tower, a steam engine and one of Germany's oldest railway turntables (still functioning), have been kept as exhibits. Walls and concrete embankments have been declared fair game for graffiti artists, and there are nearly three kilometres (two miles) of tracks and boardwalks. The tranquillity is punctuated by modern-day trains whizzing past nearby, but that's just part of the magic.

Britzer Garten is perhaps the best option with small children. You can even (sometimes) hire a small handcart to wheel them around in. Built for a national garden show in 1985, the manicured lawns and futuristic architecture look like something out of *Teletubbies*. Apart from the undulating gardens, the park has some farm animals,

an adventure playground, a mud-hut village built and maintained by kids, a wonderful water playground complete with an Archimedes screw, a narrow-gauge railway, a working 19th-century windmill, and plenty of food and drink options.

Another beautifully landscaped park, **Erholungspark Marzahn**, opened in 1987. The focus here is on oriental gardens. There's a Chinese garden (with restaurant and tea-house), a Korean garden, a Balinese garden and an oriental garden combining horticultural philosophies of various Far Eastern lands. The 'rhododendron grove' features miniature statues of popular figures from the tales of Hans Christian Andersen and the Brothers Grimm. There's also a 'garden of stones' with fountains, ponds and various boulders. An Italian Renaissance garden and a hedge maze are under construction, and the place is dotted with playgrounds, kiosks and cafés.

Britzer Garten
Mohriner Allee, Neukölln. U6 Alt-Mariendorf or U7 Britz-Süd, then bus 181 to Windröschenweg. **Open** 9am-dusk daily. **Admission** €2; €1 6-14s.

Erholungspark Marzahn
S7 Marzahn or U5 Cottbusser Platz, then bus 195 to Erholungspark Marzahn. **Open** 9am-dusk daily. **Admission** €2; €1 6-14s.

Naturpark Schöneberger Südgelände
S2, S26 Priesterweg. **Open** *Summer* 9am-8pm daily. *Winter* 9am-5pm daily. **Admission** €1; under-14s free.

cars to explore, computers and gadgets to play with, and a new 'Maritime Wing' with boats. Tickets include access to 'Spectrum', which has fantastic hands-on experiments and exhibitions.

New City Bowling Hasenheide (*see p248*) has 12 lanes for children and is open from 10am daily. The Hasenheide park next door has a great adventure playground and crazy golf.

Leafy **Viktoriapark** is a landscaped hill with fine views from the top. In summer, a waterfall cascades to street level; in winter toboggans hurtle down the slopes. The park also has playgrounds and a tiny zoo. Stroll down nearby Bergmannstrasse for hot dogs, kebabs, bagels or sit-down snacks and meals in

one of the many cafés and restaurants. Nearby is the huge supervised indoor playground **Jolo** (Am Tempelhofer Berg 7D, 6120 2796, www.jolo-berlin.de). It has amazing facilities, including an inflatable mountain, mini-bumper cars and a snack bar.

The banks of the canal between Carl-Herz-Ufer and Kottbusser Brücke are worth a walk. The restaurant and beer garden **Brachvogel** (Carl-Herz-Ufer 34, 693 0432) also has a crazy golf course, and there's a playground next door. Further east, on the north bank, is the **Böcklerpark** (2219 5321, www.statthaus-boecklerpark.de), which has a small petting zoo and a children's flea market on the last Sunday of the month. Staff also organise sundry other events. Still further east and back on the south side of the canal is the child-friendly Italian **Casolare** (Grimmstrasse 30, 6950 6610), which does great pizzas. For dessert, cross the road to **Isabel's Eiscafé** (Böckhstrasse 1).

At the far east end of the borough is **Görlitzer Park** with playgrounds and another petting zoo.

Schöneberg

Winterfeldplatz is a pleasant focal point at the northern end of this huge district, with an outdoor market each Wednesday and Saturday, and lots of cafés, restaurants and fast food around the square, as well as along Maasenstrasse to the north and Goltzstrasse to the south. There are plenty of parks and playgrounds, but not many specific attractions.

The **Volkspark Wilmersdorf** has several playgrounds (including one with running water in summer and a ski-lift ride). Near the park's eastern end is **Stadtbad Schöneberg**, a swimming pool perfect for kids (*see p253*).

There are child-friendly restaurants dotted all over in Schöneberg. Try the hearty pasta at **Petite Europe** (*see p138*), for example, or burgers, bagels and muffins at **Tim's Canadian Deli** (*see p156*).

South of Schöneberg, in Friedenau, the children's bookshop **Storytime Books** (*see p161*) is worth a look. Also to the south, near S-Bahn Priesterweg (S2, S26), is the **Planetarium am Insulaner** (Munsterdamm

90, 790 0930), which has a programme for children with events several times a week. The nearby **Naturpark Schöneberger Südgelände** offers an unusual walk in the woods (*see p88* **Paradise regained**).

Tiergarten

The major draw in Tiergarten is the park itself with its obligatory playgrounds and welcoming open spaces. Paddle and rowing boats can be hired on the **Neuer See**. Meanwhile, along Strasse 17. Juni, which is the main road leading through the park, there is a cramped but interesting art and flea market on Saturdays and Sundays (*see p176*).

In the park's south-western corner is Berlin's beautiful **Zoo** and, good for rainy days, the sizeable **Aquarium** (for both, *see p105*). The excellent **Gemäldegalerie** (*see p105*) in Matthäikirchplatz runs Sunday afternoon tours for children.

Charlottenburg

Away from the hustle and bustle of Zoologischer Garten and the Ku'damm, the atmosphere here is pleasant, with good restaurants, shops and outdoor markets. The Saturday market at Karl-August-Platz, for example, is a popular gathering point for families, with a playground, cafés and top-notch ice-cream at **Micha's Eisdiele** (Pestalozzistrasse 85).

There's always the **Zoo**.

Arts & Entertainment

Fifteen minutes' walk west is the small but pretty **Lietzenseepark**, with a lake, playgrounds, cafés (open Apr-Oct) and sports areas. If the weather's not great, take the kids to **Toka-Tohei indoor playground** (Wintersteinstrasse 22, 3454 0346, www.tokatohei.de).

There are child-friendly restaurants all over Charlottenburg, particularly in the east part. The kids will be welcome at **La Cantina** (Bleibtreustrasse 17, 883 2156) or **Toto** (corner of Bleibtreustrasse & Pestalozzistrasse, 312 5449). At **Charlottchen** (Droysenstrasse 1, 324 4717) parents eat in the dining room (the food is nothing special) while their kids let their hair down in a rumpus room. There are theatre performances on Sundays (11.30am, 3.30pm).

Daydreaming in **Domäne Dahlem**.

Other districts

The **UFA Fabrik cultural centre** (Viktoriastrasse 10-18, 755 030, www. ufafabrik.de) in the southern district of Tempelhof has a farm for kids, a circus and a variety of courses and workshops. It's right by U-Bahn Ullsteinstrasse (U6) and has several cafés and restaurants.

South-west of the city, the vast **Grunewald** woods (*see p117*) are great for long walks, and the Kronprinzessinnenweg that runs through the middle is perfect for in-line skating and cycling. On a breezy day, fly a kite and enjoy the view from the **Teufelsberg**; on a sunny day, take a dip in the **Teufelssee** or another of the area's numerous lakes. **Strandbad Wannsee** (*see p118*) is Europe's largest inland beach; there's a playground, cafés and pedalos for hire.

To the east of the Grunewald, **Domäne Dahlem** (*see p116*) is a 17th-century-style working farm, featuring demonstrations by blacksmiths, carpenters, bakers and potters. At weekends children can ride ponies, tractors and hay-wagons. Going further back in time, **Museumsdorf Düppel** (*see p119*) is a reconstructed 14th-century village, based around archaeological excavations near the Düppel forest. Kids can ride ox-carts or see demonstrations of medieval technology, crafts and farming techniques (Apr-Oct).

In the district of Gatow to the west of the Havel is the small **British-German Yacht Club** (Kladower Damm 217A, 365 4010), which runs a range of sailing courses (4pm Tue, 11am Sat, closed Nov-Mar). There's also a British pub at the waterside, where parents can relax while the youngsters splash about. In the centre of Gatow, the children get to clamber in and out of the fighters and bombers at the **Luftwaffenmuseum** (*see p115*).

To avoid summer crowds on the Havel and Wannsee, try the **Tegeler See** to the north-west of the centre. In bad weather, take refuge in **Jacks Fun World** (Miraustrasse 38, 4190 0242, www.jacks-fun-world.de), but be warned: the extra fees for the best attractions at this indoor playground can add up. North-east of Tegel, in the quaint village of Alt Lübars, is **Jugendfarm Lübars** (415 7027, closed Oct-Mar, Mon, Sat), where kids can see farm animals, watch craftspeople and eat at the restaurant.

From the centre, it's a half-hour trip on the S3 to Wuhlheide. There, in the woods south-east of the city, you'll find **FEZ in der Wuhlheide** (An der Wuhlheide 197, 5307 1504). This communist-era children's park has a narrow-gauge railway, swimming and wading pools, forts, trampolines and picnic areas. The **Mellowpark** in nearby Köpenick (Friedrichshagener Strasse 10-12) offers supervised play for older children. Activities, daily from 2pm in summer, include skating, boarding, basketball and breakdancing on the banks of the Spree.

Also to the east is the **Tierpark Berlin-Friedrichsfelde** (*see p120*), a lovely park and zoo, featuring grassland animals such as giraffes and deer, playgrounds, a petting zoo and snack stands. Still further east, the **Müggelsee** (*see p120*) is another beautiful sailing and swimming area. Day trips by boat come here from Mitte in the summer.

Babysitters

There's a good online search engine (in German) for babysitters at www.berlinonline.de/mamas-und-papas/babysitter.

Biene Maja
344 3973/www.babysitteragentur.de.
Rates €9.50-€13/hr. **No credit cards**.

Film

Despite the multiplexes, English-language cinema remains healthy in Berlin.

Anyone returning to Berlin after a few years away will find a cinema landscape changed as drastically as the rest of the city. Before, during and for several years after the fall of the Wall, Berlin had a network of charming and idiosyncratic neighbourhood repertory cinemas in both east and west. Now, like everywhere else in the western world, the city's been multiplexed, with over 260 screens all showing the same old stuff – the latest from Hollywood, a sprinkling of British or French crossover 'hits', and mainstream German product just about holding down a modest niche.

One result has been that English-language programming, once the speciality of the small and daring, has become the domain of the large, and largely conservative, multiplex chains. Even the **Internationale Filmfestspiele Berlin** (*see p194* **Berlin International Film Festival**) – both one of the world's most important film festivals and one of Berlin's major cultural events – has forsaken historic landmark venues for two new multiplexes in the glorified mall that is Potsdamer Platz.

Those with mainstream tastes will feel at home in the modern multiplex of Cinestar (all eight screens in English) or its competing neighbour, CinemaxX Potsdamer Platz (two or three of its 19 screens in English). Though the historically less conservative all-English houses such as an **Odeon** or **Babylon** have become more middle of the road, their old-style atmosphere remains a welcome change of pace.

For rabid cineastes, all is not totally lost. Berlin is a city with not one, but two cinematheques: the **Arsenal** and the **Filmkunsthaus Babylon**, the latter under new management apparently keen on more original-language programming. Also, the **Zeughaus Kino** of the Deutsches Historisches Museum has reopened with a programme including many English-language classic movies (www.dhm.de/kino). And despite all the closures, some small off-cinemas have managed to hold on. The current list even includes one new addition: the **Dokument Kino**, devoted exclusively to documentaries, many in English.

One lasting Berlin phenomenon is a fascination with silent films, often presented with live musical accompaniment, ranging from simple piano to full symphony orchestra, with the occasional hardcore band for variety.

Recurring favourites include German historical hits such as *Metropolis*, *Berlin: Die Sinfonie der Grosstadt* and *The Cabinet of Dr Caligari*, though almost anything could show up. The most likely venues are Arsenal, Filmkunsthaus Babylon or any of the outdoor cinemas, and the Filmfest inevitably has at least one major special event of this kind.

The outdoor cinema, the Frieluftkino, is another popular tradition, though with Berlin's unpredictable weather the screen count varies from year to year. Unfortunately, almost everything, apart from silent films, is shown synchronised into German, but original English programming seems to be on the rise again at the **Freiluftkino Kreuzberg**, and on a clement night it can be fun.

FESTIVALS

A more reliable way to while away summer evenings is the **Fantasy Film Festival** (www.fantasyfilmfest.com), held at the CinemaxX (*see p193*) in mid August and showing the latest in fantasy, splatter, horror and sci-fi from America, Hong Kong, Japan and Europe. Films are often premières, with occasional previews, programmed retrospectives and assorted rarities. Aside from the occasional German film, all shows have been in English or with English subtitles.

In the spring it's **Britspotting**, the British Independent Film Festival (www.britspotting. de), an annual compilation of the freshest low-budget contributions to celluloid coming out of the UK. Organised by the British Council, it appears in April and May. Check the website for venues.

There are two film festivals, both in autumn, that spotlight gay and lesbian cinema. The more elaborate of the two is **Verzaubert: The International Queer Film Festival** (www.verzaubertfilmfest.com), run by the same bunch who do the Fantasy Film Fest. Presented in November and December at Kino International (Karl-Marx-Allee 33, Mitte, 2475 6011, www.yorck.de), it offers a high-profile survey of gay and lesbian cinema from around the world. The **Lesben Film Festival** (www.lesbenfilmfestival.de) manifests itself every October at the Arsenal with a wide international selection of films from the distaff side of queer cinema. Many events are for women only.

Wilder at heart

If ever there was a favourite Berliner in film history, it might be the writer and director **Billy Wilder**, who would have been 100 in 2006. Never mind that his fame derives from Hollywood films such as *Some Like It Hot*, *The Apartment* or *Sunset Boulevard*. Or that, like many famous Germans in Hollywood, he was actually Austrian. Wilder found his place in this city's heart with his two post-war Berlin films, *A Foreign Affair* (1948) and *One, Two, Three* (1961). And Wilder's name has been given to the cocktail bar next to the **Arsenal** (*see p192*) and **Filmmuseum** (*see p104*) and at the entrance to the Sony Center.

Wilder came of age in the wild days of Weimar Berlin, where he made his way as a journalist and gigolo. A career as a screenwriter was cut short by the rise of the Nazis. The Jewish Wilder beat it out of town with $1,000 and the address of a rich girlfriend living abroad. He arrived in Hollywood in 1934 as a complete unknown, roomed with fellow Berliner Peter Lorre, and worked a series of odd jobs, earning $75 for jumping fully clothed into a swimming pool at a Hollywood party. He learned English by listening to radio soap operas and baseball commentary, the latter no doubt contributing to his later wisecracking style. Like many émigrés, Wilder found the best way to success was minimising his foreignness and assimilating himself into the American scene. But as American as he became, his films, even the serious ones, are strongly marked by his irreverent, and sharply cynical, Berlin sense of humour.

This was the case with his two signature Berlin films, actually American productions, each of which captured the city in a defining historical moment. *A Foreign Affair* starred Marlene Dietrich singing 'Black Market' amid the post-war ruins and cast a satirical eye on the Allied occupation. *One, Two, Three* cast Mickey Rooney as a soft-drink exec and Horst Buchholz as a sloganeering young communist to poke fun at divided Berlin at the height of the Cold War. Both films were rich in local colour but Wilder's prodigal-son response to his old hometown and its strange relationship with its American occupiers cut a little too close to the bone, rubbing Berlin audiences the wrong way.

Nonetheless it was Wilder, as always, who got the last laugh. Both films were eventually adopted by the city they portrayed and both are now oft-revived cult favourites. Interestingly enough, Wilder himself got caught in the middle of the Berlin Crisis of 1961. When the Wall shot up overnight during the making of *One, Two, Three*, it nixed his planned shoot at the Brandenburg Gate. The location in the movie is actually a set built at Bavaria Studios in Munich.

Billy Wilder's

Sony Center, Potsdamer Strasse 2, Potsdamer Platz, Tiergarten (2655 4860/ www.billywilders.de). U2, S1, S2, S26 Potsdamer Platz. **Open** noon-2am daily. **Credit** AmEx, MC, V. **Map** p306/p311 K7/L7. Classic cocktail bar serving classic cocktails at the heart of Berlin's central cinema district. Wilder lends his name to Billy's Bellini (€9). There's a 6-8pm happy hour and a midnight-1am 'blue hour'. Snacks and sandwiches are available too.

Newest on the horizon is the **One World Medienfest**, which takes place in November as an extension of its namesake in Prague. Nominally centred on human rights issues, it also includes films on politics, religion, music, art and culture, with some live performances and events. At least half of the programme is in English or with English subtitles. For information on the original One World festival, visit www.oneworld.cz; check www.oneworld-fest.de or local listings for programme updates.

INFORMATION

The best way to find out what's going on is to check the listings in *tip* and *Zitty*, as well as *[030]*, which is available free in most bars. You can also look at the English-language monthly *Exberliner*, but be aware some listings info is dodgy. Check for the notation OF or OV ('Originalfassung' or 'original version'), OmU ('original with subtitles', which could be a French or Chinese movie with German titles) or OmE ('original with English subtitles'). The cinemas listed are those most likely to show films in English.

Cinemas

Arsenal

Sony Center, Potsdamer Strasse 2, Potsdamer Platz, Tiergarten (2695 5100/www.fdk-berlin.de). U2, S1, S2, S26 Potsdamer Platz. **Tickets** €6.50; €4.50 concessions. **No credit cards. Map** p306/p311 K7/L7.

This is the Berlin Cinematheque in everything but name. Its brazenly eclectic programming ranges from classic Hollywood flicks to contemporary Middle Eastern cinema, from Russian art films to Italian horror movies, from Third World documentaries to silent films with live accompaniment. It shows many English-language films and sometimes also screens foreign films with English subtitles. Occasionally filmmakers show up to present their work and answer questions. The Arsenal's two state-of-the-art screening rooms are in the Sony Center, placing it in the belly of the great Hollywood Beast – probably right where we need it. Like its bigger neighbours, the Arsenal is a major venue for the Internationale Filmfestspiele Berlin (*see p194* **Berlin International Film Festival**).

Babylon Kreuzberg (A&B)

Dresdener Strasse 126, Kreuzberg (6160 9693/ www.yorck.de). U1, U8 Kottbusser Tor/bus 247. **Tickets** €4.90-€7. **No credit cards**. **Map** p307 P9.
This twin-screen theatre runs a varied programme of off-Hollywood, indie crossover and UK films. Formerly a neighbourhood Turkish cinema, its programme now consists almost entirely of English-language movies; the place offers a cosy respite from all the multiplexes. Beware: Babylon Kreuzberg should not to be confused with Filmkunsthaus Babylon (for which, *see p194*).

Central

Rosenthaler Strasse 39, Mitte (2859 9973/www.kino-central.de). U8 Weinmeisterstrasse or S5, S7, S9, S75 Hackescher Markt. **Tickets** €4.50-€6.50. **No credit cards**. **Map** p303/p310 N5.
Not as much English as it once had, it is still one of the more innovatively programmed cinemas in town. On the edge of busy Hackesche Höfe, it's definitely worth a look in.

CinemaxX Potsdamer Platz

Potsdamer Strasse 5, Potsdamer Platz, Tiergarten (2592 2111/www.cinemaxx.de). U2, S1, S2, S26 Potsdamer Platz. **Tickets** €4.50-€7.30. **No credit cards**. **Map** p306/p311 L7.
The biggest multiplex in town with 19 screens, two or three of which usually show something in English. Bland mall surroundings for programming that is strictly Hollywood mainstream. A main venue for the Internationale Filmfestspiele Berlin (*see p194* **Berlin International Film Festival**).

CineStar Sony Center

Potsdamer Strasse 4, Potsdamer Platz, Tiergarten (2606 6400/www.cinestar.de). U2, S1, S2, S26 Potsdamer Platz. **Tickets** €4.50-€7.50; €4.50-€5.50 concessions. **No credit cards**. **Map** p306/p311 K7/L7.
Programming is much the same as its Potsdamer Platz neighbour, CinemaxX (*see above*), but showing films exclusively in their original languages, mostly English. Despite a few random sparks of creativity, it is basically mainstream fare. A 5-Star ticket permits you five entries for €30. Also a main venue for the Internationale Filmfestspiele Berlin (*see p194* **Berlin International Film Festival**).

Dokument Kino

Rungestrasse 20, Mitte (2759 5895/www.dokument-kino.de). U8 Heinrich-Heine-Strasse or U8, S5, S7, S9, S75 Jannowitzbrücke. **Tickets** €3-€4. **No credit cards**. **Map** p307 P7.
This newest addition to Berlin's off-cinemas features all documentaries all the time, on potentially any subject you can name. Located in a cosy upstairs cinema on the border of Mitte and Kreuzberg.

Eiszeit

Zeughofstrasse 20, Kreuzberg (611 6016/www.eiszeit-kino.de). U1 Görlitzer Bahnhof. **Tickets** €5-€6; €3 concessions. **No credit cards**. **Map** p307 Q9.

CineStar Sony Center – mainstream but exclusively original-language screenings.

Berlin International Film Festival

The **Internationale Filmfestspiele Berlin** (*see also p186*) is the city's biggest annual, and international, event. Born out of the Cold War, it developed from a propaganda showcase, supported by the Allies, into a genuine meeting place – or maybe collision point – for East and West during the post-War, Cold War and post-Cold War periods. Whether it was the French boycott over Stanley Kubrick's *Paths of Glory* in 1959, the jury revolt over the pro-Vietnamese *OK* in 1970, or the East Bloc walkout over the depiction of Vietnamese people in *The Deer Hunter* in 1979, the drama of the festival was never confined to the screens. The years following the fall of the Wall were particularly exciting, reflecting the joy and chaos of the changing city.

Now settled into its new home in Potsdamer Platz, the festival has taken on more of the glamour and celebrity of its two major rivals, Cannes and Venice. The **Filmmuseum Berlin** (*see p104*) in the nearby Sony Center has increased the profile of the Retrospective section and added opportunities for special exhibitions and events. The festival's director, Dieter Kosslick, energetically added sidebars and symposiums, an outreach programme for developing filmmakers (Talent Campus) and, most recently, a co-production market for film financing. Berlin also offers arguably the widest and most eclectic mix of any film festival, and is at least as much about the audiences as the industry. Every February, it seems the entire city has turned out to see the hundreds of films, presented in eight sections – the most important are given below.

THE INTERNATIONAL COMPETITION

If the most visible part in terms of glamour and publicity, this is also by nature the most conservative in selection. Concentrating on major, big-budget productions from all over the world, with a heavy (and often heavily criticised) accent on America, these films often make it to general release. Films compete for the Gold and Silver Bears, and there can sometimes be a furore accompanying the announcement of the winners. Since the evening galas are the most expensive and most likely to sell out, go for the afternoon shows or the repeats in neighbourhood cinemas. All shows in the Berlinale Palast come with simultaneous translation over headphones. Repeats are at the **Urania** (An der Urania 17, Schöneberg, 218 9091) and **Kino International** (Karl-Marx-Allee 33, Mitte, 2475 6011, www.yorck.de).

THE INTERNATIONAL FORUM OF YOUNG CINEMA

Some devotees claim this is the real Berlin festival, and the place where discoveries are made. Born out of the revolt that dissolved the Competition in the 1970 festival, the Forum provides challenging and eclectic fare that you wouldn't see elsewhere. Anything can happen here, from the latest American indie film, to African cinema, to midnight shows of Hong Kong action films. The likes of George Clooney can look pretty small waving from the stage of the Berlinale Palast, but at the Forum dialogue between audience and filmmaker is de rigueur. Shows at **CineStar** (*see p193*), **Arsenal** (*see p192*) and the **Delphi** (Kantstrasse 12A, Charlottenburg, 312 1026) have simultaneous translation.

PANORAMA

Intended to showcase films that fell outside the strict guidelines of the Competition, the Panorama now gives the Forum a run for its money in terms of innovative programming.

Once the most energetic cinema in town, now not as self-consciously weird but still offering some welcome changes from multiplex fare.

Filmkunsthaus Babylon

Rosa-Luxemburg-Strasse 30, Mitte (242 5076/ www.fkh-babylon.de). U2, U5, U8, S5, S7, S9, S75 Alexanderplatz or U2 Rosa-Luxemburg-Platz. **Tickets** €5.50-€6.50; €5.50 concessions. **No credit cards. Map** p303/p310 O5.

Not to be confused with Babylon Kreuzberg (*see p193*), this was once a premier East German theatre, housed in a landmark building by Hans Poelzig, who designed the classic German silent film *The Golem*.

After years of renovation, the cinema is back to its full Weimar glory and it's worth a visit just for that. The place was recently taken over by new management and programming policy was still refining itself at press time, though English-language fare seemed on the increase. Its cosy auxiliary *kino* around the corner is likely to offer more original-language programming and assorted surprises.

Freiluftkino Kreuzberg

Mariannenplatz 2, courtyard of Haus Bethanien, Kreuzberg (www.freiluftkino-kreuzberg.de). U1, U8 Kottbusser Tor or S3, S5, S7, S9, S75 Ostbahnhof. **Tickets** €6. **No credit cards. Map** p307 Q8.

But Panorama films are less rigorous than the Forum, with a spotlight on world independent movies, gay and lesbian, and political films. Panorama films show in the **CineStar** (*see p193*) and **Zoo Palast** (Hardenbergstrasse 29A, Charlottenburg, 2541 4777), with special premières at **International** (Karl-Marx-Allee 33, Mitte, 2475 6011), with repeats at **CinemaxX** (*see p193*), CineStar and **Colosseum** (Schönhauser Allee 123, Prenzlauer Berg, 01805 2463 6299). Most have English subtitles.

PERSPEKTIVE DEUTSCHES KINO AND NEW GERMAN CINEMA

Both New German Cinema and its baby brother Perspektive reflect the festival's increased focus on current German cinema, with a range of interesting and provocative fare. If German cinema has a bad rep, these sections are here to overturn it. Screenings are at **CinemaxX** (*see p193*) and **Colosseum** (Schönhauser Allee 123, Prenzlauer Berg, 01805 2463 6299); all films have English subtitles.

RETROSPECTIVE

Perhaps the surest bet for sheer movie-going pleasure. While the Retrospective often concentrates on the established mainstream, it's a not-to-be-missed opportunity to see classics, as well as rarities, on the big screen. Themes have ranged from great directors such as Fritz Lang, Erich von Stroheim or William Wyler, to subjects such as Production Design, Cinemascope, Hollywood Mavericks or Nazi entertainment films. There is also an *hommage* section, which celebrates the work of stars such as Kirk Douglas, Shirley MacLaine or Jeanne Moreau. It's often accompanied by an exhibition and daily seminars (mostly in English) at the nearby **Filmmuseum** (*see p104*). Films show at **CinemaxX** (*see p193*) and **Zeughaus Kino** (*see p196*).

TALENT CAMPUS

Not a film series per se, this newly created event offers a chance for young filmmakers from all over the world to come together, show their work and learn from world-class professionals. Guest speakers and participants have included Anthony Minghella, Ken Adam (designer of the James Bond films), Wim Wenders and even John Cale, who did a lecture/demo on film scoring.

TICKETS

Tickets can be bought up to three days in advance (four days for Competition repeats) at the main ticket office in the **Arkaden am Potsdamer Platz** (Alte Potsdamer Strasse, Tiergarten, 259 2000), as well as yearly changing locations around the city and online. On the day they must be bought at the theatre box office and last-minute tickets are often available. Queues for advance tickets can be long and online tickets can go fast, so plan ahead. Competition and Panorama films are described in a catalogue, which you can pick up for a nominal price at the main ticket office. The Forum has its own programme booklet, available free at every Forum theatre. There is also a free daily *Festival Journal,* with news, articles and screening info, available at all theatres. Films usually screen three times.

Tickets are usually €7-€16, but Berlinale Palast is cheaper during the day and on the last day all films showing are reduced. There are group discounts and 50 per cent off for students, unemployed and disabled. From January, check for updates and programme information at **www.berlinale.de**.

This big-screen Dolby Stereo outdoor summer cinema (open June through August), offers a decent mix of past cinema hits, cult films and independent movies. Bring a pillow. And maybe an umbrella.

FSK

Segitzdamm 2, Kreuzberg (614 3195/www.fsk-kino.de). U1, U8 Kottbusser Tor or U8 Moritzplatz. **Tickets** €5-€6.50. **No credit cards. Map** p307 O9. This two-screen cinema is in the heart of Turkish Kreuzberg – handy for the bars and cafés. It mostly gets German versions, but has some American and British indie films and documentaries, and Taiwanese or Hong Kong films with English subtitles.

Hackesche Höfe

Rosenthaler Strasse 40-41, Mitte (283 4603/www.hackesche-hoefe.org). U8 Weinmeisterstrasse or S5, S7, S9, S75 Hackescher Markt. **Tickets** €5-€7.50; €6.50 concs. **No credit cards. Map** p303/p310 N5. Being a four-flight walk-up hasn't stopped this from being one of the area's best-attended cinemas. It shows mostly foreign films, with feature-length docs and some indie features in English. Tickets are available from 2.30pm Mon-Sat, from 10.30am Sun.

High End 54 im Kunsthaus Tacheles

Oranienburger Strasse 54-6, Mitte (283 1498/Tacheles office 282 6185). U6 Oranienburger Tor

The old-school **Odeon** just about holds its own in the multiplex era.

or S1, S2 Oranienburger Strasse. **Tickets** €5-€6.
No credit cards. Map p302/p310 M5.
Once the screening room for the GDR State Film
Archive, this two-screen cinema is part of the multi-
purpose Tacheles centre. Programming is a mish-
mash of independent and off-Hollywood films, plus
some interesting foreign movies. Films in original
English seem to show as often as not.

Moviemento
*Kottbusser Damm 22, Kreuzberg (692 4785/
www.moviemento.de). U7, U8 Hermannplatz or
U8 Schönleinstrasse*. **Tickets** €4.50-€6.50; €5.50
concessions. **No credit cards**. Map p307 P10.
A Kreuzberg institution, this laid-back upstairs
cinema shows a few films in English in three small
screening rooms (232 seats altogether).

Odeon
*Hauptstrasse 116, Schöneberg (7870 4019/www.
yorck.de). U4, S41, S42, S45, S46 Innsbrucker
Platz or S1, S41, S42, S45, S46 Schöneberg*.
Tickets €4.90-€7.50; €5 concessions. **No
credit cards**. Map p305 H11.
Deep in the heart of Schöneberg, this is one of the
last big, old, single-screen neighbourhood cinemas,
it should be supported just for that. Still exclusively
English-language, providing a reasonably intelligent
selection of Hollywood and UK fare.

Xenon
*Kolonnenstrasse 5-6, Schöneberg (782 8850/www.
xenon-kino.de). U7 Kleistpark*. **Tickets** €4-€6; €2.50
concessions. **No credit cards**. Map p306 J11.
A snug cinema mostly dedicated to gay and lesbian
programming, largely from the US and the UK. The
films are predominantly in English.

Zeughaus Kino
*Unter den Linden 2, Mitte (203 0421/tickets 2030
4670/www.dhm.de/kino). U8 Weinmeisterstrasse
or S5, S7, S9, S75 Hackescher Markt*. **Tickets** €5.
No credit cards. Map p303/p311 N6.

The recently renovated Zeughaus Kino at the
Deutsches Historisches Museum (*see p79*) often
hosts travelling retrospective shows. It makes a concerted effort to get the original versions.

Video rental

If home video can be blamed for the decline
of repertory cinema, Berlin has several video-
rental outlets that almost make up for the loss.
(All outlets demand ID and proof of residency
when you open an account.) The **Amerika-
Gedenkbibliothek** (Blücherplatz, Kreuzberg,
9022 6105, www.zlb.de, closed Sun) has a
good range of classics, silents, musicals, sci-fi,
westerns and war films, mostly on video,
but more and more DVDs. All can be borrowed
free with a library card (a one-off €10, €5
concessions). The **British Council Library**
(Hackescher Markt 1, Mitte, 3110 9910, www.
britishcouncil.de, closed Sun) has a large
collection of British classic and contemporary
films and TV shows. **Film Galerie 451**
(Torstrasse 231, Mitte, 2345 7911, www.film
galerie451.de) has a decent selection of English-
language fare, including foreign films and TV
series. **Incredibly Strange Video** (Eisenacher
Strasse 1, Schöneberg, 215 1770, www.incredibly.
de, closed Sun) covers sci-fi, horror, crime,
comedy, foreign films and many TV shows.
Negativeland (Dunkerstrasse 9, Prenzlauer
Berg, 447 7447, www.negativeland.de, closed
Sun) has a meaty selection of biker, cult hit,
Japanimation, lesbian vampire, foreign, *Star
Trek*, documentary and music films. The
amazing **Videodrom** (Mittenwalder Strasse
11, Kreuzberg, 695 740 611) offers over 20,000
titles, encompassing mainstream, Japanimation,
splatter, Hong Kong and women-in-prison films,
as well as cult and current TV shows.

Galleries

The money's too tight to mention, but growing international credibility fuels a dogged optimism on the Berlin art scene.

The local art market remains impossibly sluggish, but despite the uncertain economic future of Germany in general and Berlin in particular, there is still a certain optimism in the air. This is due, in part, to Berlin's finally – and firmly – established credibility as an International Capital of Art. Not only do Berlin gallerists enjoy an increasing presence internationally (take, for example, the worldwide success of Gerd Harry 'Judy' Lybke and the **Eigen + Art** crew), but the continued success of the city's own major international fair, the **Berlin Art Forum** (www.art-forum-berlin.de), brings the increasing participation of galleries (and buyers) from abroad. And now, in response to all the high-powered proceedings at the Forum, the same autumn weekend sees three fledgling homegrown events: the alternative **Kunstsalon** (www.berliner kunstsalon.de); the even more alternative **Berliner Liste** (liste@voelker.de), representing smaller, independent galleries from all over Europe; and the more cohesive and upscale **Preview** (www.previewberlin.de), which premiered this year at the Brotfabrik (*see p239*) to great acclaim.

Additionally, among the thousand-plus exhibitions and events that took place in 2005 were the first and second exhibitions drawn from the massive (and controversial) **Frick Collection**, currently on loan at the Hamburger Bahnhof (*see p85*) and seeing the light of day in carefully curated instalments. Add to that the **Biennale** (www.berlinbiennale.de) and the plans of several major galleries to up sticks in other capitals and decamp to Berlin, and you have a surefire recipe for international success.

Chaotic geographic trends, which in the past had the scene in a never-ending state of flux, have settled at last. **Charlottenburg**, though quieter, still remains the classic showplace for some of Berlin's oldest established dealers, specialising in classic contemporary pre-1990s art. Mitte's historic **Scheunenviertel** sees many of the city's galleries still clustering in and around its main drag, Auguststrasse, with some important alternative spaces holding the fort on Brunnenstrasse to the north. But the area around **Checkpoint Charlie**, resettled by some of the city's finest galleries as an alternative to the Viertel's busloads of non-

buying tourists and bar-hoppers, is still breathing new life into Berlin art. The **DAADgalerie** and **Jette Rudolph** (*see p200* **Zimmerstrasse's newest recruit**) have recently joined the roster of luminaries in this area, and more will soon follow. Similarly, the galleries clustered under the arches of **Jannowitzbrücke** station – including **BüroFriedrich, Mehdi Chouakri, Carlier/Gebauer** and the second **Max Hetzler** – have wonderful new neighbours from out-of-town in the tower block across the street. Add to that the large art deco building on Rosa-Luxemburg-Platz across from the Volksbühne (*see p238*) – shared by **MagnusMüller, Johann König** and **Christian Nagel** – and you've got a good, focused start on the grand tour.

A **Galerienrundgang**, or walkabout, takes place three times a year for galleries around Auguststrasse, and a less formal collective called KunstMitteNord now sponsors an **Open Weekend** (www.kunstmittenord.de); check local listings for exact dates and times. There are also guided tours through the galleries in Charlottenburg and Mitte every autumn. More information is available at **www.kunstherbst.de**.

LISTINGS AND INFORMATION

Artery is the most complete art guide for Berlin and environs. It is published every two months and sold at galleries, bookstores and some newsagents. *Berliner Galerien* serves all of Berlin but is more selective, and *Index* lists only those galleries in Mitte; both of these are free and available in most galleries and museums. *Zitty* and *tip*, the two Berlin listings fortnightlies, cover most current showings throughout the city. Almost every gallery has a website, with many in English. For those with serviceable German, www.art-in-berlin.de provides up-to-date information on current events and the inner workings of the market.

Mitte

Alexander Ochs Galleries
Sophienstrasse 21 (2839 1387/www.alexanderochs-galleries.de). U8 Weinmeisterstrasse or S5, S7, S9, S75 Hackescher Markt. **Open** 11am-6pm Tue-Sat. **No credit cards. Map** p303/p310 N5.

Begun in 1997 by Ochs and his partner Jaana Prüss as part of a European cultural exchange with China, this gallery features important young Chinese artists such as Fang Lijun, Yin Xiuzhen and Xu Bing. There are also some showings from other South-east Asian countries.

Arndt & Partner

Zimmerstrasse 90-91 (280 8123/www.arndt-partner. com). U6 Kochstrasse. **Open** 11am-6pm Tue-Sat. **Credit** MC, V. **Map** p306/p311 M8.

At this high-powered, high-quality establishment, gallerist Matthias Arndt shows excellent examples from the more accessible side of experimental work. Artists represented here include Sophie Calle, Thomas Hirschhorn, Mathilde ter Heijne, Keith Tyson and Massimo Vitali.

Galerie Barbara Thumm

Dircksenstrasse 41 (2839 0347/www.bthumm.de). U2, U5, U8, S5, S7, S9, S75 Alexanderplatz. **Open** 11am-6pm Tue-Fri; 1-6pm Sat. **Credit** MC, V. **Map** p303/p311 O5.

A respected gallerist in Berlin and abroad, Barbara Thumm delivers a solid programme of established names, such as (e.) Twin Gabriel, Sabine Hornig and Alex Katz, and newer artists Martin Dammann, Christian Hoischen and Ralf Ziervogel.

Galerie Barbara Weiss

Zimmerstrasse 88-91 (262 4284/www.galeriebarbara weiss.de). U6 Kochstrasse. **Open** 11am-6pm Tue-Sat. **No credit cards.** **Map** p306/p311 M8.

This beautiful gallery's rather spare, modest atmosphere is reflected in its style of exhibition. Gallerist Barbara Weiss specialises in serious-minded, no-frills presentations of such international conceptually oriented artists as Jonathan Horowitz, Frederike Feldmann and Eric Steinbrecher.

Galerie Berinson

Auguststrasse 22 (2838 7990/www.berinson.de). S1, S2 Oranienburger Strasse. **Open** 11am-6pm Tue-Sat. **No credit cards.** **Map** p303/p311 N5.

A tiny, classic gem on the main drag, Hendrik Berinson's gallery is best known for exhibits of fine vintage photography by such 20th-century masters as Weegee and Peter Hujar. Other photographers in his collection include Lee Miller, Laszlo Moholy-Nagy and even Stanley Kubrick.

BüroFriedrich

Holzmarktstrasse 15-18, S-Bahn Arches 53/54 (2016 5115/www.buerofriedrich.org). U8, S5, S7, S9, S75 Jannowitzbrücke. **Open** noon-6pm Tue-Sat. **No credit cards.** **Map** p307 P7.

Waling Boers began this non-profit venue as somewhere to house internationally collaborative 'projects' with an interesting cultural-studies bent. Highlights have included *Higher Truth 2 (A Project on Fashion)* and work by Kurdish videographer Fikret Atay, and there's an upcoming show by Susan Phillips. BüroFriedrich is now planning to open its second space in Beijing.

Capri

Brunnenstrasse 149 (6956 5383/www.capri-berlin. de). U8 Bernauer Strasse. **Open** 4-7pm Thur-Sat; or by appointment. **No credit cards.** **Map** p303 N3.

Ina Bierstadt, Bettina Carl and Alena Meier established Capri in 2001 as a purely non-commercial showcase for themselves and other independent artists such as Geka Heinke, Tina Habor and Thomas Ravens of WBD (*see p202*). Formerly a florist's shop (some of the fixtures remain from this previous incarnation), the venue hosts project-oriented showings fortnightly.

Carlier/Gebauer

Holzmarktstrasse 15-18, S-Bahn Arches 51/52 (280 8110/www.carliergebauer.com). U8, S5, S7, S9, S75 Jannowitzbrücke. **Open** 11am-6pm Tue-Sat. **No credit cards.** **Map** p307 P7.

Ulrich Gebauer and co-director Marie Blanche Carlier present a truly varied programme of larger-scale installations and work in various media by international and politically minded contemporary artists such as Tracey Emin, Luc Tuymans, Thomas Schütte and Aernout Mik.

Galerie Christian Nagel

Weydinger Strasse 2-4 (4004 2641/www.galerie-nagel.de). U2 Rosa-Luxemburg-Platz. **Open** 11am-7pm Tue-Sat. **No credit cards.** **Map** p303/p310 O5.

Opened in 2002, this offspring of the original Galerie Christian Nagel in Cologne continues to further its somewhat austere and socially conscious position with installations by Kai Althoff and Mark Dion, and paintings by Gang Zhao.

C/O Berlin

Linienstrasse 144 (2809 1925/www.co-berlin.com). U6 Oranienburger Tor or S1, S2 Oranienburger Strasse. **Open** 11am-7pm Wed-Sun. **Admission** €5; €4 concessions. **No credit cards.** **Map** p302/p310 M5.

Co-founded by photographer Stephan Erfurt, this magnificent building contains studios, a rooftop lounge and a first-class space for exhibits by internationally known photographers such as Margaret Bourke-White, Alfred Eisenstaedt, André Rival and James Nachtway.

Contemporary Fine Arts

Sophienstrasse 21 (288 7870/www.cfa-berlin.com). U8 Weinmeisterstrasse or S5, S7, S9, S75 Hackescher Markt. **Open** 10am-6pm Tue- Fri; 11am-5pm Sat. **No credit cards.** **Map** p303/p310 N5.

Well-established off a quiet courtyard in the Sophie-Gips-Höfen, Contemporary Fine Arts is where Brunno Brunnet and Nicole Hackert exhibit contemporary works by such solid representative artists as Cecily Brown, Daniel Richter, Raymond Pettibon, Juergen Teller, plus the collaborative work of Albert Oehlen and Jonathan Meese.

Galerie Crone Andreas Osarek

Kochstrasse 60 (2589 9370/www.cronegalerie.de). U6 Kochstrasse. **Open** 10am-1pm, 2-6pm Tue-Fri; 11am-6pm Sat. **No credit cards.** **Map** p306/p311 M8.

Championing Leipzig School luminaries – **Galerie Eigen + Art**.

In a new storefront space not far from Checkpoint Charlie and Zimmerstrasse, Andreas Osarek continues the tradition begun in Hamburg by his late partner, Ascan Crone. A wide spectrum of contemporary work that ranges from Rosemarie Trockel and Gilbert & George to Hanne Darboven and Cosima von Bonin.

DAADgalerie

Zimmerstrasse 90-91 (261 3640/www.daad-berlin.de). U6 Kochstrasse. **Open** 11am-6pm Mon-Sat. **No credit cards**. **Map** p306/p311 M8.
Formerly above the Café Einstein (*see p156*), the brand new and highly visible shopfront gallery of the 40-year-old Berlin Artists-in-Residence Program continues to invite important and aspiring artists to Berlin. Stan Douglas, Rachel Whiteread and Damien Hirst are among the alumni.

Galerie Eigen + Art

Auguststrasse 26 (280 6605/www.eigen-art.com). S1, S2 Oranienburger Strasse. **Open** 11am-6pm Tue-Sat. **No credit cards**. **Map** p303/p311 N5.
Now a star of the international art world (and a far cry from his Leipzig living-room gallery in the early 1980s), the ubiquitous Gerd Harry 'Judy' Lybke continues to champion Leipzig School luminaries such as Neo Rauch and Tim Eitel, as well as presenting startling newer talents such as Martin Eder.

Esther Schipper

Linienstrasse 85 (2839 0139/www.estherschipper. com). U8 Rosenthaler Platz. **Open** 11am-6pm Tue-Sat. **No credit cards**. **Map** p302/p310 N5.
Since beginning in the early 1990s with partner Michael Krome, Esther Schipper has always had a penchant for heady projects and cutting-edge greats, and the tradition continues with, among others, Angela Bulloch, Liam Gillick and Carsten Höller.

Galerie Giti Nourbakhsch

Rosenthaler Strasse 72 (4404 6781/www.nourbakhsch. de). U8 Rosenthaler Platz. **Open** 11am-6pm Tue-Sat. **No credit cards**. **Map** p303/p310 N5.
This former hair salon remains as refreshing and brash as a quasi-established gallery can get, with a continuous – often difficult – mix of known and emerging artists such as Piotr Janas, Zoe Leonard, Vincent Tavenne and Hayley Tompkins. Though perhaps not quite as loud as in earlier days, the effect is often no less startling.

Johann König

Weydingerstrasse 10 (3088 2688/www.johann koenig.de). U2 Rosa-Luxemburg-Platz. **Open** 11am-7pm Tue-Sat. **No credit cards**. **Map** p303/p310 O5.
A newer but active presence on the domestic and international scene, Johann König often presents sparse, politically oriented and conceptualised

Arts & Entertainment

Zimmerstrasse's newest recruit

In a rarefied but accessible part of Mitte, the enclave at Zimmerstrasse 88-91 sits all by itself, just a stone's throw from Checkpoint Charlie. Bordered by a wide, empty lot where the Wall once stood, this turn-of-the-century business complex now houses some of Berlin's most prestigious contemporary galleries, including **Arndt & Partner** (see p198), **Barbara Weiss** (see p198), **Volker Diehl** (see p202), **Max Hetzler** (see p201) and **Klosterfelde** (see p200). It all began here in 2001, when savvy dealers chose to leave the now over-hyped theme park of Mitte's Scheunenviertel and the staid, forgotten streets of Charlottenburg, consolidating into one of the liveliest and most interesting views of the Berlin scene.

Though the atmosphere is undoubtedly professional, there is a certain relaxed charm to it all, and while the work itself can often be risky and challenging, it never strays too far from the accessible. This one city block offers not only a selection of the tried and true, but also a glimpse of tomorrow's hopefuls. This is perhaps best exemplified by the most recent addition to the premises: the **Galerie Jette Rudolph**.

Born in 1971, Jette Rudolph (*pictured*) grew up near the American military bases of Frankfurt/Main, where first tastes of rock 'n' roll would lead her to organise the biker-rock art events for which she became known. After studying art history in Bonn and the Belgian city of Leuven, she moved to Berlin in 1998 and once again began producing art events. The first Galerie Jette Rudolph opened in 2000 in small, neat rooms off Auguststrasse. Among early offerings was a show by Marcus Sendlinger, with bold rally stripes of auto-paint, and accompanying video, to reference a motorcycle-run in Brandenburg. This mix of popular culture and academic approaches has always been characteristic (she continues to introduce events with dissertation-like extracts). And it was also here that she began her ongoing exchange with galleries in England and North America.

With a programme that is decidedly not media-determined, Jette Rudolph highlights the newer tendencies by showing an international group of young independent artists that she describes as 'individual, personal and media-savvy'. But this is no Pop-Fest, despite the imagery – though the work can be humorous and light, it also delves deeper. Lea Pagenkemper, for example, often depicts dark, graffiti-layered spaces that are disturbingly isolated. The classical inks and etchings of Dennis Rudolph prove achingly wistful. And even the brashness of Sendlinger's new work does little to hide a certain frustration (or is it anger?), as if suggesting a map full of dead ends and impossible routes.

After finally getting fed up with the Scheunenviertel – and only after receiving the unanimous approval of her new co-tenants – Jette Rudolph moved into her Zimmerstrasse

---

works by artists such as Tue Greenfort, Jeppe Hein and Micol Assaël. A recent installation by Manuel Graf was a surprising treat.

Johnen Galerie
Schillingstrasse 31 (2758 3030/www.johnen galerie.de). U8, S5, S7, S9, S75 Jannowitzbrücke. **Open** 11am-6pm Tue-Sat. **No credit cards.** **Map** p303 P6.

In a former post office below the tower blocks at Jannowitzbrücke, the new Berlin branch of Cologne's Johnen + Schöttle gallery has a simply breathtaking roster of conceptual and photoconceptual greats. This is a beautiful space for the likes of Jeff Wall, Thomas Ruff and Rodney Graham, and a class act all the way.

Klosterfelde
Zimmerstrasse 90-91 (283 5305/www.klosterfelde. de). U6 Kochstrasse. **Open** 11am-6pm Tue-Sat. **No credit cards.** **Map** p306/p311 M8.

Among the more varied of gallery menus, with occasional showings by invited guests and seemingly little method to the madness. Martin Klosterfelde focuses principally on younger artists in as interesting and wide a range as Vibeke Tandberg, Matt Mullican and Christian Jankowski.

Kuckei + Kuckei
Courtyard of Linienstrasse 158 (883 4354/www. kuckei-kuckei.de). U6 Oranienburger Tor or S1, S2 Oranienburger Strasse. **Open** 11am-6pm Tue-Fri; 11am-5pm Sat. **No credit cards.** **Map** p303/p310 M5.

Ben and Hannes Kuckei continue to present young, concept-related artists, including Barbara Probst, Lois Renner, Michael Laube and Oliver van den Berg. The sensibility is uniformly interesting, clean and sparse.

Kunst-Werke
Auguststrasse 69 (243 4590/www.kw-berlin.de). U6 Oranienburger Tor or S1, S2 Oranienburger

space in 2005. From here, her gallery exchange continues: she and her artists appeared at Toronto's Greener Pastures Gallery in 2004, and she presented Canadian work in Berlin. Her opening bash was a days-long event still true to the esprit. She may now be Jette Rudolph GmbH, but her presence at the recent Art Forum (with a large installation by

Tine Benz) was no less bold and successful. Now she's got the address to prove it.

Galerie Jette Rudolph

Zimmerstrasse 90-91, Mitte (6130 3887/ www.jette-rudolph.de). U6 Kochstrasse. **Open** 11am-5.30pm Tue-Sat. **No credit cards. Map** p306/p311 M8.

Strasse. **Open** noon-6pm Tue-Sun. **No credit cards. Map** p303/p311 N5.
Housed in a baroque former factory (with a court-yard designed by Dan Graham), this co-host of the Biennale has been a major non-profit showcase since the early 1990s. KW puts on culturally themed exhibits of contemporary artists, such as 2004's controversial RAF show. A good starting point for a gallery walk in Mitte. **Photo** *p202.*

Galerie Max Hetzler

Zimmerstrasse 90-91 (229 2437/www.maxhetzler. com). U6 Kochstrasse. **Open** 11am-6pm Tue-Sat. **No credit cards. Map** p306/p311 M8.
With two differently dramatic and versatile spaces, this wonderful gallery (in business long before its Berlin days began in 1994) represents an amazing roster of talent, including Darren Almond, Cady Noland, Christopher Wool and Kara Walker. **Other locations**: Holzmarktstrasse 15-18, S-Bahnbogen 48 (2404 5630).

Mehdi Chouakri

Schlegelstrasse 26 (2839 1153/www.mehdi-chouakri. com). U6 Zinnowitzer Strasse. **Open** 11am-6pm Tue-Sat. **No credit cards. Map** p302/p310 M4.
In sleek, sparse surroundings, Mehdi Chouakri features both emerging artists and established international names such as Sylvie Fleurie, John M Armleder, Gitte Schäfer and the recent National Gallery Award-winner Monica Bonvicini.

MagnusMüller

Weydingerstrasse 10 (3903 2040/www. magnusmuller.com). U2 Rosa-Luxemburg-Platz. **Open** noon-7pm Tue-Sat. **No credit cards. Map** p303/p310 O5.
Formerly with partner Laurie De Chiara, a New York gallerist, Berlin art historian Sönke Magnus Müller is now going it alone in his presentation of young international conceptual artists, including exciting and difficult work by Christoph Draeger, Jenny Rosemeyer, Ellen Harvey and Piotr Nathan.

Kunst-Werke – red faces all round. *See p200.*

Murata & Friends

*Rosenthaler Strasse 39 (2809 9071/www.murataand
friends.de). U8 Weinmeisterstrasse or S5, S7, S9,
S75 Hackescher Markt.* **Open** 1-7pm Wed-Fri; noon-
6pm Sat. **No credit cards. Map** p303/p310 N5.

In this tiny, romantically warm atelier, tucked above
a courtyard next to the Hackesche Höfe, Manabi
Murata primarily features the work of young emerging Japanese artists such as Tatsuya Higuchi,
Yoshiaki Kaihatsu and Tsuneo Shinano.

Neuer Berliner Kunstverein

*Chauseestrasse 128-9 (280 7020/www.nbk.org). U6
Oranienburger Tor.* **Open** noon-6pm Tue-Fri; 2-6pm
Sat, Sun. **No credit cards. Map** p302/p310 M5.

This non-profit organisation was founded in 1969
through a citizens' initiative with the purpose of
bringing contemporary art to a much wider public.
In addition to lectures, a video archive and a lending library for works of art, it features exhibitions
by young talent in all media, but with an emphasis
on photography and video.

neugerriemschneider

*Linienstrasse 155 (2887 7277). U6 Oranienburger
Tor or S1, S2 Oranienburger Strasse.* **Open** 11am-
6pm Tue-Sat. **No credit cards. Map** p303/p310 N5.

At the back of the courtyard, Tim Neuger and
Burkhard Riemschneider have made a bright, friendly viewing space in which to show the latest and

hippest art from America and Europe, plus a host of
works by local talent. Names include Franz
Ackermann, Jorge Pardo, Elizabeth Peyton and the
brilliant Rirkrit Tiravanija.

Galerie Rafael Vostell Berlin

*Friedrichstrasse 134 (885 2280/www.vostell.com).
U6 Oranienburger Tor.* **Open** 2-7pm Wed-Sat.
No credit cards. Map p303/p310 M5.

Recently relocated in the new Art-Center-Berlin,
Rafael Vostell continues to champion such 1960s
luminaries as Yoko Ono, Naim June Paik and his
own father, Fluxus pioneer Wolf Vostell. You'll also
find work by emerging international artists such as
Qin Yufen and Salustiano.

Galerie Volker Diehl

*Zimmerstrasse 88-91 (2248 7922/www.dv-art.
com). U6 Kochstrasse.* **Open** 11am-6pm Tue-Sat.
No credit cards. Map p306/p311 M8.

One of the original organisers of the Berlin Art
Forum, Volker Diehl has long been an established
and prominent member of the international art
world, concentrating his efforts on younger contemporary artists including Angela Dwyer, Marcel
Dzama and Jaume Plensa. **Photo** *p203.*

WBD

*Brunnenstrasse 9 (2180 4657/www.webede.com).
U8 Rosenthaler Platz.* **Open** 4-7pm Thur-Sat.
No credit cards. Map p303/p310 N4.

A commercial gallery since 2000, WBD was started and is run by artists Martin Städeli, Michael Dethleffsen and Thomas Ravens. With six shows a year, they feature not only their own work, but that of other young artists such as Thaddäus Huppi, Joachim Grommek and Rudi Molacek.

Wohnmaschine

Tucholskystrasse 35 (3087 2015/www.wohnmaschine. de). S1, S2 Oranienburger Strasse. **Open** 11am-6pm Tue-Sat. **No credit cards. Map** p302/p310 M5.
Begun in his nearby apartment in 1988, Friedrich Loock's gallery (which is named after Le Corbusier's *machine à habiter*) now offers often minimal exhibitions of work by young Japanese artist Yoshihiro Suda, as well as Robert Lippok, Holly Zausner and Anton Henning.

Zwinger Galerie

Gipsstrasse 3 (2859 8907). U8 Rosenthaler Platz. **Open** 2-7pm Tue-Fri; noon-6pm Sat. **No credit cards. Map** p303/p310 M5.
In this tiny and intimate courtyard gallery, Werner Müller, a long-established member of the art community, turns his enthusiastic eye towards younger talents such as Margarethe Hahner, Tobias Hauser, Theresa Lükenwerth and Susi Pop.

Prenzlauer Berg

Akira Ikeda Gallery Berlin

Pfefferberg, Schönhauser Allee 176 (4432 8510/ www.akiraikedagallery.com). U2 Senefelderplatz. **Open** 11am-6pm Tue-Sat. **No credit cards. Map** p303/p310 O4.

Akira Ikeda is hidden at the back of the Pfefferberg, a dilapidated 19th-century brewery turned cultural centre. This magnificent third branch of the gallery (other outposts are in Taura, Japan, and New York) specialises in work post-1945, with room enough to display the mammoth di Suveros, older and new, and a variety of works by the Starn Twins, Mel Bochner and On Kawara.

Kreuzberg

Künstlerhaus Bethanien

Mariannenplatz 2 (616 9030/www.bethanien.de). U1, U8 Kottbusser Tor or U1 Görlitzer Bahnhof. **Open** 2-7pm Wed-Sun. **No credit cards. Map** p307 P8.
Housed in a former 19th-century hospital complex, this Berlin institution began as an art squat in the 1970s and has since developed a major studio residency programme for foreign artists staying in Berlin. With open studios and three full galleries, it remains a lively endeavour despite the looming threat of budget cuts.

Laura Mars Group

Sorauer Strasse 3 (6107 4630/www.lauramars.de). U1 Schlesisches Tor. **Open** noon-7pm Tue-Fri. **No credit cards. Map** p308 R9.
In this wonderful surprise of a space, Gundula Schmitz has a clear, brilliant eye for bringing young, extraordinarily talented artists such as Philip Wiegard, Christoph Ziegler, Ursula Döbereiner and the fabulous Kerstin Drechsel to a once art-neglected corner of Kreuzberg.

Galerie Volker Diehl – contemporary work by young artists. *See p202.*

NGBK

*Oranienstrasse 25 (616 5130/www.ngbk.de). U1,
U8 Kottbusser Tor.* **Open** noon-6.30pm daily.
No credit cards. Map p307 P9.
Begun in the smoky haze of the late 1960s, the
NGBK is still confrontational and energetic, continuing its group-based projects with a social conscience (legal/illegal featured work by Dennis
Oppenheim and Abbie Hoffman), in addition to running a public project series on the platform of the U2
at Alexanderplatz U-Bahn. The gallery entrance is
through the bookstore.

Tiergarten

Galerie Eva Poll

*Lützowplatz 7 (261 7091/www.poll-berlin.de).
U1, U2, U3, U4 Nollendorfplatz.* **Open** 10am-1pm
Mon; 11am-6.30pm Tue-Fri; 11am-3pm Sat.
No credit cards. Map p306 J8.
Opened in 1968 with her collection of critical realists
from the 1960s, Eva Poll's beautiful gallery (her private apartment is still in the back) includes, among
others, Sabina Grzimek, Peter Sorge and Peter
Chevalier. Stiftung Eva Poll exhibits photography.
Other locations: Stiftung Eva Poll, Gipsstrasse 3,
Mitte (2849 6250).

Haus am Lützowplatz

*Lützowplatz 9 (261 3805/www.hausamluetzow
platz-berlin.de). U1, U2, U3, U4 Nollendorfplatz.*
Open 11am-6pm Tue-Sun. **No credit cards.**
Map p306 J8.
Though exhibits were held in this building as early
as 1949, the non-profit society that has occupied it
since the early 1960s (Elvira Bach is on the board)
maintains a pledge to present both unknown Berlin
artists and guests such as Dorothy Iannone, Mario
Mertz and Emmett Williams.

Charlottenburg

Galerie Anselm Dreher

*Pfalzburger Strasse 80 (883 5249/www.galerie-
anselm-dreher.com). U1 Hohenzollernplatz.* **Open**
2-6.30pm Tue-Fri; 11am-2pm Sat. **No credit cards.**
Map p305 F9.
Since opening his gallery on the Wilmersdorf border in 1967, Anselm Dreher continues the lonely task
of championing hardcore minimalist and concrete
works by newcomers and old masters such as
Dennis Oppenheim, Joseph Kosuth and Carl Andre.
He does it wonderfully.

Camera Work

*Kantstrasse 149 (310 0773/www.camerawork.de).
S5, S7, S9, S75 Savignyplatz.* **Open** 10am-6pm
Tue-Sat. **No credit cards. Map** p305/p312 F8.
Named for the magazine started by Alfred Stieglitz,
this magnificent courtyard space offers prime viewing of some of the 20th-century's most important
photographic work, including Irving Penn, Leni
Riefenstahl, Peter Beard and Man Ray.

Galerie Georg Nothelfer

*Uhlandstrasse 184 (881 4405/www.galerie-nothelfer.
de). U1 Uhlandstrasse.* **Open** 11am-6.30pm Tue-Fri;
10am-2pm Sat. **Credit** V. **Map** p305/p312 F8.
Long-time doyen Nothelfer quietly and importantly
pursues his love of Informel and Tachist work, best
exemplified by artists such as Walter Stöhner, Henri
Michaux and Jan Voss.
Other locations: Corneliusstrasse 3, Tiergarten
(575 9806).

Galerie Haas & Fuchs

*Niebuhrstrasse 5 (8892 9190/www.haasundfuchs.
de). U1 Uhlandstrasse or S5, S7, S9, S75
Savignyplatz.* **Open** 9.30am-6.30pm Tue-Fri; 11am-
2pm Sat. **No credit cards. Map** p305/p312 E8.
Next door to his original Galerie Michael Haas
(www.galeriemichaelhaas.de), which now specialises in classic contemporary art post-1945, Michael
Haas and his partner Michael Fuchs here feature
such varied artists as Howard Hodgkin, Richard
Jordan and Frank Thiel.

Raab Galerie Berlin

*Fasanenstrasse 27 (261 9217/www.raab-galerie.de).
U1 Uhlandstrasse.* **Open** 10am-7pm Mon-Fri; 10am-
4pm Sat. **No credit cards. Map** p305/p312 F9.
Since her monumental first show of Jungen Wilden
in 1978, Ingrid Raab has been a grand champion of
work by young artists such as Paul Vergier, Ben
Henriques and Christian Sauer, as well as stalwarts
such as Lüpertz, Fetting and the wonderful Odd
Nerdrum. Two gallery spaces later (this newest venture was only a year old when we went to press), her
enthusiasm remains contagious.

Galerie Springer & Winckler

*Fasanenstrasse 13 (315 7220). U2, U9,
S5, S7, S9, S75 Zoologischer Garten or U1,
U9 Kurfürstendamm.* **Open** 10am-1pm, 2-6pm
Tue-Fri; 11am-3pm Sat. **No credit cards. Map**
p305/p312 F9.
Originally the gallery of Rudolph Springer (one of
the grand old men of Berlin's art world, who'd been
in the business since 1948), this space is now run by
his son Robert and partner Gerald Winckler. These
days, the pair concentrate mainly on lush German
post-war artists such as Georg Baselitz, Markus
Lüpertz, Sigmar Polke and Gerhard Richter.

Galerie Thomas Schulte

*Mommsenstrasse 56 (324 0044/www.galeriethomas
schulte.de). U7 Adenauerplatz or Wilmersdorfer
Strasse or S5, S7, S9, S75 Charlottenburg.*
Open 11am-6pm Mon-Fri; 11am-3pm Sat. **No**
credit cards. Map p305/p312 P8.
New Yorker Thomas Schulte and Swiss-born Eric
Franck opened their doors in 1991, hoping to breathe
some new life into the local art market. Since those
early days the gallery has become one of Berlin's
finer, more upmarket venues, featuring excellent
work by the likes of Richard Artschwager, Rebecca
Horn, Robert Mapplethorpe, Gordon Matta-Clark
and Tony Oursler.

Gay & Lesbian

Queer culture thrives in Berlin – even the mayor is out and proud.

A high level of tolerance coupled with a strong and open sense of gay pride means that in Berlin it's possible to live an almost exclusively gay or lesbian existence – from partying to hiring a plumber. Same-sex couples now also have the right to a civil registration of their union and though the attached rights don't go as far as in some other European countries, around 2,000 couples have already signed up.

Appropriate, then, that Berlin also has an out gay city mayor, the charismatic Klaus Wowereit who, in 2001, before being nominated by his party to be the new mayor of Berlin, winded the tabloids by openly declaring his homosexuality with a phrase that has entered the local vernacular: 'I am gay, and that's OK!' ('Ich bin schwul, und das ist auch gut so!').

As long ago as the 18th century, Berlin had the reputation of being tolerant towards people of other faiths and sexual orientation, being the capital of a kingdom whose king, Frederick the Great, was himself rumoured to love 'in the Greek Fashion'. In 1897 the first institution in the world with an emancipatory homosexual agenda was founded in Berlin – the Wissenschaftlich-Humanitäres Komitee (Scientific-Humanitarian Committee). Its main aims were legal reform, scientific research into the 'Third Gender' and the publication of supporting literature. In the 1920s Berlin became the first city in the world to have what we might recognise as a large gay and lesbian community, frequented by such diverse people as Marlene Dietrich, Ernst Röhm and Christopher Isherwood. Hitler put a stop to all that, of course. Gays were persecuted and forced to wear the Pink Triangle in concentration camps. They are commemorated on a plaque outside Nollendorfplatz station, and there are plans for another memorial in the Tiergarten (*see p82* **Monumental debate**). In the late 1960s Berlin resumed its role as one of the world's gay meccas.

The gay and lesbian scenes today are big and bold, mostly concentrated in Schöneberg, Mitte, Kreuzberg and Prenzlauer Berg. Summer is the most exciting time of year, when all contingents come together and enjoy themselves. Mid June's **Schwul-Lesbisches Strassenfest** is followed by the **Christopher Street Day Parade** (for both, *see p183*), a flamboyant annual event where up to 500,000 gays and lesbians commemorate the Stonewall riots.

The scene includes much more than just the venues listed here, especially with such cultural events as plays, drag shows or the Gay Teddy award for the best gay film at the **Berlin International Film Festival** (*see p186*). Queer films can be seen on Mondays at **Kino International** (Karl-Marx-Allee 33, Mitte, 2475 6011). Gay art and history is documented at the **Schwules Museum** (*see p98*), the sports club **Vorspiel** is in 2006 celebrating its 20th anniversary (*see p211* **Keep fit with foreplay**) and, of course, there is gay sex, any time of the day or night, any day of the week.

INFORMATION AND PUBLICATIONS

For helplines, information and counselling services, *see p275*. *Sergej* (www.sergej-berlin.de) and *Siegessäule* (www.siegessaeule.de) are monthly listings freebies, found at most venues. In addition to a what's-on calendar, both list all gay and lesbian venues and pinpoint them on a map. Should you want to live an exclusively gay lifestyle, *Siegessäule* also publishes *Kompass* (www.siegessaeule-kompass.de), a classified directory of everything lesbian or gay. Comprehensive information in English is available on www.gaymap.info/berlin/index.html. The English-language monthly *Exberliner* (www.ex-berliner.com) has a funny gay column by Maurice von Ritz.

Mixed

In West Berlin gays and lesbians trod separate paths for decades, but in the East things were different. Homosexuals of both genders shared bars and clubs, making common cause under the communists, and the tradition hasn't disappeared in the last decade and a half. That said, the western half of the city has changed. There has been an increase in the number of mixed gay and lesbian venues, and one-nighters now usually target both groups.

Bars & cafés

Prenzlauer Berg

Café Amsterdam

Gleimstrasse 24 (448 0792/www.pension-amsterdam. de). U2, S8, S41, S42, S85 Schönhauser Allee. **Open** 8-11am, 3.30pm-2am Mon-Sat; 8am-2am Sun. **Credit** AmEx, MC, V. **Map** p303 O2.

No longer Bowie's Nemesis, **Neues Ufer** is Berlin's oldest extant gay café. *See p207.*

Nice café in daytime, offering snacks and salads, which becomes a popular bar to get wrecked in at night, with loud house and techno music. Mostly youngish crowd. Central location.

Schall & Rauch

Gleimstrasse 23 (443 3970/4433 9722/www. schall-und-rauch-berlin.de). U2, S8, S41, S42, S85 Schönhauser Allee. **Open** 9am-3am daily. **No credit cards. Map** p303 O2.

Relaxed and friendly, good selection of food, central location – an ideal place to spend the afternoon or kick off an evening. Wireless internet available.

Friedrichshain

Himmelreich

Simon-Dach-Strasse 36 (7072 8306). U5 Frankfurter Tor or U1, S3, S5, S7, S9, S75 Warschauer Strasse. **Open** 7pm-2am Mon-Thur; 7pm-4am Fri; 2pm-4am Sat; 2pm-3am Sun. **No credit cards. Map** p308 S7.

Colourful, comfortable lounge café and bar. Regular women-only nights, but with men in drag admitted.

HT

Kopernikusstrasse 23 (2900 4965/www.ht-berlin.de). U5 Frankfurter Tor or U1, S3, S5, S7, S9, S75 Warschauer Strasse. **Open** 6pm-2am daily. **No credit cards. Map** p308 F7.

Comfortable but quiet café and bar in a popular nightlife district. Good service, friendly staff.

Kreuzberg

Barbie Bar

Mehringdamm 77 (6956 8610/www.barbiebar.de). U6, U7 Mehringdamm. **Open** from 4pm Mon-Fri; from 2pm Sat, Sun. **No credit cards. Map** p306 M10.

Adorned with dolls and pictures of drag queens on the walls, this is a camp and stylish place, with comfortable easy chairs and quiet music, which makes it good for chatting. Small terrace in summer; two drinks for the price of one on Tuesday from 8pm.

Roses

Oranienstrasse 187 (615 6570). U1, U8 Kottbusser Tor. **Open** 10pm-5am daily. **No credit cards.** **Map** p307 P9.
Whatever state you're in (the more of a state, the better) you'll fit in fine at this boisterous den of glitter. Customers from across the sexual spectrum come to mingle and indulge in excessive drinking amid plush, kitsch decor. No place for uptights, always full.

Schöneberg

Neues Ufer

Hauptstrasse 157 (7895 7900). U7 Kleistpark. **Open** 11am-2am daily. **No credit cards.** **Map** p306 J10.
Established in the early 1970s as Café Nemesis, this is the city's oldest extant gay café and was a favourite of David Bowie's when he lived two doors down the road. Relaxed daytime scene.

Clubs & one-nighters

Friedrichshain

Berghain/Panorama Bar

Am Wriezener Bahnhof (no phone/www.berghain.de). U5 Weberwiese or S3, S5, S7, S9, S75 Ostbahnhof. **Open** midnight-late Fri, Sat. **Admission** €10. **No credit cards. Map** p308 R7.
The hippest and hardest electronic music club in Berlin. The building is a former power station transformed into a concrete cathedral of techno on two floors, with the mixed Panorama Bar upstairs and Berghain (successor to the legendary Ostgut club) below. Saturday night's Klubnacht sees Berghain awash with pumped-up, shirtless gay men sweating it out on the dancefloor – and in the darkroom at the back. Once on Am Wriezener Bahnhof, follow the stream of taxis to find it. Cameras are prohibited and confiscated at the door to be returned later. But you won't need photos to remember it.

Black Girls Coalition

Samariterstrasse 32 (0179 381 4363/www.black girlscoalition.de). U5 Samariterstrasse. **Open** 8pm-4am Mon, last Thur of mth. **Admission** varies. **No credit cards. Map** p309 T6.
Owned by a black drag queen from New York, BGC is a unique synthesis of punk and queer sensibilities. Mondays are indie rock and punk, while the monthly Thursday party features drag shows and electronic dance. Staff also offer resettlement advice for incoming kindred spirits (call for appointment), plus German classes at 6pm on Tuesdays.

Die Busche

Mühlenstrasse 11-12 (296 0800/www.die busche.de). U1, S3, S5, S7, S9, S75 Warschauer Strasse. **Open** 10pm-5am Wed, Sun; 10pm-7am Fri, Sat. **Admission** €3.50-€6. **No credit cards. Map** p308 R8.

Café Melitta Sundström

Mehringdamm 61 (692 4414). U6, U7 Mehringdamm. **Open** noon-late daily. **No credit cards. Map** p306 M10.
During the day this place serves as a cosy café for students; in the evening it's full of gays too lazy to go to Schöneberg and lesbians who wouldn't go to Schöneberg anyway. Then at weekends it becomes the entrance to SchwuZ (*see p212*), and the place is hectic and fun.

Möbel Olfe

End of Dresdener Strasse/Kotbusser Tor (6165 9612/www.moebel-olfe.de). U1, U8 Kottbusser Tor. **Open** 6pm-late Tue-Sun. **No credit cards. Map** p307 P9.
Odd location for a gay bar, wedged among Turkish businesses in a down-at-heel 1960s development and visible to the world through large glass windows on both sides, but this place has been packed since it opened, mainly with gay and lesbian beer-lovers. Unpretentious, crowded, fun. Regular DJ nights.

Arts & Entertainment

An East German relic: loud, tacky, mixed and packed, this is one of east Berlin's oldest discos, full of stylish lesbians, gay teens and their girlfriends. A must for kitsch addicts and Abba fans; a no-go area for guys who like a masculine atmosphere.

Kreuzberg

SO36

Oranienstrasse 190 (6140 1306/www.so36.de). U1, U8 Kottbusser Tor. **Open** varies. **Admission** *Parties* €3-€8. *Concerts* €8-€20. **No credit cards**. **Map** p307 P9.

A key venue for both gays and lesbians. Monday (Electric Ballroom, from 11pm) isn't completely gay, but the hard techno sounds draw a largely male following. Last Saturday in the month is Gay Oriental Night (Gayhane, from 10pm), with belly dancing, transvestites and Turkish hits. Women now have their own version, Ladyhane (every month on Fri or Sat, from 9pm). Monthly m.appeal parties (first Fri or Sat of the month, from 8pm) bring together every imaginable manifestation of womanhood (plus gay friends) to dance to house and disco. Sunday is Café Fatal (7pm-2am May-Sept, 6pm-2am Oct-Apr), at which gays and lesbians get into ballroom dancing. Every second Tuesday from 7pm, Bingo Bar attracts a colourful mixture of guys and girls, who cross out numbers read out by trash-queen announcers.

Gay

You don't need to look for the gay scene in Berlin. It'll find you in about ten minutes. Some areas, however, are gayer than others, especially Schöneberg's **Motzstrasse** and **Fuggerstrasse**, and around **Schönhauser Allee** station in Prenzlauer Berg.

The age of consent is 16, the same as for everyone else. Gays making contact in public are rarely of interest to passers-by, but bigots do exist and so does anti-gay violence. In the west it tends to be by gangs of Turkish teenagers, in the east by right-wing skinhead Germans. But violence is rare compared to other cities.

Where to stay

Most hotels know gays are important to the tourist industry and are courteous and helpful. Below are some catering specifically for gay men. In addition, **Schall & Rauch** (*see p206*) has rooms to rent.

ArtHotel Connection Berlin

Fuggerstrasse 33, Schöneberg, 10777 (210 218 800/fax 210 218 830/www.arthotel-connection.de). U1, U2, U3 Wittenbergplatz. **Rates** €54-€88 single; €76.50-€110 double; €117-€140 apartment. **Credit** AmEx, MC, V. **Map** p305 H9.

Comfortable and spacious rooms (most en suite), sumptuous breakfast included, prime location right in the middle of Schöneberg's gay area. The SM room is fitted with a sling, stocks and a cage.

Eastside

Schönhauser Allee 41, Prenzlauer Berg, 10435 (4373 5484/fax 4373 5485/www.eastside-gayllery.de). U2 Eberswalder Strasse. **Rates** from €36 single, €66 double. **Credit** AmEx, MC, V. **Map** p303/p312 O3.

Quiet guesthouse in the centre of Prenzlauer Berg. All rooms have TV/VCR and private bath.

Enjoy Bed & Breakfast

Mann-O-Meter, Bülowstrasse 106, Schöneberg, 10783 (2362 3610/fax 2362 3619/www.ebab.de). U1, U2, U3, U4 Nollendorfplatz. **No credit cards**. **Map** p306 J9.

This excellent accommodation service caters to both gays and lesbians, and can fix you up with a room in the private apartment of fellow gays for as little as €20 a night. You can both view and book rooms on its website.

LGHEI

Contact: J Wiley, Schönleinstrasse 20, Kreuzberg, 10967 (691 9537/fax 691 9537/www.lghei.org). U8 Schönleinstrasse. **Map** p307 P10.

The Lesbian & Gay Hospitality Exchange International is a worldwide network of lesbians and gay men who offer each other the gift of short-term hospitality on the basis of reciprocity. No sex.

RoB Leather Apartments Berlin

Contact: RoB, Fuggerstrasse 19, Schöneberg, 10777 (2196 7400/www.rob.nl). U1, U2, U3 Wittenbergplatz. **Open** noon-8pm Mon-Sat. **Rates** (min 3-night stay) €79-€139. **Credit** AmEx, MC, V. **Map** p305 H9.

Two apartments to rent, including kitchen, bathroom, TV, VCR, internet access, own mobile telephone number – and a playroom.

Tom's House

Eisenacher Strasse 10, Schöneberg, 10777 (218 5544/www.toms-house-alster-berlin.de). U1, U2, U3, U4 Nollendorfplatz. **Rates** €35-€65 single; €65-€85 double. **Credit** DC, MC, V. **Map** p305 H10.

An eccentric establishment deep in the heart of gay Schöneberg, with seven double rooms, one single, and first-rate buffet brunches from 10am to 1pm.

Bars, cafés & restaurants

Prenzlauer Berg

Flax

Chodowieckistrasse 41 (4404 6988/www.flax-berlin. de). S8, S41, S42, S85 Greifswalder Strasse. **Open** 5pm-2am Mon-Fri; 3pm-2am Sat; 10am-2am Sun. **No credit cards**. **Map** p303/p312 Q3.

Although on the edge of the Prenzlauer Berg scene, this is one of the most popular café/bars in the east, pulling in a young, mixed crowd.

Heile Welt – 'Do you come here often?' *See p210.*

Greifbar

Wichertstrasse 16 (444 0828/www.greifbar.net).
U2, S8, S41, S42, S85 Schönhauser Allee. **Open**
10pm-late daily. **No credit cards. Map** p303 P2.
Cruisy bar with a younger crowd looking for adventure and pleasure, either by picking someone up or by roaming about in the large darkrooms.

Guppi

Gleimstrasse 31 (4373 9611). U2, S8, S41,
S42, S85 Schönhauser Allee. **Open** from 4pm
Mon-Fri; from 2pm Sat, Sun. **No credit cards.**
Map p303 O2.
Stylish two-storey bar with high ceilings and easy chairs. Low music and warm colours make it a relaxing place for coffee in daytime or drinks at night.

Pick Ab!

Greifenhagener Strasse 16 (445 8523). U2, S8, S41,
S42, S85 Schönhauser Allee. **Open** 10pm-6am Mon-Fri, Sun; 10pm-noon Sat. **No credit cards. Map**
p303/p312 O2.
Late-night cruise bar decorated in camp taste. Fills up best during winter, when heated backrooms are more comfortable for cruising than freezing parks.

Stiller Don

Erich-Weinert-Strasse 67 (4437 6747/www.
stillerdon.de). U2, S8, S41, S42, S85
Schönhauser Allee. **Open** 8pm-late daily.
No credit cards. Map p303 P1.
Formerly home to the avant-garde, now attracting a mixed crowd from all over Berlin. Like a cosy café, but it gets high-spirited at weekends and on Mondays.

Kreuzberg

Rausch Gold

Mehringdamm 62 (7895 2668/www.rauschgold-
berlin.de). U6, U7 Mehringdamm. **Open** 8pm-late
daily. **No credit cards. Map** p306 M10.
This plush and somewhat tacky bar opposite Café
Melitta Sundström (*see p207*) is a good place to
prolong night into morning, or take a first drink on
an evening out.

Schöneberg

Berio

Maasenstrasse 7 (216 1946/www.cafe-berio.de). U1,
U2, U3, U4 Nollendorfplatz. **Open** 8am-midnight
Mon-Thur, Sun; 8am-1am Fri, Sat. **No credit cards.**
Map p306 J9.
One of the best daytime cafés, full of good-looking,
trendy young men (including the waiters), with a
good terrace for people-watching in summer.

Hafen
Motzstrasse 19 (211 4118/www.hafen-berlin.de). U1, U2, U3, U4 Nollendorfplatz. **Open** 8pm-late daily. **No credit cards. Map** p305 H9.

A red, plush and vaguely psychedelic bar in the centre of Schöneberg's gay triangle. Popular with the fashion- and body-aware, especially for the Quizz-o-Rama, with questions in English from 10pm on the first Monday of the month.

Heile Welt
Motzstrasse 5 (2191 7507). U1, U2, U3, U4 Nollendorfplatz. **Open** 6pm-4am daily. **No credit cards. Map** p306 J9.

Stylish café, lounge and cocktail bar for the fashion-conscious. The front has a 1970s feel, the back lounge is all plush leather seating. A good place to practise chat-up lines and decide whether to go clubbing. **Photo** *p209*.

Mutschmanns
Martin-Luther-Strasse 19 (2191 9640/www. mutschmanns.de). U1, U2, U3 Wittenbergplatz. **Open** 10pm-5am Wed, Thur; 11pm-late Fri, Sat. **No credit cards. Map** p305 H9.

This well-frequented hardcore bar with a large basement darkroom is suitable for either cruising or hanging out, but there is a dress code – wear leather, rubber or uniform.

Prinzknecht
Fuggerstrasse 33 (2362 7444/www.prinzknecht.de). U1, U2, U3 Wittenbergplatz. **Open** 3pm-3am daily. **No credit cards. Map** p305 H9.

With a large but underused darkroom out back, this huge, open bar draws in local gays and leather types. A bit provincial in feel, but nice for a chat and a beer.

Tom's Bar
Motzstrasse 19 (213 4570/www.tomsbar.de). U1, U2, U3, U4 Nollendorfplatz. **Open** 10pm-6am daily. **No credit cards. Map** p305 H9.

Something of a cruising institution. The front bar is fairly chatty but the closer you get to the darkroom the more intense things become. Popular with men of all ages and styles.

Clubs & one-nighters

With only a few real discos (**Die Busche**, *see p207*; **SchwuZ**, *see p212*; **Connection**, *see p212*), one-nighters are all the rage. Some come and go, others run and run. Check *Siegessäule* and *Sergej*, or look out for flyers.

Mitte

Chantal's House of Shame
Kinzo Club, Karl-Liebknecht-Strasse 11 (www. siteofshame.com). U2, U5, U8, S5, S7, S9, S75 Alexanderplatz. **Open** from 11pm Thur. **Admission** €6; €3 before midnight. **No credit cards. Map** p303/p311 O6.

Hosted by well-known drag queen Chantal, this popular early weekend house night is an anything-goes mishmash of top dance tunes, united by their 'Ossi' feel. Impromptu naked stage-dancers mix with new romantic 'elegentsia' wearing top hats. The boys in tight T-shirts are there, too, but they're overshadowed by everyone else.

GaymeBoy
Kino International, Karl-Marx-Allee 33 (6900 1731/ www.daddy-cool-party.de). U5 Schillingstrasse. **Open** 11pm-late 1 Sat of mth. **Admission** €6-€8. **No credit cards. Map** p303 P6.

Saved by Kino International after its previous home closed, GaymeBoy's electro and disco night for young bucks under 26 enjoys a once-a-month spot, often shared with the likes of Studio 69 (*see p210*). The venue is a 1950s GDR cinema and worth a look for the interior alone.

GMF
Nachtbar Moskau, Karl-Marx-Allee 34 (2809 5396/ www.gmf-berlin.de). U5 Schillingstrasse. **Open** 10pm-late Sun. **Admission** €8. **No credit cards. Map** p303 P6.

For those who want to stick up a finger at Monday mornings, this is the ultimate Sunday Tea Dance, located in the Café Moskau in all of its 1950s glory. The downstairs dancefloor is intense and the cocktail lounge upstairs sociable and buzzing, with a second pop-based dancefloor. Always packed with a young, stylish, energetic crowd.

Klub International
Kino International, Karl-Marx-Allee 33 (2475 6011/ www.kino-international.com). U5 Schillingstrasse. **Open** 11pm-late 1st Sat/mth. **Admission** €9. **No credit cards. Map** p303 P6.

One of the biggest parties in town, Klub International regularly attracts up to 1,500 youngish guests in their tightest T-shirts. The cinema building has two dancefloors, where the DJs play a mix of house and chart dance.

Nite Club
Sage Club, Köpenicker Strasse 76 (278 9830/www. sage-club.de). U8 Heinrich-Heine-Strasse. **Open** 11pm-late Sun. **No credit cards. Map** p307 P7.

There are those for whom a whole weekend of partying is never enough. Such people cannot sleep, they have nothing to do, they do not have to get up on Monday. And so it is that they go to Sage, to enjoy wicked techno and house in an interestingly styled club. Fullest around 5am, when GMF (*see above*) usually tips out.

Studio 69
Kino International, Karl-Marx-Allee 33 (2475 6011/ www.dissentertainment.de). U5 Schillingstrasse. **Open** 11pm-late 1 Sat/mth. **Admission** €6-€8. **No credit cards. Map** p303 P6.

Studio 69 offers a wicked mix of music from the 1960s, '70s and '80s. It mostly attracts a shrieking, youngish crowd.

Keep fit with foreplay

In November 2006 Berlin's gay and lesbian sports club, cheekily named **Vorspiel** ('foreplay'), celebrates its 20th anniversary. This doesn't make it the oldest such sports club in Germany – that honour goes to SC Janus in Cologne, now 25 years old – but it has now overtaken its rivals in terms of membership. When Vorspiel was launched in 1986 it had just 150 members playing a handful of traditional sports – volleyball, football, squash, swimming; two decades down the track it has 1,200 full-time members, a further 300 who pay on the day, and more than 30 sports on offer.

It was the first Gay Games in San Francisco in 1982 that sparked the establishment of gay and lesbian sports groups in the 1980s. Vorspiel came into being alongside groups in other northern European countries – Denmark, Holland, Austria and Switzerland – where forming clubs for anything and everything is also a national pastime.

Vorspiel has always had an open-door policy and, as well as gays and lesbians, members include heterosexuals, transsexuals, bisexuals, older people and people with HIV and AIDS. It is essentially a leisure club rather than a centre for serious training, but ambitious athletes can compete as Team Vorspiel.

The list of sports on offer reflects recent popular trends. While football and volleyball are still on the menu, the last five years have seen a marked increase in wellness sessions: yoga, massage, health sports, fitness for older people and people with HIV and AIDS.

'We are very proud,' says Vorspiel's Dirk Alex. 'A club of 1,500 members offering lots of activities for little money is a great opportunity for members to meet other gays, lesbians and their straight friends who are into playing sport together. Vorspiel has also earned a professional reputation at home and abroad. We are on the board of the European Gay and Lesbian Sport Federation (EGLSF) and the Federation of Gay Games (FGG).'

The next two decades are likely to be tougher for the organisation, with funding cuts affecting the number of public sporting facilities available. Private locations cost more and the money will have to be found somewhere, whether from Vorspiel's members or private sponsorship. Dirk says: 'We are definitely at a turning point and we will have to think of a new way forward. But that is our challenge for the next 20 years.'
For more details, see www.vorspiel-berlin.de.

Classy clobber for boys of all ages at **Boyz 'R' Us**. *See p215.*

Prenzlauer Berg

Irrenhouse

*GeburtstagsKlub, Am Friedrichshain 33
(4202 1406/www.ninaqueer.com). Tram M4
Am Friedrichshain.* **Open** 11pm-late 3rd Sat
of mth. **No credit cards. Map** p303 Q5.
True to its name, 'Madhouse', this popular one-
nighter is a bizarre mixture of party kids, trashy
drag queens and nocturnal flotsam partying to
house and chart music under even more bizarre porn
installations. Don't hesitate to misbehave – hostess
Nina Queer does it all the time.

SchwuZ

*Mehringdamm 61 (629 0880/www.schwuz.de).
U6, U7 Mehringdamm.* **Open** 11pm-late Fri, Sat.
Admission from €5-€6. **No credit cards. Map**
p306 M10.
Saturday is the main disco night at the Schwulen
Zentrum ('Gay Centre'), Berlin's longest-running
dance institution. The club attracts a mixed crowd
of all ages and styles. There are two, sometimes
three dancefloors, and much mingling between the
three bars and Café Melitta Sundström (*see p207*) at
the front. Friday hosts an assortment of one-
nighters: first Friday of the month is London Calling
with independent and pop music; second Friday
there's subterra (*see p216*); third Friday, SubworxX
offers indie and rock music; and on the fourth Friday

the vibe is R&B, hip hop, soul and funk at
Bootylicious. The Madonnamania party (usually the
third or fourth Sat of Oct, Jan, Apr and July) plays
the hits from the last 20 years in two rooms.

Schöneberg

Connection

*Fuggerstrasse 33 (218 1432/www.connection-
berlin.com). U1, U2, U3 Wittenbergplatz.* **Open**
11pm-late Fri, Sat. **Admission** €7 (incl drink
ticket). **Map** p305 H9.
On Saturdays, a popular men-only club with DJs
playing mainly electronic sounds. The dancefloor is
usually packed and, if you're bored with that, you
can cruise the vast flesh-dungeons of Connection
Garage (*see p215*), which is where most guests end
up. First Friday of the month is now mixed.

Leather, sex & fetish

The hardcore and fetish scene in Berlin is
huge. Places to obtain your preferred garb
are plentiful, as are opportunities to show it
off, including the eternally crowded **Leather
Meeting** over the Easter holidays, the annual
Gay Skinhead Meeting and various fetish
parties or events. Most of the parties are men-
only and have a strict dress code.

Prenzlauer Berg

Midnight Sun
Paul-Robeson-Strasse 50 (4471 6395/www.
themidnightsun.de). U2, S8, S41, S42, S85
Schönhauser Allee. **Open** 10pm-late daily.
Credit AmEx, MC, V. **Map** p303 O1.
Cruising fetish bar, popular with skinheads and
hardcore types. There are also sex parties (7-9pm
Tue, 5-6.30pm Sun), utilising a second darkroom in
the basement. Sunday themes vary: Coffee & Cream
(first of the month); Fist Afternoon (second Sun);
Gang Bang (third); Fist and Fuck Weekend (fourth).

Stahlrohr
Greifenhagener Strasse 54 (4473 2747/www.
stahlrohr.com). U2, S8, S41, S42, S85 Schönhauser
Allee. **Open** 10pm-late Mon-Sat; 6pm-late Sun.
Admission €5 (incl 1 drink). **No credit cards.**
Map p303/p312 O2.
Stahlrohr is a small hardcore pub in the front and a
huge darkroom in the back. The sex parties here
cater for every taste, including Fist and Fuck (Sun);
Sneakers and Boots (alternate Fri); Underwear,
Naked and Fetish (Thur); and the Youngster party
for those aged 18-26 (Tue).

Kreuzberg

Bodies in Emotion
AHA, Mehringdamm 61 (692 3600/www.aha-
berlin.de). U6, U7 Mehringdamm. **Open** 9pm-5am
every 2nd Fri. **Admission** €6. **No credit cards.**
Map p306 M10.
This sex party is popular with guys under 30 (or who
look it – no hairy chests). What you wear is your
business, but most put on sexy shorts, to be taken
off in the sex area. There mattresses and slings invite
you to have fun, if you can find an empty one.

Club Culture Houze
Görlitzer Strasse 71 (6170 9669/www.club-culture-
houze.de). U1 Görlitzer Bahnhof. **Open** 7pm-late
Mon, Thur; 8pm-late Wed, Fri; 10pm-late Sat.
Admission €7.50. **Map** p307 Q9.
Diverse sex parties (some of them mixed), ranging
from Naked to SM and Fetish. Exclusive gay nights
on Monday (Naked Sex), Thursday (After Work),
Friday (Fist and Fuck Factory) and Saturday (Gay
Sex Party). Mostly body-conscious night owls visit
these kitsch rooms. Mattresses encourage people to
lie down, but actually they do it everywhere.

Quälgeist
Mehringdamm 51 (4th backyard, ground floor)
(788 5799/www.quaelgeist-berlin.de). U6, U7
Mehringdamm. **Open** varies. **Admission**
€8-€15. **No credit cards.** **Map** p306 M10.
First institution established solely to organise SM
parties. Themes include SM for beginners, bondage,
slave-market and fist nights. Pick up flyers at any
leather bar or Mann-O-Meter (*see p275*). There is
usually a dress code.

Triebwerk
Urbanstrasse 64 (6950 5203/www.triebwerkberlin.
com). U7, U8 Hermannplatz. **Open** 10pm-late Mon,
Thur-Sat; 9pm-late Tue, Wed; 4pm-late Sun. **No**
credit cards. **Map** p307 P10.
Small comfortable bar with a huge video screen, a
darkroom maze and Kreuzberg gays of every
denomination. Mondays are two drinks for the price
of one; Naked and Underwear Parties happen on
Tuesdays, Fridays and Sundays; Wednesdays are
Young Love (for boys aged 18-28).

Schöneberg

Ajpnia
Eisenacher Strasse 23 (2191 8881/www.ajpnia.de).
U1, U2, U3, U4 Nollendorfplatz. **Open** 7pm-2am
Wed; 9pm-7am Fri; 9pm-midnight Sat. **Admission**
€5-€6. **No credit cards.** **Map** p305 H9.
Two-storey, intimate sex club frequented by men
of all ages. First and third Saturdays are Posithiv
verkehr, a party by and for HIV-positives; second
and fourth are Nachtverkehr (Night Traffic).
Wednesdays are Feierabendverkehr (After Work
Traffic). Note: *verkehr* also means 'intercourse'.

Kit Kat Club
Bessemerstrasse 2-14 (no phone/www.kitkatclub.de).
U6 Alt-Tempelhof or S2, S26 Papestrasse. **Open**
11pm-late Fri, Sat; 8am-7pm Sun. **No credit cards.**
Essentially a mixed/straight sex and techno club
with a gay night on the first Monday of the month.
Saturday parties are also frequented by gays but the
most popular regular event is Peepshow (8am-7pm
Sun). Most parties have a dress code; the least you
have to do is take off your shirt. The club is also used
for the annual men-only Hustlaball, a major gay
dance and sex extravaganza, usually in October,
which attracts the beautiful, toned and scantily clad.
The stage shows and vast downstairs basement
cruising area leave nothing to the imagination.

New Action
Kleiststrasse 35 (211 8256/www.new-action-
berlin.de). U1, U2, U3, U4 Nollendorfplatz. **Open**
8pm-late Mon-Fri; continuously 10pm Sat-7am Mon.
No credit cards. **Map** p305 H9.
Atmospheric, custom-designed hardcore bar with
small darkroom. Eccentrics who haven't got to bed or
just got up appear in the early morning. Leather, rubber, uniform, jeans, but also the odd woollen pullover
create a casual atmosphere. Don't be sober. Naked Sex
Party on Thursday and Sunday from 10pm.

Scheune
Motzstrasse 25 (213 8580/www.scheune-berlin.de).
U1, U2, U3, U4 Nollendorfplatz. **Open** 9pm-7am
Mon-Thur, Sun; 9pm-9am Fri, Sat. **Admission**
varies. **No credit cards.** **Map** p305 N9.
Small and welcoming leather hardcore bar. Action
in the cellar is late and heavy. Entrance to the
Sunday afternoon Naked Sex Party is from 4pm to
6.30pm and costs €3. Occasional rubber nights.

Apollo City Sauna

*Kurfürstenstrasse 101, Schöneberg (213 2424).
U1, U2, U3 Wittenbergplatz.* **Open** 1pm-7am daily.
Admission €14.50/day with locker; €20.50 with
cabin. **Credit** AmEx, MC, V. **Map** p305 H8.
A sprawling labyrinth of sin with 130 lockers and 60
cabins, dry and steam saunas, porn-video den, TV
lounge, weights room, sunbeds and a well-stocked
bar. If you don't end up in a cabin, there's lots of
action in the dark, cruisy steam bath downstairs.

Steam Sauna

*Kurfürstenstrasse 113, Tiergarten (218 4060/www.
steam-sauna.de). U1, U2, U3 Wittenbergplatz.* **Open**
11am-7am Mon-Thur; continuously 11am Fri-7am
Mon. **Admission** €14-€17.50; €6 small cabin; €8.50
large cabin. **No credit cards. Map** p305 H8.
Classic sauna with 180 lockers and 38 cabins. Sex is
plentiful, sometimes hardcore. Clientele of all ages,
plus sauna and steam rooms, whirlpool, bar and TV
room showing porn. Clubbers drift along early on
Sunday mornings. Steam Night Specials are cheaper
(from 10.30pm Mon-Thur).

Treibhaus Sauna

*Schönhauser Allee 132, Prenzlauer Berg (448 4503/
449 3494/www.treibhaussauna.de). U2 Eberswalder
Strasse.* **Open** 1pm-7am Mon-Thur; continuously
1pm Fri-7am Mon. **Admission** from €10 (incl
locker & €3 drink ticket). **No credit cards**.
Map p303/p312 O3.
Tucked in the first courtyard (buzz for entry), this
has become a big favourite, especially with students
and youngsters. Facilities include dry sauna, steam
room, whirlpool, cycle jet, solarium, a shop stocked
with toys and lubricants, and cabins equipped with
TV and VCR. During the week, there's a variety of
health treatments on offer.

Comedy night
at **Begine**. *See p216.*

Cruising

Cruising is popular and legal in Berlin. Don't
panic when you encounter the police – they are
actually there to protect you from gay bashers
and never hassle cruisers – so it's quite safe to
go roaming about at night in Berlin. Summer
seems to bring out all of Berlin's finery and
there is no taboo attached to nudity in parks.

Grunewald

S7, S9 Grunewald.
Head into the woods behind the car park at
Pappelplatz. This is a popular daytime spot, but it's
also well frequented at night, when bikers and harder guys mingle among the trees.

Tiergarten

S5, S7, S9, S75 Tiergarten. **Map** p305 H7.
The Löwenbrücke (where the Grosser Weg crosses
the Neuer See) is the focal point – but the whole corner south-west of the Siegessäule is a bit of a gay
theme park. Summer sees hundreds of gays sunning
themselves on the 'Tuntenwiese' ('faggots meadow').

Other districts

Böse Buben

*Lichtenrader Strasse 32 (2nd backyard),
Neukölln (6270 5610/www.boesebubenberlin.de).
U8 Leinestrasse.* **Open** 5pm-4am Wed; 9pm-4am
Fri, Sat. **Admission** €5. **No credit cards**.
Fetish sex party club with imaginatively furnished
and decorated rooms. Tiled piss room, sling room,
bondage cross and cheap drinks make this quite a
grotto of hedonism. Wednesday is the After Work
Sex Party; weekends have different parties, such as
hard SM, fist, bondage or spanking.

Saunas

Saunas are popular and you may have to queue,
especially on cheaper days. In-house bills are
run up on your locker or cabin number and
settled on leaving. There are no open cabins,
only personal ones.

Volkspark Friedrichshain

U2, U5, U8, S5, S7, S9, S75 Alexanderplatz, then tram M4 Am Friedrichshain. **Map** p303 Q5.
After sundown, the area around and behind the Märchenbrunnen fills with horny lads. Busy at night, it has a friendlier feel than Berlin's other hunting grounds. Some activity by day, but you will have to search the nearby slopes for it.

Shops

Books & art

Bruno's

Bülowstrasse 106, Schöneberg (6150 0385/www.brunos.de). U1, U2, U3, U4 Nollendorfplatz. **Open** 10am-10pm Mon-Sat; 1-9pm Sun. **Credit** AmEx, MC, V. **Map** p306 J9.
Large and rather plush shop with an extensive selection of reading and viewing material, plus cards, calendars, videos and other paraphernalia.
Other locations: Schönhauser Allee 131, Prenzlauer Berg (6150 0387).

Prinz Eisenherz Buchladen

Lietzenburger Strasse 9A, Schöneberg (313 9936/fax 313 1795/www.prinz-eisenherz.com). U1, U2, U3 Wittenbergplatz. **Open** 10am-8pm Mon-Sat. **Credit** MC, V. **Map** p305 H9.
One of the finest gay bookshops in Europe, and among its large English-language stock are many titles unavailable in Britain. There's a good art and photography section, plus magazines, postcards and news of readings and other events.

Clothes

Boyz 'R' Us

Maasenstrasse 8, Schöneberg (2363 0640/www.boyz-r-us.de). U1, U2, U3, U4 Nollendorfplatz. **Open** 11am-8pm Mon-Fri; 10am-8pm Sat. **No credit cards. Map** p306 J9.
For discerning gays who like to be noticed and don't mind paying for it. Think G-Star, Diesel, Calvin Klein. Ladies' store GOLDelse (www.goldelse.net) is accessed through the back. **Photo** p212.

LadeRaum

Maasenstrasse 8, Schöneberg (2363 0640). U1, U2, U3, U4 Nollendorfplatz. **Open** 11am-8pm Mon-Fri; 10am-8pm Sat. **No credit cards. Map** p306 J9.
Walls full of tight T-shirts and tops for day and night, many at bargain prices. If you're still not satisfied, adapt your own – with print costs from €6.

Waahnsinn

Rosenthaler Strasse 17, Mitte (282 0029/www.waahnsinn-berlin.de). U8 Rosenthaler Platz or Weinmeisterstrasse. **Open** noon-8pm Mon-Sat. **Credit** AmEx, MC, V. **Map** p303/p310 N5.
Men's sequinned hot pants and tank tops are among the stand-out new items in this stylish and theatrical 1950s-70s second-hand clothes shop.

Toys & fetish outfits

Black Style

Seelower Strasse 5, Prenzlauer Berg (4468 8595/www.blackstyle.de). U2, S8, S41, S42, S85 Schönhauser Allee. **Open** 1-6.30pm Mon-Wed; 1-8pm Thur, Fri; 11am-4pm Sat. **Credit** AmEx, DC, MC, V. **Map** p303 O1.
From black fashion to butt plugs – if it's made out of rubber or latex, this shop's got it. High quality, reasonable prices and big variety. Mail order.

Butcherei Lindinger

Motzstrasse 18, Schöneberg (2005 1391/www.butcherei-lindinger.de). U1, U2, U3, U4 Nollendorfplatz. **Open** 2-8pm Mon-Sat. **No credit cards. Map** p305 H9.
Smart, new workshop producing tailor-made leather clothing and offering toys and rubber gear, including some of the biggest dildos on the market.

Connection Garage

Fuggerstrasse 33, Schöneberg (218 1432/www.connection-berlin.com). U1, U2, U3 Wittenbergplatz. **Open** 10am-1am Mon-Sat; 2pm-1am Sun. **Credit** MC, V. **Map** p305 H9.
Huge selection of leather novelties, clothing, SM accessories and magazines. Also a porn cinema (entry €7 incl 2 drinks). The cruising area comes alive at weekends, when it amalgamates with the Connection disco (see p212).

Leathers

Schliemannstrasse 38, Prenzlauer Berg (442 7786/www.leathers.de). U2 Eberswalder Strasse. **Open** noon-7.30pm Mon-Fri; noon-4pm Sat. **Credit** AmEx, MC, V. **Map** p303/p312 P3.
A workshop that produces leather and SM articles of the highest quality. No smut here – just helpful staff and a range of well-presented products.

Mr B

Motzstrasse 22, Schöneberg (2199 7704/www.misterb.com). U1, U2, U3, U4 Nollendorfplatz. **Open** noon-8pm Mon-Fri; 11am-8pm Sat. **Credit** AmEx, DC, MC, V. **Map** p305 H9.
This smart place is known particularly for its leather and rubber outfits, metal accessories and toys, SM articles, lubricants and clothing. Also hosts the occasional art exhibition.

Lesbian

There are few cities that can compete with Berlin's network of lesbian institutions, but there aren't that many lesbian-only bars. Mixed bars and club nights are listed in Siegessäule or L-mag (www.L-mag.de), a free lesbian quarterly. Many young lesbians favour the city's mixed venues such as **SchwuZ** (see p212), **SO36** (see p208) or **Die Busche** (see p207).

Bars & cafés

Mitte

Café Seidenfaden
Dircksenstrasse 47 (283 2783/www.frausucht zukunft.de). U8 Weinmeisterstrasse or S5, S7, S9, S75 Hackescher Markt. **Open** noon-9pm Mon, Tue, Thur, Fri; noon-9pm Wed; 11am-8pm Sat. **No credit cards. Map** p303/p311 O5.
Run by women from a therapy group of former addicts. There are readings and exhibitions, but no drugs or alcohol. Packed at lunchtime, quiet at night.

Friedrichshain

Frieda Frauenzentrum
Proskauer Strasse 7 (422 4276/www.frieda-frauenzentrum.de). U5 Samariterstrasse. **Open** 9am-8pm Tue, Thur; 9am-6pm Wed; 2-8pm Fri; 11am-2pm every 1st & 3rd Sat. **No credit cards. Map** p309 T6.
Centre for women's well-being and interests, with a full programme of lesbian, mother and senior events.

Kreuzberg

Schoko Café
Mariannenstrasse 6 (backyard) (615 1561/ www.schokofabrik.de). U1, U8 Kottbusser Tor. **Open** 5pm-late Mon, Wed-Sun. **No credit cards. Map** p307 P9.
Part of the Schoko-Fabrik women's centre, mostly frequented by lesbians. Snacks, occasional parties.

Schöneberg

Begine
Potsdamer Strasse 139 (215 1414/www.begine.de). U2 Bülowstrasse. **Open** 6pm-late Mon, Tue, Fri; 7pm-late Thur; times vary according to events Wed, Sat. **No credit cards. Map** p306 J9.
Women-only café frequented by lesbians. Part of the 'Meeting Point and Culture for Women' centre. **Photo** *p214.*

Charlottenburg

neue Bar
Knesebeckstrasse 16 (3150 3062/www.neuebar.de). S5, S7, S9, S75 Savignyplatz. **Open** 6pm-late Tue-Sat. **No credit cards. Map** p305/p312 F8.
Small, talkative pub for women and lesbians.

Clubs & one-nighters

Prenzlauer Berg

Frauenparty
EWA eV Frauenzentrum, Prenzlauer Allee 6 (442 8023/www.ewa-frauenzentrum.de). U2

Rosa-Luxemburg-Platz. **Open** 8pm-late 1st Fri of mth. **No credit cards. Map** p303 P5.
The venue hosts regular dance parties, but it's always worth checking the website and local press for other events here.

Kreuzberg

m.appeal
SO36, Oranienstrasse 190 (6140 1306/www.so36. de). U1, U8 Kottbusser Tor. **Open** 10pm-late 1st Fri of mth. **No credit cards. Map** p307 P9.
Every first Friday of the month, m.appeal sees youngish, progressive lesbians party in a slightly trashy atmosphere. Drag welcome, but gays are only admitted when accompanied by lesbians.

subterra
SchwuZ, Mehringdamm 61 (693 7025/www. megadyke.de). U6, U7 Mehringdamm. **Open** 10pm-late every 2nd Fri. **Admission** €6-€8. **No credit cards. Map** p306 M10.
This is a mixed party, albeit with distinctly more lesbians than gays, held downstairs in SchwuZ and organised by Megadyke Productions. In addition to the two dancefloors, there's a massage corner in the candlelight lounge, where a professional masseuse will knead anyone's flesh. Subterra often fills SchwuZ to capacity.

Shops & services

Lustwandel
Raumerstrasse 20, Prenzlauer Berg (4404 0860/ www.lustwandel.de). U2 Eberswalder Strasse. **Open** noon-8pm Mon-Fri; 11am-4pm Sat. **Credit** MC, V. **Map** p303/p312 P3.
Lustwandel is a women's book store that sells erotic literature catering to every taste. You'll also find various works of fiction, art books and illustrated publications.

Playstixx
Waldemarstrasse 24, Kreuzberg (6165 9500/ www.playstixx.de). U1, U8 Kottbusser Tor. **Open** 2-6pm Wed, Thur; 2-5pm Fri; noon-3pm 2nd & 4th Sat of mth. **No credit cards. Map** p307 P8.
The dildos on offer at this workshop, run by sculptress Stefanie Dörr, come in the form of bananas, whales, fists or dolphins rather than phalluses. Most are made of non-allergenic, highly durable silicon. The premises open only for women on Wednesdays, Fridays and fortnightly Saturdays.

Sexclusivitäten
Contact: Laura Méritt, Fürbringerstrasse 2, Kreuzberg (693 6666/www.sexclusivitaeten.de). U7 Gneisenaustrasse. **Open** by appointment only, noon-8pm Fri. **No credit cards. Map** p307 N10.
Laura Méritt calls herself a feminist linguist and sexpert, offering sex counselling, conflict mediation and a big selection of sex toys. Shop for a variety of dildos, vibrators and other items.

Music: Rock, World & Jazz

The scene might be a muddle, but music matters in Berlin.

Knaack. *See p219.*

Berlin is a city of musical paradox. For decades there was little innovation in the eastern half of the city, while on the western side there was almost too much. West Berlin tried to make the most of skewed demographics, encouraging youth culture and effectively subsidising rock bands. Many of those drawn to the city, at least in part because residency eliminated military service requirements, settled in Kreuzberg, and the effects of those inspired by Bowie, Iggy, Cave and Neubauten are felt to this day. So, on the one hand, low rents, makeshift clubs, active nightlife and a tradition of youthful dissent led to a density of musical activity – this is a city where music is important.

On the other hand, the continual paucity of disposable income among Berlin's younger residents means some of the lowest band guarantees in western Europe. Add that to the city's distance from other urban centres and you have a situation where big-name acts that might play Würzburg or Kiel often skip Berlin when touring the country. Also, somewhere in the techno-powered 1990s, Berlin managed to

get a reputation as an anti-rock city, something which has only recently begun to dissipate.

As well it might. Berlin audiences are some of the most enthusiastic in the world. Perhaps too enthusiastic. Normally mild-mannered Berliners will carry on demanding an encore long after the lights have been turned on. Yes, Berlin does rock, even if its signature sound for the time being remains a minimalist electro take on techno – as exemplified by DJs such as Kaos or bpitch control label head Ellen Allien.

In the past few years, however, just as the boundaries between East and West have blurred, so has there been a heavy overlap between live performance and dance venues, with many major clubs featuring a live act along with DJs on their most popular nights. Much of this has to do with Canadian settler Peaches, who broke biggish (her debut album on Berlin's Kitty-Yo label sold 50,000 copies in the USA alone). Since then there has been a glut of lascivious, 1980s-tinged, art-school playback singers hopping around to relatively primitive electronics, ranging from the leathered irony of long-timers such as Boy from Brazil and Cobra Killer, to theatrical expats like Snax and Angie Reed. Add to this electro-cabaret the influx of club-influenced rock acts such as The Robocop Kraus, and in the end it's all about dancing. And Berliners do love to dance, even if they're not terribly good at it.

But all sorts of music get aired here, and once a trend starts, it never dies. Kreuzberg retains an anarcho-punk aesthetic. East German hippies strum Beatles songs in Friedrichshain. British post-punk has taken over Mitte. Hip hop dominates suburban working-class estates. And white rastas are all over the place. Sometimes everyone in this city appears to consider themselves a DJ, even if all they're doing is letting side two of Bowie's *Hunky Dory* play out while they're off in the toilets inhaling a line. Meanwhile, several major labels have moved their German or European headquarters to Berlin, and the city also hosts PopKomm (*see p185*), the German music industry's annual trade fair, talking shop and showcase.

As for the regular *Volk*, the likes of Chris De Burgh or A-Ha still have viable careers here (both played the Berlin Live8), and there's a strain of *Schlager* that can still be heard in a lot of mainstream music. This can make radio difficult for the non-initiated, though RadioEins (95.8 FM, www.radioeins.de), Radio Multikulti (96.3 FM, www.multikulti.de), RadioFritz (102.6 FM, www.fritz.de) and MotorFM (106.8 FM, www.motormusic.org/radio) are all above average, if middlebrow.

Rock venues

The sports venues **Max-Schmeling-Halle** and **Velodrom** (for both, *see p244*) also host occasional music events.

Arena Berlin
Eichenstrasse 4, Treptow (533 2030/www.arena-berlin.de). S6, S8, S9, S41, S42, S85 Treptower Park. **Open** *Box office 10am-7.30pm Mon-Fri. Performances varies.* **No credit cards.** **Map** p308 S9.
It's a former bus garage and often sounds like it, but Arena hosts A-list concerts by acts such as Bob Dylan or Björk, and its moveable stage also allows for some smaller acts. The surrounding entertainment complex includes the Badeschiff (*see p253*), a swimming pool popular with the gay crowd, and the party boat MS Hoppetosse (*see p230*).

Ausland
Lychener Strasse 60, Prenzlauer Berg (447 7008/www.ausland-berlin.de). U2 Eberswalder Strasse/bus N2. **Open** *varies.* **Admission** €3-€5. **No credit cards.** **Map** p303/p312 P2.
A tiny basement space run by nutty bohos offering experimental music – noise, free jazz, avant-folk and

live electronica – plus film and installations. It can get packed when a top act, such as Acid Mothers Temple, stops by. Note that concerts begin one hour later than the time posted – on principle, apparently. There's usually a DJ after the show, though he or she may not be concerned with making you dance.

Bastard@Prater
Kastanienallee 7-9, Prenzlauer Berg (247 6772/www.praterteam.de). U2 Eberswalder Strasse/bus N52. **Open** *Box office noon-6pm Tue-Fri (& 1hr before show). Performances varies.* **Admission** varies. **No credit cards.** **Map** p303/p312 O3.
Connected to the Prater theatre (*see p238*) and Prater beer garden (*see p149*), this many-chandeliered spot veers between first-rate indie rock, over-the-hill and up-and-coming underground hip hop, and DJ nights that favour hardcore gabba, ragga and jungle.

Café Zapata in Tacheles
Oranienburgerstrasse 54-6A, Mitte (281 6109/www.cafe-zapata.de). U6 Oranienburger Tor. **Open** varies. **Admission** varies. **No credit cards.** **Map** p302/p310 M5.
Though part of the squatted Tacheles complex, Café Zapata stands on its own, booking top-flight folk and indie from Joanna Newsom to local heroes such as Bruno Adams. It's a small space, but opens up into a beer garden in summer.

Columbiaclub
Columbiadamm 9-11, Tempelhof (Trinity Ticketing 7809 9810/www.columbiaclub.de). U6 Platz der Luftbrücke. **Open** *Box office 10am-7pm Mon-Fri; 12.30-6pm Sat.* **Admission** varies. **No credit cards.** **Map** p307 N11.
This former US Forces cinema is a little impersonal once you get past the old-fashioned box office, but showcases mid-size acts of every genre, from John Cale to Morgan Heritage. There's been less on here of late via RadioFritz, which used to run it, has moved its shows to the Postbahnhof (*see p219*).

Columbiahalle
Columbiadamm 13-21, Tempelhof (tickets 6110 1313/www.columbiahalle.de). U6 Platz der Luftbrücke. **Open** 9am-7pm Mon-Fri; 10am-2pm Sat. **Admission** varies. **No credit cards.** **Map** p307 N11.
Next door to Columbiaclub, this unappealing, roomy venue with a reputation for the best sound in town hosts larger acts that haven't made it to stadium status, such as Moby, the White Stripes or Goldfrapp. Drinks cost too much, but it's a good place to see superstar hip hop acts, such as Jay-Z and Eminem, that would be playing amphitheatres in other cities.

Festsaal Kreuzberg
Skalitzer Strasse 130, Kreuzberg (6165 6003/www.festsaal-kreuzberg.de). U1, U8 Kottbusser Tor. **Open** varies. **Admission** varies. **No credit cards.** **Map** p307 P9.
It looks an unlikely place to go raving, but, thanks to a westward-moving scene and an eclectic booking policy, this has become one of Kreuzberg's most

Kulturbrauerei: always something brewing.

popular venues, featuring indie acts and DJs from Wolf Eyes to Miss Kittin and all over the map.

Frannz Club

Schönhauser Allee 36, Prenzlauer Berg (7262 7930/ www.frannz.de). U2 Eberswalder Strasse. **Open** 9pm, 11pm Wed; 10pm Fri, Sat; 3pm, 8pm Sun. **Tickets** free-€8. **No credit cards. Map** p303/p312 O3.

A former GDR youth club, Frannz has reopened as an anonymous black box with decent sound, pricey drinks and overzealous doormen. Musically, it lacks an identity, and is heavy on German acts that don't really translate culturally, though they have booked some rockabilly stars such as Wanda Jackson.

Fritzclub im Postbahnhof

Strasse der Pariser Kommune 3-10, Friedrichshain (tickets 6110 1313/www.fritzclub.com). S3, S5, S7, S9, S75 Ostbahnhof. **Open** 9am-7pm Mon-Fri; 10am-2pm Sat. **Admission** varies. **No credit cards. Map** p308 R7.

This restored industrial building is a newcomer, but its association with RadioFritz gives it the clout to book on-their-way indie acts such as Arcade Fire and Maximo Park, as well as mid-level names such as Luka Bloom and Fun Lovin' Criminals.

Kalkscheune

Jannisstrasse 2, Mitte (5900 4340/www.kalkscheune. de). U6 Oranienburger Tor. **Open** Box office noon-7pm Mon-Fri. **Admission** varies. **No credit cards. Map** p302/p310 M5.

This elegantly restored 19th-century factory building is a popular venue for *Schlager* parties and cabaret acts, but also gets booked with a few interesting and offbeat bands, such as Devendra Banhart and Nouvelle Vague.

Knaack

Greifswalder Strasse 224, Prenzlauer Berg (concerts 442 7061/club 442 7060/www.knaack-berlin.de). S8, S41, S42, S85 Greifswalder Strasse. **Open** *Bar* 6pm-late daily. *Club* 8pm-late Wed; 9pm-late Fri, Sat. **Admission** *Club* €1; €5 after 11pm. *Concerts* free-€18. **No credit cards. Map** p303 Q4.

Follow the Rammstein-ish bar to the back, enter a narrow hallway, and you'll find a dark, small and anonymous club. Knaack books an eclectic array of excellent acts, from the Rapture to RA the Rugged Man to Michael Hurley. It also hosts free nights of local bands, which are usually less impressive. There's an upstairs discotheque. **Photo** *p217*.

Kulturbrauerei

Schönhauser Allee 35 (443 1515/www.kesselhaus- berlin.de). U2 Eberswalder Strasse. **Open** Box office noon-6pm Mon-Wed, Sun; noon-8pm Thur-Sat. **Tickets** €5-22. **No credit cards. Map** p302/p310 O3.

There is an assortment of different venues within this enormous former brewery which, with its outdoor bars and barbecues, can resemble a cross between a medieval fairground and a school disco. Kesselhaus, Maschinehaus and Palas are the three venues linked to the Kulturbrauerei proper (unlike nbi; *see p220*) and host diverse acts in a similar vein. Kesselhaus is the largest, drawing its biggest crowds for reggae concerts. Some jazz and German acts also show up, but booking is eclectic.

Magnet

Greifswalder Strasse 212/3, Prenzlauer Berg (4400 8140/www.magnet-club.de). S8, S41, S42, S85 Greifswalder Strasse/tram M4, N54. **Open** 8pm-late daily. **Admission** €1-€14. **No credit cards. Map** p303/p312 Q4.

Once a jazz club, this venue has become one of the biggest bookers for the kind of up-and-coming indie bands featured in the *NME* – catch them here before they hit the stadium circuit. Recent renovations have improved the sight lines, though it can still be difficult to navigate a peek when the place fills up.

Maria am Ostbahnhof

An der Schillingbrücke, Friedrichshain (2123 8190/ www.clubmaria.de). S3, S5, S7, S9, S75 Ostbahnhof. **Open** 8pm-late daily. **Admission** €8-€15. **No credit cards. Map** p307 Q7.

The premier venue for hipper live acts not quite ready for Columbiahalle (*see p218*) also hosts dance nights that, although eclectically booked with top-notch DJs, don't come off very glam in the concrete bunker environs. Other attractions are the stylish post-industrial design and labyrinth of lounges that swell and shrink depending on the organisers' whim.

Mudd Club

Grosse Hamburger Strasse 17, Mitte (4403 6299/ www.muddclub.de). S5, S7, S9, S75 Hackescher Markt. **Open** varies. **Tickets** varies. **No credit cards. Map** p303/p310 N5.

This brick-lined basement is owned by Steve Mass, who founded the original, NYC club of yore. He's more besotted by Russendisko than No Wave these days, with a self-conscious attempt to ape the success of Kaffee Burger (*see p224*), complete with Russian beer and DJs with moustaches. Band booking emphasises loveable losers such as Mark Lanegan or the Dirty Three.

nbi

Kulturbrauerei, Schönhauser Allee 36, Prenzlauer Berg (4405 1681/www.neueberlinerinitiative.de). U2 Eberswalder Strasse/bus N2. **Open** 6pm-late daily. **Admission** varies. **No credit cards. Map** p302/p310 O3.

Recently moved to the Kulturbrauerei, the latest space for this electroclub pioneer is a pink box sprinkled with furniture in the current *Wohnzimmer* style. The bartenders can't stop talking about the excellent sound system, though, and several nights per month are given to labels and promoters such as Monika and RepeatRepeat, which leads to such surprises as Einstürzende Neubauten popping in. The space doesn't lend itself to dancing, so electronic music has been de-emphasised, but the booking remains interesting. Sometimes there's ping-pong.

Passionskirche

Marheinekeplatz 1-2, Kreuzberg (tickets 6959 3624/ 6940 1241/www.akanthus.de). U7 Gneisenaustrasse. **Open** varies. **Admission** varies. **No credit cards. Map** p307 N10.

The likes of Beck, Ryan Adams and Marc Almond have graced the stage of this deconsecrated church – the best place for acts whose amplifiers don't go past 4. But get there early, as it's the only church in Berlin whose pews regularly overflow. And the only one where you can drink more than wine.

SO36

Oranienstrasse 190, Kreuzberg (tickets 6110 1313/ 6140 1306/www.so36.de). U1, U8 Kottbusser Tor. **Open** 9pm-late daily. *Box office* noon-4pm daily. **Admission** varies. **No credit cards. Map** p307 P9.

Berlin's legendary punk club continues to book the biggest names in DIY, from Bolt Thrower to Killing Joke, as well as edgy up-and-comers such as The Streets. Also hosts reggae nights, gay parties (*see p208*) and more.

Volksbühne/Roter Salon

Rosa-Luxemburg-Platz, Mitte (tickets 4171 7512/4401 7400/www.roter-salon.de). U2 Rosa-Luxemburg-Platz. **Open** *Box office* noon-6pm Fri. **Admission** €5-€8. **No credit cards. Map** p303/p310 O5.

Two to three times a month the main stage at east Berlin's premier avant-garde theatre hosts arty acts such as Animal Collective or Tom Zé. And sometimes they open up the wood-panelled stage to such curator-approved DJs as Aphex Twin. The same complex contains the likeable Roter Salon, where you can hear a wide-ranging array of DJs and see indie-style live acts.

Wabe

Danziger Strasse 101, Prenzlauer Berg (902 953 850/www.wabe-berlin.de). S8, S41, S42, S85 Greifswalder Strasse. **Open** varies. **Admission** varies. **No credit cards. Map** p303 Q3.

A GDR-era community centre in Ernst-Thälmann-Park, this octagonal space provides young local bands with an opportunity to perform live – partly by hosting its own 'battle of the bands' contest and co-operating with MTV.

World music

It only takes a few minutes' listening to Radio Multikulti (note new frequency: 96.3 FM) to get an aural impression of Berlin's global music scene. From indie pop to Brazilian acoustic, Klezmer remix to oriental crossover, the palette of worldbeat offerings seems to be shrinking and expanding at the same time. While big-name performers made fewer appearances in Berlin in 2005 (recent concerts included Amadou & Mariam from Mali, New York-based Richard Bona from Cameroon, and the legendary Skatalites from Jamaica), a profusion of lesser-known hybrid acts fills Berlin's cultural calendar with dizzying diversity.

Anyone visiting in late spring shouldn't miss the **Karnival der Kulturen** (*see p182*), a four-day festival of multiculturalism. Just outside of Berlin, Potsdam's **Afrika Festival** in early July is growing in popularity and quality.

World music acts are often also booked at the Kesselhaus or Maschinenhaus in the **Kulturbrauerei** complex (*see p219*).

Haus der Kulturen der Welt

John-Foster-Dulles Allee 10, Tiergarten (397 870/ www.hkw.de). S5, S7, S9 S75 Bellevue. **Open** 10am-9pm Tue-Sun. **Admission** varies. **No credit cards.** Map p302 K6.

Berlin's largest world music venue, a sort of global cultural centre, houses several auditoriums and exhibition spaces. *See p101.*

Havanna Club

Hauptstrasse 30, Schöneberg (784 8565/www. havanna-berlin.de). U7 Eisenacher Strasse. **Open** 9pm-late Wed; 10pm-late Fri, Sat. **Admission** €2.50 Wed; €6.50 Fri; €7 Sat. **No credit cards.** Map p306 J11.

Three dancefloors with salsa, merengue and R&B. It's a popular place with expatriate South Americans and Cubans. One hour before opening, there's a salsa class for €4, which is reckoned to be a good place to meet people, as well as learn a few steps.

Werkstatt der Kulturen

Wissmannstrasse 32, Neukölln (609 7700). U7, U8 Hermannplatz. **Open** 9am-5pm Mon; 9am-6pm Tue-Fri. **Admission** €12; €8 concessions. Price varies for special concerts. **No credit cards.** Map p307 P11.

This intimate venue usually presents traditionally ethnic music acts or local collaborations that blend jazz, trance or folk elements.

So far so Gut

Musician, producer, label-owner and DJ, **Gudrun Gut** (*pictured*) has been a prime mover on the Berlin scene for over 20 years. She arrived from West Germany at 17, attracted by the 'breath of freedom' Berlin promised. After enrolling in art school, she played with an early incarnation of Einstürzende Neubauten and co-founded the all-female band Malaria! with Bettina Köster. Despite (or because of) the band's severe, very German aesthetic, it gained international notice, including support gigs with New Order and John Cage. Gut describes 1980s Berlin as 'a city of young people and pensioners', and says it has always attracted misfits.

After Malaria!, Gut began exploring electronic music technology with the band Matador and numerous other projects. In the mid 1990s she started the Ocean Club (www.oceanclub.de), a loose collective of like-minded artists. Gut and collaborator Thomas Fehlmann also began hosting and producing a weekly radio programme of the same name on RadioEins (Friday 11pm-1am, repeated Sunday 1-3am; 95.8 FM) to showcase an eclectic selection of music. And she founded the label Monika Enterprise (www.monika-enterprise.de), whose excellent releases by artists such as Barbara Morgenstern, Quarks and Contriva she describes as 'poppy electronica with an edge'.

When asked what makes the Berlin scene unique, Gut describes the city as a 'grey oasis', pointing to its relative affordability and

tolerance as factors in attracting artists. That tolerance, she says, has helped create a multi-layered musical culture that offers 'many niches to be filled'. But rather than having a typical sound or genre, Berlin's music scene is distinguished more by a subversive attitude, a Berlin tradition she sees as dating back to at least the 1920s.

Perhaps that attitude feeds what Gut sees as the rigorous criticism musicians in Berlin can expect from their peers. Artists get feedback quickly and directly. For that reason, Berlin musicians tend to start tours elsewhere, wanting the set to be perfect before it reaches the hometown crowd. But that, says Gut, doesn't mean there's no sense of community. While every label does its own thing, there's a sense of co-operation rather than competition.

'There's still that communist perspective, where you say, "Together we're stronger than on our own."'

Gut regards the creeping yuppification of Berlin and the recent closings of illegal clubs with concern, pointing out that the renegade spirit of those places is part of what makes the city's scene what it is. But in general her view of the future is positive: the crisis in the music business appears to have been overcome, with major labels and independents now each doing their own thing. And she's unfazed by Berlin's financial crisis, saying she's 'never experienced a prosperous Berlin'. After more than 20 years helping to shape Berlin music, she's not about to let budget cuts get in the way.

B-Flat: jam with everything.

Jazz

After a post-Wall upswing in activity, many of the city's better jazzfolk have joined forces with their experimental or electronic brethren. Berlin has never been big on genre purity. That said, a rule of thumb for clubs here is jazz+blues = mouldy, jazz+weird = fun. World-class musicians such as avant-gardist Peter Brötzmann and Australian drummer Tony Buck make their homes here, and each autumn boasts two fantastic, overlapping jazz festivals, the larger **Berlin JazzFest** (*see p185*), and the more free-rooted **Total Music Meeting**.

Rather than sticking to the jazz clubs, search out galleries, artist-run venues, social clubs and cultural houses. The famed GDR-era **JazzKeller Treptow** (www.jazzkeller69.de) continues to promote many interesting shows in a variety of small spaces. Berlin also features Germany's only 24-hour jazz radio (101.9 FM) but bean counters and bureaucrats have rendered it sadly inoffensive.

A-Trane

Bleibtreustrasse 1, Charlottenburg (313 2550/ www.a-trane.de). S5, S7, S9, S75 Savignyplatz. **Open** 9pm-2am Mon-Thur, Sun; 9pm-late Fri, Sat. *Performances* 10pm daily. **Admission** €6-€25. **Credit** AmEx, DC, MC. **Map** p305/p312 E8.
A bit ostentatious, but the place usually gets at least one top-flight act a month for an extended stay.

B-Flat

Rosenthaler Strasse 13, Mitte (283 3123/www.b-flat-berlin.de). U8 Rosenthaler Platz. **Open** from 9pm daily. **Admission** €4-€12; €4-€8 concessions. **No credit cards. Map** p303/p310 N5.

Maintaining a large piano-bar feel, B-Flat manages to get a decent local hero in once in a while, but its strongest nights tend to feature singers. Free Wednesday night jam session from 9pm.

Quasimodo

Kantstrasse 12A, Charlottenburg (312 8086/www. quasimodo.de). U2, U9, S5, S7, S9, S75 Zoologischer Garten. **Open** *Performances* 10pm Tue-Sun (doors open 1hr before show). **Admission** €5-€25. **No credit cards. Map** p305/p312 F8.
This basement spot appears close to severing its connections to jazz entirely, preferring the 'jazzy'. It still gets some good acts, both local and international, as well as heroic singers such as Terry Callier.

Tränenpalast

Reichstagsufer 17, Mitte (office 206 100/tickets 2061 0011/www.traenenpalast.de). U6, S1, S2, S5, S7, S9, S75 Friedrichstrasse. **Open** *Box office* 6pm-performance begins. *Performances* varies. **No credit cards. Map** p303/p311 M6.
This roomy, fascinating location – it's the building people passed through when leaving East Berlin – mostly books comedy and cabaret (*see p242*), but sometimes also hosts jazz greats such as Pharoah Sanders, Don Byron and Nils Petter Molvaer.

Yorckschlösschen

Yorckstrasse 15, Kreuzberg (215 8070/www. yorckschloesschen.de). U6, U7 Mehringdamm. **Open** 9am-3am Mon-Thur, Sun; 9am-4am Fri, Sat. **Admission** free. **Credit** AmEx, DC, MC, V. **Map** p306 L10.
The music at this century-old *Eck-Kneipe* is a faintly ridiculous mix of German Dixieland and long-in-the-tooth beat music. But in the old-world environment (and after several *Weizenbiers*) it can actually get pretty groovy.

Nightlife

Enough edgy entertainment to satisfy even the most jaded of night owls.

Bohannon: 'Are you ready for some soulful electronic clubbing?' *See p224.*

It's difficult to be late for an event in Berlin. This is a town where nightlife is everything. And why not? Hardly anyone has a job (and those that do are serving the beer) and things often don't even begin to stir until one in the morning. Bars are open all night long, moveable parties are everywhere, venues open and close in spaces rediscovered or repurposed. The city has long been an insomniac's dream and a recovering addict's nightmare.

But the DIY spirit of old has abated. With the city's continuing renovation, rents have increased and many of the famed squatter bars, as well as the legendary techno club Tresor and even chi-chi nightspot Cookies, have disappeared. Berlin's egalitarian spirit has been tested by a new wave of clubs with door policies and doormen – even though, compared to London or New York, these remain rather informal. And prices are rising, though they will still seem cheap to many visitors.

Still, even with decreased options, Berlin overflows with nocturnal activity and boundary-erasing nightlife. Electro clubs will host live acts, while it seems that almost every bar has a DJ booth – and following the DJ to the next bar after he finishes his set is not an uncommon occurrence. A literary salon, such as **Kaffee Burger**, turns into a wild disco that

closes after dawn, while the decadent **Panorama Bar** might host a reading of Banana Yoshimoto's work.

Though the trend in Mitte is more toward a fashion-y, exclusive vibe, it's still not usually much of a problem to get in anywhere – they need your money. Prenzlauer Berg, Friedrichshain and Kreuzberg offer a more down-to-earth approach. There's no longer much happening in Tiergarten and Schöneberg these days, and Charlottenburg is a desert.

Finding out where the party is can be a haphazard affair. Clubs often don't update their websites, or only post the next weekend's events, while party promoters can move from venue to venue. It's not a bad idea to go into shops, bars and cafés that look interesting and hunt for flyers. Listings magazines will cover the basics, but there is always an underground party or some last minute goings-on. Then again, you might just want to stand on the street at three in the morning and listen for a ruckus. There's sure to be one somewhere.

But remember, nothing stays the same for very long. Some clubs stick around for years, others wink in and out of existence. These listings were as correct as we could make them at the time of going to press. But it's worth checking that places are still in business.

Club der polnischern Versager.
See p225.

This marvel of socialist architecture was once the hotspot for party apparatchiks. These days its assortment of spaces host an assortment of regular one-nighters and one-off events, from left-field fashion shows to world-class DJs – and the downstairs dancefloor is a surprisingly intimate place to see them. There's an outside area for summer.

Delicious Doughnuts

Rosenthaler Strasse 9 (2809 9274/www.delicious. doughnuts.de). U8 Rosenthaler Platz/bus N8, N84. **Open** 9pm-late daily. **Admission** €3. **No credit cards. Map** p303/p310 N5.

This pioneer club of the east – a long, dark room with intimate booths – has seen better days, but its time may come again. There's been a recent move towards soul/house derivatives, though sometimes the music is a bit too uptempo for the loungey environment.

Golden Gate

Dircksenstrasse 77-8 (no phone/www.goldengate-berlin.de). U8, S5, S7, S9, S75 Jannowitzbrücke. **Open** from 11pm Fri, Sat. **Admission** €5-€8. **No credit cards. Map** p303/p310 O5.

Trickily located beneath the Jannowitzbrücke U-Bahn, Golden Gate is accessed from that station's exit in Schicklerstrasse – look for where the bicycles are all parked. Down below you'll find plenty of drunken locals crowded into a small space with an informal living-room feel. There's a varied selection of DJs and a tiny stage that sometimes hosts surprisingly popular bands, such as Comets on Fire, as well as electro-cabaret events. Sometimes there is a Saturday afternoon lounge, with DJs starting at 1pm.

Kaffee Burger

Torstrasse 60 (2804 6495/www.kaffeeburger.de). U2 Rosa-Luxemburg-Platz/bus N2/tram N54. **Open** 8pm-late Mon-Thur; 9pm-late Fri, Sat; 7pm-late Sun. **Admission** €3-€5. **No credit cards. Map** p303/p310 N5.

Best known as home of the popular twice-monthly Russendisko (*see p227* **One Russian under a groove**), Kaffee Burger's programme runs the cultural gamut. Early evenings may see readings, lectures, film screenings or live music. Later on, local and expat DJs play anything from old-school country to something called Global Hungarian Dancehall, as well as the more common indie, rock, soul or Britpop fare. The club's decor has been left intact from GDR days, and the relatively bright lighting facilitates interaction with strangers. To go with the eclectic programming, Burger draws a mixed, international crowd, and it's recently undergone a renaissance as a somewhat sleazy all-night joint that still retains some of the degeneracy that made post-Wall Berlin so much fun. Drinks are cheap.

Kinzo Club

Karl-Liebknecht-Strasse 11 (9700 4820/www. kinzo-berlin.de). U2, U5, U8, S5, S7, S9, S75 Alexanderplatz/bus N5, N7, N65, N92. **Open** 11pm-late Thur-Sat. **Admission** €4-€6. **No credit cards. Map** p303/p311 O6.

Mitte

Berlin Bar

Alte Schönhauser Strasse 28 (9700 5058/www.berlin bar.org). U8 Weinmeisterstrasse/bus N2, N5, N8, N65, N84. **Open** 8pm-late daily. **Admission** €3 Tue, Thur-Sat. **Credit** AmEx, MC, V. **Map** p303/p310 O5.

This large, basement club is one of the new wave of upscale spots sneaking into Mitte. The decor is bland, the door policy is snooty and the place tries too hard to be exclusive. The weekend DJs are OK, though, as they're pulled from the same group of talented Berlin regulars that spin everywhere.

Bohannon

Dircksenstrasse 40 (6950 5287/www.bohannon.de). U2, U5, U8, S5, S7, S9, S75 Hackescher Markt/bus N2, N5, N8, N65, N84. **Open** 10pm-late Mon, Thur-Sat. **No credit cards. Map** p303/p310 O5.

The club's name, a nod to funk legend Hamilton Bohannon, indicates its driving musical principle. Billed as offering 'soulful electronic clubbing', this basement location features two dancefloors and regular sets by the likes of Berlin's own Jazzanova or guest DJs such as Keb Darge. **Photo** *p223.*

Café Moskau

Karl-Marx-Allee 34 (2463 1626/www.das-moskau. com). U2, U5, U8, S5, S7, S9, S75 Alexanderplatz or U5 Schillingstrasse/bus N5, N8, N65. **Open** varies. **Admission** varies. **No credit cards. Map** p303 P6.

Sage Club.

Minimalist, cutting-edge club on the cusp of nightlife and media arts, boasting top DJs such as Chica and the Folder, Erobique, Le Hammond Inferno or Eric D of Whirlpool Productions, plus VJ sets, film screenings and sound art. Has a gay vibe, though all types show up, and on Thursdays hosts Chantal's House of Shame (*see p210*). Booking has slid a bit recently.

Club der polnischen Versager

Torstrasse 66 (2809 3779/www.polnischeversager. de). U2 Rosa-Luxemburg-Platz/bus N2/tram N54. **Open** 8pm-late Mon-Sat. **Admission** varies. **No credit cards. Map** p303/p310 N5.
The Club of Polish Losers maintains a semi-legal feel – it looks like someone's living room – while putting on a winning, if seat-of-the-pants, mix of film, readings and live music with, naturally, a Polish emphasis. Rarely have the avant-garde and always-drunk mixed with such a sense of purpose. Plenty of vodka and Baltika beer assist the process. **Photo** *p224*.

Rio

Chausseestrasse 106 (no phone/www.rioberlin.de). U6 Zinnowitzer Strasse/bus N6, N84. **Open** 11.30pm-late Sat. **Admission**: €6. **No credit cards. Map** p302 L4.
The DJs in the front room of this former restaurant can sometimes be a bit indulgent, but the dancefloor in the back usually moves to the best electro in Berlin, as well as hosting local heroes such as Cobra Killer and Kissogram. It's a big and well-liked place, perhaps because it contrives to retain the gritty, debauched charm of the city while also managing to glam it up a bit.

Sage Club

Köpenicker Strasse 76 (278 9830/www.sage-club.de). U8 Heinrich-Heine-Strasse/bus N8. **Open** 10pm-late Thur; 11pm-late Fri-Sun. **Admission** €6-€11. **No credit cards. Map** p307 P7.
Warrenous complex of half-a-dozen dancefloors and bars under Heinrich-Heine-Strasse station, catering to a youngish, fashion-conscious crowd. Nights are themed: Thursday is rock, Friday R&B and hip hop, Saturday house and electro, Sunday techno. In a separate part of the same complex, the Cantina Berlin Barcelona also hosts an assortment of club nights.

Sophienclub

Sophienstrasse 6 (282 4552). U8 Weinmeisterstrasse or S5, S7, S9, S75 Hackescher Markt/bus N2, N8, N54, N92. **Open** 10pm-late Tue-Sat. **Admission** €3-€5 Tue-Fri; €6-€8 Sat. **No credit cards. Map** p303/p310 N5.
A survivor from the old east, this space has a reputation for ignoring musical trends. But the boys from Karrera Klub are now doing their indie/Britpop thing here on Thursdays, a popular night with teenagers and twentysomethings. Other nights feature disco, house, R&B. Good for people looking to party but not concerned about being fashionable.

Sternradio

Alexanderplatz 5 (2472 4982/www.sternradio-berlin.de). U2, U5, U8, S5, S7, S9, S75 Alexanderplatz/bus N5, N8, N65, N92. **Open** 11pm-late Thur-Sat. **Admission** €4 Thur; €8 Fri; €10 Sat. **No credit cards. Map** p303/p311 O5.

Named after an old East German radio brand and located in a typical late 1960s edifice, this place was considered déclassé until punters started grooving on the *Ostalgie* of the architecture. So now it has become popular, even sort of hip. The DJ menu varies from techno to hip hop.

2BE

Ziegelstrasse 23 (2630 9610/www.2be-club.de). U6, S1, S2, S5, S7, S9, S75 Friedrichstrasse, S1, S2 Oranienburger Strasse or U6 Oranienburger Tor/ bus N6, N84. **Open** 11pm-late Fri, Sat. **Admission** €7.50-€8; women free 11pm-midnight Sat. **No credit cards. Map** p303/p310 M5.

Regular DJs specialise in hip hop, with some reggae and dancehall thrown in as well. There's also usually a live act or two every month, and big-name spinners such as Grandmaster Flash and DJ Premier do pass through. It's a big space with a dancefloor, an outside area and several understaffed bars; some may remember it as the third location of WMF. The basic crowd is young and enthusiastic, and, during summer when they all start milling around in the courtyard, it can feel a bit like a circus.

Week12End Club

Alexanderplatz 5, 12th floor (no phone/www. week-end-berlin.de). U2, U5, U8, S5, S7, S9, S75 Alexanderplatz/bus N8, N65, N92. **Open** 11pm-late Thur, Fri, Sat. **Admission** €6-€8. **Map** p303/p311 O5.

Super-chic but only moderately pretentious club on the 12th floor of an office building. Biggish names often take the turntables, such as the 2ManyDJs and DFA crews, and very occasionally there are live acts, too, usually in a danceable vein. It also sometimes hosts Yellow Lounge DJ/performance classical nights. Whatever's on, it's almost worth visiting just for the location and view.

White Trash Fast Food

Schönhauser Allee 6-7 (no phone/www.whitetrash fastfood.com). U2 Senefelderplatz. **Open** 4pm-late daily. **Admission** varies. **No credit cards. Map** p303/p310 O4.

Recently relocated from a small, poky place to this enormous red-draped edifice, the drunken expat white trash of White Trash appear set on world domination, with multiple floors, a Flintstones-style cave in the basement, nightly DJs (who can finally crank up the country and electro without the neighbours complaining), gutter-dwelling live acts and the usual, above-average American cuisine (hamburgers €5.50) of sadly shrinking proportions. It remains to be seen how well they fill the place without altering a formerly quite snooty door policy.

Prenzlauer Berg

Acud

Veteranenstrasse 21 (449 1067/www.acud.de). U8 Rosenthaler Platz or S1, S2, S25 Nordbahnhof/ bus N8, N84. **Open** varies. **Admission** varies. **No credit cards. Map** p303/p312 N4.

Massive complex with alternative pedigree containing a cinema, a theatre and a gallery as well as a dancefloor mostly devoted to reggae, breakbeat and drum 'n' bass. It's a popular spot for stoners, particularly the dingy bar. The cinema programme is interesting, mostly independent and low-budget films. The place has recently undergone a makeover that blanded it out somewhat. There's something on most nights, but time and admission prices vary according to what it is. The website has details.

Duncker

Dunckerstrasse 64 (445 9509/www.dunckerclub.de). U2 Eberswalder Strasse or S8, S41, S42, S85 Prenzlauer Allee. **Open** 9pm-late Mon; 10pm-late Tue, Thur, Sun; 11pm-late Fri, Sat. **Admission** €1.50-€4; free Thur. **Map** p303/p312 P2.

Dig the 1980s revival but sick of Mitte-style irony? Then head to Duncker, a GDR-era institution in a neo-Gothic building, where time seems to stand still. Monday is Goth night, while the rest of the week is devoted to music ranging from the 1960s to modern-day indie and electro.

GeburtstagsKlub

Am Friedrichshain 33 (4202 1406/ www.geburtstagsklub.de). Tram M4/bus N54. **Open** 11pm-late Mon, Fri, Sat. **Admission** €5-€8. **No credit cards. Map** p303 Q5.

House, breakbeats, electro, funk and disco boom loud in this subterranean establishment, decorated with light and slide projections. Reggae, ragga and dancehall feature on Monday nights. There are also monthly drag performances.

Icon

Cantianstrasse 15 (4849 2878/www.iconberlin.de). U2 Eberswalder Strasse. **Open** 11pm-late Tue; 11.30pm-late Fri, Sat. **Admission** €3-€6. *Special events* €10. **No credit cards. Map** p303/p312 O2.

A tricky-to-locate entrance in the courtyard just north of the junction with Milastrasse leads to an interesting space cascading down the levels into a long stone cellar. It's a well-ventilated little labyrinth, with an intense dancefloor space, imaginative lighting, good sound and a separate bar. Sounds vary from breakbeat and drum 'n' bass to reggae and hip hop. Best when the core crowd of locals is augmented by a wider audience for some special event. Ninja Tune DJs have a monthly night, and jungle legends such as Grooverider often spin. **Photo** *p229*.

Pfefferbank

Schönhauser Allee 176A (281 8323/www.pfefferbank.de). U2 Senefelderplatz/bus N2. **Open** 11pm-late Fri, Sat. **Admission** €5-€8. **No credit cards. Map** p303/p311 O4.

Located behind a semi-hidden booking near the main entrance of the massive Pfefferberg, a recently revivified booking policy is bringing au courant DJs and live acts, such as Optimo and The Locust, to this under-attended, bunker-like spot. With nightlife starting to pool along the bottom of Schönhauser Allee, this place may finally find its feet.

One Russian under a groove

While **Wladimir Kaminer** may be better known abroad for his short-story collection *Russian Disco*, in Berlin the Moscow native is famous as one-half (along with Ukrainian Yuriy Gurzhy) of the DJ team that launched the infamously successful Russendisko.

Kaminer came to Berlin in 1990, during the period of upheaval following the collapse of communism. The aspiring writer began reading his work at cafés around town, including one run by a group who bought up abandoned or struggling bars and revived them. Their next project was called **Kaffee Burger** (*see p224*), which they envisaged as a space for young creative types to try out their latest work, be it writing or music.

Kaminer began programming events there and started DJing in 2000. What began as a small dance night for his friends featuring the daft Russian rock and pop that he enjoyed – Kaminer says he has a particular taste for hard yet melodic ska-punk – has grown into a twice-monthly event that threatens to burst out of its original venue. Kaminer and Gurzhy are regularly invited to DJ in other European cities, but invitations to hold Russendisko evenings in Russia have always failed – Kaminer says potential organisers inevitably wind up emigrating before the event.

The thing has also spawned a host of imitators eager to profit from the growing interest in east European music. But Kaminer reckons those efforts are carried out with too much respect for the musical culture being presented. For him, the point is not simply to play contemporary Russian music, but to have fun and play the music he likes: 'If I dance, then everyone else dances too.' The densely packed dancefloor at Kaffee Burger seems to prove him right.

But both Kaminer and the owners of Kaffee Burger recognise that Russendisko has become a victim of its own success: the Berlin evenings are always packed, with a long queue waiting to get in. (Kaminer says it was the Russendisko queue that prompted the opening of nearby **Club der polnischen Versager**; *see p225*.) So they've come up with an ambitious solution: a whole Russendisko club is planned to open at Jannowitzbrücke in early 2006.

Kaminer and the other organisers want to programme bands and events that would attract too large a crowd for Kaffee Burger. And they hope to draw people who might be turned off by what Kaminer calls Burger's 'trashy' aspects. But don't expect the new club to appeal only to suits. Along with Russendisko evenings, events such as a sort of 'fight club', where punters can throw punches to music, are also planned. That sounds like a concept suited for Berlin, a city Wladimir Kaminer considers 'ballsy and adventurous, almost like in Russia'.

Roadrunners Club

Saarbrücker Strasse 24 (448 5755/www.roadrunners-paradise.de). U2 Senefelderplatz/bus N2. **Open** Fri, Sat. **Admission** €5-€10. **No credit cards.** **Map** p303/p310 O4.

It takes a bit of wandering around the grounds of a disused brewery to find this club, but it's worth it, especially for fans of rockabilly, country, surf, burlesque and suchlike. The small stage can seem a bit overwhelmed by the high ceilings, but there's plenty of room for dancing, and the decoration was obviously done by a keen enthusiast of 1950s American kitsch. Programming features both live acts and DJs.

Zentrale Randlage

Schönhauser Allee 172 (no phone/www.zentrale-randlage.de). U2 Senefelderplatz. **Open** varies. **Admission** free-€12. **No credit cards.** **Map** p303/p311 O4.

A prime exponent of the clubhouse trend, with old couches and a serving hatch rather than a bar. It wouldn't immediately strike you as a party space – the entrance suggests a high-school gym – but it packs for live acts and local DJs. Music ranges from avant-jazz to electro-rock, but weekends are for dancing. There's tango on the first Monday of the month and the Thursday-night Globus bar is free.

Friedrichshain

Berghain/Panorama

Am Wriezener Bahnhof (no phone/www.berghain.de). S3, S5, S7, S9, S75 Ostbahnhof/bus N44. **Open** 11pm-late Thur; midnight-late Fri, Sat. **Admission** €10. **No credit cards.** **Map** p308 R7.

Successor to the legendary Ostgut, considered by some to be the best club in the world, this is a place for serious fans of the best in electronic music. Ambitious booking brings DJs from around the world, and the club attracts an eclectic, daring mix of people. Though not exclusively a gay club, it does draw a large gay crowd, and has a reputation for no-holds-barred hedonism – one of the reasons for its strictly enforced no-cameras policy. Housed in a converted power station, Berghain has an impressive industrial interior and features some serious artwork.

K17

Pettenkofer Strasse 17 (4208 9300/www.k17.de). U5, S8, S9, S41, S42, S85 Frankfurter Allee/bus N5. **Open** 10pm-late Tue-Fri. **Admission** free-€15. **No credit cards.** **Map** p309 U6.

Goth, EBM, industrial and metal are undead and well in this three-floor club. Parties have names such as House of Pain and Schwarzer Donnerstag, and the midweek Jailbreak concert series features live earaches from hardcore, nü-metal and crossover bands.

lovelite

Simplonstrasse 38/40 (no phone/www.lovelite.de). U1, U3, S5, S7, S9, S75 Warschauer Strasse. **Open** from 11pm daily. **Admission** €4-€12. **No credit cards.** **Map** p308 T7.

Low-key, unfinished-looking late-night space that offers an eclectic selection of bands and DJs – usually of a local bent for a local crowd, but interesting smaller acts do arrive from the outside world, such as Rogers Sisters and the Poets of Rhythm. We like the funk nights. Weekends feature a GDR-era truck outside selling waffles.

Pavillon im Volkspark Friedrichshain

Friedenstrasse, corner with Platz der Vereinten Nationen (0172 750 4724/www.pavillon-berlin.de). Tram M5, M6, M8, N92. **Open** 9pm-late Tue; 10pm-late Fri, Sat. **Admission** €5-€6. **No credit cards.** **Map** p303 Q5.

Shake away your blaxploitation booty to a mix of funk, disco, dancehall and house in this East German-style parkside pavilion. Soul Explosion nights of rare funk 45s are extremely popular, and there are regular, debauched gay parties. Summer beer garden and barbecue.

Raumklang

Libauer Strasse 1 (2930 9802/www.raum-klang.de). U1, S3, S5, S7, S9, S75 Warschauer Strasse. **Open** 11pm-late daily. **Admission** varies. **No credit cards.** **Map** p308 S7.

Simple, 1970s chic and drenched in multicoloured light, Raumklang resembles its neighbour lovelite (*see above*) after a shower and shave. Boasting a sophisticated, ear-saving sound system suspended over the crowd, the DJs tend toward techno perhaps a bit better suited for a larger spot, emphasising locals such as Suzi Wong and Kotai. But there are also ragga nights and live acts from all over the map.

Rosi's

Revaler Strasse 29 (no phone/www.rosis-berlin.de). S3, S5, S7, S8, S9, S41, S42, S75, S85 Ostkreuz/bus N40, N44. **Open** 9pm-late Thur; 11pm-late Fri, Sat. **Admission** €5. **No credit cards.** **Map** p308 T8.

The sort of place eastern Berlin seemed to be full of in the early to mid 1990s: a rambling former industrial space decorated with flea-market furniture and graffiti, with a comfortable, unpretentious vibe. Music is provided by live acts and DJs, and runs the gamut from indie, punk and electro to drum 'n' bass, reggae/dancehall and even wacky Norwegian country-cabaret. The beer garden is a popular neighbourhood hangout in the summer.

Kreuzberg

Cake Club

Oranienstrasse 31 (6165 9399/www.cakeclub.de). U1, U8 Kottbusser Tor/bus M29, N8, N29. **Open** 8pm-late daily. **Admission** free. **No credit cards.** **Map** p307 P9.

Another one of those hybrids so common in Berlin: a bar with a regular DJ programme (genres run to funk, electro and Britpop; they start spinning at 10pm) and a small dancefloor. There's also groovy, retro 1960s decor and an impressive cocktail menu.

Jail

Ohlauer Strasse 3 (6663 9901/www.phonocaster. com/jail). U1 Görlitzer Bahnhof/bus N29, N44. **Open** 10pm-late Wed-Sat. **Admission** free. **No credit cards. Map** p307 Q9.

Don't let the ominous name and slightly forbidding exterior put you off: once you're inside, this three-day-a-week bar run by booking agent and record label owner Jens Czopnik offers a friendly, unpretentious living room (complete with pinball machine) for fans of rock, punk and metal. He also hosts record-release parties for the likes of Mötley Crüe (with special guests Tommy Lee and Nikki Sixx) as well as aftershow parties for metal bands who come through town.

Konrad Tönz

Falkensteinstrasse 30 (612 3252/www.konrad toenzbar.de). U1 Schlesisches Tor/bus N29, N65. **Open** 8.15pm-2am Tue-Thur; 8.15pm-late Fri-Sun. **Admission** free. **No credit cards. Map** p308 R9.

Named after the Swiss correspondent of the popular true crime show *Aktenzeichen XY ungelöst*, this quirky lounge with small dancefloor also embraces a retro, shaken-not-stirred aesthetic with patterned wallpaper and suave jazzy and twangy grooves from mono record players. DJs play from 9pm at weekends.

103 Club

Falkensteinstrasse 47 (no phone/www.103club.de). U1 Schlesisches Tor/bus N29. **Open** 11.30pm-late Fri, Sat. **Admission** €6-€8. **No credit cards. Map** p308 R9.

A spin-off from the 103 bar on Kastanienallee (*see p146*), this place is huge and weirdly proportioned, with a variety of rooms connected by a cramped hallway. Sometimes there are as many as three different sets of DJs in the building, playing anything from Baile Funk to easy listening, though there appears to be an emphasis on housier styles. Live acts such as Simian Mobile Disco or Schneider TM show up quite regularly, but the feel is generally down-to-earth and you can stretch out in the upstairs lounge.

Privat Club

Pückler Strasse 34 (611 3302/www.privatclub-berlin.de). U1 Görlitzer Bahnhof/bus N29, N44. **Open** 11pm-late Fri, Sat. **Admission** €5. **No credit cards. Map** p307 Q8.

This long, low space in the basement of the Markthalle restaurant (*see p135*) hosts a variety of events, from occasional live acts to retro parties, avant performances and dance music of all persuasions. Worth a look, though it's hard to predict just what you'll find.

Watergate

Falkensteinstrasse 49 (6128 0396/www.water-gate.de). U1 Schlesisches Tor/bus N29, N65. **Open** 11pm-late Wed, Fri, Sat; check website for occasional Tue, Thur events. **Admission** €6-€10. **No credit cards. Map** p308 R9.

Underground at **Icon**. *See p226.*

This two-floor club, next to the Oberbaumbrücke, has a slick feel, a panoramic view of the Spree and a better-than-average sound system. Both floors open up on weekends, and usually host two different sets of acts, often label nights, and sometimes label battles. Music tends toward electro, house and minimal techno, such as Ricardo Villalobos, though left-field acts, such as a classical ensemble playing Einstürzende Neubauten, appear from time to time.

Schöneberg

Ex 'n' Pop

Potsdamer Strasse 157 (2199 7470/www.ex-n-pop. de). U2 Bülowstrasse/bus N48. **Open** 10pm-late daily. **Admission** free Mon-Thur, Sun; €2.50 Fri, Sat. **No credit cards. Map** p306 J9.

The last direct descendant of the 1980s black-leather, noise-underground, speed-and-dope scene that Nick Cave and Neubauten once inhabited still rocks through the night, every night. It's a somewhat insalubrious dive full of rowdy intellectuals, off-duty drag queens and local bohos, with intense activity around the Kicker table, a 50-seat cinema in the back (independent and offbeat movies every Wednesday and Thursday), occasional bands on the small stage, and an eclectic music policy that spreads in all directions from a heartland of left-field country and rock. Not usually much happening before 3am. At weekends the party carries on until the following afternoon.

Goya

Nollendorfplatz 5 (2639 1439/www.goya-berlin.de).
U1, U2, U3, U4 Nollendorfplatz/bus M19, M29,
187, N5, N19, N26. **Open** 6pm-late Thur, Fri, Sat.
Admission €10. **No credit cards. Map** p306 J9.
This massive undertaking in the former Metropol is
an attempt to bring a continental-style high-end club
to Berlin, which may be like Fitzcarraldo dragging a
ship up a mountain, but several hundred investors
have gone to considerable expense to make the
dream a reality. Resident DJs spin in a world music/
trip hop vein and there are plans to create a Hotel
Costes-style brand, but it's as much about dining as
dancing. Door policy is apparently to encourage an
older crowd. The place had just opened at press time
and it was unclear whether this would all work out.

KitKatClub

Bessemer Strasse 4 (no phone/www.kitkatclub.de).
Bus 204, N6, N46. **Open** 11pm-late Fri, Sat; 8pm-
late Sun. **Admission** varies. **No credit cards.**
You thought the days of true Berlin decadence were
a thing of the past? Think again. Although the city's
best-known sex club is not in the least bit seedy, this
is still no place for the narrow-minded, with half the
crowd in fetish gear, the other half in no gear at all,
and every kind of sexual activity taking place in full
view. In its way KitKat is the most relaxing club in
Berlin. No one has anything to prove and everyone
knows why they're there, and will almost certainly
get it. But on most nights, if you're not dressed up
(or down) enough, you probably won't get in. Crap
sound system.

Tiergarten

Adagio

Marlene-Dietrich-Platz 1 (2592 9550/www.adagio.de).
U2, S1, S2, S26 Potsdamer Platz/bus N2, N5, N19.
Open 7pm-2am Wed-Thur, Sun; 10pm-4am Fri;
10pm-5am Sat; occasionally closes for private
events. **Admission** €5-€10. **Credit** AmEx, V.
Map p306/p311 K8.
Spin-off of a chi-chi Zurich disco, its 'medieval' decor
and Renaissance frescos are jarringly at odds with
the Renzo Piano-designed Musicaltheater whose
basement it occupies. Pricey drinks, abundant mem-
bers-only areas and a music policy of disco, polite
house and oldies cater to fortysomething tourists
and locals willing to shell out for a semblance of
exclusivity. Dress code (no jeans or sports shoes).

Kapital

Potsdamer Strasse 76 (no phone/www.club-kapital.
com). U1 Kurfürstenstrasse. **Open** 11pm-late
Fri, Sat. **Admission** €5-€15. **No credit cards.**
Map p306 K8.
Inhabiting a long-abandoned bank, Kapital started
out as an art collective, and still hosts occasional
exhibitions and installations. But it has recently
commited itself to clubbing, with name DJs such as
King Britt and Souls of Mischief performing in a
determinedly unadorned space. The bar is attrac-

tive, though, and there's table football. Sometimes
there are concerts and these start at 9pm.

Trompete

Lützowplatz 9 (2300 4794/www.trompete-berlin.de).
U1, U2, U3, U4 Nollendorfplatz/bus N5, N19. **Open**
6pm-late Thur; 10pm-late Fri, Sat. **Admission** free.
Dance events €5-€6.
Credit AmEx, DC, MC, V. **Map** p306 J8.
Actor Ben Becker is the not-so-silent partner in this
nightlife joint venture, which has found its niche
thanks to the hugely popular After Work Lounge on
Thursdays, from 6pm, with DJs from RadioEins
spinning sounds to forget the day's stress by.

Charlottenburg

Abraxas

Kantstrasse 134 (312 9493). U7 Wilmersdorfer
Strasse or S5, S7, S9, S75 Savignyplatz/bus N49.
Open 10pm-late Tue-Sat. **Admission** free Tue-
Thur; €5 Fri, Sat. **Credit** V. **Map** p304 D8.
A dusky, relaxed disco where you don't have to
dress up to get in and where academics, social work-
ers, bank clerks and midwives populate the floor.
Flirtation rules. Dance to funk, soul, Latino and jazz.

Big Eden

Kurfürstendamm 202 (882 6120/www.big-eden.
de). U1 Uhlandstrasse/bus N10, N19, N21, N29.
Open 10pm-late Wed, Thur; 11pm-late Fri, Sat.
Admission €10. **Credit** MC, V. **Map** p305/p312 F8.
What was once West Berlin's prime discotheque for
would-be playboys today provides a decadently old-
school backdrop for occasional club nights programmed by Kitty-Yo, Ministry of Sound, Yellow
Lounge and Alexander Hacke of Neubauten.

Other districts

Insel

Alt-Treptow 6, Treptow (5360 8020/www.insel-
berlin.com). S8, S9, S85 Plänterwald/bus N65.
Open 7pm-1am Wed; 10pm-late Fri, Sat.
Admission free Wed; €5-€10 Fri, Sat.
No credit cards.
Out of the way, but brilliant – like a miniature castle on a tiny Spree island, with several levels and a
top-floor balcony. Once a communist youth club,
now a live venue/colourful club – with lots of neon
and ultra-violet, crusties and hippies, techno and hip
hop, punk and metal. Great in summer.

MS Hoppetosse

Eichenstrasse 4, Treptow (533 7169/www.arena-
berlin.de/hoppetosse.aspx). S1 Schlesisches Tor or
S8, S9, S41, S42, S85 Treptower Park/bus N65.
Open 10pm-late Thur-Sun. **Admission** varies.
Credit MC, V. **Map** p308 S9.
This docked boat on the Spree near Arena Treptow
is a café/restaurant by day and a disco by night.
Music centres on reggae, ragga and dancehall, with
occasional indie and electropop nights.

Performing Arts

Whether it's classical music, opera, theatre, dance or (of course) cabaret, Berlin remains a major centre for anything you do on a stage.

Music: Classical & Opera

Berlin quite literally has enough classical music for any two normal cities. It's as much the result of Cold War division as of artistic heritage, but no city anywhere can compete with the number of orchestras (seven, plus various private ones), opera houses (three, not counting several independent houses and companies) and venues (two major concert halls, plus a myriad of smaller venues). And it's not only quantity. The Berlin Philharmonic is arguably the world's finest symphony orchestra, and there are usually several top-notch performances to choose from pretty much any night of the year.

But how long can an increasingly bankrupt city continue to afford all this? Belt-tightening has already begun. In March 2004 the **Berlin Symphoniker** closed after being refused further public funding, reducing the city's major orchestra count from eight to seven. Meanwhile, rationalisation of Berlin's opera houses was begun by Federal Minister of Culture Christina Weiss and it remains to be seen how her successor Bernd Neumann will continue this policy.

A TALE OF THREE HOUSES

The three houses are now incorporated into one foundation, the so-called Opernstiftung headed by Michael Schindhelm, former Intendant of the Theater Basel. Apart from a few attempts at joint marketing, not much has changed. Coordination of programmes between the three houses is still an issue, as is their simultaneous closure during the summer when tourists fill Berlin. But rumours that one house will close have died down.

The **Deutsche Oper** still does not seem to have got over the 2000 death of long-time intendant Götz Friedrich. Although a successor was eventually found in Kirsten Harms – after a brief appearance by Udo Zimmermann – her goal of giving the house an unmistakeable artistic profile has not yet been reached. Faced with critical press and occasional audience resistance, the appointment of Renato Palumbo as new musical director was generally not

perceived as a masterstroke. Still, there are hopes that the new musical director will spend more time in Berlin than his often absent predecessor Christian Thielemann – for the benefit of both orchestra and ensemble.

Meanwhile, the **Staatsoper Unter den Linden** seems to be leaping from one success to the next under intendant (and neurologist) Peter Mussbach. Musically, all performances are of the finest quality, though often marred by overly spectacular rather than gripping productions. While comfortably situated in Mitte and enjoying its proximity to the German government, the house itself remains in desperate need of renovation. The underground passage connecting the main house and administrative offices is regularly flooded and the public has almost got used to performances being stopped midway due to security hazards. Quite who will pay to sort all this out and where productions will be staged during the necessary closure remains unclear. Its orchestra, the Berliner Staatskapelle, founded in 1570 by royal decree and today directed by Daniel Barenboim, is regarded as Berlin's finest opera orchestra and in 2005 was once again voted Orchestra of the Year by critics of *Opernwelt* magazine.

The **Komische Oper**, under the direction of Kyrill Petrenko and Andreas Homoki, regularly pushes itself into the public eye by staging controversial productions such as Mozart's *Entführung aus dem Serail*. Directed by Catalan Calixto Bieto, this production saw porn, sex and crime on stage, which provoked a little outrage. Efforts to be different and appear sexy also involve projects such as *Hip H'opera*, a production uniting young people from four different nations with opera houses, opera singers, hip hoppers and graffiti artists, as well as four youth chamber orchestras. Even the World Cup will be given its share with the performance of a football oratorio written by Moritz Eggert and recently premièred at the Ruhrtriennale.

For more independent operatic fare, don't neglect the **Neuköllner Oper** (*see p235* **No ordinary opera house**), which puts on witty and imaginative productions. Other companies worth checking out are the **Neue Opernbühne**, **Zeitgenössische Oper**, the **Berliner Kammeroper** and the newly

About as classical as it gets – the **Konzerthaus**. See p234.

founded company **Novoflot** (www.novoflot.de), which usually performs at the **Sophiensaele**. Expect innovative music and theatre of surprising quality despite low budgets.

ORCHESTRAL MANOEUVRES

Despite the closure of the Berliner Symphoniker, Berlin's orchestral scene is as vibrant as ever. The **Deutsches Symphonie Orchester** (www.dso-berlin.de) still boasts fairly substantial subsidies and remains one of the best places in town to hear avant-garde compositions and unusual programmes. Kent Nagano's successor from July 2006 is Ingo Metzmacher, former musical director at the Hamburgische Staatsoper.

Ground-breaking 20th-century composers, from Hindemith to Prokofiev and Schönberg to Penderecki, have conducted their own work with the **Rundfunk-Sinfonieorchester Berlin** (www.rsb-online.de). Founded in 1923 to provide programming for radio, the orchestra continues drawing attention to contemporary works under the competent hand of musical director Marek Janowski. It also aims to establish new locations for its concerts, such as the Schlüterhof in the **Deutsches Historisches Museum** (see p79), where a music festival is planned for late summer 2006.

Fans of the old masters are still well served by the **Berliner Sinfonie-Orchester** (www.berliner-sinfonie-orchester.de), which plays at the splendid **Konzerthaus**. From the

season 2006/7, chief conductor Eliahu Inbal will be succeeded by Lother Zagrosek, formerly of the Staatsoper Stuttgart. The feisty group – founded after the building of the Wall as the East's answer to the Philharmonic – has a loyal following, but one that prefers more familiar works. How Zagrosek, especially admired for his interpretations of contemporary music, will influence the musical scope and direction of the orchestra remains to be seen.

Berlin's chamber orchestras also offer a steady stream of first-rate concerts. One of the finest groups is **Ensemble Oriol** (www. ensemble-oriol.de) with a strong emphasis on contemporary music. The **Kammerorchester Berlin** (www.koberlin.de) remains popular but predictable, with works usually ranging from Vivaldi to Mozart and back again. The **Deutsches Kammerorchester Berlin** (www.dko-berlin.de) under manager Stefan Fragner has acquired an excellent reputation for working with rising star conductors and soloists, and providing innovative though still audience-friendly programmes.

Finally, there's the mighty **Berliner Philharmoniker** (www.berliner-philharmoniker.de), going from strength to strength under Sir Simon Rattle. He is joined in 2006 by new intendant Pamela Rosenberg, formerly at the San Francisco Opera. Rattle had promised to bring adventure to the programme and attract younger audiences. From his very first concert, he introduced an emphasis on contemporary composers such as Thomas Adès and Heiner Goebbels. He's also worked with jazz musicians and improvisers. But at the same time Rattle has put the ensemble through more traditional paces via an emphasis on Haydn and an early performance of Schubert's Eighth. He's also launched a successful education programme with projects that aim to integrate youngsters from different backgrounds and to get them hooked on classical music. One of these was even turned into the award-winning film *Rhythm is It*. Right now, everyone loves him to bits.

FESTIVALS & EVENTS

Music festivals pepper Berlin's calendar. **MaerzMusik – Festival für aktuelle Musik** (*see p186*) takes place annually over two to three weeks in March at various venues, and showcases trends in contemporary music. The **UltraSchall** (*see p186*) festival of new music, organised by DeutschlandRadio and Rundfunk Berlin Brandenburg every January, presents many of the world's leading specialist ensembles. The biennial **Zeitfenster – Biennale für alte Musik** (*see p182*) at the Konzerthaus focuses on 17th-century baroque music for one week in April (2008). Major-name orchestras and soloists often open the **Classic Open Air** concert series (*see p183*) on Gendarmenmarkt over several days in early July. There is less focus on food, drink and socialising at **young.euro.classic** (*see p185*), which assembles youth orchestras from across Europe over a couple of weeks in August and offers tickets for just €9. In September 2006 talented pianists from all over the world will take part in the first **International Piano Amateur Competition** in Berlin (www.ipac-berlin.com), planned as an annual event at the Philharmonie from then on. The Berliner Festspiele (www.berlinerfestspiele.de) organises the annual **Musikfest** (*see p185*) from August until September, bringing some of the world's finest orchestras to Berlin.

Finally, for classical music in a refreshingly different context, look out for the **Yellow Lounge** club events (www.yellowlounge.de) that take place on the first Monday of the month at a variety of venues including **Week12End Club** (*see p225*), **Big Eden** (*see p230*) and **103 Club** (*see p229*). There are DJs spinning anything from Gesualdo to Gorecki, visual effects from top-class VJs, and a live performance to anchor the evening. Performers have included the Deutsches Kammerorchester, Yundi Lee, the Emerson String Quartet, Hilary Hahn and Anne-Sofie von Otter. At the turntables have been Matthew Herbert, Rupert Huber of Tosca and Pet Shop Boy Neil Tennant.

TICKETS

Getting seats at the Philharmonie can still be difficult, especially to see big-name stars or when the Berlin Phil itself is in residence; tickets for concerts by visiting performers are often easier to come by. It's worth scanning the listings in daily papers or *tip* and *Zitty*, and phoning venues to see what's available. If all else fails, try positioning yourself outside the venue with a sign reading '*Suche eine Karte*' ('seeking a ticket'), or chatting up arriving concert-goers ('*Haben Sie vielleicht eine Karte übrig?*' means 'Got a spare ticket?'). You may also see people with extras for sale ('*Karte(n) zu verkaufen*'), but beware of ticket sharks.

Some of the former East Berlin venues – especially the Konzerthaus and the Komische Oper – remain more affordable than their western counterparts, but the days of socialist subsidies and dirt-cheap tickets are long gone. Standing-room at the top of the Konzerthaus actually gives a decent view, but before buying cheap seats for the Staatsoper ask how much of the stage you can see.

Most venues offer student discounts; students can save even more by queuing 30 minutes before performance time at the Staatsoper, when leftover balcony seats are sold for €10.

The **ClassicCard** is worth considering; if younger than 28, you can get one for €15, valid for one year and entitling the holder to excellent seats for a mere €8 for concerts and €10 for opera and ballet. Participating institutions are the Deutsche Oper, the Komische Oper, the Konzerthaus, the Rundfunk Orchester, the State Ballet and the Staatsoper Unter den Linden. A card can be ordered at the Staatsoper.

TICKET AGENCIES

Tickets are sold at concert hall box offices or through ticket agencies, called *Theaterkassen*. At box offices, seats are generally sold up to one hour before the performance. You can also make reservations by phone, except for concerts by the Berlin Phil. *Theaterkassen* provide the easiest means of buying a ticket, but be prepared to pay for the convenience as commissions can run as high as 17 per cent. **Hekticket** is probably the best bet, or check www.ticketonline.de. For the 50 or so other options around the city, look in the *Gelbe Seiten* (Yellow Pages) under 'Theaterkassen'. Many may not accept credit cards.

Hekticket

Hardenbergstrasse 29D, Charlottenburg (last minute 230 9930/tickets 2309 9233/www.hekticket.de). U2, U9, S5, S7, S9, S75 Zoologischer Garten. **Open** 10am-8pm Mon-Sat; 2-6pm Sun. **Credit** AmEx, DC, MC, V. **Map** p305/p312 G8.

Arts & Entertainment

Hekticket offers discounts of up to 50% on theatre and concert tickets, so should be your first choice if using a ticket agency. For a small commission, its staff will sell you tickets for the same evening's performance. Tickets for Sunday matinées are available on Saturday. You can check ticket availability online, though not everything is listed. The Mitte branch is open from noon and closed all day Sunday. **Other locations**: Karl-Liebknecht-Strasse 12, Mitte (2431 2431).

Major venues

Deutsche Oper

Richard-Wagner-Strasse 10, Charlottenburg (343 8401/www.deutscheoperberlin.de). U2 Deutsche Oper. **Open** *Box office* 11am-1hr before performance Mon-Sat; 10am-2pm Sun. **Tickets** €12-€114. **Credit** AmEx, DC, V. **Map** p305 E7.

With roots dating back to 1912, the Deutsche Oper built its present 1,900-seat hall in 1961, just in time to carry the operatic torch for West Berlin during the Wall years. It has lost out in profile to the more elegant and central Staatsoper since Reunification, but retains a reputation for blockbuster productions of the classics. Unsold tickets are available at a discount half an hour before performances.

Komische Oper

Behrenstrasse 55-7, Mitte (walk-in ticket office Unter den Linden 41) (202 600/tickets 4799 7400/www. komische-oper-berlin.de). U6 Französische Strasse. **Open** *Box office* 11am-7pm Mon-Sat; 1-4pm Sun. **Tickets** €6-€62. **Credit** AmEx, MC, V. **Map** p302/p311 M6.

Despite its name, the Komische Oper puts on more than just comic works, and, after its founding in 1947, made its name by breaking with the old operatic tradition of 'costumed concerts' – singers standing around on stage – and putting an emphasis on 'opera as theatre', with real acting skill demanded of its young ensemble. Outgoing artistic director Harry Kupfer strove for intelligent opera that speaks to the public – one reason why the Komische sings most of its productions in German. Telephone bookings can be made 9am-8pm Mon-Sat and 2-8pm Sun. Discounts available for tickets sold immediately before performances.

Konzerthaus

Gendarmenmarkt 2, Mitte (203 092 101/www. konzerthaus.de). U6 Französische Strasse. **Open** *Box office* noon-7pm Mon-Sat; noon-4pm Sun. **Tickets** €7-€99; some half-price concessions. **Credit** AmEx, MC, V. **Map** p306/p311 M7.

Formerly the Schauspielhaus am Gendarmenmarkt, this 1821 architectural gem by Schinkel was all but destroyed in the war. Lovingly restored, it was reopened in 1984 with three main spaces for concerts: the Grosser Konzertsaal for orchestras, the Kleiner Saal for chamber music, and the recently opened Werner-Otto-Saal, named after the businessman who financed its construction. Organ

recitals in the large concert hall are a treat, played on the massive Jehmlich organ at the back of the stage. The Berliner Sinfonie-Orchester is based here, presenting a healthy mixture of the classic, the new and the rediscovered. The Deutsches Sinfonie Orchester and Berliner Staatskapelle also play here, and there are occasional informal concerts in the cosy little Musik Club in the depths of the building. In 2005 the Konzerthaus for the first time opened its doors to an after-show party with DJs. It was after a concert by the Junge Deutsche Philharmonie and is planned as an annual event. **Photo** *p232.*

Philharmonie

Herbert-von-Karajan-Strasse 1, Tiergarten (2548 8999/www.berlin-philharmonic.com). U2, S1, S2, S26 Potsdamer Platz. **Open** *Box office* 9am-6pm daily. **Tickets** €15-€120. **Credit** AmEx, MC, V. **Map** p306 K7.

Berlin's most famous concert hall, home to the world-renowned Berlin Philharmonic Orchestra, is also the city's most architecturally daring; a marvellous piece of organic modernism, sadly now a little dwarfed by its new neighbours at Potsdamer Platz. The hall, with its golden vaulting roof, was designed by Hans Scharoun and opened in 1963. Its reputation for superb acoustics is accurate, but it does depend on where you sit. Behind the orchestra the acoustics leave plenty to be desired, but in front (where it is much more expensive) the sound is heavenly. The structure also incorporates a smaller hall, the Kammermusiksaal, about which the same acoustical notes apply.

The unique Berliner Philharmoniker was founded in 1882 by 54 musicians keen to break away from the penurious Benjamin Bilse, in whose orchestra they played. Over the last 120 years it has been led by some of the world's greatest conductors, as well as by composers such as Peter Tchaikovsky, Edvard Grieg, Richard Strauss and Gustav Mahler. Its greatest fame came under the baton of Herbert von Karajan, who led the orchestra between 1955 and 1989. Since 2002 it has been under the leadership of the popular Sir Simon Rattle. The Berlin Phil gives about 100 performances in Berlin during its August to June season, and puts on another 20 to 30 concerts around the world. Some tickets are available at a discount immediately before performances.

Staatsoper Unter den Linden

Unter den Linden 7, Mitte (203 540/tickets 2035 4555/www.staatsoper-berlin.de). U2 Hausvogteiplatz. **Open** *Box office* 11am-7pm Mon-Fri; 2-7pm Sat, Sun (by phone 10am-8pm Mon-Sat; 2-8pm Sun). **Tickets** €7-€80. **Credit** AmEx, MC, V. **Map** p303/p311 N6.

The Staatsoper was founded as Prussia's Royal Court Opera for Frederick the Great in 1742, and designed along the lines of a Greek temple. Although the present building dates from 1955, the façade faithfully copies that of Knobelsdorff's original, twice destroyed in World War II. The elegant interior gives an immediate sense of the house's past glory, with huge chandeliers and elaborate wall

No ordinary opera house

Anyone who knows their Brecht and Weill knows that Germans take their popular musical theatre seriously. Far from the fashionable stages of Berlin, in the working-class suburb of Neukölln, the **Neuköllner Oper** carries on this tradition. Once upon a time this place might have been called the 'Workers' Music Hall'. It's certainly no ordinary opera house, and even begs a redefinition of the term. Productions walk a tightrope between musical and operetta, and are original attempts to address themes such as consumerism, media overkill, chatrooms, mass hysteria and obesity. And in keeping with their populist objective, there are also condensed versions of major productions shown during the day for schoolchildren.

Neuköllner Oper was founded in 1972 and moved into its current premises in 1988, making it Berlin's youngest opera house. Because it is not a civic theatre (it's run as a society) and has no ensemble, touring is not an option and all works are created specifically to be performed in this house. The only place to see its productions – each very much a labour of love – is here.

It's no great shakes as a building – connected to a complex of dingy shops, fast-food stands and a cinema. It looks a little grungy at first and it's hard to believe you're in the right place. Then you look up and spot the sign. Walk up the long, wide, majestic staircase and finally at the top you find an oasis with a fabulous view.

There is a classy but unpretentious café, which also occasionally has a dinner programme. The main stage is small with a fringe feel and the quality of productions varies, but the acting is always top notch, an impressive range of musical styles is presented, and the place never loses its integrity. Even the poster artwork is good.

All in all, this is a house offering work that is accessible, original, relevant and political – an informal, down-to-earth alternative to both the champagne-and-chandeliers atmosphere of the major opera houses, and the austerely avant-garde approach of the bigger civic theatres. Popular theatre is alive and well and living on Karl-Marx-Strasse. Brecht and Weill would surely have approved.

Neuköllner Opera

Karl-Marx-Strasse 131-3, Neukölln (6889 0777/www.neukoellneroper.de). U7 Karl-Marx-Strasse. **Open** *Box office* 3-7pm Tue-Sat. **Tickets** €12-€18; €9 concessions. **No credit cards. Map** p308 R12.

A down-to-earth alternative to champagne, chandeliers and the avant-garde.

Arts & Entertainment

paintings. Chamber music is performed in the small, ornate Apollo Saal in the main building, which is now also open for occasional club nights. Half an hour before performances, unsold tickets are available to students under 30 for €12.

Other venues

Many churches offer organ recitals. It's also worth enquiring if concerts are to be staged in any of the area's castles or museums, especially in summer. Telephones are often erratically staffed, so check *tip* or *Zitty* for information.

Akademie der Künste
Hanseatenweg 10, Tiergarten (390 760/www.adk. de). U9 Hansaplatz or S5, S7, S9, S75 Bellevue. **Open** 11am-6pm Mon, Tue, Fri-Sun; 10am-8pm Thur. **Tickets** €5-€8. **No credit cards.** **Map** p300 H6.
Founded by Prince Friedrich III in 1696, this is one of the oldest cultural institutions in Berlin. By 1938, however, the Nazis had forced virtually all of its prominent members into exile. It was re-established in West Berlin in 1954, in this fine new building from architect Werner Duttmann, to serve as 'a community of exceptional artists' from around the world. Apart from performances of 20th-century compositions, its programme offers a variety of other events, from jazz and poetry readings to film screenings and art exhibitions. Despite portions of the now reunified Akademie moving into a new building at Pariser Platz 4, its pre-war address, most performances and exhibitions remain here at Hanseatenweg.
Other locations: Pariser Platz 4, Mitte.

Ballhaus Naunynstrasse
Naunynstrasse 27, Kreuzberg (347 459 844/ www.kunstamtkreuzberg.de). U1, U8 Kottbusser Tor. **Open** *Box office* 1hr before performance Mon-Fri. **Tickets** €6-€12. **No credit cards.** **Map** p307 P8.
Don't expect to hear anything ordinary at this Kreuzberg cultural centre. A varied assortment of western and oriental music is on the menu, with drinks and snacks in the café out front. The long, rectangular hall, which seats 150, plays host to the excellent Berliner Kammeroper, among others.

Berliner Dom
Lustgarten 1, Mitte (308 785 685/www.berliner-dom.de). S5, S7, S9, S75 Hackescher Markt. **Open** *Box office* 10am-8pm daily. **Tickets** €7-€30. **No credit cards.** **Map** p303/p311 N6.
Berlin's restored cathedral now hosts some recommendable concerts, usually of the organ or choral variety. *See also p80.*

Meistersaal
Köthener Strasse 38, Kreuzberg (5200 0060/www. meistersaal.de). U2, S1, S2, S26 Potsdamer Platz. **Open** *Box office* 10am-5pm Mon-Fri. **Tickets** varies. **Credit** MC, V. **Map** p306 L8.

What was once the Hansa recording studio now hosts solo instrumentalists and chamber groups that can't afford to book the Kammermusiksaal of the Philharmonie (*see p234*). Don't be fooled: music-making of the highest rank occurs in this warm and welcoming salon, notable for its superb acoustics.

Musikhochschule Hanns Eisler
Charlottenstrasse 55, Gendarmenmarkt, Mitte (203 092 101/www.hfm-berlin.de). U2, U6 Stadtmitte. **Open** *Box office* 2-7pm Mon-Sat; noon-4pm Sun. **Tickets** varies (usually free). **No credit cards.** **Map** p306/p311 M7.
Opposite the Konzerthaus, this musical academy was founded in 1950 and named after the composer of the East German national anthem. It offers students the chance to study under some of the stars of Berlin's major orchestras and operas. Rehearsals and master classes are often open to the public for free, and student performances, some of them top notch, are held in the Konzerthaus. Other events are held in the annexe at Wilhelmstrasse 53, Mitte.

St Matthäus Kirche am Kulturforum
Matthäikirchplatz, Tiergarten (262 1202/www. stiftung-stmatthaeus.de). U2, S1, S2, S26 Potsdamer Platz. **Open** *Box office* noon-6pm Tue-Sun. **Tickets** varies. **No credit cards.** **Map** p306 K8.
Concerts here might be anything from a free organ recital to a chorus of Russian Orthodox monks. Exquisite acoustics.

Universität der Künste
Hardenbergstrasse 33, corner of Fasanenstrasse, Charlottenburg (3185 2374/www.udk-berlin.de). U2, U9, S5, S7, S9, S75 Zoologischer Garten. **Open** *Box office* 3-6pm Tue, Wed, Fri; 11am-2pm Sat. **Tickets** varies. **No credit cards.** **Map** p305/p312 F7.
This place may be grotesquely ugly, but it is nonetheless a functional hall, hosting both student soloists and orchestras, as well as performances by lesser-known professional groups.

Theatre

Berlin revels in its long-standing reputation as a city of immense artistic potential with a large international scene. After the fall of the Wall there was a rapid increase of people moving to Berlin to work in theatre. The result has been a rich and colourful mixture of styles and techniques, which have together become an integral part of the Berlin theatre scene.

In particular, the crossover between theatre, dance and performance art has become so complex and enmeshed that it is almost impossible to separate them any more. In theatres such as **HAU** and **Sophiensaele** they share relatively equal time and space. For over six years the **Schaubühne** has successfully meshed contemporary dance and theatre under one roof by supporting both

Colourful shows and art deco architecture at the **Renaissance**. *See p238.*

the theatre ensemble of Thomas Ostermeier and the dance company of world-renowned choreographer Sasha Waltz. But no more. Due to serious personal disagreements and financial issues this partnership ended in January 2006. Although it is hard to imagine the Schaubühne without Waltz, she is optimistic about the future and sees her new independence as challenging her to find other partners and fresh ways of working on a much smaller budget. Ostermeier, on the other hand, sounds bitter about the rift and consequent serious cut in funding. Although his contract continues in the Schaubühne, he is threatening to leave Berlin completely in search of greener pastures. We shall see. The Schaubühne will supposedly still be showing Waltz's work, although less frequently.

Performers and public alike have benefited greatly from the amalgamation of the **Hebbel Theatre**, **Theatre am Halleschen Ufer** and **Theatre am Ufer** into one unit called HAU. This has provided much-needed support for new directors, playwrights, dance companies and performance artists. Independent companies such as She She Pop, Gob Squad (English) and Riminiprotokoll have also flourished. These young companies are all constantly creating timely new works using elements of dance, video and docu-drama.

FESTIVALS

Berlin has a bewildering assortment of theatre festivals. In mid November, **Sehnsucht – Festival Politik im Freien Theater** (www.politikimfreientheater.de) is a ten-day festival of political fringe theatre. **100° Berlin – Das Lange Wochenende des Freien**

Theaters is a long weekend in February at the Sophiensaele and HAU to showcase the work of fringe theatre companies. In March at the Schaubühne (www.schaubuehne.de) there's **FIND – Festival Internationale Neue Dramatik**, which in 2006 focused on new drama from the Middle East. May's **Theatertreffen Berlin** (*see p182*) remains the major festival for German-language work. **Freischwimmer** (www.freischwimmer-festival.com), in October and November at the Sophiensaele, features new works from young German writers and directors. And the winter-long **Spielzeiteuropa** (www.berlinerfestspiele.de; *see p185*) cherry-picks work from around Europe.

Civic theatres

Theatre box offices usually open one hour before the show.

Berliner Ensemble

Bertolt-Brecht-Platz 1, Mitte (2840 8155/www. berliner-ensemble.de). U6, S1, S2, S5, S7, S9, S75 Friedrichstrasse. **Open** *Box office* 8am-6pm Mon-Fri; 11am-6pm Sat, Sun. **Tickets** €5-€30; €7 concessions. **Credit** AmEx, DC, MC, V. **Map** p302/p311 M5.

Constructed in 1891, and still with an elaborate period interior, this place is best known for its association with Brecht – first during the Weimar period (this was where *The Threepenny Opera* was first staged in 1928) and later under the Communists when Brecht ran the place from 1948 until his death in 1956. Under current intendant Claus Peymann, expect a repertoire where modern productions of Brecht rub shoulders with pieces by living German and Austrian writers.

Deutsches Theater

Schumannstrasse 13A (284 410/tickets 2844 1225/ fax 282 4117/www.deutsches-theater.berlin.net). U6, S1, S2, S5, S7, S9, S75 Friedrichstrasse. **Open** *Box office* 11am-6.30pm Mon-Sat; 3-6.30pm Sun. **Tickets** €4-€43. **Credit** AmEx, MC, V. **Map** p302/p311 L5.

With new interpretations of classics mixed with high-class contemporary and international dramas, the former East German state theatre was voted Theatre of the Year 2005 by German critics. Increasing audience support means it's necessary to book months in advance for such shows as Michael Thalheimer's production of Goethe's *Faust*.

HAU

Main office, HAU2, Hallesches Ufer 32, Kreuzberg (box office 2590 0427/information 259 0040/www. hebbel-am-ufer.de). U1, U7 Möckernbrücke or U1, U6 Hallesches Tor. **Open** *Box office* noon-7pm daily. **Tickets** €10-€15; €6 concessions. **Credit** AmEx, MC, V. **Map** p306 M9.

With the amalgamation of the former Hebbel Theatre (HAU1), Theatre am Hallesches Ufer (HAU2) and Theatre am Ufer (HAU3) under intendant Matthias Lilienthal, it is now possible to develop, rehearse and present internationally renowned guest ensembles, innovative theatre projects and dance productions – all at the same time. The plus for artists is that while working on concurrent projects they are able to view and discuss each others' work. This is what creates the whirlwind of excitement around HAU. A festival for new Polish theatre – Polski Express – is set to become an annual spring event here and thematic weekends will continue throughout the year with discussions, debates and docu-dramas on a wide range of social issues. Within its first year of operation in 2003, HAU was voted Theatre of the Year by German critics – unusual for such a young institution.

Other locations: HAU1, Stresemannstrasse 29, Kreuzberg; HAU3, Tempelhofer Ufer 10, Kreuzberg.

Maxim Gorki Theater

Am Festungsgraben 2, Mitte (box office 2022 1115/ information 2022 1129/www.gorki.de). U6, S1, S2, S5, S7, S9, S75 Friedrichstrasse. **Open** *Box office* noon-6.30pm Mon-Sat; 4-6.30pm Sun. **Tickets** €13-€30. **Credit** MC, V. **Map** p303/p311 N6.

The primary house for progressive Russian and east European drama, known for its naturalistic, down-to-earth style. The production of *The Threepenny Opera* directed by Brecht's granddaughter Johanna Schall is a real crowd-pleaser. Actress and director Katharina Thalbach is also a major attraction. Autumn 2006 will bring big changes when the highly successful writer and director Armin Petras arrives as new intendant, along with a new ensemble.

Prater

Kastanienallee 79, Prenzlauer Berg (247 6772/ www.volksbuehne-berlin.de). U2 Eberswalder Strasse. **Open** *Box office* noon-6pm daily. **Tickets** €12; €6 concessions. **Credit** MC, V (no credit cards by phone). **Map** p303/p312 O6.

Artistic director Rene Pollesch has developed a reputation as a non-conformist, both here and overseas. Under his leadership, Prater has stepped out from the shadow of the Volksbühne, which still manages it, and into its own limelight. To create contact with wider audiences, a summer project has been launched along with Volksbühne, the Rollende Road Schau. This mobile event steps outside genre limitations through audience participation as it visits Berliners in their suburbs.

Renaissance

Hardenbergstrasse 6, Charlottenburg (312 4202/ www.renaissance-theater.de). U2 Ernst-Reuter-Platz. **Open** *Box office* 10am-7pm Mon-Fri; 10am-6pm Sat; 1-6pm Sun. **Tickets** €12-€39. **Credit** AmEx, MC, V. **Map** p305/p312 F8.

If you want famous actors and a classy location, then this is the place. Some of Germany's best-known performers appear in shows here, with a major hit being Judy Winter's one-woman show about Marlene Dietrich. The building is one of only two remaining examples of work by Oskar Kaufmann, premier Berlin theatre architect of the early 20th century. It claims to be the only art deco theatre left in Europe, which makes it a great backdrop to the chansons evenings that are served up with a full dinner in the upstairs salon. **Photo** *p237*.

Schaubühne am Lehniner Platz

Kurfürstendamm 153, Charlottenburg (890 023/ www.schaubuehne.de). U7 Adenauerplatz or S5, S7, S9, S75 Charlottenburg. **Open** *Box office* 11am-6.30pm Mon-Sat; 3-6.30pm Sun. **Tickets** €6.50-€35.50; €8 concessions. **Credit** AmEx, MC, V. **Map** p304 D9.

One of the places to be for the theatrical in-crowd, offering modern drama from young authors played by great stage actors. The programme is almost exclusively contemporary drama and dance, including some English-language works (plays by Sarah Kane, Nicky Silver, Mark Ravenhill and Caryl Churchill have all been featured) and Thomas Ostermeier's internationally renowned productions of Ibsen.

Volksbühne

Rosa-Luxemburg-Platz, Linienstrasse 227, Mitte (247 6772/www.volksbuehne-berlin.de). U2 Rosa-Luxemburg-Platz. **Open** *Box office* noon-6pm daily. **Tickets** €10-€30; €5-€15 concessions. **Credit** AmEx, MC, V (no credit cards by phone). **Map** p303/p310 O5.

This massive landmark theatre on Rosa-Luxemburg-Platz was hovering on the brink of closure before Frank Castorf became intendant. His provocative interpretations restored the popularity of the 'People's Stage', but his deconstructions and modernisations of Russian novels and American plays have now become a bit predictable – it's not easy to shock Berlin audiences for long. Christoph Schlingensief's productions, however, guarantee a love/hate reaction every time. The theatre is also home to a gallery, a small studio theatre (Parasit), and the hip, eclectic Roter and Grüner Salons. Former after-hours hangouts for the East German theatre elite, these two very different halls retain their old-style decor and reek of nostalgia in spite of the frequent indie-record-release parties held there.

Fringe & English-language

Berlin once boasted 100 fringe companies; only about two dozen exist today. The profile of fringe theatre, known to Germans as *Off-Theater*, has been growing over the past several years, but remains dangerously reliant on shrinking public funds. The spaces occupied are often rough and ready, but performances can be revelatory. Quality does vary considerably, but prices will always be lowish and the audience unstuffy.

The English-language theatre scene is still vibrant, although it has seen a lot of comings and goings. A lot of American, British and Irish theatre enthusiasts came to taste the artistic flavour of Berlin, shone briefly – and disappeared. But some have remained. Platypus Theater, Australian expat actor Peter Scollin's successful youth and children's company, is still putting on exciting shows for youngsters. Friends of Italian Opera, which has been producing and hosting quality English-language productions since the early 1990s, has now changed its name to English Theatre Berlin and finally moved to a larger venue. The company has become partners with Theater Thikwa (www.thikwa.de*)*, a company that works with disabled actors, and together they have opened a brand new 140-seater – **F40** – in the same building as the old theatre.

Two other small fringe theatres that occasionally have English-language productions are still hanging in there, located within the complexes of alternative cultural centres: **Brotfabrik** and **Acud** do not have artistic directors and show exclusively guest productions, so the quality varies greatly.

Unless otherwise indicated, box offices open one hour before a performance and sell tickets for that performance only. Tickets are around €8-€15 and an international student ID card should get you a discount at most local and fringe theatres on the night.

Brotfabrik

Caligariplatz, Weissensee (4714 0012/fax 473 3777/www.brotfabrik.de). Tram M2, M13 Prenzlauer Allee/Ostseestrasse. **Open** *By phone* 8am-7pm Mon-Fri; 4-7pm Sat, Sun. **Tickets** €12; €8 concessions. **Credit** MC, V. **Map** p303 Q1.

In its current incarnation this former bread factory houses a cinema and a smaller, experimental theatre, where productions are performed in a variety of languages. The café has a congenial summer courtyard.

F40

Fidicinstrasse 40, Kreuzberg (box office 691 1211/information 693 5692/www.fidicin40.de). U6 Platz der Luftbrücke. **Open** *Box office* 1hr before performance. **Tickets** €7-€15; €8 concessions. **No credit cards. Map** p306 M11.

Finally, after 15 years in a small backyard venue, Berlin's English-language theatre – formerly Friends of Italian Opera, now just known as English Theatre Berlin – has moved to a new, larger, posher space on the same premises. It is continuing with the same high-quality programme that directors Günther Grosser and Bernd Hoffmeister have been presenting from the start: a mixture of internation-

Kleine Nachtrevue. *See p241.*

al guest shows, co-productions and staged readings of new works. The organisation shares this new space with Theater Thikwa, one of Europe's most renowned companies working with disabled actors. The old theatre was in the building's second courtyard; F40 is in the first one.

Orphtheater

Ackerstrasse 169-70, Mitte (441 0009/www. orphtheater.de). U8 Rosenthaler Platz. **Open** *Box office* 10am-4pm daily. **Tickets** €12; €8 concessions. **Map** p303/p310 N4.
In the back courtyard of Schokoladen, a former squatted house turned cultural centre, lurks a hardcore East German theatre company – probably one of the few left untarnished by globalisation. You'll witness precise directing with an eye for detail and a company that shows a true love of their craft. The work is often overtly existential, sometimes provocative and always intelligent.

Sophiensaele

Sophienstrasse 18, Mitte (information 2789 0030/tickets 283 5266/www.sophiensaele.com). U8 Weinmeisterstrasse or S5, S7, S9, S75 Hackescher Markt. **Open** 1hr before performance daily. **Tickets** €13; €8 concessions. **No credit cards. Map** p303/p310 N5.
Expect a contemporary programme of dance, theatre, music and opera, with up-and-coming groups from around the world. If avant-garde is ever crowd-pleasing, then this is where you'll find it. The largest of the off-theatres and with still more room for expansion (even though it looks like it is falling apart), Sophiensaele is the perfect venue for an assortment of theatre and dance festivals. Nico and the Navigators and Lubricat, two young fringe ensembles, are the artists in residence.

Theaterdiscounter

Monbijoustrasse 1, Mitte (4404 8561/www. theaterdiscounter.de). S1, S2 Oranienburger Strasse. **Open** *Box office* from 7pm daily. *Performances* 8pm. **Tickets** €9.99; €7.99 concessions. **No credit cards. Map** p303/p310 N5.
Opened in 2003 in an old telegraph office, this is where an intense group of ten actors and various directors performs original pieces. It's anti-illusion theatre with interactive possibilities – very casual and fresh. Shows are for audiences of up to 50.

Theater unterm Dach

Danziger Strasse 101, im Kulturhaus im Ernst-Thälmann-Park, Prenzlauer Berg (902 953 187/ www.kulturamt-pankow.de). S8, S41, S42, S85 Greifswalder Strasse/tram M4, M10. **Open** (phone bookings only) from 7pm daily. **Tickets** €8; €5 concessions. **No credit cards. Map** p303 Q3.
In the large attic of a converted factory, this is the place to see new German fringe groups. The artistic director searches for the country's most promising young directors or companies and gives them a chance in the capital. Productions are always full of energy and can be quite inspiring.

Cabaret

Although cabaret in Berlin now bears little resemblance to the cabaret of the Weimar years, there are some great performers here who can recreate an entire era in one night. The town is teeming with acts that can sometimes be more sexually adventurous (or ambiguous) than most other places and still manage to titillate the cool Berlin audiences.

Some good acts to watch out for include **Die O-Tonpiraten** (clever drag musical theatre that montages famous film dialogues into irreverent storylines), the charming American entertainer **Gayle Tufts** ('denglish' stand-up comedy with pop) and **Bridge Markland**'s gender-bending dance/poetry.

Don't confuse *Cabaret* with *Varieté*; the latter is more of a circus-like show, minus the animals but with a lot of dancing girls. *Kabarett* is different again – a unique kind of German entertainment with a strong following in Berlin. It's basically political satire sprinkled with songs and sketches, sometimes intellectual and sometimes crass. It can be found at venues such as Stachelschweine, Wühlmäuse, Mehringhof Theatre, Kartoon or Kneifzange (check local listings for details), but most of it will be over your head if you don't have perfect German and a thorough understanding of local politics. When it comes to *Travestie* – drag revue – Berlin offers some of the best you can get, from fabulous to tragic, and in places where you might not expect it. For the more progressive and intelligent drag acts, the **BKA** is a safe bet.

Venues come in all sizes and styles, from small and dark to huge and glittery. Remember that the look and price of a venue is not always an indication of the quality of the show.

Varieté & revue

Chamäleon

Hackesche Höfe, Rosenthaler Strasse 40-41, Mitte (ticket hotline 400 0590/www.chamaeleon berlin.de). S5, S7, S9, S75 Hackescher Markt. **Open** *Box office* 10.30am-8pm Mon-Fri; 10.30am-10pm Sat; noon-7pm Sun. *Performances* 8.30pm Mon, Wed, Thur; 8.30pm, midnight Fri, Sat; 7pm Sun. **Tickets** €25-€32, €21-€26 concessions Tue-Thur, Sun; €25-€37 Fri, Sat. **No credit cards. Map** p303/p310 N5.
Beautiful old theatre with a touch of decadence in the heart of Mitte. The focus here is on stunning acrobats combined with music theatre. As Hackesche Höfe becomes increasingly commercialised and touristy, there's a risk this club may become a sort of Wintergarten-Ost (*see p241*). For now it attracts a very diverse audience and is the most comfortable and affordable revue house.

Friedrichstadtpalast

Friedrichstrasse 107, Mitte (2326 2326/www.
friedrichstadtpalast.de). U6, S1, S2, S5, S7, S9,
S75 Friedrichstrasse. **Open** 6pm-1am daily. *Box*
office 10am-6pm Mon, Sun; 10am-7pm Tue-Sat.
Performances 8pm Tue-Fri; 4pm, 8pm Sat; 4pm
Sun. **Tickets** €18-€62. **Credit** AmEx. **Map**
p303/p310 M5.
An East Berlin institution where stars like Marlene
Dietrich and the Comedian Harmonists played to
packed houses. Since Reunification it has mainly featured big, Las Vegas-style musical revues with
Vegas-style prices to match. Mostly packed with
coachloads of German tourists.

Pomp, Duck & Circumstance

Spiegelpalast Salon Zazou, Möckernstrasse 26,
Kreuzberg (2694 9200/www.pompduck.de). U1, U7
Möckernbrücke. **Open** *Box office* 9am-8pm Mon-Fri;
noon-8pm Sat, Sun. *Performances* 8pm Mon-Sat; 7pm
Sun. **Tickets** €45 Mon, Tue; €110 Wed-Thur, Sun;
€120 Fri, Sat. **Credit** MC. **Map** p306 L9.
A variety extravaganza in an old-fashioned tent,
where the show comes with a four-course meal – yes,
usually including duck. Performers work the audience constantly and are first rate; the food is less reliable. Very expensive, but always packed.

Wintergarten Varieté

Potsdamer Strasse 96, Tiergarten (250 0880/hotline
2500 8888/www.wintergarten-variete.de). U1
Kurfürstenstrasse. **Open** 10-11am, noon-
6pm Mon-Fri; 1-8pm Sat, Sun. *Performances* 8pm
Mon, Tue, Thur, Fri; 4pm, 8pm Wed; 5pm, 9pm Sat;
3pm, 6pm Sun. **Tickets** *Show & dine* €17-€57. *Show &*
dine €68-€83. **Credit** AmEx, MC, V. **Map** p306 J8.
Prussia meets Disney with shows that are slick and
professional and a little boring. Excellent acrobats
and magicians, but some questionable comedy acts.
Fancy decor and more busloads of tourists.

Cabaret

Bar jeder Vernunft

Spiegelzelt, Schaperstrasse 24, Wilmersdorf
(883 1582/www.bar-jeder-vernunft.de). U3, U9
Spichernstrasse. **Open** *Box office* noon-7pm daily;
3-6pm Sat, Sun. *Performances* 8.30pm Mon-Thur;
8pm Fri, Sun. **Tickets** €15-€30. **Credit** AmEx,
MC, V. **Map** p305/p312 F9.
In this snazzy circus tent of many mirrors, you can
see some of Berlin's most celebrated entertainers,
and some polished English entertainers too. A new
adaptation of *Cabaret* continues to be a box office
hit. This is the perfect place to see it, but watch out
for the drink prices. A three-course meal costs €29
per person.

BKA Theater

Mehringdamm 34, Kreuzberg (2022 0044/www.
bka-luftschloss.de). U6, U7 Mehringdamm.
Open *Box office* 11am-8.30pm Mon-Fri; 2-8.30pm
Sat. *Performances* 8pm daily. **Tickets** €9-€24.
Credit AmEx, MC, V. **Map** p306 M10.

With a long tradition of taboo-breaking acts, BKA
still features some of the weirdest and most progressive acts in town: intelligent drag stand-up,
freaky chanteuses and power-packin' divas. Fresh
performances and good theme parties.

Cafe Theater Schalotte

Behaimstrasse 22, Charlottenburg (341 1485/
www.schalotte.de). U7 Richard-Wagner-Platz.
Open *Box office* varies. *Performances* (usually)
8.30pm Thur-Sat. **Tickets** €8-€15. **No credit**
cards. Map p300 D6.
Nice café, dedicated staff and some excellent shows.
The O-Tonpiraten, a very clever drag theatre troupe,
plays here often. The theatre hosts some brilliant
acts in November during its annual international a
cappella festival. Entrance is just €8 on Thursdays.

Kleine Nachtrevue

Kurfürstenstrasse 116, Schöneberg (218 8950/www.
kleine-nachtrevue.de). U1, U2, U3 Wittenbergplatz.
Open 7pm-3am Tue-Sat. *Performances* 10.45pm
Tue-Sat. **Admission** €15-€25. **Credit** AmEx, DC,
MC, V. **Map** p305 H8.
Used as a location for many a film, this is as close
as you can get to real nostalgic German cabaret –
intimate, dark, decadent but very friendly. Nightly
shows consist of short song or dance numbers sprinkled with playful nudity and whimsical costumes.
Special weekend shows at 9pm vary from erotic
opera or a four-course meal to songs sung by the
male reincarnation of Marlene Dietrich. **Photo** *p239.*

Scheinbar

Monumentenstrasse 9, Schöneberg (784 5539/
www.scheinbar.de). U7 Kleistpark. **Open** *Box*
office from 7.30pm daily. *Performances* 8.30pm.
Admission €5-€12. **No credit cards.**
Map p306 K11.
Experimental, fun-loving cabaret in a tiny club
exploding with fresh talent. If you like surprises,
try the open-stage nights, where great performers
mix with terrible ones, creating a very surreal
evening for all.

Tipi Das Zelt

Grosse Querallee, between the Bundeskanzleramt &
Haus der Kulturen der Welt, Tiergarten (0180 327
9358/www.tipi-das-zelt.de). Bus 100, 248 Platz der
Republik. **Open** *Box office* noon-7pm Mon-Sat; 3-6pm
Sun. *Performances* 8.30pm Tue-Sat; 3pm, 8pm Sun.
Tickets €18.50-€42. **Credit** AmEx, MC, V.
Map p302 K6.
A circus tent in the Tiergarten, near the Federal
Chancellery, with cool international performers,
such as Italian Ennio and his amazing paper cos-
tumes, and England's Tiger Lillies. Similar fare to
Bar jeder Vernunft except twice the size.

Tränenpalast

Reichstagufer 17, Mitte (2061 0011/www.
traenenpalast.de). U6, S1, S2, S5, S7, S9,
S75 Friedrichstrasse. **Open** 10am-9pm Mon-Sat;
10am-6pm Sun. *Performances* varies. **Tickets**
varies. **No credit cards. Map** p302/p311 M6.

The Batsheva Company from Israel beg for a response at **Tanz Im August.**

In the days of division this was the entrance to the Friedrichstrasse checkpoint, scene of many a sad farewell, hence the name: 'Palace of Tears'. A historical landmark to see, especially since it might not be in business for much longer. Shows here range from *Kabarett* and stand-up to chansons, concerts and tango evenings, but none are especially daring.

Travestie

Chez Nous
Marburger Strasse 14, Charlottenburg (213 1810/ www.cabaret-chez-nous.de). U2, U9, S5, S7, S9, S75 Zoologischer Garten. **Open** *Box office* 10am-1pm, 1.30-6.30pm Mon-Sat. *Performances* 8.30pm, 11pm daily. **Admission** €35. **Credit** AmEx, MC. **Map** p305 G8.
Standard *travestie* revue, performed by international drag artists.

Theater im Keller
Weserstrasse 211, Neukölln (623 1452/www. theater-im-keller.de). U7, U8 Hermannplatz. **Open** *Box office* 11am-10pm daily. *Performances* 8pm daily. **Admission** €24-€30. **Credit** AmEx, MC, V. **Map** p307 Q11.
Cosy neighbourhood drag club with a touch of grandma and a passable drag revue.

Dance

Berlin has become a major destination for both young and established choreographers, and on the international stage there is hardly a major festival that doesn't feature a production from the German capital. Indeed, during the last 15 years, the city has reasserted itself as one of the world's leading centres for dance – its institutions are rewarded with more funding than most other artistic endeavours.

Much of this reputation comes as a result of a thriving independent dance scene, in which a constant influx of international dancers serves to sharpen the competitive edge. In addition, there is a bounty of professional training opportunities. The city's schools have a sturdy international profile, with Dock 11 leading the way, and one of the city's main dance venues, **HAU** (*see p238*), offers an innovative artist-in-residence programme.

Berlin offers myriad possibilities for staging productions in incongruous settings, such as anonymous apartments (Two Fish), leftover bomb shelters (Ausland) and culturally charged venues such as the looming, ex-Communist Volksbühne (Constanza Macras) or the doomed hulk of the Palast der Republik. And then there is the cross-fertilisation phenomenon. Choreographers frequently team up with leading lights in new media, fine art or music, giving Berlin dance an adventurous edge.

For information on current performances, check *tip* or *Zitty* or the free *Tanzkalender*, which can be picked up across town.

For ticket agencies, *see p233*.

Major venues & festivals

HAU and **Sophiensaele** are the two most important venues for the Berlin contemporary dance world. Interestingly, neither are exclusively dance institutions – both also focus heavily on theatre, with literature and visual arts also on their horizons. This says something about the collaborative nature of Berlin dance and, indeed, the city also has a strong tradition of dance theatre, a wave led first by **Sasha Waltz** at the Schaubühne and now by independent innovator **Constanza Macras.**

HAU is the force behind the three-week **Tanz im August** festival (*see p183*) – the most exciting dance event in Berlin, which takes place at HAU and Sophiensaele as well as some smaller venues around town. HAU invites international and often more established artists,

Arts & Entertainment

offering an artist-in-residence programme and funding long-term projects that tour worldwide. Sophiensaele hosts its own two-week **Tanztage** (*see p186*) in January, focusing on new and local talent. Developing talent is the current raison d'être, as well as offering local dancers from all mediums their first choreographic experiences.

Dock 11 (Kastanienallee 79, Prenzlauer Berg, 448 1222, www.dock11-berlin.de) is the only venue in town dedicated entirely to dance. It combines a small, cosy stage and a well-reputed, dynamic school. There's a community feel to the place, which is frequented by big and small names from the Berlin dance scene.

Tanzwerkstatt, another important local organisation, lost its base at the Podewil cultural centre last year, but continues to collaborate with HAU and Sophiensaele, scouting out fresh talent and organising an important artist-in-residence programme.

In Transit (*see p182*) is a relative newcomer to the festival scene, launched in 2002 by the Haus der Kulturen der Welt. It commissions a different, non-European curator every two years to travel the world and book dance and performance artists who then come to the city to work with Berlin groups during a three-week period in early summer. Interestingly, audiences can not only watch completed evening performances, but also watch the collaborative pieces being developed.

Contemporary companies & choreographers

Constanza Macras

Born in Buenos Aires, Macras is an anti-conceptualist working in a conceptualist era – and hugely popular in Berlin for it. She came to this city via New York and Amsterdam, and leads the company Dorky Park, a group of dancers who are also actors and singers. She works in often unlikely venues around Berlin, including old shopfronts and tacky nightclubs. Her 2004 *Wonderland* was an autobiographical piece, which she danced herself (for the first time in years) to standing ovations at Tanz im August. In the past few years she has worked in Korea, Japan, the United States and India. Her 2003 *Back to the Present* was a hit throughout Europe and in 2006 she will present a piece produced for Nike.

Felix Ruckert

Based at Dock 11 (*see above*), French-born Ruckert (formerly a dancer with Pina Bausch) and his company explore all aspects of audience participation – including nudity, touch and the infliction of pain. Ruckert's company tours extensively, but he has also worked for Strasbourg's National Ballet Company with great success.

Jerome Bel

Frenchman Bel lives in Berlin and Paris, and is considered one of the most important European choreographers working today. A conceptualist, he works with light, music and movement in such productions as *Jerome Bel and the Show Must Go On*, the second instalment of which ran at Berlin's Schaubühne in 2005. His work sits somewhere between classical ballet, modern and contemporary dance, causing frequent uproar in more conservative European cities.

Jochen Roller

German-born Roller is one of the hottest choreographers on the Berlin scene and a rising international star. He gained fame in 2002 with *Perform, Performing*, a three-hour solo piece about the sense and senselessness of pursuing dance as a career, the success of which allowed him to do just that. In 2005 he premièred *Mnemonic Nonstop*, a piece based on the biographies of four cities, in Paris; he will perform it at Sophiensaele in 2006.

Sasha Waltz

Germany's leading proponent of postmodern dance-theatre, Sasha Waltz is now independent after co-directing the Schaubühne am Lehniner Platz (*see p238*) for many years. Her site-specific projects took audiences on to the roof of the Schaubühne and inside the shell of Libeskind's Jüdisches Museum (*see p97*) before it opened. In 2004 Waltz produced a hugely successful show of *Dido and Aeneas* at the Staatsoper, one of Berlin's two main classical stages.

Thomas Lehmen

Born in the Ruhr and trained in Amsterdam, Lehmen bridges performance and choreographic art. Since 2003 he has been working on *Stationen*, for which he invites people of all types of professions to join in and talk about their work. His *Schreibstück* is a written score for a dance piece that is handed out to different choreographers for interpretation.

Ballet

In recent years, budget cuts have changed the face of ballet in Berlin. In August 2004 three main companies became one, when half of the Deutsche Oper dancers and all but one at the Komische Oper lost their jobs. Those remaining joined the existing Staatsoper Ballet to form the **Staatsballett Berlin** (www.staatsballett-berlin.de). Thankfully, 'dancer of the century' Vladimir Malakhov remained at the helm and, with his roots in the Russian academic tradition, continues to uphold the reputation of Berlin ballet. Malakhov's now 90-member company performs from September until June at both the **Deutsche Oper** and the **Staatsoper Unter den Linden**. Diana Vishneva from the Kirov Ballet is a regular guest artist, while Russian Polina Semionova thrives as the company's 'baby ballerina'.

Sport & Fitness

Beach volleyball, windsurfing, climbing and curling are just some of the unlikeliest attractions.

In Berlin you can find every activity from American football to Zen meditation. For the serious player, there are countless organisations and clubs. For the more informal, there are the parks. In summer you're bound to come across some motley crew playing football, chucking a frisbee or throwing themselves around at a volleyball net. If there's a game going on with uneven sides, you'll probably be welcomed if you want to join in.

Spectator sports are reasonably priced and you can often just show up and pay at the door; only the really big events sell out in advance.

Major stadiums & arenas

Max-Schmeling-Halle

Am Falkplatz, Prenzlauer Berg (443 045/tickets 4430 4430/www.max-schmeling-halle.de). U2 Eberswalder Strasse or U2, S8, S41, S42, S85 Schönhauser Allee. **Map** p303 O2.
Named after the German boxer who knocked out the seemingly invincible Joe Louis in 1936, this state-of-the-art indoor arena is better known as the home of Berlin's basketball hotshots ALBA (*see below*). The 11,000-capacity hall hosts a variety of international sporting events, rock concerts and conferences.

Olympiastadion

Olympischer Platz 3, Charlottenburg (2500 2322/tickets 01805 189 200/www.olympiastadion-berlin.de). U2 Olympia-Stadion or S5, S75 Olympiastadion. Centrepiece for the 1936 Olympics, this is one of the best surviving examples of Nazi monumentalism. And after years of neglect, the stadium was given extensive renovations and a new roof for the 2006 FIFA World Cup Final (*see p39* **The final stadium**). The 76,000-seater bowl hosts Berlin's top football club, Hertha BSC (*see below*), the German Cup Final (Deutschland Pokal-Endspiele; *see p182*), American football's Berlin Thunder (*see below*) and the ISTAF annual athletics meeting (*see below*), as well as rock concerts and other events. **Photo** *p245*.

Velodrom

Paul-Heyse-Strasse 26, Prenzlauer Berg (office 443 045/tickets 4430 4430/www.velomax.de). S8, S41, S42, S85 Landsberger Allee. **Map** p309 S4.
Opened in 1997, this multifunctional sports and entertainment venue was designed by Dominique Perrault for the annual six-day cycling race, and boasts a track made from Siberian spruce. It also accommodates equestrian and super-cross events, as well as pop concerts, trade fairs and conferences.

Spectator sports

American football

Berlin Thunder

Friesenhof 1, Hanns-Braun-Strasse, Charlottenburg (3006 4400/www.berlin-thunder.de). U2 Olympia-Stadion or S5, S75 Olympiastadion. **Tickets** €8-€31.50. **Credit** (advance bookings only) AmEx, V.
The NFL Europe has grown in stature and popularity since it started in the early 1990s. Initially viewed as a last-chance saloon for players who couldn't make it in the NFL, it has earned a reputation as something of a finishing school, especially for quarterbacks. Berlin Thunder won the World Bowl in 2001, 2002 and 2004 and went to the final in 2005. They now play at the Olympiastadion (*see above*) and draw crowds approaching 20,000.

Athletics

ISTAF Athletics Meeting

243 1990/www.istaf.de. **Tickets** €8-€69; 10% off for concessions.
First held in 1937, this international one-day meet at the Olympiastadion (*see above*) is the last of four events in the IAAF's Golden League. The $1 million prize money is shared between athletes who win their disciplines at all four Golden League meetings. With that kind of wealth and prestige at stake, the crowd is often treated to world records.

Basketball

ALBA

01805 300 777/www.albaticket.de. **Tickets** €7.50-€32. **Credit** AmEx, MC, V.
Berlin's representatives in the top division of German basketball take their name from their sponsors, a waste disposal and recycling firm. They won seven domestic league titles in a row in the late 1990s and early 2000s and, although 2005 was a barren year, the club's loyal followers can be counted on to fill the Max-Schmeling-Halle (*see above*).

Football

Germany won the bidding to host the 2006 FIFA World Cup Finals, with the final being played at Berlin's **Olympiastadion** (*see above*). That stadium is also host to Berlin's biggest club, **Hertha BSC**, one of the country's

Olympiastadion – roofed and renovated after years of neglect. *See p244.*

top teams, enjoying regular top-six finishes and forays into Europe. The only other club of much consequence is **FC Union**.

Hertha BSC

0180 518 9200/www.herthabsc.de. **Tickets** €10-€45. **Credit** (online bookings only) MC, V.
After a disastrous 2003-04 season, Hertha returned to European competition in the 2004-05 UEFA Cup. At the time of going to press, the club was also doing all right in both the Bundesliga and Deutschland Pokal. Repeatedly touted as title contenders, Hertha so far haven't found the strength in depth to claim any significant silverware. Their home ground is the Olympiastadion (*see p244*).

1. FC Union

Stadion An der Alten Försterei 263, Köpenick (6566 8856/www.fc-union-berlin.de). S3 Köpenick. **Tickets** €7-€18. **No credit cards.**
Strugglers under communism, 'Iron Union' aren't faring too well under capitalism, either. A German Cup Final appearance in 2001 earned them a UEFA Cup slot, but since then Union have slipped into the third division and seriously into the red. Their fan base, however, drawn from the industrial working class, is still arguably the city's best.

Horse racing

Galopprennbahn-Hoppegarten

Goetheallee 1, Dahlwitz-Hoppegarten (0334 238 930/tickets 780 111/www.galopprennbahn-hoppegarten. de). S5 Hoppegarten. **Tickets** €5-€30. **Credit** AmEx, MC, V.
Thoroughbred races are held between April and October. Betting is run along the lines of the British tote system: all money bet on a race goes into a 'pot' that is shared by those who placed a winning bet.

Pferdesportpark

Treskowallee 129, Karlshorst (5001 7121/www.psp-sportpark.de). S3 Karlshorst. **Tickets** *Daytime* €2. *Evening* free. **No credit cards.**
Trotting (harness racing) events are held all year round on Wednesdays at about 6pm.

Trabrennbahn Mariendorf

Mariendorfer Damm 222-98, Mariendorf (740 1212/www.berlintrab.de). U6 Alt-Mariendorf, then bus X76, 176, 179. **Tickets** free Mon-Fri; €2.50 Sat, Sun. **No credit cards.**
Irregular trotting meetings (check the website) on Sundays at 1.30pm and Tuesdays at 6pm. Derby Week in August is now a major international event.

Berlin Marathon – gateway to record-breaking performances. *See p247*.

Ice hockey

Since German ice-hockey clubs set up a private national league in 1994, the sport has become big business. For now, Berlin's **Eisbären**, the old eastern club, have seen off their western rivals, the **Capitals** (*see p250* **The corrugated iron palace of dreams**).

EHC Eisbären Berlin

Wellblechpalast, Steffenstrasse, Hohenschönhausen (971 8400/tickets 9718 4040/www.eisbaeren.de). S8, S41, S42, S85 Landsberger Allee, then tram M5 Simon-Bolivar-Strasse. **Tickets** €15-€30. **No credit cards.**
Survived communism and the transition to capitalism, as well as the loss of their big city rivals.

Tennis

The **Qatar Total Ladies German Open**, as it is now called, is held each May as a warm-up tournament for the French Open and usually attracts most of the big names. *See also p182.*

LTTC Rot-Weiss

Gottfried-von-Cramm-Weg 47-55, Grunewald (tickets 8957 5520/www.rot-weiss-berlin.de). S7, S9 Grunewald. **Open** 8am-5pm Mon-Thur; 8am-noon Fri. **Tickets** €15-€65; €7.50-€10 concessions. **No credit cards.**
Venue for the Qatar Total Ladies German Open, played on clay courts. In 2004 Centre Court was named after German tennis legend Steffi Graf.

Active sports/fitness

Berlin is a dream for the DIY athlete. This chapter only covers a fraction of what's on offer; if you don't find what you're looking for, contact one of the organisations listed.

Landessportbund Berlin (LSB)

Jesse-Owens-Allee 2, Charlottenburg (300 020/ www.lsb-berlin.org). U2 Olympia-Stadion or S5, S75 Olympiastadion. **Open** 9am-3pm Mon-Thur; 9am-2pm Fri.
The Berlin Regional Sports Association's central office provides general information and co-ordinates other offices in charge of specific sports. The Landesauschuss Frauensport (Regional Committee for Women's Sport) is at the same address.

Turngemeinde in Berlin 1848

Columbiadamm 111, Neukölln (611 0100/www. tib1848ev.de). U7 Südstern or U8 Boddinstrasse.
The city's oldest sports club is also perhaps its most diverse, with a list of activities almost as long as its history. As suggested by the name ('Gymnastics Community in Berlin'), it was founded in 1848. It's based beside the Hasenheide park, where Friedrich Ludwig Jahn, 'the father of German gymnastics', established the country's first physical education

facility in 1811. It offers outdoor and indoor tennis courts, badminton courts, beach volleyball and sundry other facilities.

Athletics

Berlin Marathon

Glockenturm 23, Charlottenburg (3012 8810/www. berlin-marathon.com). **Entrance fee** €50-€90. **Date** last Sun in Sept.
With almost 60,000 participants, this is one of the world's largest marathons, spread over two days to fit in all the runners, wheelchair athletes and in-line skaters. Because Berlin is flat and the weather moderate in September, the race is conducive to record-breaking performances. The less ambitious can try the Berlin Half-Marathon in April or 'City Night' in August, a 10km (six-mile) trot on the Ku'damm. There's also the New Year Fun Run on 1 January, starting near the Brandenburg Gate. **Photo** *p246.*

Badminton

See p253 **Tennis.**

Beach volleyball

Land-locked Berlin is, oddly, a major centre for beach volleyball and one of the four cities that hosts a grand slam tournament. Permanent facilities for the sport are listed on the website of umbrella organisation **Volleyball-Verband Berlin** (3199 9933, www.vvb-online.de).

Beach Mitte

Caroline-Michaelis-Strasse, Mitte (0177 280 686/ www.beachmitte.de). S1, S2, S25 Nordbahnhof. **Map** p302 M4.
This new facility (opening hours unavailable at press time) boasts outdoor courts and a beach bar atmosphere, with cocktails and a bonfire at night.

City Beach Berlin

Michelangelostrasse/Hanns-Eisler-Strasse, Prenzlauer Berg (0177 247 6907/www.city-beach-berlin.de). S8, S41, S42, S85 Greifswalder Strasse. **Open** 10am-11pm daily. **Rates** €20-€22/hr. **Map** p309 R2/S2.
Indoor facility with three courts. **Photo** *p249.*

City Beach am Friedrichshain

Kniprodestrasse/Danziger Strasse, Prenzlauer Berg (0177 247 6907/www.city-beach-berlin.de). Tram M10 Kniprodestrasse/Danziger Strasse. **Open** call for details. **Rates** €10/hr. **Map** p309 R4.
Outdoor nine-court facility with a beach bar in summer; they also have an indoor facility. Call in advance to book a court.

Bowling

There are more than 50 bowling alleys in Berlin, all listed at www.bowling-zone.de.

Bowling Center am Alex

Rathausstrasse 5, Mitte (242 6657). U2, U5, U8, S5, S7, S9, S75 Alexanderplatz. **Open** 11am-midnight Mon-Thur; 11am-late Fri, Sat; 10am-midnight Sun. **Rates** €10.80-€17.40/hr; €1.50 shoes. **No credit cards. Map** p303/p311 O6.
This GDR relic boasts all mod cons: 18 lanes with scorers, pool tables, darts, pinball and a restaurant. Look for the big neon sign and go down the steps.

New City Bowling Hasenheide

Hasenheide 107-9, Kreuzberg (622 2038/www. bowling-hasenheide.de). U7, U8 Hermannplatz. **Open** 10am-midnight daily. **Rates** €1.80-€3.30 per person/game. **No credit cards. Map** p307 P11.
Top international competitions are hosted at this 28-lane facility. There are also 12 lanes for children and a bar/restaurant.

Canoeing & kayaking

Der Bootsladen

Brandensteinweg 8, Spandau (362 5685/www. der-bootsladen.de). Bus 149. **Open** *Mar-Oct* noon-7pm Tue-Fri; 9am-7pm Sat, Sun. *Nov-Feb* 1-4pm Fri; 10am-4pm Sat. **Rates** *Kayak* €5.50/hr. *Canadian double* €6.50/hr. **Credit** V.
Berlin's urban waterway network is unique in central Europe. This is a good place for canoe and kayak tours of the western river and canal system. If you want a boat for more than three hours, you'll save money by booking for a whole day.

Kanu-Connection

Köpenicker Strasse 9, Kreuzberg (612 2686/www. kanu-connection.de). U1 Schlesisches Tor. **Open** 10am-7pm Mon-Fri; 9am-1pm Sat. **Rates** €20-€28 per person/day; €46-€61/wknd; €90-€112/wk. **No credit cards. Map** p308 R8.
Kreuzberg itself is a nice area to paddle through, or you could head east to the forests. This outfit can provide you with maps and guides.

Climbing

Either go to one of the commercial halls or join a club – the clubs offer good-value introductory courses and access to some fantastic outdoor venues such as the World War II-era flak tower in Humboldthain. Official and unofficial climbing venues are listed at www.klettern-in-berlin.de, with a colour-coded legality guide. **Himaxx** (*see p252*) allows you to train in an atmosphere that mimics this mountain air.

Deutscher Alpenverein (DAV)

Markgrafenstrasse 11, Kreuzberg (251 0943/www. alpenverein-berlin.de). U6 Kochstrasse. **Open** 2-7pm Mon, Wed; 9am-1pm Fri. **Admission** *Membership* €80; €45 18-26s; €36 under-18s. **No credit cards. Map** p307 N8.
Information, courses and access to an assortment of cool climbing venues.

Magic Mountain

Böttgerstrasse 20-26, Wedding (8871 5790/www. magicmountain.de). U8, S1, S2, S25, S41, S42, S46 Gesundbrunnen. **Open** noon-midnight Mon-Wed, Fri; 10am-midnight Thur; 11am-10pm Sat, Sun. **Admission** €12-€14; €9-€11 concessions. **Credit** MC, V. **Map** p302 L2.
Indoor climbing hall, featuring a range of walls and a 'donut boulder' for experts.

T-Hall

Thiemannstrasse 1, Neukölln (6808 9864/www.t-hallberlin.de). U7 Karl-Marx-Strasse or S41, S42 Sonnenallee. **Open** *June-Sept* 2pm-midnight Mon, Wed, Thur; 11am-midnight Tue, Fri; 11am-9pm Sat, Sun. *Oct-May* 2pm-midnight Mon, Wed, Thur; 11am-midnight Tue, Fri-Sun. **Rates** €10-€14/day; €8-€11.50/day concessions. **No credit cards.**
Spacious indoor climbing facility where the 36ft-high (11m) ceiling's the limit.

Cricket

Cricket has been played in Berlin since the mid 19th century and though history has bowled it repeated googlies, it's still at the crease. The sport is run by the **Berlin Cricket Komitee** (8867 2710, www.berlin-cricket.de). Six teams currently play competitively and in summer there are games every Saturday and Sunday. The **Berlin Cricket Club** (6950 9065, www.berlincc.de), 'the Refugees', is an English-speaking team of expats and locals who are always on the lookout for new members. Games start at 11am in one of the most beautiful grounds in mainland Europe (Körner Platz, Hanns-Braun-Strasse, Charlottenburg, U2 Olympia-Stadion).

Cycling

Cycling is an ideal way to get around Berlin, as the city is flat and well supplied with cycle lanes. It can be a particularly scenic way to see the city, as lanes run through parks and alongside canals. Competitive cycling is also popular, and Berlin has produced several internationally renowned riders. The city's level hinterland is also ideal for touring. For bike rental, *see p273*.

Allgemeiner Deutscher Fahrrad-Club

Brunnenstrasse 28, Mitte (448 4724/www.adfc-berlin.de). U8 Bernauer Strasse. **Open** noon-8pm Mon-Fri; 10am-4pm Sat. **Map** p303 N3.
Has an information and meeting point for cyclists, and a DIY repair station. Contact the club for a map of cycle paths or details of routes in and around Berlin.

Berliner Radsport Verband

Paul-Heyse-Strasse 29, Prenzlauer Berg (4210 5145/www.bdr-radsport.de/ber). S8, S41, S42,

Ain't that a beach? Suitably sandy surfaces at **City Beach Berlin**. *See p247.*

S85 Landsberger Allee. **Open** 9am-1pm Tue,
Fri; 2-5pm Thur. **Map** p309 S4.
Information on clubs, races and events. The Tour de
Berlin, a five-stage, 600km (375-mile) race, is held
annually at the end of May.

Disabled

There are dozens of clubs and organisations for
disabled athletes in Berlin. For details, contact
Behinderten-Sportverband Berlin (3009
9675, www.bsberlin.de).

Fitness centres

There are hundreds of health and fitness
clubs in Berlin – from sweaty body-building
basements to luxurious spa-like penthouses.
Courses offered match those in any big city,
and there are branches of all the chains, such
as **Kieser**, **Swiss Training** and **Gold's**.

Aspria

Karlsruher Strasse 20, Wilmersdorf (890 688 810/
www.aspria.de). S41, S42, S45, S46, S47 Halensee.
Open 6am-11pm Mon-Fri; 9am-10pm Sat, Sun.
Rates from €70/mth (no day pass). **Credit** AmEx,
DC, MC, V. **Map** p304 C9.
Luxurious five-floor complex with a health and
beauty centre, 25m (82ft) pool, saunas, steam room,

ice room, restaurants, bars, sun terrace with solari-
ums and a view of central Berlin. The club offers
massages, fitness courses and customised workouts.

Axxel City Fitness

Bülowstrasse 57, Schöneberg (2175 3000/www.
axxel24.de). U2 Bülowstrasse or U7, S1, S2, S26
Yorckstrasse. **Open** 24hrs daily. **Rates** €55/mth
(2yr contract €37). **No credit cards**. **Map** p306 K9.
For insomniac fitness freaks.

Club Olympus Spa & Fitness

Marlene-Dietrich-Platz 2, Tiergarten (2553 1890/
www.berlin.grand.hyatt.com). U2, S1, S2, S26
Potsdamer Platz. **Open** 6.30am-10.30pm Mon-Fri;
7.30am-9pm Sat, Sun. **Rates** €60/day. **Credit**
AmEx, DC, MC, V. **Map** p306/p311 K8.
Luxurious, expensive fitness centre on the roof of
the Grand Hyatt hotel (*see p60*).

Jason's City Fitness

Wilmersdorfer Strasse 82-3, Charlottenburg (324
1025). U7 Adenauerplatz. **Open** 8am-midnight Mon-
Fri; 10am-10pm Sat, Sun. **Rates** vary. **No credit**
cards. **Map** p304 G9.
Once a men-only joint, this place has opened its
doors to women. It's still popular with gays, but now
draws a more mixed clientele.

Jopp Frauen Fitness

Tauentzienstrasse 13A, Charlottenburg (210 111/
www.jopp.de). U1, U9 Kurfürstendamm or U1,

The corrugated iron palace of dreams

In April 2005 Berlin's top ice-hockey team, the **Eisbären** ('Polar Bears') achieved the impossible: having survived the transition from communism to capitalism in a ruthlessly professional sport, they went on to become champions of Germany.

Their existence under communism was down to a caprice of Erich Mielke, head of the Stasi. In 1970, when the Politburo decided to stop promoting hockey, two teams were kept going for Mielke's entertainment, creating the world's smallest league. One of them was the Eisbären, known back then as Dynamo Berlin.

Then came the fall of the Wall and a whole new threat: big bucks. In their first season in the top flight, the Eisbären were relegated. Though they bounced back straight away, they continued to struggle financially. Fans were happy as long as their club survived – and beat their cross-town rivals, the Preussen ('Prussians') of West Berlin, later the Capitals. In their first league appearance against the Preussen in 1990, the Eisbären lost 12-nil at home. A bitter rivalry began.

'Dy-Na-Mo' is a chant still heard from Eisbären fans, despite efforts to ban it for the sake of respectability – 'Dynamo' was the name given to teams sponsored by secret police all across communist Europe. The fans treat this heritage with a mixture of pride and irony, and take the abuse they get in the west

with a healthy pinch of salt. And they inspire similar feelings among their players. This sense of identity went full circle one day in Kassel, when an Eisbären player was being abused as a 'Stasi swine' by opposing supporters. The Canadian Scott Metcalfe jumped to his team-mate's aid and, to the bewilderment of reporters, bawled into their microphones: 'Yes – I'm 100 per cent Stasi!'

Now the Capitals have gone bust and the Eisbären are having the last laugh. The fans, a tight-knit but friendly bunch, will tell you they miss the derbies. Those in charge see it differently: the Eisbären have flourished in the absence of their rivals.

There has been some movement of fans from west to east, but the club is far from embracing, or being embraced by, the whole city. That could be partly down to the obscure location of its arena, the evocatively named Wellblechpalast ('Palace of Corrugated Iron'). But since 1999, when the club's professional operations were bought by the US-based Ansbach Entertainment Group, the days of the Wellblechpalast have been numbered. A new state-of-the-art arena is planned for the north (read east) bank of the Spree at Ostbahnhof, a more central location. That may well help attract more west Berliners and make the club more popular, but it's unlikely the core fans will care.

U2, U3 Wittenbergplatz. **Open** 7am-11pm Mon-Fri; 10am-8pm Sat, Sun. **Rates** €66/mth (3mth contract). **Map** p306 G8.
A women-only chain.
Other locations: Friedrichstrasse 50, Mitte (2045 8585); Karl-Liebknecht-Strasse 13, Mitte (2434 9355).

Gay & lesbian sports

The rift in international GLBT sports that resulted in the Gay Games and the Outgames being held almost back-to-back in 2006 has filtered down to Berlin, which was also hoping to hold a major event. Berlin's gay mayor Klaus Wowereit saw no option but to withdraw official backing for either faction. The Outgames 2009 went to Copenhagen and, at the time of writing, Cologne was in the running for the 2010 Gay Games. Berlin, meanwhile, is out

in the cold and the gay sporting community is split. But you can still visit www.vorspiel-berlin.de (*see p211* **Keep fit with foreplay**) for details of local sports.

Golf

Golfpark Schloss Wilkendorf

Am Weiher 1, OT Wilkendorf, Gielsdorf (03341 330 960/www.golfpark-schloss-wilkendorf.com). S5 Strausberg Nord, then walk or taxi. **Open** *Nov-Feb* 9am-5pm daily. *Mar-Oct* 8am-8pm daily. **Rates** *Westside Platz* (18 holes) €30 Mon-Fri; €45 Sat, Sun. *Sandy-Lyle-Platz* (18 holes; members only) €30-€38 Mon-Fri; €55 Sat, Sun. *Public course* (6 holes) €10-€15. **Credit** MC, V.
Westside Platz is the only 18-hole course in the area open to non-members; at weekends, you'll need a Platzreife – 'German Golf Certificate' – obtainable with membership or by taking a course and/or test.

Global Golf Berlin

*Schöneberger Ufer 1, Kreuzberg (2269 7844/
www.globalgolfberlin.de). U1, U2 Gleisdreieck, U2
Mendelssohn-Bartholdy-Park, U7 Möckernbrücke
or S1, S2, S26 Anhalter Bahnhof.* **Open** 7am-10pm
daily. **Rates** *Club rental* €1.50. *Ball hire* eg 40 for €4.
Map p306 L9.

Spectacular inner-city driving range with members'
and non-members' areas. The clubhouse, snack bar
and shop are open to all. The members' driving
ranges offer computerised swing-analysis and auto-
matic teeing, along with chipping and putting
greens. There's also a non-members' putting green
and courses for all levels. **Photo** *p252.*

Öffentliches Golfzentrum Berlin-Mitte

*Chausseestrasse 94, Mitte. Office: Habersaathstrasse
34, Mitte (2804 7070/www.golfzentrum-berlin.de).
U6 Zinnowitzer Strasse.* **Open** 7am-11pm daily.
Rates *Club rental* €1. *Ball hire* eg 40 for €3, 20
for €1, happy hour until noon. **Credit** AmEx, V.
Map p302 L4.

An older and more down-to-earth alternative driving
range, with lower rates. Also features chipping and
putting greens, floodlights and coaching offers (free
for kids on Thursday afternoons).

Ice skating

The Christmas market at Alexanderplatz has a
small outdoor rink, and you can try your hand
at curling in the Sony Center at Potsdamer Platz
from late November to early January.

Eisstadion Berlin Wilmersdorf

*Fritz-Wildung-Strasse 9, Wilmersdorf (8973 2734/
www.eissport-service.de). S41, S42, S45, S46, S47
Hohenzollerndamm.* **Open** *Oct-mid Mar* 9am-6.30pm,
7.30-10pm Mon, Wed, Fri; 9am-5.30pm, 7.30-10pm
Tue, Thur; 9am-10pm Sat; 10am-6pm Sun. **Rates**
€3.30/2hrs; €1.60/2hrs concessions. **No credit
cards.** **Map** p304 D11.

With an outer ring for speed skating and an inner
field for figure-skaters. Skate rental too.

Erika-Hess-Eisstadion-Mitte

*Erika-Hess-Stadion, Müllerstrasse 185, Wedding
(200 945 550). U6 Reinickendorfer Strasse.* **Open**
Oct-Mar 9am-noon, 3-5.30pm Mon, Tue; 9am-noon,
3-5.30pm, 7.30-9.30pm Wed, Thur; 9am-noon, 3-
5.30pm, 7.30-10pm Fri, Sat; 9am-noon, 2-5pm Sun.
Admission €3.30; €1.65 concessions. **No credit
cards.** **Map** p302 K3.

Cheapest public rink in town. Admission gets you
up to three hours of skating. The venue also holds
important skating competitions.

Sailing & motor boating

Berlin boasts 50 lakes and a 200-kilometre (125-
mile) network of navigable rivers, estuaries and
canals. The city is bordered on the west by the
Havel river and to the south by the Dahme; the

Spree forms an east–west axis through the
centre. If you're planning a longer stay, you
might join one of the clubs or associations listed
at www.wassersport-in-berlin.de. But there are
also opportunities for the short-term visitor.
You need a licence for boating and sailing.
If you have one, bring it. Boat rental places
may then issue you a charter pass for sailboats
or motor boats.

The **Berlin-Brandenburg Water
Sports Association** (Wassertourismus
Förderverband, www.wtb-brb.de) publishes
a waterway map with speed limits and
landings. The **Berliner Segler-Verband**
(3083 9908, www.berliner-segler-verband.de)
has info on sailing in and around Berlin.

The **Wassersportzentrum Berlin**
(www.wassersportzentrum.de) runs two centres
with marinas at the Müggelsee in south-east
Berlin. For the Wannsee, to the south-west,
try www.yachthafen-marina-wannsee.de.

Sauna & Turkish baths

Many of Berlin's public baths, including those
listed below, have affordable saunas and
cheapish massage.

Hamam Turkish Bath

*Schoko-Fabrik, Naunynstrasse 72, Kreuzberg (615
1464/www.hamamberlin.de). U1, U8 Kottbusser Tor.*
Open *Sept-Apr* 3-11pm Mon; noon-10pm Tue-Sun.
May-June call for hours. **Rates** €12/3hrs; €21/5hrs.
No credit cards. **Map** p307 P9.

Under the glass cupola of the main hall, women sit
in alcoves, soaking in warm water. A friendly and
laid-back place, attracting a mixed clientele. Enjoy
Turkish tea and a reviving massage afterwards.
Thursday is kids' day, but no children are allowed
in on Tuesdays and Fridays; although the place is
women only, boys up to the age of six can visit too.

Sultan Hamam

*Bülowstrasse 57, Schöneberg (2175 3375/www.
sultan-hamam.de). U2 Bülowstrasse.* **Open** noon-
11pm daily. **Rates** €14/3hrs; €11 peel; €16 massage.
No credit cards. **Map** p306 J9.

Traditional massages and peelings, as well as more
modern cosmetic treatments. It's women only,
except for Mondays (men) and Sundays (families).

Thermen am Europa-Center

*Europa-Center, Nürnberger Strasse 7,
Charlottenburg (257 5760/www.thermen-berlin.de).
U1, U2, U3 Wittenbergplatz.* **Open** 10am-midnight
Mon-Sat; 10am-9pm Sun. **Rates** €17.90/day; €9.20
1st hr; €4.10 2nd hr; €154 10 admissions. **No credit
cards.** **Map** p305 G8.

Big, central, mixed facility offering Finnish saunas,
steam baths, hot and cool pools, and a garden (open
until October). There is a rooftop pool where you can
swim outside, even in winter. Thermen also boasts
a café, pool-side loungers, table tennis and billiards.

Arts & Entertainment

Plenty of clubs, even for non-members, such as at **Global Golf Berlin**. *See p251.*

Skateboarding, in-line skating & BMX

Berlin is a skater-friendly city, with small facilities dotted across town and several bigger complexes, all listed by district at www.skate spots.de. The city's in-line skaters occasionally disrupt street traffic with demonstrations for equal rights. Routes vary; check www.berlin parade.de for dates and starting points.

Erlebniswerkstatt des Projektes Erlebnisräume

Sterndamm 82, Treptow (631 0911/www. erlebnisraeume.de). S8, S9, S45, S46, S47, S85 Schöneweide. **Open** call for appointment. **Admission** free.

This is a trial track with jump ramps, and its a good place to make contact with what's going on. The project builds and maintains skateboarding, skating and climbing facilities around town as well as organising events.

Squash

See also p253 **Tennis**.

Sportoase, Lady Line & Himaxx

Stromstrasse 11-17, Tiergarten (390 6620/ www.sportoase.de). U9 Turmstrasse. **Open** 8am-11.30pm Mon-Thur; 8am-10pm Fri; 10am-8pm Sat; 9am-10pm Sun. **Rates** €10-€18. **No credit cards**. **Map** p301 H5.

This impressive complex, in a former brewery, has badminton and squash courts, saunas, a mixed fitness room, a women-only fitness centre called Lady Line, and Himaxx, a high-altitude training centre where oxygen levels are dosed to reproduce the thin air of the mountains. There's also a pleasant pub/restaurant if that's too much health for you.

Swimming (indoor)

Every district has an indoor pool. Check the phone book under 'Stadtbad' or visit www.berlinerbaederbetriebe.de for the nearest.

SSE Europa-Sportpark

Paul-Heyse-Strasse 26, Prenzlauer Berg (4218 6120). S8, S41, S42, S85 Landsberger Allee. **Open** 6.30am-10.30pm Mon, Tue, Thur; 8am-10.30pm Wed; 9am-10.30pm Fri; noon-7pm Sat; 10am-6pm Sun. **Admission** €4; €2.50 concessions. **No credit cards**. **Map** p309 S4.

One of the largest swimming pools in Europe. It often hosts international swimming competitions, and is next door to the Velodrom (*see p244*).

Stadtbad Mitte

Gartenstrasse 5, Mitte (3088 0910). S1, S2, S25 Nordbahnhof/tram M8, 12 Nordbahnhof. **Open** 6.30am-10pm Mon, Wed, Fri; 10am-4pm Tue; 6.30am-8pm Thur; 6.30-10pm Fri; 2-9pm Sat; 10am-6pm Sun. **Admission** €4; €2.50 concessions. **No credit cards. Map** p302 M4.
This impressive place was built in 1928. It has a 50m (164ft) pool.

Stadtbad Neukölln

Ganghoferstrasse 3, Neukölln (6824 9812). U7 Rathaus Neukölln. **Open** 2-5pm Mon; 6.45am-6.30pm Tue, Wed; 6.45am-10pm Thur, Fri; 8am-8pm Sat; 8am-2pm Sun. **Admission** €4; €2.50 concessions. **Map** p308 R12.
Described as 'Europe's most beautiful baths' when opened in 1914, they survived the 20th century unscathed and beautiful they remain. Built in Greco-Roman style, the complex features two pools flanked by Ionic columns, with original tiling and mosaics, wood panelling and stained-glass windows.

Stadtbad Schöneberg

Hauptstrasse 39, Schöneberg (780 9930). U7 Eisenacher Strasse. **Open** 10am-10pm Mon; 7am-10pm Tue-Fri; 9am-10pm Sat, Sun. **Admission** €4; €3 concessions for 1hr; €4-€5 concessions for 2hrs. **Map** p306 J11.
Great mixture of old and new. Kids can play in the wave pool while you recharge batteries in the sauna. Busy at peak times, such as Saturday afternoon.

Swimming (open-air)

Before setting out to a pool, phone to make sure it's open (the Berlin service hotline is 0180 310 2020) as the city's financial woes affect opening times. Details of all outdoor public pools can be found at www.berlinerbaederbetriebe.de. There is also plenty of lake swimming. Schlachtensee and Krumme Lanke in the west are attractive, clean and easily accessible by public transport.

Badeschiff Berlin

Eichenstrasse 4, Treptow (533 2030/www.arena-berlin.de). S8, S9, S41, S42, S85 Treptower Park/ bus 265, N48. **Open** 8am-midnight daily. **No credit cards. Map** p308 S9.
This popular commercial operation features a barge converted into a swimming pool, moored on the river Spree. It belongs to the Arena cultural centre (*see p218*), which also has a restaurant, beergarden and concert venue. At press time, the owners were building a sauna and bar to make it a year-round facility.

Freibad Müggelsee

Fürstenwalder Damm 838, Rahnsdorf (648 7777). S3 Rahnsdorf. **Open** *Summer* call for times. **Admission** €4; €2 concessions. **No credit cards.**

North shore bathing beach, complete with nudist camp, on the bank of east Berlin's biggest lake.

Sommerbad Kreuzberg

Prinzenstrasse 113-119, Kreuzberg (616 1080). U1 Prinzenstrasse. **Admission** €4; €2 concessions. **No credit cards. Map** p307 O9.
Known as Prinzenbad, a popular outdoor complex for swimming and sunbathing. It has a 50m (164ft) pool, and one for non-swimmers. Disabled access, nudist area and refreshments.

Strandbad Wannsee

Wannseebadweg, Nikolassee (803 5450). S1, S7 Nikolassee. **Admission** €4; €2.50 concessions. **No credit cards.**
Europe's largest inland beach, with sand, sunbeds, water slides, pedalos, snack stalls and beer garden.

Tennis

An expensive sport in Berlin. Mornings are cheapest, and even then it can cost €15-€30 an hour for an indoor court. **Tennis-Verband Berlin-Brandenburg** (8972 8730, www.tvbb.de) has info on local leagues and clubs.

Tennis Center Weissensee

Roelckestrasse 106, Weissensee (927 4594/ www.tcwsports.com). Bus X54, 155, 156, 158 Rennbahnstrasse. **Open** 7am-midnight Mon-Fri; 8am-midnight Sat, Sun. **Rates** €11-€25. **No credit cards.**
Tennis, badminton and fun ball courts, all indoors. Prices include use of the sauna (open 10am-10pm).

TSB City Sport

Brandenburgische Strasse 53, Wilmersdorf (873 9097/www.citysports-berlin.com). U7 Konstanzer Strasse. **Open** 8am-11pm daily. **Rates** *Tennis* €21-€26. *Squash* €12.50-€19.50. *Badminton* €10.50-€17.50. *Sauna* €2.50-€7.50. **Credit** V. **Map** p305 E10.
Tennis, squash and badminton courts, plus a sauna, solarium, restaurant and beer garden. Coaching is available, along with aerobics and dance classes.

TSF

Richard-Tauber-Damm 36, Marienfelde (742 1091/ www.tsf-sport.de). U6 Alt-Mariendorf. **Open** 7am-11pm daily. **Rates** *Winter* €16-€24. *Summer* €12-€19. **No credit cards.**
Indoor tennis and squash courts, gymnastics, massage, sauna and a restaurant. No membership fee.

Windsurfing, waterskiing, wakeboarding & surfing

The **Müggelsee** in the south-east of Berlin is a popular lake for watersports, as are the **Wannsee** in the south-west and the **Tegeler See** in the north-west. The website www.wassersport-in-berlin.de has loads of information on venues and clubs, all in German.

Arts & Entertainment

WE DON'T JUST DO CITIES

Croatia

'And the winner is...
Time Out, of course'
The Sunday Times

Trips Out of Town

Rügen Island. *See p263.*

Trips Out of Town

Seek out meandering waterways, the solitude of the Baltic or cities crammed with handsome architecture.

All gates lead to Brandenburg – Potsdam's **Brandenburger Tor**. *See p259.*

Berlin is a city in the middle of nowhere. For miles around, fields, lakes and dense woods are scarcely interrupted by a scattering of small towns and villages (*see p258* **The empty quarter**). In fact, water and greenery crowd into the city from all sides, providing a wealth of opportunities for walking, cycling and swimming (*see pp113-120* **Other Districts**).

By far the most popular day trip is to **Potsdam**, which is to Berlin what Versailles is to Paris. There's easily enough there to fill a couple of days. Neighbouring **Babelsberg** has the old UFA film studios, Germany's answer to Hollywood. Another worthwhile, though more sombre, trip is just north of the city to the former concentration camp **Sachsenhausen**.

The **Spreewald**, a forest scattered with small streams, is good for a stroll or boat ride, and can be reached in an hour by train. For the seaside, head north to the Baltic coast and the island of **Rügen**, but plan on staying at least overnight. Two other good trips are south to the historic cities of Saxony: **Leipzig** and **Dresden**.

LEAVING BERLIN

At press time the new Berlin **Hauptbahnhof** (*see p102* **Hub, bub**) and the north–south railway tunnel had yet to open, and Deutsche Bahn had not yet published any timetables that took them into account. However, trains to all destinations will depart from Berlin Hauptbahnhof beginning June 2006, and in many cases journey times should be reduced.

Depending on where they're going, trains will also stop at the new **Nordkreuz** station (formerly Gesundbrunnen), the new **Südkreuz** station (formerly Papestrasse) and also at **Berlin-Spandau**. Once Berlin Hauptbahnhof has opened, only S-Bahn and Regionalbahn trains will stop at Bahnhof Zoo and Ostbahnhof, though at the time of writing there is an energetic campaign for **Bahnhof Zoo** to retain its inter-city status.

Check the Deutsche Bahn website at www.bahn.co.uk for updated information. It also has a useful timetable search facility, with information provided in English.

Around Berlin

Potsdam & Babelsberg

Just outside the city limits to the south-west of Berlin, **Potsdam** is the city's most beautiful neighbour and capital of the state of Brandenburg. Known for its 18th-century baroque architecture, it's a magnet for tourists; summer weekend crowds can be overwhelming, so visit outside peak times if you can.

For centuries, Potsdam was the summer residence of the Hohenzollerns, who were attracted by the area's gently rolling landscape, rivers and lakes. Despite the damage wrought during World War II and by East Germany's socialist planners, much remains of the legacy of these Prussian Kings. The best-known landmark is **Sanssouci**, the huge landscaped park created by Frederick the Great, one of three royal parks flanking the town.

Potsdam has changed considerably in the years since Reunification. In East German times Potsdam's associations with the monarchy were regarded with suspicion; the lack of political will and economic means led to much of the town's historic fabric falling into disrepair or being destroyed. But in 1990 Potsdam was assigned UNESCO World Heritage status; some 80 per cent of the town's historic buildings have been subsequently restored.

The end of East Germany also marked the end of Potsdam's historic role as a garrison town. Until the Soviet withdrawal, some 10,000 troops were stationed here. With their departure, vast barracks and tracts of land to the north of the town were abandoned. The area is currently being redeveloped for civilian use, including the BUGA or Volkspark, with its nature museum, the **Biosphäre**.

THE OLD TOWN

One of the most dominant – if not the prettiest – buildings of historical interest in the old town is the 19th-century **Nikolaikirche**. It is hard to miss the huge dome. Rather more graceful is the mid 18th-century **Altes Rathaus**, diagonally opposite, whose tower was a prison until 1875. Nowadays, the former town hall is used for exhibitions and lectures. Both the Nikolaikirche and the Altes Rathaus were badly damaged in the war and rebuilt in the 1960s. They are all that remain of the original Alter Markt, once one of Potsdam's most beautiful squares.

The **Stadtschloss**, in the centre of town, was substantially damaged during the war and the East German authorities demolished the rest of it in 1960. There are plans to rebuild it, but funding problems mean this is unlikely to

Trips Out of Town

Rügen
Sassnitz
Bergen
Baltic Sea
Binz
Stralsund
Peenemünde
Usedom

Neubrandenburg
Szczecin

Sachsenhausen
POLAND

See pp298-299
BERLIN

Brandenburg
FRANKFURT/ODER
Potsdam

Spreewald
Lübben
Lübbenau
Cottbus

GERMANY

LEIPZIG

DRESDEN

CZECH REPUBLIC

| 0 | | 80 miles |
| 0 | | 120 km |

© Copyright Time Out Group 2006

PRAGUE

Plzeň

happen soon. Private sponsors have already funded the reconstruction of the Fortunaportal, one decorative former entrance to the palace, in the Alter Markt. To get an impression of this square before 1945, take a look at the model in the foyer of the Altes Rathaus.

The area behind the gargantuan Hotel Mercure was once part of the palace gardens. Later, Friedrich Wilhelm I, the Soldier King, turned it into a parade ground. Now it has become a park. If you walk up Breite Strasse, you can see all that is left of the old Stadtschloss. The low red building that now houses the **Filmmuseum Potsdam** is the former *Marstall*, or royal stables. Dating from 1685 and originally an orangery, it is one of the oldest buildings in the town.

The nearby Neuer Markt survived the war intact. At No.1 is the house where Friedrich Wilhelm II was born. The *Kutschstall*, originally a royal stables, now houses the new **Haus der Brandenburgisch-Preussischen Geschichte** with its exhibition charting 800 years of Brandenburg history.

THE BAROQUE AND DUTCH QUARTERS

Potsdam's impressive **baroque quarter** is bounded by Schopenhauerstrasse, Hegelallee, Hebbelstrasse and Charlottenstrasse. Some of the best houses can be found in Gutenbergstrasse and Brandenburger Strasse, Potsdam's pedestrianised shopping drag. Note the pitched roofs with space to accommodate troops – the Soldier King built the quarter in the 1730s. Around the corner is Lindenstrasse 54, once the house of a Prussian officer, later a Stasi detention centre; nowadays visitors to the cells are there of their own volition.

The empty quarter

No other European capital is surrounded by such a sparsely populated landscape as Berlin. This is a region of rare and delicate beauty, too often ignored by visitors. Flat it may be, but the *Land* of Brandenburg deserves more attention than it gets. Forests and lakes are interspersed with water meadows and low gravelly ridges that speak of glaciers that came this way thousands of years ago.

Speeding along the Autobahn, it may seem a boring landscape. But leave the main highways and you'll find empty tree-lined secondary roads that twist and turn through forests and fen to come unexpectedly upon unspoilt villages with neat brick barns, ponds with the statutory quota of ducks and, more often than not, a traditional *Gaststätte* serving beers and improbably large portions of pork with dumplings. At some of the best such hostelries, look for local freshwater fish, notably pike-perch or carp, and off-dry Müller-Thurgau wines from eastern Germany. Against all odds, decent white wines are produced in the region south-west of Berlin, and though rarely found in the capital, they often pop up in the countryside.

Some of the finest country is about 70 kilometres (40 miles) north of the city in an arc from Rheinsberg via Furstenberg to Templin. But travel out of Berlin in any direction to find exquisite unspoilt forests and lakes and, at the right time of year, storks that preside majestically over a village from a manicured nest. On minor roads, expect ferries rather than bridges at the major river crossings, and even the odd stretch of gravel or dirt highway.

Even without a car, it is perfectly feasible to get a flavour of Berlin's hinterland. The **Ostdeutsche Eisenbahn Gesellschaft** (ODEG, www.odeg.info) runs comfortable, modern, glass railway carriages that afford panoramic views from its routes running out of the city to the east. The OE36 runs hourly from Lichtenberg (U5, S5, S7, S75) and Betriebsbahnhof Schöneweide (S8, S9, S45, S46, S85) to Frankfurt-an-der-Oder. The full journey takes 150 minutes, and traverses some of Germany's most unspoilt scenery. Break the journey midway at Wendish-Rietz for boat trips (from Easter until the end of October) on the Scharmützelsee (timetables can be viewed at www.scharmuetzelsee.de/schiffahrt). At Frankfurt there is much GDR-era architecture and the pleasure of wandering over the river into Poland. Those with a real appetite for train travel can return to Berlin on ODEG's other main route, OE60, which loops north through the hills of the Oderbruch to regain the capital from the north-east. This alternative route runs once every two hours, also takes 150 minutes, and terminates at Lichtenberg station.

The fares for these trips aren't very expensive (€10 one-way) – and come even cheaper with a €24 **Brandenburg Ticket**, which allows up to five people to travel together for the price. Further information is available at www.vbbonline.de.

Three baroque town gates – the Nauener Tor, Jäger Tor and the Brandenburger Tor (**photo** *see p256*) – stand on the northern and western edges of the quarter. The latter predates its Berlin namesake by 18 years. On the quarter's eastern edge, two churches bear witness to Potsdam's cosmopolitan past. The Great Elector's 1685 Edict of Potsdam promised refuge to Protestants suffering religious persecution in their homelands, sparking waves of immigration. The Französische Kirche was built for the town's Huguenot community, while St Peter and Paul's in Bassinplatz was built for Catholic immigrants who came to this Protestant area in answer to the Prussian King's call for skilled workers and soldiers.

The **Holländisches Viertel**, or Dutch quarter, is the most attractive part of Friedrich Wilhelm I's new town extension. As part of a failed strategy to attract skilled Dutch immigrants to the town, the King had Dutch builders construct 134 gable-fronted houses. But in this era, Brandenburg was backward and sparsely populated, as a result of war and epidemics, while Holland was one of Europe's most progressive nations. In the **Jan Bouman Haus** in Mittelstrasse 8 you can see an original interior. Today this quarter is filled with upmarket boutiques and restaurants.

THE RUSSIAN INFLUENCE

Another Potsdam curiosity is the Russian Colony of Alexandrowka, 15 minutes' walk north of the town centre. The settlement consists of 13 wood-clad, two-storey dwellings with steeply pitched roofs laid out in the form of a St Andrew's Cross. There is even a Russian Orthodox church with onion dome on the rise behind the houses. Regular services are still held in the Alexander-Newski-Kapelle.

Alexandrowka was built in 1826 by Friedrich Wilhelm III to commemorate the death of Tsar Alexander I, a friend from the Wars of Liberation against Napoleon. The settlement became home to surviving members of a troupe of Russian musicians given into Prussian service by the Tsar in 1812. Two of the houses are still inhabited by the descendants of these men. At the **Teehaus Russische Kolonie** (Alexandrowka 1, 0331 200 6478, closed Mon, main course €8-€14.60), Russian specialities are served by waitresses in folkloric costume.

The area around and to the north of Alexandrowka became the focus of a different Russian presence during the Cold War. The late Wilhelmine villas served as offices for the Soviet administration or as officers' homes. Soviet forces took over buildings used by the Prussian army in the 19th century and later by the Nazis.

One such is the castle-like **Garde-Ulanen-Kaserne** in Jäger Allee, close to the junction with Reiterweg. The recently restored Belvedere, at the top of the hill to the north of Alexandrowka, is the town's highest observation point. It fell into disuse after the Wall went up in 1961, when people were banned from enjoying views over West Berlin.

POTSDAM'S ROYAL PARKS

Back towards the town centre is Potsdam's biggest tourist magnet, **Park Sanssouci**. It's beautiful, but be warned: its main avenues can become overrun and it is not always easy to get into the palaces (guided tours are compulsory and numbers limited).

The park is a legacy of King Frederick the Great, who was attracted to the area by its fine views. He initially had terraced gardens built here, before adding a palace. *Sans souci* means 'without worries' and reveals the King's desire for a sanctuary where he could pursue his philosophical, musical and literary interests. Voltaire was among his guests. His nearby Bildergalerie was the first purpose-built museum in Germany.

After victory in the Seven Years War, Frederick built the huge **Neues Palais** on the park's western edge. Friedrich II's sumptuous suite, as well as the Grottensaal (Grotto Room), Marmorsaal (Marble Room) and Schlosstheater (Palace Theatre), are worth a visit. Other attractions in the park include the Orangery; the Spielfestung, or toy fortress, built for Wilhelm II's sons, complete with a toy cannon that can be fired; the Chinesisches Teehaus (Chinese Teahouse) with its collection of Chinese and Meissen porcelain and the Drachenhaus (Dragonhouse), a pagoda-style café. In the park's south-west corner lies Schloss Charlottenhof, with its blue-glazed entrance and Kupferstichzimmer (copper-plate engraving room), built in the 1830s on the orders of Crown Prince Friedrich Wilhelm IV. Outside Sanssouci in the Breite Strasse is the Dampfmaschinenhaus that pumped water for Sanssouci's fountains, but was built to look like a mosque.

North-east of the town centre is yet another large park complex, the Neuer Garten, designed on the orders of Frederick the Great's nephew and successor to the throne, Friedrich Wilhelm II. In the neo-classical **Marmorpalais** the King died a premature death allegedly as a result of his dissolute lifestyle. At the park's most northern corner is **Schloss Cecilienhof**, the last royal palace to be built in Potsdam. This incongruous, mock-Tudor mansion was built for the Kaiser's son and his wife. Spared wartime damage, in summer 1945 it hosted the Potsdam Conference, where Stalin, Truman and Churchill (replaced by Clement Attlee) met to discuss Germany's future. Inside, you can see the round table where the settlement was negotiated.

During the conference, the Allied leaders lived across the Havel in one of the secluded 19th-century villa districts of Babelsberg. Stalin stayed in Karl-Marx-Strasse 27, Churchill in the Villa Urbig at Virchowstrasse 23 (one of Mies van der Rohe's early buildings) and Truman in the Truman-Villa in Karl-Marx-Strasse 2. These buildings can be viewed from the outside only.

Potsdam's third and most recent royal park, **Park Babelsberg**, also makes for a good walk. In East German times this fell into neglect because it lay so close to the border. Schloss Babelsberg, a neo-Gothic extravaganza inspired by Windsor Castle, nestles among its wooded slopes. Another architectural curiosity is the Flatowturm, an observation point in mock-medieval style close to the Glienicker See.

Also on the east side of the Havel, not too far south of Potsdam's main station, is the Telegraphenberg – once the site of a telegraph station. In 1921 it became the site of Erich Mendelsohn's expressionist **Einsteinturm**, commissioned to house an observatory that could confirm the General Theory of Relativity. A wonderfully whimsical building, it was one of the first products of the inter-war avant-garde.

On the nearby Brauhausberg, there is one last reminder of Potsdam's complex, multi-layered past. The square tower rising up from the trees is the present seat of Brandenburg's state parliament. In East German days, the building was known as the Kremlin because it served as local Communist Party headquarters. Originally, it was the 'Kriegsschule' – the war school – where young men trained to be officers in the German imperial army.

HOLLYWOOD BABELSBERG

The main attraction in Potsdam's eastern neighbour, Babelsberg, is the film studio complex, sections of which are open to the public in theme-park form. In the 1920s this was the world's largest studio outside Hollywood and it was here that Fritz Lang's *Metropolis*, Josef von Sternberg's *The Blue Angel* and other masterpieces of the era were produced. During the Nazi period it churned out thrillers, light entertainment and propaganda pieces such as Leni Riefenstahl's *Triumph of the Will*. And more than 700 feature films were made here in the communist era.

The studios were privatised after Reunification and now there are state-of-the-art facilities for all phases of film and television production, and offices for all manner of media and production companies. The **Filmpark** has an assortment of attractions, ranging from themed restaurants and rides to set tours and stunt displays, but it's all pretty tacky stuff.

Altes Rathaus

Am Alten Markt (0331 289 6336/www.altesrathaus potsdam.de). Tram X98, 90, 92, 93, 96 Alter Markt. **Open** 10am-6pm Tue-Sun. **Admission** €3; €2 concessions. **No credit cards.**

Biosphäre

Georg-Hermann-Allee 99 (0331 550 740/www. biosphaere-potsdam.net). **Open** 9am-6pm (last entry 4.30pm) Mon-Fri; 10am-7pm (last entry 5.30pm) Sat, Sun. **Admission** €9.50; €8 concessions; €6.50 under-14s. **No credit cards.**

Filmmuseum Potsdam

Marstall (0331 271 810). Tram X98, 90, 92, 93, 96 Alter Markt. **Open** 10am-6pm daily. **Admission** €3; €2 concessions. **No credit cards.**
The museum's permanent exhibition opened in April 2004. Exploring 90 years of filmmaking at the Babelsberg studios, it focuses on the history of DEFA, East Germany's sole filmmaking company.

Filmpark Babelsberg

August-Bebel-Strasse 26-53, entrance on Grossbeerenstrasse (0331 721 2717/www. filmpark.de). S1 Babelsberg/bus 601, 602, 618, 619, 690. **Open** Apr-Oct 10am-6pm daily. **Admission** €17; €15.50 concessions. **No credit cards.**

Gedenkstätte Lindenstrasse

Lindenstrasse 54 (0331 289 6136). Tram 94, 96 Dortusstrasse. **Open** 10am-6pm Tue, Thur, Sat. **Admission** €1.50. **No credit cards.**
East German secret police once interrogated people in this warren of cells.

Haus der Brandenburgisch-Preussischen Geschichte

Kutschstall, am Neuen Markt (0331 620 8549/www. hbpg.de). Tram X98, 90, 92, 93, 96 Alter Markt. **Open** 10am-6pm Tue, Thur-Sun; 10am-8pm Wed. **Admission** €5; €4 concessions. **No credit cards.**

Jan Bouman Haus

Mittelstrasse 8 (0331 280 3773). Tram 90, 92, 95 Nauener Tor. **Open** 1-6pm Mon, Fri; 11am-6pm Sat, Sun. **Admission** €3; €1 concessions. **No credit cards.**

Marmorpalais

Im Neuen Garten (0331 969 4246). Bus 692. **Open** Apr-Oct 10am-5pm Tue-Sun. Nov-Mar 10am-4pm Sat, Sun. **Admission** €3; €2.50 concessions. **No credit cards.**

Nikolaikirche

Am Alten Markt (0331 291 682/www.nikolaipotsdam. de). Tram X98, 90, 92, 93, 96 Alter Markt. **Open** 2-5pm Mon; 10am-5pm Tue-Sun. **Admission** free.

Sanssouci

Potsdam (0331 969 4202/www.spsg.de). Bus X15, 695. **Open** Palace & exhibition buildings Apr-Oct 9am-5pm Tue-Sun; Nov-Mar 9am-4pm daily. Park

Incongruous conference venue **Schloss Cecilienhof**.

9am-dusk daily. **Admission** *Palace & exhibition buildings* €8; €5 concessions. *Park* free. **Credit** MC, V. Each of the palaces and buildings has its own closing days each month and some are only open mid May to mid October. Phone for details. **Photo** *p262*.

Schloss Cecilienhof

Im Neuen Garten (0331 969 4244/www.spsg.de). Bus 692. **Open** *Apr-Oct* 9am-5pm Tue-Sun. *Nov-Mar* 9am-4pm Tue-Sun. **Admission** €5; €4 concessions. **No credit cards**.

Where to eat & drink

B-West (Zeppelinstrasse 146, 0331 951 0798, main course €5-€10) attracts a lively, young crowd and serves simple German cuisine. The cosy **Café Heider** (Friedrich-Ebert-Strasse 29, 0331 270 5596, main course €3-€15) offers excellent coffee and cake, plus a wide range of main dishes. **Kinocafé Melodie** (Friedrich-Ebert-Strasse 12, 0331 620 0699, admission €3) serves no food, but is a popular watering hole. **Matschkes Galerie Café** (Alleestrasse 10, 0331 270 1210, main course €4-€8) serves good simple German and Russian cooking at a reasonable price and has some outdoor courtyard seating. There is an assortment of cafés, pubs and restaurants along pedestrianised Brandenburger Strasse, most of which have tables outside in summer.

Theatre & nightlife

Lindenpark (Stahnsdorfer Strasse 76-8, 0331 747 970, www.lindenpark.de) in Babelsberg has regular club nights and gigs. **Theater Schiff** (Lange Brücke, 0331 280 0100, www.theater schiff-potsdam.de), moored close to the Hans-Otto-Theater, is a vessel offering theatre, cinema, cabaret and discos. **Waschhaus** (Schiffbauergasse, 0331 271 560, www. waschhaus.de), a large club just outside Potsdam centre, has both DJs and live acts.

Getting there

By train

Both Potsdam and Babelsberg can be reached via the S1 S-Bahn line. It takes just under an hour from Mitte and you will need a ticket that covers the C zone. From some parts of Berlin it's easier to take the S7 to Wannsee, and change to the S1 there. There is also a direct, hourly Regionalbahn train to Medienstadt Babelsberg that takes just 20mins from Mitte, and a number of Regional trains to Potsdam Hauptbahnhof. The station is across the river from the centre of town.

Getting around

Potsdam is small compared to Berlin, but it's still too big and spread out to do everything on foot. The tram and bus network covers everything, however, and the routes aren't difficult to figure out. A **Potsdam Card**, available from the tourist office for €9.80, provides free public transport as well as discounted entry to most attractions.

Tourist information

Potsdam Tourismus Service

Brandenburger Strasse 3 (0331 275 580/www. potsdam-tourism.com). Tram 94, 96/bus X15, 695 Luisenplatz. **Open** *Apr-Oct* 9.30am-6pm Mon-Fri; 9.30am-4pm Sat, Sun. *Nov-Mar* 10am-6pm Mon-Fri; 9.30am-2pm Sat.

Trips Out of Town

Sanssouci – the palace in the park. *See p260.*

Sachsenhausen

Many Nazi concentration camps have been preserved and opened to the public as memorials and museums. Sachsenhausen is the one nearest to Berlin.

Immediately upon coming to power, Hitler set about rounding up and interning his opponents. From 1933 to 1935 an old brewery on this site was used to hold them. The present camp received its first prisoners in July 1936. It was designated with cynical euphemism as a *Schutzhaftlager* ('Protective Custody Camp'). The first *Schutzhaftlagern* were political opponents of the government: communists, social democrats, trade unionists. Soon, the variety of prisoners widened to include anyone guilty of 'anti-social' behaviour, gays and Jews.

About 6,000 Jews were forcibly brought here after Kristallnacht alone. It was here that some of the first experiments in organised mass murder were made: thousands of POWs from the Eastern Front were killed at Station Z.

The SS evacuated the camp in 1945 and began marching 33,000 inmates to the Baltic, where they were to be packed into boats and sunk in the sea. Some 6,000 died during the march before the survivors were rescued by the Allies. Another 3,000 prisoners were found in the camp's hospital when it was captured on 22 April 1945.

The horror did not end here. After the German capitulation, the Russian secret police, the MVD, reopened Sachsenhausen as Camp 7 for the detention of war criminals; in fact, it was filled with anyone suspected of opposition. Following the fall of the GDR, the remains of some 10,000 prisoners were found in mass graves.

On 23 April 1961 the partially restored camp was opened to the public as a national monument and memorial. The inscription over the entrance, *Arbeit Macht Frei* ('Work Sets You Free'), could be found over the gates of all concentration camps.

The parade ground, where morning roll-call was taken and from where inmates were required to witness executions on the gallows, stands before the two remaining barrack blocks. One is now a museum and the other a memorial hall and cinema, where a film about the history of the camp is shown. Next door stands the prison block.

There are another couple of small exhibitions in buildings in the centre of the camp (no English labelling), but perhaps the grimmest site here is the subsiding remains of Station Z, the surprisingly small extermination block.

A map traces the path the condemned would follow, depending upon whether they were to be shot (the bullets were retrieved and reused) or gassed. All ended up in the neighbouring ovens. Note: it's a good idea to hire an audio guide (available in English) at the gate.

KZ Sachsenhausen

Strasse der Nationen 22, Oranienburg (0330 120 00/ www.gedenkstaette-sachsenhausen.de). **Open** *Apr-Sept* 8.30am-6pm Tue-Sun. *Oct-Mar* 8.30am-4.30pm Tue-Sun. **Admission** free.

Getting there

By train

Oranienburg is at the northern end of the S1 S-Bahn line (40mins from Mitte). From the station follow signs to 'Gedenkstätte Sachsenhausen'. It's a 20min walk.

Further Afield

Spreewald

This filigree network of tiny rivers, streams and canals, dividing patches of deciduous forest and farmland, is one of the loveliest excursions from Berlin. German author Theodor Fontane described the Spreewald as how Venice would have looked 1,500 years ago. It gets crowded in season, particularly at weekends, giving the lie to its claim to be one of the most perfect wilderness areas in Europe. Still, out of season, you can have the area to yourself.

About 100 kilometres (60 miles) south-east of Berlin, the Spree bisects the area into the **Unterspreewald** and Oberspreewald. For the former, Schepzig or Lübben are the best start points; Lübben is 15 kilometres (nine miles) beyond Schepzig on the train to Lübbenau.

The character of both sections is very similar. The **Oberspreewald** is perhaps better, for its 500 square kilometres (190 square miles) of territory contain more than 300 natural and artificial channels, called *Fliesse*. You can travel around these on punts – rent your own or join a larger group – and also take out kayaks. Motorised boats are forbidden. Here and there in the forest are restaurants and small hotels. The tourist information centres in Lübbenau will provide you with maps and walk routes.

The local population belongs to the Sorbish minority, a Slav people related to Czechs and Slovaks. Their own language is found in street names, newspapers and so on. This adds an air of exoticism, unlike the folk festivals laid on for tourists in the high season.

Where to eat & drink

There are plenty of eating and drinking options in Lübben and Lübbenau, and little to choose between most of them. Follow your nose.

Getting there

By train
There are regular trains to Lübben and Lübbenau. Journey time is around an hour to Lübben and an extra 15mins to Lübbenau.

Tourist information

Tourist websites (www.spreewald-info.com or www.spreewald-online.de) are good sources of information about the area and allow you to book hotel rooms online.

Haus für Mensch & Natur
Schulstrasse 9, Lübbenau (0354 289 210/892 130). **Open** *Apr-Oct* 10am-5pm daily. **Admission** free.
In an old schoolhouse, the 'House for Mankind & Nature' is the visitor centre for the Spreewald Biosphere Reservation. It has an exhibition about the environmental importance of the Spreewald.

Spreewald Information
Ehm-Welk-Strasse 15, Lübbenau (0354 236 68/www. spreewald-online.de). **Open** *Apr-Oct* 9am-6pm Mon-Fri; 9am-4pm Sat. *Nov-Mar* 9am-4pm Mon-Fri.

Rügen

The Baltic coast used to be the favoured holiday destination of the GDR citizen; post-Reunification it is still the most accessible stretch of seaside for Berliners. The coast forms the northern boundary of the modern state of Mecklenburg-Vorpommern. Bismarck famously said of the area: 'When the end of the world comes, I shall go to Mecklenburg, because there everything happens a hundred years later.'

The large island of Rügen (**photo** *p264*) is gradually resuming its rivalry with Sylt in the North Sea – both claim to be the principal north German resort. The island is undoubtedly beautiful, with its white chalk cliffs, beechwoods and beaches. Most people stay in east-coast resorts such as Binz (the largest and best known), Sellin and Göhren. In July and August Rügen can get crowded (be sure to pre-book accommodation), and the island's handful of restaurants and lack of late-night bars mean visitors are early to bed and early to rise. Go out of season and enjoy the solitude.

Where to stay & eat

Most accommodation on Rügen is in private houses. Your best bet is to contact the local tourist office (*see below*), which will help you find a room. Camping is very popular on Rügen. Binz offers the best selection of places to eat.

Getting there

By train
There are some direct trains to Bergen on Rügen, but the journey usually involves changing trains at Stralsund. Journey time is 3-4hrs.

Tourist information

The head office in Bergen provides information, but cannot book rooms; try the other offices if you need your accommodation to be sorted out. For general information, there is also the website www.ruegen.net.

Old-school summer fun on **Rügen**.
See p263.

Bergen *Bahnhofstrasse 15 (0383 880 770).* **Open** *Summer* 8am-6pm Mon-Fri; 9am-noon Sat. *Winter* 9am-4.30pm Mon, Wed, Thur; 9am-noon, 1-6pm Tue; 1am-3pm Fri.

Binz *Heinrich-Heine-Strasse 7 (0383 9314 8148).* **Open** *Summer* 9am-6pm Mon-Fri; 10am-6pm Sat, Sun. *Winter* 9am-4pm Mon-Fri; 10am-4pm Sat, Sun.

Göhren *Postrasse 9 (0383 086 6790).* **Open** *Summer* 9am-noon, 1-6pm Mon-Fri; 9am-noon Sat. *Winter* 9am-noon, 1-4.30pm Mon, Wed, Thur; 9am-noon, 1-6pm Tue; 9am-noon, 1-3pm Fri.

Sellin *August-Bebel-Strasse 5 (0383 038 7006).* **Open** *Summer* 9am-7pm Mon-Fri. *Winter* 9am-4pm Mon-Fri.

Dresden

Destroyed twice and rebuilt one and a half times, the capital of Saxony – 100 kilometres (60 miles) south of Berlin – boasts one of Germany's best art museums and many historic buildings. A few more pieces of the city, including the Frauenkirche, have been restored for the city's 800-year anniversary in 2006, a year that sees a host of festivals and cultural events.

Modern Dresden is built on the ruins of its past. A fire consumed Altendresden on the bank of the Elbe in 1685, and the city was rebuilt. On the night of 13 February 1945 the biggest of Sir Arthur 'Bomber' Harris's raids caused huge firestorms that killed up to 100,000 people. After the war, Dresden was twinned with Coventry, and Benjamin Britten's *War Requiem* was given its first performance in the Hofkirche by musicians from both towns. Under the GDR reconstruction was erratic,

but a maze of cranes and scaffolding sprang up in the 1990s and the city started to make up for lost time.

An unappealing resemblance to Coventry is apparent walking from the station to the centre along hideous Prager Strasse. But press on through the tower blocks and 1960s shopping arcades (stopping at the tourist office for a map) and the older city starts to assert itself.

Dresden's major attractions are the buildings from the reign of Augustus the Strong (1670-1733). The Hofkirche and the Zwinger complex are fine examples of the city's baroque legacy.

The main draw for art lovers is the **Gemäldegalerie Alte Meister** in the Zwinger. There's usually more art at the **Albertinum**, which contains the Grünes Gewölbe, a collection of Augustus's jewels and trinkets, but it's closed for a refurb until 2008.

Building was continued by Augustus's successor, Augustus III, who then lost to Prussia in the Seven Years War (1756-63). Frederick the Great destroyed much of the city during the war, though not the lovely riverside promenade of the Brühlsche Terrasse in the old part of town. A victorious Napoleon ordered the demolition of the city's defences in 1809.

By the Zwinger is the Semperoper, an opera house – fully restored to its earlier elegance in 1985 – named after its architect Gottfried Semper (1838-41).

The industrialisation of Dresden heralded a new phase of construction that produced the Rathaus (Town Hall, 1905-10) at Dr-Külz-Ring; the Hauptbahnhof (1892-5) at the end of Prager Strasse; the Yenidze cigarette factory (1912) in

Könneritzstrasse, designed to look like a mosque; and the grandiose Landtagsgebäude (completed to plans by Paul Wallot, designer of Berlin's Reichstag, in 1907) at Heinrich-Zille-Strasse 11. The finest example of inter-war architecture is Wilhelm Kreis's Deutsches Hygienemuseum (1929) at Lingner Platz 1, built to house the German Institute of Hygiene.

The Neue Synagoge (Rathenauplatz) was dedicated in Dresden in November 2001, 63 years after its predecessor (built by Semper in 1838-40) was destroyed in the Nazi pogroms.

Reconstruction of the domed **Frauenkirche** at Neumarkt was finally completed and the restored cathedral reconsecrated in October 2005. The Communists had left it as a heap of rubble throughout the Cold War period as a reminder of Allied aggression. In the end its restoration was funded partly by private donations from the UK and US. The golden orb and cross that top the dome were built by goldsmith Alan Smith, son of one of the British pilots who took part in the 1945 bombings.

The **Striezelmarkt**, founded in 1434, is the oldest Christmas market in Germany. It is held on Altstädtermarkt every December and is named after the savoury pretzel you will see everyone eating. Dresden is also home to the best Stollen, a German variety of yuletide cake.

The Neustadt – on the Elbe's north bank – literally means 'new town', although it is over 300 years old. Having escaped major war damage, the Neustadt has much of its original architecture intact. When Augustus the Strong commissioned the rebuilding of Dresden in 1685, he pictured a new Venice. The Neustadt doesn't quite measure up, but the 18th-century townhouses in Hauptstrasse and Königstrasse are charming.

To avoid the tourist spillover from the Altstadt, head north and east of Albertplatz. Recently, a wealth of boutiques, cafés and bars has sprung up here in the cobblestone streets.

Albertinum

Brühlsche Terrasse (0351 491 4622/ www.skd-dresden.de).
The Albertinum is closed for renovation until 2008. Until then, the paintings of the Gemäldegalerie will be at the Residenzschloss on Sophienstrasse and some sculpture will join the Gemäldegalerie Alte Meister (*see below*) at the Zwinger.

Gemäldegalerie Alte Meister

Zwinger, Theaterplatz (0351 491 4622/www.skd-dresden.de). **Open** 10am-6pm Tue-Sun. **Admission** €6; €3.50 concessions. **No credit cards**.
A superb collection of Old Masters, particularly Italian Renaissance and Flemish. There is also porcelain from nearby Meissen, and collections of armour, weapons, clocks and scientific equipment.

Semperoper

Tickets: Aldstädter Wache, Theaterplatz (0351 491 10/www.skd-dresden.de). **Open** Box office 10am-6pm Mon-Fri; 10am-1pm Sat. **Tickets** vary. **Credit** AmEx, MC, V.

Where to stay

The trendy **Arthotel Dresden** (Ostra-Allee 33, 0351 49220, www.artotel.de, rates €160-€215) is decorated with 600 works by local

Dresden – classier than Coventry, but not quite Venice. *See p264.*

painter AR Penck. **Bastei/Königstein/ Lilienstein** (0351 4856 6388/6442/7777, www.ibis-hotel.de, rates €62-€95) are three functional tower-block hotels on Prager Strasse between the railway station and Altstadt. The **Hotel Bayerischer Hof Dresden** (Antonstrasse 33-5, 0351 829 370, www.bayerischer-hof-dresden.de, rates €85-€160) has comfy rooms and a personal feel; the **Bülow-Residenz** (Rähnitzgasse 19, 0351 800 30, www.buelow-residenz.de, rates €120-€395) offers elegant, old-world luxury. In the Neustadt, the **Hostel Mondpalast** (Katharinenstrasse 11-13, 0351 563 4050, www.mondpalast.de, rates €13.50-€34) is a decent budget option. **Hotel Smetana** (Schlüterstrasse 25, 0351 256 080, www. hotel-smetana.de, rates €59-€129) is a pleasant three-star, east of the centre.

Where to eat & drink

Caroussel, Caroussel (Bülow-Residenz, Rähnitzgasse 19, 0351 800 30, closed Mon & Sun, main course €30-€40), a contemporary German restaurant, has fine cooking and a leafy courtyard for summer. **Piccola Capri** (Alaunstrasse 93, 0351 801 4848, closed Sun, main course €6.50-€15.50) is one of Neustadt's best Italians. In the same part of town, there are good bars and cafés on and around Alaunstrasse in the area north-east of Albertplatz.

Nightlife

The Neustadt is best for nightlife. Clubs such as **Déjà-Vu** (Rothenburgerstrasse 37, 0351 802 3040) and **Flower Power** (Eschenstrasse 11, 0351 804 9814) have different DJs every night.

Getting there

By train
Regular direct trains take about 2hrs from Berlin.

Tourist information

Dresden Tourist Information
Ostra-Allee 11 (0351 491 920/www.dresden-tourist.de). **Open** 10am-6pm Mon-Fri; 10am-4pm Sat. **Other locations**: Schinkelwache, Theaterplatz (0351 491 920).

Leipzig

One of Germany's most important trade centres and former second city of the GDR, Leipzig is Bach's city, a centre of education and culture, and the place where East Germany's mass movement for political change began. Set in north-west

Saxony, some 130 kilometres (80 miles) south-west of Berlin, Leipzig traces its origins back to a settlement founded around AD 800 by the Sorbs, a Slavic people who venerated the lime tree. They called the place *Lipzk*, 'place of limes'.

Today's city contains a pedestrianised old centre, with Renaissance and baroque churches, narrow lanes and an ancient university. Bombed to bits during World War II, it is undergoing further renovation thanks to its role as one of 12 host cities of the 2006 World Cup. Much of it, from its vast central train station to the focal Markt itself, is currently under construction, the spacious market square off-limits to pedestrians while builders put in a huge roadway beneath the city to free the centre of traffic.

Leipzig Hauptbahnhof (photo *p267*) stands on the north-east edge of the centre, surrounded by a ring road that follows the course of the old city walls. Much of the ring road is lined with parks; most of the city's attractions can be found within its limits.

The first place to head is the Leipzig Tourist Service office, diagonally left across tram-strewn Willy-Brand-Platz from the front of the train station. Pick up a guide to the city in English (which includes a map) and head for Markt, the old market square, to get your bearings. The eastern side of the square is occupied by the lovely Altes Rathaus (Old Town Hall), built in 1556-7. It now houses the **Stadtgeschichtliches Museum** (Town Museum). On the square's south side are the huge bay windows of the Könighaus, once a haunt of Saxony's rulers when visiting the city (the notoriously rowdy Peter the Great of Russia also once stayed here).

The church off the south-west corner of Markt is the **Thomaskirche**, where Johan Sebastian Bach spent 27 years as choirmaster of the famous St Thomas's Boys Choir; the great man is buried in the chancel and his statue stands outside the church. Here, too, is the prefab Thomasshop, which details on its side a Bach-themed stroll around the city. Opposite the church in the Bosehaus is the **Bach-Museum**.

South from the Thomaskirche towards the south-west corner of the ring road is the Neues Rathaus (New Town Hall), whose origins are 16th century, though the current buildings are only about 100 years old.

Back at the Altes Rathaus, immediately behind the building, is the delightful little chocolate box of the Alte Börse (Old Stock Exchange), built in 1687, and fronted by a statue of Goethe, who studied at Leipzig University. Follow his gaze towards the entrance to Mädler Passage, Leipzig's finest shopping arcade, within which is Auerbachs

The vast **Leipzig Hauptbahnhof**. *See p266*.

Keller, one of the oldest and most famous restaurants in Germany. It was in Auerbachs, where he often used to drink, that Goethe set a scene in *Faust*, which saw Faust and Mephistopheles boozing with students before riding off on a barrel.

North of the Alte Börse is Sachsenplatz, site of the city's main outdoor market, and new home of the **Museum der Bildenden Künste** (Museum of Arts Picture Gallery).

Just south-east of here is the **Nikolaikirche**, Leipzig's proud symbol of its new freedom. This medieval church, with its baroque interior, is the place where regular free-speech meetings started in 1982. These evolved into the 'Swords to Ploughshares' peace movement, which led to the first anti-GDR demonstration on 4 September 1989 in the Nikolaikirchhof.

West of here, on the edge of the ring road, is the **Museum in der 'Runden Ecke'** (Museum in the 'Round Corner', nickname of the building that once housed the local Stasi headquarters and now has an exhibition detailing its nefarious methods). North of here, outside the ring road, is **Leipzig Zoo**.

In the south-east corner of the ring road rises the drab tower block of Leipzig University. Rebuilt in 1970 to resemble an opened book on its side, this modern monstrosity is ironically one of Europe's oldest centres of learning; besides Goethe, alumni include Nietzsche, Schumann and Wagner. The university is responsible for running the **Ägyptisches Museum**; nearby is the **Grassi Museum für Kunsthandwerk**.

The university tower stands at the south-eastern corner of Augustplatz, a project of GDR Communist Party leader Walter Ulbricht, himself a Leipziger. Next door to it are the brown glass-fronted buildings of the **Gewandhaus**, home of the Leipziger Gewandhaus Orchester, one of the world's finest orchestras. On the square's northern side stands the **Opernhaus Leipzig** (opened in 1960), which also has an excellent reputation.

Ägyptisches Museum
Burgstrasse 21 (0341 973 7010/www.uni-leipzig.de/ ~egypt). **Open** 1-5pm Tue-Sat; 10am-1pm Sun. **Admission** €2; €1 concessions. **Credit** AmEx, MC, V.

Bach-Museum
Thomaskirchhof 16 (0341 913 7202/www.bach-leipzig.de). **Open** 10am-5pm daily. **Admission** €3; €2 concessions. *Tour* €6; €4 concessions. **No credit cards**.
A collection of documents, instruments and furniture from Bach's time, used to illustrate his work and influence on others.

Gewandhaus
Augustusplatz 8 (0341 127 0309/www.gewandhaus. de). **Open** *Box office* 10am-6pm Mon-Fri; 10am-2pm Sat. **Tickets** vary. **Credit** AmEx, DC, MC.

Grassi Museum für Kunsthandwerk
Neumarkt 20 (0341 213 3719/www.grassi museum.de). **Open** 10am-6pm Tue, Thur-Sun; 10am-8pm Wed. **Admission** €4; €2 concessions. **No credit cards**.
Founded in 1874 and now in a temporary home, this was a major centre for applied art in the 1920s.

Trips Out of Town

Leipzig Zoo

Pfaffendorfer Strasse 29 (0341 593 3500/www.zoo leipzig.de). **Open** 9am-dusk daily. **Admission** €10; €5-€8.50 concessions. **No credit cards.**
All the usual family favourites are here: lions, tigers, orang-utans, polar bears and hippos.

Museum der Bildenden Künste

Katarienen Strasse 10 (0341 216 9914/www. mdbk.de). **Open** 10am-6pm Tue, Thur-Sun; noon-8pm Wed. **Admission** €2.50; €1 concessions; free 2nd Sun of mth. *Temporary exhibitions* €6; €4 concessions. **No credit cards.**
The gallery's 2,200-strong collection stretches from 15th- and 16th-century Dutch, Flemish and German paintings to expressionism and GDR art. Artists include Dürer, Rembrandt and Rubens.

Museum in der 'Runden Ecke'

Dittrichring 24 (0341 961 2443/www.runde-ecke-leipzig.de). **Open** 10am-6pm daily. *Tour* 3pm daily. **Admission** free. *Tour* €3; €2 concessions. **No credit cards.**
An interesting look at the Stasi's frightening yet ridiculous methods – collecting scents of suspected people in jars, say – and a hilarious section on Stasi disguises. No English labelling.

Nikolaikirche

Nikolaikirchhof 3 (0341 960 5270/www. nikolaikirche-leipzig.de). **Open** 10am-noon Mon, Tue, Thur, Fri; 4-6pm Wed. **Admission** free.

Opernhaus Leipzig

Augustusplatz 12 (0341 126 10/www.oper-leipzig.de). **Open** *Box office* 10am-8pm Mon-Fri; 10am-4pm Sat; 1hr before performances Sun. **Tickets** varies. **No credit cards.**
Call for information about tours of the building.

Stadtgeschichtliches Museum

Altes Rathaus, Markt 1 (0341 965 130/www. stadtgeschichtliches-museum-leipzig.de). **Open** 10am-6pm Tue-Sun. **Admission** €2.50; €2 concessions. **No credit cards.**

Thomaskirche

Thomaskirchhof 18 (0341 212 4681/www. thomaskirche.org). **Open** 9am-6pm daily. **Admission** free.

Where to stay

Leipzig regularly holds major trade fairs, during which time rooms are in shorter supply and rates increase by at least 15 per cent. The following prices are standard rates, not applicable to trade fairs or during the 2006 World Cup in mid June.
Accento Hotel Leipzig (Taucher Strasse 260, 0341 926 20, www.accento-hotel.de, rates €59-€165) has stylish rooms and polite staff. **Adagio Minotel Leipzig** (Seeburgstrasse 96, 0341 216 699, www.hotel-adagio.de, rates

€67-€160) offers individually furnished rooms and a central location. **Hotel Vivaldi** (Wittenburger Strasse 87, 0341 903 60, www.hotel-vivaldi.de, rates from €60) is a friendly, comfortable three-star only a short tram hop from the station. Rooms have baths and breakfast is taken on a pleasant terrace. For art nouveau luxury, try the **Seaside Park Hotel** (Richard-Wagner-Strasse 7, 0341 985 20, www.parkhotelleipzig.de, rates €100-€178). The tourist office (*see below*) can help you out with budget options.

Where to eat

Apels Garten (Kolonnadenstrasse 2, 0341 960 7777, main course €8-€17) is a pretty restaurant that serves imaginative German cooking. **Auerbachs Keller** (Mädlerpassage, Grimmaische Strasse 2-4, 0341 216 100, set menus €11-24), set in a 1525 beerhall, has a gourmet menu and a cheaper version: both have classic Saxon cuisine (schnitzel, dumplings, pork and sauerkraut). **Barthels Hof** (Hainstrasse 1, 0341 141 310, main course €9.20-€17.60) offers hearty Saxon cooking in a cosy panelled *Gasthaus*. **El Matador** (Friedrich-Ebert-Strasse 108, 0341 980 0876, closed Sun, main course €8-€15) serves decent Spanish food.

Nightlife

The central nightlife hub around the Markt is on the short, cobbled stretch of Barfussgäschen, but apart from the attractive café/restaurant **Spizz** (Markt 9, 0341 960 8043) on the corner, the terrace bars here are pretty standard. You're better off exploring bar-lined Gottschedstrasse, a short walk west of the old town, with venues such as **Barcelona** (No.12, 0341 212 6128) and upmarket cocktail bar **Chocolate** (No.1, 0341 225 2727). After hours, try the huge **Tanzpalast** (Bosestrasse 1, 0341 960 0596, admission €5), where there's live music on Wednesdays and Fridays.

Getting there

By train

Regular trains from Berlin will take only an hour to reach Leipzig once the new Berlin Hauptbahnhof (*see p102* **Hub, bub**) is up and running.

Tourist information

Leipzig Tourist Service

Richard-Wagner-Strasse 1 (0341 710 4260/4265/ www.leipzig.de). **Open** 9am-6pm Mon-Fri; 9am-4pm Sat, Sun.

Directory

Features

Directory

Getting Around

As we went to press in early 2006, the old Hauptbahnhof Lehrter Bahnhof had not yet reopened as the new **Berlin Hauptbahnhof** (Central Station; *see p102* **Hub, bub**). This was to happen at the end of May 2006. New official maps of the city's transport system were not ready but it seems there will be few radical changes to Berlin's internal public transport. A north–south rail link opens between Hauptbahnhof and Potsdamer Platz, and a short new section of U-Bahn between Hauptbahnhof and the Brandenburg Gate is set to begin shuttling in late 2007. Two S-Bahn stations are reinvented as intercity stop-offs: Gesundbrunnen becomes Nordkreuz; Papestrasse becomes Südkreuz. These changes are not reflected on the public transport map on pp318-319.

Arriving & leaving

By air

Until the new **Berlin-Brandenburg International Airport** is ready in 2011, Berlin is served by three airports: **Tegel**, **Schönefeld** and **Tempelhof**. Information in English on all of them (including departure and arrival times) can be found at www.berlin-airport.de.

Tegel Airport

Airport information: 0180 500 0186/www.berlin-airport.de. **Open** 4am-midnight daily. **Map** p301 C1.
Most flights to and from Berlin use the compact Tegel Airport, just 8km (5 miles) north-west of Mitte. The airport contains tourist information, exchange facilities, shops,

restaurants, bars and car rental desks. A cab can drop you right by the check-in desk and departure gate.
Buses 109 and X9 (the express version) run via Luisenplatz and the Kurfürstendamm to Zoologischer Garten (also known as Zoo Station, Bahnof Zoo or just Zoo) in western Berlin. Tickets cost €2.10 (and can also be used on U-Bahn and S-Bahn services). Buses run every five to 15 minutes, and take 30-40 minutes to reach Zoo. At Zoo there are rail and tourist information offices (*see p271*), and you can connect to anywhere in the city (same tickets are valid). You can take bus 109 to Jakob-Kaiser-Platz U-Bahn (U7), or bus 128 to Kurt-Schumacher-Platz U-Bahn (U6), and proceed on the underground from there. One ticket can be used for the combined journey (€2.10).
The JetExpressBusTXL is the direct link to the new Hauptbahnhof and Mitte. This runs from Tegel to Alexanderplatz with useful stops at Beusselstrasse S-Bahn (connects with the Ringbahn), Berlin Hauptbahnhof (regional and intercity trains, as well as the S-Bahn), Unter den Linden S-Bahn (north and south trains on the S1 and S2 lines). It costs €2.10, runs every 15 or 20 minutes between 6am-11pm, and takes 30-40 minutes.
A taxi to anywhere central will cost around €20-€25, and takes 20-30 minutes, depending on traffic and precise destination.

Schönefeld Airport

Airport information: 0180 500 0186/www.berlin-airport.de. **Open** 24hrs daily.
The former airport of East Berlin is 18km (11 miles) south-east of the city centre. It's small, and much of the traffic is to eastern Europe and the Middle and Far East, but UK budget airlines also use it. The usual foreign exchange, shops, snack bars and car hire facilities can be found here.
Train is the best means of reaching the city centre. S-Bahn Flughafen Schönefeld is a five-minute walk from the terminal (a free S-Bahn shuttle bus runs every ten minutes between 6am-10pm; at other times, bus 171 also runs to the station). From here, the Airport Express train runs to Mitte (25 minutes to Alexanderplatz), Berlin Hauptbahnhof (30 minutes) and Zoo (35 minutes) every half hour from 5am-11.30pm. Be warned that the final

destination of the trains varies, so check the timetable for your stop. You can also take S-Bahn line S9, which runs into the centre every 20 minutes (40 minutes to Alexanderplatz, 50 minutes to Zoo) stopping along the way. The S45 line from Schönefeld connects with the Ringbahn, also running every 20 minutes. Bus 171 from the airport takes you to Rudow U-Bahn (U7), from where you can connect with the underground.
Tickets from the airport to the city cost €2.10, and can be used on any combination of bus, U-Bahn, S-Bahn and tram. There are ticket machines at the airport and at the station.
A taxi to Zoo or Mitte is pricey: €30-€35, and takes 45-60 minutes.

Tempelhof Airport

Airport information: 0180 500 0186/www.berlin-airport.de. Flight information: 6951 2288. **Open** 5am-11pm daily. **Map** p307 M11.
Berlin's third airport, Tempelhof, is just 4km (2.5 miles) south of Mitte, but few airlines use it. The airport has basic shops, snack bars, currency exchange and car hire desks.
Connections to the rest of Berlin are easy. Platz der Luftbrücke U-Bahn station (U6 – direct to Mitte in around ten minutes) is a short walk from the terminal building.
Tickets to the centre from Tempelhof cost €2.10, and can be used on any combination of bus, U- and S-Bahn.
A taxi to Mitte or Zoo will cost €12-€18, and will take about 15 minutes and 20 minutes respectively.

Airlines

From outside Germany dial the international access code (usually 00), then 49 for Germany, then the number (omitting any initial zero). All operators speak English.
Air Berlin 0180 573 7800/ www.airberlin.com
British Airways 0180 526 6522/ www.britishairways.com
DBA 0180 535 9322/www.flydba.com
EasyJet 0180 365 4321/ www.easyjet.com
German Wings 0180 595 5855/www.germanwings.com
Iberia 0180 544 2900/www.iberia.de
Lufthansa 0180 5838 4267/www.lufthansa.de
Ryanair 0190 170 100/www.ryanair.com

Directory

By rail

Berlin Hauptbahnhof

118 61/www.bahn.de. **Map** p302 K5.
As of June 2006 the new Berlin
Hauptbahnhof (*see p102* **Hub, bub**)
is the central point of arrival for all
long-distance trains, with the
exceptions of night trains from
Moscow, Warsaw and Kiev, which
will start and end at Berlin
Lichtenberg (U5, S5, S7, S75).

Hauptbahnhof is inconveniently
located in a no-man's land just north
of the government quarter, and is
linked to the rest of the city by S-
Bahn (S5, S7, S9, S75), but not yet by
U-Bahn. The line U55, which will run
two stops to the Brandenburger Tor,
is set to open in late 2007. Eventually,
the line will extend to connect to the
U5 at Alexanderplatz, but work on
the second stage may not commence
until 2010. For now, Berlin has two
airports and one central station, none
of which connect to its underground.

At press time, few details were
available as to what services would
be available at Berlin Hauptbahnhof,
but there will be information
counters, currency exchange, shops
and restaurants, left-luggage
facilities and everything you'd expect
to find in a large, modern,
international railway interchange.

On their way in and out of town,
intercity trains will now also stop at
Nordkreuz (formerly Gesundbrunnen),
Südkreuz (formerly Papestrasse) and
Spandau, depending on destinations.

By bus

Zentraler Omnibus Bahnhof (ZOB)

*Masurenallee 4-6, Charlottenburg
(information 301 0380).* **Open** 6am-
9pm Mon-Fri; 6am-3pm Sat, Sun.
Map p304 B8.
Buses arrive in western Berlin at the
Central Bus Station, opposite the
Funkturm and the ICC (International
Congress Centrum). From here, U-
Bahn line U2 runs into the centre.
There's also a left luggage office.
East Berlin has no bus station.

Getting around

The city of Berlin is served
by a comprehensive network
of buses, trains, trams and
ferries, which all interlink.
It's efficient and punctual,
but not that cheap.

With the completion of the
inner-city-encircling Ringbahn
in 2002, the former East and

West Berlin transport
systems were finally sewn
back together, although
travelling between eastern
and western destinations
can still sometimes prove
a complicated task. Even
within one half of the city,
journeys can involve several
changes of route or mode of
transport. But services are
usually regular and frequent,
timetables can be trusted,
and one ticket can be used
for two hours on all legs
of the journey and all
forms of transport.

The Berlin transport
authority, the BVG,
operates bus, U-Bahn
and tram networks, and
a few ferry services. The
S-Bahn (overground railway)
is run by its own authority,
but services are completely
integrated within the same
three-zone tariff system (*see
p271* **Fares & tickets**).

Information

BVG information centres
are at Turmstrasse U-Bahn
(U9; open 6am-10pm Mon-Fri,
8.45am-4.15pm Sat) and at
Zoo Pavillon, Hardenberger
Strasse, outside Bahnhof Zoo
(open 6am-10pm daily). There
will likely also be one at Berlin
Hauptbahnhof. In addition,
www.bvg.de has a wealth
of information (in English)
on city transport. The S-Bahn
has its own website at
www.s-bahn-berlin.de.

The **Liniennetz**, a map
of U-Bahn, S-Bahn, bus and
tram routes for Berlin and
Potsdam, is available free
from info centres and ticket
offices. It includes a city
centre map. A map of the
U- and S-Bahn can also be
picked up free at ticket offices
or from the grey-uniformed
Zugabfertiger – passenger
assistance personnel – who
can be found wandering
about the larger U-Bahn
and S-Bahn stations.

Fares & tickets

The bus, tram, U-Bahn, S-Bahn
and ferry services operate on an
integrated three-zone system.
Zone A covers central Berlin,
zone B extends out to the edge
of the suburbs and zone C
stretches into Brandenburg. See
the public transport map at the
back of this guide for specific
details of precisely what area is
covered by each zone.

The basic single ticket is the
€2.10 *Normaltarif* (zones A and
B). Unless going to Potsdam,
few visitors are likely to travel
beyond zone B, making this in
effect a flat-fare system.

Apart from the *Zeitkarten*
(longer-term tickets, *see p272*),
tickets for Berlin's public
transport system can be
bought from the yellow or
orange machines at U- or S-
Bahn stations, and by some
bus stops. These take coins and
sometimes notes, give change
and have a limited explanation
of the ticket system in English.
Once you've purchased your
ticket, validate it in the small
red or yellow box next to the
machine, which stamps it with
the time and date. (Tickets
bought on trams or buses are
usually already validated.)

If an inspector catches you
without a valid ticket, you will
be fined €40 on the spot.
Ticket inspections are
frequent, particularly at
weekends and at the beginning
of the month.

Single ticket (Normaltarif)

Singles cost €2.10 (€1.40 for 6-14s)
for travel within zones A and B, €2.30
(€1.60) for zones B and C, and €2.60
(€1.90) for all three zones. A ticket
allows use of the BVG network for two
hours, with as many changes between
bus, tram, U-Bahn and S-Bahn as
necessary travelling in one direction.

Short-distance ticket (Kurzstreckentarif)

The *Kurzstreckentarif* (ask for a
Kurzstrecke) costs €1.20 (€1
concessions) and is valid for three U-
or S-Bahn stops, or six stops on the
tram or bus. No transfers allowed.

Day ticket (Tageskarte)

Zones A and B costs €5.80 (€4.20 concessions); all three zones cost €6 (€4.50). A day ticket lasts until 3am the day after validating.

Longer-term tickets (Zeitkarten)

If you're in Berlin for a week, it makes sense to buy a *Sieben-Tage-Karte* ('seven-day ticket') at €25.40 for zones A and B, or €31.35 for all three zones (no concessions).

A stay of a month or more makes it worth buying a *Monatskarte* ('month ticket'), which costs €67 for zones A and B, or €83 for all three zones.

U-Bahn

The first stretch of Berlin's U-Bahn was opened in 1902 and the network now consists of nine lines and 170 stations. (Many of the most interesting old stations – such as Wittenbergplatz – were renovated for the U-Bahn's 100th birthday in 2002.) The first trains run shortly after 4am; the last between midnight and 1am, except on Fridays and Saturdays when trains run all night on lines U1, U2, U5, U6, U7, U8 and U9. The direction of travel is indicated by the name of the last stop on the line.

S-Bahn

Especially useful in eastern Berlin, the S-Bahn covers long distances faster than the U-Bahn and is a more efficient means of getting to outlying areas. The 2002 completion of the Ringbahn, which circles central Berlin in around an hour, was the final piece of the S-Bahn system to be renovated, though there are still temporary disruptions here and there.

Buses

Berlin has a dense network of 150 bus routes, of which 54 run in the early hours. The day lines run from 4.30am to about 1am the next morning. Enter at the front of the bus and exit in the middle. The driver sells only individual tickets, but all tickets from machines on the U- or S-Bahn are valid. Most bus stops have clear timetables and route maps.

Trams

There are 21 tram lines (five of which run all night), mainly in the east, though some have now been extended a few kilometres into the suburbs and western half of the city, mostly in Wedding. Hackescher Markt is the site of the main tram terminus. Tickets are available from machines on the trams, at the termini and in U-Bahn stations.

Other rail services

Berlin is also served by the Regionalbahn, which once connected East Berlin with Potsdam via the suburbs and small towns left outside the Wall. It still circumnavigates the city. The Regionalbahn is run by Deutsche Bahn and ticket prices vary according to the journey.

For timetable and ticket information in English, go to Deutsche Bahn's website at www.bahn.de and click on 'Internat. Guests'.

Travelling at night

Berlin has a comprehensive *Nachtliniennetz* ('night-line network') that covers all parts of town via 59 bus and tram routes running every 30 minutes between 12.30am and 4.30am. Before and after these times the regular timetable for bus and tram routes applies.

Night-line network maps and timetables are available from BVG information kiosks at stations, and large maps of the night services are usually found next to the normal BVG map on station platforms. Ticket prices are the same as during the day. Buses and trams that run at night are distinguished by an 'N' in front of the number.

The N11, N35 and N41 buses will actually take you right to your front door if it's close to the official route. The BVG also operates a *Taxi-Ruf-System* ('taxi-calling service') on the U-Bahn for female passengers and people with disabilities from 8pm every evening until the network closes. Ask the uniformed BVG employee in the platform booth to phone, giving your destination and method of payment.

Truncated versions of U-Bahn lines U1, U2, U5, U6, U7, U8 and U9 run all night Fri and Sat, every 15mins. The S-Bahn also runs on weekend nights, with S1, S2, S3, S5, S7, S8, S9, S25, S26, S41, S42, S46, S47 and S75 in service.

Boat trips

Getting about by water is more of a leisure activity than a practical means of getting around the city, but the BVG network does include a handful of boat services on Berlin's lakes. There are also several private companies offering water tours. *See also p108* **Berlin by boat**.

Reederei Heinz Riedel

Planufer 78, Kreuzberg (693 4646). U8 Schönleinstrasse. **Open** *Mar-Sept* 6am-9pm Mon-Fri; 8am-6pm Sat; 10am-3pm Sun. *Oct* 8am-5pm Mon-Fri; 8am-6pm Sat; 10am-3pm Sun. *Nov-Feb* 8am-4pm Mon-Fri. **Map** p307 P9.

This company operates excursions that start in the city and pass through industrial suburbs into rural Berlin. A tour through the city's network of rivers and canals costs €7-€16.

Stern & Kreisschiffahrt

Puschkinallee 15, Treptow (536 3600/ www.sternundkreis.de). S8, S9, S41, S42, S85 Treptower Park. **Open** 9am-4pm Mon-Thur; 9am-2pm Fri. Offers around 25 different cruises along the Spree and lakes in the Berlin area. Departure points and times vary. A 3hr 30min tour costs €16.

Taxis

Berlin taxis are pricey, efficient and numerous, yet sometimes hard to find. The starting fee is €2.50 and thereafter the fare is €1.53 per kilometre (about €3 per mile). The rate remains the same at night. For short journeys ask for a *Kurzstrecke* – up to two kilometres for €3, but only available when you've hailed a cab and not from taxi ranks. Taxi stands are numerous, especially in central areas near stations and at major intersections.

You can phone for a cab 24 hours daily on 261 026. Cabs ordered by phone are charged at the same rates. Most taxi firms can transport people with disabilities, but require advance notice. Cabs accept all credit cards except Diners Club, subject to a €0.50 charge.

The majority of cabs are Mercedes. If you want an estate car (station wagon), ask for a *Combi*. As well as normal taxis, Funk Taxi Berlin (261 026) operates vans capable of transporting up to seven people and has two vehicles for people with disabilities.

Driving

Despite some congestion, driving in Berlin, with its wide, straight roads, presents few problems. Visitors from the UK and US should bear in mind that, in the absence of signals, drivers must yield to traffic from the right, except at crossings marked by a diamond-shaped yellow sign. Trams always have right of way. An *Einbahnstrasse* is a one-way street.

Breakdown services

The following garage offers 24-hour assistance at a rate of about €65 an hour. But it won't take credit cards.

ADAC
Bundesallee 29-30, Wilmersdorf (0180 222 2222).

Filling stations

Both of the places below are open 24 hours a day.

Aral
Holzmarktstrasse 12, Mitte (2472 0748). **Credit** AmEx, MC, V. **Map** p307 P7.

BP-Oil
Kurfürstendamm 128, Wilmersdorf (8909 6972). **Credit** AmEx, MC, V. **Map** p304 C9.

Parking

Parking is free in Berlin side streets, but spaces are hard to find. On busier streets you may have to buy a ticket (€1 per hour) from a nearby machine. Without a ticket, or if you park illegally (pedestrian crossing, loading zone, bus lane), you risk getting your car clamped or towed away.

There are long-term car parks at Schönefeld and Tegel airports (*see p270*). Otherwise, there are numerous *Parkgaragen* and *Parkhäuser* (multi-storey and underground car parks) around the city, open 24 hours, that charge around €2 an hour.

Schönefeld Airport Car Park
0180 500 0186. **Rates** €18-€20/day; €70-€80/wk. **Credit** V.

Tegel Airport Car Park
0180 500 0186. **Rates** €18-€22/day; €95-€125/wk. **No credit cards.**

Tempelhof Airport Car Park
0180 500 0186. **Rates** €12/day; €70/wk. **No credit cards.**

Vehicle hire

Car hire in Germany is not expensive and all major companies are represented in Berlin. There are car hire desks at all three of the city's airports, including the major

international names. Look under 'Autovermietung' in the *Gelbe Seiten* (*Yellow Pages*).

Cycling

The western half of Berlin is wonderful for cycling – flat, with lots of cycle paths, parks to scoot through and canals to cruise beside. East Berlin has fewer cycle paths and more cobblestones and tram lines.

Cycles can be taken on the U-Bahn, up to a limit of two at the end of carriages that have a bicycle sign on them. Bikes may not be taken on the U-Bahn during rush hour (6-9am and 2-5pm). More may be taken on to S-Bahn carriages, and at any time of day. In each case an extra ticket (€2.60) must be bought for each bike. The ADFC Fahrradstadtplan, available in bike shops (€6.50), is a good guide to cycle routes. Contact the companies below or see 'Fahrradverleih' in the *Yellow Pages*.

Fahrradstation
Dorotheenstrasse 30, Mitte (2045 4500/www.fahrradstation.de). U6, S1, S2, S5, S7, S9, S75 *Friedrichstrasse.* **Open** *Summer* 8am-8pm daily. *Winter* 10am-7pm Mon-Sat. **Rates** from €15/day; €30 for 3 days. **Credit** AmEx, MC, V. **Map** p302/p311 M6.
Other locations: Bergmannstrasse 9, Kreuzberg (215 1566); Hackesche Höfe, Mitte (2838 4848).

Pedalpower
Grossbeerenstrasse 53, Kreuzberg (5515 3270/www.pedalpower.de). U1, U7 *Möckernbrücke.* **Open** 10am-6.30pm Mon-Fri; 11am-2pm Sat. **Rates** from €10/day. **No credit cards. Map** p306 L10.
Other locations: Pfarrstrasse 115, Lichtenberg (5515 3270).

Walking

Berlin is a good walking city, but it's spread out. Getting around, say, Mitte is most pleasant on foot, but if you then want to check out Charlottenburg, you'll need to take a bus or train.

Directory

Resources A-Z

Addresses

The house/building number always follows the street name (eg Friedrichstrasse 21), and numbers sometimes run up one side of the street and back down the other side. Strasse (street) is often abbreviated to Str and not usually written separately but appended to the street name, as in the example above. Exceptions are when the street name is the adjectival form of a place name (eg Potsdamer Strasse) or the full name of an individual (eg Heinrich-Heine-Strasse).

Within buildings: EG means *Erdgeschoss*, the ground floor; 1. OG (*Obergeschoss*) is the first floor; VH means *Vorderhaus*, or the front part of the building; HH means *Hinterhaus*, the part of the building off the *Hinterhof*, the 'back courtyard'; SF is *Seitenflügel*, stairs that go off to the side from the *Hinterhof*. In big, industrial complexes, stairwells are often numbered or lettered. Treppenhaus B, or sometimes just Haus B, would indicate a particular staircase off the courtyard.

Age restrictions

The legal age for drinking is 16; for smoking it is 16; for driving it is 18; and the age of consent for both heterosexual and homosexual sex is 16.

Business

Conferences

Messe Berlin
Messedamm 22, Charlottenburg (303 80/www.messe-berlin.de). U2 Theodor-Heuss-Platz. **Open** 10am-6pm Mon-Fri; 10am-2pm Sat. **Map** p304 A8/B8.
The city's official trade fair and conference organisation can advise on setting up small seminars and congresses, or big trade fairs.

Couriers

A package up to 5kg delivered within Germany costs about €7; to the UK about €12; and to North America about €30. The post office (*see p281*) runs a cheaper express service.

DHL
Linkstrasse 10, Tiergarten (0180 5345 2255/www.dhl.de). U2, S1, S2, S26 Potsdamer Platz. **Open** 9am-6pm Mon-Fri; 9am-noon Sat. **No credit cards. Map** p306 L8.
Delivers to 180 countries worldwide.

Office hire

Regus Business Centre
Kurfürstendamm 21, Charlottenburg (887 060/fax 887 061 200/www.regus.de). U2, U9, S5, S7, S9, S75 Zoologischer Garten. **Open** 8.30am-6pm Mon-Fri. **Map** p305/p312 F8.
Offices for rent, secretarial services and conference facilities.
Other locations: Friedrichstrasse 50, Mitte.

UPS
Lengeder Strasse 17-19, Reinickendorf (0800 882 6630/www.ups.com). S25 Alt-Reinickendorf. **Open** 8am-7pm Mon-Fri. **Credit** AmEx, MC, V.
Office hire and secretarial services.

Relocation services

Hardenberg Concept GmbH
Von-Luck-Strasse 13, Zehlendorf (805 8660/www.hardenberg-relocation.de). S1, S7 Nikolassee. **Open** 10am-4pm Mon-Fri.
Help looking for homes and schools, and with residence and work permits.

Translators & interpreters

See also 'Übersetzungen' in the *Gelbe Seiten* (*Yellow Pages*).

Intertext Fremdsprachendienst
Greifswalder Strasse 5, Prenzlauer Berg (4210 1777/www.intertext.de). Tram M4 Am Friedrichshain. **Open** 8am-4.30pm Mon-Fri. **Map** p303 P5.

K Hilau Übersetzungsdienst
Innsbrucker Strasse 58, Schöneberg (781 7584). U4, U7 Bayerischer Platz. **Open** 1-6pm Mon-Fri. **Map** p305 G11/H11.

Useful organisations

American Chamber of Commerce
Charlottenstrasse 42, Mitte (2887 8920). U2, U6 Stadtmitte. **Open** 9am-5pm Mon-Fri. **Map** p302/p311 M6.

American Embassy Commercial Dept
Neustädtische Kirchstrasse 4-5, Mitte (8305 2730). U6, S1, S2, S5, S7, S9, S75 Friedrichstrasse. **Open** 8.30am-5.30pm Mon-Fri. **Map** p302/p311 M6.

Berlin Chamber of Commerce
Fasanenstrasse 85, Charlottenburg (315 100). **Open** 8am-5pm Mon-Thur; 8am-4pm Fri. **Map** p305/p312 F8.

Berlin Partner GmbH
Charlottenstrasse 65, Mitte (2024 0196). U2, U6 Stadtmitte. **Open** 9am-5.30pm Mon-Fri. **Map** p302/p311 M7.

British Embassy Commercial Dept
Wilhelmstrasse 70, Mitte (204 570/fax 245 7577). S1, S2 Unter den Linden. **Open** 9-11am, noon-4pm Mon-Fri. **Map** p302/p311 L6.

Customs

EU nationals over 17 years of age can import limitless goods for personal use, if bought tax paid. For non-EU citizens and duty-free goods, the limits are:
● 200 cigarettes or 50 cigars or 250 grams of tobacco
● 1 litre of spirits (over 22% alcohol), or 2 litres of fortified wine (under 22%), or 2 litres of wine
● 50 grams of perfume
● 500 grams of coffee
● Other goods to the value of €175 for non-commercial use
● The import of meat, meat products, fruit, plants, flowers and protected animals is restricted

Disabled

Only some U- and S-Bahn stations have wheelchair facilities; the map of the transport network (see p318; look for the blue wheelchair symbol) indicates which ones. The BVG is improving things slowly, adding facilities here and there, but it's still a long way from being a wheelchair-friendly system.

Berlin Tourismus Marketing (see p284) can give details about which of the city's hotels have disabled access, but if you require more specific information, try the **Beschäftigungswerk des BBV** or the **Touristik Union International**.

Beschäftigungswerk des BBV

Bizetstrasse 51-5, Weissensee (924 0050). S8, S41, S42, S85 Greifswalder Strasse. **Open** 8am-4.30pm Mon-Fri.
The Berlin Centre for the Disabled provides legal and social advice, together with a transport service and travel information.

Touristik Union International (TUI)

Unter den Linden 17, Mitte (2005 8550/www.tui.com). S1, S2 Unter den Linden. **Open** (by appointment) 9am-9pm Mon-Fri; 10am-6pm Sat. **Map** p302/p311 M6.
This service provides information on accommodation and travel in Germany for the disabled.

Drugs

Berlin is relatively liberal in its attitude towards drugs. In recent years, possession of hash or grass has been effectively decriminalised. Anyone caught with under ten grams is liable to have the stuff confiscated, but nothing more. Joint smoking is tolerated in some of Berlin's younger bars and cafés. It's usually easy to tell whether you're in one. Anyone caught with small amounts of hard drugs will net a fine, but is unlikely to be incarcerated.

For the Emergency Drug Service (*Drogen Notdienst*), see p277.

Electricity

Electricity in Germany runs on 220V. Change the plug or use an adaptor for British appliances (240V); US appliances (110V) need a converter.

Embassies & consulates

Australian Embassy

Wallstrasse 76-9, Mitte (880 0880). U2 Märkisches Museum. **Open** 8.30am-5pm Mon-Thur; 8.30am-4.15pm Fri. **Map** p303/p311 O7.

British Embassy

Wilhelmstrasse 70, Mitte (204 570). S1, S2 Unter den Linden. **Open** 9-11am, noon-4pm Mon-Fri. **Map** p302/p311 L6.

Irish Consulate

Friedrichstrasse 200, Mitte (220 720). U2, U6 Stadtmitte. **Open** 9.30am-12.30pm, 2.30-4.45pm Mon-Fri. **Map** p306/p311 M7.

US Consulate

Clayallee 170, Zehlendorf (832 9233/visa enquiries 0190 850 055). U3 Oskar-Helene-Heim. **Open** *Consular enquiries* 8.30am-noon Mon-Fri. *Visa enquiries* 8.30-11.30am Mon-Fri.

US Embassy

Neustädtische Kirchstrasse 4, Mitte (830 50). S1, S2 Unter den Linden. **Open** 24hrs daily. **Map** p302/p311 M6.

Emergencies

Police 110
Ambulance/Fire Brigade 112
See also p277 **Helplines**.

Gay & lesbian

Help & information

Lesbenberatung e.V.

Kulmer Strasse 20A, Schöneberg (215 2000/www.lesbenberatung-berlin.de). U7, S1, S2, S26 Yorckstrasse. **Open** 4-7pm Mon, Tue, Thur; 10am-1pm Wed; 2-5pm Fri.
The Lesbian Advice Centre offers counselling in all areas of lesbian life as well as self-help groups, courses, cultural events and an info-café.

Mann-O-Meter e.V.

Bülowstrasse 106, Schöneberg (216 8008/www.mann-o-meter.de). U1, U2, U3, U4 Nollendorfplatz. **Open** 5-10pm Mon-Fri; 4-10pm Sat, Sun. **Map** p306 J9.
Drop-in centre and helpline. Advice about AIDS prevention, jobs, flats, gay contacts, plus cheap stocks of safer sex materials. English spoken.

Schwulenberatung

Mommsenstrasse 45, Charlottenburg (office 2336 9070/counselling 194 46/www.schwulenberatungberlin.de). U7 Adenauerplatz. **Open** 9am-8pm Mon-Thur; 9am-6pm Fri. **Map** p304 D8.
The Gay Advice Centre provides info and counselling about HIV and AIDS, crisis intervention and advice on all aspects of gay life.

Travel advice

For up-to-date information on travel to a specific country – including the latest news on safety and security, health issues, local laws and customs – contact your home country government's department of foreign affairs. Most have websites packed with useful advice for would-be travellers.

Australia
www.dfat.gov.au/travel

Canada
www.voyage.gc.ca

New Zealand
www.mft.govt.nz/travel

Republic of Ireland
www.irlgov.ie/iveagh

UK
www.fco.gov.uk/travel

USA
http://travel.state.gov

Directory

Health

In January 2006 the **European Health Insurance Card (EHIC)** was introduced, allowing travellers from EU countries to access healthcare in Germany. British travellers should apply for one of these online at www.dh.gov.uk (providing name, date of birth and NHS or NI number), at least ten days before leaving home. It does not cover all medical costs (for example dental treatment), so private insurance is not a bad idea.

Citizens from non-EU countries should take out private medical insurance. The British Embassy (*see p275*) publishes a list of English-speaking doctors and dentists, as well as lawyers and interpreters.

Should you fall ill in Berlin, take your EHIC to your doctor or to the hospital in an emergency. If you require non-emergency hospital treatment, the doctor will issue you with a *Notwendigkeitsbescheinigung* ('Certificate of Necessity'), which you must take to the AOK (*see below*). Staff there give you a *Kostenübernahme-schein* ('Cost Transferral Certificate'), which entitles you to hospital treatment. All hospitals have a 24-hour emergency ward.

AOK Auslandsschalter

Karl-Marx-Allee 3, Mitte (253 10/ www.aokberlin.de). U2, U5, U8, S5, S7, S9, S75 Alexanderplatz. **Open** 8am-2pm Mon, Wed; 8am-6pm Tue, Thur; 8am-noon Fri. **Map** p303 P6.

Accident & emergency

Hospitals are in the *Gelbe Seiten* (*Yellow Pages*) under 'Krankenhäuser/Kliniken'. These are the most central.

Charité

Schumann Strasse 20-21, Mitte (450 50/www.charite.de). U6, S1, S2, S5, S7, S9, S75 Friedrichstrasse/ bus 147. **Map** p302 L5.

Klinikum Am Urban

Dieffenbachstrasse 1, Kreuzberg (6970). U7 Südstern. **Map** p307 O10.

St Hedwig Krankenhaus

Grosse Hamburger Strasse 5, Mitte (231 10). S5, S7, S9, S75 Hackescher Markt or S1, S2 Oranienburger Strasse. **Map** p303/p310 N5.

Complementary medicine

There is a long tradition of alternative medicine (*Heilpraxis*) in Germany, and medical insurance will usually cover treatment. Practitioners are listed as 'Heilpraktiker' in the *Gelbe Seiten* (*Yellow Pages*). There you'll find a complete list of chiropractors, osteopaths, acupuncturists, homeopaths and healers of various kinds. Homeopathic medicines are harder to get hold of and much more expensive than in the UK, and it's generally harder to find an osteopath or chiropractor.

Contraception, abortion & childbirth

Family-planning clinics are thin on the ground in Germany, and generally you have to go to a gynaecologist (*Frauenarzt*).

The abortion law was amended in 1995 to take into account the differing systems that had existed in East and West. East Germany had abortion on demand; in the West, abortion was only allowed in extenuating circumstances, such as when the health of the foetus or mother was at risk.

In a complicated compromise, abortion is still technically illegal, but is not punishable. Women wishing to terminate a pregnancy can do so only after receiving certification from a counsellor. Counselling is offered by state, lay and church bodies.

Feministisches Frauengesundheitszentrum (FFGZ)

Bamberger Strasse 51, Schöneberg (213 9597). U4, U7 Bayerischer Platz. **Open** 10am-1pm Mon, Tue, Fri; 10am-1pm, 5-7pm Thur. **Map** p305 G10.
Courses and lectures are offered on natural contraception, pregnancy, cancer, abortion, AIDS, migraines and sexuality. Self-help and preventative medicine are stressed. Information on gynaecologists, health institutions and organisations can also be obtained.

ProFamilia

Kalkreuthstrasse 4, Schöneberg (2147 6414/www.profamilia-berlin. de). U1, U2, U3 Wittenbergplatz. **Open** 9am Mon, Tue, Thur; 9am-noon Wed, Sat. **Map** p305 H9.
Free advice about sex, contraception and abortion is offered here. Call for an appointment.

Dentists

Dr Andreas Bothe

Kurfürstendamm 210, Charlottenburg (882 6767). U1 Uhlandstrasse. **Open** 8am-2pm Mon, Wed, Fri; 2-8pm Tue, Thur. **Map** p305/p312 F8.

Mr Pankaj Mehta

Schlangenbader Strasse 25, Wilmersdorf (823 3010). U1 Rüdesheimer Platz. **Open** 9am-noon, 2-6pm Mon, Tue, Thur; 8am-1pm Wed, Fri.

Doctors

If you don't know of any doctors, or are too ill to leave your bed, phone the Emergency Doctor's Service or *Ärztlicher Bereitschaftdienst* (310 031). This service specialises in dispatching doctors for house calls. Charges vary according to treatment.

In Germany, you choose your doctor according to his or her speciality. You don't need a referral from a GP. The British Embassy (*see p275*) can provide a list of English-speaking doctors, but many doctors can speak some English. All will be expensive, so either have your EHIC (*see above*) at hand, or your private insurance document.

The following doctors both speak good English.

Frau Dr I Dorow
Rüsternallee 14-16, Charlottenburg (302 4690). U2 Neu-Westend. **Open** 9-11.30am, 4-6pm Mon, Tue, Thur; 9-11.30am Fri. **Map** p304 A7.

Dr Christine Rommelspacher
Bochumer Strasse 12, Tiergarten (392 2075). U9 Turmstrasse. **Open** 9am-noon, 3-6pm Mon, Tue, Thur; 9am-noon Fri. **Map** p301 G5.

Gynaecologist

Dr Lutz Opitz
Tegeler Weg 4, Charlottenburg (344 4001). U7 Mierendorffplatz. **Open** 8am-2pm Mon; 4-7pm Tue; 5-7pm Thur; 8am-noon Fri. **Map** p300 C5.

Pharmacies

Prescription and non-prescription drugs (including aspirin) are sold only at pharmacies (*Apotheken*), which have a red 'A' outside. A list of pharmacies open on Sundays and in the evening should be displayed at every pharmacy, and can also be found under www.apothekennotdienst.de.

STDs, HIV & AIDS

For most STDs, see a doctor.

Berliner Aids-Hilfe (BAH)
Büro 15, Meinekestrasse 12, Wilmersdorf (885 6400/advice line 194 11). U1, U9 Kurfürstendamm. **Open** noon-6pm Mon, Wed; 10am-6pm Thur; 10am-3pm Fri. *Advice line* 10am-midnight daily. **Map** p305/p312 F9.
Information on all aspects of HIV and AIDS. Free consultations, condoms and lubricant are also provided.

Helplines

Berliner Krisendienst
Mitte, Friedrichshain, Kreuzberg, Tiergarten & Wedding (390 6310). Charlottenburg & Wilmersdorf (390 6320). Prenzlauer Berg, Weissensee & Pankow (390 6340). Schöneberg, Tempelhof & Steglitz (390 6360).
For most problems, this is the best service to call. It offers help and/or counselling on a range of subjects,

and if staff can't provide exactly what you're looking for, they'll put you in touch with someone who can. The phone lines, organised by district, are staffed 24 hours daily. Counsellors will also come and visit you in your house if necessary.

Drogen Notdienst
Ansbacher Strasse 11, Schöneberg (192 37). U1, U2, U3 Wittenbergplatz. **Open** 8.30am-10pm Mon-Fri; 2-9.30pm Sat, Sun. **Map** p305 H8.
At the 'drug emergency service', no appointment is necessary if you're coming in for advice, and the phone line is staffed 24 hours daily.

Frauenkrisentelefon
615 4243 (Mon-Fri)/615 7596 (Sat, Sun). **Open** 10am-noon Mon, Thur; 7-9pm Tue, Wed, Fri; 5-7pm Sat, Sun. Offers advice and information for women on anything and everything.

ID

By law you are required to carry some form of ID, which, for UK and US citizens, means a passport. If police catch you without one, they may accompany you to wherever you've left it.

Internet

There's a free wireless network in the Sony Center (map *p311 L7*) and at Barcomi's (*see p144*). For an ISP, try www.snafu.de or www.gmx.de. For Berlin-related websites, *see p289*.

British Council
Hackescher Markt 1, Mitte (311 0090/www.britishcouncil.de). S5, S7, S9, S75 Hackescher Markt. **Open** 9am-6pm Mon-Fri. **Map** p303/p310 N5.
Half an hour of internet access is free at the terminals left of reception.

easyInternetCafé
Dunkin' Donuts, Sony Center, Tiergarten (www.easy internetcafe.com). U2, S1, S2, S26 Potsdamer Platz. **Open** 7am-11pm Mon-Thur, Sun; 7am-midnight Fri, Sat. **No credit cards.** **Map** p306/p311 K7/L7.
Dozens of computers, no staff, mechanised system to buy time online, and plenty of doughnuts to hand. Other branches are similarly lodged with Dunkin' Donuts.
Other locations: Hardenbergplatz 2, Charlottenburg; Kurfürstendamm

224, Charlottenburg; Rathaus Passagen, Rathausstrasse 5, Mitte; Karl-Marx-Strasse 78, Neukölln; Schlossstrasse 102, Steglitz.

Internet Café Alpha
Dunckerstrasse 72, Prenzlauer Berg (447 9067/www.alpha-internetcafe. de). U2 Eberswalder Strasse. **Open** noon-1am Mon-Fri; 2pm-1am Sat, Sun. **No credit cards.** **Map** p303/p312 P2.
Using one of the 15 computers costs €2 per hour. Wine, beer and a range of snacks can fuel your surfing. Also available: CD burners, scanners and games.

Left luggage

Airports
There is a left luggage office at **Tegel** (*see p270*; 0180 500 0186; open 5am-10.30pm daily) and lockers at **Schönefeld** (*see p270*; in the Multi Parking Garage P4) and **Tempelhof** (*see p270*; in Parking Area P1).

Rail & bus stations
There are lockers and left luggage facilities at **Bahnhof Zoo**, and 24-hour lockers at **Friedrichstrasse** and **Alexanderplatz** stations. There will probably be some kind of provision at **Berlin Hauptbahnhof** as well. **Zentraler Omnibus Bahnhof** (ZOB; *see p271*) also has facilities.

Legal help

If you get into legal difficulties, you should contact the British Embassy (*see p275*): it can provide you with a list of English-speaking lawyers based in Berlin.

Libraries

Berlin has hundreds of *Bibliotheken/Büchereien* (public libraries). To borrow books, you will be required to bring two things: an *Anmeldungsformular* ('Certificate of Registration'; *see p284*) and your passport.

Directory

Amerika-Gedenkbibliothek

Blücherplatz 1, Kreuzberg (9022 6105/www.zlb.de). U1, U6 Hallesches Tor. **Open** 10am-8pm Mon-Fri; 10am-7pm Sat. **Membership** €10/yr. *Students* €5/yr. **Map** p306 M9.
This library only contains a small collection of English and American literature, but it has an excellent collection of English-language videos and many DVDs.

British Council

Hackescher Markt 1, Mitte (3110 9910/www.britishcouncil.de). S5, S7, S9, S75 Hackescher Markt. **Open** 1-7.30pm Mon, Tue, Thur, Fri; 1-4pm Sat. **Membership** €50/yr. *Students, teachers & journalists* €40/yr. **Map** p303/p310 N5.
The Information Centre at the British Council holds 2,500 English-language videos, plus DVDs and CD-ROMs.

Staatsbibliothek

Potsdamer Strasse 33, Tiergarten (2660/www.sbb.spk-berlin.de). U2, S1, S2, S26 Potsdamer Platz. **Open** 9am-9pm Mon-Fri; 9am-7pm Sat. **Map** p306 K8.
Books in English on every subject are available at this branch of the State Library, which featured in Wim Wenders's *Wings of Desire*.

Staatsbibliothek

Unter den Linden 8, Mitte (2660/www.sbb.spk-berlin.de). U6, S1, S2, S5, S7, S9, S75 Friedrichstrasse. **Open** 9am-9pm Mon-Fri; 9am-5pm Sat. **Map** p302/p311 M6.
A smaller range of English books than the branch above, but it's still worth a visit, not least for its café.

Lost/stolen property

If your belongings are stolen, go immediately to the police station nearest to where the incident occurred (listed in the *Gelbe Seiten/Yellow Pages* under 'Polizei') and report the theft. There you will be required to fill in report forms for insurance purposes. If you can't speak German, don't worry: the police will call in one of their interpreters, a service provided free of charge.

For information about what to do concerning lost or stolen credit cards, *see p280*.

BVG Fundbüro

Potsdamer Strasse 180-2, Schöneberg (194 49). U7 Kleistpark. **Open** *Office* 9am-6pm Mon-Thur; 9am-2pm Fri. *Call centre* 24hrs daily. **Map** p306 J10.
You should contact this office if you have any queries about property lost on Berlin's public transport system. If you are robbed on one of BVG's vehicles, you can ask about the surveillance video.

Zentrales Fundbüro

Platz der Luftbrücke 6, Tempelhof (7560 3101). U6 Platz der Luftbrücke. **Open** 7.30am-2pm Mon; 8.30am-4pm Tue; noon-6.30pm Wed; 1-7pm Thur; 7.30am-noon Fri. **Map** p306 M11.
Central police lost property office.

Media

Foreign press

International publications are available at larger stations and Internationale Presse newsagents around town. Book retailers **Dussmann** (*see p162*) and **Hugendubel** (*see p161*) also carry international titles. The monthly *Exberliner* magazine (*see p279*) offers listings as well as articles on cultural and political topics in English.

National newspapers

BILD

Flagship tabloid of the Axel Springer group. Though its credibility varies from story to story, *BILD* leverages the journalistic resources of the Springer empire and its four-million circulation to land regular scoops, so even the German intelligentsia pays attention to its daily riot of polemic.

Financial Times Deutschland

Since hitting newsstands in 2000, the FTD's circulation has been steadily increasing, and though it's not likely to dethrone *Handelsblatt*, its success proves there's room for different approaches within the business trade market.

Frankfurter Allgemeine Zeitung

Germany's de facto newspaper of record. Stolid, exhaustive coverage of daily events, plus lots of analysis, particularly on the business pages.

The relaunched Sunday edition has become one of the best-edited papers in the country.

Handelsblatt

The closest thing Germany can offer to the *Wall Street Journal*, the *Handelsblatt* co-operates with that paper's European offshoot. Competition from the *Financial Times Deutschland* has shaken *Handelsblatt* out of its complacency and energised its reporting.

Sueddeutsche Zeitung

Based in Munich, the *Sueddeutsche* blends first-rate journalism with enlightened commentary and, not unusual in the German press, uninspired visuals. On Mondays there is an English-language feature supplement called *The New York Times International Weekly*.

die tageszeitung

Set up in Berlin's rebellious Kreuzberg district in the 1970s, the *taz* was an attempt to balance the provincial world view offered by West German newspapers and give coverage to alternative political and social issues. Today, with many of its charter readers now making mainstream policies in the Bundestag, the *taz* seems to be floundering. Still, the Berlin edition keeps watch on crooks in local government.

Die Welt

Springer's *Die Welt* moved its main editorial office to Berlin in advance of the government's arrival, appointed a new editor-in-chief and enjoyed a redesign. The previously lacklustre mouthpiece of provincial thinking now has wider political horizons. But at a circulation of around 17,000 for its Berlin edition, it's a non-starter in the capital. Recently pooled its personnel with the Springer-owned local daily *Berliner Morgenpost* (*see below*) to cut costs.

Local newspapers

Berliner Morgenpost

Fat, fresh and self-conscious, this broadsheet is the favourite of the petty bourgeois. Good local coverage, and gradually gaining readers in the east through the introduction of neighbourhood editions, but no depth on the national and international pages and not helped by the fusion of the paper's staff with that of *Die Welt*. Comprehensive employment opportunities section on Saturday.

Berliner Zeitung

This East Berlin paper has passed through the hands of a number of owners since it was relaunched in the early 1990s, the latest being a consortium led by Britain's David Montgomery. Though it is profitable and its journalistic ambitions less sullied than those of its West Berlin competitor *Der Tagesspiegel*, it remains a local read, with a circulation largely confined to the eastern districts, where its editorial offices are located.

BZ

The daily riot of polemic and pictures hasn't let up since it was demonised by the left in the 1970s – but its circulation has. Although still Berlin's largest seller with 270,000 copies daily, *BZ* sales are down by over 70,000 copies since 1991.

Der Tagesspiegel

Owned by the conservative Holzbrinck publishing empire, this paper has fallen from the pre-eminent position it once held in West Berlin, and is now bleeding both cash and editorial talent. Driven by the business department instead of the newsroom, the paper has dumbed down to boost circulation, and in the process lost the intellectual underpinnings that once attracted well-educated, upmarket readers.

Weekly newspapers

Freitag

'The East-West weekly paper' is a post-1989 relaunch of a GDR intellectual weekly. Worth a look for its political and cultural articles.

Jungle World

Defiantly left, graphically switched-on and commercially undaunted, this Berlin-based weekly can be relied on to mock the comfortable views of the mainstream press. Born of an ideological dispute with the publishers of *Junge Welt*, a former East Berlin youth title, it lacks sales but packs a punch.

Die Zeit

Every major post-war intellectual debate in Germany has been carried out in the pages of *Die Zeit*, the newspaper that proved to a suspicious world that a liberal tradition was alive and well in a country best known for excesses of intolerance. Unfortunately, the wandering style of its elite authors makes for a difficult read.

Magazines

Focus

Once, its spare, to-the-point articles, four-colour graphics and service features were a welcome innovation.

But the gloss has faded, and *Focus* has established itself as a non-thinking man's *Der Spiegel*, whose answer to the upstart was simply to print more colour pages and become warm and fuzzy by adding bylines.

Der Spiegel

Few journalistic institutions in Germany possess the resources and clout to pursue a major story like *Der Spiegel*, one of Europe's best and most aggressive news weeklies. After years of firing barbs at ruling Christian Democrats, *Der Spiegel* was caught off guard when the Social Democrats were elected in 1999, but remains a must-read for anyone interested in Germany's power structure.

Stern

The heyday of news pictorials may have long gone, but *Stern* still manages to shift around a million copies a week of big colour spreads detailing the horrors of war, the beauties of nature and the curves of the female body. Nevertheless, its reputation has never really recovered from the Hitler diaries fiasco in the early 1980s.

Listings magazines

Berlin is awash with German-language listings freebies, notably *[030]* (music, nightlife, film), *Partysan* (club guide), *Siegessäule* and *Sergej* (both gay). These can be picked up in bars and restaurants. Two newsstand fortnightlies, *Zitty* and *tip*, come out on alternate weeks and, at least for cinema information, it pays to get the current title.

Exberliner

Berlin's current English-language monthly is a lively mix of listings, reviews and commentary, mostly by and for the young American expat community. It's based on the US 'alternative press' model, except it's not free. And its view is detached, almost self-absorbed, rather than engaged, as one might expect from a magazine put together by outsiders.

tip

A glossier version of *Zitty* in every respect, *tip* gets better marks for its overall presentation and readability, largely due to higher quality paper, full colour throughout and a space-saving TV insert. This makes it more appealing to display advertisers – a double-edged sword depending on why you buy a listings magazine in the first place.

Zitty

Having lost some countercultural edge since its foundation in 1977, *Zitty* remains a vital force on the Berlin media scene, providing a fortnightly blend of close-to-the-bone civic journalism, alternative cultural coverage and comprehensive listings. The *Harte Welle* ('hardcore') department of its Lonely Hearts classifieds is legendary.

Television

Germany cabled up in the late 1970s, so there is no shortage of channels. But television has never been viewed as an art form, and there is no federal broadcasting standards bureau. That means programming revolves around bland, mass market entertainment, except for political talk shows, which are pervasive, but often very good. At its worst, the television schedule consists of cheesy 'erotic' shows, vapid folk-music programmes with studio audiences that clap in time, and German adaptations of reality TV and casting shows such as *Big Brother* and *Star Search*. Late-night TV is chock-a-block with imported action series and European soft porn, interspersed with ads for phone sex numbers.

There are two national public networks, **ARD** and **ZDF**, some no-holds-barred commercial channels, and loads of special-interest channels. *Tagesschau*, daily at 8pm on ARD, is the most authoritative news broadcast nationally.

N-tv is Germany's all-news cable channel, owned partly by CNN, but lacking the satellite broadcaster's ability to cover a breaking story. **TVBerlin** is the city's experiment with local commercial television and, though more ambitious under new management, it's still catching up with ARD's local affiliate **RBB** (a merger of the Berlin and Brandenburg stations SFB and ORB), which covers local news with more insight than its rival.

Directory

RTL, **Pro 7** and **SAT.1** are privately owned services offering a predictable mix of Hollywood re-runs and imported series, plus their own sensational magazine programmes and sometimes surprisingly good TV movies.

Special interest channels run from **Kinderkanal** for kids to **Eurosport**, **MTV Europe** and its German-language competitors **Viva** and more offbeat **Onyx**, to **Arte**, an enlightened French-German cultural channel with high-quality films and documentaries.

Channels broadcasting regularly in English include **CNN**, **NBC**, **MTV Europe** and **BBC World**. British or American films on ARD or ZDF are sometimes broadcast with a simultaneous soundtrack in English for stereo-equipped TV sets.

Radio

Some 33 stations compete for audiences in Berlin, so even tiny shifts in market share have huge consequences for broadcasters. The race for ratings in the greater metropolitan area is thwarted by a clear split between the urban audience, in both east and west, and the rural one in the hinterland. The main four stations have their audiences based in either Berlin (**Berliner Rundfunk**, 91.4; **r.s.2**, 94.3) or Brandenburg (**BB Radio**, 107.5; **Antenne Brandenburg**, 99.7). No single station pulls in everyone.

Commercial stations **104,6 RTL** (104.6), **Energy 103,4** (103.4) and **Hundert,6** (100.6) offer standard chart pop spiced with news. **RadioEins** (95.8) and **Fritz** (102.6) are a bit more adventurous but still far from cutting edge. Jazz is round the clock on **Jazz Radio** (101.9). Information-based stations such as **Info Radio** (93.1) are increasing in

popularity. The **BBC World Service** (90.2) is available 24 hours a day. **Radio MultiKulti** (96.3) broadcasts in 19 languages and serves up global sounds. In April 2006 **US National Public Radio** (87.9) began broadcasting from the former frequency of the American Forces Network and Voice of America.

Money

One euro (€) is made up of 100 cents (¢). There are seven notes and eight coins. The notes are of differing colours and sizes (€5 is the smallest, €500 the largest) and each of their designs represents a different period of European architecture. They are: €5 (grey), €10 (red), €20 (blue), €50 (orange), €100 (green), €200 (yellow-brown), €500 (purple).

The eight denominations of coin (€2, €1, 50¢, 20¢, 10¢, 5¢, 2¢, 1¢) vary in colour, size and thickness – but not enough to make them easy to tell apart. They share one common side; the other features a country-specific design (all can be used in any participating state).

For more information on the euro, see www.euro.ecb.int. At the time of going to press, the exchange rate was £1 = €1.46 and US$1 = €1.21.

ATMs

ATMs are found throughout central Berlin, and are the most convenient way to get cash. Most major credit cards are accepted, as well as debit cards that are part of the Cirrus, Plus, Star or Maestro systems. You will normally be charged a fee for withdrawals, but the exchange rate is usually good.

Banks & bureaux de change

Foreign currency and travellers' cheques can be exchanged in most banks.

Wechselstuben (bureaux de change) are open outside normal banking hours and give better rates than banks, where changing money often involves long queues.

Reisebank AG

Zoo Station, Hardenbergplatz, Charlottenburg (881 7117). U2, U9, S5, S7, S9, S75 Zoologischer Garten. **Open** 10am-6pm Mon, Tue, Thur; 10am-4pm Wed, Fri; 10.30am-2pm Sat. **Map** p305/p312 G8.
The *Wechselstuben* of the Reisebank offer good exchange rates. There are branches at Alexanderplatz, Ostbahnhof and Lichtenberg.

Credit cards

Many Berliners prefer to use cash for most transactions, although larger hotels, shops and restaurants often accept major credit cards (American Express, Diners Club, MasterCard, Visa) and many will take Eurocheques with guarantee cards, and travellers' cheques with ID. In general, German banking and retail systems are less enthusiastic about credit than their UK or US equivalents, though this is changing.

If you want to take out cash on your credit card, some banks will give an advance against MasterCard and Visa cards. But you may not be able to withdraw less than the equivalent of US$100. A better option is using an ATM.

American Express

Bayreuther Strasse 37, Schöneberg (214 9830). U1, U2, U3 Wittenbergplatz. **Open** 9am-7pm Mon-Fri; 10am-1pm Sat. **Map** p305 H8.
Holders of an American Express card can use the company's facilities here, including the cash advance service.

Lost/stolen cards

If you've lost a credit card, or had one stolen, phone one of the 24-hour emergency numbers listed below.

American Express 0180 523 2377
Diners Club 069 6616 6123
MasterCard/Visa 0697 933 1910

Tax

Non-EU citizens can claim back German value-added tax (*Mehrwertsteuer* or *MwSt*) on goods purchased in the country (it's only worth the hassle on sizeable purchases). Ask to be issued with a Tax-Free Shopping Cheque for the amount of the refund and present this, with the receipt, at the airport's refund office before checking in bags.

Opening hours

Most banks are open 9am to noon Monday to Friday, and 1pm to 3pm or 2pm to 6pm on varied weekdays.

Shops can stay open until 8pm on weekdays, and 6pm on Saturdays, though many close earlier. Most big stores open their doors at 9am, newsagents a little earlier, and smaller or independent shops open around 10am or later.

An increasing number of all-purpose neighbourhood shops (*Spätkauf*) open around 5pm and close around midnight. Many Turkish shops are open on Saturday afternoons and on Sundays from 1pm to 5pm. Many bakers open to sell cakes on Sundays from 2pm to 4pm. Most 24-hour fuel stations also sell basic groceries.

The opening times of bars vary, but many are open during the day, and most stay open until at least 1am, if not through until morning.

Most post offices are open 8am to 6pm Monday to Friday and 8am to 1pm on Saturdays.

Police stations

You are unlikely to come in contact with the *Polizei*, unless you commit a crime or are the victim of one. There are very few pedestrian patrols or traffic checks (and local radio news often announces where to look out for them).

The central police HQ is at Platz der Luftbrücke 6, Tempelhof (466 40), and there are local stations at: Jägerstrasse 48, Mitte (466 433 2700); Bismarkstrasse 111, Charlottenburg (466 422 7700); Friesenstrasse 16, Kreuzberg (466 455 2700); Hauptstrasse 44, Schöneberg (466 444 2700); Eberswalder Strasse 6-9 (466 411 5700). But police will be dispatched from the appropriate office if you just dial 466 40.

Postal services

Most post offices (simply *Post* in German) are open from 8am to 6pm Monday to Friday, and 8am to 1pm Saturday.

For non-local mail, use the *Andere Richtungen* ('other destinations') slot in post-boxes. Letters of up to 20 grams (7oz) to anywhere in Germany and the EU need 55¢ in postage. Postcards require 45¢. For anywhere outside the EU, a 20-gram airmail letter costs €1.55, a postcard €1.

Postamt Friedrichstrasse

Georgenstrasse 12, Mitte. U6, S1, S2, S5, S7, S9, S75 Friedrichstrasse. **Open** 8am-10pm daily. **Map** p303/p311 M6. Berlin has no main post office. This branch, actually inside Friedrichstrasse station, has the longest opening hours.

Poste restante

Poste restante facilities are available at the main post offices of each district. Address envelopes to the recipient 'Postlagernd', followed by the address of the post office, or collect them from the counter marked 'Postlagernde Sendungen'. Take your passport.

Public holidays

On public holidays (*Feiertagen*) it can be difficult to get things done in Berlin. However, most cafés, bars and restaurants stay open – except on the evening of 24 December, when almost everything closes.

Public holidays are: **New Year's Day** (1 Jan); **Good Friday** (Mar/Apr); **Easter Monday** (Mar/Apr); **May/Labour Day** (1 May); **Ascension Day** (May/June); ten days before Whitsun/Pentecost, the 7th Sun after Easter); **Whit/Pentecost Monday** (May/June); **Day of German Unity** (3 Oct); **Day of Prayer and National Repentance** (3rd Wed in Nov); **Christmas Eve** (24 Dec); **Christmas Day** (25 Dec); **Boxing Day** (26 Dec).

Religion

For lists of places of worship for the major religions, the website **www.berlinfo.com** is useful (click on the link for 'community'). *See p282* **Not so godless after all**.

Safety & security

Though crime is increasing, Berlin remains a safe city by western standards. Even for a woman, it's pretty safe to walk around alone at night in most central areas. Avoid the eastern working-class suburbs if you look gay or non-German. Pickpockets are not unknown around major tourist areas. Use some common sense and you're unlikely to get into trouble.

Smoking

Many Berliners smoke, and, though the habit is in decline, there is less stigma attached than in the UK or US. Smoking is banned on public transport, in theatres and many public institutions, but is tolerated almost everywhere else.

Study

Germany's university system is currently in a state of flux. Under the Bologna Process

Directory

(the EU's initiative to create a unified standard of education throughout Europe), the traditional *Magister* degree – which lasts between nine and 12 terms, during which time students can take a wide variety of courses – is being replaced by the internationally recognised Bachelors and Masters degrees. The gradual changeover has created a two-tiered system, and students of the same age at different universities (or even different courses at the same university) are receiving grossly discrepant levels of education and qualification. The proposed introduction of tuition fees, along with the competitive frenzy as departments vie to be part of the government's 'elite universities' scheme (which will award financial assistance to a few select institutions) have also helped create a mood of uncertainty. Nevertheless, Berlin retains its pull on scholars from across the world. There are currently almost 150,000 students in the city – approximately 10 per cent of whom are foreigners – divided between four universities and 16 subject-specific colleges.

Language classes

Goethe-Institut

Neue Schönhauser Strasse 20, Mitte (259 063/www.goethe.de). U8 Weinmeisterstrasse or S5, S7, S9, S75 Hackescher Markt. **Map** p303/p310 O5.
Considerably more expensive than most of its competitors (a four-week course costs €950, or €1,405 with accommodation), the Goethe-Institut offers the most systematic and intensive language courses in the city. Enrolled students can benefit from extra-curricular conversation classes, as well as a Cultural Extension Programme that organises regular cinema, theatre and museum visits. Exams can be taken (with certificates awarded) at the end of every course.

Not so godless after all

Berlin is a pretty godless place, a far cry from Bavaria or the Rhineland where Catholicism oozes out of every lintel. But, on closer examination, the city is home to an eclectic religious mix. Berlin's Turkish population ensures a hefty dose of Islam, and there are about 30 neighbourhood mosques. Among the most attractive is the **Ahmadiyya Mosque** (Brienner Strasse 7-8, Wilmersdorf). A useful starting point for investigating Berlin's Islamic life is the **Islamic Federation of Berlin** (www.islamische-foederation.de).

The texture of Berlin life remains deeply influenced by its Jewish history and, over the last dozen years, the city's Jewish population has grown in both size and confidence. Jewish social and religious life focuses on the **Neue Synagoge** (*see p87*) and Centrum Judaicum on Oranienburger Strasse. In the nearby community offices (Oranienburger Strasse 28-9, Mitte), there is a wealth of information on modern Jewish life in Berlin. For a real taste of Jewish Berlin, though, head for the **Jüdisches Gemeindehaus** (Jewish Community Centre, Fasanenstrasse 79-80, Charlottenburg) where, beyond the security cordon, there is a superb library and research centre that's open to the public. The facility hosts lectures, an extensive cultural programme, an annual film festival (in June) and, upstairs at the **Gabriel** restaurant (*see p143*), some of the best kosher food in town.

Berlin's Roman Catholics have been going through a tough time recently. Budget cuts forced the Berlin Archdiocese to halve the number of parishes in 2004, and more cuts are on the way. But the community is unusual for its international character. A high percentage of Berlin's Catholics are foreign, and every Sunday and feast day services are celebrated in some 20 languages. A network of foreign-language missions serves this mixed bunch, the largest ministering to the needs of over 20,000 devout Polish migrants. There is an active English-language RC mission, based at **St Bernhard Church** (Königin-Luise-Allee, Dahlem, 813 2026), with its main Sunday Mass at 11am.

Berlin hosts an unlikely outpost of the Anglican Church, based at **St George's Church** (Preussenallee, Charlottenburg, 304 1280, www.stgeorges.de). It's not all British expats; the community has members from over 30 nations, plus Berliners whose Lutheran affections have been transferred to the Anglican communion. The main Sunday service at St George's is at 10am.

Finally, the city has a remarkable **Russian Orthodox Cathedral** (Hohenzollerndamm 166, Wilmersdorf, 873 1614). Here the thriving local Russian community are joined each Sunday at 10am by Orthodox believers from all over the world. The informality and absence of seating mean visitors can easily mingle with the faithful, who come and go at will. Ultra-casual, but for those with no experience of Orthodox services, it offers an opportunity to sample something truly exotic – as well as some intriguing insights into Berlin's Russian community.

Directory

Tandem

*Lychener Strasse 7, Prenzlauer Berg
(441 3003/www.tandem-berlin.de).
U2 Eberswalder Strasse.* **Map**
p303/p312 O3/P3.
For a single payment of €15 Tandem
will put you in touch with two
German speakers interested in
conversation exchange. Formal
language classes are also available
at €300 a month.

Universities

Freie Universität Berlin

*Central admin: Kaiserswerther
Strasse 16-18, Dahlem (information
838 700 00/www.fu-berlin.de). U3
Dahlem-Dorf.*
Germany's largest university was
founded in 1948, after the Humboldt
fell under East German control.
Centre of the 1969 student
movement, as well as the quieter
radicalism of the Green Party, the FU
was for a long time a hotbed of
romantic left-wing dissent. A
founding constitution ensured that
students were represented on the
university's governing body and
given a vote on all major decisions.
Sadly, though, not much of this
idealism remains. The Student
Committee still exists, but retains no
decision-making powers, and the
vast, anonymous campus is
embroiled in the same bureaucratic
structures as any other modern
university. Since the Wall came down
the FU has lost much of its prestige
and influence to the newly
restructured Humboldt, and
competition between the two
universities is fierce.

Humboldt-Universität zu Berlin (HUB)

*Unter den Linden 6, Mitte (209
30/www.hu-berlin.de). U6, S1, S2,
S5, S7, S9, S75 Friedrichstrasse.*
Map pp302-3/p311 M6/N6.
Founded in 1810 by the humanist
Wilhelm von Humboldt, the HU was
the first university in the world
where teachers were expected, as a
term of their employment, to further
their own research. Hegel and
Schopenhauer both taught there, Karl
Marx was a student, and other
departments have included the likes
of Albert Einstein, Werner
Heisenberg, Heinrich Heine and Max
Planck. The HU entered a dark
period in the 1930s, when professors
and students joined enthusiastically
in the Nazi book-burning on
Bebelplatz. After 1945 the university
fell into decline under communism.
Since 1989, though, the HU has
regained much of its former

reputation, and a variety of new
courses are being offered. The Centre
for British Studies holds regular
Monday evening lectures in English,
which are open to the general public
– recent speakers have included
Richard Dawkins on evolution and
Timothy Garton Ash on Germany's
place in Europe.

Technische Universität Berlin (TU)

*Strasse des 17. Juni 135, Tiergarten
(3140/www.tu-berlin.de). U2 Ernst-
Reuter-Platz.* **Map** p305 F7.
The TU began life in 1879 when the
former Building and Vocational
Academies merged into a single
institution. Since 1916 the former
Mining Academy has also been
included. The university is strong
in chemistry, engineering and
architecture, and counts Schinkel
among its graduates. In the 1930s the
emphasis on development, business
and construction made the TU a
priority for the Nazi government,
which allocated it more funds than
any other university in the country.
After the war, the TU was reopened
under its current name and expanded
to include philosophy, psychology
and the social sciences. It is now
(with 30,000 students, 19% of whom
are foreigners) one of Germany's
largest universities. A new library,
with almost three million books,
was recently built on the campus.

Universität der Künste Berlin (UdK)

*Hardenbergstrasse 33, Charlottenburg
(318 50/www.udk-berlin.de). U2, U9,
S5, S7, S9, S75 Zoologischer Garten.*
Map p305/p312 F7.
Formerly the Hochschule der Künste
(a name most Berliners still use), and
founded in 1975 as a single vocational
academy comprising the former
Colleges of Art, Drama, Music and
Printing. The range of subjects has
been further broadened over the
years, and courses are now offered in
everything from Fashion Design to
Experimental Film and Media. The
eclecticism of artistic and academic
disciplines, along with the
appointment of some high-profile
teachers – such as Vivienne
Westwood, Professor of Fashion since
1992 – have secured the UdK a well-
deserved reputation as one of the best
establishments of its kind in Europe.

Useful organisations

Sprach- & Kulturbörse an der TU Berlin

*Ernst-Reuter-Platz 7, Charlottenburg
(3142 2730/www.skb.tub-fk1.de). U2
Ernst-Reuter-Platz.* **Open** 2.30-

3.30pm Tue, Thur; 3.30-5.30pm
Tue, Thur by telephone only.
Map p305 F7.
The TU's Language and Cultural
Exchange Programme for foreigners,
the SKB, is open to students from
any university in Berlin. It offers a
range of services, including language
courses, informal conversation
groups, and seminars on
international issues.

Studentenwerk Berlin

*Hardenbergstrasse 34, Charlottenburg
(311 20/information 311 2317/www.
studentenwerk-berlin.de). U2, U9,
S5, S7, S9, S75 Zoologischer Garten.*
Open 8am-6pm Mon-Fri. **Map**
p305/p312 F7.
The central organisation for students
in Berlin will give advice and provide
information about accommodation,
finance, employment and various
other essentials.

Telephones

All phone numbers in this
guide are local Berlin numbers
(other than in **Trips Out of
Town**) but note that numbers
beginning with 0180 have
higher tariffs. To call from
outside the city, *see below*.

Dialling & codes

To phone Berlin from abroad,
dial the international access
code (00 from the UK, 011 from
the US, 0011 from Australia),
then 49 (for Germany) and 30
(for Berlin), followed by the
local number.
  To phone abroad from
Germany dial 00, then the
appropriate country-code:

  Australia 61
  Canada 1
  Ireland 353
  New Zealand 64
  United Kingdom 44
  United States 1

And then the local area code
(minus the initial zero) and the
local number.
  To call Berlin from
elsewhere in Germany, dial 030
and then the local number.

Making a call

Calls within Berlin from 9am-
6pm cost 10¢ per minute.

Directory

Numbers prefixed 0180 are charged at 12¢ per minute.

A call from Berlin to the UK and Ireland costs 60¢ per minute, to the US and Canada 90¢ per minute and to Australia €2.60 per minute.

Both local and international calls can be a lot cheaper if you simply dial a prefix before the international code. There are various numbers and they change from time to time. Look in local newspapers or visit www.tariftip.de.

Public phones

At post offices you'll find both coin- and card-operated phones, but most pavement phone boxes are card-only.

You can sometimes find a coin-operated phone in a bar or café. Phonecards can be bought in newsagents and at post offices for various sums from €5 to €50, and you'll find phonecard machines in both Alexanderplatz and Zoo stations.

To make international calls, look for phone boxes marked 'international' and with a ringing-bell symbol – you can be called back on them.

Operator services

For online directory enquiries (available in English), go to www.teleauskunft.de.
Alarm calls/Weckruf 0180 114 1033 (automated, in German)
International directory enquiries 118 34
Operator assistance/German directory enquiries 118 33 (118 37, English-speaking only)
Phone repairs/ Störungsannahme 080 0330 2000
Telegram/Telegrammaufnahme 0180 512 1210

Mobile phones

German mobile phone networks operate at 900MHz, so all UK and Australian mobiles should work in Berlin (if roaming is activated). US and Canadian cellphone users (whose phones operate at 1900MHz) should check whether their phones can switch to 900MHz. If they can't, you can rent a 'Handy' (as the Germans call them) at www.edicom-online.com. They'll deliver to your hotel, and pick the phone back up from there up when you're gone.

Time

Germany is on Central European Time – one hour ahead of Greenwich Mean Time. Summer time (daylight-saving time) starts on the last Sunday in March (clocks go forward one hour) and lasts until the last Sunday in October (clocks go back one hour).

When summer time is in effect, London is one hour behind Berlin, New York is six hours behind, San Francisco is nine hours behind, and Sydney is nine hours ahead.

Germany uses a 24-hour system. 8am is '8 Uhr' (usually written 8h), noon is '12 Uhr Mittags' or just '12 Uhr', 5pm is '17 Uhr' and midnight is '12 Uhr Mitternachts' or just 'Mitternacht'. 8.15 is '8 Uhr 15' or 'Viertel nach 8'; 8.30 is '8 Uhr 30' or 'halb 9'; and 8.45 is '8 Uhr 45' or 'Viertel vor 9'.

Tipping

A 17 per cent service charge will already be part of your restaurant bill, but it's common to leave a small tip too. In a taxi round up the bill to the nearest euro.

Toilets

Single-occupancy, coin-operated, self-cleaning 'City Toilets' are becoming the norm. The toilets in main stations are looked after by an attendant and are pretty clean. Restaurants and cafés have to let you use their toilets by law and legally they can't refuse you a glass of water either.

Berlin Tourismus Marketing (BTM)
Europa-Center, Budapester Strasse, Charlottenburg (250 025/www.btm. de). U2, U9, S5, S7, S9, S75 Zoologischer Garten. **Open** 10am-7pm Mon-Fri; 10am-6pm Sat, Sun. **Map** p305 G8.
Berlin's official (though private) tourist organisation. The branch below is open 10am-6pm daily.
Other locations: Brandenburg Gate.

EurAide
Main hall, Bahnhof Zoologischer Garten, Charlottenburg (www. euraide.de). U2, U9, S5, S7, S9, S75 Zoologischer Garten. **Open** *June-Oct* 8am-noon, 1-6pm Mon-Fri. *Nov-May* 8am-noon, 1-4.45pm Mon-Fri. **Map** p305/p312 G8.
Behind the Reisezentrum in Bahnhof Zoo, this excellent office offers info in English. Staff can advise on sights, hostels, tours and local transport, and can sell you rail tickets.

Visas & immigration

A passport valid for three months beyond the length of stay is all EU, US, Canadian and Australian citizens need for a stay in Germany of up to three months. EU citizens with valid national ID cards need only show their ID cards.

Citizens of other countries should check with their local German Embassy or consulate.

As with any trip, you should confirm visa requirements well before you plan to travel.

Residence permits

For stays of longer than three months, you'll need a residence permit. To obtain one, EU citizens (and those of Andorra, Australia, Canada, Cyprus, Israel, Japan, Malta, New Zealand and the US) should first register at the local Anmeldungsamt. There is one in the Bürgeramt of every district – they're listed at www. berlin.de/buergerberatung. You don't need an appointment, but expect to wait. Bring proof of address in Berlin and your passport. You'll be issued with an *Anmeldungsbestätigung* – a form confirming you have registered. Take your *Anmeldungsbestätigung* to the Landesamt für Bürger & Ordnungsangelegenheiten Ausländerbehörde in the Moabit district of Tiergarten. Also bring your passport, two passport photos and something to read. There are always huge queues and it takes forever – people start queuing hours before the office opens – but all you can do is take a number and wait. Eventually, you will be issued with an *Aufenthaltserlaubnis* – a residence permit. If you have a work contract, bring it – you may be granted a longer stay.

If unsure about your status, contact the German Embassy in your country of origin, or your own embassy or consulate in Berlin. *See p275* **Embassies & consulates**.

Landesamt für Bürger & Ordnungsangelegenhei ten Ausländerbehörde

Friedrich-Krause-Ufer 24, Tiergarten (information 902 694 000). U9, S41, S42, S45, S46, S47 Westhafen. **Open** 7am-2pm Mon, Tue; 10am-6pm Thur; 9am-noon Wed, Fri (telephone only) & then by appointment. **Map** p301 H3.

When to go

Berlin has a continental climate, hot in summer and cold in winter. In January and February Berlin often ices over. Spring begins in late March/April. For more detailed information, *see p285* **Weather report**.

Women

See also p277 **Helplines** and *p276* **Health**.

Women's centres

EWA Frauenzentrum

Prenzlauer Allee 6, Prenzlauer Berg (442 5542/www.ewa-frauenzentrum. de). U2 Senefelderplatz. **Open** 10am-6pm Mon-Fri; 10am-11pm Sat (disco 1st Fri of mth). *Café & gallery* 6-11pm Mon-Thur. **Map** p303 P4. Offers legal advice and counselling, courses, readings and discussion groups. The media workshop has PCs, a darkroom, an editing suite, archive and library.

Working in Berlin

Although Berlin offers a decent range of working opportunities, the job market is beginning to shrink.

The small ads in *Zitty, tip* (*see p279*) and *Zweite Hand* are good places to look for work. Teaching English is popular: there is always a demand for native English speakers.

If you're studying in Berlin, try the Studenten Vermittlung Arbeitsamt ('Student Job Service'). You'll need your passport, student card and a *Lohnsteuerkarte* ('tax card'), available from your local Finanzamt ('tax office' – listed in the *Yellow Pages*). Tax is reclaimable. Students looking for summer work can contact the Zentralstelle für Arbeitsvermittlung.

The German equivalent of the Job Centre is the Arbeitsamt ('Employment Service'). There are very few private agencies. To find the address of your nearest office in Germany, look in the *Gelbe Seiten* under 'Arbeitsämter'.

EU nationals have the right to live and work in Germany without a work permit.

Studenten Vermittlung Arbeitsamt

Hardenbergstrasse 35, Charlottenburg (8340 9930/www.studentenwerk-berlin.de). U2 Ernst-Reuter-Platz. **Open** 10am-3.45pm Mon, Tue, Wed, Fri; 10am-5.45pm Thur. **Map** p305/p312 F7.

Weather report

	Average max temperature (°C/°F)	Average min temperature (°C/°F)	Average daily sunshine (hrs/dy)	Average rainfall (mm/in)
Jan	2°C/36°F	-3°C/27°F	2hrs	43mm/0.17in
Feb	3°C/37°F	-2°C/28°F	3hrs	38mm/0.15in
Mar	8°C/46°F	0°C/32°F	5hrs	38mm/0.15in
Apr	13°C/55°F	4°C/39°F	6hrs	43mm/0.17in
May	18°C/64°F	8°C/46°F	8hrs	56mm/0.22in
June	22°C/72°F	11°C/52°F	8hrs	71mm/0.28in
July	23°C/73°F	13°C/55°F	8hrs	53mm/0.21in
Aug	23°C/73°F	12°C/54°F	7hrs	66mm/0.26in
Sept	18°C/64°F	9°C/48°F	6hrs	46mm/0.18in
Oct	13°C/55°F	6°C/43°F	4hrs	36mm/0.14in
Nov	7°C/45°F	2°C/36°F	2hrs	51mm/0.20in
Dec	3°C/37°F	-1°C/30°F	1hr	56mm/0.22in

Vocabulary

Pronunciation

z – pronounced **ts**
w – like English **v**
v – like English **f**
s – like English **z**, but softer
r – like a throaty French **r**
a – as in f**a**ther
e – sometimes as in b**e**d, sometimes as in d**a**y
i – as in s**ee**k
o – as in n**o**te
u – as in l**oo**t
ch – as in Scottish lo**ch**
ä – combination of a and e, sometimes as in p**ai**d and sometimes as in s**e**t
ö – combination of o and e, as in French **eu**
ü – combination of u and e, like tr**u**e
ai – like p**ie**
au – like h**ou**se
ie – like fr**ee**
ee – like h**ey**
ei – like f**i**ne
eu – like c**oi**l

Useful phrases

hello/good day – guten Tag
goodbye – auf Wiedersehen
goodbye (informal) – tschüss
good morning – guten Morgen
good evening – guten Abend
good night – gute Nacht
yes – ja; (emphatic) jawohl
no – nein, nee
maybe – vielleicht
please – bitte
thank you – danke
thank you very much – danke schön
excuse me – entschuldigen Sie mir bitte
sorry! – Verzeihung!
I'm sorry, I don't speak German – entschuldigung, ich spreche kein Deutsch
do you speak English? – sprechen Sie Englisch?
can you please speak more slowly? – können Sie bitte langsamer sprechen?
my name is... – ich heisse…
open/closed – geöffnet/geschlossen
with/without – mit/ohne
cheap/expensive – billig/teuer
big/small – gross/klein
entrance/exit – Eingang/Ausgang
push/pull – drücken/ziehen
I would like... – ich möchte…
how much is...? – wieviel kostet… ?
could I have a receipt? – darf ich bitte eine Quittung haben?
how do I get to...? – wie komme ich nach… ?
how far is it to...? – wie weit ist es nach… ?
where is...? – wo ist… ?
airport – der Flughafen
railway station – der Bahnhof
petrol – das Benzin
lead-free – bleifrei
do you come here often? – sind Sie oft hier?
please leave me in peace! – lass mir bitte im Rühe!
can you call me a cab? – können Sie bitte mir ein Taxi rufen?
left – links
right – rechts
straight ahead – gerade aus
far – weit
near – nah
street – die Strasse
square – der Platz
help! – Hilfe!
I feel ill – ich bin krank
doctor – der Arzt
pharmacy – die Apotheke
hospital – das Krankenhaus

Numbers

0 null; 1 eins; 2 zwei; 3 drei; 4 vier; 5 fünf; 6 sechs; 7 sieben; 8 acht; 9 neun; 10 zehn; 11 elf; 12 zwölf; 13 dreizehn; 14 vierzehn; 15 fünfzehn; 16 sechszehn; 17 siebzehn; 18 achtzehn; 19 neunzehn; 20 zwanzig; 21 einundzwanzig; 22 zweiundzwanzig; 30 dreissig; 40 vierzig; 50 fünfzig; 60 sechszig; 70 siebzig; 80 achtzig; 90 neunzig; 100 hundert; 101 hunderteins; 110 hundertzehn; 200 zweihundert; 201 zweihunderteins; 1,000 tausend; 2,000 zweitausend.

It goes around the sausage

Ever since Mark Twain's 'The Awful German Language', *Deutsch* has had something of a bad press. But everyday German is rich in beguiling idiom, as in the following crucial colloquialisms:

Wurst

The centrality of the sausage in German culture is reflected in a wealth of idiom. If you really don't care, say *Mir ist alles Wurst!* ('It's all sausage to me!'). When it comes to the crunch, *Es geht um die Wurst!* ('It goes around the sausage!'). And if someone's sulking, tell them *Sei keine beleidigte Leberwurst!* ('Don't be an insulted liver sausage!').

Arsch

Arsch ('arse') is German's most common amplifier. Weather can be *arschkalt* (very cold), goods are often *arschteuer* (extremely expensive) and someone who talks crap is an *Arschgeige* ('arse violin'). When everything's going wrong you say there's an *Arschprogramm* going on. Be warned: *Arschloch* ('arsehole') is a more serious insult than it is in English. Don't use it unless you want to end up *am Arsch* (fucked up).

Schwein

When fed up at home alone, complain that *Kein Schwein ruft mich an!* ('No pig phones me!'). Had a stroke of luck? Say *Ich habe Schwein gehabt!* ('I have had pig!'). To convey incredulity, try *Ich glaube mein Schwein pfeift!* ('I believe my pig whistles!'). *Schweinarbeit* is really crap work, a *Schweinerei* is a real mess, and if a stranger's getting over-familiar, ask them: *Haben wir mal zusammen Schweine gehütet?* ('Have we sheltered pigs together?').

Further Reference

Books

We've chosen these books for quality and interest as much as availability. Most are in print, but some will only be found in libraries or second-hand. The date given is that of first publication in English.

Fiction

Baum, Vicki *Berlin Hotel* (London 1946)
Written in 1944, this pulp thriller anticipates the horror of the collapsing Reich via the story of a German resistance fighter trapped in a hotel with a lurid cast of Nazi bigwigs.
Deaver, Jeffrey *Garden of Beasts* (New York 2004)
American hit man sets out on a kill during the 1936 Olympics in this slightly naïve thriller.
Deighton, Len *Berlin Game, Mexico Set, London Match* (London 1983, 1984, 1985)
Epic espionage trilogy with labyrinthine plot set against an accurate picture of 1980s Berlin. The next six books aren't bad either.
Döblin, Alfred *Berlin-Alexanderplatz* (London 1975)
Devastating Expressionist portrait of the inter-war underworld in the working-class quarters of Alexanderplatz.
Eckhart, Gabriele *Hitchhiking* (Lincoln, Nebraska 1992)
Short stories viewing East Berlin through the eyes of street cleaners and a female construction worker.
Grass, Gunther *Local Anesthetic* (New York 1970)
The angst of a schoolboy threatening to burn a dog in the Ku'damm to protest the Vietnam War is firmly satirised, albeit in Grass's irritating schoolmasterly way.
Harris, Robert *Fatherland* (London 1992)
Alternative history and detective novel set in a 1964 Berlin as the Nazis might have built it.
Isherwood, Christopher *Mr Norris Changes Trains, Goodbye to Berlin* (London 1935, 1939)
Isherwood's two Berlin novels, the basis of the movie *Cabaret*, offer finely drawn characters and a sharp picture of the city as it tipped over into Nazism.
Johnson, Uwe *Two Views* (New York 1966)
Love story across the East–West divide, strong on the mood of Berlin in the late 1950s and early 1960s.

Kaminer, Wladimir *Russian Disco* (London 2002)
Best-selling collection of short tales from cult Kaffe Burger DJ.
Kerr, Philip *Berlin Noir* (London 1994)
The Bernie Gunther trilogy, about a private detective in Nazi Berlin, now in one volume.
Markstein, George *Ultimate Issue* (London 1981)
Stark thriller of political expediency leading to uncomfortable conclusion about why the Wall went up.
McEwan, Ian *The Innocent* (London 1990)
Tale of naïve young Englishman recruited into Cold War machinations with tragi-comic results.
Nabokov, Vladimir *The Gift* (New York 1963)
Written and set in 1920s Berlin, where a Russian émigré dreams of writing a book very like this one.
Porter, Henry *Brandenburg* (London 2005)
Decent fall-of-the-Wall spy thriller, even if the author does get street names wrong.
Regener, Sven *Berlin Blues* (London 2003)
Irresponsibility and childhood's end in the bars of late 1980s Kreuzberg – a western version of Ostalgic thinking.
Schneider, Peter *The Wall Jumper* (London 1984)
Somewhere between novel, prose poem and artful reportage, a meditation on the madhouse absurdities of the Wall.

Children

Kästner, Erich *Emil and the Detectives* (London 1931)
Classic set mostly around Bahnhof Zoo and Nollendorfplatz.

Biography & memoir

Baumann, Bommi *How It All Began* (Vancouver 1977)
Frank and funny insider's account of the Berlin origins of West German terrorism.
Bielenberg, Christabel *The Past Is Myself* (London 1968)
Fascinating autobiography of an English woman who married a German lawyer and lived through the war in Berlin.
Funder, Anna *Stasiland* (London 2003)
Brutal stories of individuals and the East German state, reconstructed through the author's conversations with friends. Reads like a novel, both horrifying and touching.

Libeskind, Daniel *Breaking Ground* (London 2004)
Reflections on the building of Berlin's Jüdisches Museum.
Newton, Helmut *Autobiography* (London 2003)
Begins with an absorbing account of growing up Jewish in Weimar Berlin, and Newton's apprenticeship with fashion photographer Yva.
Parker, Peter *Isherwood* (London, 2004)
Enormous biography includes a well-researched section on the author's Berlin trouble.
Rimmer, Dave *Once Upon a Time in the East* (London 1992)
The collapse of communism seen stoned and from ground level – tales of games between East and West Berlin and travels through assorted east European revolutions.
Schirer, William L *Berlin Diaries* (New York 1941)
Foreign correspondent in Berlin 1931-41 bears appalled witness to Europe's plunge into Armageddon.

History

Friedrich, Otto *Before the Deluge* (New York 1972)
Vivid portrait of 1920s Berlin, based on interviews with those who survived what followed.
Garton Ash, Timothy *We the People* (London 1990)
Instant history of the 1989 revolutions.
Kellerhoff, Sven Felix *The Führer Bunker* (Berlin 2004)
The bare facts about Hitler's last refuge and what became of it.
Levenson, Thomas *Einstein in Berlin* (New York 2003)
Absorbing mainstream account of the historical deal between physicist and city.
McElvoy, Anne *The Saddled Cow* (London 1992)
Lively history of East Germany by a former Berlin *Times* correspondent.
Read, Anthony & Fisher, David *Berlin – The Biography of a City* (London 1994)
Readable, lightweight history.
Richie, Alexandra *Faust's Metropolis* (London 1998)
Best one-volume history of Berlin, but too heavy for holiday reading and with a too-conservative agenda.

Architecture

Berlin: Open City (Berlin 2001)
Excellent guide to both new building and extant architectural curiosities, built around walks detailed in fine fold-out maps.

Ladd, Brian *The Ghosts of Berlin: Confronting German History in the Urban Landscape* (Chicago 1997)
Erudite and insightful look into the relationship between architecture, urbanism and Berlin's violent politics.

Miscellaneous

Dax, Max & Defcon, Robert *Einstürzende Neubauten: No Beauty without Danger* (Berlin 2005)
Engaging oral history of the group also serves as a funny and illuminating picture of West Berlin's rock underground from 1980 through the fall of the Wall.
Friedrich, Thomas *Berlin – A Photographic Portrait of the Weimar Years 1918-1933* (London 1991)
Superb photographs of lost Berlin, its personalities and daily life.

Film

Cabaret (Bob Fosse, 1972)
Liza Minelli as Sally Bowles, the very definition of the Berlin myth, and the last great Hollywood musical.
Christiane F (Uli Edel, 1981)
To hell and back in the housing estates and heroin scene of late 1970s West Berlin, with Bowie soundtrack.
A Foreign Affair (Billy Wilder, 1948)
Marlene Dietrich sings 'Black Market' among the romantically rendered ruins of post-war Berlin.
Funeral in Berlin (Guy Hamilton, 1966)
Adaptation of Len Deighton's novel: Michael Caine in entertaining, puzzling Cold War yarn.
Good Bye Lenin! (Wolfgang Becker, 2003)
Ostalgia, the movie – a comic eulogy for the GDR, in which socialism gets a different kind of send-off.
It Is Not the Homosexual Who Is Perverse, But the Society in Which He Lives (Rosa von Praunheim, 1973)
The best of von Praunheim's many films, a laundry list of the follies of Berlin's gay population.
The Legend of Paul and Paula (Heiner Carow, 1974)
Cult GDR love story banned by the unromantic regime. Soundtrack by the also legendary Puhdys.
M (Fritz Lang, 1931)
Paedophilia and vigilantism as Peter Lorre's child murderer stalks an Expressionistic Weimar Berlin.
The Man Between (Carol Reed, 1953)
James Mason stars in *The Third Man*'s Berlin cousin.
Olympia (Leni Riefenstahl, 1937)
In filming the 1936 Olympics, the Nazis' favourite director invented the conventions of modern sportscasting.

One, Two, Three (Billy Wilder, 1961)
James Cagney is brilliant as the Pepsi exec whose daughter falls for East Berlin communist Horst Buchholz. Hilarious torture scene involving 'Itsy Bitsy Teeny Weeny Yellow Polka Dot Bikini'.
Possession (Andrzej Zulawski, 1981)
Sam Neill and Isabelle Adjani star in cult psychosexual horror flick that uses its West Berlin backdrop to compellingly weird effect.
The Spy Who Came In From the Cold (Martin Ritt, 1965)
Intense atmosphere, brilliant Richard Burton performance, and an ending that shatteringly brings home the obscenity of the Wall.
Westler (Wieland Speck, 1985)
Low-budget gay romance between West and East Berliners and all you need know about the Wall in one checkpoint strip-search scene.
Wings of Desire (Wim Wenders, 1987)
Bruno Ganz in love, Peter Falk in a bunker, Nick Cave in concert, and an angel on the Siegessäule – Wenders has never surpassed his (double) vision of the divided city.

Music

AG Geige *Raabe?* (Zensor)
One of the first post-1989 discs to emerge from the East Berlin underground came from a bizarre electronica outfit rooted in The Residents and Die Tödliche Doris.
Ash Ra Tempel *Join Inn* (Temple/Spalax)
The 1972 hippie freakout incarnation of guitarist Manuel Göttsching, before he was reborn as techno's most baffling muse.
Meret Becker *Noctambule* (Ego)
Actress/chanteuse Becker restages Weimar alongside Berliner Krankheit classics like Neubauten's 'Schwarz'.
The Birthday Party *Mutiny/The Bad Seed EP* (4AD)
Nick Cave and cohorts escaped drab London for the fevered creativity of early 1980s Berlin to record their two most intense EPs, here compressed into one volatile CD.
David Bowie *Heroes* (EMI)
In which Bowie romanticises the Wall and captures the atmosphere of (misspelt) Neuköln.
David Bowie *Low* (EMI)
Begun in France but completed at Hansa Studios, the album that soundtracked Bowie's new career in a new town.
Brecht/Weill *Die Dreigroschenoper Berlin 1930* (Teldec)
Historic shellac transcriptions from 1930 featuring a young and shrill Lotte Lenya, who also contributes a brace of *Mahagonny* songs.

Caspar Brötzmann/FM Einheit *Merry Christmas* (Blast First/Rough Trade Deutschland)
Guitarist son Caspar is no less noisy than *père* Brötzmann, especially on this frenzy of feedback and distortion kicked up with ex-Neubauten man-mountain FM Einheit on, er, stones.
Peter Brötzmann *No Nothing* (FMP)
Uncharacteristically introspective recording from the sax colossus of German improvisation for Berlin's vital Free Music Production label, which he co-founded 30 years ago.
Ernst Busch *Der Rote Orpheus/Der Barrikaden Tauber* (BARBArossa)
Two-CD survey of the revolutionary tenor's 1930s recordings covers Brecht, Eisler and Weill.
Nick Cave *From Her to Eternity* (Mute)
Cave in best Berlinerisch debauched and desperate mode, with a title track later featured in *Wings of Desire*.
Comedian Harmonists *Ihre grossen Erfolge* (Laserlight)
Sublime six-part harmonies from the Weimar sensations whose career was cut short during the Third Reich.
Crime & the City Solution *Paradise Discotheque* (Mute)
Underrated Berlin-Australian group's finest disc (1990) is an oblique commentary on the heady 'neo-black market burnt-out ruins' amorality of the immediate post-1989 era.
DAF *Kebabträume* (Mute)
Exhilarating German punk satire of Berlin's Cold War neuroses, culminating in the coda 'We are the Turks of tomorrow'.
Marlene Dietrich *On Screen, Stage and Radio* (Legend)
From 'I Am the Sexy Lola' through 'Ruins of Berlin', the sultry Schöneberg songstress embodies the mood of decadent Berlin.
Einstürzende Neubauten *Berlin Babylon Soundtrack* (Zomba)
More Neubauten 'Strategies Against Architecture' accompanying a highly watchable documentary about the head-spinning changes in Berlin's urban landscape and the movers and shakers behind them.
Alec Empire *The Geist of…* (Geist)
Wonderful triple CD compilation of ATR mainman Empire's less combative electronica explorations for Frankfurt brainiac label Force Inc/Mille Plateaux.
Manuel Göttsching *E2-E4* (Racket)
Great lost waveform guitar album by ex-Ash Ra Tempel leader.
Die Haut *Head On* (What's So Funny About)
Avantish Berlin equivalent of The Ventures lay down Morricone-meets-Loony Tunes backdrops for such guest singers as Alan Vega, Lydia Lunch, Kim Gordon and Jeffrey Lee Pierce.

Liaisons Dangereuses *Liaisons Dangereuses* (Roadrunner)
Formed by ex-DAF member Chrislo Haas, this 1982 album of chipped beats and industrial atmospheres was a key influence on Detroit techno.
Malaria! *Compiled* (Moabit Musik)
With suffocating synth swirls, heavy-stepping beats and song titles like 'Passion', 'Power' and 'Death', Malaria! was girl-pop, Berlin-style.
Maurizio *M* (M)
Essential CD compilation of Basic Channel mainman Moritz von Oswald's vinyl releases, which lights up Chicago house with beats diverted from the Berlin-Detroit techno grid.
Monolake *Momentum* (Imbalance)
Robert Hencke's post-techno pulses in some vast acoustic space, like last night's riffs still echoing around a distant corner of the club.
Barbara Morgenstern *Vermona ET-61* (Monika)
Morgenstern's everywoman voice, simple lyrics and clever accompaniment on a GDR home organ grow after repeated listenings, but the achingly beautiful instrumentals are the true highlights.
Pole *CD1* (Kiff SM)
Ex-Basic Channel engineer Stefan Betke is now at the cutting edge of the digidub school of blunted beats and vinyl glitches.
Iggy Pop *The Idiot* (Virgin America)
With Bowie in the producer's chair, Iggy begins to absorb the influence of early German electronica and the city of bright, white clubbing.
Iggy Pop *Lust for Life* (Virgin America)
Way back in West Berlin, Iggy the passenger cruises through the divided city's ripped-back sides and finds himself full of lust for life.
Rhythm & Sound w/ the artists (Indigo)
Techno meets reggae at the mixing desk of Mark Ernestus and Moritz von Oswald. Eight singles (and vocalists) compiled on this and companion B-side CD *the versions*.
Spacebow *Big Waves* (Noteworks)
Extraordinary reverberating metallic sound sculptures hewn from Berlin-based American expatriate artist Robert Rutman's steel cellos.
Stereo Total *My Melody* (Bungalow)
Demented chansons with cheesy lounge backing – Mitte's kitsch aesthetic plus a francophone spin.
Tangerine Dream *Zeit* (Jive Electro)
Where cosmic consciousness and electronic minimalism first met by the Wall.
Ton Steine Scherben *Keine Macht für Niemand* (David Volksmund)
Ernst Busch reincarnated as the early 1970s rock commune that provided Kreuzberg's anarchists with their most enduring anthems.

U2 *Achtung Baby!* (Island)
It took Zoo Station and post-Wall Berlin to inspire the U2 album for people who don't like U2.
Christian van Dorries *Wagnerkomplex* (Masse und Macht)
Spooky, powerful examination of 'music and German national identity' carried out in the shell of the Palast der Republik using live and recorded orchestral and techno elements, electronic treatments and the building's acoustics.
Various *Das Beste aus der DDR parts I-III* (Amiga)
Three-part DDR rock retrospective, divided into rock, pop and 'Kult', including Ostalgia stalwarts like Puhdys, Silly and Karat plus Sandow's alt anthem 'Born in the GDR' and an early Nina Hagen ditty.
Various *Berlin 1992* (Tresor)
On the first of several Tresor compilations, Berlin techno is captured in its early, apocalyptic phase. Includes Love Parade anthem 'Der Klang der Familie' by 3Phase (at that time, Dr Motte and Sven Röhrig).
Various *Berlin Super 80* (Monitorpop)
CD/DVD/book set documenting the West Berlin underground 1978-83. Features all the usual musical suspects, plus scratchy Super 8 celluloid from Jörg (Nekromantic) Buttgereit, among many others.
Various *Freischwimmer* (Kitty-Yo)
Sampler covering five years of work on Mitte's premier post-rock indie label. Acts include Laub, Tarwater, Raz O'Hara, Gonzalez.
Various *Die Grosse Untergangshow: Festival Genialer Dillentanten* (Vinyl-On-Demand)
Lovingly assembled double LP/CD and DVD set from the 1981 show that launched the likes of Neubauten, Gudrun Gut, Die Tödliche Doris, Mark Reeder and more.
Various *Hotel-Stadt-Berlin* (Hausmusik/Kompakt/Indigo)
Label showcase bodes well for the future, with local electronica musicians exploring paths off the beaten track of techno and trance.
Various *Pop 2000* (Grönland/Spiegel Edition)
Eight-CD companion to TV chronicle of post-war German culture in East and West. Ostrock is a bit under-represented, but otherwise an engaging compilation.
Various *Russensoul* (Trikont)
Wladimir Kaminer and Yuriy Gurzhy's survey of Russian and east European emigré musical activity in Berlin, with the likes of Leonid Soybelman and Rotfront, as viewed from their Kaffee Burger DJ console.
Various *Tranceformed from Beyond* (MFS)
Compilation that defined Berlin trance. Includes Cosmic Baby, Microglobe and Effective Force.

Westbam *A Practising Maniac at Work* (Low Spirit)
Effectively summarises the best of Berlin's best-known DJ, veering from stomping techno to twisted disco.
Wir Sind Helden *Die Reklamation* (Reklamation Records)
Simple but addictive tunes, lyrics asking modern consumer culture to 'give me my life back', touched a nerve with leftish alterna-teens and charmed older intelligentsia into believing that music still matters.

Websites

Time Out
www.timeout.com/berlin
General information and history, plus shop, restaurant, café, bar and hotel reviews, all written by residents.
berlinfo.com
www.berlinfo.com
Up-to-date information about life in Berlin, designed for residents and visitors alike. It contains film and theatre listings, as well as lists of professionals – doctors, lawyers, tax accountants – who speak English.
Berlin Info
www.berlin-info.de/index_e.html
Fairly comprehensive source of information and links, but the English translation is often painful (and sometimes missing). Operated by the official tourist board BTM (*see p284*) and oriented to upmarket tourism.
berlin.de
www.berlin.de
Berlin's official site – run by the tourist board (BTM) – is inevitably not its most objective but is nonetheless well written.
HotelGuide
berlin.hotelguide.net
A commercial site that sends you to the most expensive hotels, but then they're the ones that have online reservation services.
SPK
www.smb.spk-berlin.de
Smart bilingual site with information on more than 20 Berlin museums.
stadtplandienst
www.stadtplandienst.de
An interactive map that can pinpoint any address in the city; zoomable so you can figure out how to get there.
Stadtmuseum Berlin
www.stadtmuseum.de
Comprehensive information on Berlin's museums and useful links.
BVG
www.bvg.de
Online timetable and public transport information for Berlin/Brandenburg.
Zitty
www.zitty.de
The online sister of Berlin's main listings publication. This rather crowded site contains listing information and has search functions. In German only.

Directory

Index

Advertisers' Index

Index

Please refer to relevant sections for
contact details

Place of interest and/or entertainment	▮
Railway station	▮
Park	▮
Hospital/university	▮
Pedestrian Area	▮
Autobahn	═
Main road	
Airport	✈
Church	✛
S-Bahn Station	Ⓢ
U-Bahn Station	Ⓤ
S-Bahn line	S1
U-Bahn line	U1
District boundary	▬
Course of Wall	▬
Area	MITTE
Hotels	❶
Restaurants	❶
Cafés, Pubs & Bars	❶

Maps

Berlin & Around

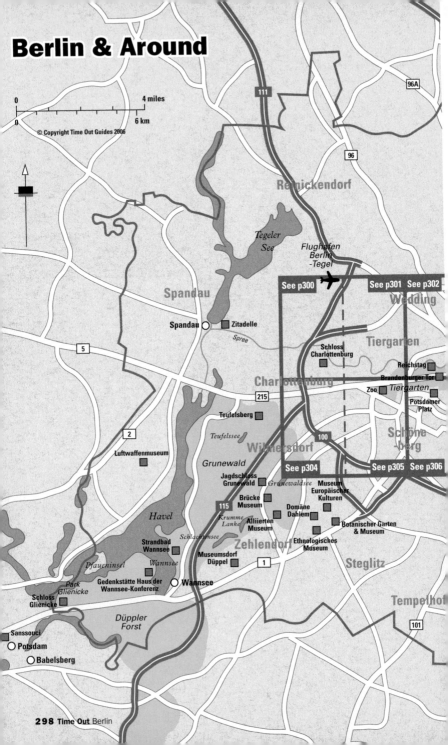

0   4 miles

0   6 km

© Copyright Time Out Guides 2006

111

96A

96

Reinickendorf

Tegeler See

Flughafen Berlin -Tegel

See p300   See p301   See p302

Wedding

Spandau

Spandau   Zitadelle

Spree

Tiergarten

Schloss Charlottenburg

Reichstag

Brandenburger Tor

5

Charlottenburg

Zoo   Tiergarten

215

Potsdamer Platz

Teufelsberg

Schöne- berg

Teufelssee

2

Wilmersdorf

100

Luftwaffenmuseum

Grunewald

See p304   See p305   See p306

Jagdschloss Grunewald

Grunewaldsee

Museum Europäischer Kulturen

Brücke Museum

115

Domäne Dahlem

Havel

Krumme Lanke

Alliierten Museum

Botanischer Garten & Museum

Schlachtensee

Ethnologisches Museum

Strandbad Wannsee

Zehlendorf

Steglitz

Museumsdorf Düppel

1

Pfaueninsel

Wannsee

Gedenkstätte Haus der Wannsee-Konferenz

Wannsee

Park Glienicke

Schloss Glienicke

Tempelhof

Düppler Forst

101

Sanssouci

Potsdam

Babelsberg

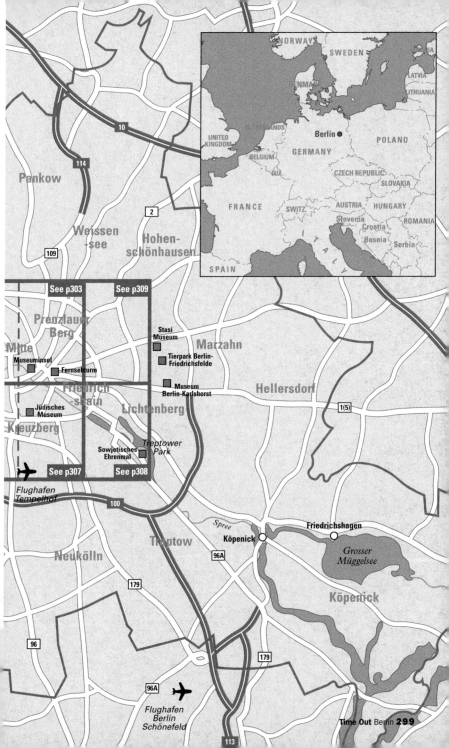

NORWAY
SWEDEN
DENMARK
LATVIA
LITHUANIA
NETHERLANDS
UNITED
KINGDOM
Berlin
POLAND
BELGIUM
GERMANY
LUX.
CZECH REPUBLIC
SLOVAKIA
FRANCE
SWITZ.
AUSTRIA
HUNGARY
Slovenia
ROMANIA
Croatia
Bosnia
Serbia
ITALY
SPAIN

Pankow

10

114

Weissen
-see

2

109

Hohen-
schönhausen

See p303   See p309

Prenzlauer
Berg

Mitte

Museuminsel   Fernsehturm

Stasi
Museum

Marzahn

Tierpark Berlin-
Friedrichsfelde

Hellersdorf

1(5)

Friedrich
-shain

Museum
Berlin-Karlshorst

Jüdisches
Museum

Lichtenberg

Kreuzberg

Sowjetisches
Ehrenmal

Treptower
Park

See p307   See p308

Flughafen
Tempelhof

100

Spree

Köpenick

Friedrichshagen

Treptow

Grosser
Müggelsee

Neukölln

96A

179

Köpenick

96

179

96A

Flughafen
Berlin
Schönefeld

113

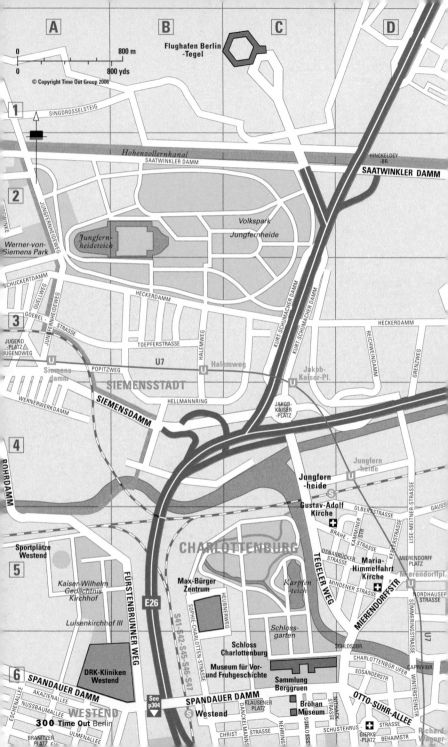

A   B   C   D

0 ⌐ 800 m
0 ⌐ 800 yds
© Copyright Time Out Group 2006

1

SINGDROSSELSTEIG

Flughafen Berlin
-Tegel

Hohenzollernkanal
SAATWINKLER DAMM

2

Werner-von-
Siemens Park

HINCKELDEY
-BR

SAATWINKLER DAMM

JUNGFERNHEIDEWEG

*Jungfern-
heideteich*

*Volkspark
Jungfernheide*

SCHUCKERTDAMM

QUELLWEG

HECKERDAMM

KURT-SCHUMACHER DAMM

KURT-SCHUMACHER DAMM

HECKERDAMM

REICHWEINDAMM

GRENZWEG

3

GOEBEL-
STRASSE

JUNGFERNHEIDEWEG

JUGEND
-PLATZ
JUGENDWEG

TOEPFERSTRASSE

HALEMWEG

U7   **Halemweg**

POPITZWEG

Jakob-
Kaiser-Pl.

U *Siemens
damm*

SIEMENSSTADT

HELLMANNRING

JAKOB-
KAISER-
PLATZ

SIEMENSDAMM

WERNERWERKDAMM

4

ROHRDAMM

*Jungfern
-heide*

**Jungfern
-heide**
S

**Gustav-Adolf
Kirche**
✚

OLBERSSTRASSE

BRAHE STR.

KAMMINER STRASSE

KEPPLERSTRASSE

LISE-MEITNER-STRASSE

GAUSS

**Sportplätze
Westend**

*Kaiser-Wilhelm
Gedächtnis
Kirchhof*

FÜRSTENBRUNNER WEG

CHARLOTTENBURG

OSNABRÜCKER
STRASSE

TEGELER WEG

**Maria-
Himmelfahrt
Kirche**
✚

MINDENER STRASSE

MIERENDORFF
PLATZ

U **Mierendorffpl.**

5

**Max-Bürger
Zentrum**

HEUBNERWEG

*Karpfen
-teich*

NORDHAUSER
STRASSE

SÖMMERINGSTRASSE

E26

S41–S42–S45–S46–S47

SOPHIE-CHARLOTTEN-STRASSE

*Schloss-
garten*

MIERENDORFFSTR

U7

Luisenkirchhof III

**Schloss
Charlottenburg**

SCHLOSSBR.

CHARLOTTENBGR UFER

CAPRIVIBR

6

SPANDAUER DAMM

ESCHENALLEE

AKAZIENALLEE

NUSSBAUMALLEE

**DRK-Kliniken
Westend**

See
p304
▽

SPANDAUER DAMM

KLAUSENER
PLATZ

Westend
S

**Museum für Vor-
und Frühgeschichte**

**Sammlung
Berggruen**

**Bröhan
Museum**

NITHACK STRASSE

EOSANDERSTR

OTTO-SUHR-ALLEE

WINTERSTEINSTR

SCHLOSSSTR

NEHRINGSTR

DANCKELMANNSTR

WESTEND

BRANITZER
PLATZ

ULMENALLEE

300 Time Out Berlin

CHRIST STRASSE

SCHUSTEHRUS

GIERKE-
PLATZ

BEHAIMSTR

STRASSE

*Richard
Wagner Pl.*

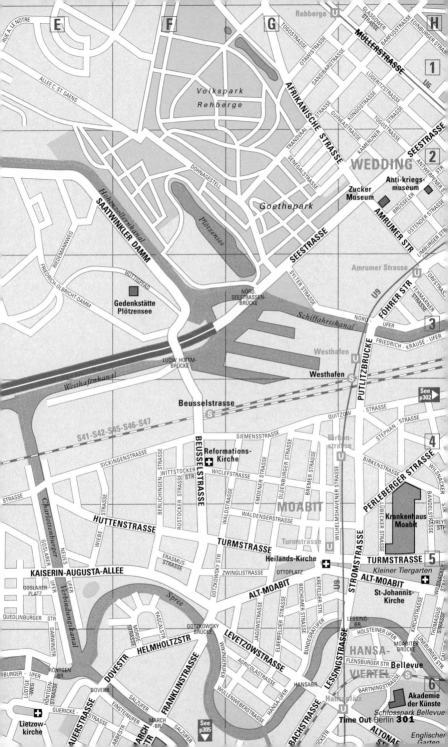

Time Out Berlin **301**

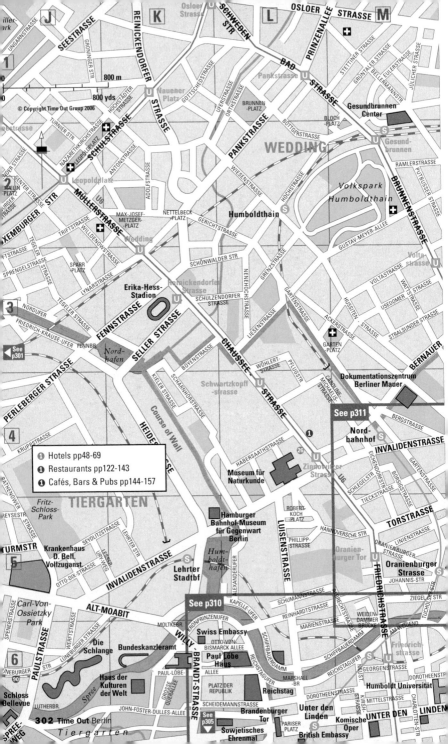

① Hotels pp48-69
① Restaurants pp122-143
① Cafés, Bars & Pubs pp144-157

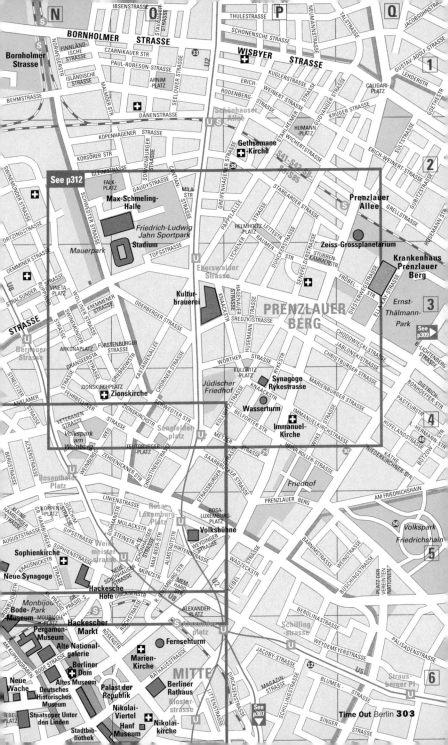

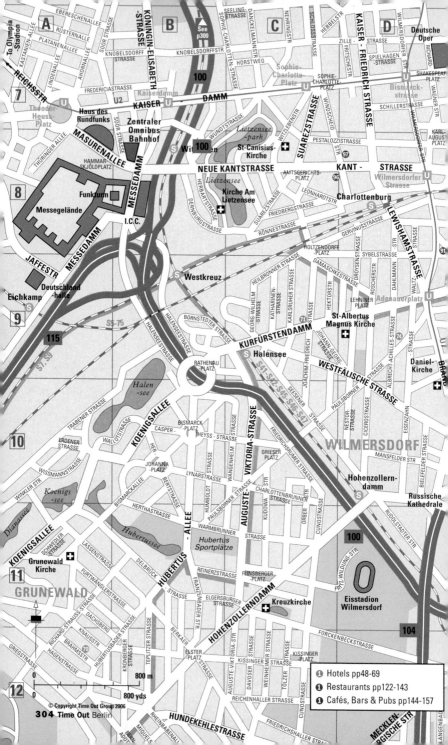

© Copyright Time Out Group 2006

- Hotels pp48-69
- Restaurants pp122-143
- Cafés, Bars & Pubs pp144-157

● Hotels pp48-69
● Restaurants pp122-143
● Cafés, Bars & Pubs pp144-157

0   800 m
0   800 yds

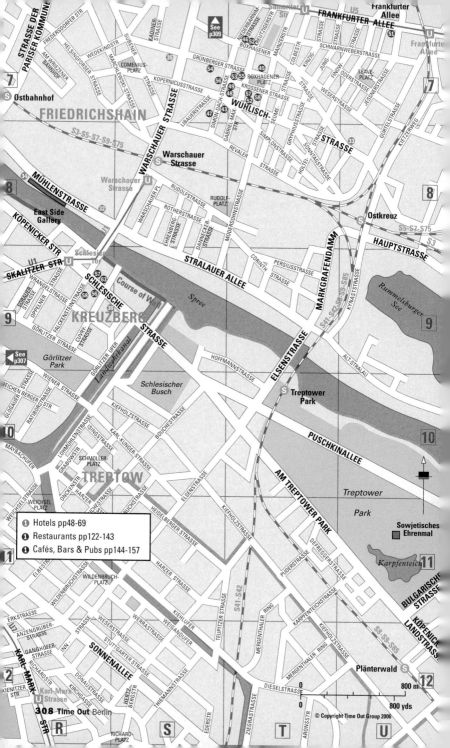

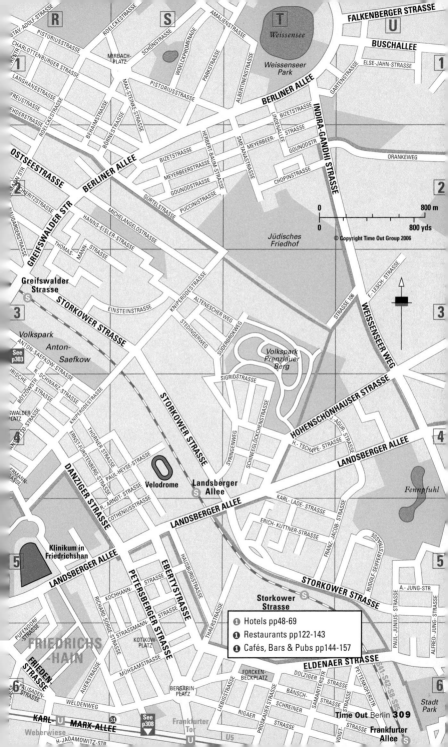

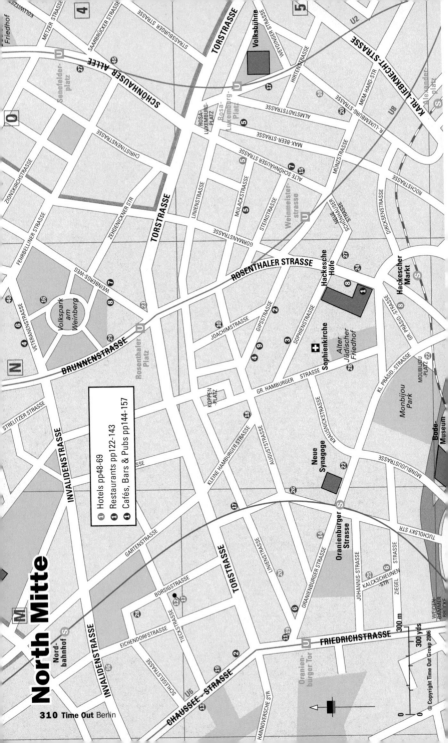

North Mitte

Hotels pp48-69
Restaurants pp122-143
Cafés, Bars & Pubs pp144-157

© Copyright Time Out Group 2006

300 m
300 yds

Street Index

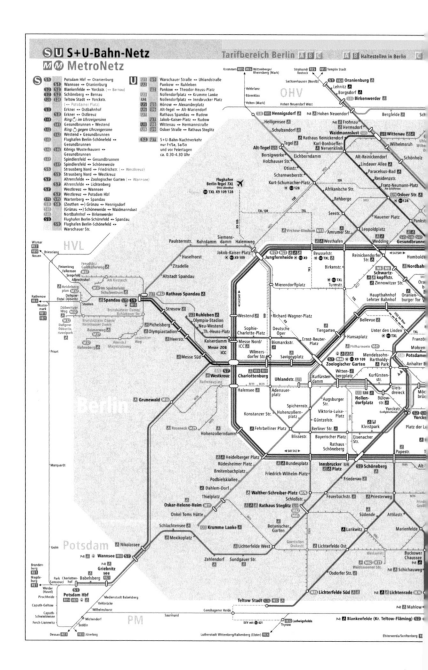

⊗⊍ S+U-Bahn-Netz
ⓜⓜ MetroNetz

Tarifbereich Berlin Ⓐ Ⓑ Ⓒ   Ⓐ Ⓑ Haltestellen in Berlin Ⓒ

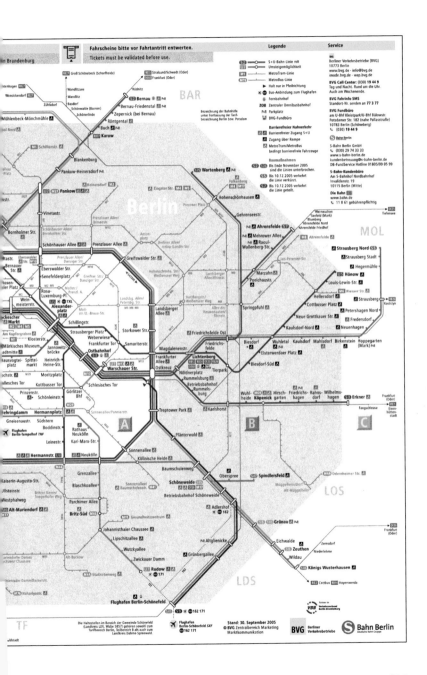

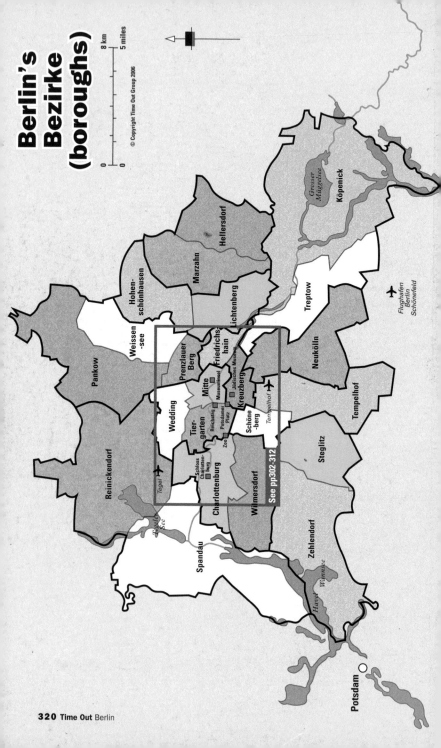

Berlin's Bezirke (boroughs)

© Copyright Time Out Group 2006

Köpenick

Grosser
Müggelsee

Hellersdorf

Marzahn

Hohen-
schönhausen

Lichtenberg

Treptow

Weissen-
see

Pankow

Friedrichs-
hain

Prenzlauer
Berg

Neukölln

Mitte

Museuminsel

Jüdisches Museum

Reichstag

Kreuzberg

Tempelhof

Wedding

Tier-
garten

Potsdamer
Platz

Schöne-
berg

Zoo

Tempelhof

Flughafen
Berlin
Schönefeld

Reinickendorf

Schloss
Charlotten-
burg

Charlottenburg

Wilmersdorf

Steglitz

See pp302-312

Tegel

Tegeler
See

Spandau

Zehlendorf

Havel

Wannsee

Potsdam

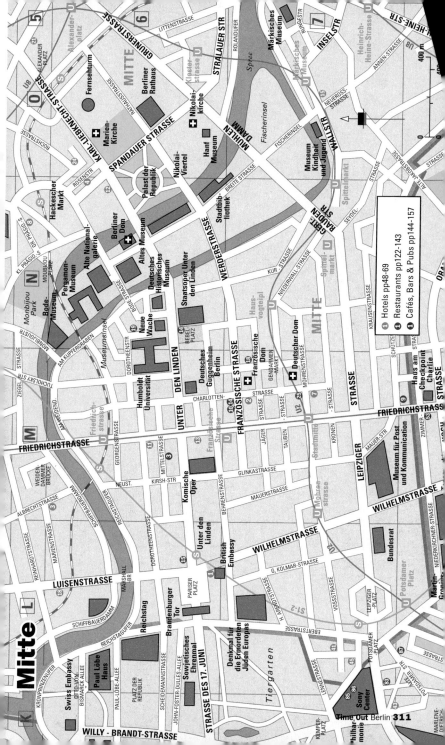

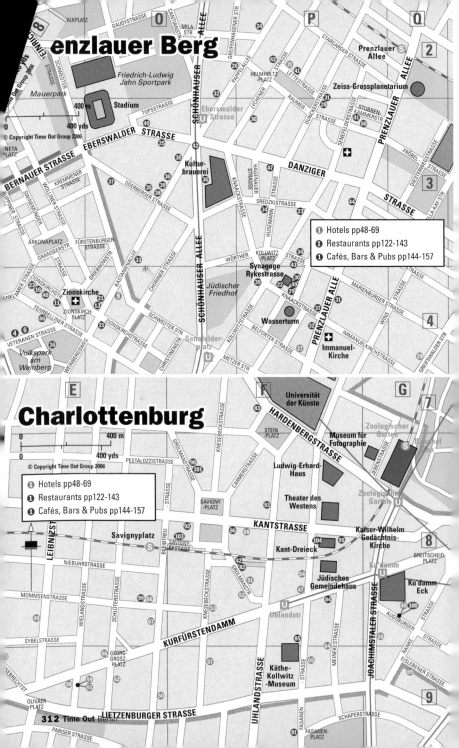